CW01270963

Additional praise for
Divine Wrath and Salvation in Matthew

"What happens if we attend to Matthew's *inception* history, rather than to its *reception* history? If we read it not within the New Testament but alongside of other late first-century Jewish texts (4 Ezra, 2 Baruch)? If we see this 'passionately angry' Gospel not as an instance of 'Christian origins,' but as a witness to Jewish origins? In *Divine Wrath and Salvation in Matthew*, Anders Runesson accomplishes exactly such a historical reimagining. The result is a profound work of ethical reasoning and a clear summons to theological courage."

—**Paula Fredriksen**
The Hebrew University of Jerusalem

"For students of Matthew's Gospel, Anders Runesson's *Divine Wrath and Salvation in Matthew: The Narrative World of the First Gospel* presents a strong and challenging interpretation. Matthew, he insists, originates as a thoroughly Jewish text and, contrary to many later Christian readings, is primarily concerned with the salvation of Israel, particularly those 'lost sheep' so led astray by their leaders who, in a particular way, have earned God's judgement. Not all will agree with Runesson's assessment, but no one should ignore it."

—**Donald Senior**
Catholic Theological Union

"I know of no other book that approaches the Gospel of Matthew from a strictly historical point of view in the consistent and masterful way that Runesson does. He shows that Matthew can be explained as a document whose origins lie fully within its first-century Jewish context. This is a stimulating and insightful book that the next generation of Matthean specialists will not be able to ignore."

—**Donald A. Hagner**
Fuller Theological Seminary

Divine Wrath and Salvation in Matthew

Divine Wrath and Salvation in Matthew

The Narrative World of the First Gospel

Anders Runesson

Fortress Press
Minneapolis

DIVINE WRATH AND SALVATION IN MATTHEW
The Narrative World of the First Gospel

Cover design: Alisha Lofgren

Library of Congress Cataloging-in-Publication Data
Print ISBN: 978-0-8006-9959-8
eBook ISBN: 978-1-4514-5225-9

The paper used in this publication meets the minimum requirements of American National Standard for Information Sciences — Permanence of Paper for Printed Library Materials, ANSI Z329.48-1984.

Manufactured in the U.S.A.

This book was produced using Pressbooks.com, and PDF rendering was done by PrinceXML.

For Anna
Fellow traveller, loving wife, incisive theologian

Contents

Part II. Judging and Saving the Nations

Tables and Figures

Preface

μακάριοι οἱ δεδιωγμένοι ἕνεκεν δικαιοσύνης,
ὅτι αὐτῶν ἐστιν ἡ βασιλεία τῶν οὐρανῶν.

This study began its life on a somewhat dusty backstreet in Nairobi more than 20 years ago. My wife and I had completed a semester of undergraduate study at the Swedish Theological Institute in Jerusalem and had then backpacked our way around the world for an additional seven months. After traveling mostly through the so-called two-thirds world, observing on a daily basis the ever-present results of the exploitation by the powerful of the less fortunate, the question became palpably acute whether the God of the Hebrew Bible and the New Testament had anything to say about this intolerable state of affairs. Why are the perpetrators of injustice allowed to continue their abuse unhindered, flourishing in their endeavors, while those who fight corruption and its devastating consequences are made targets of mistreatment and violence? Is there no end to the suffering that the poor and defenseless must endure because of other people's greed and indifference? Why doesn't the biblical God interfere, condemning the oppressors and restoring justice to the destitute? And where did all the prophets of the Hebrew Bible go? Was their call for individual integrity and just laws—their insistence on the protection of orphans, widows, the poor, and the immigrants[1]—silenced as the Messiah of the

---

1. E.g., Isa 1:15–17; 10:1–3; Jer 7:5–7; Ezek 9:9–10; 22:29; Amos 5:10–24; Zech 7:9–10; cf. Lev 19:17–18, 34; Deut 10:16–19; 24:17; Ps 68:6 [Eng. 68:5]; 82:1–8.

New Testament entered the scene, seemingly proposing a non-political and "religious" solution to the constant crisis we are encouraged to call "world order"? Did these proclaimers of rightful divine wrath and judgment vanish, never to return, superseded by doctrinal concerns in a community that, when faced with despotism and persecution, adjusts and withdraws from direct interaction, washing its hands with abstract theological constructs formulated to secure a heavenly salvation utterly divorced from the earthly deliverance of the downtrodden and demoralized? What is it, really, that the notion of the kingdom of heaven is trying to convey, and what does it mean to ask in prayer for its urgent realization, for the divine will to prevail upon earth as much as it does in heaven?[2]

Such were the questions that forced themselves upon me, and since I was a university student at the time, I thought it natural, first of all, to apply academic tools to see how the ancients would have dealt with these and similar issues; to seek insight by listening to voices from the past. Once we had returned to Lund University, the idea developed into an essay on divine judgment in the Hebrew Bible and Matthew's Gospel (1994), which led to a licentiate thesis on the same topic (1997). Parallel to my work on ancient synagogues, Paul, and other aspects of Matthew, I have since continued to explore judgment discourse in biblical and related texts.[3] The present study is an attempt to present parts of the research I have undertaken on and off over the years whenever I have found the time. I have focused here exclusively on one of the books included in the New Testament: the Gospel of Matthew. The reason for this limitation is that Matthew's Gospel differs significantly from the other Gospels, not only in its fierce emphasis on divine wrath and judgment, unmatched by any other New Testament text with the possible exception of Revelation, but also in its coherent, almost systematic treatment of this theme throughout the narrative.

In addition to the uniqueness of Matthew's Gospel, and perhaps

---

2. Matt 6:10.

3. See, e.g., Anders Runesson, "Judgment," in *NIDB* (vol. 3; Nashville: Abingdon press, 2008) 457–66, for an overview and discussion of the theme of judgment in the Hebrew Bible and the New Testament, as well as in the Apocrypha and Pseudepigrapha.

counterintuitively, considering the rather orderly nature of its theo-ritual[4] pattern, the diverse reception history of the First Gospel in both church and academy suggests that this text is in need of special attention, particularly with regard to nuances that would have been apparent to its first-century audiences, but which may since have been forgotten. There is one peculiarity, though, that stands out in the midst of this interpretive heterogeneity due to its remarkable historical consistency, from late antiquity until very recently. Regardless of whatever diversity human creativity has produced in its search for divine requirements of salvation, there is, in Christian interpretations of Matthew, one group of people that has been singled out for divine—and human—condemnation more often than not: the Jewish people. One does not have to engage in more than a cursory investigation into the reception of Matt 27:25 to become horrified at the ingenuity of humans as interpretive beings when it comes to developing divinely ordained pretexts for violence—textual as well as physical and psychological—against this, from a Christian perspective, specific "other."[5]

In light of the fact that Matthew's narrative, more than the other Gospels, seems to place the reader in a Jewish world in order to communicate the meaning of Jesus, this interpretive consistency in which the Jews *as a people* are theologically destined for eradication appears to disrupt the fundamental stability of the plotline. In this regard, Matthew's intriguing reception history triggered early on in

---

4. By "theo-ritual," I mean to refer to a pattern of practice and thought in which what we term "theology" and "ritual" cannot be understood as separate issues, with the implication that they need to be analyzed in conjunction with each other. The nature of the text is such that "theology," as this term is often defined in academic discourses, seems to reduce what really is an expression of a ritually determined Second-Temple Jewish worldview to an attempt at systematizing religious thought as disentangled from cultic praxis.

5. For recent discussion, see Anders Runesson, "Judging the Theological Tree by its Fruit: The Use of the Gospels of Mark and Matthew in Official Church Documents on Jewish-Christian Relations," in *Mark and Matthew. Comparative Readings II: Hermeneutics, Reception History, Theology* (edited by Eve-Marie Becker and Anders Runesson; Tübingen: Mohr Siebeck, 2013) 189–228, and literature referred to there. For a comprehensive study of the reception of this verse in the west until the fifth century, see Rainer Kampling, *Das Blut Christi und die Juden: Mt 27,25 bei den lateinischsprachigen christlichen Autoren bis zu Leo dem Großen* (Münster: Aschendorf, 1984). See also John Nolland, "The Gospel of Matthew and Anti-Semitism," in *Built Upon the Rock: Studies in the Gospel of Matthew* (edited by Daniel M. Gurtner and John Nolland; Grand Rapids: Eerdmans, 2008), 154–69, here 163–69.

my studies a curiosity about basic thematic structures in the text. This, in turn, led to a focus on how the identity of "the other" is construed, since answers to such questions seemed to me to be a key to a first-century understanding of the notion of divine judgment in the Gospel. How would those who first read the Gospel have pictured "the other," and how is divine judgment construed in relation to them? From such considerations follows what is perhaps an even more important issue: Who are the insiders? Are they so easily identified, as is usually assumed? Are they all considered "saved" (and if so, on the basis of which criteria?), or is the threat of condemnation or punishment directed also, or even primarily, against the insider? Why?

Such questions lead to further interpretive problems related to the judgment of collectivities in the text: What is the role in this narrative of "Israel," an entity which is allowed to identify not only the land in which the story takes place (2:20–21; 10:23), but also the people among whom the Messiah carries out his mission (2:6; 10:6), and the God whose Spirit establishes the kingdom through the Christ (15:31)? If "Israel" is, as is so often assumed, condemned and superseded as God's people, what are the criteria on the basis of which such punishment is meted out? Or is "Israel" rather referring to the people at whose center the saved are found, a nation into which even non-Jews are invited for protection as the final judgment is fast approaching, the time when justice and divine rule will be established globally?

If this is so, what, then, is the role of the other nations in this story, whose customs and politics are deplorable (5:47; 6:7, 32; 20:25–26), whose representatives torture and crucify the Messiah (20:19), and who, as a general category, are said to hate Jesus's followers (24:9), but among whom are also found heroes of compassion who will be welcomed into the eschatological kingdom quite apart from any consideration of their "faith" (25:31–46)? Do we find in Matthew that divisions are made not only, or even primarily, between individuals who are approved or not for life in the kingdom, but, on a basic level, between "Israel" and "the nations"? If so, we would have identified here a fundamental challenge as we aim to understand what a first-century reading of the text may have looked like, as opposed to its later reception in (Christian) settings. If the reception of Matthew, in both church and academy, concludes that "Israel" as an ethno-religious collectivity has ceased to carry within it any theological or salvific meaning, divine judgment can, after it has dissolved the (Abrahamic) covenant which brought "Israel" into being, only be concerned with individuals, whatever their background might be.[6] But such an approach to judgment seems to be at odds with how the text is actually formulated, from basic matters (such as the terminology used) to larger issues concerned with narrative progression.

An analysis of the notion of divine wrath and salvation thus leads us deeper into the nature of the text than the topic might at first have caused us to believe. As we aim to answer questions about judgment, we are pulled into and forced to deal with key issues concerning the fundamental theo-ritual structure of the text, which carries within it implications for the identification of the Gospel as an expression of first-century Judaism.

For the historian, the results of the present study point to a need to re-categorize the Gospel of Matthew as a text that belongs among other (diverse) Jewish texts from around the turn of the era, such as the Psalms of Solomon, the Dead Sea Scrolls, 4 Ezra, 2 Baruch, and the Tannaitic literature, rather than placing it along interpretive trajectories leading into what is properly understood as (mainstream, i.e., non-Jewish) Christianity. Indeed, while the churches have favored Matthew more than most other texts in the New Testament, historically the basic patterns of thought and practice revealed in the Gospel follow a rather different trajectory, one which moves in a direction similar to that of later rabbinic Judaism, the mother of all

---

6. While scholars who argue that "Israel" or "the Jewish people" have been abolished in Matthew's Gospel often point to individual salvation beyond any ethno-religious categories as its replacement, it is rare to see in such studies any discussion of the fact that this would also, by theo-logical necessity, imply the abolishment of the covenant of Abraham. The reason for this is simply that it is with this covenant, not the Mosaic covenant, that the Jewish people were brought into being; if the peoplehood of the Jews is abolished that implies the end of the Abrahamic covenant. One may suspect that the importance of Abraham in Christian tradition, and in Paul's letters, has contributed to the reluctance of many interpreters to follow their argument through to its logical conclusion in this particular case.

mainstream forms of Judaism today. Even if Matthew's main character, Jesus, connects the narrative with later forms of Christianity on what, in this context, is best called a superficial level, rather than with modern mainstream forms of Judaism, it is somewhat misleading to conceptualize the study of this Gospel within the framework of 'Christian origins,' and speak about Matthew as a Christian text.[7] After all, in antiquity, belief in Jesus as the Messiah in no way defined "Christianity" as something other than "Judaism"; the term "Christianity" was not even invented until the second century, decades after the completion of Matthew's Gospel.[8] The study of Matthew's importance for the church belongs, arguably, to the reception history of the text, not its inception history.[9] Matthew's inception history, which includes pre-textual traditions, the process of textualization, as well as the final form of the text,[10] should, in my opinion, primarily be conceptualized within the study of Second-Temple Judaism, just as much as the study of the historical Jesus should.[11] Indeed, in the case of Matthew one may even go further; based on Matthew's hermeneutical techniques and fundamental focus on the interpretation of Jewish law as salvifically significant, interests which this text shares with later

7. As most scholars, and Christians, do. See, e.g., Douglas R. A. Hare, "How Jewish is the Gospel of Matthew?" *CBQ* 62 (2000), 264–77, as he aims to refute the Jewish readings of Matthew by Anthony Saldarini, Andrew Overman, and Amy-Jill Levine.

8. For discussion of this point and the so-called parting of the ways between Judaism and Christianity, see Anders Runesson, "Inventing Christian Identity: Paul, Ignatius, and Theodosius I," in *Exploring Early Christian Identity* (edited by Bengt Holmberg; Tübingen: Mohr Siebeck, 2008), 59–92. For the relationship between later forms of Jesus-centered Judaism and rabbinic Judaism, see also most recently Karin Hedner Zetterholm, "Alternative Visions of Judaism and Their Impact on the Formation of Rabbinic Judaism," *JJMJS* 1 (2014), 127–53 [http://www.jjmjs.org/].

9. The distinction is similar to what most would agree would be the case with texts included in the Hebrew Bible; the fact that (non-Jewish) Christians included this collection in their canon does not mean that the texts themselves are to be labeled "Christian" when we consider them in their original historical settings.

10. If such a form can indeed be found. As the continuously (more or less) revised versions of the Greek text still today indicate, a "final form" of the text has never existed in any absolute sense of that word. There is a point in history, however, when we can talk about Matthew as a text containing a full narrative with certain characteristics. While some scholars (legitimately) prefer to work on extant full manuscripts, which are then quite late, for access to this narrative, it is, in my view, both as legitimate and necessary (and interesting) to engage in the task of reconstructing earlier forms of the text, which have since been lost. The present study is based on such a reconstruction, which aims at restoring the earliest form of Matthew's Gospel, namely the 28th edition of Nestle–Aland's *Novum Testamentum Graece* (Deutsche Bibelgesellschaft, 2nd corrected printing, 2013).

11. Again, as with the Hebrew Bible texts, few, if any, would identify Jesus as a Christian.

forms of rabbinic Judaism,[12] the study of Matthew may be best thought of as a topic in Jewish origins.[13]

From a historical point of view, the present analysis of the notion of divine wrath and salvation thus aims at revealing an ancient pattern of thought and practice, a theo-ritual perspective, that has been silenced by centuries of later reception taking place in religio-cultural and political settings that, while connected in many ways with Christianity as we know it today, have been radically different from the first-century context in which the text came into being. In other words, the book seeks to tell a story rarely told, and in this way engage contemporary historical claims about Matthew that are, seen from the perspective of the present study, tainted both by anachronism and anatopism, reading into the text assumptions from the wrong time and the wrong place.[14] As with all history, the present analysis emerges from within our own world, the place where our questions

12. One may note here Ulrich Luz's brief comparison between Matthew and Yohanan Ben Zakkai (*Matthew*, 1.55–56); cf. also David C. Sim, "Introduction," in *Matthew and His Christian Contemporaries* (edited by David C. Sim and Boris Repschinski; London: T&T Clark, 2008), 1–10, here 1–3. While there are some problems in Luz's overview, not least with regard to his use of "synagogue" and "church" as two separate entities at this time, comparisons such as these are instructive, and should be further explored, as Sim also notes. As in the case of Matthew and Yohanan ben Zakkai, what is interesting is not the question of a direct (genetic) relationship between the different corpora of texts, but rather the similarities in the thematic deep structures of the texts, which originated, in all likelihood, in similar cultural contexts. On the latter point, see also Serge Ruzer, *Mapping the New Testament: Early Christian Writings as a Witness for Jewish Biblical Exegesis* (Leiden: Brill, 2007).

13. As Rebecca Runesson succinctly puts it on her blog, *The Angry Theologian*: "[I]f you pick up the New Testament looking for a sugar-coated fairy tale about a nice Jewish-yet-not-too-Jewish man and his faithful friends road-tripping through Galilee, you've come to the wrong place." (https://theangrytheologian.wordpress.com/2015/05/12/diet-jesus-is-not-a-thing/). This could certainly be said about Matthew's Gospel and the way it presents Jesus.

14. Looking at the history of interpretation over the centuries, it seems clear, as others have also noted (See, e.g., Tord Fornberg, "Matthew and his Readers: Some Examples from the History of Interpretation," *Religio* 48 [1997]: 25–39 [in Swedish], here 32; referring to Gerhard Ebeling, *Wort Gottes und Tradition* [Göttingen: Vandenhoeck and Ruprecht, 1964]: 9–27), that the reception of Matthew has, by and large, mirrored church history. I would venture to say that, in some ways, this is true also of some modern academic studies of the First Gospel, as these have often been linked to the churches not only institutionally but also through individual interpreters. Some scholars have suggested that interpretations of Matthew as a first-century Jewish text is a concession to post-holocaust sensitivities, implying or stating explicitly that such readings have negotiated the strict historical rules of academia. I would suggest, though, that the short time span of a few decades since the horrifying events of World War II, while important as a time for asking new kinds of historical questions, are dwarfed in comparison with centuries of pre-critical interpretation in church settings, the influence of which is still felt in academia today. In the end, though, such rhetoric is less meaningful; what matters are the arguments put forward and how well they can be defended using sound historical-critical tools.

are necessarily born (we cannot inhabit, by definition, any other place than the here and now). It aims, though, to the degree that it is at all possible, at visiting the past, bringing back for the reader, in as non-technical language as possible, a translation into Western academic idiom of an intellectual and ritual culture that is not our own, but which we desire to understand.[15]

Now, as focus is put on the theme of judgment and salvation in Matthew, there will emerge what for many who are immersed in Christian and Jewish traditions, respectively, will be unexpected and perhaps even unwelcome news. Traditional boundaries between the saved and the lost may be re-drawn; sometimes they may even dissolve, and this for reasons unfamiliar to those who are not used to reading Gospels within their ancient Jewish settings. I am not going to pretend that the academic study of texts included in the New Testament takes place in a vacuum, as if its results would be unrelated to discourses nurtured by those 2.18 billion people, one-third of the world's population, who identify themselves as Christians and the Gospels as normative narratives.[16] Matthew's Gospel, as much as other texts of the New Testament, "has become a classic text, one that has transcended the historical circumstances of its original composition."[17] A few words on the relationship between the academic historical study of canonical texts, truly a minority mode of reading both historically and in the world today, and contemporary normative discourses may therefore be permissible in order to clarify what the present study

---

15. As with all translation, the terminology used is of crucial importance, as it may carry within it anachronistic ideas that threaten to mislead both writer and reader in their attempts to understand the historical other. While some such anachronistic terms have been avoided here altogether (e.g., "Christian" and "church"), I have signaled the significance of some ancient notions through (terminological) references to discourses common in Matthew's later reception history. Examples of this type of "translation" include the use of words/concepts such as "works" (of law), or "works righteousness," as well as "grace." Using these words and phrases, I do not mean to say, however, that the theology that usually comes with them is applicable to the first century. Rather the opposite; I have aimed at drawing attention to how such themes and issues, often discussed in contemporary scholarship using this type of terminology, are in need of nuanced elaboration if we seek historical understanding.

16. The estimate of the number of Christians in the world today is taken from a report by *Pew Research Center*, published in 2011: http://www.pewforum.org/2011/12/19/global-christianity-exec/.

17. Daniel J. Harrington, *Meeting St. Matthew Today: Understanding the Man, His Mission, and His Message* (Chicago: Loyola Press, 2010), 99.

does and does not intend to do, and what it may achieve beyond its immediate historical concerns; transparency is a virtue, after all, though celebrated more often than acted upon.[18]

It is my opinion that reconstructed meanings of a text belong, ultimately, to history, not to us, even if we mold such meanings through the very language we use as we translate a message from one culture to another. What I mean by this is that we should not mistake our urge to understand the other—and historical texts and subjects are always representations of the other—with a will to domesticate the ancients, forcing them to serve us within systems of beliefs and practices that are fundamentally foreign to them, and into which they never spoke. History is, by definition, always active in both concealed and discernible ways in the present, as much as the present is the

18. As the historical study of Matthew has increasingly come to the realization that conclusions drawn about the patterns of thought and practice in the First Gospel are truly alien to later forms of mainstream Christianity, scholars concerned also with the interpretation of Matthew outside the academic scene have begun to suggest ways to deal with what they have found in the contemporary contexts in which they live. See, e.g., Wolfgang Reinbold, "Das Matthäusevangelium, die Pharisäer und die Tora," *Biblische Zeitschrift* 50:1 (2006), 51–73, here 70–73; "Für christliche Theologie heute birgt dieses Ergebnis ein Problem, das nicht verschwiegen sei. Die Vorstellung des Matthäus von der rechten christgläubigen Praxis hat wenig mit dem zu tun, was in unseren Gemeinde gang und gäbe ist. Wir verzehnten nicht nur nicht nach den Regeln der Rabbinischen Weisen, wir verzehnten überhaupt nicht, obwohl es in der Torah des Mose ausdrücklich angeordnet wird. Unsere Kirche ist in einer Weise eine Kirche der Heiden geworden, die sich Matthäus vermutlich kaum hätte vorstellen können. Hätte er nur anderthalb Jahrhunderte später gelebt, wäre er Gefahr gelaufen, als Häretiker bezeichnet zu Verden" (71). See also Harrington, *Meeting St. Matthew Today*, esp. chs. 8 and 9, entitled "A Jewish Book" and "A Christian Gospel," respectively. As Harrington notes, "[w]e can be enlightened by reading Matthew's Gospel as a historical document of late first-century Judaism and Early Jewish Christianity. But Christian believers cannot simply leave it in the past" (99). This type of discussion goes beyond more common attempts at making the Gospel accessible to modern readers, such as, e.g., Mark Allan Powell, *God With Us: A Pastoral Theology of the Gospel of Matthew* (Minneapolis: Fortress, 1995); Powell structures his texts using five key words—mission, worship, teaching, stewardship, and social justice—all of which require serious hermeneutical work to be applicable outside the world of the text in modern non-Jewish settings. Cf., from a different perspective, Lloyd Gaston, "The Messiah of Israel as Teacher of the Gentiles," *Interpretation* 29:1 (1975), 24–40, who calls on redaction criticism for hermeneutical assistance: "The redaction of the Gospel is not itself kerygma but it shows us how the kerygma can be transmitted and applied" (40). See also the recent two-volume commentary edited by Cynthia A. Jarvis, and E. Elizabeth Johnson, *Feasting on the Gospels: Matthew* (Louisville: Westminster John Knox Press, 2013). These volumes approach the interpretive task by structuring the commentary in four distinct parts for every passage: theological, pastoral, exegetical, and homiletical. In the end, the very definition of "exegesis" can be stated to be, according to the *Anchor Bible Dictionary*, "the process of careful analytical study of biblical passages undertaken to produce *useful* interpretations of those passages" (Douglas Stuart, "Exegesis," *ABD*, vol. 2, 682–88, here 682; my emphasis). What counts as "useful" is, obviously, dependent on the socio-academic or religio-political location of the reader, regardless of his or her personal religious or non-religious convictions.

matrix within which we communicate and thus form the past. But the way the present is imagined and continuously reinvented and acted upon is not to be constrained by images of the past, just as the present moments of the past never were snapshots of their own histories; the past, as we reconstruct it, must not be made prisoner of and slave to the present and vice versa.

History, academically defined, is, then, best understood as a conversation between the past and the present. As such, the first-century voice of Matthew's Gospel can never be more than one voice in contemporary religious, theological, and scholarly conversations. Original meanings, as much as we can talk about such, are never the only meanings carried by a text, since meaning is triggered in the contextually defined space between text and reader, but they constitute a contribution, nevertheless, to modern reflection on the past in relation to contemporary issues, political, theological, or otherwise. In other words, a historical reconstruction of a religious text cannot, in my opinion, be understood as religiously authoritative in and of itself, just as reconstructions of the historical Jesus can never be normative from a Christian perspective; after all, that which is created by human hands must not be worshiped, lest roles are reversed and humans emerge as rulers of the universe.[19]

Neither the worshipper nor the theologian lives by history alone. The Christian may relate to the divine as he or she would engage someone with whom they live; there is a dependency between the parties, based on daily contact in the here and now. The historical interactions of the other person in such a relationship are one part of the link that nurtures both, but it cannot define exhaustively the bond between them, since God is the God not of the dead, but of the living.[20] In a corresponding way, the theologian needs his or her thinking to be nurtured by insights from a wider spectrum of human experience than can be provided by the historian.[21] The present reconstruction of

---

19. Cf. Exod 20:4–6; 32:23; Deut 9:12. On the historical Jesus as non-normative, cf. John P. Meier, *A Marginal Jew: Re-Thinking the Historical Jesus*, vol. 1: *The Roots of the Problem and the Person* (New York: Doubleday) 197: "[T]he Jesus of history is not and cannot be the object of Christian faith."
20. Matt 22:32.

a specific first-century understanding of divine judgment does not aim, therefore, to provide ready-made normative material to be applied in contemporary theology; it simply attempts to translate a specific aspect of the theo-ritual pattern of an ancient text into modern academic idiom. Indeed, it has been important for this entire investigation precisely to disregard any normative reception of Matthew in cultures foreign to the context in which the traditions behind the text, as well as the text itself, were born.

Having said this, as noted in the introductory paragraphs above, the very impulse to write the book came from personal experiences of and theological reflection on the flagrant injustices indisputably inherent in the current "world order." The turning to biblical, and more specifically New Testament texts for illumination and theological elaboration of the basic insights that experience and preliminary contemplation had provided is, in and of itself, a move that reveals aspects of the ethos within which the initial steps of the analysis were undertaken. While ultimately, the historical conclusions of the study were, to me, unanticipated as I launched the first stages in this investigation many years ago, the end result may nevertheless speak to some issues that may be of relevance to people for whom Matthew's Gospel or the New Testament texts more generally carry significance in their personal and/or communal projects of making (religio-ethical) sense of human (co-)existence.

First, I think it wise to remind oneself that a theological theme such as that of divine judgment may be a dangerous tool with which ideologies of death, destruction, and persecution may be forged, as surely has been done in all too many religio-politically charged settings throughout history and across continents. For some, this fact alone would lead to the hermeneutical verdict that all such notions of judgment are to be viewed as (embarrassing) remains from an unenlightened dark past of human existence that should be relegated

---

21. I have suggested a way to conceptualize the process of constructing theology in Anders Runesson, *O That You Would Tear Open the Heavens and Come Down! On the Historical Jesus, Jonas Gardell, and the Breath of God* (Örebro and Skellefteå: Libris and Artos, 2011 [in Swedish]) 131–65; see esp. 150–58 and the charts there.

to whatever museums would be interested in displaying how far human progress has reached since these texts were authored. I believe that this would be a theological mistake, however. The notion of divine judgment is so intertwined with Matthew's Gospel that any attempt at untangling it from the fabric of the text would tear apart the entire narrative and leave us only unintelligible disjointed and incoherent fragments of lettering with little interpretive value. Further, billions of people, both within and outside Christian communities, have been and are still, for good and for bad, influenced or affected in one way or another by interpretations of Matthew's notion of judgment. It would mean little to them, in the bigger scheme of things, to attempt to excise this all-pervasive theme from the text. Better, it seems to me, in terms of identifying the sense-making and problem-solving power of the study of the New Testament in the life of real people (rather than in abstract intellectual conversation rooms) would be to work on hermeneutical strategies that may be applied to the canonical texts in general, and then the judgment theme in particular. As Elna Mouton writes:

> We have seen that the authority of the sacred texts we study lies in their referential power, in their ability to point beyond themselves to an ultimate reality which they could only describe in limited and provisional ways. Their authority for subsequent readers *likewise* resides in the continuing encounter with the God mediated and stimulated by them. Ethically responsible interpretation of these texts therefore calls for a continuous wrestling, for imaginative, Spirit-filled, *faith*-full and rigorously critical reflection on the radically active presence and will of God in ever changing times and circumstances.[22]

She suggests as a way forward a hermeneutic and theology of listening:

> A hermeneutic of listening will pay attention to all the voices represented in the epicentre of New Testament interpretation, refusing mentally to block out the voices that have not been considered important in the past, including the silenced voices within the biblical texts themselves. "Such openness does not eliminate a hermeneutics of suspicion and elevation,

22. Elna Mouton, *The Pathos of New Testament Studies: Of What Use Are We to the Church?* (Stellenbosch: University of Stellenbosch, 2005), 17.

but it does eliminate a hermeneutic of arrogance and of accusation and a presumption that prejudges and presumes the ancient world should look like the modern or that we already have the truth. Humility is part of a hermeneutics of hearing; it seeks to know rather than profess to know."[23]

A basic insight that may be gained from such radical listening to voices silenced is that the very otherness which is restored to the Gospel through historical study is from a theological perspective sacred, as it is part of canonized scripture. For what John P. Meier writes about Jesus is true also of Matthew: "The more we appreciate what Jesus meant in his own time and place, the more 'alien' he will seem to us."[24] Regardless of how we choose to hermeneutically interact with this "other," theological use of historical reconstructions should remind us on a fundamental level that respect for the sacred means respect for the other. Indeed, any interpretive practices that mold the (historical) other in our own image are perhaps best described as an act of hubris in which we attempt to appropriate divine prerogatives.[25]

Second, accepting the basic approach above would mean that readers of Matthew as a normative text should consider theologically the fact that this narrative endorses a life as a follower of Jesus *within Judaism*, with strict law observance in specific Second-Temple period format as its main focus. Again, this does not mean that mainstream Christianity today, which has moved in other directions, should adopt a Matthean way of life. However, if history is to be part of theology at all,[26] it does provide a hermeneutical opportunity for theological

23. Mouton, *Pathos*, 18. The quote within the quote is taken from Klyne Snodgrass, "Reading to Hear: A Hermeneutics of Hearing," *Horizons in Biblical Theology* 24 (2002), 1–32, here 28.

24. Meier, *Marginal Jew*, 1.200. Albert Schweitzer wrote in a similar vein: "There is a deep significance in the fact that whenever we hear the sayings of Jesus we have to enter a realm of thought which is not ours" (*Out of My Life and Thought: An Autobiography. Postscript 1932-1949* by Everett Skillings [translated by C.T. Campion; New York: Mentor Books, 1953], 47–48). Cf. E.P. Sanders, *Jesus and Judaism* (London: SCM Press, 1985), 334: "I am a liberal, modern, secularized Protestant, brought up in a church dominated by low christology and the social gospel. I am proud of the things that that religious tradition stands for. I am not bold enough, however, to suppose that Jesus came to establish it, or that he died for the sake of its principles."

25. Gen 1:27; 5:1–2. Considering human history and sacred scripture in tandem, diversity seems inscribed in the nature of the divine.

26. This, of course, has been part of the protestant project from its very beginnings, and it is also the official Catholic approach to the study of the Bible; see, e.g., *The Interpretation of the Bible in the Church*. Presented by the Pontifical Biblical Commission to Pope John Paul II on April 23, 1993 (as published in *Origins*, January 6, 1994): "[The Bible's] proper understanding not only admits the

efforts to reconsider the concept of "heretic," as well as the exclusion mechanisms and forms of violence that have accompanied it since the time of the church fathers. Just as the canon includes diverse, even contradictory, approaches to Jewish law and religio-ethnic identities, a Christianity that professes to embrace the canon as normative should be able to move beyond attempts at harmonization that ultimately erode the richness of the texts, as well as what, from this perspective, may arguably be understood as God's intentions with them. Such theological procedures, however, require of us the courage to de-center ourselves and our hierarchies, renegotiating our position as the ultimate defenders of the faith in favor of a willingness to share responsibility for truth with those who are not like us. Just as the canon does.

Third, if the story of Jesus is a story about love, as Christianity often insists, then it is also, in Matthew, a story about passionate anger. This pattern of wrath runs through the narrative from beginning to end, and results in a focus on divine judgment. From a theological point of view, it might be of some interest to note the direction of this anger, since its target, if de-individualized, may be understood as transcending the ethno-religiously and culturally specific, whereas the criteria of judgment, based on strict observance of Jewish law, are more firmly rooted in context. Time and again, Matthew's Jesus defines his purpose as not only saving his people (1:21), but more specifically as tending to the crowds, the lost sheep of the house of Israel, the people abused by their leaders (4:23; 9:36; 10:6; 15:24). Divine wrath is, then, primarily unleashed in this story against people embodying various forms of authority in the communities within which we also find the crowds, the victims of what is presented as maladministration (23:1–3); against policy-makers and administrators with both indirect and direct religio-political power, these who are accused of misleading the people (15:14; 23:15–22), judging the innocents (12:7), and even

---

use of this [historical-critical] method but actually requires it." Cf. *Dei Verbum*, 12. Again, this, of course, does not mean that history is, can, or should be the only component as theology is formed.

plotting to eliminate the one whom God had sent to set things right for the oppressed (16:21; 21:38, 45–46; 26:3–5).

Due to this mismanagement of religious and political affairs by characters identified as leaders, confusion is caused among the people, which leads to suffering for all as the land comes under foreign powers (and their gods). As a consequence, the temple, the place where heaven and earth meet, becomes defiled, later to be destroyed. If there is anything that seems theologically applicable in this classic text, which transcends its original setting, it would seem to have to do with a critique of leadership as well as with the divine will to save the people through a process of judgment. From a canonical perspective, this aligns Matthew's message with the prophets of the Hebrew Bible, and forms a bridge between the initial theological questions that triggered this study and the historical analysis undertaken to gain insight into the fundamental problem of oppression as a plight of human societies that transcends the historically particular.

Matthew's story aims ultimately to provide a solution to this problem, through a narrative written for the defeated, those who lack access to positions of power. It is not a text for those in control, for those who run daily business, wherever they may be in society. In God's judgment, the author claims, apparently fixed realities will be reversed, so that the first will be last, and the last will be first (19:30). While such statements surely refer to the final verdict that immediately precedes the new Spirit-infused world order called the kingdom of heaven, things will change already in the here and now as soon as people, regardless of their status, start seeking the righteousness that includes but also reaches beyond the mundane (6:33; 25:34–40). Like the covenant with Abraham, then, and in ways Matthew could not possibly have foreseen, the First Gospel cuts through the boundaries of its own narrative and points beyond itself as salvation, like a seed hidden within the wrath of God, is unleashed and reaches beyond the people of God. The forms this process has taken and will take as it comes to fruition are as contextually circumscribed as Matthew's Gospel itself; there is no theological—or historical—

reason to pretend otherwise. If anything, this may indicate to historian and theologian alike the value of studying each other's work.

* * *

No book is an island; all text is a part of the main, a piece of the continent, made to stand by itself only superficially through the illusion created by the covers of the artifact. Below the surface, signaled only partially by footnotes and other allusions to works consulted and discussions had, the present study is, as much as any, indebted to untold discourses and encounters nurturing its arguments and conclusions. A note, thus, on the context of the book is in order, beginning with my discussion partners as found in published form.

I have aimed at avoiding intellectual ageism, attempting to draw on and integrate insights regardless of whether they were put in writing last year or last century. Spending time, I find, with works whose copyright has long since vanished at least partially circumvents the wheel-inventing industry, destabilizes paradigms of unidimensional interpretive evolution, and inspires humility. To some degree, I have also pursued interaction with research in languages which are less commonly quoted in English scholarship, such as the Scandinavian languages. This reflects, of course, the context of my own academic socialization in Sweden, but I am hoping, too, in this way to widen the conversation and point to shared concerns and connections between continents.

Considering the time during which the research presented in this book has been in the making, it is, with regard to non-published formal and informal conversations, impossible to mention all individuals who have, in different ways, contributed to its argument. Still, aware that any list would necessarily be incomplete, I would be remiss not to mention some of the colleagues and friends that, in special ways, have generously shared with me their time and expertise. I have learned from all, perhaps most from those with whom I disagree.

From Lund University and the early phases of the work I am especially grateful to Birger Olsson, whose encouragement and persistent emphasis on the importance of methodology, sharp eye for textual detail, and interpretive courage have been and continue to be an inspiration. In many ways, Birger embodies the classic academic ideal, in which intellectual curiosity, hermeneutical sensitivity, and simply a wide-ranging knowledge of all things philological, historical, and theological are brought together, creating a space where wisdom is nurtured. Thank you, Birger.

I am very grateful also to Bengt Holmberg, Samuel Byrskog, and the late Birger Gerhardsson, who read and commented on my work as it first took form. Sections of the research were presented at the New Testament Higher Research Seminar in the Department of Theology and Religious Studies in Lund; I am grateful to friends and colleagues, who contributed comments and criticism during these discussions. I benefitted from learning Second-Temple Judaism, Rabbinics, and medieval Judaism under the guidance of Hanne Trautner Kromann, who held the Chair in Jewish studies in Lund, as well as from Göran Larsson, then director at the Swedish Theological Institute in Jerusalem where I studied in 1993. In Lund I also had the privilege of studying and doing research together with Karin Hedner Zetterholm, from whose expertise in Rabbinic literature I have learnt a lot and continue to learn, as we presently work together with Magnus Zetterholm and Cecilia Wassen within the same research project: *Beyond Theology: Ancient Polemics, Identity Formation, and Modern Scholarship*, funded by the Swedish Research Council. I am especially grateful to Karin as she read and commented on parts of the penultimate draft of the manuscript. Funding for the research, as it was first formulated in 2002 as part of a larger project on early Christian Identity formation, which I co-authored with Bengt Holmberg and Dieter Mitternacht, was generously provided by Riksbankens jubileumsfond (The Swedish Foundation for the Humanities and Social Sciences). While I had to leave this funding behind when I moved to Canada in 2003, I remain grateful for the financial support during the critical time when the idea of the monograph began to take concrete form.

From this period in the making of the book, I would also like to mention the late Krister Stendahl, who unexpectedly called me after I had defended my licentiate in 1997 to discuss my interpretation of Matthew and encouraged me to continue on the path I had taken. Subsequently, our conversations extended into other fields as well, and I am grateful to him for generously sharing his insights with a junior scholar. I regret that he never got to see how this particular (reconstructed) story ended, and that we will not be able to continue discussions of the school of Matthew in light of this story and recent developments in synagogue and association studies.

From McMaster University, where I spent twelve good years, I am indebted to several friends and colleagues, especially Stephen Westerholm, Eileen Schuller, and Daniel Machiela, as well as graduate and undergraduate students, for many a discussion of Matthew and Second-Temple Judaism. I am, indeed, grateful to everyone who contributed to inspire the exceptional academic milieu at the department of Religious Studies, including its outstanding administrators, Sheryl Dick, Doreen Drew, and Jennifer Nettleton, whose cheerful professionalism and efficiency are simply amazing. A special thanks to Mark Rowe for running countless of miles with me, in arctic snowstorms, tropical rainstorms, boiling heat—and sometimes quite lovely weather—occasionally joined by the stray coyote and zigzagging between giant squirrels as we prepared for the iconic Around the Bay and other (in)sane but quite compatible alternatives to deskwork. I cannot imagine a better context for critical reflection on the academic study of religion, be it on the Buddha or the Christ. While in Canada, generous funding supporting the research resulting in this book was provided by the Social Sciences and Humanities Research Council (SSHRC); for this I am very grateful.

I arrived at the Faculty of Theology in the University of Oslo in July 2015 just in time to teach a course on Matthew while finalizing the last revisions and conclusions before submitting the manuscript. I am grateful for the very warm welcome I have received from colleagues, students, and administrators here, and I look forward to continuing exploring not only Matthew but Christian and Jewish origins more widely and from a variety of perspectives in this dynamic research and teaching setting.

In addition to the above institutional settings, I have benefitted from conversations with and comments from a range of scholars over the years, whose insights and advice on Matthew have contributed in various ways to the conclusions drawn. I am particularly grateful to Terence L. Donaldson and David C. Sim, who both read and commented on the penultimate draft of the manuscript. I also owe gratitude to E. P. Sanders and Adele Reinhartz, who read and commented on my earlier work on Matthew, and to Donald A. Hagner, Michael P. Knowles, Amy-Jill Levine, Rikard Roitto, and the late Sean Freyne for discussions of the First Gospel and its setting. I would like to extend, too, a word of thanks to my colleagues on the steering committee of the SBL Matthew section: Daniel M. Gurtner, Joel Willitts, Catherine Hamilton, and Michael Barber. Finally, for many and stimulating discussions of theology and history, and the relationship between these modes of seeking knowledge, I am grateful to Rune and Lisbeth Svenson, Maria Holm, Per-Rune Svenson, Karl G. Anderberg, Torbjörn Sjöholm, and Per Anders Sandgren.

Substantial parts of the manuscript were finalized during a month-long research fellowship at the Galilee Center for Studies in Jewish–Christian Relations at the Max Stern Yezreel Valley College, Israel, in July 2014. I am grateful to the Center, and to its Director Faydra Shapiro, for their generosity and the care they took to provide me with an ideal environment for this stage of my work.

I am grateful to Nick Meyer for assistance with putting together the bibliography. A very warm thank-you also to Wally Cirafesi, who not only compiled the indices but also helped with proof-reading and did a final check of bibliographic details. I owe a great debt of gratitude to Neil Elliott at Fortress Press, for his unwavering support and patience as I finalized and submitted the manuscript, and for his careful reading and constructive criticism of my text. Any remaining errors are, of course, my own.

Last but not least my greatest appreciation goes to my wife Anna and to our children Rebecca, Noah, and Rachel, who were all born subsequent to the launch of this research project and have literally spent all their lives with this mysterious fourth sibling "Matthew." Ironically—or not—all four will have flown the nest by September 2016. I am glad, though, that it took me so long to finish the book, since this has allowed me to benefit from their insights as we have discussed difficult Matthean passages and exegeted life together doing so. The book is dedicated to my beloved Anna, who was there from the beginning and is still here. As it happens, her commentary on the Gospel of Mark will be published synchronously with the present study.[27] I have greatly appreciated and learnt from our many discussions of these two earliest portraits of Jesus. My gratefulness, though, goes deeper than theological and historical deliberations, even as they grow from reading texts that lead beyond themselves. Indeed, Anna, μετὰ τὸν θεὸν ἡ σωτηρία μοῦ εἶ σύ.

While I hope the reader will find on the pages to follow analyses that constructively challenge previous scholarship, and perhaps even be convinced by some of the arguments made, I am very much aware of the difficulties involved in a historical endeavor like the present. The problem, I believe, in the reconstruction of a world of ideas and practices that has long been lost lies as much in our own entanglement with our personal and other histories and concerns, conscious and/or subconscious, as it does in complications in the text itself. In the end, after more than two decades of reflection on this Matthean theme, it is clearer to me than ever that "I must ask for my writing the indulgence of the kindly, since it is beyond my capacity to promise a complete and perfect work."[28]

Oslo, St. Lucia's Day, 2015

27. Anna Runesson, *The Kingdom of God has Come Near! The Gospel of Mark* (Örebro: Libris, 2016 [in Swedish]).
28. Eusebius, *Hist. eccl.* 1.3.

Introduction: To Distinguish Good from Evil

> Let us go on toward perfection, leaving behind the basic teaching about
> Christ, and not laying again the foundation: repentance from dead works
> and faith toward God, instruction about baptisms, laying on of hands,
> resurrection of the dead, and eternal judgment. (Heb 6:1–2)

It seems as if the author of Hebrews counted among the simple and
foundational teachings the idea that divine judgment is a reality that
all followers of Jesus should be aware of before even attempting to
move forward toward perfection.[1] The modern reader of the texts
included in the New Testament, a collection unknown to the author
of Hebrews, may be excused, however, for pointing out that there
was considerable disagreement among early Christ-believers regarding
most of these elementary teachings, including the theme of divine
judgment. While counted among the foundational beliefs by all—and
perhaps, for that very reason—divine judgment and its (non-
apocalyptic and apocalyptic) consequences was a reality considered
from different perspectives.

The basic conviction behind all ideas about divine judgment is the
simple but, for most people in the ancient Mediterranean world,
crucially important claim that a god or gods have an interest in and
claim authority over human beings, the world, and events taking place
in history.[2] Such beliefs may take various forms, depending on the

---

1. The author compares these teachings to food for infants, as opposed to solid food for the mature,
who have been "trained by practice to distinguish good from evil" (Heb 5:12–14).
2. Cf. Hermann Spieckermann, "Wrath and Mercy as Crucial Terms of Theological Hermeneutics,"
in *Divine Wrath and Mercy in the World of Antiquity* (edited by Reinhard G. Kratz and Hermann

religio-cultural and social context in which individuals and groups happen to live. What is so intriguing about these discourses on divine wrath and judgment is, however, that such notions, often harshly articulated, tend to mark the boundaries not only of mental constructs of an ideal world, but also of the social worlds in which the concepts are formed and incarnated.[3] This means that judgment discourse becomes inherently important for authorities in various religious settings, since they may refer to such traditions or texts in order to mark the boundaries of their communities, outline what distinguishes the good life from its opposite, and emphasize the importance of obedience. Indeed, assertions making reference to divine judgment orient the reader toward the heart of fundamental issues of identity in any given text or community.

The analysis of ideas about divine wrath will therefore prove essential to the understanding of the overall pattern of thought of a specific text, as well as of core aspects of the identity and social practices of a religious group. It goes without saying that an understanding of the former, the pattern of the text, must precede insights into the latter, the social setting in which the text came into being, although it is true that only limited understanding can be achieved without reference to context. This book has its focus on the primary task of understanding the pattern of divine judgment in the text, and I have chosen to put the spotlight on what is probably the single most influential New Testament text of all times—the Gospel of Matthew. As it happens, this narrative is also more concerned with

Spieckermann; FAT 33; Tübingen: Mohr Siebeck, 2008), 3–16: "Wrath and mercy of gods are among the most significant divine features of any religion in antiquity. [...] In any religious system the relation of wrath and mercy is considerably dependent on the interplay of authoritative texts and individual experiences treasured in the collective memory and interpreted by philosophical and theological experts" (3).

3. Cf. the more general discussion of the relationship between text and the formation of lifestyle in Warren Carter, *Matthew and the Margins: A Socio-Political and Religious Reading* (London: T & T Clark, 2000), 9–14. See also, Stephen Westerholm, *Understanding Matthew: The Early Christian Worldview of the First Gospel* (Grand Rapids: Baker Academic, 2006), 141–44, who discusses the implications of the fact that Matthew is a story about the past for the impact it may have on later readers as they understand their own lives in light of the story. See also idem, "Hearing the Gospels of Matthew and Mark," in *Mark and Matthew. Comparative Readings II: Hermeneutics, Reception History, Theology* (edited by Eve-Marie Becker and Anders Runesson; WUNT 304; Tübingen: Mohr Siebeck, 2013)m 245–58.

divine judgment than any other early text written by believers in Jesus.[4]

Divine Judgment in Church and Academy

Over the centuries, the diversity found in the New Testament texts has inspired thinkers within both church and academy to describe, analyze, and claim as theologically or historically authoritative a variety of understandings of why and how the God of Israel would be judging the world. In the history of the church, certain periods have seen interest in divine judgment peak, often as such notions have become intertwined with other doctrines against the background of more general understandings of salvation and its requirements. It seems, for example, that God's judgment of the Jewish people and their "religion" became particularly important for the (non-Jewish) church fathers in late antiquity.[5] Another illustration of this phenomenon, with enormous influence on the church theologically, and, as it turned out, organizationally, is the controversies during the Reformation in the sixteenth century, which related, in one way or another, to practices and debates in which ideas about divine judgment were a defining element.[6]

---

4. On the centrality of divine judgment in Matthew's Gospel, see, e.g., Gerhard Barth, "Matthew's Understanding of the Law," in *Tradition and Interpretation in Matthew* (edited by Günther Bornkamm, Gerhard Barth, and Heinz Joachim Held; London: SCM Press, 1963), 58–164, 62; Daniel Marguerat, *Le jugement dans l'évangile de Matthieu* (2nd ed.; Geneva: Labor et Fides, 1995), 13; Blaine Charette, *The Theme of Recompense in Matthew's Gospel* (Sheffield: Sheffield Academic press, 1992), 13; David C. Sim, *Apocalyptic Eschatology in the Gospel of Matthew* (Cambridge: Cambridge University Press, 1996), 110. The correlation between this concern for divine judgment—and thus, also boundary-marking—on the one hand, and the extraordinary success of Matthew's Gospel in terms of its reception in various communities and societies as the Jesus movement spread and developed into what we know as Christianity, is intriguing, but lies beyond the parameters of the present study. It is, however, a topic worthy of further social-scientifically-oriented reception-historical analyses. For discussion of this theme as it relates to the production of the Gospel in the first century, see Anders Runesson, "Rethinking Early Jewish–Christian Relations: Matthean Community History as Pharisaic Intragroup Conflict," *JBL* 127:1 (2008): 95–132.
5. See discussion in Anders Runesson, "Judging the Theological Tree by its Fruit: The Use of the Gospels of Mark and Matthew in Official Church Documents on Jewish–Christian Relations," in *Mark and Matthew. Comparative Readings II: Hermeneutics, Reception History, Theology* (edited by Eve-Marie Becker and Anders Runesson; WUNT 304; Tübingen: Mohr Siebeck, 2013), 189–228, esp. 189–93.
6. Most famously, these debates orbited the sale of indulgences and Martin Luther's insistence on the doctrine of righteousness through faith alone (*sola fide*), without works.

Many of these debates have been replicated over the centuries in academic discursive trajectories focused on the New Testament texts, although the university setting has given birth to an understanding of authority as dependent on the proper use of historical-critical methodologies, rather than on rulings issued by ordained bishops and priests. For example, it has been quite common among Protestant scholars to assume, without discussion, the existence in the first century of "Jews" and "Christians" as distinct groups, and then to move on to construe their respective views on judgment, reward, punishment, and salvation as antithetical. First-century Jews, on the one hand, are said to have believed in "works righteousness" based on the ability of individuals to uphold the law; Christians (i.e., followers of Jesus), on the other hand, are claimed to have embraced a theological worldview in which judgment is not based on "the law," or "works," but on Jesus's sacrifice, which is to be accepted in faith.[7] Such interpretive procedures and the results they have produced have matched quite closely, and sustained, Protestant–Catholic debates that originated in the sixteenth century. "The Jews" or "the Pharisees" of the Gospel narratives have been understood to incarnate judgment-related doctrines ascribed to contemporary Catholics, and the hero of the texts (Jesus) has been made to conform to Protestant convictions.

Hermeneutically, there are, thus, two larger problems here that

---

7. See, e.g., the chapter entitled "Der Lohngedanke im Neuen Testament" in Günther Bornkamm, *Studien zu Antike und Urchristentum. Gesammelte Aufsätze*, band II (Munich: Chr. Kaiser Verlag, 1959) especially 69–71. See also Wilhelm Pesch, *Der Lohngedanke in der Lehre Jesu vergleichen mit der religiösen Lohnlehre des Spätjudentums* (Munich: Karl Zink, 1955), 143: "An die Stelle eines Gesetzeskodex tritt jetzt die unbedingte Nachfolge Jesu, an die Stelle der Selbsterlösung durch Gesetzeswerke die Erlösung durch das Blut des Erlösers Jesu. Damit ist jeder Formalismus und Legalismus für alle Zeit verurteilt." Cf. the more general critique of similar perspectives by Charette, *Recompense*, 13: "Evidence of scholarly unease is seen in the fact that discussions of Jesus' teaching on reward are frequently dominated by the issue of 'grace versus merit' and are concerned to highlight the differences of the teaching of Jesus and the teaching of early Judaism." Of course, the seminal work of E.P. Sanders, *Paul and Palestinian Judaism: A Comparison of Patterns of Religion* (London: SCM Press, 1977), especially the first part of the book, which is dedicated to understanding Second-Temple Judaism, has been of tremendous importance for the development of a new interpretive paradigm with regard to issues relating to judgment and salvation in Judaism. Still, there is always the risk even when painting a positive portrait of "the other" (in relation to Christ-believers) to create this "other" in one's own (Christian/protestant) image, so that similarity is what constitutes the basis for appreciation. Cf. the recent critical discussion of Sanders's main conclusions in Chris VanLandingham, *Judgment and Justification in Early Judaism and the Apostle Paul* (Peabody: Hendrickson, 2006).

stand in the way for the historian interested in first-century ideas about divine judgment and salvation: inter-church debates as they took form in the Western churches during the Reformation and which have been replicated in academic discourses, on the one hand, and Christian anti-Jewish traditions with roots in late-antique concerns about construing and sustaining separate (non-Jewish) Christian and (Rabbinic) Jewish identities, on the other.[8] These hermeneutical obstacles are related to several other key issues that tend to obstruct our view as we try to understand the New Testament, one of the most important and persistent being that of distinct Jewish and Christian identities. Scholars today, regardless of whether they are Jews or Christians or belong to or identify with any other denominational or non-denominational worldview and/or community, live in societies in which there are clearly identifiable institutional boundaries between mainstream Judaism and Christianity, between synagogue and church. Our own immediate context undoubtedly affects, unconsciously, the way we talk about and construe ancient groups and their convictions.

Further, it is also important to recognize the fact that since history is often perceived as playing a role in contemporary identity formation and preservation, and the first-century texts under investigation are considered sacred by Christians, it has been and continues to be all too easy for both Christian and Jewish scholars of the New Testament to identify in these texts beliefs which, in one way or the other, support present-day denominational boundaries. In such hermeneutical processes, the terminology used by the historian ("Jews" and

---

8. On the formation of Christian identity during the early centuries, including discussion of terminology, see Anders Runesson, "Inventing Christian Identity: Paul, Ignatius, and Theodosius I," in *Exploring Early Christian Identity* (edited by Bengt Holmberg; WUNT 226; Tübingen: Mohr Siebeck, 2008), 59–92. The problem of protestant convictions coming through in historical research on Matthew has been noted by Ulrich Luz, *The Theology of the Gospel of Matthew* (Cambridge: Cambridge University Press, 1995), 49–50, who, as he comments on the Sermon on the Mount, writes: "[I]ts central thrust is the justification by grace alone of those who strive for righteousness. Such paraphrases may puzzle people who have been trained to think in terms of Protestant theology of justification. However, they will be familiar to those who proceed from Jewish thought." Similar Protestant influence on the research process is also present in many studies on Paul and judgment. See David W. Kuck, *Judgment and Community Conflict: Paul's Use of Apocalyptic Judgment Language in 1 Corinthians 3:5–4:5* (Leiden: Brill, 1992), 1–7. Regarding the question of anti-Judaism as related to judgment discourse in Matthew's Gospel, see the discussion in Marguerat, *Jugement*, 575ff.

"Christians," "Judaism" and "Christianity," "synagogue" and "church") often complicates matters further, since it replicates modern ideas about distinct and even irreconcilable identities as if these were present in the first-century, an (often unstated) assumption, which is demonstrably false.[9]

Related to such mechanisms of interpretation is the tendency among some scholars to stress a single harmonizing perspective when investigating the various texts included in the canon.[10] Such inclinations may be ascribed to more general human leanings toward uniformity rather than diversity as analytical work is to be synthesized and ancient meaning translated into modern sense. This interpretive habit may also, however, be understood as related to a theological paradigm in which theology is thought of as building more on a uniform construal of historical meaning than on the often ambiguous and diverse voices of the historical "other."[11] When combined with the above problem of modern identity-sustaining hermeneutical mechanisms, this preference for uniformity in thought and practice, as applied to texts included in the Christian canon, is perhaps one of the more difficult obstacles to overcome for the historian.

Considerations such as these should lead, in my view, to a realization

---

9. "Christianity" (Greek: *christianismos*) as a term appears for the first time in the second century in the writings of Ignatius of Antioch. The term *christianos*, however, occurs only three times in the New Testament, and, arguably, does not mean what we today mean when we use the English term "Christian"; the term should, rather, be understood as a designation comparable to "Pharisee," or "Sadducee," indicating Jewish messianic convictions and lifestyles. See discussion in Runesson, "Inventing Christian Identity"; cf. idem "The Question of Terminology: The Architecture of Contemporary Discussions on Paul," in *Paul Within Judaism: Restoring the First-Century Context to the Apostle* (edited by Mark Nanos and Magnus Zetterholm; Minneapolis: Fortress, 2015), 53–77. Further, "Church" is erroneously used to translate *ekklēsia* in most English bibles; this term was one of many used in the first century, in addition to Greco-Roman uses, to designate synagogue institutions. For synagogue terminology and sources, see Anders Runesson, Donald D. Binder, and Birger Olsson, *The Ancient Synagogue From its Origins to 200 C.E.: A Source Book* (AJEC 72; Leiden: Brill, 2008). For a comprehensive analysis of Greco-Roman, Jewish, and Christ-follower uses of the term *ekklēsia*, see Ralph Korner, "*Before 'Church': Political, Ethno-Religious and Theological Implications of the Collective Designation of Pauline Christ-Followers as Ekklēsiai*" (Ph.D. diss., McMaster University, 2014).
10. A recent example of this may be found in Alan P. Stanley, *Did Jesus Teach Salvation by Works? The Role of Works in Salvation in the Synoptic Gospels* (Eugene: Pickwick Publications, 2006). Such tendencies, however, have been around for more than a millennium in the interpretation of biblical texts.
11. On the relationship between history and theology, see the discussion in Anders Runesson, *O That You Would Tear Open the Heavens and Come Down! On the Historical Jesus, Jonas Gardell, and the Breath of God* (Örebro and Skellefteå: Libris and Artos, 2011 [in Swedish]), especially 131–65.

of the necessity of abandoning—on historical and theological (and ethical) grounds—any attempts at harmonizing the obvious diversity that inescapably must exist in all human societies and within all worldviews that individuals and groups happen to entertain. Indeed, the present study of judgment discourse in the Gospel of Matthew began as a study of divine wrath in the Synoptic Gospels. Very soon, I realized, however, that Matthew's perspective differed in significant ways from Mark's and, especially, Luke's. This made it necessary to narrow down the investigation to deal with Matthew only, as a first step in a larger investigation. The First Gospel, it seemed to me then as it does now, has, contrary to the other Gospels, a very structured and coherent approach to divine judgment, as if this theme were at the heart of what the text is trying to communicate. As many have pointed out before and as we noted above, Matthew is more concerned with the judgment theme than any other New Testament text. Divine judgment is, indeed, at the center of the proclamation of the good news, according to this Gospel. This, in turn, means that if we can reconstruct Matthew's perception of divine judgment, we will have reached a fuller understanding of the historical nature and aim of this text as a whole, which may then clarify its relationship to the other Gospels within which such care regarding consistency and emphasis is not discernable. In other words, renewed study of the judgment theme in Matthew's Gospel will not only have implications for our appreciation of a fundamental concern in the theo-ritual pattern of this text, but will also contribute insights to the wider discussion of how to locate this narrative in relation to other contemporary texts and the socio-political and religious settings in which the Jesus movement emerged.

Some notes on Matthew's Judgment in Recent Discussion

As can be expected, the present book is not the first to realize the importance of judgment discourse for the understanding of Matthew's Gospel. While several studies have recently been published that focus on divine judgment and its function in particular texts, especially Paul and the historical Jesus,[12] and while the judgment theme in Matthew was dealt with in several important articles in the twentieth century,[13] our Gospel has received more comprehensive treatment, from different perspectives, in five monographs of particular interest to the present study, authored by Daniel Marguerat, Blaine Charette, David C. Sim, Petri Luomanen, and, most recently, Nathan Eubank.[14]

David Sim's survey of research on Matthew's apocalyptic eschatology and judgment still gives the best concise overview of the state of research, covering the most important studies and trends

12. For the historical Jesus, see Marius Reiser, *Jesus and Judgment: The Eschatological Proclamation in its Jewish Context* (Minneapolis: Fortress, 1997); Steven Bryan, *Jesus and Israel's Traditions of Judgment and Restoration* (Cambridge: Cambridge University Press, 2002). In studies on Paul, analysis of the judgment theme is often interrelated with questions raised by the so-called New Perspective (or even more recently, the Radical New Perspective, now also called the Paul-within-Judaism perspective) and the problem of justification. Studies specifically addressing judgment include Kuck, *Judgment and Community Conflict*; Kent L. Yinger, *Paul, Judaism, and Judgment According to Deeds* (Cambridge: Cambridge University Press, 1999); Matthias Konradt, *Gericht und Gemeinde: Eine Studie zur Bedeutung und Funktion von Gerichtsaussagen im Rahmen der paulinischen Ekklesiologie und Ethik im 1 Thess und 1 Kor* (Berlin: Walter de Gruyter, 2003); VanLandingham, *Judgment and Justification*. For discussion of the theme of divine judgment in the Hebrew Bible and Early Jewish texts, including the New Testament, see Anders Runesson, "Judgment," *New Interpreters Dictionary of the Bible* (edited by Katharine Doob Sakenfeld; Nashville: Abingdon, 2008), 457–66. The relationship between the motif of judgment, according to works in Ps 62 and the New Testament as well as other Jewish texts, is analyzed in Kyong-Shik Kim, *God will Judge Each One According to Works: Judgment According to Works and Psalm 62 in Early Judaism and the New Testament* (Berlin: Walter de Gruyter, 2011). The study of divine judgment in 1 Enoch and Sirach receives in-depth treatment in chapters five and six of Randal A. Argall, *1 Enoch and Sirach: A Comparative Literary and Conceptual Analysis of the Themes of Revelation, Creation and Judgment* (Atlanta: Scholars Press, 1995), 165–247. Argall argues not only that these two works take different approaches to divine judgment, but also, that they do so in awareness of one another's traditions, presenting rival ideas on the matter. A wider approach to judgment in various ancient cultures (Israelite, Hittite, Babylonian, Iranian, Egyptian, Greek, Roman, Christian, as well as aspects of Indian and Chinese traditions) is found in J. Gwyn Griffiths, *The Divine Verdict: A Study of Divine Judgment in the Ancient Religions* (Leiden: Brill, 1991). See also, more recently, Reinhard G. Kratz and Hermann Spieckermann (eds.), *Divine Wrath and Mercy in the World of Antiquity* (FAT 33; Tübingen: Mohr Siebeck, 2008). This volume addresses the relevant theme moving from the ancient Near East to Plato and the New Testament, and from there, into Late Antiquity, including also studies of Early Christianity and Islam, respectively. A more theologically-oriented approach was published very recently, indicating continued keen interest among scholars and students in these types of questions: Alan P. Stanley (ed.), *Four Views on the Role of Works at the Final Judgment* (Grand Rapids: Zondervan, 2013).

13. But see also Luz special section on this theme in his commentary, *Matthew*, 3.285–96.

14. Marguerat, *Jugement*; Charette, *Recompense*; Sim, *Apocalyptic Eschatology*; Petri Luomanen, *Entering the Kingdom of Heaven: A Study on the Structure of Matthew's View of Salvation* (WUNT 2.101; Tübingen: Mohr Siebeck, 1998); Nathan Eubank, *Wages of Cross-Bearing and Debt of Sin: The Economy of Heaven in Matthew's Gospel* (Berlin: Walter de Gruyter, 2013). On the history of research, note also the helpful discussion of the role of grace and works by Luomanen, *Entering the Kingdom*, 7–36. In addition to these studies, a doctoral thesis on the theme of soteriology was defended in 2014 at Murdoch University: Mothy Varkey, "Salvation in Continuity: A Reconsideration of Matthew's Soteriology" (Ph.D. diss., Murdoch University, 2014). This thesis has a special focus on the law and its salvific function in Matthew.

before 1996.[15] Sim begins his discussion by noting Johannes Weiss' and Albert Schweitzer's emphasis on the apocalyptic theme more generally in New Testament scholarship, which relates closely to judgment discourse. Their approach, in turn, influenced key studies on Matthew, such as Burnett H. Streeter's 1924 publication.[16] Streeter understood Matthew's emphasis on apocalyptic judgment and imminent end-time expectation to be the creation of an apocalyptic sect in the postwar period, dating the Gospel to ca. 85 CE and locating it in Antioch. This analysis of Matthew, which provides an important point of departure for Sim's own perspective on the nature and location of the Gospel,[17] was, however, soon to become neglected.

Perhaps the most influential of all studies on Matthew with regard to our topic has been Günther Bornkamm's article "End-Expectation and Church in Matthew."[18] Bornkamm argued that the eschatological orientation of Matthew's Gospel had the purpose of exhorting Christ-believers to attain the higher righteousness required by Jesus's teaching, in this way domesticating the apocalyptic theme of the Gospel in the service of community-building. The major effect of Bornkamm's work on scholarship was precisely this: Matthew's eschatology came to be seen as intertwined with his ecclesiology, and the function of judgment discourse was reduced to paraenesis meant to instruct Christ-believers in Matthew's present; Matthew's community was transformed into a non-apocalyptic, well-established group. In this context, Sim's quote from Howard C. Kee is worth repeating: "The

---

15. Sim, *Apocalyptic Eschatology*, 3–14. See also Luomanen, *Entering the Kingdom*, 7–34. For a recent discussion of scholarship on Matthew more broadly, see David C. Sim, "Matthew: The Current State of Research," in *Mark and Matthew. Comparative Readings I: Understanding the Earliest Gospels in the First-Century Settings* (edited by Eve-Marie Becker and Anders Runesson; WUNT 271; Tübingen: Mohr Siebeck, 2011), 33–51, and Daniel M. Gurtner, "The Gospel of Matthew from Stanton to Present: A Survey of Some Recent Developments," in *Jesus, Matthew's Gospel, and Early Christianity: Studies in Memory of Graham N. Stanton* (edited by Daniel M. Gurtner, Joel Willitts, and Richard A. Burridge; London: T & T Clark, 2011), 23–38. The following discussion will draw upon Sim's 1996 work to structure previous scholarship.

16. Burnett Hillman Streeter, *The Four Gospels: A Study of Origins* (London: Macmillan, 1924).

17. See also David C. Sim, *The Gospel of Matthew and Christian Judaism: The History and Social Setting of the Matthean Community* (Edinburgh: T&T Clark, 1998).

18. Günther Bornkamm, "End-Expectation and Church in Matthew," in *Tradition and Interpretation in Matthew* (edited by Günther Bornkamm, Gerhard Barth, and Heinz Joachim Held; London: SCM Press, 1963), 15–51. See also Bornkamm, *Studien zu Antike und Urchristentum*.

church of Matthew, with the apostolic foundation going back to Peter as sovereign and arbiter . . . is an established institution, not an apocalyptic sect."[19]

Daniel Marguerat's extensive treatment of the judgment theme in Matthew continues the research trajectory established by Bornkamm, and does so in a very comprehensive way.[20] There is much in his study to be commended. The judgment theme is rightly stated to be the center of Matthew's thought,[21] and the focus on the criteria of judgment, as based on Jesus's interpretation of Jewish law, is certainly to the point, although such a claim does not exclude an interest on the part of the evangelist in the actual judgment act itself, as well as its consequences.[22] It is also clear that divine judgment applies to all, including Jesus's disciples. On this point, however, Marguerat's use of terminology, in my view, leads the investigation in a problematic direction.

Marguerat's argument takes as point of departure a terminological distinction between Israel and the disciples, as if for Matthew, Jesus and his followers would not be "Israel," but rather, a new category, "the church."[23] Matthew's Gospel, however, does not support such a distinction.[24] As far as the criteria of judgment are concerned, there is only one major distinction between groups in Matthew, and that is between Jews and non-Jews.[25] The fact that the narrative then distinguishes between individuals and groups *within* Israel as either

---

19. Howard C. Kee, *Christian Origins in Sociological Perspective* (London: SCM Press, 1980), 143, as quoted in Sim, *Apocalyptic Eschatology*, 7.
20. Marguerat, *Jugement*. Cf. discussion of Marguerat's analysis in Sim, *Apocalyptic Eschatology*, 6–9; Luomanen, *Entering the kingdom*, 21–23.
21. Marguerat, *Jugement*, 13.
22. Cf. the critique of Sim, *Apocalyptic Eschatology*, 6–7, 9. On the extreme representations of violence in Matthew's Gospel, see most recently, John S. Kloppenborg, "The Representation of Violence in Synoptic Parables," in *Mark and Matthew. Comparative Readings I: Understanding the Earliest Gospels in the First-Century Settings* (edited by Eve-Marie Becker and Anders Runesson; WUNT 271; Tübingen: Mohr Siebeck, 2011), 323–51.
23. The same problem is present in Wolfgang Trilling, *Das Wahre Israel: Studien zur Theologie des Matthäusevangeliums* (3rd edition; Munich: Kösel, 1964). This leads Trilling to assume that "Israel" is rejected as "the Church" takes over. As we shall see, such conclusions are based on the use of modern terminology inconsistent with Matthew's text.
24. On terminological issues, see above note 9. Similar terminological problems are present in Charette, *Recompense*, and many other studies on Matthew.
25. On this distinction, see further discussion below.

good or bad is a different issue altogether; the same criteria are valid for all who are Jews, including Jesus's disciples. It follows, therefore, that it would be incorrect to conclude, as Marguerat does, that "Israel" has been replaced by the "church."[26] The fact that *ekklēsia* was used as a synagogue term by other Jews in the first century further problematizes any such claims.[27] The importance for Matthew's judgment theme of the distinction between Jews and non-Jews, and the non-existence of a third category "church" in between, warrant further discussion and we shall therefore return to this issue below.

In addition, the fall of the Jerusalem temple, which Marguerat interprets as a key indication of God's rejection of Israel, must be re-considered. In Matthew's narrative, the temple's destruction is a catastrophe.[28] It is described as the ultimate, although by Jesus predicted, tragedy, since the temple is God's dwelling place (23:21) and its destruction is part of the devastation of the city of the great king (5:35), the holy city (4:5; 27:53). The Gospel blames the Pharisees and scribes associated with them for this cataclysmic event,[29] and the destruction of the city and the temple is understood as God's judgment, which, while caused primarily by the Pharisees, is affecting the entire people (cf. 21:33–46[30]). Matthew's point, indeed the very heart of Matthew's message, would, in fact, be the opposite of Marguerat's claim: *despite* the fall of the temple—which most Jews would interpret not as Rome's triumph but as God's judgment on Israel[31]—Israel is *not*

---

26. Marguerat, *Jugement*, 239–407.
27. See, e.g., most recently, Ralph Korner, "*Ekklēsia* as a Jewish Synagogue Term: Some Implications for Paul's Socio-Religious Location," *JJMJS* 2 (2015): 53–78 (http://www.jjmjs.org/). The interpretive dilemma created when ancient Jewish synagogue terminology is not taken into account can also be seen in the interesting, but problematically entitled edited volume by Charles E. Carlston and Craig A. Evans, *From Synagogue to Ecclesia: Matthew's Community at the Crossroads* (WUNT 334; Tübingen: Mohr Siebeck, 2014).
28. On the place of the Temple in Matthew's Gospel, see Daniel M. Gurtner, *The Torn Veil: Matthew's Exposition of the Death of Jesus* (Cambridge: Cambridge University Press, 2007) especially 98–126.
29. As implied by the narrative progression in Matt 23:1–24:2. Jesus's death, however, is presented in the passion narrative as largely unrelated to the Pharisees, and instead blamed on the priests and the elders of Jerusalem. See further discussion below, chapter 3.2.1.
30. It should be noted that Matthew combines in this parable accusations against Pharisees, on the one hand, and chief priests, on the other.
31. This pattern of thought goes back to the interpretation of the fall of the first temple in the prophetic literature and continues in Josephus, who is blaming Jewish "bandits" for the fall of the second temple. In Rabbinic literature (cf. *b. Yoma* 9b), "baseless hatred" is said to have caused God's wrath and the ensuing destruction in 70 CE. The same basic pattern of grave sin leading to

rejected. In fact, Jesus's sacrificial death (26:28) becomes necessary precisely *because* of the (narratively predicted[32]) fall of the temple, "for he will save *his people* [*laos*] from their sins" (1:21).[33]

Having evaluated Marguerat's study as the most comprehensive and final representative of the type of redaction-critical investigation that Bornkamm initiated, and building on the work of Graham Stanton, Donald A. Hagner, and O. Lamar Colpe,[34] David Sim approaches the topic from the wider perspective of apocalyptic eschatology with the ultimate aim of not only descriptively analyzing Matthew's text, but also offering an explanatory model for understanding why the text was composed the way it was.[35] His study is divided into three parts. Part one deals with apocalyptic eschatology and apocalypticism in general, with a special focus on its social setting and function. Part two presents an analysis of Matthew's Gospel, arguing convincingly that it presents us with imminent end-time expectations. Here, chapter five is dedicated specifically to the judgment theme and its connection especially to the resurrection and the re-creation of the cosmos. The third and final part proceeds to reconstruct the social setting of the Matthean community and the function of apocalyptic eschatology within such a setting. Sim paints a harsh picture of the situation in

the destruction of the temple, interpreted as punishment, is present in 4 Ezra, 2 Baruch, and the Apocalypse of Abraham. See further below, chapters 3.2.1.2 and 3.2.2.1.

32. Craig A. Evans, "Predictions of the Destruction of the Herodian Temple in the Pseudepigrapha, Qumran Scrolls and Related Texts," *JSP* 10 (1992): 89–147, has argued convincingly that it is likely that the historical Jesus (as several other groups and individuals) claimed that the temple would be destroyed. When Matthew's Gospel is being written in the late first century, followers of Jesus probably experienced the destruction that occurred in 70 CE as "proof" that the eschatological events had begun, and this affected how the Gospel was composed, especially the emphasis on judgment in the text. But such theorizing is beyond the scope of the present study, which focuses on Matthew's narrative world. On the Jerusalem temple as defiled and rejected according to other Jewish groups, see also Jonathan Klawans, *Purity, Sacrifice, and the Temple: Symbolism and Supersessionism in the Study of Ancient Judaism* (Oxford: Oxford University Press, 2006), chapter 5 (145–74).

33. For discussion of this point, see Anders Runesson, "Purity, Holiness, and the Kingdom of Heaven in Matthew's Narrative World," in *Purity, Holiness, and Identity in Judaism and Christianity: Essays in Memory of Susan Haber* (edited by Carl Ehrlich, Anders Runesson, and Eileen Schuller; WUNT 305; Tübingen: Mohr Siebeck, 2013), 144–80.

34. Graham N. Stanton, "The Gospel of Matthew and Judaism," *BJRL* 66 (1984): 264–84; Donald A. Hagner, "Apocalyptic Motifs in the Gospel of Matthew: Continuity and Discontinuity," *HBT* 7 (1985): 53–82; O. Lamar Cope, "To the Close of the Age: The Role of Apocalyptic Thought in the Gospel of Matthew," in *Apocalyptic and the New Testament: Essays in Honour of J. Louis Martyn* (edited by Joel Marcus and Marion L. Soards; Sheffield: Sheffield Academic Press, 1989), 113–24.

35. Sim, *Apocalyptic Eschatology*.

which the Mattheans lived in postwar Antioch. Alienated from other Jews ("formative Judaism") and the gentile world, as well as from other Christ-believers who adhered to a law-free gospel, the Mattheans embraced apocalypticism and apocalyptic eschatology in order to legitimize their sectarian group, explain its current circumstances, and invalidate any alternative symbolic universes.

Sim's study is refreshingly perceptive and cogently argued, not shying away from conclusions that make sense historically, but which may be perceived as theologically problematic by many today. Most of Sim's insights are of lasting value, especially the insistence on the Jewish nature of the text and the community behind it, as well as the emphasis on Matthew's acute sense of the imminent coming of the end times.[36] Sim's approach does not, however, address all the problems in earlier redaction-critically oriented studies on divine judgment in Matthew. His study serves a partly different purpose, presenting the most thorough argument for an apocalyptic-eschatological reading of Matthew published so far. But this approach does not, in itself, invalidate attempts at understanding the pattern of thought and practice as it may be reconstructed from within Matthew's narrative world itself; neither does it undermine a redaction-critical, or composition-critical, approach as such.

The two different approaches represent overlapping but ultimately different types of investigations, and results originating from one approach need not necessarily contradict conclusions drawn on the basis of the other. Rather, while not denying the intense apocalyptic eschatology of the text (indeed, I would argue that the text was authored precisely in such a mindset), we need to re-read Matthew, paying close attention to what are often considered non-apocalyptic features. Contra Kee, there is no obvious conflict between the idea of an organized community, which entertains views on judgment as active in the community in the present, on the one hand, and intense eschatological expectations, on the other, as also the sectarian writings

---

36. Regarding the social setting in which Matthew's Gospel was authored, I have argued for a slightly different scenario in "Re-Thinking Early Jewish–Christian Relations," 95–132, where I locate the origin of the text in the Galilee, rather than in Antioch.

among the Dead Sea Scrolls indicate. The parenetic function of judgment discourse, and whatever role such may play in community-building, does not, in and of itself, exclude an imminent end-time expectation, but may be seen as an integral component of it.

The discussion of how Matthew narratively construes divine wrath and judgment is thus in need of further analytic-descriptive elaboration beyond Marguerat's study in order to address problems that can be solved within the same, or similar, methodological discourse. A new perspective is needed, based on more recent research on the relationship between Jews and non-Jews in the Gospel. In fact, such an investigation may produce further support, in addition to the exploration of the larger context of the apocalyptic theme, for an understanding of Matthew's Gospel as a first-century Jewish text, and so contribute to the current more general shift away from reading the New Testament against the *background* of Jewish texts, towards, in my view, the more historically attuned approach, in which these texts are seen as (diverse) *expressions* of Second-Temple Judaism.[37]

---

37. For such approaches see, e.g., John W. Marshall, *Parables of War: Reading John's Jewish Apocalypse* (Waterloo: Wilfrid Laurier University Press, 2001), who identifies and argues extensively for the book of Revelation as a Jewish, not a Christian text. See also Marshall's terminological discussion in "John's Jewish (Christian?) Apocalypse," in *Jewish-Christianity Reconsidered: Re-Thinking Groups and Texts* (edited by Matt Jackson McCabe: Minneapolis: Fortress, 2007), 233–56. Cf. the methodology of Serge Ruzer, *Mapping the New Testament: Early Christian Writings as a Witness for Jewish Biblical Exegesis* (Leiden: Brill, 2007), who explores the New Testament, especially Matthean passages, in search of common Jewish interpretive techniques, which later reoccurs in rabbinic writings. For Paul see, e.g., Mark Nanos, *The Irony of Galatians: Paul's Letter in First-Century Context* (Minneapolis: Fortress, 2002), 3; Neil Elliott, *The Arrogance Nations: Reading Romans in the Shadow of Empire* (Minneapolis: Fortress, 2008), 15. One of the latest contributions in this area is Daniel Boyarin's *The Jewish Gospels: The Story of the Jewish Christ* (New York: New Press, 2012), a book that deserves careful attention. Boyarin argues that Mark's Gospel "is best read as a Jewish text, even in its most radical Christological moments" (127); indeed "Gospel Judaism was straightforwardly and completely a Jewish-messianic movement, and the Gospel the story of the Jewish Christ" (156). The "creativity" of Jesus and the Gospels, he further states, "is most richly and compellingly read within the Jewish textual and intertextual world, the echo chamber of a Jewish soundscape of the first century" (160). While I have worked on the present monograph (and earlier studies on Matthew) independently of Boyarin's book, I have come to similar general conclusions based on different types of analyses. I would certainly agree with Boyarin that these texts are best read from within a Jewish textual and intertextual landscape, if what we aim for is a historical understanding of them. See also Thomas R. Blanton IV, "Saved by Obedience: Matthew 1:21 in Light of Jesus' Teaching on the Torah," *JBL* 132:2 (2013): 393–413, who states that the author of Matthew "draws his inspiration" from "the symbolic world of early Judaism" (394), and Craig A. Evans, "The Jewish Christian Gospel Tradition," in *Jewish Believers in Jesus: The Early Centuries* (edited by Oskar Skarsaune and Reidar Hvalvik; Peabody: Hendrickson, 2007), 241–77, who argues that "[t]he Jewishness of Matthew is profound and systemic" (244).

As we address such issues, it is important, as Luomanen has pointed out, that Matthew's understanding of judgment and salvation is not analyzed through the lens provided by (traditional) readings of the Pauline literature, especially with regard to the themes of grace and works and their interrelationship in the judgment process. Luomanen, who introduces his analysis of the structure of Matthew's view of salvation as the first monograph devoted entirely to the soteriology of Matthew,[38] finds E. P. Sanders's comparison of patterns of religion to be useful in limited analyses such as those of the pattern of salvation in Matthew, *if* the approach is slightly modified in terms of the suggested "getting in – staying in" paradigm. As will be discussed below in chapter 2.8, I generally agree that what Sanders calls "covenantal nomism" provides an important theo-ritual matrix for understanding Matthew.[39] Luomanen's approach differs from the present study, though, in that it aims at relating the textual analysis to the socio-religious setting of Matthew's community,[40] and so lets the two tasks inform one another. In terms of conclusions, he focuses on Matthew's relationship with Judaism and argues that Matthew has broken with the local Jewish community and also shows "isolationist attitudes towards other Christian communities as well."[41] For Luomanen, while Matthew seeks to legitimize his community through drawing on Jewish traditions, Jesus and his followers ultimately break "traditional Jewish law."[42] Matthew's view on salvation aligns to some degree with Jewish covenantal nomism, but the role ascribed to Jesus leads Luomanen to conclude that "Matthew was not 'a proper Jew' any more."[43]

While there is much in Luomanen's analysis that is insightful and valuable, the present study departs from his work, both in terms of

---

38. Luomanen, *Entering the Kingdom*, 3.
39. For a definition of covenantal nomism, see E. P. Sanders, *Paul and Palestinian Judaism*, 75.
40. As does David Sim's monograph discussed above.
41. Luomanen, *Entering the Kingdom*, 5.
42. Ibid.
43. Ibid., 5; on Luomanen's understanding of covenantal nomism in Matthew, see 281–84. Luomanen concludes that "Matthew's covenantalism is not Jewish anymore nor is it yet clearly Christian" (283). While the present study certainly supports the conclusion that Matthew's theo-ritual pattern of thought cannot be described as "Christian," I have not been convinced by Luomanen's arguments that it would not qualify as Jewish.

approach and some key conclusions, especially with regard to Matthew's take on Jewish law and its salvific efficacy. As will be argued throughout, *pace* Luomanen's assertions,[44] Matthew's Jesus complains not that his opponents are too strict in their observance of the law, but, on the contrary, that they are not rigorous enough. This inability of his interlocutors, primarily identified as Pharisees, to obey the Jewish law is the very reason why they will be condemned on the day of judgment.[45] In other words, the Matthean Jesus can hardly be described as entertaining a "liberal" attitude toward Jewish law, but should rather be thought of as belonging to a strict school of thought, according to which law observance carries within it salvific significance.[46]

In terms of methodology, it is clear that understanding cannot be had beyond context. I have, however, aimed in this book to focus on the narrative world, as a first-century audience familiar with the socio-cultural and religious setting within which the text was authored would likely have interpreted it. Thus, the pattern of thought and practice in the text as it applies to the theme of divine wrath and salvation will not be explained primarily through references to the socio-cultural and religious location of the Matthean community/ies. Still, however, in order to achieve a plausible first-century reading of the Gospel, contemporary Jewish texts and traditions will have to be dealt with in comparative fashion since they provide a conceptual

---

44. Luomanen, *Entering the Kingdom*, 283.

45. Cf., e.g., Matt 5:20, and cf. discussion in Benno Przybylski, *Righteousness in Matthew and his World of Thought* (Cambridge: Cambridge University Press, 1980). Note that not only Jesus's opponents, but also his followers are warned that lack of observance of the law (as Jesus interprets it) will result in condemnation, regardless of whether these followers acknowledge Jesus as their lord or not; not even their prophecies or their (successful) exorcisms invoking Jesus's name will do on the day of judgment if such observance is lacking (Matt 7:21–23).

46. As Matt 5:17–19 indicates early on in the Gospel, a perspective maintained through the narrative, as we shall see. For discussion, see also William R. G. Loader, *Jesus' Attitude towards the Law: A Study of the Gospels* (Grand Rapids: Eerdmans, 1997), 137–272. Loader, correctly in my opinion, emphasizes the continued validity of the law, including cultic law, although the latter is subordinated under the more important commandments requiring acts of compassion (271). As Loader writes: "Matthew's Jesus upholds Torah and sees his ministry in terms of both fulfilling the law and the prophets and making sure that Torah is rightly understood and fully obeyed. [...] For Matthew, Jesus is the judge to come, offering the grace of forgiveness and instruction, and warning of the consequences of rejection" (271, 272). Varkey, "Salvation in Continuity," develops this theme in even greater detail, showing that the law in Matthew has salvific efficacy. See also Blanton IV, "Saved by Obedience," 393–413.

context within which the Gospel text emerges as theo-ritually logical. Further, in order to understand Matthew's narrative references to groups such as the Pharisees, scribes, and the chief priests, it will be necessary to explain how these groups would have been placed on a first-century socio-political and religious map, since Matthew uses these characters to conceptualize the limits of salvation, and the location of these groups in Jewish society will shed light on Matthew's understanding of divine judgment.[47] My focus will remain, though, on the world of the text and how divine wrath and salvation is construed within this world.[48]

While Sim and Luomanen work with both the text and its socio-religious location, Nathan Eubank's recent study directs our attention exclusively to the textual world and provides a detailed exegesis of the theme of divine judgment in Matthew. His analysis further supports, in my opinion, an inner-Jewish reading of the Gospel, which is, in some parts, similar to the conclusions of the present study. The book is divided into five chapters, beginning with a contextualization of Matthew's theology of recompense within Judaism and Christianity (chapter 1). The study then analyzes notions of heavenly treasures and debts (chapter 2), and the idea of filling up all righteousness as a way of achieving salvation through a process of re-payment of debts (chapter 3). Cross-bearing is conceptualized as work resulting in wages, and the wages earned include eternal life and positions of prominence (chapter 4). Part of this overall picture is also the idea of a ransom price being paid for those in debt, with reference to Matt 20:28: "[I]t is Jesus' active, obedient giving of his life that earns a surplus of heavenly treasure."[49] This surplus in wages with God is then used to repay the debt of sin for the many. This theme is then developed further in the final chapter, which deals with the passion and resurrection.

---

47. This will be addressed especially in chapter 3 below.
48. While the issue of the identity of the author and/or the communities using Matthew's Gospel will not be dealt with at any length in the present study, I would argue, based on previous studies, that the text was produced by an individual or small group identifying themselves as Jews and presenting their text as a form of (messianically oriented) Judaism to their audience. For details, see Runesson, "Rethinking Early Jewish–Christian Relations."
49. Eubank, *Wages of Cross-Bearing*, 157.

Eubank's analysis is detailed, and in most cases, convincing. His insistence in particular that the nature of a person's actions (or "works") is such that deeds performed in accordance with Jesus's interpretation of Jewish law, including the suffering that may follow from such life-choices ("cross-bearing"), will lead to an accumulation of "wages" to be paid to the doer primarily in the world to come.[50] Failure to live obediently will, conversely, incur "debt," which must be repaid.[51] Still, while all this makes Matthean sense, I believe that further consideration of key concepts such as the covenant and its place in Matthew would have contributed to slightly different conclusions, in which what is often called grace ("to get something for nothing") would have infused the language of wages and debt with important nuances, especially in the case of the mechanisms affecting the possibility of salvation.

A theological theme such as that of judgment and recompense often leads scholars to approach their analysis of concepts as if they were stable throughout the text, as if the text were a map upon which themes are inscribed, so that wherever they would be found, they would signal and repeat established meaning. However, while mapping territory is an important part of the analysis, in my view, the text is better approached as a world in which the progression of the story,

---

50. On the language of debt (in the Q version of the Lord's prayer), cf. Giovanni Battista Bazzana, "*Basileia* and Debt Relief: The Forgiveness of Debts in the Lord's Prayer in the Light of Documentary Papyri," *CBQ* 73 (2011): 511–25. See also Gary A. Anderson, "From Israel's Burden to Israel's Debt: Towards a Theology of Sin in Biblical and Early Second Temple Sources," in *Reworking the Bible: Apocryphal and Related Texts at Qumran. Proceedings of a Joint Symposium by the Orion Center for the Study of the Dead Sea Scrolls and Associated Literature and the Hebrew University Institute for Advanced Studies Research Group on Qumran, 15-17 January, 2002* (edited by Esther G. Chazon et al.; STDJ 58; Leiden: Brill, 2005), 1–30. On "wages" as a biblical metaphor, cf. Tzvi Novik, "Wages From God: The Dynamics of a Biblical Metaphor," *CBQ* 73 (2011): 708–22, whose analysis covers the Hebrew Bible and Ben Sira.

51. An additional point is that, at least in my opinion, Matthew's language of wages and debts should be regarded as metaphorical in the sense that it points beyond itself to a reality, which is anchored in cult. That is, the cultic system as it exists within the law, and upon which the law is dependent (the purpose of the law is, ultimately, to make possible God's presence among his people), is what governs the human–divine relationship, including the reality of divine judgment and salvation. The imagery of "wages" and "debts" functions to point the audience to that reality, explaining in economic terms a cultic truth. While Anderson ("Israel's Debt," 1–2) is certainly correct that metaphors and their use structure the way phenomena are perceived, the opposite is also true, namely, that metaphors grow from specific cultural contexts within which they present things in certain ways, and on some level, make sense to those involved in conversation. This dynamic will be further explored in the analysis to follow in Part I.

in and of itself, is a carrier of meaning.[52] In the narrative world into which the audience is invited, theological themes and concepts need to be understood dynamically in context, since theology is brought to the reader only through the mental picture of the world generated by the author. Thus, I would argue, we must be open to the possibility that Matthew's depiction of judgment and the criteria of judgment change as a consequence of key events taking place in the narrative (cause and effect). After all, the author wants to tell his audience something that cannot be communicated in the "sayings" style of the Gospel of Thomas. As I hope to show in the pages to follow, the fall of the temple and the resurrection of Jesus are two such game-changing events that explain the Gospel and its focus on divine judgment within and beyond the covenant between God and Israel.

The purpose of the present study, which will focus on the narrative progression of the story as well as utilize the developed form of redaction criticism often called composition criticism,[53] is to contribute to the descriptive-analytical discussion of the pattern of thought and practice in Matthew's Gospel as it applies to its central theme of divine judgment.[54] This approach, which will consequently not engage sociological issues or put forward explanatory models related therewith, recognizes that meaning is to be sought on the basis of the composition of the text as a whole, not only of the changes made in redacted material.[55] The basic premise accepted here is that

---

52. Cf. Luz, *Matthew*, 1.9, who asserts that "the Gospel of Matthew intends to be a *book of narration*" (emphasis original). It is appropriate, then, if we seek to recover first-century understandings of this text, to pay methodological attention to narrative aspects of the Gospel.

53. This methodology is presented well by Charette, *Recompense*, 16–19, who locates the approach between (traditional) redaction criticism and narrative criticism.

54. On the composite approach to methodology in investigations concerned with issues of a thematic nature, cf. most recently, Robert H. Gundry, *Peter: False Disciple and Apostate According to Saint Matthew* (Grand Rapids: Eerdmans, 2015), 4. In Gundry's study, "Matthew's Petrine texts will undergo treatment seriatim with the use of redaction, composition, and narrative criticism (although without their terminological paraphernalia)." For this type of approach, he finds support in Pheme Perkins' *Peter: Apostle for the Whole Church* (Columbia: University of South Carolina Press, 1994); see p. 54, where she states that she applies "an eclectic method of analysis that combines results of redaction criticism and narrative criticism" (Gundry, *Peter*, 4n9).

55. Cf. Charette, *Recompense*, 17: "Composition criticism is the product of a recent trend in redaction criticism which, admitting the limitations of earlier forms of the method, recognizes that the concerns of the evangelist are to be found not merely in the study of the changes he has made to his sources but also in the study of the completed work he has produced."

Matthew's Gospel can be read as a highly structured and coherent text that makes (ancient) narrative and theological sense.[56]

The composition-critical approach, applied in tandem with more general concerns focusing on the text as narrative, is important for several reasons. In terms of the meaning(s) triggered by the text, even passages retained verbatim from Mark receive new significance in the story as a whole, based on the literary context in which they have been placed. There is, further, no consensus regarding the sources used by Matthew. While most agree that Mark was the earliest Gospel, and that, in some form, it was used by the author of Matthew,[57] the existence of the hypothetical source Q is disputed.[58] Even if we acknowledge Markan priority, which is, in my view, the most plausible explanation of the material, this does not automatically result in the (historically very unlikely) scenario that Matthew would have known about traditions that occur in Mark's Gospel only from Mark's Gospel. Such considerations complicate any theory about the nature of Matthew's dependence on and use of Mark, without disputing that Matthew did indeed have access to Mark. In this situation, which is further problematized by recent research on the transmission of oral tradition in the first century, continuing into the second century alongside the

---

56. For a recent interpretation of Matthew's structure, see Anders Runesson, "Matthew, Gospel According to," in *The Oxford Encyclopedia of the Books of the Bible* (edited by M. D. Coogan; 2 vols.; Oxford: Oxford University Press, 2011), 2.59–78. The perspective here differs from the otherwise influential entry by John P. Meier in *ABD* 4.622–41, which is mirrored rather closely in the entry on Matthew in the *New Interpreters Dictionary of the Bible* by Michael Joseph Brown (3.839–52).

57. There are some exceptions to this majority view. Recent studies by Armin Baum contest literary interdependence between the Synoptic Gospels. See his *Der mündliche Faktor: Analogien zur synoptischen Frage aus der antiken Literatur, der experimentalpsychologie, der Oral Poetry-Forschung und dem rabbinischen Traditionswesen* (Tübingen: Franke, 2008). Regarding Matthew's sources more specifically, see idem, "Matthew's Sources – Written or Oral? A Rabbinic Analogy and Empirical Insights," in *Built Upon the Rock: Studies in the Gospel of Matthew* (edited by Daniel M. Gurtner and John Nolland; Grand Rapids: Eerdmans, 2008), 1–23.

58. See Mark Goodacre, *The Case Against Q: Studies in Markan Priority and the Synoptic Problem* (Harrisburgh: Trinity Press International, 2002). See also Francis Watson, *Gospel Writing: A Canonical Perspective* (Grand Rapids: Eerdmans, 2013), 117–285. For discussion of some implications for Matthew from a slightly different perspective, see Anders Runesson, "Giving Birth to Jesus in the Late First Century: Matthew as Midwife in the Context of Colonisation," in *Infancy Gospels: Stories and Identities* (edited by Claire Clivaz, Andreas Dettwiler, Luc Devilliers, and Enrico Norelli; WUNT 281; Tübingen: Mohr Siebeck, 2011), 301–27, here 304–6. For the setting in which Matthew's Gospel was composed and used, including discussion of the Didache, see Anders Runesson, "Building Matthean Communities: The Politics of Textualization," in *Mark and Matthew. Comparative Readings I: Understanding the Earliest Gospels in their First-Century Settings* (edited by Eve-Marie Becker and Anders Runesson; WUNT 271; Tübingen: Mohr Siebeck, 2011), 379–408.

written texts, it makes best sense in light of the purpose of the present study to build an understanding of Matthew's narrative on the text as we have it, rather than relying too heavily on hypothetical redactional activity, based on a disputed hypothetical source (Q) or on the assumed restricted access to Markan traditions from the Markan text alone.[59]

Having said this, it is, of course, not possible to isolate a text and read it ahistorically, assuming that such a procedure would generate meaning in any absolute sense of that word; understanding evolves, always, in context. Whichever way we read, the text will instantly become embedded in ideas, concepts, and worldviews, which may or may not relate to the historical setting in which the Gospel was produced and first read. In order to attempt a historical understanding of Matthew's judgment theme, we need, therefore, to pay attention to various ways of understanding the world and God's wrath in the first century. Charette has rightly recognized that, "[a] thorough analysis which contributes to a more complete assessment of the subject requires the introduction of other elements from the Gospel [i.e. other than those passages which employ the vocabulary of recompense] which are related to the same framework of thought even though they utilize different terminology."[60] This leads him to widen the scope of his study to include "a significant part of the Old Testament."[61] Thus, one of the objectives of his study is "to demonstrate that Matthew's conception of recompense can be understood fully in terms of his understanding of the Old Testament."[62] He continues, consequently—and problematically—to state that "[t]he question as to whether (and if so, how) other writings subsequent to the Old Testament may have influenced Matthew is not of interest to the present study."[63]

Charette's argument assumes that limiting the scope of the material

59. A renewed discussion of Matthew's sources is also of major importance for the reconstruction of the socio-religious and political setting in which the text was produced. I will address this issue in a comprehensive study on the Gospel of Matthew and its origin (in preparation). See also Runesson, "Rethinking Early Jewish–Christian Relations"; idem, "Politics of Textualization."

60. Charette, *Recompense*, 16.

61. Ibid.

62. Ibid., 19.

63. Ibid.

used to historically embed his reading of Matthew's Gospel to the Hebrew Bible produces the best first-century understanding of "the purpose and function of the recompense theme within Matthew's Gospel" available to us.[64] However, as Sim's study has shown, since recompense language is part and parcel of later apocalyptic discourse, and Matthew shares many of the components of such language with other contemporary Jewish texts, such a limited choice of contextual material is methodologically problematic. Our understanding of Matthew's narrative needs to be informed by the ways the texts of the Hebrew Bible were read by Matthew's contemporaries, rather than by the ways they were originally meant to be understood.[65] Unfortunately, the reluctance of Charette to use other ancient Jewish texts in his investigation has led to some less-than-convincing results when he sums up his findings and relates them to "covenantal nomism."[66] This does not mean, of course, that the Hebrew Bible, whose books were considered holy by Matthew, can be ignored when Matthew's ideas and concepts are analyzed; only that we need to expand the material to include later Jewish texts.

Charette's approach, especially its strategy of taking into account notions related to the judgment theme in order to shed light on the latter, is well-argued and indispensable for the topic at hand. However, of the related themes that he deals with, some key areas have not, in my view, been satisfactorily treated, such as the sacrificial cult and atonement as mechanisms integral to Jewish law. If these aspects of Jewish life are not treated as essential components of the law, the problem of grace, so elusive in Matthew, but so important in the history of scholarship on this Gospel, will become difficult to address. As David E. Holowerda has pointed out, "[w]hereas Matthew's emphasis on righteousness is apparent to all, his structures of grace are more implicit and thus more difficult to discover."[67] He notes that

---

64. Ibid., 20.
65. The wish to understand the Hebrew Bible texts historically in their original contexts is a modern phenomenon unknown to (pre-Enlightenment) ancient writers.
66. Charette, *Recompense*, 166.
67. David E. Holowerda, *Jesus and Israel: One Covenant or Two?* (Grand Rapids: Eerdmans, 1995), 114.

already Augustine saw this problem, and provided as a solution the suggestion that Matthew's Gospel assumed that readers had already, by grace, been given the spirit of God. For Augustine, then, the requirements of the Beatitudes were made possible for humans to live up to only after they had received the free gift of the spirit.[68] The question is, though, if Matthew merely assumes grace, or if the Gospel actually develops such structures. In order to answer this question, Holowerda focuses on Matthew's first chapters and the person of Jesus. Jesus himself manifests, according to him, God's act of grace toward his people: Immanuel. Once this gift has been given, the demands of the Sermon of the Mount follow. Obedience in relation to these demands constitutes the answer of the people to the gracious act of God.[69] In Matthew, Holowerda claims, "eschatology has become the barrier to legalism."[70]

In a similar way, Ulrich Luz argues that the Gospel does indicate a pattern of grace, despite its heavy emphasis on works as the central criterion of judgment. He turns to the portrayal of God as father (pater), as well as the fact that the judge will be Jesus, the son of man, in order to claim that Matthew is not promoting "works-righteousness."[71] It seems, however, as if the nature of Matthew's pattern of thought resists this type of explanation, leading Luz to conclude that, ultimately, "[w]e remain in a quandary."[72] The reason for this is Luz's foundational (Christian) convictions, which seem difficult to reconcile with Matthew's judgment discourse. He writes: "It seems to me that the notion of judgment according to works is a *theological impossibility* for the God who abides in Jesus of Nazareth and who defined himself in the resurrection. But it may be, that we as human beings need the idea of judgment to take God seriously as God. The idea may be an *anthropological necessity*."[73] While this may be true for Christians on a contemporary religious level, in my view, this type of discussion does

68. Ibid., 115.
69. Ibid., 115–16.
70. Ibid., 117.
71. Luz, *Matthew* 1.379, commenting on Matt 7:21; idem, *Theology*, 61, 131–32.
72. Luz, *Theology*, 132.
73. Ibid.

little to explain what Matthew might have meant when he emphasized to such a degree the importance of divine wrath and weaved his story so intricately that whatever is meant by "good news" cannot be communicated beyond judgment discourses.

As noted above in relation to David Sim's work, the eschatological character of Matthew's Gospel cannot be ignored; end-time expectations play a critical role in the narrative. The evidence suggests, however, that God's covenant relationship with his people Israel provides the basis for the eschatological activities of Jesus, and thus, for the judgment discourse of the Gospel. As we shall see, *pace* Holowerda, it is the Mosaic covenant, rather than eschatology, that provides the theological structure within which grace may be activated. In brief, there are some key concepts in the Hebrew Bible and in various forms in Second-Temple texts, which need to be part of our *Vorverständnis*, our pre-knowledge, as we approach Matthew's construal of divine judgment. These include, especially, grace (which carries within it the related "compassion," "unwavering love," "favor," and "'mercy"),[74] covenant, law, atonement, and righteousness.[75] These concepts may be seen as the basic building blocks of the matrix in which Second-Temple period Jews expressed their various responses to the world around them referring to divine judgment. Our question

---

74. As Stephen Westerholm, "Grace," in *New Interpreters Dictionary of the Bible* (edited by Katharine Dood Sakenfeld; Nashville: Abingdon Press, 2007), 2.657, points out, "the notion of grace is abundantly present even when the word is not used [in the Gospels and Acts]." In the case of Matthew, however, this is less clear than in, e.g., Luke, due to the former's emphasis on judgment. On the meaning of "grace" in the Hebrew Bible, see Katharine Doob Sakenfeld, *The Meaning of Hesed in the Hebrew Bible* (Missoula: Scholars Press, 1978).

75. For discussion of the dynamics of these concepts in Second-Temple and Rabbinic (Tannaitic) texts, see Sanders, *Paul and Palestinian Judaism*. Studies pre-dating Sanders's work, which convey important insights with regard to our topic, include George Foot Moore, *Judaism in the First Centuries of the Christian Era.* Vol. 1: *The Age of the Tannaim* (Cambridge: Cambridge University Press, 1927); Erik Sjöberg, *Gott und die Sünder im palästinischen Judentum. Nach dem Zeugnis der Tannaiten und der apokryphisch-pseudepigraphischen Literatur* (Stuttgart: W. Kohlhammer, 1939); Henrik Ljungman, *Guds barmhärtighet och dom: Fariséernas lära om de två 'måtten'* (Lund: C W K Gleerup, 1950). Michael Winninge, *Sinners and the Righteous: A Comparative Study of the Psalms of Salomon and Paul's Letters* (Stockholm: Almqvist & Wiksell International, 1995) identifies the Psalms of Solomon as a Pharisaic text, and is supported in this by Simon J. Gathercole, *Where is Boasting? Early Jewish Soteriology and Paul's Response in Romans 1-5* (Grand Rapids: Eerdmans, 2002), 63. If this identification is accepted, this text should be regarded as especially important for the study of Matthew (cf. Runesson, "Rethinking Early Jewish–Christian Relations," for a connection between the Mattheans and the Pharisees).

as we approach Matthew's Gospel is, then, how this matrix may or may not help us as we try to reconstruct historically its narrative construal of divine judgment.[76] As will become evident, while it is difficult to paint a consistent picture of the judgment theme in the text if these concepts, so central to Jewish identity, are ignored, Matthew's theological pattern emerges as coherent once it is embedded and allowed to "move" within and be defined by this conceptual context.

Before we proceed to present the analytical work itself, a few words must be said about Jews and non-Jews as these categories are depicted in the Gospel in settings communicating ideas of divine wrath, judgment, and salvation. As we shall see, Matthew's view of judgment is dependent on this distinction to such a degree that the Gospel can hardly be understood without structuring the analysis accordingly.

Judging Jews and Non-Jews in Matthew

There is evidence in the Hebrew Bible as well as in several Jewish texts roughly contemporary with Matthew that non-Jews were often understood to be treated separately from Jews in various settings of divine judgment. Examples of this can be found, e.g., in Ezek 39:21; Joel 4 [Eng. 3]; Amos 1–2;[77] Zech 7:8–14; 9:1–8; Mic 7:11–13; Pss. Sol. 17:26–30 (cf. 17:43); 1 En. 91:7–16; 4 Ezra 13:33–49; 2 Bar. 72; T. Benj. 10:7–9.[78] A distinction between the judgment on Jews and non-Jews may also

---

76. It should be noted that the present study is not aiming at establishing a genetic connection between any of these texts, but rather to work with a theological theme within a historically plausible and more general conceptual setting.

77. Amos has separate judgments also for Judah and Israel. Note, especially, the shift in the criteria of judgment between the nations and Judah. The criteria concerning Judah are based explicitly on the Law, whereas this is not the case regarding non-Jews.

78. It is of some interest here to note the discussion of the passage from T. Benj. in Graham N. Stanton, *A Gospel for a New People: Studies in Matthew* (Edinburgh: T & T Clark, 1992), 213. Stanton quotes the following translation, with its second-century CE interpolation by a Christ-believer: "Then, too, all men will rise, some to glory and some to disgrace. And the Lord will judge Israel first for the wickedness done to him; for when he appeared as God in the flesh, as a deliverer, they did not believe him. And then he will judge all the Gentiles, everyone of them who did not believe him when he appeared on earth" (T. Benj. 10:8–9; cf. Robert H. Charles' translation in *The Apocrypha and Pseudepigrapha of the Old Testament in English. With Introduction and Critical and Explanatory Notes to Several Books* [vol. 2; Oxford: Clarendon Press, 1913], as well as Howard C. Kee's edition in James H. Charlesworth, ed., *The Old Testament Pseudepigrapha* [vol. 1; New York: Doubleday, 1983] 828). As Stanton notes, while this passage is written or redacted by a Christ-believer, "it may well be an expansion of an earlier Jewish tradition" (213n2). Important here, though, is the fact that the text *in this form* is evidence that some believers in Jesus in the early

be found, with some modifications, in New Testament writings such as Rom 2:9–10 and 1 Pet 4:17.[79] As Daniel Harrington has noted, in some texts, it is also clearly stated that the criteria of judgment regarding non-Jews will be dependent on their treatment of Israel.[80] 2 Bar. 72:4–5 proclaims that "[e]very nation which has not known Israel and which has not trodden down the seed of Jacob will live."

As Harrington points out, these and similar texts provide a context in which to understand Matthew's perspective on judgment, especially Matt 25:31–46 where the same principle is active with regard to who is being judged and why. We shall discuss this text in more detail in Part II of the study.[81] Suffice it to say here that the *panta ta ethnē* ("all the nations"; 25:32), i.e., those who are being judged in this scene, refers specifically to non-Jews (who are not followers of Jesus).[82] This judgment scene is thus distinguished from the many other statements on divine judgment, which apply to individuals and groups clearly identified as Jewish in the Gospel. Matthew, thus, seems to stand firmly in the Jewish tradition in which Jews and non-Jews will be judged separately. Further, we may note that the basic criterion of judgment in this text is how these non-Jews have treated "the least of my brothers" (25:40), meaning Jesus's followers. This compares well with the quote from 2 Bar. 72 above, but also with the pattern of thought that surfaces in Gen 12:3, where those who bless Abraham will receive blessings from God, and those who curse him will be cursed.[83] The

second century maintained the distinction between Jews and gentiles in divine judgment, just as the original author of the text did in the second century BCE.

79. In 1 Pet 4:17, the common distinction between Jews and non-Jews is modified, stated instead to be between the "the household of God" and those who do not "obey the gospel of God." By contrast, Romans maintains the language of Jew and non-Jew, but uses it to stress that judgment will befall both of these groups. See also 1 Cor 6:2–3, where *hoi hagioi* ("the holy ones," i.e., the followers of Jesus addressed in the letter) are said to be the future judges of the world as well as of the angels; cf. Matt 19:28, where the disciples are to judge and rule the twelve tribes of Israel.

80. Daniel J. Harrington, *The Gospel of Matthew* (Collegeville: Liturgical Press, 1991), 359. Cf. Sim, *Apocalyptic Eschatology*, 127: "the criteria for judgment are usually tied up with the treatment of the righteous."

81. See also Anders Runesson, "Judging Gentiles in the Gospel of Matthew: Between 'Othering' and Inclusion," in *Matthew's Gospel and Early Christianity: Studies in Memory of Professor Graham Stanton* (edited by Joel Willitts and Daniel M. Gurtner; London: T & T Clark, 2011), 133–51.

82. Cf. Stanton, *New People*, 214. The understanding of this passage is difficult, and the expression *panta ta ethnē* has been debated among scholars for decades. The position taken here is argued at some length in chapter 7.3, but see also chapters 5.2.3 and 5.3.

difference is, of course, that the Messiah is identified with those who follow him, and therefore, ultimately, the criterion of judgment is not concerned with behavior toward Israel, but toward that part of Israel which belongs to the messianic movement. Based on its affinity with the pattern of Gen 12:3, this criterion may be called the "Abrahamic principle," or "a theology of the benevolent other,"[84] and we shall have occasion to return to this theme also with regard to Matt 10:40–42, which deals with positive Jewish attitudes toward (Jewish) followers of Jesus and the consequences of such attitudes.

Taken together, the evidence suggests that the theme of judgment in Matthew should be analyzed separately with regard to Jews and non-Jews. In my view, there is nothing in Matthew's narrative that justifies Charette's claim that, in the end, Israel's "unique status is annulled."[85] As we shall see, based on an analysis of the judgment theme, paying close attention to the terminology used, Matthew displays no interest in erasing the basic Jewish worldview in which all other nations (*ethnē*) are understood as "the other,"[86] a notion which later (non-Jewish) Christian interpreters, for obvious reasons, have had difficulties accepting. The harsh judgment on some individuals and groups identified as Jewish in the narrative,[87] even when compared to non-Jews, is best explained on the basis of statements of severe judgment in the prophetic literature: it is precisely because these people are Jewish and have a covenant relationship with the God of Israel within which the law has been given that they will be judged harder than non-Jews, who repent or otherwise perform acts of loving-kindness toward Jesus's followers.[88] Although often misrepresented in the literature, it

---

83. Cf. Deut 30:7; *Jub.* 31:17. For the connection between Gen 12:3 and Matt 25:31–46, see Charette, *Recompense*, 158–59 and discussion below in chapter 7.3.

84. See Runesson, "Matthew," in *The Oxford Encyclopedia of the Books of the Bible*, 2.59–78, here 67.

85. Charette, *Recompense*, 160.

86. It is of some importance to keep in mind that this type of worldview does not in and of itself result in a negative view of outsiders. Righteous non-Jews could be thought of as having a share in the world to come, which is also the dominant perspective in rabbinic literature and later mainstream Judaism. We shall return to this below. The idea that only "insiders" would be able to attain salvation is more related to theological tendencies in later "particularistic" non-Jewish Christianity. See discussion in Anders Runesson, "Particularistic Judaism and Universalistic Christianity? Some Critical Remarks on Terminology and Theology," in *JGRChJ* 1 (2000): 120–44.

87. Cf., e.g., Matt 11:20–24.

88. Cf. Josephus, who emphasizes that the fact that all Jews have been so thoroughly educated

is key to the interpretation of Matthew that divine condemnation is not understood as connected to a rejection of the Jewish people's status as the people of God; on the contrary, judgment is pronounced on the very basis of this status, which distinguishes them from other nations.

It is not uncommon, however, that scholars conflate pronouncements of judgment on various Jewish groups mentioned in the narrative into a single description of condemnation, and then use the name "Israel," or "the Jews," to identify the people judged. Whatever is said about, e.g., the Pharisees, tend to be seen as applicable to "Israel." Such interpretive practices, conscious or unconscious, inevitably lead to predictable conclusions regarding not only God's judgment on the people of God, but also God's rejection of God's people. We have already noted such tendencies in relation to Marguerat's study. Charette writes: "Within the context of the Sermon on the Mount the warning implicit in these words are addressed both to Israel and the disciples."[89] This use of terms implies the supposition that Jesus's followers are not included in "Israel," despite several clues in the text that seem to prevent such a conclusion.

The disciples are unquestionably depicted as Jews, and thus, by necessity, included in the category "Israel."[90] Further, no mission beyond "Israel" is permitted by the pre-risen Jesus (Matt 10:5–6, 23; 15:24), which means that any characters in the narrative that are portrayed as positive toward Jesus as a consequence of such mission must be considered to be identified as "Israel."[91] Indeed, that which

in Jewish laws makes, in case someone broke the law, "evasion of punishment by excuses an impossibility" (C. Ap. 2.178).

89. Charette, Recompense, 81.

90. Cf. Bornkamm, "End-Expectation," 39, who likewise identifies, more generally, Matthew's perspective as Jewish, although seemingly lamenting this fact, using the word "imprisoned" to describe the situation of the "church" within Jewish tradition. See also J. D. G. Dunn, The Partings of the Ways: Between Christianity and Judaism and their Significance for the Character of Christianity (London: SCM Press, 2006), 204. Discussing ekklēsia in Matthew, Dunn argues that "behind it lies the familiar OT concept of the qahal Israel, 'the congregation of Israel.' In other words, we see a claim that the Matthean community represents the eschatological people of God (cf. also Matt. 19:28). This is clearly a claim from within the heritage of second temple Judaism, not from 'outside'" (emphasis original).

91. This excludes, of course, the Canaanite woman in Matt 15:21–28 and other clearly identified non-Jewish characters, which have not been the object of mission either by Jesus or his disciples, but nevertheless understand the power of the kingdom around the protagonist and want to have a share in it.

happens around Jesus, i.e., the first indications of the coming Kingdom of Heaven, are said to happen "in Israel" (Matt 9:33), and when these extraordinary events occur, "the God of Israel" is praised (Matt 15:31[92]). In one of the Beatitudes, the land[93] is promised to "the meek" (Matt 5:5); this land was identified in 2:20, 21 as "the land of Israel." Indeed, Matthew's text does not say that the message of the Sermon on the Mount is addressed to "Israel" and the disciples, but to "the crowds" (*hoi ochloi*) and the disciples (5:1; 7:28). Once this use of terms to identify who is being the target audience in the various settings of the narrative as a whole is taken seriously, it becomes clear that not only do the two groups of disciples and crowds together make up Israel,[94] but also various other groups which are identified as Jesus's opponents, such as the Pharisees. This will have implications for how we understand the judgment theme in Matthew as it is applied to different groups within the Jewish people. The disciples are not less "Israel" because they are assumed to be accepted by God, and other Jewish groups are not more "Israel" because they are assumed to be sinners and rejected by God.[95]

---

92. As elsewhere in Jewish tradition, the God of Israel is also identified as "the God of Abraham, the God of Isaac, and the God of Jacob" (Matt 22:32).

93. The Greek word translated here as "land" is *gē* (Hebrew: *'eretz*), which can also refer to the earth. In this context, and in the light of Deut 4:1, Ps 37:11 (LXX 36:11), and Isa 61:7, it seems clear that what is referred to is the land of Israel. Cf. the interest in the land in Matt 4:13–16, 25; 10:23, and the wording of Did. 3:7: "Those who are mild tempered will inherit the land" (see Kurt Niederwimmer, *The Didache: A Commentary* [Minneapolis: Fortress, 1998] 100). The later (non-Jewish) church has had an interest in spiritualizing land in ways detaching theology from politics; see, e.g., Jerome, *Comm. Matt.* on 5:4 [sic]: "He does not mean the Land of Judea or the land of this world." See also discussion in John Nolland, *The Gospel of Matthew: A Commentary on the Greek Text* (Grand Rapids: Eerdmans, 2005), 201–2. The language of inheriting the land was not uncommon in other Second-Temple Jewish texts, including the Dead Sea Scrolls. For sources, see W. D. Davies and Dale C. Allison, *The Gospel According to Saint Matthew* (3 vols.; London: T & T Clark, 1988–1997), 1.450. This focus on the land and who will inherit it does not exclude the global perspective that is one of the outcomes of the resurrection in Matt 28:18–20. Clearly, the world has a center in Matthew, and this center is the land and Jerusalem, just like Rome was the center of the empire which the disciples are eventually called upon to engage. (On Matthew's complicated relationship to Jerusalem, see most recently, Anders Runesson, "City of God or Home of Traitors and Killers? Jerusalem According to Matthew," in *Cities of God? An Interdisciplinary Assessment of Early Christian Engagement with the Ancient Urban Environment(s)* [edited by David Gill, Paul Trebilco, and Steve Walton; Grand Rapids: Eerdmans, 2016, forthcoming].)

94. This also means that when Jesus states in his conversation with the centurion in Matt 8:10, that he has not seen such faith anywhere in Israel, this includes the disciples, who are elsewhere accused of being of "little faith" (Matt 8:26; 14:31; 16:8). Both the disciples and the crowds, who together make up the audience of the Sermon on the Mount, are said to be of "little faith" in Matt 6:30, despite the fact that they are positive toward Jesus. Lack of faith is not a distinguishing feature for "Israel" as opposed to Jesus followers; it is characteristic for many in Israel, including the disciples.

Since Matthew's main concern is divine judgment as it relates to the Jewish people, which can easily be seen from the frequency of judgment texts dealing with individuals and groups that are clearly identified as Jewish, we shall begin our investigation with judgment related to Israel (Part I). This means that the followers of Jesus will be dealt with under this heading too, as per the above discussion.[96] As we shall see, while Matthew's construal of judgment discourse related to Jewish characters in the text is quite complex and founded on certain principles, allowing for a coherent picture to emerge, non-Jews, who will be discussed in Part II, are dealt with in a much less developed way, as if the author's theological worldview only allowed them a marginal existence.

But, someone may protest, can we not argue on the basis of, e.g., Matt 28:18–20, that non-Jews have a more positive and prominent place in Matthew, even to the degree that what has been said about judgment on Jews up until that point in the narrative should be valid also in relation to non-Jews? Such considerations bring us to the issue of circumcision and the status of non-Jewish followers of Jesus in the text, and we therefore need to say a few preliminary words on this issue before we proceed to the detailed analysis of Matthew's judgment.[97] Did, in the narrative world of Matthew, non-Jews who in

---

95. Robert H. Gundry, *Matthew. A Commentary on His Literary and Theological Art* (Grand Rapids: Eerdmans, 1982), 293, is certainly correct in stating that "Israel" does not mean the "Church." However, among the texts he refers to in order to support his claim (Matt 8:11–12; 21:43; 22:7; 23:32–36; 27:25), not one contains the word "Israel." It seems as if Gundry, as so many other scholars, simply assumes that all people, or groups, that are rejected are "Israel," whereas those who are accepted in the narrative cannot be referred to by that name.

96. Cf. Bornkamm, "End-expectation," 39: "The Messiahship of Jesus and the validity of his teaching are, therefore, as we have already seen, presented and defended throughout in the framework of Judaism. [...] The struggle with Israel is still a struggle within its own walls. Thus Matthew's conception of the Church remains imprisoned in the Jewish tradition."

97. The issue of circumcision of non-Jewish converts to Matthean Judaism has been debated in several studies which are concerned with the social location of the Matthean community. See, e.g., Amy-Jill Levine, *The Social and Ethnic Dimensions of Matthean Salvation History: 'Go Nowhere among the Gentiles...' Matt. 10:5b* (Lewiston: Mellen Press, 1988), 181–85; David C. Sim, "The Gospel of Matthew and the Gentiles," *JSNT* 57 (1995): 19–48, here 45. The question is, however, what can be said based on the text: what would a first-century audience have assumed with regard to this issue in the narrative world Matthew has created, and what would this imply for the construal of divine judgment? Cf. the discussion and critique in Douglas R. A. Hare, "How Jewish is the Gospel of Matthew?" *CBQ* 62 (2000): 264–77. Since these questions are important for understanding the worldview implicit in the narrative, as well as Matthew's conception of the covenant, we shall have occasion to return to this issue.

some way related to Jesus or wanted to join the movement have to become Jews first, and keep the Jewish law, which would have required circumcision for males, before they received a share of the blessings that followed in the footsteps of the kingdom?

The Question of Circumcision in Matthew's Story World

The only Gospels mentioning circumcision at all are Luke and John, the former noting that John the Baptist and Jesus were circumcised, and the latter presenting a halakhic discussion on the relative weight of the Sabbath commandment, on the one hand, and the commandment to circumcise, on the other.[98] For John's Jesus, the command to circumcise is self-evidently more important than the Sabbath, a conviction presented as being shared between Jesus and his audience; this common conviction can therefore function as a hermeneutical platform from which other arguments about what constitutes "work" on the Sabbath may be launched.[99] Although Luke's brief references to his heroes' circumcisions may seem to be of relatively minor consequence, these references play a significant role when understood within the larger two-volume work of Luke-Acts, as is seen from how the latter book construes the place of circumcision in the early Jesus movement.

The author of Acts clearly maintains that Jews, including those who have become Christ-followers, need to observe the ritual of circumcision, since this practice is related to the covenant and the law. Non-Jews who want to join the Jesus movement, on the contrary, should not be circumcised.[100] The key problem that Acts aims to solve here is how salvation relates to circumcision, a question which is intertwined with the role of the covenant and the law. The author of Acts represents the opinion in the early movement that the net of

---

98. Luke 1:59; 2:21; John 7:21–24.
99. For John's Jesus, the issue is healing, which should not be understood as work, and thus should be allowed on the Sabbath (John 7:23). Cf. the similar type of argument in Matt 12:1–8, 11–12.
100. See, e.g., Acts 15:1–35; 16:3; 21:17–26. Cf. 1 Cor 7:17–24. Cf. discussion in Matthew Thiessen, *Contesting Conversion: Genealogy, Circumcision, and Identity in Ancient Judaism and Christianity* (Oxford: Oxford University Press, 2011), 111–41.

salvation is cast wider than, and is not restricted by, circumcision, and thus, the law. Such an argument retains the basic distinction between Jews and non-Jews, but makes a case for a salvation-inclusive theology, which is similar to what we find in other Jewish texts, including later rabbinic Judaism.[101] For the author of Acts, this conclusion is drawn by the leaders of the movement, notably Peter, James, and Paul, when they discover that God's spirit had already been poured over non-Jews before they had been circumcised. God acts first and people adjust their theology and ritual practice based on what is presented as empirical evidence.[102] The question is now whether Matthew's Gospel presents us with a similar hermeneutical strategy.

Matthew never mentions the word "circumcision." No one would argue, however, that this would mean that the characters in the text identified as Jewish were thought of by the author or earliest audience of the Gospel as uncircumcised. Much of the discussion of the judgment theme in Matthew has been, in one way or the other, related to whether or not the Jews, *as a people*, have been rejected and whether the status of the Jesus movement as a "new" people of God implies the eradication of the distinction between Jew and non-Jew. The mission of Jesus in Matthew is often interpreted as construing all people as equal before God by making them all non-Jewish. Such a scenario would necessarily affect the criteria of judgment, which could then not be based on the Jewish law, or the covenant between God and Israel. Is this what Matthew is trying to communicate, meaning that the message would be very similar to what became mainstream Christian theology in later centuries, as formulated by the church fathers? Or are there indications in Matthew of the pattern present in Luke-Acts, that a distinction is maintained within the messianic community between Jews, who are circumcised, and non-Jews who are not?[103] In my view, neither of these models fit Matthew's text. We shall return to this

101. For terminology and discussion, see Runesson, "Universalistic Christianity?"
102. Acts 10:45–47; 11:17; 15:8–9, 12. James is presented as the one theologizing what has happened, based on a passage from the book of Amos that is interpreted as shedding light on what has transpired: Acts 15:14–18.
103. So, e.g., Isaac W. Oliver, *Torah Praxis after 70 CE: Reading Matthew and Luke-Acts as Jewish Texts* (WUNT 2.355; Tübingen: Mohr Siebeck, 2013).

issue in Part II of the study, just mentioning briefly here some key considerations that motivate and explain the structure and organization of the current investigation.

First, there are no non-Jewish disciples of Jesus in Matthew's story; nor are there any followers of Jesus in the wider sense of that word who are not Jews. Indeed, non-Jews in Matthew are depicted negatively when generalized.[104] Thus, whatever is said about judgment that applies to followers of Jesus in Matthew is based on the assumption that the concepts that come with circumcision, i.e., election, covenant, and law, are active categories. There is no sign in Matthew's characterization of Jesus's message that Jews should abandon any of these aspects of their Judaism when joining him. On the contrary, Jesus's audience in the Sermon on the Mount, the crowds and the disciples, is explicitly told that the Jewish law remains valid in all of its details (Matt 5:17–19; cf. 23:23).[105]

Having said this, there are two factors that complicate the situation. First, the narrative does make mention of a few non-Jews who are positive toward Jesus, and, in two cases, seek his help (Matt 2:1–12; 8:5–13; 15:21–28). Second, in the last two verses of the Gospel, Matt 28:19–20, the resurrected Jesus orders his disciples to actively convert all (non-Jewish) nations and make them disciples of Jesus.[106] Do any of these texts indicate that circumcision for (potential) converts is an active category, with implications for the criteria of judgment?

In the first case, the non-Jews mentioned play a marginal but

---

104. See, e.g., Matt 5:47; 6:7, 32; 10:5–6; 20:19, 25–26; 18:17; 24:9. For further discussion, see Runesson, "Judging Gentiles," especially 143–45. See also Sim, *Christian Judaism*, 245–55; Warren Carter, "Matthew and the Gentiles: Individual Conversion and/or Systemic Transformation?" *JSNT* 26 (2004): 259–82, here 280–81.

105. Cf. Marcus Bockmuehl, "The Noachide Commandments and New Testament Ethics," *RB* (1995): 72–101, 92–93: "[A]lthough Matthew clearly tries to formulate a 'Jewish halakhah' (e.g. in 5.21–48; 19.3–9), many questions remain wrapped in diplomatic silence. Thus, issues like circumcision, purity and food laws are not dealt with, although leprosy (8.2f; 10.8; 11.5), evil spirits (10.1; 12.43) and, by implication, pigs (7.6; 8.30–32) are evidently still unclean. Purity, tithing and phylacteries are significant but depend on inward purity (15.19f; 23.5, 23, 25f.). Other than the teaching of Jesus, no clear criteria for Gentiles emerge." For further discussion of ritual and moral purity/impurity in Matthew, see Runesson, "Purity, Holiness, and the Kingdom of Heaven."

106. The meaning of the so-called Great Commission with regard to which group(s) of people are meant to be missionised has been and continues to be a matter of debate. The position taken here is argued at some length in chapters 5.2.3 and 5.3 below.

important role in the narrative, since they signal the attraction and subordination of the nations to the Jewish Messiah—a phenomenon which is interpreted as an eschatological sign.[107] These characters are thus not related to the question of circumcision, since the very fact that they are not Jews, that they are outsiders, is the interpretive basis for their function in the narrative. This is, in and of itself, enough reason to treat them separately from Jews in a study on judgment. What, then, about Matt 28:19-20 and the process of including non-Jews in the movement, which is now, after the resurrection, begun?

There can be no doubt that the vision here is to make non-Jews full members of the movement around Jesus as portrayed in the Gospel. How is this done? If circumcision is not assumed to be part of the process, this may lead to an interpretation of Jesus's post-resurrection message to be one in which Jewish identity, especially the covenant and the law, had lost its theological importance. This could then be argued to shed light on Matthew's story as a whole, so that everything that preceded this passage with regard to the law as a criterion of judgment would now be seen as invalid. Is this a reasonable assumption? There are three key words in these verses that speak against such a reconstruction: *mathēteuō* ("to make disciple of"), *baptizō* ("baptise"), and *didaskō* ("teach").

The goal is to "make disciples" of all nations. This means to turn them into what Jesus's current followers already were,[108] namely Jews who were following a person they had identified as the Davidic Messiah (9:27; 20:30-31; 21:9), the son of Abraham (1:1, 17), and the son of God (14:33). Further, throughout the story we have been told that these disciples have been instructed to adhere to the Jewish law in every detail. We are now, at the very end of the story, told that making disciples of non-Jews includes teaching them (28:20) what Jesus's disciples had already been taught, namely, to adhere to the Jewish law

---

107. For discussion of such patterns of thought in Judaism, see Terence L. Donaldson, *Judaism and the Gentiles: Jewish Patterns of Universalism (to 135 CE)* (Waco: Baylor University Press, 2007). On Matthew's genealogy with regard to the presence of non-Jews in Jesus's lineage, see Runesson, "Giving Birth to Jesus," 301-27.

108. Cf. Bornkamm, "End-Expectation," 43, who notes that *mathētai* is the distinctive designation for Jesus's disciples throughout the narrative.

in ways superior to the customs and interpretations of the Pharisees (e.g., Matt 5:20; 15:6).[109] One would be hard pressed not to see in such a description of the process of making disciples a requirement, as a matter of course, of circumcision. This is so especially since, as we shall see, the law in Matthew functions within the covenant; without the covenant, whose ritual manifestation in terms of election is circumcision, the law would be without the context in which grace may be activated.[110] A reasonable historical interpretation, then, would be that there are two identity markers that accompany being a "disciple" in this story: being Jewish, implying (for men) circumcision, and following Jesus, implying baptism.[111] As Amy-Jill Levine has argued, "there is no reason to see the command to baptize as a replacement for circumcision."[112]

The baptismal formula "in the name of the Father, and of the Son and of the Holy Spirit" supports this view. Understood within the context of Matthew's Gospel, the formula is specifying the nature of the group that non-Jews are to be incorporated into, namely, a Jewish messianic movement that claimed to be the product of and having its authority from the direct intervention of the spirit of God at the end of time, as revealed in the story of Jesus.[113] From the perspective of the story world, this is what is important to emphasize, since these events, contrary to circumcision, are new and had fundamental implications not only for the people of Israel, but, as we now discover, for the whole world. There is no indication here of different criteria for Jews and non-Jews within the movement, contrary to what we noted in

---

109. Nothing in the narrative suggests that "heaven and earth had passed away" (5:18) when the Matthean Jesus commands his disciples to teach non-Jews everything they themselves had been taught. The law must, then, be seen as a narratively active category throughout the story.

110. Cf. Paul on the relationship between law and circumcision in Gal 5:3.

111. In Matthew, baptism is not mentioned in relation to Jesus's followers, and neither Jesus nor his disciples are said to baptize anyone. The suggestion here that discipleship was understood by the author and the earliest audience of the text to require baptism also of Jews who were following Jesus is inferred from the fact that Jesus himself was baptized (Matt 3:13–17). Strictly speaking, though, baptism of disciples is only explicitly mentioned once, after the resurrection and only as related to non-Jews in Matt 28:19. There are few interpreters, however, who have suggested that such silence with regard to baptism of Jews in Matthew should be understood as a statement that Jews who follow Jesus need not be baptized.

112. Levine, *Social and Ethnic Dimensions*, 181.

113. Cf. Matt 12:28.

relation to Acts. For Matthew, being a disciple takes one form only, and that form is Jewish, a religio-ethnic position closely related to that of the Pharisaic Christ-believers in Acts 15:1, 5, and, possibly, of Paul early on in his career as a (Jewish) missionary (Gal 5:11).[114] In light of ancient approaches to conversion, and the notion that it would be impossible for someone to convert to Judaism since this is an ethnic category, Matthew presents, contrary to Luke-Acts and Paul, in which conversion is impossible/undesirable, an open and inclusive stance.[115]

In sum, when Matthew's narrative is considered as a whole, there is a consistent distinction made between Jews and non-Jews, even in the last verses of the Gospel. The non-Jews, to be the object of intense missionary activities, are envisioned as potential proselytes, i.e., they are to be convinced by Jesus's disciples to adopt a Jewish ethno-religious identity when they join the movement as new disciples. Matt 28:19–20 cannot, therefore, change our approach to the judgment theme in the Gospel, in which we have to treat all Jews, followers of Jesus as well as others, as being judged according to the same basic criteria. The non-Jews that do play a role in the story are of three basic types: enemies of the movement, people attracted to the movement, or people who do not know anything about Jesus or the disciples but react either positively or with indifference to Jesus's suffering followers. These three types of non-Jews, none of which are counted among Jesus's disciples, will be dealt with in Part II of the study. The dynamics of ethnic characterization in Matthew's narrative may be summarized in Figure Int.1: Ethnic Identities in Matthew, as follows.

---

114. Cf. Terence Donaldson, *Paul and the Gentiles: Remapping the Apostles Convictional World* (Minneapolis: Fortress, 1997), 282, who argues that Gal 5:11 refers to Paul as a Jewish missionary before he became a Christ-believer.
115. See Runesson, "Universalistic Christianity?" for discussion. See also Thiessen, *Contesting Conversion*, 147, who makes a similar point with regard to Luke and Paul.

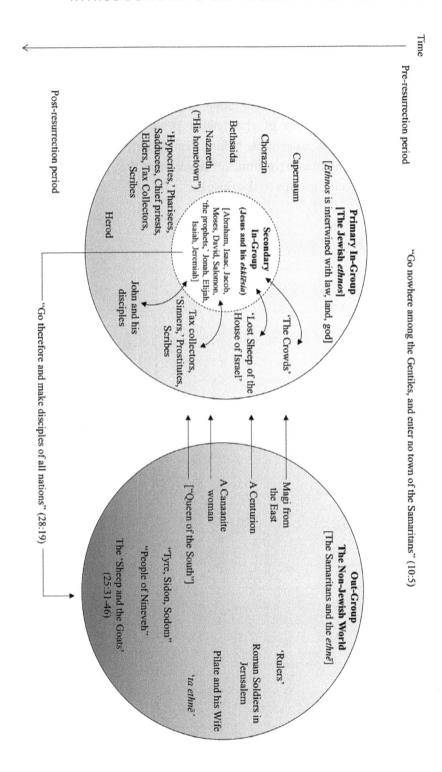

Enough has been said now about the motivation behind the basic structure of the study, and how it reflects the nature of Matthew's narrative, which carries within it a particular theology of divine wrath, judgment, and salvation. We shall begin our discussion of the eschatological situation of the Jewish people by considering the "when" and "how" questions, before dealing with, respectively, the criteria of judgment and the limits of salvation as they are construed in relation to specific groups in the Gospel.

PART I

Judging and Saving the Jewish People

1

———

When Will Israel's God Judge His People?

In order to better understand how the theme of divine judgment is developed in Matthew's narrative, it is of some importance to address the issue of *when* the God of Israel will judge his people. Such considerations will, as we shall see, shed light on the eschatological nature of the Gospel, which, contrary to claims made by some Matthean scholars, does not exclude a retained notion of judgment as implemented also in the present world. Since the scholarly discussion of the timing of divine judgment in Matthew has been made dependent on the idea that our Gospel proposes a new covenant replacing an old abolished covenant, we shall begin this chapter with some comments on Matthew's "when" in relation to Israel's covenant with God. Then we shall move on to outline three basic times of judgment, giving examples of passages that will be discussed throughout Part I. As we shall see, the criteria of judgment, of what is at stake, will differ based on which judgment we are considering. For example, while a positive outcome in the final judgment does presume obedience to the law of Moses, as Jesus interprets it, salvation ultimately depends on a covenant based on a genealogy going back to the patriarchs; it can only be inherited. Rewards and punishments in this world and in the world to come, however, are dependent entirely on what has traditionally been called works of law.

With regard to judgment and covenant, Blaine Charette has argued that Matthew's emphasis on the threat of judgment should be understood as the author's way of stressing that his people must take seriously the requirements of the law within the covenant. For Charette, however, the covenant in Matthew is a new covenant, which replaces the failed Sinai covenant. While the new covenant "operates on the same level as the old in respect of the requirement of obedience for the continuing maintenance of the covenant relationship," there is no ethnic component to the new as there was in the old: both Jews and non-Jews are now included in the covenant.[1] I agree with Charette that Matthew displays a form of covenantal nomism, based on E. P. Sanders's definition.[2] However, in terms of the relationship between covenant and law, there is, in my opinion, no support for his claim that this covenant would abolish the distinction between Jews and non-Jews. Matthew does not speak of a "new" covenant,[3] nor does he contrast "new" and "old" in such a way that "new" replaces "old."[4] Instead, as we shall see, the Matthean Jesus's task is, indeed, to make sure that the Sinaitic covenant is restored after the defilement of the temple and before the coming final judgment.

The new–old covenant distinction leads Charette to a further contrast. In the "old covenant," he argues, punishment was executed in history, whereas in the "new covenant" punishment is implemented at the end of the present age.[5] Similarly, Charette shapes his argument regarding rewards as if such will be delivered only on the day of the final judgment. He further defines reward to mean the receiving of an

---

1. Charette, *Recompense*, 166.
2. See discussion below, chapter 2.8.
3. It is Paul (1 Cor 11:25) and Luke (22:20) who identify the covenant related to Jesus as a new covenant. In addition, Luke speaks of John the Baptist's birth as related to God's faithfulness based on the covenant with Abraham (Luke 1:72). Mark speaks about "the blood of the covenant" (Mark 14:24) and Matthew does the same, adding the explicit reference that his blood effects atonement for the many (Matt 26:28).
4. Cf. Matt 13:52.
5. Charette, *Recompense*, 160. There seems to be a contradiction in his argument here, since he also claims that "Israel" is being replaced by Matthew's group for not heeding the call to repent, a punishment that is, in fact, taking place in history according to his own theory.

inheritance (i.e., the kingdom).[6] While there certainly is an emphasis on the eschatological judgment in Matthew's Gospel, such a focus does not completely exclude or replace God's intervention in this world in terms of rewards and punishments. In light of Charette's arguments, and in order to contextualize Matthew's approach to judgment, let us consider briefly passages from the Hebrew Bible before we move on to categorize the relevant Matthean passages.

In most of the texts included in the Hebrew Bible, rewards and punishments are directly related to the law and executed primarily in this world. This combination of law and continual judgment in history seems to serve the purpose of shaping Israel in the image of God:[7] as God is holy, so shall the people be holy.[8] Some prophets also relate the status of Israel to the world beyond this religio-ethnic group in the sense that the people should be a light among the nations.[9] Experiences of unremitting evil, both within Israel and as directed against Israel by the nations, lead to the development of the notion that God (and the oppressed) will ultimately triumph over the oppressor, even if that does not seem likely in the current situation. This day of final judgment often goes under the name "the day of the Lord," or simply, "that day."[10] To this notion was later attached the idea of a final judgment at the end of time,[11] and resurrection—an idea that we find among the Pharisees as well as in the Jesus movement. Neither the idea of a final judgment removing oppressors, or the notion of a final judgment following after a general resurrection, meant, however, that the idea of reward and punishment in history vanished altogether.[12]

---

6. Charette, *Recompense*, 117–18, 160. See also Eubank, *Wages of Cross-Bearing*, who argues along similar lines.

7. Cf. 2 Macc 6:12–16, where punishment in history is regarded as an expression of mercy, since it will keep the people safe on the day of the final judgment. For this author, God has a different strategy in mind for the nations: he does not punish them in history, in order that their sins may fill up their measure and result in their destruction at the final judgment.

8. Cf., e.g., Lev 11:44–45; cf. Matt 5:48.

9. See, e.g., Isa 42:6; cf. Matt 5:14.

10. E.g., Isa 10:1–4; Mica 2–3; Isa 13; Obad 15; Isa 61; Jer 23:1–4; Zech 8:12–13; Zeph 1:7; Ezek 7:7. Cf. Tobit 13:9; Ps 10:17–18 (LXX 9:38–39). See further Runesson, "Judgment," 459.

11. Dan 12; cf. Isa 65.

12. On the diverse notions of divine judgment in Jewish tradition (and in the New Testament), see also Egon Brandenburger, "Gerichtskonzeptionen im Urchristentum und ihre Voraussetzungen. Eine Problemstudie," in *Studien zur Geschichte und Theologie des Urchristentums* (edited by Egon

In the Gospel of Matthew, we can discern three different types of judgment, which may be categorized as follows: a) Punishment and reward as distributed in this world; b) Punishment and reward to be paid in the world to come; c) The final judgment. Beginning with the last of these types the final judgment will take place "chronologically" between the other two; it prepares the way for coming punishments and "payments,"[13] which will be implemented in the world to come, based on how life was lived in the present world. The main outcome of the final judgment, though, is either what we call salvation, which refers to inclusion in the world to come, or condemnation, which refers to exclusion from life in the coming kingdom. The vast majority of judgment texts in Matthew refer to the final judgment, a fact that indicates clearly the eschatological emphasis of the text.

The idea of punishment and reward in the world to come, the second category of judgment discourse in the Gospel, makes statements about how people, through the way they live in this world, prepare for their treatment after the final judgment, i.e., in the kingdom.[14] This category is distinguished from the final judgment in that all are judged on the last day, but of the ones that are allowed into the kingdom, some will be

---

Brandenburger; Stuttgart: Verlag Katholisches Bibelwerk, 1993), 289–338; Konradt, *Gericht und Gemeinde*, 10–19.

13. As Eubank, *Wages of Cross-Bearing*, 68, has pointed out, terms such as "reward" can be misleading, since there is a direct relationship in Matthew between what a person has done and the outcome of the judgment; wages would thus be a better word than "reward." Indeed, Matthew's text employs a vocabulary distinctly related to economic discourses when dealing with divine judgment, although "payment" may be conceptualized as not proportionate to the work done (e.g., Matt 19:29; 20:1–16; 25:21, 23, 29). In this study, I will, for convenience, use "reward" and "recompense" as synonymous terms, both giving voice to the same type of idea of (abundant/disproportionate) payment for work done, or compensation for suffering.

14. Cf. Sim, *Apocalyptic Eschatology*, 141, who notes that rewards will be paid in the world to come. However, Sim seems not to take into account that negative aspects will also materialize in the world to come, but understands the category of punishment to mean only eternal torture in Gehenna. While it is correct that such an outcome of judgment exists in Matthew (but see Matt 10:28, which indicates annihilation of both body and soul as a result of unfavorable judgment), it seems better to use a different term for it, in order to clarify its relationship to its opposite, which is salvation. Thus, punishment and reward should be treated separately from condemnation and salvation; the two word pairs indicate different types of phenomena. With regard to the pair reward and punishment in the world to come (the kingdom of heaven), this may refer to shifts in hierarchies depending on behavior (cf. Matt 5:19). Both groups of people have, however, passed the final judgment and have thus experienced salvation as opposed to those who have been condemned. See further below.

in a better position than others; roles will be reversed and hierarchies rearranged.

Finally, Matthew includes a few references to judgment that is executed in this world. This type of judgment is focused on punishment rather than reward. It seems Matthew generally prefers, like later Rabbinic Judaism,[15] to transfer this type of judgment to the world to come, as can be seen in the programmatic statement in parable form in Matt 13:24-30, 36-43, as well as in Matt 19:29. Beginning with the latter text, a comparison with the parallel texts in Mark and Luke is instructive. In Mark 10:29-30, those who have left the good things in life to follow Jesus will receive reward "now in this age" (*nyn en tō kairō toutō*) as well as in the world to come (*en tō aioni tō erchomenō*). The reward in relation to the world to come is defined specifically as "eternal life"/"life in the new age" (*zōēn aiōnion*).

Luke 18:29-30 has the same perspective as Mark, saying that people will be receiving already in this world "much more" than what they have given up for the sake of the kingdom; in the world to come, the reward will be eternal life. Matthew's version of this saying differs significantly from the other two with regard to two important themes. First, Matthew sets the scene by introducing an eschatological context. This is done through the claim that when the world is re-born (*en tē paliggenesia*), the twelve disciples will judge/rule[16] the twelve tribes

---

15. This was noted already by C. G. Montefiore and H. M. J. Loewe, *A Rabbinic Anthology* (London: Macmillan, 1938), 202. The evidence in the Rabbinic corpus is not, however, unambiguous. In Tannaitic literature reward and punishment are distributed both in this world and in the world to come, and the balance between these outcomes of judgment is obscure. Texts of interest include *m. Shabb.* 2:6; *m. Kidd.* 1:10; *m. Sotah* 1:7 (this text outlines the principle of "measure for measure" regarding this-worldly retribution); *m. Peah* 1:1 (cf. *t. Peah* 1:2–3); *m. Avot* 1:3; 2:7; 2:14–16; 4:2. I am grateful to Eva Maria Jansson for drawing my attention to this. Saul Lieberman, "Some Aspects of Afterlife in Early Rabbinic Literature" (reprinted in Jacob Neusner and William Scott Green [eds.], *Origins of Judaism: Normative Judaism*, vol. 1 part 2 [New York: Garland, 1990] 103–40) surveys the evidence from the first five centuries. In the first section, he deals with posthumous divine retribution and notes some (for most scholars unknown) aspects of Rabbinic thought, such as human incarnation in animals as punishment for certain sins (110). Another interesting issue is time-limited retribution in hell, *m. Eduyoth* 2:10. A. Melinek, "The Doctrine of Reward and Punishment in Biblical and Early Rabbinic Writings" (reprinted in Jacob Neusner and William Scott Green [eds.], *Origins of Judaism: Normative Judaism*, vol. 1 part 2, [New York: Garland, 1990] 297–312) shows how the Rabbis developed biblical teaching on judgment to "make it suit the experience of their own times" (304–5). For our purposes here it is of interest to note with Melinek that the Rabbis interpreted the fall of the temple in terms of this-worldly punishment (307–8). We shall have reason to return to this below.

of Israel. It is at this time, when the world is being re-born, that (abundant) rewards will be given to those who have left houses, brothers, sisters, fathers, mothers, or children for Jesus's name's sake; they will receive "hundredfold," but what exactly is to be received is, contrary to Mark, left unspecified. What in Mark and Luke is a saying about judgment resulting in this-worldly rewards is, in Matthew, a reassurance that recompense will be given in the world to come.

There is a further detail in Matthew's version of the saying, one which we shall return to, but which needs a brief comment here. While Mark and Luke seem to define eternal life as a reward, Matthew is careful to use the word "inherit" (klēronomeō) when he describes what is to take place. In fact, Matthew consistently applies this term when speaking about eternal life in judgment contexts; such a distinction between reward/recompense and inheritance is not present in Mark and Luke. It would seem that, for Matthew, eternal life cannot be "earned" as a reward, but has to be given to an individual as an

---

16. The meaning of *krinō* has been the subject of some disagreement among scholars, as Charette notes (*Recompense*, 113–14). Charette prefers the translation "to judge" rather than "to govern." This is also Luz's opinion (*Matthew*, 2.517). Gundry, *Matthew*, 392–93, argues that Matthew is referring to "govern," noting that if the meaning were "to judge," this would result in punishment only. The translation "to govern" implies that "Matthew does not regard God's rejection of Israel (21:43) as permanent." Cf. the discussion by Matthias Konradt, *Israel, Church, and the Gentiles in the Gospel of Matthew* (Waco: Baylor University Press, 2013), 259–63. Konradt suggests that the verse may be understood as "an expression of the sovereign rank of the twelve in the kingdom of God," and links this to the restitution of the twelve tribes (261). He also notes, however, that even if the reference were to the disciples taking active part in the final judgment of Israel, this does not in any way indicate that the judgment would be negative (261–62). Davies and Allison, *Matthew*, 3.55–58, argue at some length for the same view as Gundry, suggesting that Matthew's use of *krinō* should be understood against the background of the Hebrew šapaṭ, which refers to the act of ruling with authority. Just as the twelve tribes were once governed by twelve tribal leaders, the twelve disciples will govern Israel in the kingdom (under the ultimate authority of the Messiah). Perhaps the best approach would be to acknowledge the fact that governing may involve judicial procedures, and that in this specific passage we are dealing with a saying which establishes the disciples as future rulers, whose rule will begin as they judge Israel. This means that, for Matthew, Israel, *as a nation*, has a continuous existence beyond the final judgment, something which Luz does not accept based on other types of arguments elsewhere in his commentary. We shall return to this discussion below. In any case, it seems to me simply incorrect to state in absolute terms, as Luz does (*Matthew*, 2.517), that *krinō* cannot carry the meaning of governing; see, e.g., Joseph Henry Thayer, *A Greek-English Lexicon of the New Testament* (Grand Rapids: Baker Book House, 1977 [1901]), ad loc.: "Hebraistically i.q. to rule, govern; to preside over with the power of giving judicial decisions." Cf. the examples given by Thayer and note, e.g., Ps 2:10 LXX; Matt 19:28; Luke 22:29–30, Wis. 1:1; 1 Macc 9:73, and Josephus, *A.J.* 5.184. Perhaps Luz's assumption that there is just one final judgment, which includes both Jews and non-Jews in Matthew, is what complicates matters in his analysis, as he seems to conflate the scenes in Matt 19:28 and 25:31 as if they were one and the same. As we have discussed here, however, Matthew's Gospel works with the idea that there will be two such judgments: one for Israel and one for the nations.

inheritance in accordance with God's covenantal promises to the patriarchs.[17] As will be shown below, salvation is thus to be understood in Matthew as related to, or entangled with, genealogy, although this is conceptualized in ways that move beyond the world of ideas present in some other Jewish texts contemporary with the Gospel.

Now if Matt 19:29 was, unlike its parallel passages in other Gospels, transferring "wages" to the world to come, Matt 13:24–30, 36–43, i.e., the parable about the weeds and the wheat, seems to do the same with regard to punishment. Some scholars have argued that the purpose of this parable is to restrain the impatience resulting from the fact that no immediate division between good and evil had come with the first signs of the arrival of the kingdom; humans (and angels; 13:28, 38) must not get ahead of the coming judgment, but must wait patiently for God to execute judgment through his agents.[18] While this may be true, the issue of impatience is not mentioned or dealt with in the parable itself, nor in its explanation. The parable seems, rather, to contain material addressing more generally what is often referred to as the problem of evil, or theodicy. In other words, the text answers the classic question, dealt with frequently in the Psalter too,[19] why the wicked are not punished in this world if God is righteous in his judgment. Matthew's solution is to claim that God is indeed righteous, and "those who break the law" (*tous poiountas tēn anomian*) will be gathered and destroyed (Matt 13:41–42). The parable and its explanation thus respond to concerns that may arise among people socialized in a setting in which the judgment theme is defined by the writings of the Hebrew Bible; in the majority of these texts, judgment takes place in history. The parable solves what appears to be a lack of justice despite the fact that the Messiah has arrived.[20]

---

17. Eubank, *Wages of Cross-Bearing*, 70–71, argues against such an understanding of *klēronomeō*, but as we shall see when we discuss Matt 25:31–46, I believe his arguments, in this case, miss the point. See below, chapter 7.3.

18. See, e.g., France, *The Gospel of Matthew* (Grand Rapids: Eerdmans, 2007), 533; Bornkamm, "End-expectation," 44n1.

19. See, e.g., Ps 73:3–14; 82:2. See also Isa 57:1; Qoh 8:14, and note 4 Macc 3:20, which gives voice to the opposite perspective that law observance leads to prosperity. Cf. the prophecy of horror in Ezek 21:3, in which both righteous and unrighteous are struck down as punishment for the sins of, as it turns out in Ezek 22:23–31, the leaders of the nation.

These two texts, Matt 13:24–30/36–43 and 19:29, may suffice to show that there is a general tendency in Matthew's narrative to portray Jesus as postponing divine reward and punishment to the world to come. The Rabbis would eventually do the same, following a similar interpretive development of this aspect of Jewish theology. But, as mentioned, Matthew is not exclusively focused on the eschatological realization of divine judgment, and we find some texts promising reward and threatening punishment in history. All of this, it should be noted, concerns judgment related to the Jewish people. As we argued in the Introduction, Matthew's preoccupation with the people with which Jesus identifies requires us to analyze separately passages concerned with Jews and non-Jews, respectively; we shall consider the time when Israel's God will judge the nations below in Part II.

It may be helpful to list here some of the more important judgment texts relating to the Jewish people in Matthew, categorized according to the three-fold approach to judgment mentioned. Synoptic parallels will be given within brackets when applicable. (Brief preliminary comments are given in footnotes in order to contextualize the passages; full discussion will follow throughout Part I in relation to the relevant topics.)

---

20. There has been some debate regarding whom this parable deals with: the community of Jesus's followers or the world as a whole. Gundry (*Matthew*, 272) states: "'world' emphasises the widespread extension of the kingdom through evangelism (cf. 5:14; 26:13; 28:19). Matthew does not mean that all the inhabitants of the world have or will become disciples." However, the passages in Matthew that he refers to for support do not belong within the same "category." In 5:14, Jesus is exhorting the people of Israel (the crowds and the disciples) to be the light of the world. This task does not include an active proselytizing mission, however; such a perspective is not present in Matthew until 28:19–20. It is of some importance to consider the question of whether non-Jews are included in the judgment referred to by the parable. Birger Gerhardsson, "De sju liknelserna i Matteus 13," *SEÅ* 34 (1969): 77–106, here 83, has argued that the judgment in Matt 13:24–30 is on the "people of God," noting specifically the question why the "hopeless cases" are allowed to remain within the people before the final judgment. This understanding of who is being judged seems, in my view, correct. Matthew is exclusively focused on the Jewish people in the narrative at this point; Jesus (cf. 13:37: "the son of man") is said to be the sower, and he is addressing his message exclusively to Jews (cf. 15:24). Further, there has recently been a prohibition of mission outside the people (10:5–6), and the law is indicated as a criterion of judgment (13:41). Finally, as Gerhardsson points out, the parable in question is one of seven parables, all of which follow the basic pattern of the first one (13:3–9); as 13:2 indicates, these parables are spoken to Jewish crowds gathering around him by the lake. The in-group addressed here is thus best understood as the people of Israel. Consequently, the parable in 13:24–30 about divine justice and punishment may be added to other evidence in the narrative that Matthew is not replacing "Israel" with the "Church"; the people of God remains the people of God and is judged accordingly at the end of times.

Judgment, Reward, and Punishment in this World

5:22[21]; 6:33 (Luke 12:31); 7:1–2[22] (Luke 6:37); 11:23[23] (Luke 10:13–15); 12:31–32[24] (Mark 3:29; Luke 12:10); 21:18–19[25] (Mark 11:12–14, 20);

21. To be noted here is that punishment by the Sanhedrin in this verse is paralleled by punishment in Gehenna, which has led some scholars to assume that the passage describes an increase in intensity of judgment. According to Luz, *Matthew*, 1.235, however, the verse displays "a qualitative shift from human-earthly to divine-eschatological judgment." Important for our purposes is the fact that the Sanhedrin in itself functions as God's tool when judging this world, just as the courts in the Hebrew Bible. It is an expression of God's righteousness that human courts execute judgment since the law was given by God. See Runesson, "Judgment," 458–60. Cf. Roland de Vaux, *Ancient Israel: Its Life and Institutions* (2nd ed.; London: Darton, Longman & Todd, 1965), 147–58, where he notes that the law was given by God within the covenant, and it was the people's responsibility to make sure that justice prevailed through establishing effective courts. If, after examination, a court could not reach a decision the case was to be solved by the drawing of lots. In all cases, God is understood to be the judge and human beings were seen only as the performers of the necessary rituals. This verse is thus an example of the idea that the Sanhedrin in Jerusalem implements God's judgment in this world. (The fact that the example given by the Matthean Jesus as a basis for judgment by the Sanhedrin does not ring realistic due to the frequency with which such insults must have happened is beside the point; in the narrative world, this is how the [ideal?] Sanhedrin is said to be functioning.) This does not, of course, exclude an eschatological judgment, the outcome of which may be considerably grimmer.

22. It is difficult to determine whether these verses belong here or should be interpreted as referring to the outcome of judgment in the world to come. The reasons for understanding these verses as applicable to this world are as follows. First, the context seems to indicate concerns with life in this world. Matt 7:1–2 is placed between two themes dealing with peoples' everyday life: 6:25–34 (v. 33 mentioning positive outcomes as a result of seeking the kingdom), and the following verses in chapter 7, especially vv. 7–12. It may be, therefore, that these verses are intended to make clear that the relationship between human beings is inextricably connected with the relationship between the people and their God (cf. Matt 5:23–24; 6:14–15); God would then be imposing punishment in this world in accordance with how man is judging others. Second, the principle of measure for measure, which Matthew applies here, usually refers to judgment in this world. (As we see in Matt 19:29; 20:1–16, Matthew does not make use of this principle when dealing with the world to come.) This is also the case in Tannaitic literature (cf., e.g., *m. Sotah* 1:7, 8. In mishnah 7, the priests are carrying out the punishment [cf. the comment on 5:22 above], but in the following mishnah, the direct involvement of God is more obvious). Cf. Melinek, "Reward and Punishment," 386. While these considerations make a reference to judgment in this world possible, this is by no means certain. It may well be that Matthew wants to communicate a measure for measure correlation between life in this world and the next.

23. For the Matthean Jesus, Sodom's destruction is God's judgment based on the sinfulness of the city. The same fate, to take place in this world, is predicted for Capernaum. Such punishment does not mean that a final judgment will not take place.

24. Forgiveness is explicitly rejected for both this world and the world to come. The passage is therefore listed also in the category of the final judgment.

25. This pericope is often interpreted as a prophetic "parable-in-action," a symbol for the rejection of "Israel" (see, e.g., John P. Meier, *Matthew* (Collegeville: Liturgical Press, 1980), 237. The event occurs the day after the entry into Jerusalem and the temple incident. Gundry, *Matthew*, 416, has argued that Matthew has redacted his material so that it becomes clear that it is Jerusalem and the Jewish leaders that are in focus: "Thus, with the Jewish leaders in mind, a mere wish turns into a terrifying prediction of judgment." The fig-tree incident is a prophesy first and foremost of the downfall of Jerusalem and the temple, the catastrophe being described as a consequence of the neglect of the law by, as we shall see, especially the Pharisees (cf. Matt 23:1–24:2). Thus, the pericope reveals a belief in divine judgment in history.

21:33–46[26] (Mark 12:1-12; Luke 20:9-19); 23:35–36[27] (Luke 11:50–51); 23:37–24:2[28] (Luke 13:34–35; 21:5–6; Mark 13:1–2); 26:52[29]; 27:25.[30]

Reward and Punishment in the World to Come

5:12 (Luke 6:23); 5:19; 6:1–6[31]; 6:16–18; 6:20 (Luke 12:34); 10:41–42[32]

26. This parable seems to be dealing with the final judgment, but could also refer to judgment in this world. While I have previously understood the parable as related to the final judgment and the change of leadership in the kingdom, as a consequence of the wickedness of the "chief priest, the elders, and the Pharisees" (Matt 21:41, 45; Runesson, "Judging Gentiles," 141n25), I am now considering the second option as a plausible alternative. The key to this interpretation would be v. 43, where the reason for the change of leadership is based on a concern for the production of "fruit." In Matthew, bearing fruit is elsewhere related to life in this world, leading up to the final judgment and the rebirth of the world (7:19; on rebirth, see Matt 19:28). The overshadowing concern in Matthew is, further, that especially the Pharisees are not helping, but rather hindering the people from reaching the goal of a life worthy of the kingdom (3:8; 9:36; 23:4, 13). Since this will lead to the predicted catastrophe of the temple destruction, Jesus's and his disciples' task is to save as many as possible in face of the coming doom (1:21; 9:37–10:42). Thus, leadership will need to be changed before the final judgment, to a group (*ethnos*) "that produces the fruits of the kingdom." (For the meaning of *ethnos* here, see John S. Kloppenborg, *The Tenants in the Vineyard: Ideology, Economics, and Agrarian Conflict in Jewish Palestine* [Tübingen: Mohr Siebeck, 2006] 191–93.) The judgment resulting in the rejection of current leaders in favor of new leaders is thus thought of, if this argument is correct, as taking place in this world; indeed, the disciples have already been given the power to rule through correct interpretation of halakhah in Matt 16:19 (cf. 18:18–19). The full implementation of the disciples' rule over Israel will take place, however, at the rebirth of the world (Matt 19:28).

27. The context of these verses makes it clear that the outcome of divine judgment is the destruction of Jerusalem. Thus, the Matthean Jesus's attack on the "Scribes and the Pharisees" (Matt 23:1-36) comes to a climax in this prophecy about punishment in this world.

28. As we have had occasion to note above, rabbinic literature also gives expression to the view that the fall of the temple was God's punishment. Melinek, "Reward and Punishment," 285, notes that the Rabbis saw this punishment as "the liquidation of Israel's sins and left them free to look forward to restoration in the future." Referring to *b. Yom. 9b*, Melinek adds details about the cause of the punishment: "the downfall of the Jewish state is attributed specifically to the three sins of bloodshed, overbearing behaviour, and neglect of the study of the law." Interestingly, the Matthean Jesus is similarly concerned with the lack of obedience to the law (cf., e.g., Matt 23:23), bloodshed is explicitly mentioned (23:31, 35), and overbearing, or oppressive, behavior is also noted (23:4) as the narrative leads up to the destruction of the temple in 23:38, 24:1–2.

29. Cf. Gen 9:6; Isa 50:11 (in the Targum, the "kindling of fire" of Isa 50:11 is interpreted as taking up the sword. See France, *Matthew*, 1013n22). Note also, Matt 5:39.

30. As we shall argue below, this verse is likely intended to refer to the destruction of Jerusalem.

31. *Para tō patri* (6:1) indicates that the rewards for kingdom-behavior in this world will be paid in the world to come. This is true also for 6:16–18, and confirmed by 6:20.

32. These important verses should probably be understood as referring to abundant recompense in the world to come rather than as a claim that rewards will be paid in the current age. The rewards are related to acts of hospitality and compassion, seemingly following the pattern of measure for measure, which could indicate rewards in this world (see the comment above on 7:1–2). However, the rewards, or wages, are disproportionate compared to what has been done and by whom, so that this cannot be understood as a matter of measure for measure in the strict sense, although there is some level of correspondence in kind between deed and reward. Further, the immediate context makes it likely that Matthew is here speaking of heavenly rewards; see 10:32, 40. Indeed, Matt 10:40–42 corresponds to Matt 25:31–46 in terms of the hermeneutics applied, and the latter passage is explicitly describing an eschatological setting. The measure for measure principle,

(Mark 9:41); 16:27; 18:4; 19:21[33] (Mark 10:21; Luke 18:22); 19:29 (Mark 10:29–30; Luke 18:29–30); 20:1–16; 23:12

The Final Judgment

3:7–8 (Luke 3:7–8); 3:10 (Luke 3:9); 3:12 (Luke 3:17); 5:20; 5:22; 5:27–30 (Mark 9:43); 6:14–15[34] (Mark 11:25; Luke 11:14); 7:19; 7:21; 7:24–27 (Luke 6:47–49); 8:11–12[35] (Luke 13:28–29); 10:15; 10:22; 10:28 (Luke 12:4–5); 10:32–33 (Luke 12:8–9); 10:39 (Luke 17:33); 11:22–24 (Luke 10:14–15); 12:27 (Luke 11:19); 12:31–32 (Mark 3:29; Luke 12:10); 12:36–37; 12:41–42 (Luke 11:31–32); 13:24–30, 36–43; 13:47–50; 15:13;[36] 16:25 (Mark 8:35; Luke 9:24); 18:3; 18:6[37] (Mark 9:42; Luke 17:2); 18:8–9 (Mark 9:43–47); 18:23–35; 19:16–17[38] (Mark 10:17–19; Luke 18:18–20); 19:28–29 (Mark

however, should not be understood as the basis for inclusion in or exclusion from the world to come (such a principle is clearly unsuitable for such purposes), but rather, as the criterion for how things will eventually be, once the world has been reborn.

33. As the history of interpretation indicates, this verse is difficult to interpret, especially with regard to the question of judgment (for discussion, see Davies and Allison, *Matthew*, 3.47–48; Luz, *Matthew*, 2.512–14, 518–23; cf. Charles H. Talbert, *Matthew* [Grand Rapids: Baker Akademic, 2010] 236–37). For our purposes here, the crux lies in determining whether the status of *teleios* (completeness/perfection; cf. Matt 5:48) is related to rewards in the world to come, or if it should rather be understood as a requirement for entering the kingdom at all when the world is reborn after the final judgment has taken place. The question in Matt 19:16 is about entering the world to come, i.e., living according to principles which will allow for eternal life. These principles are for Jesus the same as they have always been: the law (19:17–19; cf. 5:17–20). But the law itself is not the full answer, since it is embedded within a covenant, in which for God that which is impossible for human beings is possible, namely, salvation (Matt 19:26). The question is whether to sell everything and follow Jesus is an expression referring to the law. I have argued elsewhere that it is, and that the problem for the rich man is that his refusal to give to the poor means that he breaks the law as it is stated in Matt 19:19: "You shall love your neighbor as yourself," according to the means that have been given to you (Matt 25:14–30; Runesson, "Purity and Holiness"). Had the rich man obeyed, he would have earned a treasure in heaven (Matt 19:21), which should be understood as referring to the rewards in the world to come mentioned in Matt 19:29. Thus, radically obeying the law according to one's full ability will result in recompense in the world to come.

34. The context reveals that God's forgiveness is related to the eschatological judgment, although it is dependent on the willingness of people to forgive others in the present age.

35. As with most other judgment texts involving non-Jews, this text is primarily directed to Jews; pointing to commendable characteristics displayed by a non-Jew, non-Jews being generally regarded by Matthew's Jesus as examples of how *not* to behave, is intended to shame members of God's people who should know better (cf. Matt 10:15; 11:22–24; 12:41–42). Still, however, there is information to be deduced from this text regarding the judgment on non-Jews, an issue to which we shall return in Part II.

36. The terminology of "uprooting" (*ekrizoō*) is elsewhere in Matthew related to the final judgment; see Matt 3:10; cf. 7:19. This makes it likely that what is intended here is not a shift of leadership positions in this world, although this cannot be excluded (cf. the comment on Matt 21:33–46 above).

37. Cf. Rev 18:21. See also comment below on Matt 26:24.

10:29; Luke 18:29–30); 22:1–14; 23:33; 24:13 (Mark 13:13; Luke 21:18–19); 24:22 (Mark 13:20); 24:31 (Mark 13:27); 24:37–44 (Mark 13:22–37; Luke 17:26–36); 24:45–51; 25:1–13; 25:14–30 (Luke 19:11–27); 26:24[39] (Mark 14:21).

With this basic overview of judgment texts relating to the Jewish people, including Jesus's own disciples, we can now proceed to explore if and how all of this forms a pattern in which the core elements of Matthean judgment theology are revealed. We shall begin by exploring the criteria of judgment, all of which relate quite closely to concerns present in other near contemporary Jewish texts. Based on these criteria, we shall then ask which individuals and/or groups in the narrative are excluded from or included in salvation, as it is construed in the narrative.

38. See the comment on this pericope above, note 33.
39. Cf. the expression "It would have been better for them not to have been born" in 1 Enoch 38:2, and the eschatological context in which these words refer to sinners there. Cf. Matt 18:6.

2

The Criteria of Judgment for the
Chosen People

The criteria of judgment are related to the three types and times of judgment that we have outlined and given examples of above. Consequently, the questions we now ask will have to involve consideration of the applicability of our conclusions in relation to each of these three categories. The main problem addressed in this chapter is this: on what grounds are individuals and/or groups in Matthew's narrative world punished or rewarded (in this world and the next), and under what circumstances is access to the eschatological kingdom granted? As discussed in the Introduction, such questions are related to a variety of notions providing a conceptual or discursive matrix, within which passages concerned with judgment should be understood. This discursive matrix, then, will have to inform our analysis of Matthew's criteria of judgment, as it provides us with key entry points, without which we will not be able to access Matthew's world of thought and practice. Consequently, in the following section, we shall discuss Matthean understandings of sin and guilt, of obedience and righteousness, repentance and forgiveness, as well as the roles of *pistis* ("trust"/"faithfulness"/"loyalty") and even Jesus within the larger setting provided by the notion of a covenant between the God of Israel and his people.

2.1 Sin and Guilt

When ideas about divine judgment are theologized, the understanding of sin and guilt plays a key role. It is reasonable, therefore, to begin the investigation by considering briefly the definition of sin implied in Matthew. Based on contemporary Jewish patterns of thought, two basic interpretive alternatives present themselves as possibly related to Matthew's text: either the Gospel defines sin principally as disobedience to God's law, or Matthew writes from a theological point of departure similar to the one we find in the Pauline correspondence. The former perspective would be similar to the position taken in many other near-contemporary Jewish texts, including the Qumran writings and later rabbinic literature.[1] Sin, in these texts, is thus defined as something that a person does. In the latter case, Paul's letters, sin is defined primarily, it seems, as a power from which human beings have to be delivered.[2] Sin, according to this view, is thus understood as a state in which a person lives.[3]

Although the Gospel of Matthew never outlines a theology of the nature of sin,[4] there are several clues to a Matthean understanding of sin found in passages related to the criteria on the basis of which God will execute punishment. When these criteria are taken into account, it appears that Matthew's Jesus defines sin along the lines of the non-Pauline alternative mentioned above. Sin, for Matthew, is breaking God's law, and thus, something a person does; it is not a state in which a person lives. While this would seem to be supported by statements such as those found in Matt 5:17–20; 7:21–27, some scholars have

---

1. See, e.g., Sanders, *Paul and Palestinian Judaism*, 111–12, 284, 546.
2. Sanders, *Paul and Palestinian Judaism*, 547. Cf. Winninge, *Sinners*, 212, who claims that, "In opposition to his Jewish heritage, Paul associated universal sinfulness with the status aspect."
3. This does not exclude, of course, that individual deeds are understood by Paul as expressions of sin.
4. So Walter Grundmann, "ἁμαρτάνω," *TDNT*, vol. 1, 303.

pointed to precisely the Sermon on the Mount and the (unreachable) standards for righteousness outlined there in order to argue that Matthew's Jesus is indeed thinking of sin as a state in which one lives. If no one is able to fulfill the law to perfection, to be "perfect" (*teleios*, Matt 5:48), so the logic goes, this implies that life is lived in a constant state of sin. Such arguments, however, are hardly convincing, since the premise does not necessarily lead to the conclusion.

In rabbinic literature, for example, all would agree that sin is defined as something which a person does, and that the nature of what is being done is defined through reference to law. Still, the rabbis never thought that anyone could fulfill the law perfectly, in the sense of flawlessly keeping all commandments at all times—a fact which is also implied by their concern for new ways of understanding atonement after the fall of the temple.[5] While it is possible within a Jewish worldview to draw the conclusion that if no person can fulfill the law perfectly, human existence could be explained as enslaved under the power of sin, as Paul does,[6] there is no evidence in Matthew for such a view. To be sure, Matt 1:21 ("you are to name him Jesus, for he will save his people from their sins") could, if taken in isolation, be read within the context of Pauline theology. However, if we read Matthew's story within its own horizons, this passage is best understood when related to statements such as Matt 9:13 ("I have come to call not the righteous but sinners").[7] For Matthew, not only do sins not atoned for generate

5. This was pointed out already by Ephraim E. Urbach, *The Sages: Their Conceptions and Beliefs* (Cambridge MA: Harvard University Press, 1975), 644, and Montefiore, *Anthology*, 307.
6. See, e.g., Rom 6:6, 22.
7. Cf. Davies and Allison, *Matthew*, 1.106–7. Commenting on Matt 9:13, they define the problem to be the identification of the righteous. They give four interpretive alternatives, the first of which explains that Jesus does not call the righteous because they are supposed to be saved anyway. The other alternatives are, in one way or another, stating that the righteous are not "safe" in their righteousness. Although these authors regard alternative one as unlikely, it needs to be taken seriously, especially against the background of the use of the word "righteous" in the Hebrew Bible as well as in Second-Temple texts and rabbinic literature. While salvation is often ultimately thought of as a result of God's grace, the term "righteous" designates people who, if they are Jewish, keep the law and atone for their sins, and thus, live according to the covenant obligations. Bo Johnson, *Rättfärdigheten i Bibeln* (Göteborg: Gothia, 1985 [English summary]), 118, argues that righteousness in the biblical texts, both the Hebrew Bible and the New Testament, is best understood as a gift from God, not primarily as a demand. This in no way invalidates the law, which is an integrated part of righteousness, although it is not its foundational element. It is of some importance to emphasize, due to the history of Christian theology on the topic, that a person designated "righteous" is not considered never to have sinned. Luke 15:31 may shed

and accumulate guilt, sin also defiles a person (e.g., Matt 15:18–20).[8] As Jonathan Klawans has argued persuasively, such a perspective on sin and its consequences is quite common in early Jewish texts, and does not in any way reduce the understanding of sin as the breaking of the commandments.[9] The accumulation of impurity, however, may defile the temple and lead to catastrophic consequences, including the loss of land and, as in Jubilees (and in Matthew), to apocalyptic disaster. The issue of sin in Matthew is, then, ultimately about purity, which in turn, is the key for understanding God's dwelling—or not—among his people.[10]

In sum, Matthew's narrative is dependent on an understanding of sin and guilt common in contemporary Jewish texts—namely, that sin is not a state in which a person lives, but results from disobedience to the law. Thus, in order to understand sin in Matthew, we need to understand the concept of law. The situation with regard to non-Jews is more complicated, since Jewish law is not directly applicable to them, and we shall therefore return to this issue in Part II. With regard to the Jewish people in Matthew's narrative world, which is our focus here, once we have established that sin is defined by law, so that disobedience to the law is sin, we need to consider possible nuances within this interpretive frame of sin and law, which complicates matters further. Such nuances include the distinction between intentional and unintentional sin, the way in which Jewish law is considered binding, and the notion that sin may be inherited, i.e., that the guilt accumulated by other people's sins will affect individuals and

---

some light on the problem; see discussion by C. F. Evans, *Saint Luke* (London: SCM Press, 1990), 592; Joseph Fitzmeyer, *The Gospel According to Luke* (2 vols; New York: Doubleday, 1970–1985), 2.1085–86. For comprehensive treatment of this theme, see Benno Przybylski, *Righteousness in Matthew and his World of Thought* (Cambridge: Cambridge University Press, 1980). We shall return to the problem of righteousness in Matthew below.

8. On the defilement of sin in Matthew's narrative, see discussion in Runesson, "Purity and Holiness."

9. Jonathan Klawans, *Impurity and Sin in Ancient Judaism* (Oxford: Oxford University Press, 2000). On the influence of this understanding of moral impurity on the New Testament, see also Eyal Regev, "Moral Impurity and the Temple in Early Christianity in Light of Ancient Greek Practice and Qumranic Ideology," *HTR* 97 (2004): 383–411.

10. We shall return to this issue in chapter 2.1.2, as we discuss the nature of Torah obedience in Matthew.

groups who did not commit the sins in question. We shall deal with these complicating factors in turn.

2.1.1 Intentional and Unintentional Sin: A Theology of Adjusted Guilt

The Hebrew Bible[11] and rabbinic literature[12] distinguish between intentional and unintentional sin. This distinction leads to a difference in severity in terms of the amount of guilt that will stain the sinner as a consequence of the sin. Different kinds of sacrifices apply to each type of offense. In rabbinic literature, unintentional sins are atoned for by daily offerings. Intentional sins are, according to *m. Yom.* 8:8, atoned for by sin-offerings (*ḥatt'at*) trespass-offerings (*'asham*), the Day of Atonement, and death, if accompanied by repentance. Repentance itself atones for lesser transgressions, while repentance in relation to grave sins only postpones punishment until the Day of Atonement. Further, it is understood that people will be variously able to follow the law, which, in some texts, lead to an adjustment of the amount of guilt contracted based on the status of the person sinning. Such differences in terms of contracted guilt may apply to, e.g., the scribes and the *'am ha'aretz* ("the people of the land"), respectively. In this case, the theology of adjusted guilt could be described such that unintentional sins committed by scribes are counted as intentional, and intentional sins committed by *'am ha'aretz* are regarded as unintentional.[13] Regarding examples from the Second-Temple period, the book of Jubilees is primarily interested in intentional, grave sins and their consequences. Nevertheless, it is stated that unintentional sins may be atoned for by a prayer of repentance.[14] This does not mean, though, that the author of Jubilees did not acknowledge the sacrificial cult; on the contrary, it is likely that he accepted it in its entirety.[15]

The question is now whether we have reason to believe that this

---

11. E.g., Leviticus 4–6.
12. See, e.g., discussion in Urbach, *Sages*, 643–44.
13. Urbach, *Sages*, 644.
14. *Jub* 22:14.
15. So Sanders, *Paul and Palestinian Judaism*, 380.

distinction between intentional and unintentional sins common in Jewish writings, approximately contemporary with Matthew, exists also in the Gospel, and if so, whether it affects the way the narrative is construed in terms of divine judgment. An initial observation is straightforward enough: there is no explicit mention of such a distinction in Matthew. But does this mean it is not implied as part of how sin is understood? Can we ascertain the existence of such a thought pattern based on its possible (theo-ritual) effects in the story? Like Jubilees, Matthew focuses heavily on intentional grave sins and their consequences.[16] On the other hand, as in rabbinic literature, Matthew is quite clear about people's varying ability to comply with the demands of God, and this is taken into account, as communicated in parable form in Matt 25:14-30. Those who have been given greater responsibilities will also be expected to deliver more, proportionate to their given abilities. In the final judgment, a person is expected to have made use of the gifts given to him or her (by God, the "slave owner," v. 14), so that an amount corresponding to the formula gift + investment (deeds that will benefit the master) can be delivered upon his return. If this is accomplished, the individual in question is allowed entrance into the world to come ("enter into the joy of your master," vv. 21, 23), and will receive recompense for work done.[17]

More importantly, Matthew's narrative presents the law as valid and binding, as we shall discuss in more detail below. The sacrificial cult is an integral part of the law, which means that if the law is accepted, so is the cult, unless the cult is considered to have been defiled (based on the requirements of the law not having been fulfilled) and become unacceptable to God (as we see in the sectarian writings among the Qumran texts). Matthew 5:23-24 (cf. 8:4; 23:16-22), however, indicates clearly that the Matthean Jesus accepts the temple and the sacrificial cult, at least until 23:38, at which point a prophecy of doom is uttered,

---

16. Note that Matt 25:31–46, which applies to non-Jews only, is not concerned with unintentional sins. The lack of awareness, which plays an important role in that parable, concerns the relationship between the king and the least of his brothers, not the sins committed.

17. Cf. the criticism of "the scribes and the Pharisees" in Matt 23:4, which may be interpreted as directed against a too inflexible view of the law in this regard.

based on the defilement of the temple.[18] Until that point in the story, however, acceptance of the sacrificial cult must have been thought of by the author as well as a first-century Jewish audience as implying recognition of the different types of sacrifices required by the law, which in turn distinguish between intentional and unintentional sins.[19]

In other words, as long as the temple cult is accepted in the narrative, it follows by necessity that the distinction between intentional and unintentional sins is understood as maintained. It is significant, of course, that Matthew's Jesus is exclusively focused on intentional grave sins; as we shall see, his is a mission at the end of time when the temple is about to be destroyed because of such sins. This is not a text in which legal details are discussed comprehensively. It is a narrative concentrating on that which matters the most to, and explains, the apocalyptic end which is fast approaching. This does not mean, however, that the distinction between intentional and unintentional sins is not an effective principle that affects how arguments are constructed and decides the outcome of some parts of the story. Indeed, for one group in particular, this distinction impacts their fate: the Jewish crowds (*hoi ochloi*).

The crowds in Matthew's Gospel are presented as misled and mistreated, especially by the Pharisees and their scribes, who are said to "tie up heavy burdens, hard to bear, and lay them on the shoulders of others; but they themselves are unwilling to lift a finger to move them" (Matt 23:4; cf. 7:28–29). By contrast, as Jesus walks from town to town in Galilee, he preaches the kingdom and cures the crowds from their illnesses; he feels compassion for them "because they were harassed and helpless, like sheep without a shepherd" (9:35–36). The crowds respond positively to Jesus's teaching and healing, and seek him everywhere he goes.[20] They are amazed and compare what Jesus

---

18. This will be discussed in greater detail below.

19. Even if the Matthean Jesus emphasizes repentance in his teaching, there is no contradiction between repentance and the sacrificial cult. On the contrary, as we have seen, repentance is integral to sacrificial theology in early Jewish texts. However, the fact that Jesus, in one case, forgives sins (Matt 9:6) has caused many to argue that Matthew rejects the effectiveness of the temple cult. This is, in my view, a misunderstanding of Matthew's narrative. We shall return to this below in chapter 2.4, which deals with repentance and forgiveness.

20. Matt 4:23–25; 5:1; 7:28–29; 8:1, 18; 9:8, 33; 12:15, 23; 13:2; 14:13; 15:30–31; 19:2; 21:8–11; 21:46; 23:1.

does with the teaching they have been given by their scribes, the latter receiving failing grades.

As we shall see in chapter 3, as the Matthean Jesus attacks specific groups or individuals threatening divine judgment, the crowds are exempted.[21] It seems as if the reason for this, the mechanism that causes the narrative to move in this direction regarding judgment, is the characterization of the "crowds" as misled by leaders, who should have taught differently, based on their knowledge of Torah.[22] As a consequence, the guilt contracted by the crowds when they sin cannot be considered to be equal to that of the leaders, who misled them. It appears that we have here an underlying pattern of thought similar to the distinction mentioned above between the *'am ha'aretz* and the scribes in rabbinic literature; intentional sins are dealt with as if unintentional in the case of the crowds, whereas the "scribes and the Pharisees" are condemned in the harshest way possible. The grave sins of the latter are pointed to as the very reason for the (prophesied) destruction of Jerusalem. Indeed, the Pharisaic standard of righteousness, i.e., a certain interpretation of what obedience to the commandments means, will not be enough for people to make it into the kingdom (Matt 5:20; cf. 23:35). We never see this kind of condemnation of the Jewish crowds in Matthew.[23]

The same pattern of thought seems to underlie the Matthean Jesus's pronouncements of condemnation directed against three Jewish towns, as they are compared with what for Matthew's audience were well-known examples of sinful non-Jewish cities. In Matt 11:20–24 (cf. 12:38–42), the rhetoric builds on the assumption that the guilt of these Jewish towns, Chorazin, Bethsaida, and Capernaum, which will lead

Just as the disciples, these Galilean crowds, who have followed Jesus to Jerusalem (Matt 19:2; 20:29; 21:8–11), disappear when Jesus is arrested (the crowd of Matt 27:25 refers to the people of Jerusalem, as we shall discuss in chapter 3).

21. See Terence Donaldson, *Jesus on the Mountain: A Study on Matthean Theology* (Sheffield: JSOT Press, 1985), 207–8. On the expression "this generation" and how it relates to the crowds, see discussion below, chapter 3.2.2.1.

22. Cf. Matt 23:2–3, and the discussion of this passage by Mark Allan Powell, "Do and Keep What Moses Says (Matthew 23:2–7)," *JBL* 114:3 (1995): 431–32.

23. Some scholars have argued that Matt 27:25 should be read as if Matthew here pronounces judgment on the Jewish people as a whole, including the "crowds." This is, however, an unlikely interpretation of the verse; see discussion below, chapter 3.2.2.1.

to their condemnation, is relative to the understanding that could be expected of them, based on their status as the people of God. This understanding on the part of these Jews, which the God of Israel would have the right to expect, is then contrasted with the ignorance of the non-Jews; on the basis of this ignorance (they are not the people of God, they do not have the law, and Jesus has not done any deeds of power among them), the non-Jews in these examples will be judged less harshly. If they would have had the knowledge, or experience, that the people of God have been exposed to, the argument goes, they would have repented. This type of rhetoric proceeds from a basic pattern of thought, which assumes the existence of a difference regarding the amount of guilt contracted based on a distinction between intentional and unintentional sins. Thus, while in rabbinic literature we find examples of a theology of various levels of contracted guilt as applied to scribes and 'am ha'aretz, in Matthew the distinction is applied to specific Jewish and non-Jewish towns, on the one hand, and to the crowds and the "scribes and Pharisees," on the other.

In sum, while we have no explicit mention of a distinction between intentional and unintentional sins, from the dynamics of the narrative and the rhetoric used, we may deduce a theology of sin along such lines, which is similar to what we find in other Jewish texts, both earlier and later than Matthew. The most important result of this distinction, as it is played out in Matthew's narrative, is the way in which guilt is attributed to groups and individuals, and how judgment is construed accordingly in relation to these different groups within the Jewish people. We shall return to discuss in some detail the outcome of such judgment in chapter 3. At this point, however, we need to take a closer look at the crucial issue of the law in Matthew and how it relates to divine judgment in light of how we define sin.

2.1.2 The Validity of the Law

If, in Matthew, sin is defined as disobedience of the commandments of the Torah, it follows, of course, that Jewish law must be considered binding. The topic of Matthew and the law has fascinated scholars over many decades.[24] For obvious reasons, the Sermon on the Mount, and especially, the programmatic statement in Matt 5:17–20, has been *the* center of much debate:

> Do not think that I have come to abolish the law or the prophets; I have come not to abolish but to fulfill. For truly I tell you, until heaven and earth pass away, not one letter, not one stroke of a letter, will pass from the law until all is accomplished. Therefore, whoever breaks one of the least of these commandments, and teaches others to do the same, will be called least in the kingdom of heaven; but whoever does them and teaches them will be called great in the kingdom of heaven. For I tell you, unless your righteousness exceeds that of the scribes and Pharisees, you will never enter the kingdom of heaven.

Ulrich Luz has characterized this passage as belonging among "the most difficult in the Gospel."[25] While there are, undoubtedly, difficulties involved in the historical interpretation of these verses and the so-called antitheses that follow, a look at the history of scholarship seems to indicate that some of the problems that afflict our understanding of Matthew here originate in patristic and later perceptions of the nature of Christianity as a religion that had left "Judaism," or the "synagogue," behind rather than in complexities in the text itself.[26] As a "Christian" text, a close reading of Matthew in its entirety presents us with what seems to be contradictory information, frustrating attempts at reconstructing a coherent and consistent

---

24. See, e.g., Barth, "Law," 58ff, on the interconnectedness of the emphasis on the law and judgment in Matthew. See also, his summary of previous scholarship. See also the discussion in E. P. Sanders, *Jewish Law From Jesus to the Mishnah* (London: SCM Press, 1990); Anthony Saldarini, *Matthew's Christian-Jewish Community* (Chicago: Chicago University Press, 1994), 124–64; Sim, *Christian Judaism*, 123–39 and literature referred to there. The Sermon on the Mount often plays a key role in these discussions. Luz, *Matthew*, 1.170–72, includes important bibliographies covering works dealing with the Sermon of the Mount in exegesis and history of interpretation; cf. Davies and Allison, *Matthew*, 1.481–503. See also Terence Donaldson, *Jesus on the Mountain*; Loader, *Jesus' Attitude towards the Law*, 137–272; Boris Repschinski, *Nicht Aufzulösen, sondern zu erfüllen: Das jüdische Gesetz in den synoptischen Jesuserzählungen* (FzB, 120; Würzburg: Echter Verlag, 2009), 57–142; Blanton IV, "Saved by Obedience," 393–413. A fine introduction to the issues involved is found in James G. Crossley, *The New Testament and Jewish Law: A Guide for the Perplexed* (London: T&T Clark, 2010). Most recently, Varkey, "Salvation in Continuity," deals in great detail with the salvific significance of the Jewish law in Matthew's Gospel.
25. Luz, *Matthew*, 1.213.
26. Cf. Luz, *Matthew*, 1.54.

pattern of thought and practice; understood from within a Jewish interpretive culture, however, many of these problems dissolve.[27] While a full treatment of the topic cannot be included here, the following discussion shall aim to address some of the questions that are of particular interest for the problem of divine judgment.

Gerhard Barth has argued that the author of the Gospel of Matthew is involved in a conflict with other groups of Christ-believers who consider the law obsolete. In such a setting, Matthew lets Jesus utter the words of Matt 5:17 in order to claim the "remaining validity" of the law.[28] The passage has also been understood as a defense against Jews who rejected Jesus as a messiah in Matthew's time, and who claimed that followers of Jesus negotiated the law in such a way that it, for all intents and purposes, was regarded as obsolete and abolished. While the socio-religious context is important and may offer key insights into the social dynamics which explain why the narrative was formed the way it was, what I am interested in here is the content of the narrative itself, rather than hypotheses about conflicts with other groups. While such conflicts certainly took place,[29] it is still possible halakhically and theologically to explain this passage within the overall logic of the story itself.[30]

Our first question is this: What exactly is meant by Barth's claim of the "remaining validity" of the law? Is it a *nova lex* Matthew is promoting,[31] portraying Jesus as a new lawgiver in contrast to the

---

27. It is difficult to avoid the impression, especially when reading older literature on the subject, that if statements similar to Matt 5:17–20 had been found in another Second-Temple text unrelated to later forms of Christianity, their interpretation would have seemed much more straightforward.

28. See Barth, "Law," 62–75, here 70–71.

29. Matt 7:15–21 speaks of (Jewish) followers of Jesus who are accused of engaging in empty confessions, but not doing the will of the father in heaven. Similarly, several passages describe debates with Jews who reject Jesus's authority, accusing him of breaking the law (e.g., Matt 12:1–14). Such passages may indeed mirror concerns growing from the author's experiences and/ or reveal conflicts building up around the historical Jesus and his followers (the latter certainly does not exclude the former).

30. Such a focus on the narrative should, in any case, be the primary task of any investigation into the meaning of individual pericopae.

31. Cf. Bornkamm, "End-Expectation," 25, who is of the opinion that while some of the so-called antitheses (the first, second, and fourth) sharpen the law, the others, in fact, abolish the law (the third, fifth, and sixth). According to Bornkamm, this combination of a radicalization of some parts of the law, and the abolition of other parts, represent the validity of the law, which must then, in some aspects, be regarded as new law. For Bornkamm, this is the result of the tension between the

old one, Moses? If so, the criteria of judgment would be based on a set of laws not shared between the Matthean Jesus and other Jews in the story. This, in turn, would mean that any judgment, including the divine wrath leading to the apocalyptic end of the world and the final judgment, would measure people's response to this new law rather than reflect abuse and manipulation of the law given at Sinai. The choice of such an interpretive move would mean that God is described as quite short-tempered, since "the old law" was invalid in the first place and could thus not be used as a basis for condemnation in the present.

Barth shows convincingly that such a scenario is very unlikely. Jesus is not portrayed as a "second Moses" in the sense of a giver of a new law. He argues against the view of Bacon and Kilpatrick,[32] and claims that the Moses-typology, based on the description of the location where the sermon was delivered, and other related motifs, does not mean that Jesus replaces Moses.[33] Rather, the description of the setting of the sermon triggers the understanding that here, on this mountain, the *right interpretation* of the law of Sinai was given. Barth compares this compositional strategy with an event involving Joshua ben Hananiah, a pupil of Johanan ben Zakkai, and according to the sources, a contemporary with Matthew. According to the rabbinic passage, Joshua ben Hananiah once kissed the stone where Eliezer ben Hyrcanus sat when he gave a lecture on the law and said: "This stone is like Mount Sinai, and the one that sat upon it like the ark of the covenant."[34] Barth continues:

> The law of Moses is for him [i.e. Matthew] unquestionably the law of God and also for the Church. Jesus' interpretation of the law and his

evangelist's allegiance to Jesus's own words and his own understanding of the law in the "Judaistic Jewish-Christian tradition."

32. B. W. Bacon, *Studies in Matthew* (New York: Henry Holt, 1930); George Dunbar Kilpatrick, *The Origins of the Gospel According to Saint Matthew* (Oxford: Clarendon, 1946).

33. Cf. Dale C. Allison, *The New Moses: A Matthean Typology* (Minneapolis: Fortress, 1993), whose argument goes beyond the replacement paradigm.

34. Barth, "Law," 157–58. The rabbinic quotation is taken from Songs Rabbah on 1:3. The late date of this collection of midrashim (about 500–640 CE) should be noted, even if the words are attributed to a first to second-century rabbi. The point here is not, however, to argue for a date of this saying in the first century. Rather, the intention is to show that this type imagery is not foreign to Jewish tradition in settings involving the interpretation of the law given at Sinai.

commandments are not in opposition to the law of Moses, but are rather again and again based on the Old Testament (12:1–7; 15:1–20; 19:1–9). The law which holds in the Church is identical with the 'law and the prophets.' Hence the Moses typology can only be intended to confirm the teaching of Jesus as genuine teaching from Sinai.[35]

Barth is not alone in this assessment. We find similar interpretations in studies by Anthony Saldarini,[36] David Sim,[37] Andrew Overman,[38] Phillip Sigal,[39] Birger Gerhardsson,[40] and Blain Charette.[41] Robert Banks notes when commenting on Matt 5:17: "[T]he true solution lay in the understanding of 'fulfilment' in terms of affirmation of the whole of the law [...] yet only through its transformation into the teaching of Christ, which was something new and unique in comparison with it."[42]

---

35. Barth, "law," 158.
36. Saldarini, *Christian-Jewish Community*: "Though some commentators have argued that the author supersedes the Jewish law with a new Christian law or annuls it in favour of a new spirit of the law, in fact he carefully defends his *interpretation of Jewish law* and custom by establishing Jesus as the authoritative teacher of the law and by providing arguments to support his view." (124).
37. Sim, *Apocalyptic Eschatology*: "Moreover, where Mark sets the conflict within the context of keeping the law – the Pharisees abide by the law while Jesus does not – Matthew carefully edits his source and makes clear that the issue is not whether the Torah is valid but how it is to be correctly interpreted." (190).
38. Andrew Overman, *Matthew's Gospel and Formative Judaism* (Minneapolis: Fortress 1990): "What is most characteristic about the Matthean conflict story is that these stories portray Jesus as an accurate and true interpreter of the law. This helps to distinguish Matthew's treatment of the conflict stories from that of Mark." (78–79).
39. Phillip Sigal, *The Halakhah of Jesus of Nazareth According to the Gospel of Matthew* (Lanham: University Press of America, 1986). See especially, chapter 4 on Matthew's understanding of halakhah related to divorce, which Sigal claims is unique in the first century, and chapter 5 on Matthean Sabbath halakhah.
40. Birger Gerhardsson, *The Ethos of the Bible* (London: Darton, Longman and Todd, 1982): "one thing is both clear and of great importance for the person interested in Matthew's line of reasoning: the Christian scribe who here interprets Jesus acquits him wholly of the charge of wanting to 'abolish' any of the law's commands. On the other hand, Jesus has, in his view, followed a generally accepted juridical axiom: that fundamental law take precedence over all other law...Since the legal experts of the Jews saw in God's law a great unity, this axiom became for them the principle that 'weightier' commands, when in conflict with 'lighter' commands, take precedence over them. According to Matthew, Jesus has adopted this principle" (41–42).
41. Charette, *Recompense*. Charette acknowledges that Matthew understands the law as valid, but he also modifies this view when looking at the criteria of judgment: "In the Gospel the authority of the Mosaic law is not opposed or rejected, yet neither is it regarded as final. With the establishment of a new covenant relationship between God and his people centred in Jesus, redemption is now located in one's acknowledgement of Jesus and obedience to the way prescribed by him" (165–66). This means, according to Charette, that Matthew departs from the common Jewish understanding of the relation between covenant, law, and redemption, referred to by Charette using E. P. Sanders' term "covenantal nomism." This latter conclusion is problematic and will be the object of discussion in subsequent chapters.
42. Robert Banks, *Jesus and the Law in the Synoptic Tradition* (Cambridge: Cambridge University Press, 1975), 234.

The question is, of course, how original or transformative Matthew's Jesus really is, especially since the methods used for interpreting the law were often similar to those we see in other Jewish writings, including later rabbinic literature. It is clear that the so-called antitheses of the Sermon on the Mount are not proper antitheses, since they are not opposed to or abolish the law, as also Davies and Allison insists: "Jesus does not overturn the Pentateuch."[43] Benno Przybylski's conclusion is to the point: "[T]his new interpretation of the law is representative of an extremely meticulous observance of the law. I would suggest that if this type of interpretation does not correspond directly to the hermeneutical principle of making a fence around the Torah, it has at least been strongly influenced by this particular principle."[44]

The Sermon on the Mount must therefore be understood within the context of other debates about the Torah in and around the first century, which leads us to the question: does Matthew oppose other Jewish understandings of Torah and its interpretation? Despite Matt 23:2–3, it seems that Matthew claims that Jesus sometimes does reject other interpretations, although not in principle, but in certain respects based on a specific criterion (cf. Matt 15:1–20).[45] For example, Matthew does not present Jesus as diametrically opposed to all Pharisaic interpretations of the law, which is also indicated by texts such as Matt 23:23 and 12:11. As Barth puts it, "Matthew does not reject the Rabbinic tradition in principle and as a whole."[46]

43. Davies and Allison, *Matthew*, 1.501.

44. Benno Przybylski, *Righteousness in Matthew and his World of Thought* (Cambridge: Cambridge University Press, 1980), 83.

45. Cf. Luz, *Matthew*, 2.335: "In my judgment, in this text Matthew is interested neither in basically rejecting the tradition of the elders. . . . That means that we can only say that where the tradition of the elders is in conflict with God's command itself, Matthew categorically rejects it." We shall return to this in the following section.

46. Barth, "Law," 89. See also Sigal, *Halakhah*, who primarily deals with two halakhic questions in Matthew's Gospel, on divorce and on the Sabbath, and locates them in what he calls a "proto-Rabbinic" context. Chronologically speaking, we should note that rabbinic texts are later and should only serve the purpose of illustrating the fact that the rabbis worked within a similar interpretive trajectory as Matthew did before them, and that they often came to kindred conclusions. Thus, it is anachronistic to assume, as Barth does, that Matthew did not reject rabbinic tradition, since this tradition had not yet been established, neither in the time of Jesus, nor when Matthew wrote. Rather, Matthew and the later rabbis draw from the same pool of Jewish hermeneutical resources.

There are, indeed, aspects of individual commandments about which the Matthean Jesus and the Pharisees would have agreed. The critique in such cases is, contrary to, e.g., Matt 15:3–7 and 23:16–22, not a critique of how a commandment should be interpreted, but more of how Pharisees are breaking what all agree are commandments that must be observed, such as the prohibition against the shedding of innocent blood (cf. 23:31, 34–36). Further, the accusations against, especially, the Pharisees sometimes have the character of ad hominem when the Pharisees *as a group* are condemned (23:3, 5–7).

It is of some importance to note that, in addition to the programmatic statements on the binding authority of the (Mosaic) law in Matthew, there are several examples of specific commandments that are brought up for discussion as the narrative progresses. The interpretation of such commandments has often been divided into two parts by scholars, distinguishing between moral and ritual aspects of the law. While this has sometimes led to anachronistic "Christian" readings of Matthew, such that the "ethical" parts of the law have been understood as having remaining value, whereas ritual aspects have been judged to have lost their significance, it is of some importance to pay attention to this distinction, not least in light of our concerns here with divine judgment, as we shall see.

If we summarize some of the more important examples of moral aspects of the law, we may note that the following commandments are said to be valid, although they need to be interpreted in line with the messianic authority of Jesus: adultery (5:27–30), divorce (5:31–32; 19:3–9), bloodshed (5:21–22;[47] cf. 27:6), retribution (5:38–42), honoring father and mother (15:4; 19:19), and greed (19:21–24).[48] In addition,

---

47. The point of Matthew's argument is, of course, not to abolish the law's prohibition of murder, but to widen the application of this law to cover also the related feelings of anger as well as insults (cf. Matt 24:10). The same hermeneutics of building a fence around the law apply to other commandments as well, such as the prohibition of adultery (5:27–30), and, even more sharply, vows (5:33–37), retribution (5:38–42), and love of neighbor (5:43–47).

48. That this passage is a comment on greed as a sin preventing a person from entering the kingdom may be inferred from the fact that Matthew notes specifically that the young man decides not to follow Jesus when he is asked to leave all his riches to the poor (cf. Matt 23:25). Thus, despite the many commandments he has fulfilled, the man violates the law requiring radical love for the neighbor; full loyalty to God (*teleios*; cf. Matt 5:48) is, therefore, lacking.

jealously (*phthonos*) is mentioned in association with the chief priests and the elders as they hand Jesus over to Pilate (Matt 27:18). While not previously explicitly mentioned as a sin, such emotions (and their results) are clearly viewed as forbidden and, by implication, defiling.[49] The key principles of the law, which should govern halakhic decisions, are summarized in Matt 23:23 as "the weightier matters of the law: justice and mercy and faithfulness [*pistis*]."[50] We may also note that public reading of Torah (law) in synagogues is taken for granted in the narrative, and that Jesus is said to do much of his teaching in synagogues (4:23; 9:35; 13:54). Such teaching was, judging from the Sermon on the Mount and other passages in Matthew,[51] understood to be focused on interpreting the law for the people.[52]

While the morally-oriented commandments are considered key to life in the kingdom, the focus on the moral law does not exclude the validity of the ritual aspects of law. Since this issue has been the object of some debate, it needs to be addressed in some detail.

2.1.2.1 Cult and/or "Ethics"? Human and Divine Relationships

If Jewish law is binding, according to Jesus's interpretation of it, does this mean the entire law, or is the cultic or ritual part of the law presented as obliterated, as Christian tradition has often sought to claim? In other words, are the Jewish characters in this story judged on the basis of the moral aspects of the law only, or do they need to keep both moral and ritual commandments in order to fulfill God's will?

Returning to Gerhard Barth, he discusses ritual law as a separate

---

49. Cf. Mark 7:22, which lists avarice (*pleonexia*) and envy (*ofthalmos*) as sins that defile a person. The related concept of coveting is, of course, prohibited in the Decalogue (Exod 10:17, LXX *epithymeō*; cf. Rom 13:9). Cf. Luz, *Matthew*, 3.497, who identifies envy as "the worst of all evils," referring to *Wis* 2:24; *T. Sim.* 3–4; Philo, *Spec. leg.* 3:3. In Matt 27:18, however, the main point might be to combine the accusation of the leaders who break the law with an allusion to the fate of biblical heroes, such as Daniel, along the lines of traditions appearing in 3 Macc 6:7 ("Daniel, who through envious slanders was thrown down into the ground to lions as food for wild animals, you brought up to the light unharmed"; cf. 3 Macc 6:8; Matt 12:39–40), or Joseph (cf. Acts 7:9: "The patriarchs, jealous of Joseph, sold him into Egypt; but God was with him").

50. Cf. Micah 6:8.

51. See, e.g., summarizing statements such as Matt 4:23; 9:35. Cf. Matt 7:29.

52. See Saldarini, *Christian-Jewish Community*, 124–64, which is still, together with Loader, *Jesus' Attitude*, one of the best discussions available of the law in Matthew.

issue and notes the difficulties involved in the interpretation of Matt 15:11 ("it is not what goes into the mouth that defiles a person, but it is what comes out of the mouth that defiles"). He doubts that Matthew could be interpreted as conveying the same overall message as its Markan parallel in Mark 7:15, which is followed in Mark 7:19 by the narrator's comment: "Thus he declared all foods clean." For Barth, the question regarding Matthew is this: does this attitude toward food laws break "the principle of the abiding validity of the law and the prophets? [...] Is a Jewish Christianity conceivable which in its battle for the law defends its validity most acutely, and yet abolishes the food laws?"[53]

Agreeing with Bacon,[54] Barth sees the answer in Matt 15:20. Matthew's version of this story is concerned with the ritual washing of hands before meals, not with abolishing the food laws. Mark's *katharizōn panta ta brōmata* (Mark 7:19) is missing, and Matthew ends the passage with the concluding and explanatory statement that "to eat with unwashed hands does not defile" (Matt 15:20). Further, Barth notes that the difficulty presented by Matt 15:11, that what goes into the mouth does not defile a person, does not really pose a problem with regard to the question of the validity of the law, since a rabbi such as Johanan ben Zakkai could have said the same, without thereby abolishing the law.[55] "Most probably," Barth continues, "Matthew is thinking here only of subordination" of one principle to another.[56] Referring to texts such as Matt 5:23 on sacrifice and 17:24–27 on the temple tax, Barth concludes that, "Matthew retains the ceremonial law, but it has undergone a reassessment under Christian motives."[57]

---

53. Barth, "Law," 89–90.
54. Bacon, *Studies*.
55. Barth, "Law," 90. The reference is from Buber's edition of Tanhuma from 1885, Huqqat §26: "In your life, the corps does not defile, nor does water make pure, but it is an ordinance of the King of the Kings, God spoke: I have made a law, I have established an ordinance; no man is justified in transgressing my ordinances."
56. Barth, "Law," 90. See also the discussion by Sim, *Christian Judaism*, 135, which is very much to the point.
57. Barth, "Law," 90–91. Commenting on Matt 15:1–20, Davies and Allison, *Matthew*, 2.517, states that "we do not find in Mt 15 an abolition of Old Testament purity laws." Such an interpretation would "run afoul of other Matthean texts (e.g. 5:17–20)." A similar opinion is stated by Ulrich Luz, *Das Evangelium nach Matthäus* (2. Teilband, Mt 8–17; Zürich: Benzinger, 1990), 425, who underlines that

While the word "Christian" is obviously anachronistic when used in this setting,[58] as is also the word "church" used elsewhere,[59] Barth's analysis here, which aligns well with the approaches of many later interpreters, is still valid in many respects. Barth further supports his view on the legitimacy of ritual aspects of the law with reference to Jesus's debates about the Sabbath.[60] This is interesting, not least since many later Christian writers on Matthew have claimed that Jesus's attitude precisely to the Sabbath reveals that he opposes the ("ceremonial") law. Two interrelated stories in Matthew deal with the subject: Matt 12:1-8 and 12:9-14 (cf. Matt 24:20). Reading these passages in the context of later rabbinic literature is instructive and provides us with a tool with which to identify the nature of the Matthean Jesus's claims.[61] It may be said at once that the conflict in Matt 12:1-14 is, as R. T. France states, "not on whether the sabbath should be observed (there is no suggestion that Jesus questions that) but on what that observance entailed in practical terms."[62] France, as others before him, notes that rabbinic literature provides comparative material, which can shed light on Matthew's message. Texts such as *Mek. Shab.* on Exod 31:12ff. and *m. Yoma* 8:6 present us with important comparative material discussing what constitutes "work" on a Sabbath.[63] In *m. Yoma* 8:6, the ruling is that, "[i]f anyone is seized with

it is a question of "die Überordnung des liebesgebots über die Reinheitsvorschriften." See also the extensive discussion in Nolland, *Matthew*, 606–28.

58. Matthew is, indeed, unaware of the very term.

59. For discussion and critique of these terms as used by New Testament scholars, see Runesson, "The Question of Terminology," 53–77.

60. Barth, "Law," 91. For further discussion, see also Crossley, *Jewish Law*, 26–44.

61. On the Sabbath, see the recent study by Nina L. Collins, *Jesus, The Sabbath, and The Jewish Debate: Healing on the Sabbath in the 1st and 2nd Centuries CE* (LNTS 474; New York: T&T Clark, 2014), which deals extensively with rabbinic literature.

62. R.T. France, *The Gospel According to Matthew* (Grand Rapids: Eerdmans, 2007), 455. Luomanen, *Entering the Kingdom*, 89–90, speaks, on the one hand, of Matthew as debating Jewish law with other Jews, being careful "not to give the impression that Jesus explicitly annuls some parts of the written Torah" (90), but on the other, suggests that his attitude to the Sabbath in fact is a "violation" of it, for the sake of mercy. The problem here seems to me to be a terminological one. While Luomanen is certainly correct that Matthew's Jesus judges some commandments to be "heavier" than others, so did other Jews; none of them, however, would have understood the setting aside of one commandment judged to be less important in order to be able to fulfill another considered to be more important as a "violation" of the law. Cf. Crossley, *Jewish Law*, 36ff.

63. The fact that Matthew presents Jesus's rulings embedded in a narrative, and rabbinic literature does not, should not draw our attention away from the principles underlying the rulings stated.

ravenous hunger, he is to be fed even with unclean (*teme'im*) things until his eyes become clear."[64]

The basic principle in rabbinic literature is that life always takes precedence;[65] saving life overrides the Sabbath, and this is also the principle noted in Matt 12:11–12 (applied to both animals and humans). Debates, then as now, may concern which situations should be regarded as legitimate in terms of overriding the Sabbath. For the Matthean Jesus, the decision to feed the hungry and heal the sick represent rulings, which legitimately relate to and derive from the central principle of saving life, and thus, these deeds of compassion override the Sabbath. It seems clear that while the literary characters[66] of the story did not agree with these rulings, later rabbis would have had no difficulty in seeing this line of argument as valid and would probably have agreed that this would have been one among several legitimate views.[67]

Ultimately, the conflict between Jesus and the Pharisees here is one over authority: who has the right to make rulings regarding the Sabbath? The problem is addressed in Matt 12:3–8. In this passage, the Matthean Jesus first refers to holy scriptures in which king David acts with authority, overriding the law regarding the bread of the presence due to the hunger of his men (vv. 3–4). The fact that, for Matthew, Jesus is the son of David, i.e., the Davidic king,[68] turns the incident in the grain fields into a messianic proclamation, with hunger as the connecting word between the stories. The authority of Jesus is the authority of the Davidic Messiah. Adding to this claim, the Matthean

64. Cf. *Mek.* tractate Amalek (Lauterbach, 2.169), where circumcision is said to supersede the Sabbath.
65. Cf. e.g., y. Yom 8.4.
66. The controversies may represent first-century legal debates. As Saldarini, *Community*, 126 puts it: "the Sabbath controversy in chapter 12 reflect inner Jewish conflict in the late first century." Controversies about the Sabbath were also taking place within and between the various branches of the Jesus movement; cf. Gos. Thom. 27: "if you do not observe the Sabbath as a Sabbath you will not see the Father."
67. Samuel Tobias Lachs, *A Rabbinic Commentary on the New Testament: The Gospels of Matthew, Mark and Luke* (Hoboen: Ktav Publishing House, 1987), 198, lists several passages of interest: *Mek.* on Exod 31:13, 14; *b. Yoma* 85b; Apoc. Bar. 14.18; *b. Eruv.* 43a. Note especially *Mek.* on Exod 31:14: "the Sabbath is given to you, but you are not surrendered to the Sabbath" (Lauterbach, 3.198).
68. Matt 1:1; 9:27; 12:23; 15:22; 20:30; 21:9, 15. Matt 22:41–46 does not contradict this identification, but rather, claims that Jesus's rule will transcend that of David, adding, after the resurrection, a global reach of his reign. Cf. discussion in Nolland, *Matthew*, 916–17.

Jesus refers to another example from the law: the law itself requires that the Sabbath be overridden by the more important offering of sacrifices by the priests, without the priests contracting guilt (vv. 5–6). Since that which is happening around the Messiah, i.e., the kingdom,[69] is greater than even the temple, it follows that Jesus, who is bringing the kingdom into being, has the authority to establish legitimate halakhah regarding the Sabbath. The comparison with the temple gives the Matthean Jesus an opportunity to also reveal the principle on which this ruling is based, using a quote from Hos 6:6: mercy (*eleos*; Matt 12:7; cf. 9:13; 23:23).

The climax is reached in 12:8, where Jesus states that "the son of man (*huios tou anthrōpou*) is lord of the Sabbath." The interpretation of this expression, "son of man," which, in Aramaic, may simply mean "man" (*ben 'enosh*),[70] must be based on how the expression "son of man" is used in Matthew more generally. While Matt 9:8 emphasizes that what Jesus does is interpreted within the wider frame of human power, stemming from God, other passages indicate, as France notes, "a figure with unique authority."[71]

What we have in Matt 12:1–14 is thus an inner-Jewish debate containing three interrelated, and in this context, necessary components. First, we find the rulings: feeding the hungry and healing the sick overrides the Sabbath. Second, we are informed about the hermeneutical principle leading to this conclusion: saving life overrides the Sabbath, and mercy and doing good are both understood as aspects derived from this central principle. Third, the authority of the person making the rulings is described as validating the rules: the "son of man," who, implicitly, is related to king David and said to be the bringer of things greater than the temple, namely, the kingdom of heaven.

---

69. The Greek in Matt 12:6 is in the neuter, which indicates that Jesus is not referring to himself here, but to that which is happening around him. Matthew's Gospel is quite clear about what that something is: the kingdom of heaven, which is the work of God's Spirit (Matt 12:28). Such an implied reference to the kingdom further emphasizes Jesus's messianic authority.

70. Cf. here *Mek.* on Exod 31.14.

71. France, *Matthew*, 462. 326–28; cf. Dan 7:13–14. See also Davies and Allison, *Matthew*, 2.43–52. For a full discussion of the expression "son of man," see Chrys C. Caragounis, *The Son of Man: Vision and Interpretation* (Tübingen: Mohr Siebeck, 1986).

The hermeneutical principle (mercy) used for interpreting what should count as work on the Sabbath is of importance, since it relates to the overall concern of the Gospel: the double love command (Matt 22:37–40; cf. 7:12). This is the heart of the interpretation of the law, and the method is the same as in later rabbinic literature: the weightier matters take precedence over the less weighty commandments when situations arise in which the two come into conflict. Thus, while tithing of mint, dill, and cumin must be done, the fulfillment of this commandment is meaningless if the weightier matters of the law—justice, mercy, and loyalty/faithfulness/trust (*krisis, eleos, pistis*)—are neglected (Matt 23:23). In the same way, mercy (*eleos*) determines what are acceptable activities on the Sabbath in light of the imminent coming of the kingdom and the apocalyptic calamities that will precede it. This does not abolish or violate the Sabbath; rather, as with all commandments, its status is relative to that principle that is defined as the greatest commandment in the law.[72]

Now if, in Matt 23:23, neglect of the weightier matters of the law will provoke divine wrath and lead to judgment, and, by implication, the same would be the case if mercy was neglected on the Sabbath,[73] do we have any passages in Matthew stating that neglect of the Sabbath, or of tithing or any other ritual commandment, would be condemned by God? While no explicit condemnation is narrated in relation to individual ritual commandments, the story provides enough material to support the conclusion that these commandments should, according to the Matthean Jesus, be observed as part of the covenant obligations. We may note, e.g., that Matt 5:18–19 states that anyone who breaks even the least of the commandments—which clearly refers to ritual aspects of the law, such as tithing—shall contract guilt, which will result in punishment consisting of being identified as the least in the kingdom; status displacement, in other words.

---

72. Cf. Sigal, *Halakhah*, 158–59: "What Jesus did was not to transcend the Sabbath or spiritualize its observance, an effort combated by Philo. He acted as a proto-rabbi by applying hermeneutics and other principles in the normal course of interpreting the requirements of the Sabbath."

73. Note the accusation against the Pharisees in Matt 12:7, where they are said to condemn the innocent.

Again, we see that once Matthew's story is read as an expression of Second-Temple Judaism, and compared to the culture of other near-contemporary Jewish writings, including later rabbinic texts, the logic of the narrative, and thus its aims, emerge as coherent. If we were to assume that the Mosaic law, in one way or another, had been abolished or re-written, rather than re-interpreted, Matthew's text appears to reveal contradictory statements, which in turn, need to be explained as the result of editorial work by a redactor who kept some but reworked other parts of the collection of traditions he had access to without much consistency. While it is clear that the author of this text had access to sources that he incorporated into his narrative, *reading Matthew as a Jewish text authored in a setting in which Jewish debates make sense and are important reduces the number of supplementary explanations and hypotheses that otherwise need to be adduced in order to explain the text as we have it today.* Indeed, once the perspective has begun to shift from a non-Jewish to a Jewish understanding of the law, a number of passages seem to fall into place. In addition to the Sabbath commandment, there are several other instances in Matthew's Gospel that reveal a concern for ritual aspects of the law, although these never dominate the story; as noted above, the Matthean Jesus is, like the prophets of the Hebrew Bible, driven by a passionate critique of what he believes are moral atrocities that break the law and provoke divine wrath. Nevertheless, the halakhic culture of the text gives voice to the fullness of the law. A summarizing overview of the ritual aspects of the text will support this overall picture.

Specific practices and commandments confirmed by Jesus are mentioned as they become relevant for the progression of the story. In addition to the dietary laws discussed above, these include almsgiving (6:3–4); individual prayer (in fixed form; Matt 6:5–13); fasting (6:16–18; cf. 9:14–15); the Sabbath (12:1–14[74]; 24:20); laws on purification of individuals healed from leprosy (8:4); wearing tzitzit and, most likely, tefillin[75] (9:20; 14:36; 23:5); tithing (23:23);[76] impurity related to food

---

74. See especially, Davies and Allison, *Matthew*, 2.304–22.
75. See Num 15:37–41; Deut 22:12; cf. Zech 8:23. While Jesus's tefillin (phylacteries) are not explicitly mentioned by Matthew, it is very likely that a first-century audience would have included such,

vessels and corpses (implied by the rhetoric in 23:25–26);[77] festivals (Passover, 26:2, 17–35); laws regulating or related to the sacrificial cult, including the temple tax (5:23–24; 12:3–5; 17:24–27; 23:16–22); and oaths and vows (5:33–37; 15:3–6; 23:16–22).[78] As we discussed in the Introduction, in light of the seriousness with which the law, generally, and some commandments, more specifically, are brought up and discussed in the Gospel, it is very likely that circumcision was also part of the ritual worldview which produced the perspective on law otherwise explicitly noted in the text. This means that the law and its interpretation seem to be set within the overall context of the covenant between the Jewish people and the God of Israel, a topic to which we shall return below.

The Matthean narrative thus operates with the law as a foundational principle, which is activated in divine judgment. This is true both regarding the moral and the ritual aspects of the law, although the

as they imagined the Messiah based on this story. Supporting such a conclusion is the fact that the critique in Matt 23:5 is aimed at the size of these important identity markers, not the practice itself. Indeed, it would be difficult to argue that someone who is described as wearing tzitzit would not also be accepting the practice of using tefillin.

76. While R. T. France, *The Gospel According to Matthew: An Introduction and Commentary* (Leicester: Inter-Varsity Press, 1985), correctly notes that for Matthew minor commandments lose their meaning if the weightier (moral) aspects of the law are ignored, he makes, in my view, a common mistake when he goes on to paraphrase the intention of Matt 23:23: "observe your meticulous rules *if you like*, but don't therefore neglect the things that really matter" (328; my italics). As Matt 5:17–19 clearly shows, following even the minor commandments is not a matter of choice if righteousness is sought. In France's 2007 commentary on Matthew (Eerdmans), he has removed this paraphrase, but still seems to maintain the same overall understanding of law in Matthew: "there may be an ironical element here too: 'I can't object to your tithing herbs, but what matters is that you focus on justice, mercy, and faithfulness'" (873). David Sim's position here, which is referred to by France in a footnote, is historically more in tune with the evidence: see Sim, *Christian Judaism*, 131–32. It should also be noted that tithing supported the priesthood in the Jerusalem temple. Thus, tithing even herbs (which is not part of the requirements in the Hebrew Bible, but which the rabbis—and the Pharisees according to Matthew—endorsed) is a strong indication that the Matthean Jesus regarded the temple cult as valid until Jesus's prophecy of destruction. The prophetic critique of sacrifice was done from the same perspective: the cult is only valid if the moral principles of the law are upheld, and we see this also in the Psalter, e.g., Ps 51:16–17 (Heb 18–19) and 51:19 (Heb 51:21); cf. Deut 33:19; Ps 4:5 (Heb 4:6).

77. In addition, the fact that Jesus never enters the house of a non-Jew in Matthew may be an indication of the purity concerns that are more explicitly elaborated on elsewhere in the text. See, e.g., Matt 8:5–13. Note also that while Mark 7:24 states that Jesus entered a house in the area of Tyre, Matthew's version of this passage does not include this detail, and adds the explicit statement that Jesus had only come to save "the lost sheep of the people of Israel": Matt 15:21, 24. Matthew's Jesus also instructs his disciples not to engage with non-Jews in their mission to prepare for the kingdom (10:5–6), although this is later reversed, after Jesus has been given authority over the entire world (28:18–20).

78. Cf. Deut 23:22 (23): "But if you refrain from vowing, you will not incur guilt."

moral aspects dominate the story. The evidence consists both of programmatic statements and discussion of specific commandments. The Matthean Jesus does, however, take one more step to make clear exactly where the problem lies. Several explicit statements in the Gospel stress that "lawlessness" (*anomia*) will cause divine wrath to be unleashed: 5:20; 7:23; 13:41; 23:28; 24:12.[79] Behavior identified as lawlessness excludes from the kingdom of heaven both Jesus's followers (7:23) and those who oppose the movement (13:41; 23:28; cf. 24:12). Those who lack the law altogether, the non-Jews, are regarded more generally as sinners (26:45[80]) and need to be taught the law if they are to become part of the kingdom (28:18–20).[81]

It is of fundamental importance for the understanding of the Gospel to note that, in terms of judgment, the problem in Matthew is not that "scribes and Pharisees" keep the law, or keep it too strictly. On the contrary, they simply do not keep it rigorously enough. The point in Matthew is not that the author is attacking "antinomian Christians."[82] There are no such characters in the story, and we need to explore the story itself before we aim to explain the text based on the social location in which it was authored. Rather, the key, in my opinion, lies in Matthew's critique of Pharisees and the charge that they do not keep the law of Moses. In Matt 7:23, any (Jewish[83]) follower of Jesus (7:21–22) who does not follow Matthew's strict interpretation of the law, with its emphasis on doing justice, mercy, and faith (23:23), will be the target

---

79. In Matthew, the law (*nomos*) refers to the law of Moses (Matt 5:17–18; 7:12; 11:13; 12:5; 22:36, 40; 23:23; cf. 15:3; 19:17–18). The meaning of lawlessness (*anomia*) is thus dependent on such an understanding of law and should be seen as the antithesis of keeping Moses's law. The apocalyptic setting for some of the references to *anomia*, or this concept's relationship to the concept of sin (cf. 1 John 3:4), do not contradict this interpretation of the terms as they are used in the cultural world of Matthew's perspective. Cf. *Did.* 16:3–4. See also Donald Senior, *The Gospel of Matthew* (Nashville: Abingdon, 1997), who, as he deals with Matthew's understanding of the Jewish law, notes that Jesus repeatedly "warns his disciples about those who are 'lawless' (from the Greek word *anomia*; see 7:23; 13:41; 24:12)" (40). For a recent definition of *anomia* as "failure to act in a manner that conforms to the stipulations of the Torah," see the discussion in Blanton IV, "Saved by Obedience," 393–413, here 403.
80. For discussion of Matthew's generalized view of non-Jews, see chapter 5.1.
81. There are some exceptions to this rule as we shall see below in chapter 7.3.
82. Cf. James E. Davison, "Anomia and the Question of an antinomian Polemic in Matthew," *JBL* 104 (1985): 617–33. See also Stephanie von Dobbeler, "Wahre und falsche Christen oder: An der Frage der Orthopraxie scheiden sich die Geister," *BZ* 50 (2006): 174–95.
83. Cf. Matt 10:5–6.

of the same judgment as the "scribes and the Pharisees," whose type of righteousness will not be enough, quantitatively, for the kingdom (5:20). In the same way, Matthew's Jesus attacks the "false prophets" of the movement in 7:15 by using the same kind of rhetorical distinction between the "inside" and the "outside" of a person as he does against the "scribes and Pharisees" elsewhere in the Gospel, most strongly in 23:25–28. In other words, Matthew's narrative is critiquing Jews who confess Jesus but act like Pharisees who do not.[84] In Matthew, then, the Pharisees are those who break God's law (15:3–9; 23:23, 28).[85] They can be portrayed as knowing, or having access to the law, but still not following through in interpretive practice: *legousin gar kai ou poiousin* (23:3).[86] Non-Jews generally, or non-Jewish sympathizers to the Jesus

84. As I have argued elsewhere regarding the setting in which the Gospel was produced by a group of Pharisees leaving the larger Pharisaic movement after 70 CE, on sociological grounds, the most likely scenario would be to assume that some members of the Matthean group chose to remain within the association of the Pharisees when those who produced the Gospel left. See Runesson, "Re-Thinking Early Jewish–Christian Relations," 95–132, especially 126–27, and n. 108; idem, "Building," 397–408. If this is correct, it is quite likely that the rhetoric against Christ-believing "false prophets" and "lawbreakers" is directed against these Pharisaic followers of Jesus. The same interpretation applies to Matt 5:19 too, and those who are said to break even the least of the commandments, teaching others to do the same.

85. Cf. Jerome, *Comm. Matt.* on 5:19. For Jerome, Matthew's statement that anyone who abolishes even the least of the commandments and teaches others accordingly shall be called the least in the kingdom applies to the Pharisees, "who despised God's commands and were establishing their own traditions." While this is an interesting suggestion, especially in light of Matt 15:3–9, the fact that Matt 5:20, a verse not commented upon by Jerome, claims that the Torah obedience of "the scribes and the Pharisees" is not even enough to enter the kingdom at all complicates matters further.

86. Cf. *Gen. R.* 34:6, "Good are the commandments that comes out of the mouth of those who perform them." Regarding the relationship of Matt 23:2–3 to earlier critique of Pharisaic interpretation of Torah (e.g., Matt 15:1–3; 16:11–12), several solutions have been proposed. See discussion in Mark Allan Powel, "Do and Keep What Moses Says (23:2–3)," *JBL* 114:3 (1995): 419–35, and Wolfgang Reinbold, "Das Matthäusevangelium, die Pharisäer und die Tora," *BZ* 50 (2006): 51–73. The most likely suggestion is, in my opinion, that what is communicated by the story as a whole is a position in which Pharisaic understanding of the law is accepted in cases when it does not contradict what the Matthean Jesus claims is the center of the law: the double love command, with an emphasis on mercy (Matt 22:36–40; 7:12; 9:13; 12:7). Such a solution also explains why Jesus in Matthew is keeping ritual commandments that are also accepted by the Pharisees (see above, for examples), critiquing them for, e.g., oversizing their tzitzit and tefillin rather than for wearing them at all; the critique is here based on what is claimed to be inner motivations behind making them bigger (vanity and pride). The motivation behind fulfilling these commandments should have been love of God and, in the case of moral aspects of the law, love of God and neighbor. Matt 23:2–3 thus addresses, in an inner-Jewish context, the question that a first-century Jewish audience, or anyone familiar with Pharisaic practices, would have had: Why would Jesus be portrayed as following many of the same customs as the Pharisees do, when he is so intensely and relentlessly critiquing them throughout the narrative? If the Pharisees are not to be trusted, which halakhah is advisable? Matt 23:2–3 is thus answering specifically that which is implied through many comments made in passing, that Jesus follows many of the same customs as the

group, are not really on the map when the law is discussed. While we can deduce information about a separate judgment for non-Jews (sympathizers or not), they receive very little attention in the story generally, despite the fact that many Christian commentators from Late Antiquity onwards have, understandably, tried to make the most of such passages.

A final question needs to be addressed: the "Why?" question. Why would the Gospel of Matthew insist on the validity of the law, in both its moral and ritual aspects, and why would the narrative emphasize so heavily the moral commandments? This question is rarely noted in the literature, in which Torah observance, in and of itself, is seen as something of self-evident value. Divine wrath is sparked and judgment follows simply because the law is a covenant obligation, an agreement between the Jews and their God, and thus, must be kept according to promises made in ancient times (Exodus 24). But the covenant and the law within it have a purpose: to make possible God's presence and dwelling among the people (Exod 25:8). In Exodus, the setting up of the tabernacle follows after the establishment of the covenant, the former being a precondition for the latter. The reason for this is that God is holy, and nothing impure must come in contact with the holy. The requirements of the law will ensure that the people will become and remain holy just as God is holy (e.g., Lev 19:2; 20:26; Num 15:40). Since God cannot be approached in a state of sin, and sin is defined as moral impurity, the people must obey the law. This is also related to the land, so that "[y]ou shall keep all my statutes and all my ordinances, and observe them, so that the land to which I bring you to settle in may not vomit you out" (Lev 20:22).

Matthew, as many other Second-Temple texts, understands moral and ritual commandments as protecting the people from impurity in a similar way.[87] I have dealt with this issue elsewhere and shall not

Pharisees do, including tithing herbs (Matt 23:23); the passage should not be interpreted as Jesus asking followers to embrace in an absolute way all Pharisaic teachings. On the contrary, even when certain customs are accepted by both Jesus and the Pharisees, in no case do the Pharisees meet the standard of righteousness demanded by the kingdom, since they do not comply to the law in interpretive practice (cf. Matt 5:20).

87. For discussion of moral and ritual impurity in Second-Temple Judaism, see Klawans, *Purity*,

repeat the analysis here.[88] In brief, Matthew's Jesus understands the land and the temple to have been defiled by the moral impurity of the people,[89] which may lead to exile. The mission Jesus embarks on is, therefore, to save his people from their sins (Matt 1:21), which will remove the impurity that follows when the law is broken and allow for God's presence in the land. Keeping the law in its entirety (5:17–19), then, will lead to a people prepared for God's presence, which is the reason why Jesus admonishes the crowds and the disciples to be perfect as their heavenly father is perfect, alluding to Lev 19:2 (Matt 5:48).[90] In terms of judgment, this means that purity takes central stage, and we may note how the Gospel sets up boundaries for a community of followers of Jesus in Matt 18:15–20. Those who do not fulfill the obligations that come with membership will be excluded. Love is what creates the circumstances which allows for God's as well as Jesus's (post-resurrection) presence (Matt 18:20; cf. 24:12–13), and forgiveness, which removes guilt, which in turn is an obstacle for purity, becomes crucial (Matt 6:14–15; 18:21–35).[91]

Concluding this discussion on the law as the foundation upon which divine judgment is based, I hope to have shown, for example, why, according to Matthew, it is important for someone who has been healed from leprosy to travel to the Jerusalem temple to be investigated by the priest and to offer the appropriate sacrifices (Matt 8:4). In the same way, the much more important emphasis on fulfilling the moral obligations of the law should not simply be understood as an emphasis on ethics that may later prepare for non-Jewish mission (on the assumption that only the "ethics" of the law, or the ten commandments, are valid for all nations). On the contrary, this emphasis on (moral) Torah observance is motivated by the conviction that someone who breaks commandments regulating human

---

Sacrifice, and the Temple. Klawans includes analysis of the New Testament, and this task is also taken on by Regev, "Moral Impurity and the Temple," 383–411.

88. Runesson, "Purity, Holiness, and the Kingdom of Heaven."

89. Matt 15:18–20 states explicitly that breaking the moral aspects of the law makes a person impure. The grave sins Matthew accuses the Pharisees of, including bloodshed, will cause God to leave the temple and the temple to be destroyed (Matt 23:38–24:2).

90. Cf. variants of this theology in Luke 6:36; 1 Pet 1:16.

91. See further discussion below in chapter 2.4.

relationships contracts moral impurity, and may defile land and temple, with potentially catastrophic consequences. The law as a criterion of judgment is thus at the heart of the narrative and how it develops, since breaking the moral aspects of the law defines sin and generates guilt, which must be atoned for.

In this section, we have also noted that people's different abilities to observe the law will play a role in judgment. There is, further, a distinction made in the Gospel between intentional and unintentional sins, which has implications for how people are judged. A final question regarding sin and guilt needs to be asked, however: is every individual responsible for his or her own behavior, as Jeremiah and Ezekiel would argue,[92] or can guilt be inherited, so that God would punish later generations for sins committed by their ancestors, as Exodus and Deuteronomy claim?[93]

2.1.3 Inherited Guilt

So far, we have discussed guilt that is accumulated through individual and collective sins, defined as disobedience to the Mosaic law and committed by those who are being subjected to judgment. In this section, we shall deal with the phenomenon of inherited guilt, i.e., judgment on individuals or groups that have not committed the sins for which they are judged.[94] As noted above, such notions are present, although not undisputed, in the texts included in the Hebrew Bible, texts regarded as authoritative by the author of Matthew's Gospel. Is this theological dynamic present in Matthew? If so, what would the

---

92. Jer 31:29–30; Ezek 18:1–32; but cf. Jer 32:18.
93. Exod 20:5; 34:7; Deut 5:9; but cf. Deut 24:16.
94. It should be noted at the outset that we are not dealing here, neither in the Hebrew Bible nor in Matthew's Gospel, with a doctrine, but rather, as in ancient Greece, a cultural concept. On Greece, see Renaud Gagné, *Ancestral Fault in Ancient Greece* (Cambridge: Cambridge University Press, 2013). Likewise, the notion of inherited guilt in the biblical texts has very little, or nothing, to do with the later Christian idea of original sin. On the development of the latter, from Jesus to Augustine, see Paula Fredriksen, *Sin: The Early History of an Idea* (Princeton: Princeton University Press, 2012); cf. Gary Anderson, *Sin: A History* (New Haven: Yale University Press, 2009). Frederick R. Tennant, *The Sources of the Doctrines of the Fall and Original Sin* (New York: Schocken Books, 1903; repr. 1946 with an Introduction by Mary Frances Thelen), still provides thought-provoking discussion of Jewish and Christian sources, as well as ancient Near Eastern, Greek, and Indian parallels, that have inspired the doctrine of original sin.

implications of this be for our understanding of Matthew's view of peoplehood and lineage? Or of collectivities within the people, more generally?

In the Hebrew Bible, we find two basic ways of looking at individual responsibility concerning sin. The first may be represented by Exod 20:5–6:

> [F]or I the LORD your God am a jealous God, punishing children for the iniquity of parents, to the third and the fourth generation of those who reject me, but showing steadfast love to the thousandth generation of those who love me and keep my commandments.[95]

The notion here is, simply, that when God's wrath is triggered, children will be held responsible for the sins of their parents, but also, that steadfast love will be shown to many more generations when God is loved and commandments obeyed. This type of theology of inherited guilt is, however, contested in other texts included in the Hebrew Bible. Jeremiah 31:29–30 and Ezek 18:1–32 claim the exact opposite. Jeremiah states:

> In those days they shall no longer say: "The parents have eaten sour grapes, and the children's teeth are set on edge." But all shall die for their own sins; the teeth of everyone who eats sour grapes shall be set on edge.[96]

In other words, guilt is not transferrable, according to these prophets. Tannaitic literature generally follows the view of the prophets and underlines individual responsibility.[97] While individual responsibility is the dominant theme in Matthew's narrative, there are some passages that seem to relate to the theological position found in Exodus.

In Matt 23:35–36, it is stated that "this generation" (*genean tautēn*)

---

95. Cf. Exod 34:6–7.
96. Cf. Ezek 18:1–3. Ezek 18:14–20 deals with the fate of a son who refuses to follow his father's sinful ways. In such cases, "When the son has done what is lawful and right, and has been careful to observe all my statutes, he shall surely live. The person who sins shall die. A child shall not suffer for the iniquity of a parent, nor a parent suffer for the iniquity of a child; the righteousness of the righteous shall be his own, and the wickedness of the wicked shall be his own" (Ezek 18:19–20). Cf. Ezek 14:12–20.
97. Sanders, *Paul and Palestinian Judaism*, 194.

will be held responsible for the accumulated guilt resulting from all the shedding of righteous individuals' blood, from Abel to Zechariah son of Barachiah,[98] i.e., for all the bloodshed in the Hebrew Bible, since Abel is the first righteous victim (Genesis) and Zechariah the last (2 Chronicles).[99] As in Exodus's theology, punishment for sins committed by others in history may befall later generations within the people. Interestingly, the Matthean Jesus makes sure to portray those who murdered the prophets as the "fathers" of the "scribes and Pharisees" (Matt 23:31–32), which extends the meaning of family relationships beyond the biological to refer primarily to connections established between people who act in the same or similar ways, just as he has done earlier in the story, but then in a positive sense about his disciples being his own family (Matt 12:49–50). In the case of "the scribes and the Pharisees," this identification between them and those leaders in Israel's history identified as murderers of righteous prophets sent to them by God (cf. Matt 23:34) further strengthens the connection to Exodus's theology of inherited sin.

It should be noted, however, that the application of this notion is limited to the Pharisees and the scribes associated with them, and does not apply in any straightforward way to all members of the Jewish people, as the Gospel as a whole makes clear.[100] It is the grave sins of these specific leading figures in Jerusalem that tip the scales (cf. 23:32) and provoke the outpour of divine wrath over Jerusalem. The punishment is executed because of them and nobody else, although, as Nolland suggests, the expression "this generation" may indicate that

---

98. There has been some debate over the identity of this individual (cf. Lachs, *Rabbinic Commentary*, 371–72; C. G. Montefiore, *The Synoptic Gospels: Edited with an Introduction and a Commentary* [2 vols.; vol. 2.; Second edition; London: Macmillan, 1927] 303–4). As in Jewish tradition, it is most likely that Matthew has intentionally conflated the prophet Zechariah (Zech 1:1) with the priest Zechariah, who was murdered in the temple (2 Chr 24:18–22). See discussion in Michael Knowles, *Jeremiah in Matthew's Gospel: The Rejected Prophet Motif in Matthean Redaction* (Sheffield: JSOT Press, 1993), 138–40. Knowles also notes that in Targum Lamentations, the death of Zechariah is one of the causes for the destruction of Jerusalem and the exile (139).

99. Matthew's Gospel is likely the earliest witness to the Jewish canonical arrangement that later became standard, with 2 Chronicles being the last book of the collection. See Nolland, *Matthew*, 945–48.

100. We shall discuss this in some detail below, chapter 3.2.2.1.

the outcome of the punishment will also impact the contemporaries of the scribes and Pharisees in question.[101]

What we see in Matthew is thus a concept of sin which entangles the individuals who commit evil in a family relationship that extends beyond themselves in the present and several generations into the future. This implies that guilt resulting from unatoned sin is stored, and punishment is postponed until it reaches a certain limit when the dam breaks and divine wrath is poured out over the people. There is, thus, in Matthew's theo-ritual pattern of thought, a combination of a heavy emphasis on individual responsibility and the power of deeds to create a "lineage," respectively. This produces a theology in which individuals belonging to a "family," or "lineage," can still break loose from that lineage, just like proselytes can leave behind their previous ethnic belonging when converting, through repentance and commitment to a righteous life, to following Jesus.[102] On the one hand, then, there is no sinful "genetic code," no predestinating "gene," in Matthew's Gospel, via which guilt would be transmitted to new generations. On the other hand, if an individual or group commits evil, that individual or group will be held responsible for all previously committed sin. This type of theology is, in Matthew, only applied to Pharisees and scribes associated with them, and not to the Jewish crowds, as we shall see below in chapter 3. We shall also postpone discussion of Matt 27:25 to that chapter, a passage which displays a similar pattern of thought regarding inherited sin, since this verse relates closely to the problem of who is condemned in this narrative. Important to note here with regard to 27:25 is only that this verse provides further evidence that a concept of inherited guilt is active in Matthew's story. In this case, however, we find a focus on a specific collectivity within the people of God: the city of Jerusalem, its people, and its leaders.

In Matthew, then, only sinners are held responsible for the unatoned guilt that infiltrates the present from previous generations. There is

---

101. Nolland, *Matthew*, 948.
102. Cf. Matt 10:37; 13:52.

no general concept of inherited guilt discernable; the bottom line is that all are responsible for the choices they make, although, as we have seen, the outcome of judgment will depend on people's ability to follow the law. Matthew applies lineage language to make the case that, within the people, only those who break the law are related to previous generations of sinners and carry on what their ancestors started, so that there is a filling up of a measure until divine wrath is finally triggered and apocalyptic-eschatological suffering and judgment follows. The suffering, which is irreversibly certain to come because of the leaders' adding to the cup of sin of "their fathers," will affect all within the people, including the innocent.[103] In the final judgment, however, only the guilty will be held responsible and punished in accordance with their transgressions.

If Matthew displays, then, a variant on the theme of inherited guilt found also in the Hebrew Bible and in later Jewish texts,[104] how is righteousness, the supposed opposite of the status produced by those who sin, defined in this text? This topic is of some importance for our understanding of judgment, not least when we consider centuries of especially Protestant teaching on righteousness "through faith alone," without "works," a pattern of thinking that is still visible in academic studies of the First Gospel. Is it possible to read Matthew historically from such a perspective?

2.2 Obedience and Righteousness

Based on the fact that previous scholarship on obedience and righteousness in Matthew has tended to adopt a (Protestant-) Pauline view on righteousness,[105] it would seem a good strategy to begin this

---

103. The "crowds" should be counted among these, as we shall see, but as Matthew 24 shows, the suffering will befall also Jesus's own followers.
104. The notion of filling up the measure of sins is commonly applied to collectivities; see e.g., Gen 15:16 and cf. *Tg. Ps.-J.* on Gen 15:16. In rabbinic literature, we find the idea applied to individuals too: b. *'Arak.* 15a; cf. *Gen. R.* on Gen 4:7 (22:6): "If you do good I will forgive you, but if not, your sin overflows the brim." On the idea of a "measure," see Jungman, *Guds Barmhärtighet och Dom*, 19n29; see also his discussion of the various meanings of *midda* in rabbinic literature (20–40).
105. See discussion in Przybylski, *Righteousness*, 84–85, 91–94, 105–7, and literature cited there, especially J. A. Ziesler, *The Meaning of Righteousness in Paul: A Linguistic and Theological Enquiry* (Cambridge: Cambridge University Press, 1972); Gottlob Schrenk, "*dikaiō, dikaiosynē*," *TDNT* (vol.

section with two related questions, the answer to which will carry significant theological implications: Must obedience be perfect for individuals to be identified as righteous in Matthew's Gospel, obedience being defined in relation to Jewish law (cf. Matt 5:48)? Is it only the righteous, or "perfect," who will be admitted into the world to come? In other words, must individuals display perfect obedience to God in order to escape punishment and condemnation? As we shall see, as Michael Winninge has noted, distinguishing between "status aspect" and "aspect of dynamics" will help us explain why, despite the fact that all humans commit sins, there are still people identified as righteous.[106]

Looking at the larger pattern of thought in Matthew, we have already referred to the parable of the talents in Matt 25:14–30 as evidence of the relative, rather than absolute nature of Torah obedience.[107] The point of this parable is, to be sure, that people must work for the kingdom while waiting for its full arrival, and so, be prepared for the moment when it does come.[108] However, as this overall message is communicated, other elements of the story are developed, which may reveal important patterns of thought within whose frames this central point will make sense. In this specific case, even though the talents may represent the responsibility given to the three slaves,[109] the different amounts given to these individuals reflect

2; Grand Rapids: Eerdmans, 1964), 182–210. For a historically attuned approach with a focus on contemporary comparative material, see John I. Kampen, "'Righteousness' in Matthew and the Legal Texts from Qumran," in *Legal Texts and Legal Issues: Proceedings of the Second Meeting of the International Organization for Qumran Studies, Cambridge, 1995: Published in Honour of Joseph M. Baumgarten* (edited by Moshe J. Bernstein, Florentino García Martínez and John Kampen; Leiden: Brill, 1997), 461–87. Roland Deines, "Not the Law but the Messiah: Law and Righteousness in the Gospel of Matthew: An Ongoing Debate," in *Built on the Rock: Studies in the Gospel of Matthew* (edited by Daniel M. Gurtner and John Nolland; Grand Rapids: Eerdmans, 2008), 53–84, relates righteousness to the law. Deines concludes that for Matthew, the law, while retaining important functions as God's word, can no longer contribute to the eschatological righteousness; only Jesus's commandments can do this. The role of the law is to point to the commandments of Jesus. Deines supports his conclusion with references to both Matthew and Paul. In the present section, I will argue, to the contrary, that the law *as Jesus's interprets it* is precisely what constitutes the requirement for eschatological righteousness. This does not mean, as we shall see, that those who achieve righteousness have thereby earned a place in the kingdom (although they will be rewarded); life in the world to come cannot be earned, but is, ultimately, the result of God's doing.

106. Winninge, *Sinners*, 183–84, 212. The terms distinguish between the status of a person (e.g., a person can be identified as "righteous") and the dynamics of life that are considered applicable within that status, without undermining the status.

107. See the discussion of intentional and unintentional sins above, chapter 2.1.1.

108. France, *Matthew*, 951.

their different competencies (25:15). The slaves are expected to work to the best of their abilities, which means that, objectively, the end product of their work will be different, in accordance with the resources given them. The slave owner expects different amounts of work from each slave, but regardless of that difference, if they have done what was expected of them, they will be admitted into the joy of their master upon his return, i.e., the kingdom (25:21, 23). The obedience, or loyalty, required is absolute, but the absoluteness of the loyalty takes concrete form relative to individual abilities and resources.[110] Lack of obedience (or "investment"), as indicated by the third slave who had produced nothing although he had received something, and thus failed to meet the slave owner's expectations, results in condemnation and exclusion when the master returns (25:30).

If we read this parable together with the programmatic Sermon on the Mount, especially Matt 5:48, I would suggest that achieving "perfection" or becoming "perfect" (*teleios*) should be understood not only in terms of the quantifiable results obedience produces, but rather, from the perspective that while obedience must be absolute, the outcome of a person's obedience will vary, based on individual ability and resources; everyone has to fill his or her own measure.[111] This means that "perfection" should be interpreted as a reference to the key aspect of loyalty, the word indicating that loyalty must be unconditional and absolute.[112] But if the word *teleios* in Matthew carries

---

109. So France, *Matthew*, 951. On the issue of dualism between good and evil in the parable, cf. Sim, *Apocalyptic Eschatology*, 81–82.

110. This type of hermeneutical approach to obedience is reminiscent of various adaptations or concessions with regard to sacrifices required of people in certain situations based on financial resources. For example, in Lev 12, it is stated that after childbirth, a woman must sacrifice a lamb and a pigeon (v. 6). However, if the woman cannot afford a lamb, she may sacrifice two pigeons instead (v. 8). Obedience to God's law may thus be considered absolute, independently of the financial situation of a person and the actual animals sacrificed; loyalty is defined by the act of sacrifice itself, not by the exact nature or worth of the gifts brought to the altar.

111. Cf. *Did.* 6:1–2: "See that no one leads you astray from this way of the teaching, for such a person teaches you without regard for God. For if you are able to bear the whole yoke of the Lord, you will be perfect [*teleios*]. But if you are not able, then do what you can."

112. Cf. Deut 18:13 (LXX), where *teleios* is also used. The NRSV translation captures the sense in Matthew too: "You must remain completely loyal to the LORD your God" (cf. Matt 22:37). *Teleios* is connected with the keeping of God's law and commandments in 1 Kgs 8:61, and some kings are said to have been completely loyal, or true, to God, the author of Kings using this term (David,

within it this sense of complete loyalty, in addition to referring to quantitative aspects of law observance,[113] how does this relate to individuals called righteous (*dikaios*), or to righteousness (*dikaiosynē*)? Who is righteous, and does such a status differ from that of the person who is *teleios*? Does Matthew distinguish between different levels of righteousness, and thus, acknowledge different standards for admission into the kingdom?[114] A study of the use of the word *dikaios* (Matt 1:19; 5:45; 9:13; 10: 41; 13:17, 43, 49; 20:4; 23:28, 29, 35; 25:37, 46; 27:19) and *dikaiosynē* (Matt 3:15; 5:6, 10, 20; 6:1, 33; 21:32) will shed light on these questions.[115]

A basic observation with regard to *dikaios* can be made immediately. Matthew's Gospel may classify people as "righteous" even if they do not belong to Jesus's group (Matt 1:19; 13:17; 23:29, 35; cf. 27:52).[116] Such identification of individuals as righteous is based on their status being defined by their obedience to the law of Moses, which, by implication, is regarded as a valid criterion for categorizing people, even before Jesus's birth.[117] Before we turn to the concept of *dikaiosynē* for further insights about what *dikaios* implies in Matthew, we should note how characters designated *dikaios* fare in judgment. The following table identifies the main uses of the term.

---

1 Kings 14:4; Asa, 1 Kgs 15:14). In the same sense, Noah is portrayed as "perfect" (*teleios*) in Gen 6:9 and Sir 44:17. To be completely loyal is thus related to following the law without wavering. Consequently, the use of *teleios* in Matt 5:48 should not be understood as asking the impossible; Wis 9:6 sheds some light on the ultimate dependency of the "perfect" on the wisdom of God: "for even one who is perfect (*teleios*) among human beings will be regarded as nothing without the wisdom that comes from you."

113. For the quantitative understanding of *teleios*, see Przybylski, *Righteousness*, 85–87. See also further below.

114. Cf. Matt 5:19.

115. An important contribution to the analysis of how Matthew uses these words is made by Przybylski, *Righteousness*. See especially pp. 77–89, where *dikaiosynē* is related to *teleios*.

116. Cf. Sim, *Apocalyptic Eschatology*, 200, who rightly emphasizes that not all Jews are presented as wicked in the Gospel of Matthew, giving the disciples of John the Baptist as one example. We shall return to this in chapter 3.

117. Przybylski, *Righteousness*, 101, states that "Matthew uses this term to describe those who were properly religious in the past." To be "properly religious," according to Matthew, certainly involves observing the law.

Table 2.1. The use of *dikaios* in Matthew's Gospel

Use of term *dikaios*	References in Matthew
Individuals predating Jesus	1:19; 9:13; 13:17; 23:29; 23:35
No distinction between before and after Jesus	5:45
Rewards given to people based on status	10:41
Jesus	27:19
Individuals responding positively to Jesus [and keeping the law]	13:43 (cf. 13:38, 41); 13:49
Non-Jews helping followers of Jesus	25:37, 46
Other uses	20:4; 23:28

How should we interpret the term "righteous" in light of these passages? First, "righteous" is a positive label, which is associated with rewards (Matt 10:41) as well as with salvation/eternal life (13:43; 25:46). Being "righteous" and "righteousness" are opposed to several terms that provide an interpretive context within which we may understand Matthew's use of these words: unrighteous (*adikos*; 5:45); evil (*ponēros*; 13:49); hypocrisy (*hypokrisis*; 23:28); lawlessness (*anomia*; 23:28); the accursed (*hoi katēramenoi*; 25:41). The latter case emphasizes the fact that to be righteous implies inclusion in the coming kingdom.

In the case of Matt 20:4, the term indicates what is fair and just payment for work done, maintaining the positive connotation, the (implied) opposite of which would be related to injustice. In Matt 23:28, while appearing to be righteous on the "outside," Pharisees and scribes associated with them are accused of being "lawless," based on aspects relating to the "inside." The metaphor of "outside" and "inside" builds on an assumed general agreement that Pharisees were, in fact, keeping some commandments that were seen by all, including the Matthean Jesus, as legitimate, since the opposite, the "inside," is characterized as "lawlessness" (*anomia*) and "impurity" (*akatharsia*; 23:27). In other words, the lawless and impure "inside" is contrasted with an "outside" characterized by law observance. "Appearing" to be righteous, thus, does not have to imply that the righteousness[118] is understood as false.

Rather, the verse is likely referring to "external" righteousness, i.e., the keeping of such commandments that can be seen by others while they are being performed. This interpretation fits well with the Matthean critique of people who do pious deeds in order to receive praise from others (cf. 23:5–7; 6:1–6).[119] What is doubtless in view is the distinction made in Matt 23:23 between the weightier matters of the law, which Pharisees and scribes associated with them are said to ignore, but which Jesus keeps, and ritual commandments such as tithing, which both Jesus and the Pharisees keep. If the weightier commandments are broken, however, the law as a whole is broken, regardless of how many of the other commandments are observed.[120] Thus, the expression "appearing to be righteous" implies that being righteous is something positive and that such a status is associated with law observance. The word "appearing" (*phainō*) refers to the fact that while keeping ritual aspects of the law is an expression of righteousness, this is not enough to earn the status of righteous.

The relationship between law observance and the status of being righteous needs to be addressed here briefly in relation to Matt 25:37, 46, a passage which we shall discuss in detail in Part II. Since the status of being righteous is attributed in this parable to non-Jews who are not members of the Jesus movement, there is no *direct* correlation between the designation "righteous" and law observance here; non-Jewish characters in Matthew do not keep the Jewish law. However, the connection is there, although indirect, in that the parable follows the same hermeneutical logic, as we see in Matt 10:40–42. In the latter case, positive outcomes of judgment (recompense) follow for those Jews who relate compassionately to Jesus's (Jewish) followers.[121] In Matt 25:37, 46, non-Jews who act in the same compassionate way toward

118. On the nature of 'righteousness' as a quantitative concept, see further below.
119. So also, Przybylski, *Righteousness*, 102.
120. As argued above, it is, in my view, clear that *anomia* in Matthew refers to the opposite of keeping the law of Moses. As David Sim, *Christian Judaism*, 204–6, has argued, we cannot interpret Matthew from the perspective of how other New Testament texts are using the term. For Sim, too, Matthew's Jesus is here critiquing the Pharisees for not keeping the law, since they break the weightier commandments.
121. On the three groups of Jesus followers mentioned in Matt 10:40–42 (prophet, righteous, little ones), see John P. Meier, *Matthew* (Collegeville: Liturgical Press, 1980), 115.

"the least" of Jesus's family members will receive blessing and inherit the kingdom. The followers of Jesus who have been helped by these non-Jews have elsewhere been identified as righteous and, therefore, as law-observant. On account of this status as righteous and law-observant according to Jesus's interpretation of the law, they will be admitted into the kingdom. Thus, in a measure-for-measure type of hermeneutic, the status as righteous is transferred to people who do not have the law, based on what we have called the Abrahamic principle.[122] In other words, in both Matt 10:40–42 (Jews) and 25:31–46 (non-Jews), people who are not counted among Jesus's followers, and who are not themselves known as "righteous" are given the rewards and the status of the righteous on the basis of acts of loving kindness directed towards those with whom the (righteous) Messiah identifies. We must conclude, then, that the kingdom of heaven in Matthew will welcome and even reward people who are not among those who confess Jesus as the Messiah, but who relate to his followers in compassionate ways.[123]

People identified as righteous should, thus, be understood to be included in the world to come. This is true for the righteous who predated Jesus (1:19; 9:13; 13:17; 23:29; 23:35; cf. 27:52) as well as for those who respond positively to his mission (13:43 [cf. 13:38, 41]; 13:49). Indeed, Jesus himself is identified as righteous by an outsider (27:19). The key here is that the law taught by Jesus is the same as the law of Moses, only that it is given a very strict interpretation in Matthew. Since the law is the same from Moses "until heaven and earth pass away" (Matt 5:18), and since certain people before Jesus are considered righteous, it follows that only some people have previously misunderstood the law; Jesus's mission is not brought about because of the former, neither is it directed toward them, but rather, toward

---

122. See above, p. 27.

123. This situation, which is evident from the text, speaks against a socio-historical reconstruction in which the Mattheans are described too narrowly as a sect with a salvation-exclusive worldview. Still, however, salvation is dependent on Jesus and his followers, even if only indirectly. The hermeneutics applied in Matthew is reminiscent of how later rabbis related to outsiders and the so-called righteous gentiles. See discussion Runesson, "Judging Gentiles." See further chapter 3 below as well as Part II.

"the lost sheep of the house of Israel" (Matt 15:24). This is clear with regard to the righteous of the past, but also, by implication, in the case of Joseph, who is called righteous (1:19). According to Matthew, the answer to the question why Jesus had to save his people from their sins (1:21), and consequently, why he needed to die a sacrificial death (26:28), is that elements of Jewish leadership in history and in the present had stored up a critical mass of guilt resulting from grave unatoned sins, which defiled the temple to the point where God could no longer remain in it, so that it had to be destroyed (23:37—24:2).

This means that people considered righteous in Jesus's time should not be thought of as the primary aim of his mission. His purpose was to save those who had been misled, the sinners, those who needed a doctor. It is in this context we should understand Matt 9:13: "For I have come to call not the righteous but sinners." Przybylski suggests that this verse implies that Matthew presents the Pharisees as righteous.[124] This, however, does not necessarily follow, and in fact, it is unlikely to have been Matthew's intent. Jesus's answer to the Pharisees simply states that there are two groups of people, the righteous and the sinners; the reason why he socializes with the latter is that they need guidance. Mercy, i.e., one of the weighty matters of the law, requires that he tend to their needs. Jesus is not commenting here on the status of the Pharisees specifically. The Pharisees have certainly attained a level of righteousness, as implied by 5:20, but they ignore the most important parts of the law (23:23). Most importantly, in the story, they are "in the way," so to speak; they provide an obstacle for Jesus's mission to the people whom the Pharisees and the scribes associated with them oppress (23:4). Thus, attaining a certain level of righteousness does not lead to a person being identified as righteous. Only those who stand in a positive relationship to rewards and salvation are identified as righteous in Matthew. The Pharisees, on the contrary, are explicitly said to be excluded from the kingdom, based on their limited understanding of what is important in the law (5:20; cf. 23:13, 33).

124. Przybylski, *Righteousness*, 102.

The above discussion has shown that "righteousness" (*dikaiosynē*) does not refer to a qualitative status equivalent to the status of people designated "righteous": to be identified as having attained a level of righteousness is not the same as being counted among the righteous. Przybylski has convincingly shown that "righteousness" refers to "conduct according to a norm, which in this case is the law."[125] We are not dealing in Matthew with an eschatological gift from God, which would be more of a traditional Pauline reading of the text; Matthew simply does not use *dikaiosynē* in this way. Righteousness represents God's demands on human beings.[126] Righteousness, then, does not refer to perfect obedience of the law in all its aspects, but to any fulfilling of specific commandments, including the ritual commandments. To "do righteousness" (*dikaiosynēn poiein*; Matt 6:1) means to perform individual commandments.[127]

This interpretation of *dikaiosynē* explains the comparative use of the word in Matt 5:20 with reference to the *dikaiosynē* required by the Matthean Jesus, on the one hand, and the (limited) *dikaiosynē* recorded for the Pharisees and the scribes associated with them, on the other. According to Matthew, the level of *dikaiosynē* that is ascribed to the Pharisees will not be enough for entering the kingdom. Therefore, they just "appear" to be "righteous"; in reality, they are not, since they do not have enough *dikaiosynē*, and therefore, cannot be called "righteous."[128]

It is from this perspective that Matt 5:19 should be read: "Whoever breaks one of the least of these commandments, and teaches others to do the same, will be called least in the kingdom of heaven; but whoever does them and teaches them will be called great in the kingdom of

125. Ibid., 87.
126. Przybylski, *Righteousness*, 77–101. As Przybylski points out, this does not mean that Matthew does not have a theology of grace, only that he does not outline this theology using the term righteousness. Przybylski, thus, sees no conflict between Paul and Matthew in terms of the message being salvation as gift (105–7).
127. Note the use of *eleēmosynē* for the giving of alms in Matt 6:2–4. KJV translates *dikaiosynē* in 6:1 as "alms," whereas NRSV translates the same verse as "practicing piety." Cf. the meaning of *tzedakah* in modern Hebrew (charity).
128. Cf. France, *Matthew*, (1985), 328: "it is this focus [that inward righteousness gives meaning to cultic law observance] which makes possible the righteousness exceeding that of the scribes and Pharisees (5:20)."

heaven." This verse tells us that although it is impossible to enter the kingdom if the weightier matters of the law are ignored (5:20), an individual will still be expected to enter the kingdom if only a minor commandment is broken (while the weightier are kept); punishment will follow, however, in the form of status displacement (5:19). Matthew 5:19–20 thus signals the relative importance of the two types of commandments: the moral commandments identified elsewhere as the weightier aspect of the law, and the ritual as the least of the commandments (e.g., 23:23). The situation is further explained by Matthew's use of *teleios*, "perfection," as we have discussed above. We shall return now to take a closer look at the term and its use.

The word *teleios* is used twice in Matthew, in 5:48 and 19:21. Przybylski has shown that the concept of "perfection" in Matthew may be understood in a quantitative sense rather than merely in the qualitative sense of wholeness.[129] While *dikaios* is used both for people who lived before Jesus (1:19; 9:13; 13:17; 23:29; 23:35) and people who are followers of Jesus (13:43, 49), *teleios* is used only in direct relationship with Jesus, and only in settings where the law is explicitly discussed. However, both those who are identified as *dikaios* and those who would follow Jesus's teaching and become *teleios* have access to the world to come—the kingdom. Does this mean that *teleios* refers to a higher status than *dikaios*, so that *teleios* signifies the highest rank achievable in the kingdom?[130]

We know that *teleios* represents the status achieved through doing more than the Pharisees do (5:20, 48), and we also know that Matthew's narrative suggests that people's status in the kingdom will vary, depending on how the law is observed (5:19). The implication of this seems to be that when future inhabitants of the kingdom are spoken of in general terms, they are called righteous,[131] whereas the outcome of following Jesus's interpretation of the law in particular results in the status of "perfect." If this is true, the difference between *dikaios* and

---

129. Przybylski, *Righteousness*, 86–87.
130. Ibid., 87.
131. When Pilate's wife identifies Jesus as "righteous" in Matt 27:19, these words are spoken by an outsider; the setting is, further, not dealing with the interpretation of Jewish law.

teleios is thus not so much about the different levels of righteousness that those who will enter the kingdom will have achieved, even if this may be implied, but more about emphasizing Jesus as the teacher of perfection. This interpretation receives further support in Matt 19:16–30.

The story about the rich young man in Matt 19:16–30 has been the center of much debate and divergent interpretations.[132] Ulrich Luz notes two important questions with regard to this passage:

> (1) What does the perfection that Jesus demands of the rich man in v. 21 have to do with keeping the commandments? (2) Are the "perfect" a particular group of people who then will receive a special reward (v. 28)? Or, asking the question from the other direction: To what degree does what Jesus says to the rich man (vv. 16–21) apply to all disciples (vv. 23–30)?[133]

The answer to the first question is clear: everything. Luz notes, correctly in my view, that Jesus does not reject the quantitative understanding of observing commandments that is behind the young man's question. Neither does the Matthean Jesus suggest that there is anything beyond the law of Moses that would be necessary to add in order for the man to attain "eternal life" (*zōēn aiōnion*; 19:17).[134] Of the key commandments necessary to keep in order to stay within reach of the kingdom, Jesus refers to a few examples, the strict observance of which he has explained elsewhere (5:21–30; 15:3–11): "You shall not murder; You shall not commit adultery; You shall not steal; You shall not bear false witness; Honor your father and mother" (19:18–19). Then, he adds one of the two commandments that he will soon, in 22:39, identify as the very center of the law, the core that all Torah interpretation must orbit: "Also, You shall love your neighbor as yourself" (19:19).

We are not told whether the young man has kept the other

---

132. For discussion of the history of interpretation, including Protestant – Catholic controversies, see Luz, *Matthew*, 2. 508–23.
133. Luz, *Matthew*, 2. 511.
134. Cf. Lev 18:5: "Keep my decrees and laws, for the man who obeys them will live by them." The commandments mentioned explicitly by Matthew are meant as a summary of the most important laws, but the entire law of Moses is surely in view.

commandments as radically as Jesus's teaching requires; it may well be that he is meant to be portrayed as if he has done this, since Jesus does not comment further on them. However, the last commandment of loving the neighbor now emerges as the very reason for including this story in the Gospel. Just as Jesus has built a fence around the law in the Sermon on the Mount, consistently seeking to uncover layers of meaning in the commandments which need to be brought to people's attention in order for the law not to be broken, he now states what it means to love one's neighbor: "If you wish to be perfect, go, sell your possessions, and give the money to the poor, and you will have treasure in heaven; then come, follow me" (Matt 19:21). In other words, while the man thought he had kept all commandments (19:20), in reality, his observance, his righteousness, was limited in comparison with the demands of Jesus's teaching, which is "perfection" (cf. Matt 5:48) relative to the responsibilities that come with one's status and resources (cf. Matt 25:14–30).[135]

The perfection required of the young man exceeds *quantitatively* not only the righteousness of the Pharisees, but also, what many of Jesus's other followers could hope to achieve; not everyone would have things to sell, and they could thus not contribute as much to the poor as this man could have, had he been as loyal to God as Jesus required. It also seems clear from Matthew's tenth chapter that not all of Jesus's sympathizers were required to sell everything and become itinerant preachers and healers (see especially, Matt 10:1–15),[136] even if some, like the rich young man, were chosen for such tasks (Matt 19:27–29); these latter will be given rewards accordingly in the world to come, if they do not reject the invitation.[137] The central point of the story

---

135. Cf. Jerome, *Comm. Matt.* on 19:20: "The young man is lying. For if he had fulfilled in deed what is recorded among the commandments: 'You shall love your neighbor as yourself,' why is it that when he later hears 'Go, sell what you have and give to the poor,' he went away sad, since he had 'many possessions'?" Jerome later compares the situation with the case of Ananias and Sapphira in Acts 5:1–11.

136. Selling all one's possessions necessitates taking up an itinerant lifestyle with the group. This is required of some for the spread of the good news about the kingdom, but not all of Jesus's sympathizers are portrayed as such in the Gospel.

137. The "treasure in heaven" (19:21) promised to the young man if he obeys Jesus interpretation of the law refers to such recompense for acts of righteousness. These rewards will differ between people allowed into the kingdom in accordance with their righteousness. Life in the world to

is a critique of wealth and the inability of those who have it to let it go; it is a critique of the lack of loyalty to God and failure of rich people to make use of all resources they have been given as they set their minds on obeying the commandments.[138] If perfect loyalty is not displayed in deeds, the rich will be like the slave with one talent, who did not work for the kingdom using what he had been given, and thus, could not deliver what the master had the right to expect (Matt 25:14–15, 26–30). This answers Luz's second question referred to above: the *loyalty* required by the young man is obligatory to all disciples. However, not all of Jesus's sympathizers in Matthew's story are required to sell all they have and become itinerant preachers, which highlights the aim of the present passage to be a critique specifically directed against wealth in light of the obedience necessary for the kingdom.[139]

The requirement in Matt 5:48, "Be perfect, therefore, as your heavenly Father is perfect," further indicates the function of perfection in Matthew's narrative world through its relationship to and dependence upon passages, especially in Leviticus, such as Lev 19:2, "Be holy because I, the Lord your God, am holy."[140] The formulation itself in Matt 5:48 is, without doubt, meant to signal and interpret this divine requirement that the people of God must be holy, so that the God of the people can relate to and be present among the people. Let us first note how this motif is presented and how it functions discursively within the texts included in the Hebrew Bible before we return to Matthew.

The notion of holiness and the *imitatio dei* reasoning is seen clearly in Deut 23:14, where God's presence in the wilderness camp, and help

---

come can, however, not be earned, and, contrary to Mark and Luke, Matthew never speaks of it as a reward. We shall return to discuss this in chapter 2.8.

138. Cf. Acts 4:32–5:11.

139. Cf. Moore's discussion in *Judaism*, 2.321. This conclusion thus problematizes the point of departure for understanding the passage along the lines of Protestant-Catholic debates about a "two-level morality," an approach which has been common in the history of interpretation. Note, e.g., that Barth, "Law," 95ff, rejects the idea of such a two-level morality in this pericope, but does so against the background of Catholic doctrine rather than a focus on first-century Judaism.

140. See also as Lev 11:44–45, 20:7, 26; 21:8. Cf. Luke 6:36: "Be merciful, just as your Father is merciful"; 1 Pet 1:15–16: "[A]s he who called you is holy, be holy yourselves in all your conduct; for it is written, 'You shall be holy, for I am holy.'" See also Josh 24:19–20.

against Israel's enemies, is dependent on the holiness of the camp. The same idea also translates into rulings relating to the nature of the land, and the people's presence in the land. Just as the camp must be holy, the land of Israel must be holy; if the people of God defile it, the land will "vomit them out," just as it had vomited out the people living there before them, because of their defilement (Lev 18:27–28; 20:22). There are thus two themes related to the requirement of holiness: holiness will allow divine presence among the people, and it will allow the presence of the people in the land, which is God's land. The method to make this happen is also clearly stated: observing the law will make and keep the people holy (Lev 20:22; Num 15:40). This is why the law is so important in the history of Israel as presented in these texts: it creates the conditions necessary for the good life, which is interpreted as a life lived in the land, together with the God who chose Israel as his people and gave them—under certain conditions (holiness)—the land to inhabit.

The theme of chosenness, as related to holiness, also brings forth a related issue of importance, namely, separateness. The law given to the people will, when followed, distinguish them from other people. Examples of key commandments in Leviticus 19 include keeping the Sabbath and other ritual commandments (19:3–8, 26–28), but also laws based on the fundamental principle of compassion for the poor and the immigrant (19:9–10, 34). Further, hate is prohibited and love and respect for the elderly is prescribed (19:17–18, 32, 34). Keeping such commandments makes the people holy and distinguishes them from other nations; failure to obey results in defilement and loss of land. The separation from other nations, who, according to the texts, behave in ways appalling to the God of Israel, allows the holiness of, and therefore, the divine presence among, the people (Lev 20:26). Obedience and righteousness is, therefore, the key to a life with God after God had chosen the people and made a covenant with them, which outlines the requirements for the relationship.

This pattern of thought is replicated in some detail in Matthew's Gospel, and signaled in the climax of Jesus's interpretation of the law in Matt 5:48, which deals to a significant degree with the same theme as Leviticus 19: the love of neighbor and stranger.[141] "Perfection" refers both to complete loyalty and to its result in Torah obedience, and allows for divine protection in the final judgment as the apocalyptic end is getting closer (cf. Matt 24:12–13). The theme of the land in Matthew is emphasized, as becomes clear when compared to the other evangelists, and the meek will inherit it (Matt 5:5; cf. Ps 37:11). Indeed, those who hunger for righteousness in Matt 5:6 do so in relation to how people behave in the land, rather than as an individualized expression of a sense of inner inadequacy, or a reference to God's saving gift, which would belong more within a modern, especially, perhaps, Lutheran, interpretive paradigm.[142] In other words, those who are promised to be satisfied in their hunger when the kingdom arrives in full force are those who long for the day when the people observe the law as it was meant from the beginning.[143] Such a relationship between holiness, Torah observance, and perfection is evident, then, also from the very way Matt 5:48 is worded, as an intertextual allusion to Leviticus. In addition, just as Leviticus and other Hebrew Bible texts state that the people must stay holy and not do as other nations do, Matthew uses non-Jews and people who associate with or behave like them as negative examples of behavior to be avoided (e.g., Matt 5:46–47; 6:7). Indeed, in order to keep the community of Jesus's followers separate—and, we might say, holy—sinners must be expelled

---

141. Matt 5:43–47; cf. Lev 19:17–18, 34.

142. Cf. discussion in France, *Matthew*, 167–68. For in-depth treatment of the place of the land in Matthew's Gospel, see Joel Willitts, *Matthew's Messianic Shepherd-King: In Search of 'the Lost Sheep of the House of Israel'* (Berlin: De Gruyter, 2007). See also Runesson, "Giving Birth to Jesus in the Late First Century," 301–27. Cf. the rabbinic notion that relates law observance to the coming of the Messiah: "If Israel keeps one Sabbath as it should be kept, the Messiah will come. The Sabbath is equal to all the other precepts of the Torah" (*Exod. R.* 25:12). See Jacob Neusner, *Vanquished Nation, Broken Spirit: The Virtues of the Heart in Formative Judaism* (Cambridge: Cambridge University Press, 1987), 24. While the rabbis re-framed Israel's salvation in terms of sanctification—the Messiah will come if the law is kept—Matthew's Jesus proclaims that since God is now acting *before* Israel has been sanctified, the people have to begin the path to holiness quickly (cf. Matt 5:25) in order to be saved. To hunger for righteousness in such a situation is to hunger for the world to come, in which God's will is done in the land.

143. On the nature of the law of Moses in relation to the perfection of the pristine Edenic state of things in Genesis, cf. Matt 19:4–5, 8. Note that Matthew's Jesus still operates within the law of Moses as he rules that divorce is, in fact, allowed under very special circumstances (*porneia*), indicating thereby, implicitly, that the kingdom of God, when all will return to Edenic perfection, has not yet been established in full.

and regarded as if they were non-Jews or tax collectors, i.e., people who associate with non-Jews (Matt 18:17).

Perfection, thus, functions in Matthew's story to highlight the status acquired of those who follow Jesus's strict interpretation of the law, as it is in accordance with the holiness demanded by the God of Israel. This allows for God's presence among them, through his agent Jesus: Immanuel (Matt 1:23; cf. 18:20; 28:20).[144] The keeping of the commandments, i.e., the doing of righteousness, must be an expression of a person's complete loyalty to God for this to happen. All of this leads to life in the kingdom.[145]

In sum, in Matthew, the righteous, *dikaioi*, are those individuals who have reached quantitatively (righteousness) and qualitatively (loyalty) beyond the righteousness displayed by the Pharisees and the scribes associated with them in terms of law observance, and they will, consequently, be part of the kingdom of heaven as it will be fully established after a period of apocalyptic suffering and the final judgment. Seen from a slightly different perspective, as John Kampen has shown based on a comparative study on texts from Qumran, righteousness "designates the way of life developed for the followers of Jesus in the Sermon on the Mount. [...] [T]he author of this Gospel viewed the adherents of the Jesus way of life within that Jewish community as 'the righteous.' [...] They were the 'righteous' Jews who practiced a way of life based on their understanding of 'righteousness'."[146]

Perfection, *teleios*, refers to complete loyalty to God, which is required by all disciples, but which takes different forms, depending on the abilities and resources of the individual disciple (Matt 5:19; cf.

---

144. On Jesus as God's presence (*Shekhinah*) among the people, see also David D. Kupp, *Matthew's Emmanuel: Divine Presence and God's People in the First Gospel* (Cambridge: Cambridge University Press, 1996). See also, Matt 10:20 on the presence of God's spirit with the disciples as they are persecuted.

145. As indicated by the Beatitudes, Matt 5:3–12. Cf. Lev 18:3–5: "You shall not do as they do in the land of Egypt, where you lived, and you shall not do as they do in the land of Canaan, to which I am bringing you. You shall not follow their statutes. My ordinances you shall observe and my statutes you shall keep, following them: I am the LORD your God. You shall keep my statutes and my ordinances; by doing so one shall live: I am the LORD."

146. Kampen, "'Righteousness' in Matthew," 485, 486, 487.

Did. 6:1–2). Such loyalty will also be characteristic of the individuals who will enter the kingdom. While various levels of righteousness will result in different wages in the world to come (Matt 5:19; cf. 10:41–42), nowhere does Matthew state that there is a *direct* connection between righteousness, or perfection, which represent God's demands on his people, and life in the world to come, so that *access to* the kingdom can be understood as a reward for righteousness (i.e., a quantitative measure).[147] Rather, righteousness will be rewarded in a manner resembling a measure-for-measure procedure, but which, in reality, exemplifies God's *ḥesed*, since the divine recompense will outshine any human efforts made, even a hundredfold (Matt 10:41;[148] 19:29). Life in the kingdom, however, can ultimately only be inherited (Matt 19:29; 25:34), a notion to which we shall return below.

Those who are excluded from the kingdom are those who are satisfied with the insufficient level of righteousness (i.e., law observance) represented by the Pharisees (5:20), those who are called breakers of the law (13:41), evil (Matt 13:49), and the cursed (25:41). What these literary characters have in common is that they behave disrespectfully (15:6), judge the innocent (Matt 12:7), cause others to sin (18:6–7), and oppress fellow Jews (23:4). They are, further, self-obsessed and vain (23:5–7), and prioritize minor ritual commandments above the weightier matters of the law, when both should have been taken care of (23:23–24). Such behavior is the opposite of the complete loyalty and its resulting conduct among the righteous, or perfect; there is a direct relationship between not doing enough righteousness, breaking the law, or lawlessness (*anomia*), and being excluded from the kingdom.

---

147. *Pace* Eubank, *Wages of Cross-Bearing.*

148. Based on deeds of compassion, Matt 10:40–42 assures the reader that someone who is not a "prophet" will receive a prophet's wages; someone who is not among the "righteous" will receive the wages of a righteous; someone who is not a disciple will receive, still, his or her wages. It seems as if the connection established between such compassionate individuals and Jesus's disciples is able to channel back to the doer the positive qualities of the people helped. This, in turn, may be explained as the result of the identification made between Jesus, and ultimately, God, on the one hand, and Jesus's disciples on the other (Matt 10:40); God's *ḥesed* is activated through compassionate inter-human interaction. A similar hermeneutics is applied to non-Jews in Matt 25:31–46; see discussion below, chapter 7.3.

It may seem from the above discussion that the individual characters of the narrative, weak or strong, are left to care for their own righteousness. To a certain extent, Matthew's Gospel does emphasize very strongly human accountability and capacity for loyalty to the divine, and thus, lay claim to the human dignity inherent in such an emphasis. The responsibility to comply with God's demands is, however, balanced with and measured by individual ability and resources. But the story of obligations and loyalty does not end there. Just as we noted above on the negative side of belonging to a collectivity when we discussed inherited guilt, we also find a corresponding positive pattern in the text, in which people whose righteousness and strength are not quite enough will have a share in the blessings that will be bestowed on those who are stronger—the notion of vicarious righteousness.

2.3 Vicarious Righteousness

If there is a pattern of thought in Matthew in which individuals, under certain circumstances, may be condemned for sins they did not themselves commit,[149] is there also evidence for a theology where the opposite is possible, i.e., a scenario in which punishment is not inflicted upon those who lack righteousness, due to the righteousness of others? There are a few passages in the narrative that imply that such a theme may be part of the (eschatological) worldview of the text. This type of thought pattern is present in the Hebrew Bible too, and we shall begin there in order to frame the discussion.

In Gen 18:16–32, God is about to punish with destruction the sinful cities of Sodom and Gomorrah.[150] Abraham, having physically moved closer to the rather anthropomorphic representation of God in this story, is made aware of what is about to transpire. His immediate reaction is founded upon the basic principle (*mishpat*; v. 25) of God's obligations to the righteous on earth: "Will you indeed sweep away the

---

149. See above, chapter 2.1.3.
150. For a brief, but insightful overview of important aspects of this passage, see Gerhard von Rad, *Genesis: A Commentary* (2nd edition; London: SCM Press, 1972), 210–15. Note, especially, the discussion of collective guilt and the absence of the modern concept of individualism in the story.

righteous [*tsaddiq*] with the wicked [*rasha'*]?" (Gen 18:23). It would not be appropriate, Abraham continues, for the "judge [*hashophet*] of the all the earth" to commit such an atrocity, to let the righteous be destroyed together with the wicked (Gen 18:25), and so, Abraham begins to haggle with God about the lives of the inhabitants of Sodom (Gen 18:24, 26–33). In a reversed form of Middle-Eastern style bargaining, Abraham starts off with a number of righteous he thinks will be acceptable to God for saving the city: fifty righteous individuals will prevent Sodom's destruction. As God agrees to an ever-shrinking number, Abraham finally ends at ten righteous individuals being enough to spare the city (Gen 18:32). The theology is straightforward: the life of the righteous is more important for God than the destruction of the wicked.[151] A side-effect of such theology is that due to the righteousness of the few, many sinners will be spared punishment in this world.

A similar basic theological pattern underlies Matt 24:21–22: "For at that time there will be great suffering, such as has not been from the beginning of the world until now, no, and never will be. And if those days had not been cut short, no one would be saved; but for the sake of the elect (*tous eklektous*)[152] those days will be cut short." R. T. France notes that the fact that the suffering is more destructive than anything else that may come in the future indicates that the reference is to a historical event, i.e., the fall of Jerusalem, which has just been prophesied in Matt 24:1–2; the suffering referred to is not about the eschatological end of the world.[153] Thus, what Matthew's

---

151. Cf. Jer 5:1. It is of some interest to note that some rabbis found fault with Abraham in this story; he should not have stopped at ten individuals. Moses, by way of comparison, was prepared to offer his own life in exchange for his people (Exod 32:9–14, 31–32; cf. Deut 9:14, 20, 25–29), a pattern of thought that readers of Matthew would recognize immediately as applied to Jesus, whose life also, in many other ways, is described as patterned on the life of Moses. For Jesus as the second Moses in Matthew, see Allison, *The New Moses*.

152. The "elect" is the name for those destined for salvation; these people have previously been identified as the "righteous" and the "perfect." We shall return below to the theological implications of this designation.

153. France, *Matthew*, 915. One may note here the following verses warning that many false Messiahs, saviors and prophets will come forth in the midst of these sufferings and proclaim the inauguration of the new era (cf. v. 27). This, together with the time reference in Matt 24:29–31 supports a reading of Matt 24:22 as referring to a historical event before the eschatological end will come. However, one must be careful not to distinguish too much between the historical and the eschatological, since the fall of Jerusalem is surely a sign in Matthew that the end-time tribulations have begun.

Jesus is claiming here is that when God's punishment of Jerusalem is executed, "the elect" will still be living in the land among other Jews.[154] Just as in the story about Abraham and Sodom, the sinners, including those whose love has grown cold because of the hardships (Matt 24:12), will be spared because of the elect that have endured (Matt 24:13). Thus, the life of the elect is more important for God than the immediate destruction of the sinners.[155]

There is here, again, a situation in history in which the life of the righteous and the punishment of the breakers of the law cannot be had at the same time, and God chooses life. Why would this divine choice be necessary? The narrative chronology of Matthew reveals how the eschatological end is dependent on the survival of the elect. In Matthew's vision of the events leading up to the end of the world and the final judgment, the first thing that happens is the destruction of Jerusalem. This is the signal that God has begun exercising judgment on Jerusalem, which is defiled by the shedding of innocent blood (23:35–36) and refuses to accept his prophets and his own son (cf. Matt 21:34–39, 44; 23:34, 37–38). After the destruction, there will be a period of time when the survivors, both the elect and the wicked, false prophets, and false saviors are active (Matt 24:11, 24[156]). While the latter are busy trying to deceive the people, including the elect, the followers of Jesus will travel throughout the world (*en holē tē oikoumenē*) and proclaim the kingdom "as a testimony to all the nations" (*eis martyrion pasin tois ethnesin*; Matt 24:14; cf. 28:19–20). These nations, to whom the proclamation of the kingdom will be a testimony, will, as a consequence, hate, torture, and kill Jesus's followers (Matt 24:9). Then, once all of this has been accomplished, the end will come (Matt 24:14; cf. 29–31).[157] The signal that this is happening is that the "sign of the

---

154. Matt 24:15 and the references to flight in Matt 24:16–20 suggest that the Matthean Jesus assumes that the disciples will still be living in Judea at the time when God's punishment is about to destroy Jerusalem. At that time, though, they must flee, which means that the sufferings described in the following verses are meant to refer to the situation in the land as a whole, not only to Judea.
155. The theo-eschatological logic behind such reasoning is explained in parable form in Matt 13:28–30.
156. Cf. 1 John 2:18: "Children, it is the last hour! As you have heard that antichrist is coming, so now many antichrists have come. From this we know that it is the last hour."

Son of Man will appear in heaven"; as this happens, all the tribes of the world (*pasai hai phylai tēs gēs*) will mourn,[158] as they see the Son of Man coming on the clouds of heaven with power and great glory (Matt 24:30).[159] The final judgment of the God of Israel is, for them, very bad news.

All this means that the elect are needed as the end-time events unfold. They act as God's agents, proclaiming the coming kingdom in the midst of hostile forces within and outside the people of God. When the great Day of Judgment finally arrives, but not before, evil will be removed like weeds by angels and "the righteous will shine like the sun in the kingdom of their Father" (Matt 13:29–30, 39–43). The form of vicarious righteousness implied in Matt 24:22 is, then, only providing temporary survival for the wicked in the period between the destruction of Jerusalem and the coming of the Son of Man, who will judge all according to their works, especially with regard to how they have treated the followers of Jesus living in their midst (Matt 10:40–42; 25:31–46).[160] The theological mechanism behind this temporary reprieve for the sinners is the delicate matter of God's (covenant) obligations to the righteous, who cannot be left to face the destruction brought upon the world as a result of the poor life choices of the wicked (Matt 13:29; 24:22).[161] What we see here are the implications of

---

157. The end of the world, the coming of the Son of Man, and the final judgment, are events that are then dealt with in a sequence of passages involving explanatory use of a biblical figure (Noah; Matt 24:37) and a series of parables (24:45–25:46).

158. As Nolland, *Matthew*, 984 notes, the mourning is caused by fear of judgment rather than repentance.

159. On the anti-gentile nature of Matthew's Gospel, see discussion below, Part II, chapter 5.1.

160. Cf. Dan 7:21–22, 25–27.

161. There is an interesting parallel to this pattern of thought in 4 Ezra. Here, we have the question of whether the righteous may intercede to save the lives of the wicked. The query is, however, met by the harsh statement that only individual righteousness will count in the final judgment (4 Ezra 7:102–15; cf. Ezek 14:12–23). Ezra then points out, correctly, that the righteous have always prayed for the ungodly, referring to a number of instances in the Scriptures, including Abraham in Gen 18 praying for Sodom, Moses and Joshua praying for Israel, Samuel, David, Solomon, Elijah and others, all of whose prayer involved intercession for sinners. Ezra's angelic interlocutor accepts this argument as valid for this age, but adds that in the world to come, righteousness will be complete and pervasive, and there will, consequently, be no room for sin or sinners. Therefore, they will all be destroyed before the world is reborn. Comparing this perspective to Matthew's theology, the common ground is surely that sinners have no place in the world to come. However, in Matt 24, there is no intercession on behalf of the wicked, only God's direct intervention to save his elect.

ideas that come with the covenant, ideas underlying—only in one case, surfacing explicitly[162]—and controlling much of the Gospel's theology of judgment.[163]

The second motif in Matthew's Gospel that implies a theology of vicarious righteousness is different in nature and more frequently discussed in both church and academia: the last supper. "Then he took a cup, and after giving thanks he gave it to them, saying, 'Drink from it, all of you; for this is my blood of the covenant [*to haima mou tēs diathēkēs*], which is poured out for many for the forgiveness of sins [*eis aphesin hamartiōn*]'" (26:27–28). This passage, which is placed between the identification of Judas as a traitor (26:25) and the statement that the other eleven disciples, including especially Peter, will abandon Jesus (26:30–35), is more complex and serves a different purpose than 24:22. Whereas 24:22 implies temporary reprieve in this world for the wicked due to the righteousness of the elect, Matt 26:28 gives expression to a sacrificial theology that will save "the many." Both passages share a common theme, however: God's covenant obligations to his people.

The primary theological motif in Matt 26:28 is of a dual nature: vicarious righteousness and vicarious suffering, i.e., the vicarious suffering of the righteous.[164] This motif is then embedded in and signals covenant theology, which gives the sacrifice described (the body and blood of Jesus) its specific meaning. The notion that the suffering of the righteous atones for other people's sins is not new in Judaism

---

162. Matt 26:28.

163. See further below, chapter 2.8.

164. The suffering of the righteous, especially in light of the fact that sinners often prosper, is a problem dealt with in several texts included in the Hebrew Bible, e.g., in the Psalter and the book of Job (cf. n. 160, above). Even God's messengers, the prophets, suffer and are killed (e.g., Neh 9:26; Jer 2:30; 26:20–23). In Jub 1:12, God's witnesses and those who search out the law are said to be killed and persecuted. In Matthew, prophets, both ancient ones and those sent out by Jesus, also suffer and are killed (Matt 23:30–34). The Jewish crowds believe Jesus to be a prophet (Matt 14:15; 21:11, 46), and, indeed, Jesus, as he is rejected in his hometown, identifies himself as a prophet (Matt 13:57). It is likely that traditions and experiences such as these have contributed to the development of a theology of vicarious righteousness, which invests the suffering with meaning beyond the individual. A further dimension is added when one considers the fact that the restoration of Israel in some traditions is linked to suffering, so that the suffering from which the people will be delivered also leads to the restoration of the nation (e.g., Isa 66:7–11; Dan 7; 12:1–3; T. Mos. 5–10; Jub. 23:22–31).

when Matthew writes, and this trajectory of thought also continues in later Jewish texts outside the Jesus movement. We find it in the Hebrew Bible,[165] in other forms of Second-Temple Judaism,[166] and in rabbinic literature.[167] In this Matthean passage, however, the theology of the vicarious righteousness of the righteous *par excellence* receives its full (eschatological) meaning only when considered in relation to the making of the covenant between the God of Israel and the people of Israel in Exod 24:3–8.

As both Exodus 24 and the structure of Matthew's Gospel show, the making of the Mosaic covenant involves two interrelated steps.[168] First, the law is given, representing the obligations contained in the treaty between God and people (that which establishes what righteousness is), Exod 24:3: "Moses came and told the people all the words of the LORD and all the ordinances; and all the people answered with one voice, and said, 'All the words that the LORD has spoken we will do'" (cf. Exod 24:7). In Matthew, the giving of the correct interpretation of the law, as it is claimed it was intended to be understood, is presented in particular in the first discourse, the Sermon on the Mount (Matthew 5–7), but instruction in the law continues throughout the story in the narrative sections as the author provides "real-life" examples regarding its correct fulfillment in specific situations (e.g., Matt 12:1–14; 15:1–20; 19:16–22).[169]

---

165. Isa 52:13–53:12; note especially 53:11: "The righteous one, my servant, shall make many righteous, and he shall bear their iniquities."

166. Cf. Dunn, *The Partings of the Ways*, 71–72. Important texts here include Wis 3; 5; 2 Macc 7:37–38; 4 Macc. 17:22. As Dunn notes, such theology of vicarious righteousness does not in any way replace or invalidate the temple cult (on this point, see also Nolland, *Matthew*, 1081). Most interesting for our purposes here is 4 Macc 6:27–29, where the motif of vicarious suffering is accentuated. (Cf. Exod 32:32.)

167. See Melinek, "Reward and Punishment," 309–10. The Rabbis ascribed "to the righteous in any generation a certain protective power for the whole of their generation. Thus according to them, it was for the merits of David, Esther, and Moses respectively that Israel was delivered from the Philistines, from Haman, and from drowning in the Red sea" (p. 309). Melinek also notes that after the Hadrianic persecutions, the Rabbis taught that perhaps the merits of the martyrs of Israel would "avail in God's sight to bring about the restoration." Important for our purposes here is also the Rabbinic theology of vicarious atonement, effected by "the combination of a vicarious act of merit with sincere repentance on the part of the sinner" (310). Cf. Moore, *Judaism*, 1.547ff.

168. For discussion of Matthew as one of many competitors for the heritage of Moses, see Allison, *The New Moses*.

169. Whereas in Exod 24:4, Moses writes down these words of the covenant, Matthew's Gospel leaves Jesus's instruction unwritten, indicating that it represents oral interpretation of the written law.

Second, once the people had agreed to the conditions laid out, sacrifices brought the covenant into being (Exod 24:5–6, 8). In Matthew, this is stated in Matt 26:26 ("Take, eat; this is my body") and v. 28 ("my blood of the covenant").[170] Sacrificial offerings are inextricably intertwined with the establishment of the Mosaic covenant; cult and covenant cannot be separated, and this is also what we see in Matthew's story. As it is quite clear that Matthew's text alludes to and builds upon the description of the establishment of the Mosaic covenant in Exod 24,[171] in order to understand the meaning of Jesus's sacrifice in its stated covenant context, it is important to pay attention to what type of sacrifices are offered as the Mosaic covenant is made, and how such sacrifices were understood in later Jewish tradition.

There are two kinds of sacrifices that bring the Mosaic covenant into being: the burnt offering ('ōlâ),[172] and offerings of the שלמים (shelamim) type, the latter translated variously as "peace offering," "offering of well-being," "thank offering," or "communion sacrifice."[173] While the history and understanding of the meaning of the burnt offering developed over time, it was the "highest" form of sacrifice, in which the entire animal, which had to be male and without blemish (Lev 1:3), was consumed by fire on the altar so that it may ascend to God; none of its parts were left for consumption by humans.[174] Becoming more frequently offered over time, it was performed on specific occasions, and, importantly, it effected atonement (Lev 1:4). It may be noted that when human sacrifices are mentioned, such as in the case of

This adds further to the evidence that this Gospel does not aim to replace or alter the law of Moses, but only to give it its ultimate interpretation as the eschaton is approaching.

170. Cf. A. D. A. Moses, *Matthew's Transfiguration Story and Jewish-Christian Controversy* (Sheffield: Sheffield Academic Press, 1996), 185–87.

171. See, e.g., Davies and Allison, *Matthew*, 3. 475; France, *Matthew*, 994.

172. For discussion of the *'ōlâ* sacrifice, see D. Kellermann, "עלה," in *TDOT* vol. 11 (ed. G. Johannes Botterweck, Helmer Ringgren, and Heinz-Josef Fabry; Grand Rapids: Eerdmans, 2001), 96–113.

173. On the difficulty of translation, cf. T. Seidl, "שלם," in *TDOT* vol. 15 (ed. G. Johannes Botterweck, Helmer Ringgren, and Heinz-Josef Fabry; Grand Rapids: Eerdmans, 2001), 105–16, esp. 115–16. For an in-depth analysis and discussion of this type of sacrifice, see Martin Modéus, *Sacrifice and Symbol: Biblical šĕlāmîm in a Ritual Perspective* (Stockholm: Almqvist & Wiksell International, 2005).

174. For discussion of the burnt offering, see Erhard S. Gerstenberger, *Leviticus: A Commentary* (Louisville: Westminster John Know press, 1996), 22–37.

Abraham sacrificing Isaac (Gen 22:2), the type of sacrifice stated is a burnt offering.[175]

The second type of offering mentioned as part of the sacrifices necessary for the making of the Mosaic covenant, the *shelamim* sacrifices (LXX: *thysia sōtēriou*), are more difficult to define in terms of their development and meaning. What is clear is that the sacrificial animal could be either male or female, but had to be without blemish (Lev 3:1). Only some parts of the animal, especially the fat, were to be consumed on the altar (i.e., given to God, Lev 3:3-17); the rest was consumed by the priests and those who offered the sacrifice (cf. Exod 24:11). In this way, the communal aspect of the sacrifice was focused: the sacrifice established a union between God and the people partaking in the sacrificial meal.[176] In the texts, which is what is important for us here since reconstructed historical aspects of development would have been unknown to the author of Matthew,[177] these types of sacrifices appear at peak moments in Israelite history.[178] In terms of defining more specifically their meaning, Martin Modéus argues that the very "point of the *šĕlāmîm* was that, fundamentally, it had no meaning at all. Due to this lack of meaning, it could be used in the focussing process in a wide range of *causae*."[179] This means that the *shelamim* cannot be said to be defining specifically a covenant context,[180] although they marked such settings as being of great importance, as well as indicating mutual agreement between the parties making the covenant. We may also note that there was a strong occasional aspect as the sacrifices labeled *shelamim* were performed, in contrast to sacrifices at prescribed times.

The two types of sacrifices complement each other in Exod 24:3-8.

---

175. See also Judg 11:30-40 (Jephthah's daughter); 2 Kgs 3:27 (the son of the Moabite king). See discussion in Kellermann, "107," עלה.

176. Cf., e.g., J. Philip Hyatt, *Exodus* (Grand Rapids: Eerdmans, 1980), 256. As Modéus, *Sacrifice*, 383, notes, this meaning of the sacrifice would be activated on the level of structure.

177. This is why the age of the various texts and traditions included in Exodus and Leviticus are irrelevant to our purpose here, and, consequently, not discussed.

178. Modéus, *Sacrifice*, 79-80, identifies the *shelamim* as a marking symbol.

179. Ibid., 80. *Causae* refers to specific situations, the foci, in life which trigger the performance of ritual.

180. Ibid., 176-78.

The burnt offering effects atonement, and the *shelamim* provide the context for the meal following the making of the covenant (24:11). Before the meal, though, blood from the sacrifices is collected in bowls and then sprinkled on the altar, which represents God, and on the people, respectively (Exod 24:6, 8). The blood divided and sprinkled in this way represents the union between God and people: "See the blood of the covenant [LXX: *to haima tēs diathēkēs*] that the LORD has made with you in accordance with all these words."

In later Jewish tradition, the sacrifices offered when the covenant was made were understood as expiatory.[181] This is also clear from Heb 9:18–22, where it is stated that these covenant sacrifices brought about forgiveness: "without the shedding of blood there is no forgiveness of sins" (v. 22). This means that for the covenant to be made, the people's sins have to be forgiven (cf. Ezek 16:62–63; Jer 31:34), after which they may share in the meal having been united with God through the sprinkling of blood from the sacrificial victims.

Returning to Matthew's version of the last supper, it seems as if the author combines into one the burnt offering with the *shelamim*, the former effecting atonement and the latter providing for the meal setting, in which all may share as a sign that they have accepted the obligations of the covenant as laid out by Jesus earlier in the narrative. As in Exod 24:6, 8, the blood of the covenant seals the union between God and people (Matt 26:28).[182] As the righteous *par excellence*, Jesus is equated with a sacrificial victim without blemish,[183] which is acceptable to God; it is as such, in the company of a traitor and others who will abandon him, that Jesus's perfect loyalty to God will save "many" from their sins (Matt 26:28; cf. 1:21; 20:28). His death is a

---

181. So also Davies and Allison, *Matthew*, 3. 475, referring to the targums (Onkelos and Pseudo-Jonathan). See also Nolland, *Matthew*, 1082. Kellermann, "110 ", עלה, referring to Targum Pseudo-Jonathan, notes that "the burnt offering is intended to atone for a sinful nature [...] [A]n *ʿōlâ* can atone not just for trespasses, not just for wicked plans never carried out [...], but also for the very disposition that fails to satisfy the demands of Yahweh." Matthew's insistence on the necessity of a pure heart, and that sin and the impurity that follows always begin in the heart (e.g., Matt 15:19–20), seem to require a type of atonement in line with the targumist's understanding of the burnt offering.

182. So also, Davies and Allison, *Matthew*, 3.475, who note that the author of Hebrews makes the same parallel between Moses sprinkling of blood in Exodus and Jesus's (surpassing) self-sacrifice.

183. Cf. Heb 9:14.

vicarious death, along the lines of 4 Macc. 6:27–29, where a tortured and dying Eleazar prays: "You know, O God, that though I could have saved myself I am dying in these fiery torments for the sake of the law. Be merciful to your people and let our punishment be a satisfaction on their behalf. Make my blood their purification and take my life as a ransom [*antipsychos*] for theirs."[184] The theo-ritual motif of vicarious righteousness merges here with cultic and sacrificial language.

In this way, the failings of the righteous, i.e., those who follow the law, will be atoned for by Jesus's sacrificial death, which in turn, removes the moral impurity that follows from sin and prepares for God's presence among his people as the eschaton is closing in (cf. Matt 18:20). This emphasizes the covenant relationship between God and his people even after the temple's abandonment (Matt 23:38) and (predicted) destruction (Matt 24:1–2). The concept of "righteous," thus, refers in Matthew not to a person free of sin, but to someone who accepts to follow the law *and* atone for the sins he or she will still commit.[185] It is for them that Jesus sacrifices himself, to save them from judgment.[186]

In light of the discussion above on "perfection," we may thus note here that loyalty in its complete form includes willingness to atone

---

184. Translation by H. Anderson; 4 Maccabees is probably to be dated between 19 and 54 CE (H. Anderson, "4 Maccabees: A New Translation and Introduction," 531–64 in *The Old Testament Pseudepigrapha*, vol. 2 [edited by James H. Charlesworth; New York: Doubleday, 1985] 533–34). On the offering of a righteous person's life as a "ransom" to save others, see Matt 20:28 where *lytron* is used. A variant of this pattern of thought is found in the golden-calf story (Exod 32:7–32), where Moses "threatens" God, suggesting that if God wants to destroy the people as punishment for what they have done, then he has to kill Moses too, despite the fact that he has been completely loyal to God (v. 32). This is Moses's "counter offer" after God has decided to form a new people of God based on Moses (v. 10). For Moses, however, this early variant of "replacement theology" that God suggests is unacceptable because of the promises God made to "Abraham, Isaac, and Israel" (v. 13).

185. That we are dealing here with a single sacrifice that atones also for intentional sins is shown by the fact that the sins of the disciples, who will soon abandon Jesus, are covered by this ritual. Regarding the status of the righteous, cf. Luther's famous statement, *simul iustus et peccator* ("righteous and at the same time sinner"). This idea, although colored by sixteenth-century theological discourses, indicates some aspects of what is implied in Matthew's first-century Jewish theology. Matthew would not, however, use the word "sinner" for people whose status was on a basic level defined as righteous.

186. See further the discussion below on repentance and forgiveness. Note that this saving act does not imply immunity against suffering and violent death in this world at the hands of other humans, only protection in light of the coming of the final judgment, after which the kingdom will be established.

for sins. The righteousness and perfection required of humans, i.e., the fulfillment of the Jewish law, thus involves acceptance that without God's arrangement for a sacrificial cult (and, as a consequence of its defilement, Jesus's sacrifice in its stead), through which sin is eradicated, God cannot dwell among his people, and all would perish in judgment as a result of accumulated guilt. Perfection, thus, and salvation, can only be achieved in the interplay between God's mercy and human obedience.

For Matthew, then, Jesus's death is not equated with the Passover sacrifice specifically, as Paul explicitly interprets it and as is implied in John's Gospel,[187] but with the Sinaitic covenantal sacrifice affirming the validity of the Mosaic law.[188] The timing of the ritual enactment of this sacrifice during the Passover meal, however, triggers an additional dimension of the interpretation of Jesus's death. Just as the blood of the Paschal lambs protected the people of Israel as God sent destruction and death over Egypt to liberate his people (Exod 12:12–14), Jesus's death will serve as protection when the apocalyptic disasters marking the beginning of the end are unleashed (as foretold in Matthew 24).

In sum, two quite different examples of a theology of vicarious righteousness surface in Matthew's Gospel, both of which are

187. 1 Cor 5:7; John 13:1; 18:28, 39; 19:14, 31; cf. 1:29, 36. It may also be noted that John is the only Gospel which mentions that Jesus's legs were not broken, referring to the fulfillment of a scriptural verse (John 19:33, 36). This may be a reference to Ps 34:20 (MT and LXX, 34:21), but the passage also echoes Exod 12:46, where the people are instructed not to break any of the bones of the paschal lamb. The understanding of Jesus's death as a paschal sacrifice later became the preferred interpretive path of the emerging church, in which the Mosaic covenant with the Jewish people was considered abolished. This development should not, however, prevent us from seeing diversity in the earliest sources. Cf. John P. Meier's warning against not distinguishing carefully between the agendas of the Gospels in *A Marginal Jew: Rethinking the Historical Jesus* vol. 1: *The Roots of the Problem and the Person* (New York: Doubleday, 1991), 42: "putting all four Gospels together will produce only a confused heap of theological schemas." Such an insight is valid also for the analysis of the narrativized historical Jesus according to Matthew.

188. Matthew, like Mark (14:24), does not identify the covenant as "new," like Paul and Luke do (1 Cor 11:25; Luke 22:20). Seen against the background of Matthew's Gospel as a whole, especially its emphasis on a strict interpretation of the Mosaic law, this leads to an understanding of Jesus's sacrificial offering of himself, which confirms and refreshes the covenant at Sinai at the beginning of the end times. Jesus's death, thus, becomes the logical fulfillment of the perspective that permeates Matthew's Gospel, namely that the Mosaic law, which was given within the covenant, is valid in all its aspects and details until the re-birth of the world (Matt 5:17–19; cf. 17:1–8, where Jesus is portrayed as in agreement with Moses and the prophets). What is new for Matthew is thus not the covenant in itself, but the sacrificial arrangements (atonement) within the covenant that allow the covenantal structure and mutual obligations between God and people to remain in place after the temple has been abandoned and destroyed.

ultimately examples of how God's covenantal obligations are expressed as the apocalyptic end is approaching. In the first scenario (Matt 24:22), God's protection of the righteous/elect will have temporary positive outcomes for the wicked in this world, although they will eventually be punished in the final judgment. In the second scenario (Matt 26:28), the suffering and death of Jesus is interpreted as a covenantal sacrifice atoning for the sins of "many"; these "many" will, as a consequence, be found among the righteous in the final judgment. This sacrifice of atonement by the righteous *par excellence* restores and upholds the Mosaic covenant and makes possible the continued understanding of the covenantal relationship in terms similar to what Sanders has called covenantal nomism,[189] even after God has abandoned the (morally) defiled temple (Matt 23:38), which is soon to be destroyed (Matt 24:1–2). In other words, Jesus's sacrifice is necessary because of the (predicted) fall of the temple,[190] and it will save the Jewish people from their sins (Matt 1:21). This, in turn, will protect them from destruction in the final judgment which will soon take place.

Since, in Jewish tradition, atonement is linked to repentance, we now turn to this theme in search for Matthean teaching on certain responses by humans that may avert divine wrath and its devastating consequences. What is, in other words, the role of repentance and forgiveness in Matthew's understanding of divine judgment, especially when seen in light of the above discussion of obedience and righteousness as they relate to rewards and salvation?

2.4 Repentance and Forgiveness

Until the second half of the twentieth century, there was a persistent tradition in Christian scholarship on Judaism to portray Judaism as

---

189. On this terminology, see further below, chapter 2.8.
190. According to Matthew, the fall of the temple is not to be understood as punishment for the Jewish leaders' role in Jesus's execution, as they handed him over to the Roman authorities, although this became a common interpretation in later (non-Jewish) Christianity. It is the other way around: the destruction of the temple is a consequence of the sins of especially the Pharisees and the scribes associated with them, which have polluted the temple, and this necessitates Jesus's sacrifice on behalf of his people in order to save them from God's judgment as he unleashes apocalyptic destruction and initiates the rebirth of the world. See further discussion below.

a "superficial" religion, in the sense that atonement and forgiveness were understood as almost "mechanical" processes with automatic outcomes delivered by the sacrificial cult, regardless of the inner motivation of the person seeking forgiveness. This representation of Judaism was then contrasted with the perspective of the New Testament, which was described as exclusively focused on sincere inner repentance, upon which forgiveness followed as a direct result of the inner motivation of the individual, regardless of any attempts on the part of the person seeking forgiveness to rectify what had gone wrong and provide sacrificial offerings. Such distortions of Judaism and the New Testament, on the one hand, conceal the fact that a focus on the sacrificial cult in no way excludes the requirement of repentance in order for the cult to be effective, and, on the other hand, misrepresent the New Testament as both uninterested in the temple cult and rejecting restitution as a requirement for forgiveness. As we shall see, the Gospel of Matthew exhibits a firm balance between these concerns, which, arguably, identifies its theology as an expression of a Jewish ritual worldview. The outcome of divine judgment is dependent on the inner motivations of the individual seeking forgiveness, restitution on the part of the wrongdoer in relation to the offended party, and the effectiveness of the cult. The bottom line is that, for the Matthean Jesus, repentance is not only possible; it is absolutely necessary. In order to frame our discussion, we shall begin with a brief survey of related motifs as they surface in the books cherished as holy by the scribe who authored Matthew.[191]

Repentance in the Hebrew Bible refers to a turning away from unrighteousness and wicked ways (e.g., Jer 18:11; Zech 1:2–4) and turning to God (e.g., 2 Chr 15:3–4; Isa 55:6–7; Hos 14:1 [Heb 14:2]). The process is sometimes described as being accompanied by rituals otherwise related to mourning, indicating deep remorse (e.g., Dan 9:3–5; Jonah 3:5–10). The wickedness from which the people must turn is often related to injustices committed against fellow humans,

---

191. For a different approach, see Tobias Hägerland, *Jesus and the Forgiveness of Sins: An Aspect of his Prophetic Mission* (Cambridge: Cambridge University Press, 2012); note esp. the discussion of early Judaism, 132–78.

behavior that breaks the law, and thus the covenant (e.g., Jer 34:13–18). The process of repentance may be described as involving confession (*yadah*), which must precede the actual sacrificial offering (Lev 5:5–13; cf. Nehemiah 9; Dan 9:3–19).

One of the central motifs related to repentance is that it turns away, even neutralizes God's wrath, and causes God to act with mercy and love toward his people (e.g., Hos 14:4–5 [Heb 14:5–6]; Joel 2:15–19). That such processes can be partly unrelated to the temple cult is seen from the fact that even when the people are described as in exile—a result of God's punishment—without access to the temple, repentance is the very means, the method, of reconciliation between God and people (cf. e.g., 1 Kgs 8:46–51).[192] While repentance is key to any relationship between God and humans, the notions of human remorse and turn to God seem to exist within and relate to a larger covenantal frame,[193] in which the penitent person already knows that God wants to forgive, and thus, desires the repentance that allows for such restoration of the relationship (e.g., Dan 9:4, 18).[194] The importance of repentance is emphasized by the fact that if it is lacking, divine judgment will follow (e.g., Ps 7:11–13 [Heb 7:12–14]; Jer 3:19–4:4; 5:1–19; Hos 5:1–4; 7:10–13; Amos 4:1–13). Thus, prophetic calls for repentance are often linked to threats of judgment, whether it concerns the nation as a whole or the individual (Isa 55:6–7; Ezek 14:4–7; 18:20–32; Joel 2:10–13; Mal 3:1–18). Suffering resulting from divine punishment is sometimes said to lead to repentance, which—in some cases, even if not sincere—may lead to forgiveness based on God's compassion (Ps 78:32–39; cf. Zech 1:6). Redemption shall be granted those who repent, but destruction will follow for those who remain in a state of sin (Isa 1:27–28).

Despite this emphasis on God's willingness to forgive, and the

---

192. Cf. 2 Chr 6:36–39. Although the passage describes a situation in which the people does not have access to the Jerusalem temple, the temple still plays a role in that prayer must be directed toward the land.

193. On the relationship between confession of sins, God's mercy and willingness to forgive, and the covenant, see discussion in Michael P. Knowles, *The Unfolding Mystery of the Divine Name: The God of Sinai in Our Midst* (Downers Grove: IVP Academic, 2012), 57–62.

194. Cf. Donald E. Gowan, "Repentance in the OT," *NIDB*, vol. 4 (Nashville: Abingdon, 2009), 764, who notes that Joel 2:12–13 quotes Exod 34:67 when he calls for national repentance. See also Deut 30:8–10.

necessity of repentance for this to happen, there are some texts which indicate that certain sins cannot be forgiven. As Kennedy notes, such sins are described as committed "with a high hand."[195] It seems, though, that even severe transgressions, e.g., those that led to national disaster such as the exile, will often eventually still be forgiven, after punishment has been meted out.

One of the most commonly quoted texts commenting on repentance, which includes references to a cultic setting, is Psalm 51. This hymn involves all the key components of repentance, and in many ways, summarizes what we see in other texts: confession of sins, request for forgiveness and purification (v. 7 [Heb v. 9]: *tahar*; LXX: *katharizō*), and an appeal for salvation. The key to achieve this is sincere repentance, and this is stated in direct relationship to sacrifices in order to indicate its absolute importance: "For you have no delight in sacrifice; if I were to give a burnt offering, you would not be pleased. The sacrifice acceptable to God is a broken spirit; a broken and contrite heart, O God, you will not despise" (vv. 16–17 [Heb 18–19]). Traditionally, many commentators have seen here a rejection of sacrifices as if they were meaningless, but this is based on a misunderstanding of the role of repentance. Repentance is a prerequisite without which sacrifices would be empty and in vain. Only when repentance is in place will the (necessary) sacrifices be acceptable to God, which is also stated in the final verse of the psalm: "then you will delight in right sacrifices, in burnt offerings and whole burnt offerings; then bulls will be offered on your altar" (v. 19 [Heb 21]). This pattern of thought is continued in later centuries, including in rabbinic literature.

Like Psalm 51, Sir 34:23–24 emphasizes the emptiness of sacrifices if righteousness is lacking: "The Most High is not pleased with the offerings of the ungodly, nor for a multitude of sacrifices does he forgive sins. Like one who kills a son before his father's eyes is the person who offers a sacrifice from the property of the poor."[196] Those

---

195. H.A.A. Kennedy, "The Significance and Range of the Covenant Conception in the New Testament," *The Expositor*, 8:10 (1915): 385–410, here 388–89: "The existence of the covenant is really the pledge that God is willing to forgive the sins of the penitent community in so far as they are not deliberately wilful, done 'with a high hand.'" Cf., e.g., 1 Sam 3:14.

who repent will be received by God (Sir 17:24), but if repentance is lacking, judgment will follow and may lead to exile or exclusion from the world to come (Sir 48:15; 4 Ezra 9:10–12). God wants repentance, however, and may hold back full punishment for sins committed in order to induce it (Wis 12:10). The basis for this is God's love and mercy; God does not want suffering and has therefore "appointed repentance for sinners, so that they may be saved" (Pr Man 7 [Ode 12:7]).[197]

The pattern of repentance and forgiveness within the context of God's love for his people is thus maintained in many, if not most Second-Temple Jewish texts. In some instances, though, authors identify certain sins as unforgivable, beyond the possibility of atonement. One such example is the book of Jubilees and its list of eternal sins "unto death."[198].

In rabbinic Judaism, repentance holds a central place, perhaps more so than in earlier Jewish texts; the pattern is much the same, but accentuated.[199] Without repentance, sacrifices are meaningless and atonement will not be achieved: "Be not like the fools who, when they sin, bring an offering, but do not repent. They know not the difference between good and evil, and yet venture to make an offering to God" (b. Ber 23a).[200] The place of repentance, which involves restitution, is

196. Cf. Sir 34:30–31 in terms of the correlation between ritual and inner motivation, or sincerity: "If one washes after touching a corpse, and touches it again, what has been gained by washing? So if one fasts for his sins, and goes again and does the same things, who will listen to his prayer? And what has he gained by humbling himself?"

197. See also Pr Man 13 [Ode 12:13]: "For you, O Lord, are the God of those who repent." Cf. 4 Ezra 7:62–70 [132–40], although there the vision of the forgiving God is problematized.

198. See discussion in Sanders, Paul and Palestinian Judaism, 368–71. We find a similar approach in the Dead Sea Scrolls; cf. Sanders, Paul and Palestinian Judaism, 284.

199. See especially, the following seminal works, which are still important studies in this area: Solomon Schechter, Aspects of Rabbinic Theology. Introduction to new edition by Louis Finkelstein (New York: Schocken Books, 1961 [1909]), 313–43; C. G. Montefiore and H. M. J. Loewe (eds.), A Rabbinic Anthology (Cambridge University Press, 2012 [1938]), 315–33. See also Ephraim E. Urbach, The Sages: Their Concepts and Beliefs. Translated from the Hebrew by Israel Abrahams (Cambridge MA: Harvard University Press, 1979), 462–71.

200. Cf. t. Yoma 5:9: "Sin offering and guilt offering and death and the Day of Atonement, all of them together, do not expiate sin without repentance." Cf. Schechter, Rabbinic, 342. With regard to the importance of the intention behind the sacrifice, a later rabbinic text writes: "Once a woman brought a handful of fine flour [for a meal offering], and the priest despised her saying: 'See what she offers! What is there in this to eat? What is there in this to offer up?' It was shown to him in a dream: 'Do not despise her! It is regarded as if she had sacrificed her own life'" (Lev. Rab. 3.5; cf. Mark 12:41–44). See also Urbach, Sages, 464: "Primarily repentance calls for the abandonment of the way of sin and the inner resolve never to return to it, and not the outward acts that accompany it, such as fasting and prayer."

central: "If one say, 'I will sin and repent, I will sin and repent,' he will not be given [by God] an opportunity to repent. 'I will sin and the Day of Atonement will effect atonement,' then the Day of Atonement does not effect atonement [...] For transgressions between man and his fellow man the Day of Atonement does not effect atonement until he shall have first appeased his fellow man" (m. Yoma 8:9).[201] This may be compared to the statement in Tosefta that, "[f]or tax collectors and publicans repentance is difficult; they are to give back to those they are aware of, and as for the rest, he is to use it for public requirements" (t. Baba Metsia 8:26).[202]

In a famous saying by Rabbi Eliezer, the people are advised to repent one day before death; since no one knows when they will die, this means that all "life will be spent in repentance."[203] Lack of repentance and confession, on the other hand, will result in punishment;[204] the destruction of both the first and the second temple is understood as punishment for severe sins committed there, which defiled the temple.[205] For the Tannaim, repentance, in and of itself, atones for lesser transgressions,[206] whereas more serious sins need both repentance and additional rituals. In a few cases, repentance will not be effective at all, as in the following passage from the Mishnah: "Whosoever causes the multitude to be righteous, through him shall no sin be brought about, but one that leads the many to sin, to him shall not be given the means to repentance" (m. Avot 5:18). Since repentance is necessary for forgiveness, this means that what we have here is a case of unforgivable sin.[207] Urbach suggests that the reason for such

---

201. Cf. Matt 5:23–26.
202. The implied assumption is that tax collectors commonly engaged in fraud. Cf. Luke 19:8.
203. *Midr. Ps.* on 90:12. Cf. *Mekhilta* on Exodus 20:7, where forgiveness is related to repentance even in cases of severe sin: "He [God] clears those who repent but does not clear those who do not repent." See also *b. Shabb.* 153.
204. *Midr. Ps.* on 100:1.
205. *B. Yoma* 9b, stating that pollution of the temple was caused by idolatry, sexual sins, bloodshed, and baseless hatred. Cf. Josephus, who also explains the fall of the temple by reference to its defilement: see discussion in Steve Mason, "Pollution and Purification in Josephus's Judean War," in *Purity, Holiness, and Identity in Judaism and Christianity* (edited by Carl S. Ehrlich, Anders Runesson, and Eileen Schuller; Tübingen: Mohr Siebeck, 2013), 181–207.
206. Urbach, *Sages*, 465.
207. Cf. *m. Sanh.*10:1, where it is stated that "[a]ll Israel have a portion in the world to come." The passage then goes on to list exceptions to this rule, beginning with those who do not believe in the

behavior to be counted as so severe a transgression is that it involves, by implication, the sin of "the desecration of the Divine Name"; this type of sin is unforgivable, and will be, perforce, punished.[208] The same perspective is also present in the extra-canonical tractate Avot de Rabbi Nathan, where a list of unforgivable sins is given: "Five shall obtain no forgiveness: He that is forever repenting, he that sins excessively, he that sins in a righteous generation, he that sins with the intention to repent, and he who has on his hands (the sin of) profaning the Name."[209]

While such views of unforgivable sins exist within the rabbinic corpus, they are few compared to the overwhelming emphasis on repentance from the time of the Tannaim and (even more) the Amoraim onwards. Repentance is the overshadowing and central theme in rabbinic thought as forgiveness and atonement are discussed, as is also seen from its presence in the *Shemoneh 'Esreh*, the Eighteen Benedictions.[210] Interestingly, the prayer urges God to cause the praying person to return and repent, indicating that God's help is needed in the otherwise human endeavor to seek reconciliation and avoid punishment.[211] We may note in this regard that God as the father of Israel is an important element when forgiveness is sought, implying a willingness on the part of God to forgive; the one who cleanses from the guilt following from sin is not a hostile force, but the one who is "your father in heaven."[212]

---

resurrection of the dead. Here, however, we should note that repentance is not discussed, which means that the possibility of repentance is most likely understood, and its presence will lead to a reversal of divine judgment.

208. Urbach, *Sages*, 466.

209. *'Abot R. Nat.* 39. Translation by Judah Goldin. Cf. Meier, *Matthew*, 135.

210. Cf. *b. Ber.* 28b. The origin and development of this prayer is disputed. For discussion, see Lee I. Levine, *The Ancient Synagogue: The First Thousand Years* (New Haven: Yale University Press, 2005), 540–50, and the important and comprehensive study by Ruth Langer, *Cursing the Christians? A History of the Birkat Haminim* (Oxford: Oxford University Press, 2011). For a critique of how the relationship between this prayer and communities of Christ-believers has been construed by scholars of the New Testament, especially in relation to John's Gospel and its *aposynagōgos* passages, see Jonathan Bernier, *Aposynagōgos and the Historical Jesus in John: Rethinking the Historicity of the Johannine Expulsion Passages* (Leiden: Brill, 2013).

211. The prayer, which is the fifth of the eighteen, or rather nineteen, prayers is worded as follows: "Cause us to return, our Father, unto your Torah; draw us near, our king, unto your service, and bring us back into perfect repentance unto your presence. Blessed are you, O Lord, who delights in repentance." On God's helping humans repent, see also Montefiore and Loewe, *Anthology*, 330–31.

212. So Rabbi Akiva, according to *m. Yoma* 8:9; cf. Matt 6:9, 12. See also Luz, *Matthew*, 1.379, who suggests

In the Gospel of Matthew, repentance is key to the whole process of the establishment of the kingdom of heaven, and thus directly related to the outcome of divine judgment, and more specifically, the final judgment, which is said to precede the full realization of the kingdom. Without repentance, no forgiveness; without forgiveness, no kingdom. Matthew, in fact, summarizes Jesus's proclamation of the kingdom using the same words as he did for his summary of John's preaching: "Repent, for the kingdom of heaven has come near" (Matt 3:2; 4:17). Thus, beginning our discussion with the Matthean John will serve us well as we then proceed to the Matthean Jesus.

First, the baptism of John is a ritualized form of repentance (3:11), and it is connected with confession of sins (3:6).[213] The water ritual adds to the requirements originally related to ritual impurity so that purifying rituals become effective also in relation to sin (moral impurity).[214] Beyond the water ritual, we may observe here the same connection between confession and repentance, as we have seen in the Hebrew Bible and other early Jewish texts. While in rabbinic literature, confession and repentance may be considered to have atoning force in and of themselves, effecting forgiveness for minor transgressions,[215] this is not exactly what we see in Matthew's portrait of John. For Matthew, John's baptism does not effectuate forgiveness, but is closely related to the temple cult in the sense that it prepares a person to draw near the altar without (morally) defiling it; atonement is then achieved by way of offering appropriate sacrifices. The ritual of baptism thus protects the temple from impurity, just as inter-human forgiveness does in this Gospel;[216] it does not replace it or negotiate its importance.

that Matthew's reference to God as father represents one of the few indications of the theme of grace in this Gospel, preventing us from interpreting Matthew's theology as one of "work-righteousness."

213. Neither the Matthean Jesus nor his disciples baptize anyone in Matthew. It is only after the resurrection Jesus tells his (Jewish) followers to baptize the nations and turn them into disciples (Matt 28:19–20).

214. For discussion of ritual and moral impurity in Second-Temple Judaism, including New Testament texts, as well as in Tannatic Judaism, see Jonathan Klawans, *Impurity and Sin in Ancient Judaism* (Oxford: Oxford University Press, 2000).

215. Cf. Mark 1:4, where we see the same connection between confession and forgiveness, as Mark relates baptism to such penitence and forgiveness: "John the baptizer appeared in the wilderness, proclaiming a baptism of repentance for the forgiveness of sins."

216. See also discussion below of Matt 9:1–8.

As Matthew makes clear elsewhere, no one should offer a sacrifice without first having repented and become reconciled with a person he or she might have offended (5:23–26).[217] John, too, is emphasizing that the sincerity of repentance is measured in works: "Bear fruit worthy of repentance" (3:8). Without such "fruit," condemnation will follow as divine wrath is unleashed in the immediate future (3:7, 10).[218] In other words, the Matthean John operates fully within the cultic frame of the Jerusalem temple, intensifying the demand for sincere repentance in order to enable atonement as the final judgment is approaching.

As with John, the Matthean Jesus proclaims the necessity of repentance within an eschatological setting. It is primarily in view of the coming kingdom that sins must be confessed and restitution made. However, in the Sermon on the Mount, Jesus addresses an everyday life situation as he reinforces the risk of (moral) defilement of the altar, should repentance and restitution not have been taken care of before entering the temple precincts (5:23–26). Thus, in Matthew, instruction regarding repentance relates to both the "here and now" and the "there and then" of the final judgment, and it assumes the existence and effectiveness of the temple cult. Jesus is, however, also referring to non-Jews as he aims at shaming the unrepentant within his own people. In such cases—and we shall return to the issue of non-Jews in Part II—repentance is implicitly assumed to be effective also in eschatological perspective beyond the temple-cult setting (11:20–24;

---

217. Dale C. Allison, *Studies in Matthew: Interpretation Past and Present* (Grand Rapids: Baker Academic, 2005), 65–78, offers an interesting interpretation of this passage, in which he argues that an informed reader would have thought of the story of Cain and Abel in Gen 4:1–16 rather than associated this Jesus saying with the Jerusalem temple, noting that Cyprian made this connection too in *De eccl. cath. unit.* 13 and *De dom. orat.* 23–24. While this interpretation is suggestive, it is difficult, in my view, to avoid the conclusion that a first-century reader of Matthew would have related this saying to the temple cult, which was the only Jewish cult with which he or she had experience. Indeed, even if we find here an intended allusion to Cain and Abel, this does not contradict a hermeneutic which allows this story to speak to current (or recent, understanding Matthew to be authored post-70 CE) cultic realities, regardless of whether some specific details fit or do not fit the historical circumstances of a person offering a sacrifice in the temple; the history of interpretation of biblical texts in synagogue and church are full of such examples. The point of the story in Matthew is, regardless, that no one should approach God in a state of moral impurity, so that a person's relationship with the divine is made directly dependent on his or her inter-personal relationships. The latter principle is applied in other settings too, e.g., Matt 6:14–15; 18:15–17, 21–35.

218. The Baptist points to Pharisees and Sadducees as unrepentant in this regard, since they are said to lack such works (3:7).

12:41).[219] For Jews, however, the cult functions within the Sinaitic covenant, which is why repentance in Matthew relates to the atonement achieved through the cult. Repentance is, to be sure, a universal phenomenon in Matthew, as it is also in some texts in the Hebrew Bible,[220] but it takes a specific covenantal form when it relates to the Jewish people.

As in other Jewish texts, then, in Matthew, repentance is necessary for forgiveness. Forgiveness, in turn, is one of the keys to understanding the significance of this Jesus story (1:21). For this pattern of the intertwined concepts of repentance, forgiveness, and judgment as it is played out between humans, and between humans and the God of Israel to work (6:12, 14–15; 18:21–35), the process of forgiveness needs to be constant and uninterrupted. Forgiveness must be sought (5:23–26; 18:15–17), and forgiveness must be granted (6:14–15; 18:21–35) between fellow humans. Forgiveness as a phenomenon has universal implications even when exchanged between individuals, since God's forgiveness is made conditional upon individual human forgiveness; forgiveness is relevant on a cosmic level. This notion is emphasized when repentance is lacking, since the guilt following from sin then remains and exclusion and/or punishment will follow. This is so both for Jesus's followers (18:15–17) and for all others, such as the unrepentant inhabitants of some Galilean towns (11:20–24). More importantly for Matthew's story, though, is the description of the Pharisees and the scribes associated with them (12:38, 41) as unrepentant sinners associated with all sorts of atrocities, including bloodshed (Matthew 23). What makes such sins worse is that the Pharisees and their scribes "sit on Moses' chair" (23:2) and should therefore have recognized and acted upon what Matthew's Jesus claims is the right interpretation of the law. The lack of repentance on the part of these leading figures in the story, and, more specifically, Jerusalem (23:37) is what will lead to God's punishment of the entire nation, through the destruction of the temple (23:38–24:2).

219. Cf. Luke 24:47: "and repentance and forgiveness of sins should be preached in his name to all nations."
220. See, e.g., Jonah 3:5–10.

While these concepts in Matthew—repentance, forgiveness, and judgment—align in a pattern which is observable also in other Jewish texts, we still need to address the issues that underlie Matthew's emphasis on repentance and forgiveness—namely, moral impurity and Jesus's role in the process of atonement. *Why*, more specifically, is sincere repentance and abundant and unceasing forgiveness necessary before the kingdom arrives? In order to answer this question, we need to revisit the issue of the definitions of sin, law, and righteousness. Sin is, as we have discussed above,[221] defined as violation of the law, and righteousness is defined as the opposite. Divine judgment is based on whether or not a person's deeds align with the law's requirements, as Jesus interprets it (Matt 7:21; 16:27). To prevent the impurity that results from violation of the law, correct teaching of the law is necessary.[222] As in the Torah, however, the removal of moral impurity, which results from violation of the law, requires forgiveness and sacrifice. The question is how Matthew presents Jesus's approach to these phenomena. Is forgiveness dependent on the temple cult, which we have argued is understood as valid during the (narrative) time when Jesus is proclaiming and performing his message, or does Matthew set up a new process, new mechanics, for the forgiveness of sins?[223]

First, it should be noted that, regardless of the mechanism used to bring about forgiveness (temple or extra-temple), the aim of forgiveness is to purify the people from the defilement resulting from sin (cf. Matt 15:18–20). The basic worldview is thus the same for the Matthean Jesus as for many other forms of Judaism at this time. Having

---

221. See chapter 2.1.

222. Without such teaching, the Matthean Jesus regards the people to be lost: Matt 7:29; 9:36; 16:12; 15:14; 23:15–22.

223. For ancient concepts of forgiveness, as opposed to modern ideas, see David Konstan, *Before Forgiveness: The Origin of a Moral Idea* (Cambridge: Cambridge University Press, 2010), especially the discussion of the Hebrew Bible and the New Testament on pages 91–124. See also now Charles L., Griswold, and David Konstan, eds. *Ancient Forgiveness: Classical, Judaic, and Christian* (Cambridge: Cambridge University Press, 2012). See also, most recently, Isaac K. Mbabazi, *The Significance of Interpersonal Forgiveness in the Gospel of Matthew* (Eugene: Wipf & Stock, 2013). Eubank, *Wages of Cross-Bearing*, focuses on the debt metaphor and is an important contribution to the problem of forgiveness in Matthew. Here, however, we shall aim to shed light on what is behind the metaphor; the cultically informed reality to which the metaphor of debt and debt-release refers.

said that, there is some tension in the narrative between Jesus's forgiveness of sins, Jesus's death as a sacrifice for the forgiveness of sins, and the function of the temple in Jerusalem. This tension is resolved, as we shall see, only when the progression of events in the narrative as a whole is taken into consideration and made part of the theo-ritual equation.

Second, we need to distinguish between inter-human forgiveness and forgiveness between humans and God, on the one hand, and the removal of defilement, on the other. Forgiveness between human beings is defined metaphorically as the cancelation of debt (*opheilēmata*; Matt 6:12). This process is mirrored in the human–divine relationship, which is dependent on the effectiveness of inter-human forgiveness; God will not cancel a person's debts if that person is not cancelling what others owe him or her (Matt 6:14–15; 18:23–35). The process of divine forgiveness is thus inextricably interwoven with human ability, and willingness, to forgive. This structure of forgiveness, referred to in the Gospel as the cancelling of debt, works well within the system of the sacrificial cult in the temple, and is independent of Jesus as far as the effectiveness of the cult itself is concerned; only when humans reconcile will God respond to sacrificial gifts, with which atonement is linked (Matt 5:23–24).[224] This means, by implication, that humans can, potentially, bind others in their debt, since debt can be removed only by the victim. Since this would make impossible the removal of the impurities that follow from sin, the Matthean Jesus orders his followers to always forgive, without limitation (Matt 18:21–22).[225] Based on such considerations, interpersonal forgiveness in Matthew may be defined as the removing of cultically incapacitating impurities stored up within a person, which prevents the guilty party from restoring his or her relationship with the divine.[226] It follows from such a definition that the refusal to forgive

---

224. Cf. Sir 28:2–3; *Did.* 14:1–3.

225. Cf. Sir 28:5–7. On the requirement of limitless forgiveness, see Nolland, *Matthew*, 753–55.

226. Cf. the definition given by Mbabazi, *Interpersonal Forgiveness*, 1, which focuses on the giving up of resentment related to injury and wrongdoing, or failure to live up to obligations. While such a definition does capture some of what is involved in the process of forgiveness, and while it is hermeneutically useful, in the end it fails to grasp the ultimate reason behind the need for

a person (who has repented and asks for forgiveness) would be devastating for that person in the final divine judgment.

Forgiveness must be willingly given, but the offender must also accept responsibility and thus acknowledge the need for forgiveness (Matt 18:15). If the offender refuses to acknowledge the need to be forgiven (and thus, refuses to deal with his or her impure status), after a number of steps have been taken, but have failed to make clear to the perpetrator the nature of the offence, the community of Jesus's followers must exclude him or her (Matt 18:15-17; cf. Did. 15:3). Such a procedure will ensure that the defilement caused by the sin is removed from the community, and relocated to a general category of sinners: non-Jews and tax collectors (18:17).[227] The Matthean Jesus tells his followers that they have the right to bind such a person in his or her (impure) status through exclusion (which implies absence of forgiveness, and thus, retained debt). They also have the right (or perhaps better: obligation; cf. 18:21-22) to free him or her from debt, should the offender recognize his or her offence (18:18). Forgiveness, thus, cannot be given without repentance; repentance is, by implication, a *sine qua non* for the purity required of the community.

In the Matthean narrative, all of this functions well within the sacrificial system of the Jerusalem temple. After reconciliation, a person is able to offer sacrifice without defiling the altar (5:23-24). However, Jesus is also portrayed as adding an aspect to the process of forgiveness, which is centered on himself and which goes beyond the system described so far, albeit still existing within the horizon of the sacrificial cult in Jerusalem. In Matt 9:1-8, Jesus heals a paralyzed man in Capernaum by forgiving him his sins (*hamartiai*). This is the

---

forgiveness in Matthew since it does not take into account the cultically defined interpretive frame that informs the notion and without which the concept is removed from its first-century context, within which it is culturally embedded.

227. This concern for the purity of the community may be related to the presence of Jesus in the midst of the group (Matt 18:20). It is interesting here to compare Matthean concern with the purity of the community with similar concerns in the Qumran community and in Paul's letters; see Cecilia Wassén, "Do you have to be Pure in a Metaphorical Temple? Sanctuary Metaphors and Construction of Sacred Space in the Dead Sea Scrolls and Paul's Letters," in *Purity and Holiness in Judaism and Christianity: Essays in Memory of Susan Haber* (ed. by Carl S. Ehrlich, Anders Runesson, and Eileen Schuller; Tübingen: Mohr Siebeck, 2013), 55-86.

only passage in Matthew's Gospel where Jesus explicitly forgives sins. There is no description of what the man's sins had been, nor any mention of who the offended party was. Since there is a very clear focus in Matthew on sins that relate to inter-human interaction (with consequences for the human–divine relationship), the logic that depends on the culture of the text suggests an understanding that the man's condition results from his wrongdoings to others.[228]

The logic of the pattern of forgiveness presented elsewhere in Matthew would rule that in order for the paralyzed man's sins to be forgiven, the victim(s) of his sins must first cancel his (defiling) debts. We are not told whether they have refused, and thus, bound him in his sins (and, by implication, in his [moral] impurity), or whether the paralytic has refused to acknowledge his debt. The point of the story, though, is beyond such details; the passage describes a situation in which the mechanics of forgiveness are broken in that Jesus, who was not involved in the man's previous history, steps in and extends the forgiveness that unbinds him from his "spiritual" condition, an act which has physical ramifications. By cancelling the debts that the man owes, Jesus overrides the role of the victim(s) and establishes a direct link to the forgiveness of God (which has yet to be given), which in turn results in the charge of some scribes present that this behavior amounts to "blasphemy" (blasphēmia).[229] The man is now free to bring his sacrificial gifts to God in the temple, without defiling the altar (cf. Matt 5:23–24). The passage thus reveals Jesus's authority as he sets the kingdom in motion (Matt 9:6); just as purity may be said to be accomplished through exorcisms of unclean spirits,[230] the forgiveness of sins removes a layer of defilement.

228. There is no mention here of the man being born paralyzed (cf. John 9:1–12). In addition, we may note that there is only one sin mentioned in Matthew that relates directly to God: sin against the holy spirit (Matt 12:31–33). This sin is, however, said to be unforgivable, which makes it irrelevant for the current context; for discussion of this passage see further below.

229. It should be noted that Matthew's version of this incident does not include the comment of the scribes in Mark that only God can forgive sins (Mark 2:7). Matthew also adds to the response of the crowds the summarizing comment that "they glorified God, who had given such authority [exousia] to human beings" (Matt 9:8). This emphasizes that what Matthew is dealing with here is how Jesus responds to a seemingly unsolvable issue, as a human among other humans, but with a new type of authority that has been given to him by God.

230. Matt 10:1, 8; Matt 12:43–45; cf. 8:28–34; 15:22.

So far, we have seen two ways in which Jesus's function as the Messiah (to "save his people from their sins"; Matt 1:21) is played out.[231] First, he instructs the people in the law, and commands them to allow for limitless forgiveness;[232] he also gives a strategy for expulsion of followers who do not acknowledge their debt, and thus, their (moral) impurity. Second, Jesus himself overrides the victim's role as he brings about the reconciliation required for the perpetrator to be unbound, so that he can approach the altar without defiling it, and so, restore a proper relationship with the God of Israel (cf. 5:23–26).[233] While these strategies indicate Jesus's extraordinary authority and foreshadow the interpretation of his death as atoning for sins, they do not contradict the workings of the temple cult, but function *within* its theo-ritual matrix. As the story progresses, however, this changes and Jesus offers himself in place of the now defiled temple cult in order to bring about the atonement which cannot otherwise be achieved, apart from the temple.

The Matthean Jesus predicts that the Jerusalem temple will be destroyed, and the cause of this destruction is, as we have noted, the defilement brought about by the grave sins of certain leading Pharisees and scribes associated with them, who are held responsible even for bloodshed committed in the temple in Israel's past (Matt 23:29–24:2).[234]

---

231. Luz, *Matthew*, 1. 95, notes that in some Jewish texts, the Messiah eliminates or judges sinners (Ps. Sol. 17.22–25; 1 En. 62.2; 69.27–29), but that there is also evidence of forgiveness in connection with a priestly messiah figure (T. Levi 18.9; 11 QMelch 2.6–8). In the Matthean narrative (as well as in other New Testament texts), however, forgiveness is related to a Davidic Messiah, which is unique.

232. This type of abundant forgiveness required between humans is patterned on God's willingness to always forgive the repentant, even seeking them out to achieve his purpose of inclusion and salvation. Cf. Matt 6:14; 19:26; God's willingness to actively seek out and save is evident in the very task of the Messiah, sent for this purpose, and this is repeated in various ways throughout the narrative, as applied to the Jewish people (Matt 9:36–38; 18:14). In the end (but not before), this active willingness to include as many as possible in the kingdom is applied globally to all nations (28:18–20).

233. Cf. *Pesiq. Rab.* 165a (cf. Montefiore and Loewe, *Rabbinic*, no. 824), which deals with the problem of a victim who refuses to unbind (forgive) the perpetrator despite the latter's attempts at reconciliation: "God will see that he has humbled himself, and God will forgive him; but so long as a man stays in his stiffness, God does not forgive him. And Job was forgiven by God only when he forgave, and prayed for, his friends."

234. Cf. *'Abot R. Nat.* 38. In this text, the *Shekinah*, the presence of God, withdraws from the people and exile follows as a consequence of the grave transgressions of idolatry, sexual sins, bloodshed, and neglect of the year of release of the land. On inherited guilt, see above, chapter 2.1.3.

For Matthew, like Ezekiel before him,[235] the temple cannot be destroyed as long as God dwells there.[236] In Matt 23:38, addressing Jerusalem and referring to the temple, Jesus declares: "See, your house is left to you, desolate." Then, having said this, Jesus leaves the temple, predicts that it will be destroyed (Matt 24:1–2), and walks over to the Mount of Olives east of the city (Matt 24:3), where God's presence had previously lodged after having left the first temple before its destruction (Ezek 11:23). This way of preparing the reader for Jesus's death opens up for an understanding of Jesus's status as one of extraordinary closeness to the God of Israel,[237] and foreshadows the resurrected Jesus's presence among his *ekklēsiai*, as if he himself represented the Shekinah (Matt 18:20).

As in Ezekiel, Matthew's version of God's leaving the temple is, however, described as stretched out in time, which adds further nuance to the role applied to Jesus in the process of achieving atonement for the people. In Matthew, God actually leaves the temple at the moment of Jesus's death, which is the most likely interpretation of the torn veil in Matt 26:51.[238] Jesus's leaving the temple and walking to the Mount of Olives thus initiates the process of abandonment of the temple. Matthew's story leaves little doubt that the temple, as well as Jerusalem,[239] will be destroyed, and that God leaves the temple before this happens. Since, according to Matthew, the temple is desolate

---

235. Ezekiel 10–11.
236. Cf. Josephus, who shares the same view: *B.J.* 6.124–28; 300 (cf. 300–309). Cf. *A.J.* 20.165–67; *B.J.* 2.254–57. See also Mendels, *Rise*, 301–2. Guilt for the destruction of the temple is always sought, in the Hebrew Bible, Josephus, as well as in rabbinic literature and the New Testament Gospels, within the Jewish people, since if someone else, such as the Romans, would be accused, their god(s), by implication, would have to be considered stronger than the God of Israel. By blaming the Jewish leadership (the Gospels), or Jewish "bandits" (Josephus), the Romans are transformed into a tool in the hand of the God of Israel as he punishes his people. This strengthens the view that the Gospels were written by Jews from an inner-Jewish perspective, even if they were ultimately meant to be read also by a non-Jewish audience.
237. Cf. Repchinski, "Purity," 383, who makes this claim; see also idem, "Re-Imagining," 37–49.
238. On various interpretations of this passage, see discussion by Raymond E. Brown, *The Death of the Messiah: From Gethsemane to the Grave. A Commentary on the Passion Narratives in the Four Gospels* (2 vols.; London: Geoffrey Chapman, 1994); Daniel M. Gurtner, *The Torn Veil: Matthew's Exposition of the Death of Jesus* (Cambridge: Cambridge University Press, 2007). See also, 2 Baruch 6:7; 8:2, where God leaves the temple and invites destruction after having done so. Cf. Didascalia Apostolorum 6.5.7 (the Spirit is removed from the temple), and Test. Levi 10:3 (cf. 15:1; 16:4–5), where the wickedness of the priests, who lead Israel astray, causes the veil to be torn.
239. Cf. Matt 22:7.

(*eremos*; 23:38) when Jesus dies, the cultic means to achieve atonement had already been removed from the people. This had to happen since leading figures[240] within the people had filled the measure of guilt that had been begun by former leaders, who had "murdered the prophets" (23:31–32), just as current leaders punish and kill contemporary "prophets, sages, and scribes" sent by Jesus (23:34). These leaders' shedding of innocent blood[241] thus affects the entire people in the narrative here and now ("this generation"; 23:36), since the temple can no longer function to achieve the atonement needed for the people to stay in the land and have God dwelling in their midst.

Therefore, in order to save his people from their sins—and the impurity that results from sin—Jesus is said to offer his own body as a sacrifice, taking the place of the defiled, empty, and soon to be destroyed temple (Matt 26:26–29). His blood is "poured out for many for the forgiveness of sins [*eis aphesin hamartiōn*]" (v. 28). This function of his death is already suggested in 20:28, where the life of "the Son of Man" is said to be given as "a ransom for many."[242] Jesus's death thus leads to the removal of the impurity that results from sin and offers a way for the people to be holy and "perfect" (Matt 5:48) after the temple cult has been lost.[243] Contrary to common Christian theology, in Matthew, the temple is not destroyed as a punishment for the death of Jesus. The logic goes in the opposite direction: Jesus has to die precisely

---

240. We shall discuss in chapter 3 below how Matthew construes guilt as related to specific Jewish groups.

241. On the shedding of innocent blood in Matthew, see David M. Moffitt, "Righteous Bloodshed, Matthew's Passion Narrative, and the Temple's Destruction: Lamentations as a Matthean Intertext," *JBL* 125.2 (2006): 299–320. The most comprehensive discussion to date is given by Catherine Hamilton, "Innocent Blood Traditions in Early Judaism and the Death of Jesus in Matthew" (Ph.D. diss., Wycliffe College, Toronto School of Theology, 2013); see also eadem, "'His Blood Be upon Us:' Innocent Blood and the Death of Jesus in Matthew," *CBQ* 70 (2008): 82–100.

242. Cf. the recent discussion in Eubank, *Wages of Cross-Bearing*, 148–62, which, however, does not focus on the issues of impurity, which lie behind the metaphorical language of debt and ransom-price used by Matthew.

243. It is of some interest to note that Matthew, contrary to the author of Luke–Acts, moves Jesus's followers, and Jesus himself, from Jerusalem to Galilee after the resurrection, from where the worldwide mission is to be launched. It seems, then, that for this author, just like for the Qumran community, regardless of whether the historical temple had yet been destroyed, Jerusalem was not the place to stay for Jesus's followers during the period between Jesus's death and the coming of the eschatological Son of Man, who will execute the final judgment (cf. also Matt 24:16).

because the temple has already been defiled and will, as a consequence, inevitably be destroyed.[244]

In other words, while the temple cult was still intact and functioning in the world of Matthew's narrative until chapters 23 and 24, after God has left his abode as a consequence of its defilement, caused by the sins of identified leading figures, the temple can no longer fulfill its purpose. In the same way, whereas forgiveness and atonement was related to the temple cult until Jesus's death, forgiveness and atonement in the end-time period, i.e., during the period between God's abandonment of the temple and the final eschatological judgment, is achieved apart from the temple. Since Jewish law is still to be taught after Jesus's resurrection (Matt 28:19–20), it would have to be assumed that the teaching on forgiveness, which was previously positioned in relation to the temple cult, is now centered on Jesus's atoning sacrifice for the sins of the many, and thus, on the ritualized meal in his remembrance.[245] Apocalyptic suffering will still come (Matthew 24),[246] as will the final judgment after people from all nations have been informed that the end is approaching (24:14; 25:31–46). Those who endure this suffering, the magnitude and intensity of which is said to be unlike anything in the past or in the future (24:21), in love

244. Since, as we have mentioned above, the "scribes and Pharisees" are blamed by Matthew as the cause of the destruction of the temple, Jesus's death has become necessary because of them. This may explain the consistently negative portrayal of the Pharisees in Matthew's narrative, which is not mirrored in the other Gospels. One may also note, of course, that Jesus's death in this story is for the people of Israel in its entirety, and thus, also opens up for the inclusion in the kingdom of these same groups who are accused of causing the crisis in the first place, if they repent (cf. Matt 13:52; 23:39). See further discussion below, chapter 3.

245. On the meal as related to temple cult, cf. Jacob Neusner, *The Idea of Purity in Ancient Judaism* (Leiden: Brill, 1973), 70, who argues that the Pharisees, by insisting on purity beyond the temple when they ate ordinary food, would have regarded their tables as related to the temple altar in more than a metaphorical way. (Cf. *b. Ber.* 55a, attributed to two third-century rabbis: "As long as the temple stood, the altar atoned for Israel, but now a man's table atones for him.") For the pre-70 Pharisees, then, these additional sacred meal settings did not replace the temple, but added to it. For Matthew, the meal in Jesus's remembrance is explicitly said to represent Jesus's body and blood, i.e., it is construed as a sacrificial meal, and this is done to compensate for the catastrophic loss of the temple in a way similar to how the Qumran community replaced the (defiled) temple with their own community while the temple still stood.

246. Contrary to Albert Schweitzer's reconstruction of the aims of the historical Jesus; see *Out of My Life and Thought: An Autobiography. Postscript 1932-1949* by Everett Skillings (Translated by C.T. Campion; New York: Mentor Books, 1953), 35–36. For Schweitzer, the Jesus of history knowingly sacrificed himself in order to divert God's wrath, and so, save his people from apocalyptic suffering. For Matthew, however, the suffering of the end time is inescapable for all, including Jesus's disciples.

(i.e., Torah obedience; Matt 22:36–40; cf. 24:12), repentance (3:2; 4:17; 18:15–17), and forgiveness (18:21–35; 26:28), will be saved (24:13).

There is one more aspect of repentance and forgiveness that needs discussion before we can move on to questions about more specific criteria of judgment, in addition to what has already been covered so far—the unforgivable.

2.4.1 The Unforgivable

As we have seen above,[247] the notion that some sins may not be forgiven is present in the Hebrew Bible and in later Jewish texts, including rabbinic literature. This idea may seem to reduce the force of the otherwise absolute power of repentance and its ability to transform a person's life, and let him or her evade divine punishment and destruction. Matthew, in fact, points to only one such specific sin, for which there is no forgiveness, and, consequently, in relation to which repentance is powerless: sin against the holy spirit (Matt 12:30–37).

The absolute nature of this Matthean statement has troubled many recent commentators[248] who feel that it goes against the Christian doctrine of (unconditional[249]) forgiveness.[250] The basic theological

---

247. See pp. 114–18.

248. For discussion of the early history of interpretation of this passage, see Luz, *Matthew*, 2. 206–8. The Didache, probably to be dated around the same time as the Gospel of Matthew and clearly related to it (for discussion, see Huub van de Sandt and Jürgen K. Zangenberg (eds.), *Matthew, James, and the Didache: Three Related Documents in Their Jewish and Christian Settings* (Atlanta: Society of Biblical Literature, 2008), applies a similar view on blasphemy against the Spirit in relation to the work of prophets: "Also, do not test or evaluate any prophet who speaks in the spirit, for every sin will be forgiven, but this sin will not be forgiven. However, not everyone who speaks in the spirit is a prophet, but only if he exhibits the Lord's ways. By his conduct, therefore, will the false prophet and the prophet be recognized" (*Did.* 11:7–8; cf. Matt 7:15–20).

249. With regard to repentance, however, we may observe with David Konstan, *Before Forgiveness: The Origins of a Moral Idea* (Cambridge: Cambridge University Press, 2010), 123, that "there is no evidence in the New Testament that forgiveness is understood to be unconditional." Konstan continues: "The protagonists of the biblical narrative, unlike those of the ancient Greek novels, are not innocent. Sinners, accordingly, have no choice but to confess their delinquencies frankly and commit themselves to reforming their natures, sincerely and with deep remorse, in the hope of obtaining a remission of God's anger. God is stern, but also kindly toward his creatures and mercifully disposed toward honest repentance or a change of ways."

250. See, e.g., Kennedy, "Covenant Conception," 369, and note the discussion about the weakness of the law in this regard. See also Meier, *Matthew*, 135, who argues that the Holy Spirit is the source of repentance. This means, according to him, that renunciation of the Spirit becomes, in effect, a refusal to repent. Such a reconstruction of Matthew's pattern of thought seems, however, to be at odds not only with the present passage but also with the Gospel as a whole; repentance, in Matthew, is the responsibility of human beings, not of God.

points asserted in the pericope are as follows. Except for blasphemy against the Spirit, God will forgive *all* sins and blasphemies (12:31), given, as we have seen from other passages in Matthew, that repentance is at hand. This emphasis on radical forgiveness is logical, considering the fact that Jesus's mission in Matthew's Gospel is specified as precisely this: to bring about forgiveness, and in this way, save his people and prepare for the Kingdom of heaven (Matt 1:21; cf. 26:28). This "forgiveness project," as Nolland has termed it,[251] includes even verbal attacks against Jesus himself, as the son of man (12:32). We have to conclude, then, that the Spirit is the active force as the kingdom is being established, and, as such, is distinguished from Jesus himself. When it comes to marking the absolute theological (and therefore, also socio-narrative) boundaries of the tolerable, or better, of that which can be regarded as acceptable to work with in order to make possible inclusion in the kingdom, i.e., the boundaries of forgiveness, Jesus is described more as (an extraordinary) human uniquely possessed by God's Spirit—God's tool through whom God can work via the Spirit (12:28)—than as being one with God (cf. 3:16; cf. 19:17).[252]

How, then, are we to understand this passage in light of our discussion about repentance and forgiveness? Daniel Patte has suggested the following interpretation, indicating the core issues involved.[253] Connecting 12:31–32 with 12:30, he notes that renouncing the Son of Man is not the same as renouncing the Spirit, since the Spirit is the power of God: "Rejecting the Son of Man does not necessarily involve denying the Spirit of God, God's power."[254] To be part of the process of gathering a community for the kingdom includes recognition of the fact that the gathering cannot take place without the power of God, "binding the strong man" (i.e., Satan; 12:26, 29).

---

251. Nolland, *Matthew*, 505.
252. On the historical Jesus as a spirit-possessed exorcist, see Amanda Witmer, *Jesus, The Galilean Exorcist: His Exorcisms in Social and Political Context* (London: T&T Clark, 2012).
253. Daniel Patte, *The Gospel According to Matthew: A Structural Commentary on Matthew's Gospel* (Valley Forge: Trinity Press International, 1987), 177–78.
254. Patte, *Matthew*, 178.

Blasphemy against the Spirit is the renunciation of the power of God, a denial of the need for divine intervention.[255]

On a first level, then, the criterion of judgment here is the kingdom, rather than responses to Jesus, since the kingdom is what the Spirit establishes (through "binding the strong man"; 12:29). Irreversible condemnation follows when it is suggested that the force present within the Son of Man is Beelzebul (12:24, 27), i.e., when it is denied that God's Spirit is the source of what is happening around Jesus.[256] However, the fundamental criterion of judgment is the Spirit. We shall discuss kingdom, Jesus, and the Spirit as criteria of judgment in more detail below. Our present focus must remain on the Spirit's relationship to the notion of repentance.

Nolland suggests that "[n]o doubt such blasphemy [i.e., blasphemy against the Spirit] remains unforgivable only as long as it is sustained. It too may be repented for."[257] While such a conclusion may seem to follow from the narrative's focus on the forgiveness project, this is not really what is stated in this passage. The point is rather that *despite* the Gospel's strong emphasis on forgiveness, there is one sin that generates irreversible guilt. Uniquely, Matthew's Jesus explicitly states that the unforgivability of this sin applies to both this world and the world to come (12:32). Since in this Gospel, repentance, and, in the case of inter-human relations, restitution must always precede forgiveness and atonement, it follows that if something is said to be

---

255. Cf. Evald Lövestam, "Logiet om hädelse mot den helige Ande," *SEÅ* 33 (1968): 101–17, here 108ff, who argues that the Spirit of God should be understood in relation to the notion of the Spirit in the Hebrew Bible. The Spirit is thus inextricably linked to God's salvific work, and opposition to the Spirit means rejection of God's salvation: "Hädelse mot Anden betyder opposition mot Gud i själva hans eskatologiska frälsningsingripande" (113). See also the more extensive treatment of this passage in Evald Lövestam, *Spiritus Blasphemia: Eine Studie zu Mk 3,28f par Mt 12,31f, Lk 12,10* (Lund: CWK Gleerup, 1968).

256. Cf. W. C. Allen, *A Critical and Exegetical Commentary on the Gospel According to Saint Matthew* (sec. ed.; Edinburgh: T&T Clark, 1907), 137, who paraphrases the meaning as follows: "You accuse me of satanic methods in casting out devils. In reality I cast them out by the power of God's Spirit. In substituting Satan for the Holy Spirit you are guilty of blasphemy. And this is an unpardonable sin." See also Lachs, *Rabbinic Commentary*, 112–13, who refers to Rabbinic literature and the concept of "profaning the Name." Cf. Isa 5:20: "Woe to you who call evil good and good evil, who put darkness for light and light for darkness, who put bitter for sweet and sweet for bitter!"

257. Nolland, *Matthew*, 505.

unforgivable in this world and the next, this implies that repentance is ineffective, not that it is absent.

Matthew, like the Hebrew Bible and other Jewish texts, thus emphasizes repentance as the key to forgiveness, but also reckons with the unforgivable. The saying is unique in Matthew in that it describes sin not against other human beings, but against God.[258] It should come as no surprise to the reader of this Gospel that the theology of the unforgivable is outlined in direct relation to the Pharisees (12:24; cf. 5:20).[259] At the same time, we may also note that Jesus's own disciples will have the opportunity to receive forgiveness, since they never said anything against the Spirit, only against Jesus as he was arrested (26:31, 35; Peter's role in this is especially revealing: Matt 16:22–23; 26:14–16, 30–35, 69–75; cf. 10:33).

Perhaps the case of Judas, however, is the most interesting. His sin, as he is about to betray Jesus, is described as extremely severe (26:24).[260] Yet, Judas shares in the redemptive meal with the other disciples (26:26–28), and in the moment of betrayal itself, Jesus addresses him as "friend" (hetairos; 26:50). Indeed, except for Peter's bitter weeping as he realized what he had done when he had denied Jesus (26:75; cf. 10:33), Judas is the only one of the disciples who is explicitly said to have repented once he realized the consequences of his actions (27:3–5); he even provides restitution as he hands back the money he had received from the priests (27:5). Matthew's portrait of a repenting Judas may be compared to the description of the same disciple in Acts 1:16–20, which paints him in the worst possible light.[261] While the author of Acts appears to add details intentionally to portray Judas as the archetypal villain, interpreting his gruesome death as

---

258. It may be noted that in Tannaitic literature it is more difficult to atone for sins against fellow human beings than sins against God ("cultic sins"); Sanders, *Paul and Palestinian Judaism*, 114. This is also the principle otherwise governing Matthean discourse about judgment: mercy is more important than sacrifice, meaning sacrifices are ineffective if the more important aspects of the law are not fulfilled, as discussed above. Cf. Davies and Allison, *Matthew*, 2. 320, who refer to *m. Yom.* 8:6 for comparison. Here, however, we find an exception to the general rule.

259. See further below, chapter 3.2.1.2.

260. The details of the betrayal are given in Matt 26:14–16, 20–25, 46–50.

261. The author of Luke-Acts is, however, more explicit about Peter's repentance than Matthew is: Luke 22:32.

divine punishment, Matthew's narrative—likewise deliberately— focuses on his repentance. Judas's crime is indeed described as hideous;[262] despite this, however, the Matthean narrative strategy not only avoids creating a flat character, as opposed to Acts, but also makes a theological point consistent with the Gospel's overall theme of repentance.

On the basis of the previous discussion, it seems to me that France is led astray by the horrible nature of Judas's crime—and his suicide—when he writes that: "Alongside the constant scriptural testimony to the extraordinary mercy of God, there is also, as the letter to the Hebrews insists so memorably, a point of no return, a time when it is too late to repent."[263] Matthew's Gospel has, as we have seen above, only listed one sin as unforgivable, and that is not Judas's sin, and it is not against Jesus, but against the Spirit (cf. Matt 12:32). In other words, there is nothing in Matthew that denies the effectiveness of Judas's repentance, especially since it is followed by restitution and death—the latter most likely meant to be understood as atoning.[264]

In the end, then, the force of repentance is substantial in all cases but one, neutralizing the guilt that inevitably follows from sins committed. Forgiveness is extended, regardless of the severity or the number of

---

262. A comparison with the treason committed by David's close ally Ahithophel in 2 Sam 17:23 is suggestive, not least on the basis of the fact that Ahithophel also hangs himself. (Matthew uses the same word for Judas's hanging as the LXX uses for Ahithophel's: *apagchō*. The word is used only once in the New Testament, and only twice in the LXX). For discussion of other parallels between these figures, see Davies and Allison, *Matthew*, 3.565–66.

263. France, *Matthew*, 1040.

264. Davies and Allison, *Matthew*, 3. 561–65, presents an interpretation that in my view is more sensitive than France's to the nature of Matthew's text when they suggest that Judas's death may be understood in terms of atonement for the sin committed. As they indicate, while suicide could be seen as dishonorable in some contexts in the ancient world, several Jewish texts from this and later time periods avoid such judgment (cf., e.g., Josephus' description of the suicides at Masada). In fact, there is no law against suicide in the Hebrew Bible. Indeed, not only death (cf. Abot R. Nat. 39: "Repentance atones along with the day of death, and the day of death atones when there has been repentance"), but also suicide may be understood as having an atoning effect in some Jewish traditions (Davies and Allison, *Matthew*, 3. 562–63). In Judas's case, the priests refused to deal with him, thus declining to judge him according to the law (Matt 27:4). Since Num 35:33 (cf. Lev 24:17) states that bloodshed pollutes the land, and that expiation can only be made for the land by the blood of the person who shed it, it seems Judas is presented as doing the only thing he could do at this point, when the temple authorities are corrupt, the temple is polluted, and Jesus's atoning death for the many has not yet occurred, namely to execute judgment himself. This may indeed be what the Matthean Jesus referred to in 26:24: "woe to that one by whom the Son of Man is betrayed! It would have been better for that one not to have been born."

the transgressions,[265] and it has immediate effect. This emphasizes the very real responsibility of the people addressed by the Matthean Jesus to make up their mind and choose what is good, which is also what will protect them, together with Jesus's atoning sacrifice, as the final judgment approaches. Such a theology is well-suited for proclamation directed at the many, rather than a small elite group, such as the sectarian community at Qumran; it is no coincidence, then, that the Matthean Jesus's target group is identified specifically as the lost sheep of the people of Israel (Matt 10:6; 15:24).

We have now discussed the nature of sin and its consequences (guilt and defilement) as well as the Jewish law as the basic criterion used in divine judgment. We have also examined how Matthew's narrative deals with several concepts, which in the Hebrew Bible and later Jewish texts, both predating and postdating Matthew, embed judgment discourse and may modify the outcome of divine verdicts, such as the distinctions made between intentional and unintentional sin, vicarious righteousness, and repentance. The dynamics of the Matthean narrative in this regard—especially in the case of the Jewish law—function in much the same way as other forms of Judaism as far as judgment discourse is concerned.

The question is now whether more specific notions that seem to play a significant role in the Gospel, such as *pistis* ("trust"/ "faithfulness"/"loyalty"),[266] can be understood as parameters in the larger discourse on judgment in the Gospel, and, if so, how they would function in relation to the basic criteria of judgment construed around the Jewish law. Does *pistis* in Matthew provide a way to salvation independently of the law, overriding the requirements of the commandments and so, neutralizing guilt accumulated from disobedience to the law? Further, and perhaps even more important for our understanding of Matthew's Gospel, we need to examine whether Jesus himself is portrayed as a criterion of judgment, and

---

265. Cf. Ezek 33:12. As Sanders, *Paul and Palestinian Judaism*, 147, argues, Tannaitic literature displays the same pattern of thought.

266. On the translation of *pistis* as involving the aspects of faithfulness and loyalty, cf. Steve Mason, *Life of Josephus: Translation and Commentary* (Leiden: Brill, 2003), 41.

if so, in which way. What is the role of the person of Jesus in the various processes of judgment? How does Jesus relate to the Spirit and the kingdom when divine judgment is pronounced? We shall begin with the function of trust/faithfulness/loyalty in relation to judgment, and will then proceed with the problem of Jesus, as understood from the perspectives of the kingdom, the person of Jesus, and the Spirit, respectively.

2.5 *Pistis*: A Criterion of Judgment?

As we noted above in chapter 1, judgment discourse in Matthew needs to be understood from three basic perspectives: a) Punishment and reward in this world, b) the final judgment, and c) punishment and reward in the world to come. The verdict of procedure (b) has two possible outcomes: 1) salvation (i.e., admission into the world to come), 2) condemnation (i.e., exclusion from the world to come). The question is now whether *pistis* functions as a criterion affecting the outcome of either (or all) of these processes of judgment. The answer to this question is, to a certain degree, dependent on how we define and understand *pistis* and what is said to happen as this concept is "activated" in the narrative.

Beginning with punishment and reward in this world, the word *pistis* most often occurs in contexts where healing is mentioned (Matt 8:10; 9:2, 22, 29; 15:28; 17:20). It is of some importance to note that in such cases, Matthew's Jesus makes no real distinction between Jews and non-Jews; the former (9:2, 22, 29; 17:20) as well as the latter (8:10; 15:28) may be said to display (to varying degrees[267]) this quality. Healing happens in this world, and the question is thus whether healing should be understood as a reward for *pistis*, i.e., if *pistis* is understood by Matthew as if it were part of an overall perspective on fulfilling the Jewish law. While *pistis* is, in one case, explicitly said to be part of the law (Matt 23:23; see below), there are several reasons why it would be misleading to count healing among the wages paid in this world.

---

267. Cf. Matt 9:10; 17:20.

A first indication that *pistis*-related healing in Matthew cannot be categorized as a reward for duties performed is the simple fact that it is not always the *pistis* of the sick or possessed person that brings about the healing or makes the exorcism effective.[268] While, in some cases, *pistis* is attributed to the healed individuals (9:22, 29), in other instances, it is the *pistis* of a person who cares for the sick/possessed (8:6, 10; 9:2; 15:22, 28), or even of the healers themselves (17:18–20), which results in the healing/exorcism. Faith/trust seems to be a state in which humans need to be for healing/exorcism to occur, rather than an (individual) achievement that may be rewarded with effective treatment.

Second, healings and exorcisms are closely related to the kingdom, and, as such, are part of the liberation that the kingdom brings about (10:7–8; 12:28). The dynamics involved in healings and exorcisms thus represent part of the "substance" of the eschatological future brought into the present. It is in this setting of eschatological liberation that *pistis* functions as a medium, a channel, through which the power of God brings about healing and evacuates demons from tormented bodies. This conclusion is further supported by the fact that lack of *pistis*, either on the part of the healers (17:17–20) or of those among whom extraordinary deeds otherwise could have been performed (13:58), prevents these deeds of divine origin from happening, and thus, hinders the powers of the kingdom from being unleashed in specific settings.

To be plagued by illness or possessed by demons cannot, thus, be considered examples of divine punishment without further qualification, since liberation from such afflictions cannot be considered rewards. Rather, illnesses and demon possession are primarily understood in this Gospel as the result of attacks by evil powers, indeed, ultimately by Beelzebub, i.e., the devil, himself (12:27–30; cf. 9:34). Such attacks by demons and their master not only

---

268. Note also that the healing of the sick, the raising of the dead, the cleansing of lepers and the casting out of demons are phenomena described not as rewards for duties performed, but rather, as free gifts: *dōrean elabete, dōrean dote* (Matt 10:8). Cf. F. W. Beare, "The Mission of the Disciples and the Mission Charge: Matthew 10 and Parallels," *JBL* 89 (1970), 1–13, here 8.

on the people of God, but also on non-Jews, have been facilitated by people's sinful habits (defined in Matthew as breaking the law), which has made them susceptible to the influence of such powers; these powers have then cut them off from God and "imprisoned" them in mental, bodily, and political afflictions and suffering.

The Matthean Jesus blames this pervasiveness of sin in the land on leaders who are not taking proper care of the people (*hoi ochloi*), the latter being described as "sheep without a shepherd" (9:35–36). As the God of Israel initiates the final battle to rescue his people (10:5–6)—and the world (28:18-20)—from destruction and restore an Edenic state of being in which heaven and earth have merged as a kingdom of heaven, the focus is, logically, on eliminating sin (1:21). In this process of liberation from all types of affliction, God, through his Spirit, is "binding" evil (12:29) and will judge those who have collaborated with these powers or facilitated the "imprisonment" of the people through misleading teaching. (Such accusations, though focused on the Pharisees, include the temple administration; 12:27; 23:36–24:2.)[269] The leaders who are judged, however, are not described as afflicted by suffering; those afflicted are the Jewish crowds whom they have misled (9:35–38; 16:11–12).[270] The dynamics of *pistis* in this context of liberation is thus only secondarily related to judgment, in that the liberation of the afflicted involves the judgment of those causing their affliction. *Pistis* is the posture, or attitude, among humans, including Jesus himself, that, when present, allows God's Spirit access to bodies, and the space between bodies, as this religio-political process takes place.

The role of *pistis* as the access point for the Spirit, and, by extension, as representing the context within which the potential for the extraordinary rests, is further emphasized in several other Matthean passages unrelated to healings and exorcisms. We see this in Matt 6:30–34, where food-and-clothing related anxiety is said to be an

---

269. The Matthean Jesus has already rejected all forms of collaboration with the devil and his demonic powers (4:1–11), and will, ultimately, therefore be victorious and given all powers both in heaven and on earth (28:18).

270. Cf. Ps 73:3–12; Qoh 8:14.

expression of a non-Jewish mentality (v. 32), which, in a Jewish setting, can be characterized as a lack of, or not enough *pistis* (v. 30; *oligopistos*).[271] By contrast, *pistis* is presented implicitly as *the* appropriate attitude for life within the covenant between the Jewish people and the God of Israel. In this passage, *pistis* combines with righteousness and kingdom. When *pistis* is at hand, life will begin to transform into the way it was mean to be—the ideal state of things in the eschatological kingdom of heaven.[272]

In similar ways, *pistis* as the entry point to a world of the extraordinary, a world where God's spirit is active and rules, will relieve anxiety in other situations in which life is threatened (8:23–26; 14:31). In Matt 16:5–12, lack of *pistis* is related to a lack of understanding of what can happen, extraordinarily, as the kingdom is being established. The context for this passage, though, is Jesus's contrasting of his own message with the teaching of the Pharisees, the latter not being able to open up for the extraordinary events characteristic of the kingdom, which require *pistis*. The same dynamic relationship between the extraordinary nature of developments around the kingdom, on the one hand, and *pistis* as a key for entering into that space, on the other, is present in Matt 21:21–22. In Matthew, the future powers of the kingdom are present in the here and now, but only in that special domain of the Spirit to which only *pistis* allows access. When this domain is expanded, the kingdom is gradually realized as time rushes toward the final judgment. Those men and women—both Jews and non-Jews—who live this dynamic attitude of *pistis* are thus key players through whom God is establishing his kingdom, as they mediate God's creative power in the world. This is why the Matthean Jesus admonishes his disciples, who are said to be lacking in *pistis*, with the

---

271. It should be noted, however, that non-Jews are presented as examples of everything that good Jews should not be or do only as a generalized group. There are, in Matthew's story, also examples of (individual) praiseworthy non-Jews, as we have discussed above and shall return to in Part II of the study (e.g., Matt 15:21–28), but these non-Jews are presented as exceptions to the rule, and they are used strategically to shame the Jews who reject Jesus although, according to Matthew, they should have known better since they have the law.

272. Seeking the kingdom and God's righteousness will produce justice and abundance of food etc., since this is the intent of the law and since, ultimately, this imitates the perfect Edenic state of things which will characterize the eschatological kingdom.

words: "if you have *pistis* the size of a mustard seed... nothing will be impossible for you" (17:20).

If we proceed to the relationship between *pistis* and punishment and reward in the world to come, discussion can be quite brief: There are no judgment texts in this Gospel that make claims about *pistis* as a factor for the outcome of punishment and reward in the world to come. This makes sense since we have already seen that judgment discourse is related to *pistis* on a secondary level, even in this world. The question whether *pistis* has any effect on the outcome of the final judgment is, however, a more complex issue, which is related to the concepts of both law and covenant. We shall therefore postpone this discussion to the section below, dealing with the role of the covenant for the outcome of judgment.[273] Suffice it to say here that *pistis* is not mentioned directly in any of the passages that deal with the final judgment. We may also note that despite the importance of *pistis* in Matthew, this attitude on the part of human beings is not, in itself, enough to allow access to the world to come.

There is one pericope in Matthew that presents us with a somewhat different context with regard to *pistis* and divine judgment, and we need to comment on this text before proceeding to the issue of Jesus as a criterion of judgment: Matt 23:23. *Pistis* is here said to belong among the "heavier" matters of the law (*ta barytera tou nomou*), together with justice (*krisis*) and mercy (*eleos*). Now, we have already seen above that Matthew's Gospel is quite firm on pointing to the Jewish law as *the* foundational criterion of judgment.[274] If *pistis* is understood as part of the law, would it not follow that *pistis* is a criterion of judgment after all?

First, we should refer to what has been said above about the meaning of *pistis* in Matthew; it is a human "attitude," a "space," which provides an opportunity for the extraordinary powers of the eschatological kingdom to enter into and transform various agonizing situations, often resulting from demonic afflictions current in this world. Gundry

---

273. See chapter 2.8.
274. See discussion above, chapter 2.1.2; cf. 2.2.

140

has argued that *pistis* in Matt 23:23 should be translated as "faith," rather than "faithfulness," as some scholars have argued; "faith" indicates, according to Gundry, that Matthew is referring here to the relationship between humans and God, not to inter-human relations, the latter being implied by the translation "faithfulness."[275] I wonder, though, if this is necessarily correct. Retaining the basic meaning of *pistis* as "faithfulness" and/or "loyalty" seems to me not to divert attention from the human relationship to the divine, but rather, to the contrary. Indeed, "loyalty" may merge these aspects, since we are dealing with loyalty to God through faithfulness to God's law. This means that the direction of *pistis*, here as elsewhere, is still toward God, not Jesus.[276]

As Davies and Allison have suggested, we should understand Matt 23:23 against the background of Micah 6:8: "what does the LORD require of you but to do justice (*mishpat*; LXX: *krima*) and to love kindness (*hesed*; LXX: *eleos*), and to walk humbly with your God?"[277] It seems indeed as if the Matthean Jesus echoes this passage, adapting it to emphasize where the center of the law lies.[278] In addition to justice and mercy, which are clearly stated in the Matthean text, reading *pistis* as Matthew's way of interpreting Micah's "to walk humbly with your God" aligns well with the interpretation of *pistis* given above. For Matthew, it seems, *halakhah*, to use the rabbinic term, is, ultimately, to *walk* with God, and *pistis* is the "space" in which this is to take place, since *pistis* provides access to the Spirit. In other words, *pistis*, as a necessary human attitude, is inextricably interwoven with the fulfillment of the law; the law must "happen" in the context in which *pistis* is also present, and, conversely, if *pistis* is lacking, the

---

275. Gundry, *Matthew*, 464; see also Davies and Allison, *Matthew*, 3. 294. Luz, *Matthew*, 3.124, argues for translating *pistis* as "faithfulness" here.
276. Charette, *Recompense*, 69, connects this verse with Matt 8:10–12, which may lead to the assumption that Matthew would refer to faith in relation to Jesus in both passages. But this is hardly the case, since not even 8:10–12 has its focus on the person of Jesus, but rather, the powers that work through him, i.e., the Spirit; cf. Matt 12:28. Indeed, Jesus himself, uniquely, possesses a full measure of *pistis*, which is necessary for—even the "secret" behind—the effectiveness of his healings, exorcisms, and other extraordinary deeds, as we see in Matt 17:16–18 and 21:18–21.
277. Davies and Allison, *Matthew*, 3. 294–95.
278. Cf. Matt 7:12; 22:34–40.

commandments cannot be obeyed in a way appropriate for the coming kingdom.[279] For Matthew, the aim of the law in its entirety is, after all, to allow the people to walk with their God until "all is accomplished" (Matt 5:18) and the world has been reborn (19:28). We may compare here with Matt 6:30, 33, where righteousness, i.e., obeying the commandments,[280] is closely linked with *pistis* (and kingdom). At its heart, then, the nature of the law is love (cf. Matt 22:34–39[281]), and *pistis* forms the basis for a proper understanding of how the commandments are to be interpreted and performed. This is why *pistis* may be identified as being at the core of the law. In this way, then, *pistis* is a criterion of judgment only on a secondary level, as the setting within which proper understanding and fulfillment of the law materializes, the latter being the primary criterion on which divine verdicts are based. This, again, is related to the concept of covenant, to which we, as noted, shall return shortly.

Since *pistis* is, in the passages we have discussed, a human attitude expressed in relation to the God of Israel, and not primarily to Jesus, we must now proceed to take a closer look at Jesus himself; in which way, if any, can human attitudes or reactions to Jesus be decisive in relation to divine judgment?

2.6 Jesus: A Criterion of Judgment?

In his study *Variety and Unity in New Testament Thought*, John Reumann notes with regard to Matthew that its "overall thrust is christological and more ecclesiological than any other of the four gospels."[282] The meaning and significance of Jesus in Matthew's Gospel thus deserves careful analysis. It is beyond the scope of the present study, however, to present a full examination of Matthew's Christology. Rather, what I am concerned with here are questions concerning Jesus as the Messiah

---

279. This has to do with the interpretation of how (not if) the commandments are to be fulfilled, in order that innocent people not be judged: Matt 12:7.
280. On the meaning of righteousness in Matthew, see above, chapters 2.2. and 2.3.
281. See also Matt 5:44–45; 7:12; 19:19; cf. Rom 13:8–9; 1 Cor 13:13.
282. John Reumann, *Variety and Unity in New Testament Thought* (Oxford: Oxford University Press, 1991), 53.

that arise from an examination of the criteria of judgment in the Gospel.

As Bornkamm has shown, judgment discourse is closely related to the theme of the Jewish law, which, in turn, carries within it important implications for Matthean Christology.[283] In several other texts included in the New Testament, such as the Gospel of John, Jesus is narratively positioned in such a way that divine judgment is almost exclusively dependent on how people (Jews and, less frequently, Samaritans) respond to him, and, consequently, the law plays a less prominent role in this regard.[284] Since the law is emphasized to a considerable degree in Matthew, as we have seen above, we may ask whether the person of Jesus, as a consequence, has been given a different, less emphasized position with regard to the outcome of judgment. If this is the case, though, other questions arise: Is Jesus not important enough for Matthew to represent the definitive boundary beyond which there is no salvation? In which way are or are not responses to Jesus presented by Matthew as a criterion of judgment in this, the most influential Gospel in history? In order to answer such questions, we need to distinguish between several parameters, which are active in Matthean judgment discourse.

As we have discussed above, the direction of *pistis*, i.e., of the attitude that makes possible the extraordinary events that characterize the future kingdom as it begins to take form in the land when Jesus and his followers work for its realization, is from human beings toward the God of Israel, not toward the person of Jesus.[285] This conclusion, in itself, indicates a clear distinction in the Gospel between Jesus and God.[286] The distinction between Jesus and God is, however, balanced

---

283. Bornkamm, "End-expectation," 32ff.
284. See, e.g., John 5:22–24 (but cf. 5:29); 8:24, 51; 11:25–26; 12:48; 14:6, 9; 15:22; 17:3.
285. It may be noted that this conclusion aligns with the view taken by many scholars regarding the historical Jesus; see, e.g., Werner G. Kümmel, *The Theology of the New Testament* (London: SCM Press, 1974), 63–65. On p. 64, Kümmel writes: "Did Jesus then demand belief in his person? This is unlikely, because though it is true that in the synoptic gospels faith is often spoken of, yet never in early tradition is anything said of 'faith in Jesus' or 'believing Jesus.' Jesus speaks rather of faith in God." Interestingly, Kümmel, when arguing for his opinion, cites Matthew more than Mark.
286. Cf. Matt 19:17. Note that the post-resurrection Jesus is depicted in different light in relation to God; cf. Matt 18:20; 28:18.

by claims revealing a close relationship, some would even argue an identification, between Jesus and Wisdom, a connection that signals Jesus's status as intimately related to God.[287] Would not such a close relationship between Jesus and Wisdom, and by implication, between Jesus and God, lead to a view of the person of Jesus as the key criterion of judgment, so that people who reject Jesus may be said to reject Wisdom, and thus God? As we shall see, in Matthew's narrative world, this is not necessarily the case. In order to understand the ultimate boundaries of salvation, then, beyond which condemnation awaits the sinner, one must be careful to distinguish between the person of Jesus, on the one hand, and other factors that influence the outcome of judgment, on the other. For this reason, we shall, in the following, differentiate between the themes of Jesus and the kingdom, the person of Jesus, and Jesus and the Spirit as we attempt to understand the Matthean pattern of thought.

2.6.1 Jesus and the Kingdom

For our purposes, the first and perhaps the most obvious distinction made in the narrative is that between the person of Jesus, on the one hand, and the mission of Jesus—i.e., the kingdom of heaven—on the other. In Matthew, "the gospel" (*to euangelion*) refers to the kingdom.[288]

---

287. Matt 11:19; cf. 11:25-27. In his study of the concept of wisdom and Jesus's christological self-understanding, Sverre Aalen, *Gud i Kristus: Nytestamentlige studier* (Oslo: Universitetsforlaget, 1986), 62, underlines the fact that despite the exalted picture of Jesus in the Gospels, Jesus is never presented as being identified with God. However, the connection between Jesus and Wisdom indicates that Jesus's relationship to God is the closest possible; despite the close relationship between Jesus and God, however, it is claimed, through the Wisdom analogy, that Jesus is subordinated to God: "Jesus står her på linje med visdommen. Visdommen utgjör den nærmeste analogi til denne enhet med Gud som samtidig er en underordning under Gud" (69–70). For an analysis of Wisdom and God, see James D.G. Dunn, *Christology in the Making* (2nd ed.; London: SCM Press, 1989), 163–212; for the Matthean perspective, see pages 197–206. Dunn argues that Matthew's identification of Jesus with Wisdom is done through the author's careful editing of Q. This opinion is shared by M. Jack Suggs, *Wisdom, Christology, and Law in Matthew's Gospel* (Cambridge M.A.: Harvard University Press, 1970). Cf. Samuel Byrskog, *Jesus the Only Teacher: Didactic Authority and Transmission in Ancient Israel, Ancient Judaism, and the Matthean Community* (Stockholm: Almqvist & Wiksell, 1994), 302–6, who argues that this is a question of function, rather than of identification.

288. The expression *to euangelion tēs basileias* is found several times in Matthew (4:23; 9:35; 24:14, cf. 6:10; 12:28; 13:19; 26:13), but nowhere else in the New Testament. According to Gundry, *Matthew*, 63, "Matthew's emphasis on the kingdom—i.e., God's rule—as the subject matter of the gospel scores another point against antinomianism."

This is so despite the fact that emphasis is also put on the return of Jesus, the Son of Man (Matthew 24–25),[289] since the events surrounding Jesus's return are focused on the eschatological kingdom too, as may be seen not least in the parables of Matthew 25.[290] The Matthean Jesus—and his disciples—proclaim the kingdom, not Jesus himself,[291] although Jesus, of course, has a key role to play both as the kingdom is being prepared and as the final judgment opens up for the full realization of the kingdom.

When the eschatological kingdom is proclaimed and set in motion, Jesus's focus is on the correct keeping of the Jewish law, a theme that is developed in the first of the five discourses (Matthew 5–7), and on the power of the kingdom as it is being established through healings and exorcisms, as described in the first narrative section (Matthew 8–9).[292] Of these two, the Jewish law is Matthew's primary concern, as we have discussed above,[293] which leads to the inescapable conclusion that divine judgment rests primarily on the basis of Torah observance.[294] The larger picture that emerges from such considerations is a presentation of Jesus as performing a mission with authority from God; Jesus is the only teacher (Matt 23:10).[295] This does not mean,

---

289. Cf. Reumann, *Variety*, 54.

290. See Matt 25:1, 23, 34.

291. Contra France, *Matthew*, 150, who, despite noting the continuity in the content of the proclamation of Jesus and his disciples, states that "the church's" proclamation in Matt 24:14 and 26:13 was about Jesus, rather than the kingdom. Matt 24:14 explicitly says that the gospel of the kingdom, *to euangelion tēs basileias*, is what must be proclaimed throughout the world, and nothing in 26:13 indicates that the contents of the proclamation has changed from kingdom to Jesus. While this may seem to be nitpicking, Matthew, contrary to the other Gospels, does, in fact, make this distinction; it would seem wise not to let other voices interfere with Matthew's when the evidence is unambiguous.

292. Even if Matthew's emphasis on the law is unmatched by other New Testament texts, Jesus's healings and exorcisms, as examples of the forces of the kingdom, should not be overlooked since they combine with the teaching to form a full picture of the meaning and significance of what the kingdom is about. The importance of healing in this regard is shown by the fact that it is specifically mentioned when Matthew describes Jesus's ministry in concentrated form in 4:23. Cf. Margret Davies, *Matthew* (Sheffield: Sheffield Academic Press, 1993), 48. Healing is, as France puts it in his 1985 commentary, *Matthew*, 105: "the power of the kingdom of heaven...brought into operation (cf. 12:28)." On the structure of Matthew's Gospel, see Anders Runesson, "Matthew, Gospel According to," in vol. 2 of *The Oxford Encyclopedia of the Books of the Bible* (edited by M. D. Coogan. 2 vols.; Oxford: Oxford University Press, 2011), 59–78.

293. See discussion in, chapter 2.1.2; cf. Bornkamm, "End-expectation," 35.

294. As discussed above, judgment based on law is embedded in other parameters, including a system providing means of atonement. In this system, the person of Jesus place a role as his death is interpreted in sacrificial terms; see further below.

however, that Matthew equates Jesus with the mission, that is, with the proclamation of the kingdom and the righteousness it demands.

The distinction between the mission and the person in Matthew is somewhat similar to statements on the Teacher of Righteousness in the Dead Sea Scrolls. Interpreting Hab 2:4b, "the righteous live by his faithfulness [*tsaddiq be'emunato yiḥyeh*]," the commentary on Habakkuk states:

> This refers to all those who obey the Law among the Jews whom God will rescue from among those doomed to judgment, because of their suffering and their loyalty[296] ['emunat] to the Teacher of Righteousness. (1QpHab 8:1–3)[297]

"Loyalty to," or "faith in" ('emunah), refers not to the *person* of the Teacher, but to his *interpretation* of the law: trusting the Teacher of Righteousness in this way is what will have a saving effect in the coming judgment.[298] It is, thus, of some importance not to read Pauline thought patterns into Matthew's text with regard to the distinction between the message and the person of Jesus; for Paul, contrary to Matthew, faithfulness seems to be related primarily to Jesus, rather than the kingdom.[299] As Graham Stanton argues: "Matthew takes pains to emphasise that the disciples of Jesus (and his later followers)

---

295. Cf. Byrskog, *Jesus the Only Teacher*, especially 294–96, where the authoritative *egō* and its christological significance is discussed. Byrskog concludes: "Matthew's depiction of Jesus as teaching decisive commandments, as speaking with an authoritative ἐγώ, as referring to himself as the only normative teacher and assuming the functions of the wisdom establishes a didactic christology...Jesus was to Matthew qualitatively *the only normative teacher*" (305–6).

296. Geza Vermes, *The Dead Sea Scrolls in English*, has "faith in."

297. Translation by Abegg, in Donald W. Parry and Emanuel Tov, in association with Geraldine I. Clements, *The Dead Sea Scrolls Reader. Vol. 1: Texts Concerned with Religious Law, Exegetical Texts and Parabiblical Texts* (Second revised and expanded edition; Leiden: Brill, 2014).

298. Cf. Håkan Ulfgard, "Rättfärdighetens lärare och Qumranförsamlingens historia," in *Dødehavsteksterne og Bibelen* (edited by Niels Hyldahl and Thomas L. Thompson; København: Museum Tusculanum, 1996), 129–57, here 139. See also Gert Jeremias, *Der Lehrer der Gerechtigkeit* (Göttingen: Vandenhoeck & Ruprecht, 1963), 142ff. Jeremias concludes: "Dafür garantiert nur die wahre Verkündigung der Gesetze, wie sie allein der Lehrer kann, weil er um die Geheimnisse Gottes Weiß. אמנה ist also der Glaube an seine Lehrer, besser: an seine Interpretation des Alten Testaments" (144).

299. Jeremias, *Der Lehrer*, 144, contrasts trust in the Teacher of Righteousness with Paul's insistence on trust in the person of Jesus. It should be noted that the point made here about the similarity between Matthew and the Dead Sea scrolls concerns the theme of judgment specifically; I am not arguing that Matthean Christology more generally is identical to the teaching on the Teacher of Righteousness in the scrolls.

146

proclaim the same message as Jesus (10:7, cf. 4:17; 28:20) and act in the same ways (10:8, cf. chapters 8 and 9). [...] There is a sense in which even though Jesus as Son of God is clearly set apart from his followers, his story is their story."[300]

The fact that Jesus's followers are presented as proclaiming the same message as Jesus is, of course, not unexpected; such a rhetorical strategy functions to strengthen the authority of the disciples. More interesting is perhaps the fact that Jesus's message is also said to be the same as that of John the Baptist (Matt 3:2; 4:17). It seems clear, then, that the message of the kingdom, which constitutes the basis of the criteria of judgment since the kingdom requires perfect obedience to the law and brings with it eschatological judgment, is, to some degree, independent of the person of Jesus in that characters before him (John) and after him (the disciples) are proclaiming, fundamentally, the same message as Jesus, without explicit reference to Jesus. This does not mean that Jesus does not have a unique role in bringing about the kingdom—he most certainly does. It rather means that criteria of judgment are intertwined with the message rather than the person of Jesus. In other words, despite the fact that the main character, Jesus, is elevated in the story to the highest possible status, this status does not play a role corresponding to Jesus's importance when Matthew outlines criteria of judgment. Still, as related to the mechanisms of atonement, which embed the criteria of judgment in the Gospel, the person of Jesus receives *the* central position in the narrative as his body is turned into a sacrifice for the forgiveness of sins in the passion story (Matt 26:26–29). There are also a few other passages, which shed light on the person of Jesus as a criterion of judgment.

2.6.2 The Person of Jesus

Thus far, we have argued that Matthew is careful to distinguish between Jesus and God, on the one hand, and between Jesus and the kingdom, on the other. To a certain degree, this narrative strategy

---

300. Graham N. Stanton, *A Gospel for a New People* (Edinburgh: T & T Clark, 1992), 69–70.

isolates Jesus himself as a person to whom people may react in different ways, regardless of their attitude toward God and kingdom. In other words, in terms of divine wrath and salvation, reacting to Jesus as a person is not exactly the same as reacting to God or responding to the proclamation of the kingdom. Analytically, this means that we need to treat the person of Jesus separately from these other two parameters in terms of the criteria of judgment as they are outlined in this Gospel.

One of the most common approaches to the question of the nature of the person of Jesus as portrayed in Matthew (and the other Gospels) is to isolate and analyze the so-called christological titles given to Jesus. Numerous studies have been authored from this perspective.[301] Since our focus here is the judgment of God as it relates to responses to the person of Jesus, it is not necessary to discuss them all, neither to present a full-scale investigation of these titles. However, according to some scholars, there are instances when a title will indicate the boundaries of salvation; if correct, this would have implications for our study.

Jack Dean Kingsbury has argued that the title Son of God is "the most fundamental Christological category in Matthew's Gospel."[302] As such, the title would serve as a boundary between those who believe in Jesus and those who do not, since only those who have experienced a "revelation of God" can use it.[303] If Kingsbury is correct in this regard, the title, which he calls "a 'confessional' title,"[304] would seem to point

---

301. It may be noted that even if often the same christological titles are the subject matter of such studies, scholars have drawn very different conclusions regarding which of these titles Matthew uses to describe "the essence" of Jesus as the Messiah. See discussion in Jack Dean Kingsbury, *Matthew: Structure, Christology, Kingdom* (Philadelphia: Fortress: 1975), xxv ff. While Kingsbury focuses his work on the title Son of God, Wayne Baxter's study, *Israel's Only Shepherd: Matthew's Shepherd Motif and His Social Setting* (London: T & T Clark, 2012) brings into full discussion the previously neglected Shepherd metaphor as a title of key importance for Matthew (on previous scholarship on the shepherd title, see especially, pp 9–16).

302. Kingsbury, *Structure*, 83. Cf. the discussion by James D.G Dunn, *Christology in the Making: A New Testament Inquiry into the Origins of the Doctrine of the Incarnation* (2nd ed.; London: SCM Press, 1989), 12–64, who focuses on the meaning such language would have had in the first century, as opposed to in later church history. In this regard, see also Boyarin, *Jewish Gospels*, 25–70, who argues that the title Son of God, as opposed to the title Son of Man, referred to the king of Israel, i.e., a title emphasizing not the divine, but the human aspect of authority. For a full discussion of the title Son of God in context, see Adela Yarbro Collins and John J. Collins, *King and Messiah as Son of God: Divine, Human, and Angelic Messianic Figures in Biblical and Related Literature* (Grand Rapids: Eerdmans, 2008).

303. Kingsbury, *Structure*, 82.

to Jesus as a critical criterion of judgment; those who confess are those who will be saved. However, judgment in Matthew seems not to be dependent on people's use, or not, of specific titles. In the case of the title Son of God, the so-called confession of the soldiers in Matt 27:54, where this title is used, is referred to by Kingsbury as signaling "the foundation for the emergence of the church."[305] However, as David Sim has argued convincingly, in Matthew, the centurion and the soldiers with him are not portrayed as confessing Jesus, but rather, as realizing, with great fear (*ephobēthesan sphodra*), that they, as representatives of Roman military power, had tortured and killed "God's Son" and were now facing defeat through the power of the God of Israel.[306] Thus, the realization that Jesus is the Son of God is, implicitly, connected to both condemnation and salvation in this Gospel. Explicitly, however, the so-called christological titles do not tell us very much about the boundaries of salvation, since Matthew's pattern of divine wrath and redemption is more related to "doing" than to "confessing" (cf., e.g., Matt 7:21–23). As we shall see, there are some passages, though, where acknowledgement of a relationship to Jesus seems to constitute a criterion of judgment.

The christological titles do indicate Jesus's special status, however. In addition to wisdom Christology, the story of the virginal conception, and the name Immanuel, the titles, in general, and the titles Son of God and Son of Man, in particular, portray Jesus as a person of unchallenged authority, which results from his unique relationship with God. This authority is intertwined with power (*exousia*). The extraordinary authority/power of Jesus is both related to Jesus's teaching (Matt 7:28–29), and shown through extraordinary real-life events in the story world, such as, e.g., healings (9:18–26), forgiveness (Matt 9:1–8), exorcisms (9:32–33), and the feeding of crowds (Matt 14:13–21; 15:32–19). Jesus is, in brief, portrayed as greater than anything seen before in the history of Israel, and the Jewish crowds are portrayed as

304. Ibid.
305. Ibid.
306. David C. Sim, "The 'Confession' of the Soldiers in Matthew 27:54," *HeyJ* 24 (1993): 401–24; cf. Idem, *Christian Judaism*, 225–26.

astonished and praise the God of Israel accordingly (Matt 7:28–29; 8:27; 9:8, 26, 31, 33; 13:54; 15:31; 22:33). This claim that Jesus, or rather, the events happening around him, are "greater than" other events in the history of the Jewish people is, in and of itself, an important part of Matthean (and synoptic) Christology.[307]

Such claims include that even the least in the kingdom is greater than John, who in turn is said to be greater than (*meizōn*; Matt 11:11) anyone born of a woman. Further, that which happens around Jesus is greater than the temple, just as the temple is greater than (*meizōn*; 12:5–6) the sabbath. In a similar way, the (eschatological) events taking place around Jesus are greater than (*pleion*; 12:41) the prophet Jonah as well as king Solomon (*pleion*; 12:42).[308] While this hierarchically structured language elevates that which happens around Jesus, we should note Matthew's use of the neuter in the word "greater than" (*meizōn*, *pleion*). The neuter indicates that Jesus is not presented as speaking about his own person, but about the events that the kingdom is bringing about as Jesus is fulfilling his divinely assigned role. Thus, while Jesus is the key figure around whom all of these greater things happen, Matthew avoids a narrow focus on the person of Jesus himself. As we shall see confirmed in the next section, this pattern is not a coincidence, but part of a consistent emphasis on the kingdom and, more importantly, the Spirit as the real force bringing about the eschaton. In terms of divine judgment, this nuance is quite important. It is the lack of a positive response to that which is greater than even the temple, i.e., the power of the Spirit and the establishment of the kingdom, which results in condemnation in the final judgment (Matt 12:41–42).

There are some passages, however, which seem to place Jesus, in some sense, as a breaking point between divine wrath and salvation. These passages relate in various ways to all three types of judgment, and may be categorized as follows: a) punishment and reward in this world (21:33–46); b) the final judgment (8:11–12; 10:22, 32–33, 39; 16:25

---

307. So René Kieffer, "'Mer-än'-kristologin hos synoptikerna," *SEÅ* 44 (1979): 134–47 (English summary on p. 147).
308. See also Matt 22:41–45, where even David is related to the Messiah.

[cf. 10:39]; 19:29; 26:24; 26:28). and c) punishment and reward in the world to come (5:11–12; 10:40–42; 19:29).

With regard to judgment in this world, we have already commented on the parable of the vineyard and why it seems likely to deal with status reversal already in this world, rather than only in the world to come (Matt 21:33–46).[309] The key verses here are 42–46:

> Jesus said to them, "Have you never read in the scriptures: 'The stone that the builders rejected has become the cornerstone; this was the Lord's doing, and it is amazing in our eyes'? Therefore I tell you, the kingdom of God will be taken away from you and given to a people that produces the fruits of the kingdom. The one who falls on this stone will be broken to pieces; and it will crush anyone on whom it falls." When the chief priests and the Pharisees heard his parables, they realized that he was speaking about them. They wanted to arrest him, but they feared the crowds, because they regarded him as a prophet.

Jesus is here referred to as the cornerstone from Ps 118:22, and the "chief priests and the Pharisees"[310] represent the builders who rejected it (Matt 21:46). This rejection of the cornerstone/Jesus will lead to divine punishment in the form of loss of leadership position (the kingdom will be transferred from these leaders to another group, which will govern the kingdom). Acceptance of Jesus as the cornerstone thus functions as a criterion for those who want to lead Israel as the eschaton is getting closer.

It seems, however, that this criterion is concerned more about the teachings of Jesus than about Jesus as a person, along the lines of what we discussed above with regard to the Teacher of Righteousness in 1QpHab 8:1–3.[311] The fruits of the kingdom refer to the outcome of the keeping of the law as Jesus interprets it (Matt 3:8; 7:15–21). Therefore, those whose teaching and governing produce a people worthy of the kingdom will be elevated to leadership positions by God. Much like loyalty to, or faith in, the Teacher of Righteousness means loyalty to his teachings, and that teaching is what leads to salvation, in this

---

309. For the interpretation that this parable of judgment concerns life in this world and not the final judgment, see above, ch. 1, n. 26.
310. Note, however, that the elders are also implied, as they are mentioned in Matt 21:23.
311. See above, p. 146.

parable, it is the keeping of the law that is presented as the criterion of judgment. This is further emphasized by the mention of the more dire consequences of not aiming at the righteousness that the Matthean Jesus requires: "The one who falls on this stone will be broken to pieces; and it will crush anyone on whom it falls" (Matt 21:44). Elsewhere, this threat of exclusion from the kingdom, i.e., destruction,[312] is directed only against the Pharisees (and the scribes that sympathize with them) as Jesus teaches the higher form of righteousness required for the kingdom (Matt 5:20; cf. 23:35–36).

If we proceed to look at judgment texts that deal with punishment and reward in the world to come, it seems as if there is a shift in nuance, moving toward focusing on the person of Jesus in specific contexts that involve suffering as well as compassion shown by outsiders to the movement. With Matt 5:11–12, a first step is taken in that direction. Here, the Matthean Jesus promises "great reward" in heaven for those who are reviled, persecuted, and spoken ill of because they are loyal to Jesus and his teachings. The rhetoric here rests on a claimed relationship not just between Jesus and those in the crowd that follow Jesus, but between those who suffer and the prophets, who were persecuted in the same way and who will, it is implied, receive great reward too for their faithfulness.

A similar promise of receiving rewards like the prophets and righteous is made in Matt 10:40–42. Here, however, those that will be given these rewards are not followers of Jesus, but Jews who compassionately receive Jesus's disciples, who are exposed to lethal dangers as they carry out their mission (10:38–39). The hermeneutical key behind the extending of these rewards that belong to the heroes of the movement, the prophets, the righteous,[313] and the "little ones," is an identification between the disciples and Jesus, on the one hand, and between Jesus and God, on the other, so that, ultimately, those who welcome the disciples, or even just give them a cup of water, are showing compassion to God's messengers: "Whoever welcomes you

312. Cf. Matt 24:51; 25:10–12, 30.
313. On the identity of the righteous, see above, chapter 2.2.

welcomes me, and whoever welcomes me welcomes the one who sent me" (v. 40). In other words, the rewards are based on the welcoming of God. In this rhetorical hierarchy, we see how Matthew avoids a focus on the person of Jesus as an ultimate criterion of judgment; that definitive criterion is, instead, the God of Israel. This is why violent attacks on Jesus's followers (prophets, sages, and scribes) will have devastating consequences: such rejection represents, ultimately, a rejection of God (Matt 23:34–36). In other words, we find, again, a focus not on the confession of Jesus, but on doing the right thing when it comes to reward and punishment. Christological titles, while indicating the extraordinary status of Jesus, are not activated in these contexts of judgment. Interestingly, this passage represents the first of two pericopes that explicitly claim that rewards in the world to come will be given also to people outside the Jesus movement.[314]

Finally, in Matt 19:29, Jesus promises substantial rewards, replacing in the world to come what his followers have lost in this life: "And everyone who has left houses or brothers or sisters or father or mother or children or fields, for my name's sake, will receive a hundredfold, and will inherit eternal life." We shall return below to discuss the fact that, contra Eubank, Matthew is careful not to count "eternal life" as a reward, but rather, as an "inheritance."[315] What is interesting here is that we find, again, that rewards in the world to come are directly related not to the keeping of the law in and of itself, but to the suffering that follows from proclaiming the same message as Jesus is proclaiming—the kingdom of heaven. To be sure, this proclamation involves teaching of the law, just as Jesus taught the law as he proclaimed the kingdom (cf. Matt 28:20). Indeed, the context for this passage, Matt 19:16–30, is about the correct keeping of the law. Thus, the words "for my name's sake" should be understood not as a reference to a confession of the person of Jesus, but rather, along the

---

314. As we shall see in Part II, the same hermeneutics are applied to non-Jews who act compassionately toward Jesus's suffering followers, although in that case, those who perform these acts of compassion do not know whom they are helping (Matt 25:31–46).

315. See chapters 2.8 and 7.3 and discussion of Eubank, *Wages of Cross-Bearing*, there.

lines we have discussed above, namely as referring to the hardships that follow when the disciples proclaim the teachings of Jesus.

In sum, then, while the person of Jesus is referred to in settings where rewards and punishment in the world to come are outlined, we do not find confessions involving specific christological titles, but rather, nuanced claims that either speak of Jesus's teachings, or point to God as the ultimate criterion of judgment. The overall idea in these passages is that suffering and loss in this world will be rewarded in the world to come. "Jesus" has, in these contexts, become shorthand for the message he is proclaiming. The situation changes somewhat when we consider passages making claims about the final judgment.

The role of the person of Jesus as a criterion in the final judgment is mentioned in different contexts in the Gospel. In 10:22, Jesus predicts that the disciples will be hated by everyone for their connection to him, for his "name's sake," i.e., for proclaiming and performing the same deeds of the kingdom as Jesus is now doing (cf. 10:6–8), and so, be associated with him. If they endure the suffering until the end, they will be saved (cf. 24:13). The same thought is echoed in 10:38–39 and 16:25. The implication of this message, which is directed at Jesus's own followers, not to outsiders, is that condemnation in the final judgment awaits those of his disciples who fail to endure the hardships of discipleship. Matthew 10:32–33 makes this explicit: "Everyone therefore who acknowledges me before others, I also will acknowledge (homologeō) before my Father in heaven; but whoever denies me before others, I also will deny before my Father in heaven."[316] The word translated as "acknowledge" here, homologeō, carries the sense of an announcement, or declaration, made openly in front of others.[317] In other words, those of his disciples who, for whatever reason, do not acknowledge before others their connection to Jesus will not receive

---

316. For the relationship of the Matthean text to the hypothetical document Q, see Marguerat, *Jugement*, 72–73. For the purposes of the present study, the existence of Q is of little or no concern. See discussion in the Introduction, pp. 20–21.

317. Cf. Matt 14:7, where the same verb is used to describe Herod Antipas' public announcement of his oath to give the dancing daughter of Herodias whatever she wanted after a performance (cf. v. 9).

acknowledgement by Jesus himself before his Father in heaven in the final judgment, and will thus be excluded from the kingdom.[318]

In this context, Jesus thus stands not as the judge (the Father in heaven has this role here; cf. 10:28), but rather, as the person whose voice will decide what is ultimately going to be the Father's judgment.[319] A disciple's readiness to acknowledge his or her association with Jesus before other people, including legal authorities (cf. 10:17–18, 28), will thus determine the outcome of the final judgment. It is thus quite clear that Jesus is a central criterion of judgment for his own disciples that, along with the Jewish law, will define salvation.[320] But in which way does the person of Jesus function here as a criterion of judgment? It must be emphasized that the person of Jesus does not supersede the law as the basis of which the final judgment will be carried out. Rather, the two function together to outline what is required for entry into the kingdom. For Matthew, loyalty to the person of Jesus means loyalty to Jesus's interpretation of the Jewish law and his message about the coming kingdom, as we have also seen above. This is confirmed by the literary context of Matt 10:32–33, which outlines the mission of the disciples as almost

318. Some scholars, as well as many church authorities through the centuries, have interpreted Matt 10:32-33 as an absolute statement with universal implications (see, e.g., Fornberg, *Matteusevangeliet 1:1-13-52*, 197). The idea is that this passage would give people a clear choice between heaven and hell, based on their confession or rejection of Jesus: there is no middle ground, no third option. Such an interpretation is problematic for several reasons, not only because the context of the passage is explicitly Jesus's instructions to his own disciples (not to outsiders of any kind) in a setting of persecution, but also, because we do not find other criteria of judgment in Matthew, which open up the kingdom for people who never knew Jesus. On the latter issue, see discussion in Part II below. Davies, *Matthew*, 85, seems, as so many other modern interpreters, bothered by the harshness of the words and comforts the reader by noting that despite this requirement for inclusion in the kingdom, Peter, who later in the narrative denied Jesus, is still commissioned by the same person to proclaim Jesus's teachings to the nations (Matt 28:16-20). While this is certainly correct—and we shall return to this below—Peter's story rather points to a covenantal pattern in the narrative world of Matthew's Gospel, in which repentance and forgiveness are still active parameters. We should also note with Luz, *Matthew*, 2.104, that in Church history Matt 10:31-32 have often been understood to deal with correct doctrine, as a way to distinguish between genuine and false Christians. Such ideas, however, are foreign to Matthew's text, where we never find doctrine as a criterion of judgment.

319. As Fornberg, *Matteusevangeliet 1:1-13-52*, 197, notes: "The commission discourse... give expression to a somewhat lower christology: Jesus is here clearly subordinate to the Father and does not function as judge, but rather as lawyer/prosecutor at God's judgment" (in Swedish; my translation).

320. No similar criterion for non-disciples is mentioned by Matthew. See further discussion below on Jesus and the Spirit, chapter 2.6.3.

identical to the mission of Jesus (10:5–8). This is also the reason why they must remain unwavering in their loyalty to the kingdom; as Jesus proclaimed and healed and exorcised demons, the disciples must proclaim the kingdom and heal and exorcise demons; as Jesus must suffer because of his mission, the disciples must suffer (10:38). Only those who are prepared to die for the kingdom, as Jesus is, will be seen as worthy citizens of the kingdom (10:37–39). The criterion of Jesus as a person is, thus, ultimately an *imitatio-Christi* criterion.

Such a reading is confirmed by Matt 7:23, where Matthew's Jesus uses the same verb as in 10:32, *homologeō*, in a judgment setting. Here, as the Sermon on the Mount is summed up in a final judgment scene, Jesus declares publicly (*homologeō*)—before his heavenly father, it must be assumed—that he does not even know those who openly profess to be his disciples, but fail to do "the will of my Father in heaven" (7:21). That "will of the Father" has just been explained in the same discourse to be the Jewish law, down to its most minute detail (5:17–18). In other words, public "confession," or "acknowledgement," of Jesus by his own disciples, which is required in 10:32 for life in the kingdom, means nothing if it is not expressed as, or illustrated by, perfect obedience to the law (cf. 5:48). No one can circumvent Jesus in the final judgment, since the heavenly Father, who is the judge, has made him the "gatekeeper" whose report and decision will be fully accepted by the judge. Jesus as a criterion of judgment in the final eschatological judgment, it turns out, should be understood as a person's fearless public acknowledgment, when called upon, of his or her identity as a follower of Jesus. This belonging among Jesus followers, in turn, can only be proven by perfect obedience to the Jewish law as Jesus interpreted it. "Confession" cannot be disentangled from "obedience" since the former must be an expression of the latter as far as the final judgment of Jesus's followers is concerned.[321] This means that, ultimately, it is the will of the heavenly Father, which is laid out in the Torah, that is the definite criterion of judgment, since the Matthean Jesus represents its perfect fulfillment; the person of Jesus points us,

---

321. Cf. 2 Clem. 3.4 and see discussion in Luz, *Matthew*, 2.105.

once again, to the God of Israel for the definition of the ultimate boundaries of salvation.

It is of some interest to note that the key disciple in Matthew, Peter (Matt 16:18–19), is explicitly said to have failed to acknowledge his association with Jesus, as he gives in to fear in the face of lethal danger in Matt 26:69–75. According to Matt 10:32–33, this is the exact kind of situation that would lead to Jesus's denial of Peter in the final judgment. Since such a grim outcome for Peter in the future divine judgment is not, contra Gundry,[322] suggested by the narrative—he is rather presented as among those entrusted to preach to all the nations what Jesus had taught his disciples (28:16–20)—Matthew's Gospel adds further emphasis to the power of repentance, a first stage of which is already hinted at in the passion story (26:75). Thus, while Jesus is a criterion of judgment for his disciples in terms of obedience to his teachings and fearless public acknowledgement of being associated with him, this criterion is embedded within the larger conceptual context which provides a means for forgiveness if repentance is at hand. In this regard, the Matthean Jesus thus belongs firmly and explicitly within the larger covenantal pattern of theo-ritual thought that governs the dynamics of Torah in divine judgment, i.e., within the symbolic universe of Second-Temple Judaism. Without Judaism, there will be neither grace nor mercy in judgment, as Matthew has weaved his story.

The implied message in Matthew in this specific case seems to be that if Peter, the rock on which Jesus's *ekklēsia* is to be built, cannot make it to the kingdom without reliance on the possibility of repentance and forgiveness, no one can make it without these provisions.[323] The question is, then: how is atonement achieved within

---

322. Gundry, *Peter*, argues that Peter is portrayed by Matthew as a failed disciple destined for condemnation in the final judgment (cf. Matt 13:24–30; 37–43).

323. For a discussion of Judas as repentant, see above, pp. 133–35. While Judas is most likely portrayed by Matthew as repentant, the severity of his crime stands in direct relationship to the importance of the figure of Jesus in Matt 26:24. Cf. 1 Enoch 38:2: "...when the Righteous One shall appear...where will the dwelling of the sinners be, and where the resting place of those who denied the name of the Lord of the Spirits? It would have been better for them not to have been born" (translation by E. Isaac). For the severity of experienced or expected suffering as related to the reversal of a person's birth, see also Job 3:2.

the *ekklēsia*, after a person expresses repentance? We have discussed forgiveness and atonement in Matthew at some length above.[324] Here, we shall just note briefly that in this context, the person of Jesus is at the heart of the matter, as he provides his own body as an atoning sacrifice beyond the defiled Jerusalem temple; it is in this setting, uniquely, that Jesus as an individual, rather than his teaching, is at the center (Matt 26:26–29; cf. 1:21). It is of interest to note, also, that when the focus shifts away from the law to Jesus as a person, we also move from the criteria of judgment to the mechanisms of atonement that covenantally embed and may modify, through the forgiveness of sins, the outcome of an act of judgment that has been based on the law.

In other words, in Matthew's story, Jesus is not primarily a character in relation to which divine verdicts are formulated, but rather a figure whose self-sacrifice will enable the people to survive the otherwise inescapable condemnation of the eschatological judgment. Thus, while the Matthean Jesus relentlessly proclaims the coming judgment and the necessity of keeping the law as the kingdom approaches, Jesus himself, as an embodied person, plays a different role in the end-time drama; his person complements the law, rather than opposes or annuls it, within a covenant setting. This difference between Jesus and that which happens around him is further emphasized when we shift the focus to the relationship between Jesus and the Spirit within the setting of divine judgment: apart from the sacrificial act that provides a means to retain the theo-ritual pattern of the Mosaic covenant once the temple has been defiled, that which happens around Jesus, or through him, seems to be more important than Jesus himself.

2.6.3 Jesus and the Spirit

As Birger Gerhardsson has pointed out, Matthew does not speak a lot about the Spirit, but when he does, it is in contexts of fundamental importance.[325] One such key passage is the pericope about blasphemy

---

324. See chapter 2.4.
325. Birger Gerhardsson, *"Hör, Israel": Om Jesus och den gamla bekännelsen* (Lund: LiberLäromedel, 1979), 124. (For an English version of Gerhardsson's argument, see idem, *The Testing of God's Son [Matt 4:1–11 & Par]: An Analysis of an Early Christian Midrash* [Lund: CWK Gleerup, 1966; republished by Wipf

against the holy Spirit, Matt 12:31–32, a text which has been called one of the most obscure and difficult texts in the synoptic tradition:[326]

> Therefore I tell you, people will be forgiven for every sin and blasphemy, but blasphemy against the Spirit will not be forgiven. Whoever speaks a word against the Son of Man will be forgiven, but whoever speaks against the Holy Spirit will not be forgiven, either in this age or in the age to come.

We have already discussed this text above in relation to the theme of repentance and forgiveness.[327] Here, we are concerned more with the carefully crafted distinction between Jesus and the Spirit when the ultimate boundaries of the kingdom are dealt with by the author. We are faced with a Christology in which Jesus as a person is explicitly subordinated to the Spirit, so that Jesus's importance is dependent on the Spirit's power, which works through Jesus. As Charette argues, "it is the creative force of the Spirit of God which lends to his [Jesus'] ministry its defining element."[328] It seems, thus, that while Jesus's birth is said to have come about through the power of the Holy Spirit (Matt 1:18–25), for Matthew, this does not mean that Jesus and the Spirit have merged completely in the person of Jesus. Matthew resists, explicitly, such forms of what has become known as high Christology.[329] Rather, the person of Jesus is presented more as a tool, a channel through which the powers of the Spirit can work unhindered; indeed, Jesus is

---

& Stock, 2009], ch. 7.) For a recent study on the Spirit in Matthew, see Blain Charette, *Restoring Presence: The Spirit in Matthew's Gospel* (Sheffield: Sheffield Academic Press, 2000). As Charette notes in his preface, when he was asked to write the book, his immediate response was to ask "whether the Gospel of Matthew even has a theology of the Spirit" (7). The aim of his book is to demonstrate that "Matthew's Gospel not only contains some significant insights but also offers a suggestive framework that allows for a deeper appreciation of the Spirit's role in the redemptive purpose of God" (7). A focus on the theme of divine judgment in Matthew strengthens that more general view. For a wider discussion of Jesus and the Spirit, see James D. G. Dunn, *Jesus and the Spirit: A Study of the Religious and Charismatic Experience of Jesus and the First Christians as Reflected in the New Testament* (London: SCM Press, 1975; republished by Eerdmans, 1997).

326. See, e.g., Evald Lövestam, *Spiritus Blasphemia: Eine Studie zu Mk 3,28f par Mt 12,31f, Lk 12,10* (Lund: CWK Gleerup, 1968), 3: "Das Logion von der Lästerung des heiligen Geistes gilt von alters her für eines der dunkelsten Jesusworte der synoptischen Traditionen. Bereits Augustin äusserte sich dazu: 'Forte in omnibus sanctis Scripturis nulla major queastio, nulla difficilior invenitur' (Serm. LXXI, cap. V /8/)."

327. See pp. 130–35.

328. Charette, *Restoring Presence*, 77.

329. Cf. Dunn's critique of interpretations that focus on Jesus rather than the Spirit; for Dunn, such a perspective "gives Jesus a uniqueness he did not claim" (*Jesus and the Spirit*, 48).

portrayed in this Gospel as an extraordinary individual, possessed by the Spirit of God,[330] and this is why blasphemy against the Spirit is a more serious offense than anything said against Jesus, "the Son of Man."

Mark's version of this logion (Mark 3:28–30) does not include a comparison between Jesus and the Spirit, and while Luke has this comparison, he is less extensive in his wording than Matthew. Luke 12:10 only states that no forgiveness will be given, whereas Matthew, who is more concerned with divine judgment than the other two synoptics, clarifies that no forgiveness will be given *either in this world or the world to come* (*oute en toutō tō aiōni oute en tō mellonti*). It seems as if Matthew has deliberately used this logion to create a paradigmatic statement, a statement that makes clear exactly what Jesus's position is in relation to the Spirit and the final judgment. The way the logion is worded shows that, for Matthew, the Spirit plays the leading role in the eschatological drama, and Jesus's extraordinary authority and power (*exousia*) derives from this divine power that brings the new world into being.

Mogens Müller has argued that, in Matthew's thought-world, this closeness between Jesus's *exousia* and the Spirit surfaces in passages of special importance, such as Matt 12:31–32.[331] Gerhardsson goes one step further and claims that "[i]t seems as if Matthew almost equates Jesus' exousia from heaven and his possession of the Spirit of God."[332] Further, the Matthean Jesus has the authority to give this *exousia* to his disciples (Matt 10:1, 7–8).[333] The Spirit empowers Jesus and Jesus has the ability to transfer this power to individuals whom he has chosen. Thus, it makes sense in Matthew's narrative world that the author preserves a different version of the miracle tradition in Mark 2:12, in which forgiveness is extended and healing follows; for Matthew's

---

330. Cf. Amanda Witmer's study of the historical Jesus, where she claims that Jesus was most likely perceived of as possessed by a spirit: *Jesus, The Galilean Exorcist: His Exorcisms in Social and Political Context* (London: T & T Clark, 2012). Matthew's christology seems to follow rather closely such a view of Jesus.

331. Mogens Müller, "Mattæusevangeliets messiasbillede," *SEÅ* 51 (1986–7): 168–79, here 175.

332. Gerhardsson, *Hör Israel*, 124 (my translation): "Det förefaller som Matteus närmast sätter likhetstecken mellan Jesu exousia från himlen och hans besittning av Guds Ande."

333. So Müller, "Mattæusevangeliets messiasbillede," 176.

crowds, as for the Matthean Jesus, the power to do such extraordinary things comes from God and is given to humans: "When the crowds saw it, they were filled with awe [*phobeō*], and they glorified God, who had given such authority [*exousia*] to human beings" (Matt 9:8). It is through the Spirit that Jesus is better equipped than John the Baptist to wage the war against Satan or Beelzebub.[334] Jesus's special status above his disciples comes from a combination of being God's chosen son (Matt 3:16–17) and Messiah (16:16–17) and his ability to let the Spirit work unconstrained through him.[335] This is why, while the person of Jesus is not a judgment criterion as important as the Spirit, Jesus's special status still provokes severe judgment when he is betrayed, although there will, it seems, still be room for repentance even then (26:24).[336]

The extraordinary role of the Spirit as divine judgment is to be meted out surfaces also in passages beyond Matt 12:31–32, which indicates that this perspective is thoroughly and consistently integrated in the Matthean narrative. We have already discussed Matt 12:41–42.[337] Here, we have a *qal vaḥomer* type of argument, in which the people of Nineveh and the Queen of the South will rise up at the final judgment and condemn "this generation,"[338] since the former listened to Jonah and Solomon, while the latter has not repented despite the fact that what happens around Jesus is "greater than" both Jonah and Solomon.[339] That which is "greater" (*pleion*) cannot refer to Jesus, since *pleion* is in the neuter, neither to the kingdom, which would have required a feminine form. But if we think of that which is greater in terms of the Spirit's eschatological work, the wording makes more sense.[340] To be sure, a reference to the work of the Spirit would include,

---

334. So Kieffer, "'Mer-än'-kristologin," 136: "Genom Anden är Jesus bättre rustad än Döparen för att utkämpa den viktiga kampen mot Satan eller Beelsebul".
335. The disciples, while having been given the power of the Spirit in Matt 10:1, are still portrayed as weaker than Jesus when it comes to performing acts of kingdom-related power, based on their lack of *pistis* (17:16–20).
336. See discussion of Judas above, pp. 133–35.
337. See also Matt 12:6.
338. For discussion of this expression, see below chapter 3.2.2.1.
339. Cf. Rom 2:27.
340. Gundry, *Matthew*, 246, argues that *pleion* refers to Jesus, although the neuter "emphasises quality as distinct from personal identity." See also France, *Matthew*, 461, who comes close to Gundry's reading: "it is the authority of Jesus which is immediately at issue, but not so much Jesus in his own person as in his *role*... the neuter is perhaps also intended to point beyond Jesus himself to

implicitly, both Jesus and the kingdom, since the kingdom is what the Spirit is establishing and Jesus is the agent through whom this is made possible (cf. 4:17; 12:28). We find in these verses, then, that the Spirit functions as a form of judgment criterion, since a rejection of what it establishes (through Jesus) leads to condemnation. For Matthew, saying that what happens around Jesus is the work of the Spirit, and that lack of repentance when confronted with these extraordinary deeds will lead to divine judgment, is a way to emphasize Jesus's importance, not diminish it.

What are we, then, to say about Jesus as a criterion of judgment in Matthew's version of the good news? Does reward/punishment, or salvation/condemnation in the final judgment, depend on how people respond to Jesus? As we have seen above, the answer is more complex than a simple yes or no. Indeed, in the context of the Gospel of Matthew as a whole, the author ascribes to Jesus a somewhat surprisingly low profile in judgment settings. In passages where Jesus is referred to as a criterion at all, it is either to ensure his disciples who suffer because of him that if they endure, they will be rewarded in the world to come. In such cases, though, it is not so much Jesus as a person as Jesus's message about the kingdom that is referred to; they suffer for the kingdom just as Jesus suffered for the kingdom. Indeed, when Jesus is referred to explicitly as a person to whom people around him react, Matthew is careful to declare that he is, in fact, less important than the Spirit, so that sin against the Spirit is unforgivable, whereas things said against Jesus are not. In other words, as far as judgment is concerned, the author of Matthew points away from the person of Jesus and focuses, on the one hand, on Jesus's teaching of the Jewish law, and on the other hand, on the Holy Spirit, the latter providing us with the only example of a breach of the covenant for which there is no atonement. The importance of the Spirit in judgment settings

the new principle of God's relationship with his people which will result from Jesus' ministry." I find the emphasis on the quality, or role, rather than the person to be a step in the right direction. The argument is not entirely satisfactory, however, since the Spirit's work is dealt with in a paradigmatic way just a few verses later, in 12:31–32, and thus should be allowed to impact the interpretation of these verses.

should be understood against the background of Matthean Christology, according to which Jesus receives his power, his *exousia*, from the Spirit, so that the work of the Spirit, although taking place through Jesus, is ultimately more essential than Jesus himself in the eschatologically charged world of the Gospel. This does not mean, however, that Jesus is not present at all as a criterion of judgment, since rewards will be given to those who compassionately receive his disciples, as if they had received Jesus (Matt 10:40). The reason for Jesus's role in divine judgment here, however, is that, ultimately, such individuals receive God.

Jesus's importance as a person comes to the fore independently especially in one key setting that relates to divine judgment: when he offers himself as an atoning sacrifice that will save his people from destruction as God's wrath is unleashed and the defiled temple is destroyed. Thus, the person of Jesus does not belong among the criteria of judgment, but rather with the parameters that embed and negotiate divine judgment within a covenant setting. The Jewish law is what, for the Matthean Jesus, provides the basis for judgment, and this is never changed at any point in the narrative and certainly not by Jesus's sacrificial death (or resurrection). Indeed, Jesus's death replaces the sacrificial atonement that the temple had been able to provide for the people until the cult was defiled by the moral impurity of leading individuals, and is thus, just as the temple was before Matthew 23–24, an integral part of the covenant without which the law cannot function properly. Jesus's death, then, is necessary in order to uphold the Mosaic law within the covenant.

2.7 In Which Way(s) are "Works of Law" Criteria of Judgment?

Up till now we have discussed various criteria of judgment and found that, in Matthew's Gospel, the law of Moses is the foundational criterion that decides various forms of punishments and rewards. We have also seen that Matthew's story relies upon certain theo-ritual mechanisms, which embed the function of law within a wider context, and have the ability to modify or change altogether the outcome of verdicts. These mechanisms include, primarily, repentance and forgiveness, but we also find passages where the notion of vicarious righteousness surfaces. Before we conclude chapter 2 with a discussion of the covenant theme, which we have touched upon a few times in the previous discussion, but which requires more comprehensive treatment, we need to say a few words on how "works," a designation often used in Christian contexts, may be defined in a Matthean setting. This is of some importance since much of the discussion about criteria of judgment and the possibility of salvation, not least since the Reformation in the sixteenth century, has been structured as an interpretive choice between "works" and "grace." Is such a choice reflected in Matthew's Gospel, or are we at risk of being misled by traditions unknown to Matthew, but foundational to many later forms of Christian theology and identity?

It should be noted, first, that "works" in Christian tradition, which is the tradition in which Matthew's Gospel has primarily been read and interpreted, has come to mean any type of act, or good deed, as opposed to grace, which has been defined as God's initiative to save human beings, regardless of any such good deeds. Some Christians have argued that a combination of the two is necessary for salvation; others—most famously, Luther—have claimed that only grace, without works, can save, suggesting that Paul would support this type of theology. In Matthew's narrative world, things look slightly different. What in later Christian debates is called "works" refers in Matthew not to good deeds generally, but specifically, to obedience to Torah. This means that the focus is kept strictly on the Jewish people, since the law was given only to this religio-ethnic group. The Greek word translated as "grace" (charis) does not exist in Matthew's Gospel, a striking contrast to, especially, Paul's letters.[341] However, if we understand "grace" as God's initiative to save his people from annihilation as inevitable destruction will soon strike due to the

---

341. Charis is also absent from Mark's Gospel, although it occurs several times in Luke-Acts. John's Gospel has three occurrences of charis, in the very beginning of the Gospel, and only in the narrator's voice. A vast majority of the 155 occurrences of the word in the New Testament is found in the Pauline literature, both in the undisputed and the disputed letters.

defilement of both land and temple, for which the people's leaders are ultimately responsible, then we have evidence of the notion of divine grace in Matthew's Gospel.[342]

Second, in the history of Christianity, while good deeds and/or grace are mentioned frequently, authorities have often insisted rather on the confession of the right doctrines in order to distinguish between "true Christians," who are destined for salvation, and "heretics," who are relegated to a future in hell. In Matthew's world, however, no such distinction with regard to judgment and salvation based on doctrine is ever made or referred to; doctrine is a concept foreign to the characters of the story as well as to the narrator himself.[343] Obeying the Mosaic law according to the interpretation of the Matthean Jesus—an interpretive tradition placing love of God and neighbor at the center, emphasizing justice and mercy (22:34-40; cf. 23:23)—obviously highlights the importance of "works." These "works," however, relate not only to the world around a human being, but also to the world within her. We may therefore further define Torah observance as taking place on three levels of "works" in Matthew, all of which will be scrutinized in the process of divine judgment:

a. *External Deeds.* Such actions are performed in the world external to the person and in direct relation to other people (e.g., 5:40–41; 10:40–42).

b. *Verbal Deeds.* This refers to words, which are understood as actions since they affect and influence the world around a person (e.g., 5:22; 12:36–37).

c. *Internal Deeds.* This refers to the inner landscape in which a person expresses thoughts that are related to the reality around him or her (e.g., 5:28; 15:8, 19). (It should be noted that other forms of thinking, such as intellectual endeavors, knowledge, or doctrine,

---

342. Cf. above p. 24n74.

343. Albert Schweitzer, *Out of My Life and Thought: An Autobiography. Postscript 1932-1949 by Everett Skillings* (Translated by C.T. Campion; New York: Mentor Books, 1953), argued in a similar way with regard to the historical Jesus: "Jesus never undertakes to expound the late Jewish dogmas of the Messiah and the Kingdom. His concern is, not how believers ought to picture things but that love, without which no one can belong to God, and attain to membership of the Kingdom, shall be powerful within. [...] [H]e does not think dogmatically. He formulates no doctrine" (47, 50).

are not related to either condemnation or salvation in Matthew).[344]

Verbal deeds have a prominent position between external and internal deeds, since "out of the abundance of the heart the mouth speaks" (12:34). Indeed, for Matthew, observance of the Torah begins, and must begin, in the inner world of a person, "in the heart" (cf. 5:8); if the inner dimension is found to be insufficiently pure, external deeds will, as a consequence—even if they look good "on the surface," such as almsgiving—fail to be counted as obedience (e.g., 6:2-6; 18:35; cf. the paradigmatic statement in 15:18-20). The hermeneutical principle from which such rulings emerge is grounded in what the Matthean Jesus regards as the greatest commandment of them all, the key word of which has become known in Jewish tradition as the *Shema* (Deut 6:5): "You shall love the Lord your God with all your heart, and with all your soul, and with all your mind" (Matt 22:37). In other words, external, verbal, and inner deeds all have their origin in "the heart," and thus, all ultimately depend on the pureness of the heart when they are being scrutinized in the divine judgment.

Do we find, then, with these definitions of "works" in mind, that works are the basis of judgment in this world, the world to come, and in the final judgment? Beginning with judgment in this world, we have already noted that Matthew has a tendency to postpone divine verdicts to the final judgment (and the world to come).[345] Still, Matthew's

---

344. The only indication we have of the place of knowledge in processes related to judgment is found in Matt 11:25, where the Matthean Jesus notes the disadvantage of "the wise and intelligent," as God is said to have made his revelation available to "infants" (ὅτι ἔκρυψας ταῦτα ἀπὸ σοφῶν καὶ συνετῶν καὶ ἀπεκάλυψας αὐτὰ νηπίοις). This may be compared to the emphasis on knowledge as necessary for salvation that can be observed in the Dead Sea Scrolls. For recent and comprehensive discussion of this theme, see Eric Montgomery, "A Stream from Eden: The Nature and Development of a Revelatory Tradition in the Dead Sea Scrolls" (Ph.D. diss., McMaster University 2013). For discussion of knowledge in relation to salvation as expressed by the historical Jesus, Paul and 1 John, see Anders Runesson, "Kunskap, dårskap och intighet i nytestamentlig frälsningsteologi: Jesus, Paulus och Första Johannesbrevet." ["Knowledge, Madness, and Nothingness in New Testament Theologies of Salvation: Jesus, Paul, and First John."] Pages 43-65 in Benjamin Ekman and Henrik Rydell Johnsén (red.), *Sōteria och gnōsis: Frälsning och kunskap i den tidiga kyrkan. Föreläsningar hållna vid Nordiska patristikermötet i Lund 18-21 augusti 2010.* [*Sōteria and Gnōsis: Salvation and Knowledge in the Early Church. Papers given at the Meeting of the Nordic Society for Patristic Studies in Lund August 18-21, 2010.*] Patristica Nordica VIII. Skellefteå: Artos & Norma, 2012.

345. See above, chapter 1.

Gospel reveals a pattern of thought in which God may also engage directly in this world with both punishments and rewards. The clearest example is the destruction of Jerusalem and its temple, which is dealt with in the form of a so-called miracle story (21:18–19)[346] and in prophetic statements. We see the latter in 23:35–24:2 (cf. 27:25, and the parenetic-prophetic statement in 26:52). The types of works that lie behind the punishment are forms of external deeds, as is also made clear by the reference to the lack of fruit, fruit in Matthew being a frequently used metaphor for the outcome of obedience to Torah. The destruction of cities interpreted as divine punishment is also found in 11:23, where the Matthean Jesus refers to biblical Sodom, implying that it was because of all its sins (external deeds)—and lack of repentance—that the city was destroyed.[347] External deeds, again in the form of violence and bloodshed, are also behind the punishment outlined in the parable of the tenants in the vineyard (21:33–46), which is to take place in this world, in the form of the displacement of the leaders of the people (the chief priests and the Pharisees).[348] This punishment is closely related to the destruction of the Jerusalem temple, from where the chief priests ruled (cf. 22:6–7).

There is one text of a more general character that points us to direct outcomes in this world based on human behavior. In Matt 6:33, Jesus summarizes a discourse concerning things that worry people, such as food and clothing, with the following words: "Strive first for the kingdom of God and his righteousness, and all these things will be given to you as well." As we have noted above, "righteousness" in Matthew is quantitative in nature and refers to the keeping of the commandments. Here, then, observing the Torah and seeking the kingdom of God are brought together, emphasizing that the righteousness that is required is the full fidelity to the Torah that Jesus

346. For the interpretation of this pericope as symbolic for the destruction of the temple, see the discussion in France, *Matthew*, 791–94.

347. This reference to Sodom is then used to make the point that the final judgment will mean punishment for Capernaum, since the town had not repented despite the extraordinary deeds Jesus had done there. Thus, punishment in Israel's history is used, pedagogically, to transfer the audience's focus to the final eschatological judgment, alerting them to the fact that, as God has punished in the past, he will judge in the future if repentance is lacking.

348. For this interpretation of the parable, see discussion above, pp. 50n26, 151–52; see also 219–20.

taught earlier in the Sermon on the Mount, namely, an eschatologically informed obedience that exceeds the Torah observance of the Pharisees (Matt 5:17–20). Such Torah observance, which involves obedience in the form of all types of deeds, the Matthean Jesus insists, will result in a situation, in this world, in which all the needs of the people are taken care of. Whether this ideal state of things, in which hunger and lack of clothing are non-existent should be understood as an "automatic" outcome when everyone keeps the law, or whether it should rather be thought of in terms of divine recompense for obedience, is a distinction that may prove to be artificial, since the law in and of itself is a divine gift.[349]

In addition to judgment related to these external deeds, we have two instances of verbal deeds that are condemned by God with immediate consequences in this world. In Matt 5:22, Matthew's Jesus refers to the council (*synedrion*) as the institution within which God's justice is put into practice in the case of one person insulting another.[350] A more dire proclamation of judgment relates to anyone who "speaks against the Holy Spirit" (12:32). For this sin, defined as a verbal deed, there will be no forgiveness "either in this age or in the age to come."[351] As we have discussed above, if a person's sin is not forgiven, he or she will not be

---

349. Some interpreters have commented that this type of saying reflects an "ethics of the well-to-do." However, one has to keep in mind that the radical obedience to the Jewish law that Jesus is teaching in Matthew's Gospel is centered on justice, mercy, love of God and neighbor, and a servant ideal with a special focus on the lower strata of society (e.g., Matt 23:11, 23; 22:37–39; 7:12; 12:7; 18:4). If everyone sought the kingdom through striving for this righteousness/obedience to the law, then, by necessity, a type of equality between people would emerge and no one would need to worry about meeting the demands of everyday life; it would be a first step toward realizing the vision of a return to paradise, which the eschaton will eventually bring: the re-birth of the world (19:28; cf. 25:34).

350. Just as in the Hebrew Bible, the Matthean Jesus understands human institutions as carrying out God's will, as revealed in God's law, when justice is administered. For discussion, see Runesson, "Judgment," 458–59, 462. To be sure, Matthew's scene seems hyperbolic in that even an insult can be judged in official courts. This is not the point of the passage, however. While Luz, *Matthew*, 1. 235–36, thinks the verse is structured as a progression from human courts to divine judgment, it is more likely that all instances of judgment, both those dealt with by human courts and the "Gehenna of fire," which lies beyond such judicial settings, are thought to administer God's justice. What we find in terms of progression in 5:22 is rather from divine judgment carried out in this world, in history, to the final eschatological judgment. Thus, Matthew's Jesus portrays these judgment proceedings as closely interrelated; just as judgment is administered in history, there will be a final eschatological reckoning (cf. above on the rhetoric of Matt 11:23).

351. For discussion of sin against the Spirit, see above, chapter 2.4.1.

able to offer sacrifices to God in the temple without defiling the altar (cf. 5:23–24), which effectively results in exclusion from salvation.

Finally, Matthew avoids speaking about divine judgment in this world in relation to internal deeds. Such violations of law or fulfillment of law (punishments and rewards) are dealt with in the final judgment and in the world to come only, perhaps because they are hidden from other humans, but not from God, who sees what happens in secret (e.g., 6:4, 6, 18).

Looking now at how "works" are punished or rewarded in the world to come, we find the following pattern. As with judgment in this world, the majority of passages dealing with the world to come speak of works in the form of external deeds as the criteria on which the divine verdict will be based. We see this in Matt 6:2–4, 16–18, where the Matthean Jesus promises rewards in the world to come for those who give alms and fast in secret.[352] In Matt 19:21, the language of storing up a treasure in heaven is applied to the keeping of very specific commandments, which summarize the law, and in 10:40–44, rewards are given to those who show hospitality toward Jesus's disciples. In one instance, in Matt 5:11–12, suffering is said to be rewarded in heaven. This is not explicitly related to external deeds, but as 5:44–47 indicates, the reward is intertwined with the act of loving the enemies that are reviling and persecuting those who suffer; the one who suffers must, thus, actively engage in specific ways those who cause their suffering (cf. 5:39–42). Suffering resulting from personal sacrifices will be rewarded hundredfold in the world to come (19:29).

We have several texts speaking more generally of status displacement or exaltation in the coming kingdom, based on behavior and attitudes in this life. In Matt 5:19, those who keep and teach even the least of the commandments in the law will be considered great in the kingdom, and those who do not will be seen as the least. In addition, those who humble themselves as a child (18:4), or behave

---

352. The interpretation that these rewards will be paid in the world to come is based on the fact that those who do these benevolent deeds in public are said to have already received their pay. In addition, the sayings about reward are all summed up in Matt 6:19–21, where it is explicitly stated that people should strive to store up treasures in heaven rather than on earth.

like a servant (*diakonos*; 23:11–12) in the present age will be exalted or considered the greatest in the kingdom. Again, "works" here should be defined as external deeds, based on Jewish law. Finally, while right prayer is said to be rewarded in heaven (6:5–6), just as right almsgiving and fasting, the clearest example of verbal deeds being a criterion of judgment in the world to come is the pericope about blasphemy against the Holy Spirit (Matt 12:32), as we noted above.

Moving on to divine verdicts based on "works" in the final eschatological judgment we find all types of deeds taken into account: external (e.g., 3:7–8, 10; 5:20; 7:19–23; 10:14–15; 11:21–22; 19:16–17; 23:31–33; 24:45–51; 25:14–30), verbal (e.g., 12:36–37), and internal (e.g., 5:27–28; cf. 18:9). An interesting passage which is summarizing in nature, i.e., it assumes all types of deeds, is Matt 16:27: "For the Son of Man is to come with his angels in the glory of his Father, and then he will repay everyone according to his work [*kai tote apodōsei hekastō kata tēn praxin autou*]."[353] Matthew is here likely making use of Ps 62:13,[354] as Kyoung-Shik Kim has argued.[355] The singular *praxis*,[356] which I have translated here as "work,"[357] refers to the totality of a person's deeds, his or her "praxis" in life.[358] The setting is the final judgment. The question is whether the passage refers to vindication/condemnation, i.e., entering the kingdom or not, or to status adjustments and other forms of punishments and rewards *in* the kingdom.

In my opinion, the word *apodidōmi* (here: "to pay") may be understood to indicate both. As we shall discuss in more detail below,[359] the Matthean Jesus, contrary to Mark's and Luke's portraits, avoids speaking about life in the world to come in terms of reward, as if it were given as payment for work done.[360] But Matthew also emphasizes,

353. This text caused trouble for Lutheran interpreters during the reformation; see Luz, *Matthew*, 2. 385–86.
354. But cf., e.g., Prov 24:12; Sir 35:22; *T. Job* 17:3; Rom 2:6; Rev 2:23; 22:12.
355. Kyoung-Shik Kim, *God will Judge*, 148–66, contra Marguerat, *Jugement*, 93; Luz, *Matthew*, 2. 385.
356. The Hebrew of Ps 62:13 is also in the singular כי אתה תשלם לאיש כמעשהו; the LXX has the plural of *ergon* (ὅτι σὺ ἀποδώσεις ἑκάστῳ κατὰ τὰ ἔργα αὐτοῦ).
357. NRSV has "he will repay everyone for what has been done." Luz, *Matthew*, 2. 385, suggests "behaviour."
358. So also Davies and Allison, *Matthew*, 2. 676.
359. See also the discussion of Matt 19:29 above, pp. 45–47.
360. Pace Eubank, *Wages of Cross-Bearing*.

as we have seen, that condemnation and exclusion from life in the kingdom is based upon a person's "works," i.e., on the lack of obedience to the Jewish law. Since Matt 16:27 is spoken to Jesus's disciples and the wording is open with regard to the outcome of judgment—it is either negative or positive—it makes Matthean sense to interpret the *praxis* of a person, on the one hand, to be the basis on which exclusion from the kingdom is decided (i.e., condemnation), and, on the other hand, the basis for possible rewards or punishments (e.g., status adjustments) in the kingdom for those who are allowed to enter.[361] In other words, Matt 16:27 does not comment on the criteria of salvation, but rather, summarizes a principle, which is also common in other forms of Judaism contemporary with Matthew as well as in later rabbinic literature, namely, that while condemnation is based on a person's "works," salvation can never be earned, only "inherited." Salvation, however, does not exclude punishments and rewards, either in this world or in the next.[362]

The parable of the wedding banquet in Matt 22:1–14 seems to lend further support to this pattern of thought.[363] The parable aims at illustrating how judgment relates to the kingdom of heaven (22:2). Once the banquet has begun, a person found not wearing the proper clothing is thrown out "into the outer darkness, where there will be weeping and gnashing of teeth" (22:13). As in Rev 19:8 (cf. 3:4–5; 16:15), clothing symbolizes, as Luz also argues, "the good works that are to be produced at the judgment,"[364] thus indicating that exclusion from the kingdom is based on "works," i.e., on insufficient fulfillment of the commandments (cf. 5:16, 17–19; 19:16–17).[365] Even Jesus's followers, Luz

---

361. The context seems to exclude the possibility that we are only dealing with rewards and punishments administered to those who are saved, since our verse follows immediately after a statement that threatens the disciples with loss of life: "For what will it profit a person if he gains the whole world but forfeit his life? Or what will a person give in return for his life?"

362. Cf. Sanders, *Paul and Palestinian Judaism*, 517: "[T]he distinction between being *judged on the basis of deeds* and punished or rewarded at the judgment (or in this life), on the one hand, and being *saved by God's gracious election*, on the other, was the general view in Rabbinic literature. [...] Salvation by grace is not incompatible with punishment and reward for deeds." (Cf. 426–28.)

363. On the unity of the parable, see Daniel Patte, *The Gospel According to Matthew* (Valley Forge: Trinity Press International, 1987), 301. For full discussion of the parable in relation to the Pharisees, see below, chapter 3.2.1.2.

364. Luz, *Matthew*, 3. 56.

concludes, "will receive the kingdom only to the extent that they bring their fruits (21:43)."

In sum, what we see in Matthew's Gospel is a theology of divine judgment, based on "works." "Works," in turn, should be understood as referring to fulfillment of the Jewish law on three levels, which we have called external, verbal, and internal, the latter referring to thought processes involving other human beings. We have also seen, however, that there are several divinely-ordained mechanisms at work in the narrative that embed the pattern of judgment and may modify its outcome, such as repentance and forgiveness.[366] Further, Matthew's Jesus, contrary to Mark's and Luke's portraits, avoids speaking of salvation, i.e., admittance into the kingdom after the final judgment, as payment for work that has been accomplished.

Now, these theological dynamics, taken together, point in the direction of an overall theo-ritual thought pattern that is rather closely related to a Jewish understanding of the covenant between God and Israel, a pattern which Ed Sanders has called covenantal nomism. We have had occasion to note such similarities with Jewish thought related to the covenant, as we have discussed the various aspects of Matthew's judgment theology. It is time now to focus on the notion of covenant in Matthew, more specifically, and ask whether this element of the text's thought pattern affects or complements the overall pattern of divine judgment in the Gospel. As we shall see, it is Matthew's covenant theology that explains the otherwise elusive notion of grace in this story. This conclusion is reinforced as we aim at identifying which covenant Matthew's Jesus refers to in order to claim salvation for his people.

2.8 Covenant and Grace

Matthew's text is saturated with assertions of divine judgment, reassuring the oppressed that liberation is coming, and threatening

---

365. Cf. Luz, *Theology*, 120: "[T]he guest without wedding clothes—that is, without sufficient good deeds—is thrown out of the banquet hall."
366. See above, chapters 2.1.1; 2.3; 2.4.

those who lead the people astray and who break the law with disaster, punishment, and exclusion from the kingdom of heaven.[367] But the discourse of the punishment and suffering awaiting lawbreakers is intertwined with and perforated by expressions of divine affection that are communicated through a theo-ritual mechanism allowing for forgiveness and atonement, which in turn opens up for the repentant to approach God. The question is now how to best explain this hermeneutical mechanism. What is it and where did it come from? What place does it have in Matthew's narrative? Why is this important for Matthew?

When we search for a hermeneutical matrix in Jewish tradition within which a pattern of divine love for the people may have been formed and nurtured in collective memory, the concept of covenant soon surfaces as the only likely candidate.[368] Such a "place," so frequently referred to in the Hebrew Bible and in Jewish tradition, would be able to explain in a coherent manner otherwise disconnected sayings and motifs of forgiveness and atonement in the text, and, while doing so, balance ideas of grace—i.e., getting something for nothing—against Matthew's incessant focus on divine judgment, punishment, and reward, as based on obedience to the law ("works"). While the Hebrew Bible contains references to several covenants between God and humans,[369] the most important, both within this

---

367. Cf. Matt 6:26; 7:29; 9:36; 12:7; 18:6; 13:41–42.
368. Cf. Scott W. Hahn, *Kinship by Covenant: A Canonical Approach to the Fulfillment of God's Saving Promises* (New Haven: Yale University Press, 2009). For Hahn, the covenant theme is what keeps the discreet parts of the canon together, providing cohesion to this diverse collection of texts as well as influencing the theology expressed. This should not be understood, though, to mean that the notion of covenant was always understood in the same way. For discussion, see most recently Richard J. Bautch and Gary N. Knoppers (eds.), *Covenant in the Persian Period: From Genesis to Chronicles* (Winona Lake: Eisenbrauns, 2015).
369. Although later Jewish tradition contains references to a covenant between God and Adam (see discussion below, Part II), the covenant between God and Noah is the first covenant mentioned in the Book of Genesis (Gen 9:8–17). God makes a covenant with Abraham, promising him offspring and land, and for him and Sarah to become the father and mother of many nations (Gen 15:1–21; 17:1–27). The covenant with Abraham is renewed and continues with Isaac (Gen 17:19; 26:3–5), and Jacob (28:13–15), and their descendants (e.g., Lev 26:42–45). Other covenants involve David, his son, and the Davidic kingdom (2 Sam 7:12–16; 23:5; Ps 132:11–12). In Neh 13:29 (cf. Mal 2:4–8), we find a covenant not mentioned in the Pentateuch, between God and the priesthood and the Levites. About this covenant, H.G.M. Williamson, *Ezra, Nehemiah* (Word Biblical Commentary 16; Waco: Word Books, 1985), 401, writes: "It included reverence for God, righteousness in life and speech, and a knowledge of God which the priest is then responsible for teaching to the people.

collection of texts and in later Jewish texts, is the covenant between God and Israel mediated by Moses, in which the people accept the law, the "book of the covenant," as their obligation to fulfill (Exod 24:1–11). The various covenants, however, are not talked about as replacing or contradicting each other, but rather, as being added to one another, with the Mosaic covenant at the center.[370]

The basic pattern of thought behind the notion of covenant is that God first loved the ancestors, usually but not always identified as Abraham, Isaac, and Jacob, and then made a covenant with them, promising them peoplehood and land in return for worship. Then, based on this love for the ancestors, God liberates the people from Egypt and initiates the Mosaic covenant between himself and the people. In this way, the keeping of the law becomes the response of the people to God's election—which is based on God's love rather than the people's greatness, power, or privilege (Deut 7:6–8)—as well as his liberating actions and promises, all of which preceded the giving of the law (cf., e.g., Deut 4:37–40; 6:1–9).[371] Especially Deuteronomy emphasizes that while obedience to the law within the covenant will result in blessings and a good life in abundance (e.g., Deut 7:12–8:10), disobedience will lead to disaster, punishment, and loss of land (e.g., Deut 4:25–27; 6:10–25; 8:11–20); God is both "a devouring fire, a jealous God" (Deut 4:24) and "a merciful God" (Deut 4:31).

While, for Deuteronomy as well as the prophets, anger and the resulting punishment are very real reactions of God when the people disobeys the Mosaic law and break the covenant, it is the merciful

---

This should have brought 'life and peace' to the nation." In prophetic texts such as Isaiah, the covenant between God and God's people has wider implications for the nations of the world (e.g., Isa 42:4–7; 55:3–5).

370. We see this hermeneutics of addition at play also in Paul's writings (Gal 3:17). Note that even when Jer 31:31–34 (cf. Ps 37:31) speaks of a new covenant different from the Mosaic covenant made after the liberation from Egypt, the Mosaic law is still at the center of this vision for the future; the difference is the locus of the law, which will not be stone tablets or books, but the hearts of God's people: "[T]his is the covenant that I will make with the house of Israel after those days, says the LORD: I will put my law within them, and I will write it on their hearts; and I will be their God, and they shall be my people. No longer shall they teach one another, or say to each other, 'Know the LORD,' for they shall all know me, from the least of them to the greatest, says the LORD; for I will forgive their iniquity, and remember their sin no more" (Jer 31:33–34). For discussion of the covenant in Jeremiah, see, e.g., John Bright, *Covenant and Promise*.

371. Cf. Kennedy, "Covenant Conception," 388.

nature of God that overcomes anger and opens up for new life and restoration of the broken covenant. The key, on the human side of things, for this to happen, is repentance: "In your distress, when all these things have happened to you in time to come, you will return to the LORD your God and heed him. Because the LORD your God is a merciful God, he will neither abandon you nor destroy you; he will not forget the covenant with your ancestors that he swore to them" (Deut 4:30–31; cf., e.g., Isa 1:27; Ps 7:12 [Heb 7:13]; Ezek 18:26–32; Dan 9:4–19; Sir 17:24; 21:6).[372]

But God's mercy and benevolence to his people go beyond even repentance, as the Deuteronomist explains how the people were given a land that was taken away from other nations. It is explicitly noted, repeatedly, that God's giving of the land to the people of Israel was not done as a reward for their righteousness (*tsedaka*; LXX: *dikaiosynē*), because the people were, in fact, lacking in this regard (Deut 9:6); it became their possession because of: a) the "wickedness" of the nations living there, and b) God's promise to the patriarchs, Abraham, Isaac, and Jacob (Deut 9:5). Indeed, on one occasion the people had broken the most important commandment within the covenant—that is, not to worship any other god than the God of Israel. God's response was a decision to destroy the people and create a new people based on Moses. Moses, however, even before the people had repented, refused this type of replacement paradigm and prayed for Israel until God's mercy was activated through reference, again, to Abraham, Isaac, and Jacob (Deut 9:7–10:11). *Thus, there is a distinct and consistent pattern in these texts of underserved rescue and deliverance, based on God's love for, promise to, and covenant with the patriarchs, even when the Mosaic covenant has been broken by a disobedient people.*[373] Peoplehood, which is what is referred to when

---

372. Pr Man 13 summarizes this perspective well: "For you, O Lord, are the God of those who repent." Repentance functions in the same way even beyond God's people, as shown by, e.g., Isa 19:22 and the Book of Jonah.

373. Cf. Jer 31:3: "I have loved you with an everlasting love; therefore I have continued my faithfulness to you." The same pattern is active in Paul's theology, as he addresses the question of the redemption of "all Israel" and refers to God's love for the patriarchs as the reason why God will not abandon his people even when they have rejected the Messiah (Rom 11:28–32). God's love, peoplehood, and covenant are thus key concepts retained in Paul's world of thought and they govern his theology of salvation. Paul's hermeneutical principle with regard to covenants and

the patriarchs are mentioned, is at the heart of notions of grace and mercy in the Hebrew Bible and later forms of Judaism, including the Gospel of Matthew.

While there is an aspect of vicariousness to this pattern, such a notion may be properly categorized under the rubric of grace: despite disobedience, i.e., a lack of merits or righteousness, a process of forgiveness and deliverance may be set in motion by God, based on God's mercy.[374] While God's mercy and grace may be activated independently of the sacrificial cult on the basis of God's promises to the patriarchs, the cult itself, which is part of the Mosaic covenant, represents a ritualized version of the same basic pattern. As is clear from the Psalter and the prophets, without repentance and "a broken and contrite heart," without justice in society, sacrifices will be meaningless (Ps 51:17 [Heb 51:18]; cf. Amos 5:21–24; Isa 10:1–4);[375] with repentance, the sacrificial cult provides God's people with a mechanism which makes available the atonement necessary for God's presence in the temple and among God's people, as well as for the good life in the land.

The patterns of grace and law as they are played out within the context of the covenant—meaning the covenantal setting that is created by the merging of various covenants with the all-important Mosaic covenant—are described in narratives, rulings, hymns, and prophetic oracles in the Hebrew Bible and may be summarized in the following way.[376] To the pattern of grace belongs God's election of the

their validity is explicitly stated in Gal 3:17: "My point is this: the law, which came four hundred thirty years later, does not annul a covenant previously ratified by God, so as to nullify the promise." This conviction represents one of few agreements between Paul and Matthew, although Matthew's emphasis is on Moses rather than Abraham as he lets Jesus address his own people.

374. Cf. Dan 9:18: "We do not present our supplication before you on the ground of our righteousness, but on the ground of your great mercies."

375. Cf. *m. Yoma* 8:8–9, where the importance of penitence and repentance are emphasized in order for atonement to be effective on Yom Kippur. (The sacrificial and other rituals pertaining to Yom Kippur are described in Leviticus 16.)

376. We are talking here, of course, about a generalization. While the patterns surface in most texts, not all texts deal with issues that evoke these motifs, and texts also display individual nuances and emphases. The patterns described, however, provides, as Sanders, *Paul and Palestinian Judaism*, 75, has defined it, "an account of the basic motivating forces of the religious life and of how the participants perceived the religion to function." We are not, thus, dealing with systematic theology.

patriarchs as well as the election of Israel as God's people. Also, the giving of the law is an act of grace, enabling a relationship between God and the people. In addition, we find within this pattern of grace, the motif of God's mercy and deliverance as activated even when the covenant has been broken by the people; sometimes God's deliverance is based on the people's repentance, sometimes on the prayers and supplication of a Moses or a Daniel. The pattern of law, on the other hand, requires obedience, and, when obedience fails, repentance and atonement through the sacrificial cult is still necessary. The cult functions as a bridge between and negotiates the patterns of grace and law within the covenant. To the pattern of law, further, belong punishments and rewards, based on obedience or disobedience ("works").

Grace, thus, is based on God's love and (eternal) promises, and therefore, precedes, indeed initiates, the making of covenants in general and the Mosaic covenant in particular. The pattern of grace also transcends the pattern of law in that God's mercy may be, ultimately, independently activated despite people's disobedience to the law; the covenant can be renewed and deliverance set in motion in settings where righteousness is conspicuous by its absence and divine punishment is about to be or has been implemented.[377] God's renewal of broken covenants is one of the major themes in the prophetic literature.[378] Indeed, even repentance among the nations, who were never given the law in the first place, may motivate and trigger God's mercy.[379]

The patterns of grace and law within the covenant described here as generally prevalent in the Hebrew Bible and fundamental to the workings of the Mosaic covenant as it is interpreted in different texts

---

377. Cf. John Bright, *Covenant and Promise* (Philadelphia: The Westminster press, 1976), who, commenting on Jeremiah, states: "So it is that God, who has condemned his people by the terms of his covenant, will come to them again in the wilderness of exile and will make with them a new and eternal covenant. The awful chasm between the demands of covenant by which the nation was judged, and the sure promises of God which faith could not surrender, is bridged from the side of the divine grace" (196).

378. Cf. Origen, CER 7.13, where Origen notes how Israel's sins led, repeatedly, to her being disinherited, but also that Israel repeatedly had her covenant renewed.

379. Cf. Jonah 3:5–10.

included in this diverse collection of writings are well described by the term "covenantal nomism."[380] Election and invitation to the covenant is by grace, but remaining within the covenant requires obedience to the law as well as repentance and atonement for transgressions. Atonement, according to Sanders, "implies the restoration to a pre-existing relationship, and that relationship is best called covenantal."[381] Further, as Sanders notes, while election is an important category in Tannaitic literature, "simple heredity did not ensure salvation."[382] With the exception of 4 Ezra,[383] Sanders concludes that the pattern of covenantal nomism is prevalent in all of the texts he has investigated,[384] which means that, if we accept Sanders's results, we find a basic consistency with regard to this pattern of religion from the writings of the Hebrew Bible to the early rabbis.[385]

While Sanders's interpretations of some individual texts and passages, perhaps especially the Dead Sea Scrolls with their many unresolved tensions, must be given more attention and nuance in light of recent research,[386] I remain unconvinced by the categorical critique by some scholars of his overall thesis regarding the presence of a covenantal-nomism pattern in Second-Temple Judaism.[387] It is my

---

380. For the definition of covenantal nomism, see Sanders, *Paul and Palestinian Judaism*, 75, 236.

381. Ibid., 236.

382. Ibid., 237–38.

383. Ibid., 409.

384. See the concluding discussion, with some reservations, in Sanders, *Paul and Palestinian Judaism*, 419–28.

385. While Sanders critiques George W. Buchanan, *The Consequences of the Covenant* (Leiden: Brill, 1970; see *Paul and Palestinian Judaism* 13–14), for not being detailed enough in his analysis of the Hebrew Bible and later Jewish texts, it seems clear that, with regard to Judaism and the pattern of covenantal nomism, Sanders would agree with him that this type of "religion" was maintained from earliest times to the rabbis. This impression is reinforced as Sanders summarizes his findings and quotes with approval the part of H. A. A. Kennedy's study "Covenant Conception," which establishes the importance of understanding the law within the context of the covenant in the Hebrew Bible: *Paul and Palestinian Judaism*, 419–20; the problem, Sanders notes correctly, with Kennedy's conclusions concerns later Jewish texts.

386. See, e.g., the discussion by Markus Bockmuehl, "1QS and Salvation in Qumran," in *Justification and Variegated Nomism. Vol. 1: The Complexities of Second Temple Judaism* (edited by D. A. Carson, Peter T. O'Brien, and Mark Seifrid; Tübingen: Mohr Siebeck and Grand Rapids: Baker Academic, 2001), 381–414. A critical discussion of rabbinic material is offered by Friedrich Avemarie, "Erwählung und Vergeltung: Zur Optionalen Struktur Rabbinischer Soteriologie," *NTS* 45 (1999): 108–26; cf. James D. G. Dunn, "A Response to Peter Stuhlmacher," in *Auferstehung/Resurrection: The Fourth Durham-Tübingen Research Symposium: Resurrection, Transfiguration and Exaltation in Old Testament, Ancient Judaism and Early Christianity* (edited by Friedrich Avemarie and Hermann Lichtenberger; Tübingen: Mohr Siebeck, 2001), 363–68, here esp. 366–67.

387. Cf. the recent attempt at a comprehensive refutation of Sanders's thesis leveled by Chris

contention that when we ask the question of grace and covenant in relation to Matthew's Gospel, the basic components of covenantal nomism may function as a general context within which we may understand the text as either departing from or affirming God's covenant with Israel, which in turn, will shed light on the theme of judgment according to "works." In order to address these issues in Matthew, we may take Sanders's summary of these basic components—he has eight of them—as a point of departure:

> (1) God has chosen Israel and (2) given the law. The law implies both (3) God's promise to maintain the election and (4) the requirement to obey. (5) God rewards obedience and punishes transgression. (6) The law provides for means of atonement, and atonement results in (7) maintenance or re-establishment of the covenantal relationship. (8) All those who are maintained in the covenant by obedience, atonement and God's mercy belong to the group which will be saved. An important interpretation of the first and last points is that election and ultimately salvation are considered to be by God's mercy rather than human achievement.[388]

Can such a pattern of covenantal nomism, which exists both in the texts treated as authoritative in Matthew's narrative and in texts

VanLandingham, *Judgment and Justification in Early Judaism and the Apostle Paul* (Peabody: Hendrickson, 2006). In my opinion, not only does VanLandingham fail to consider fully the interpretive frame provided by the notions of election and covenant in these texts, his treatment of the Hebrew Bible also leaves something to be desired. While I would agree with VanLandingham, contra Sanders, that "Paulinism is better described as one spoke among many on the wheel that is Judaism" (335), I would do so from a different perspective. But this is not the place for further discussion of Paul. For a more balanced point of departure for discussion of Sanders's covenantal nomism and Second-Temple Judaism, see the contributions in *Justification and Variegated Nomism. Vol. 1: The Complexities of Second Temple Judaism* (edited by D. A. Carson, Peter T. O'Brien, and Mark Seifrid; Tübingen: Mohr Siebeck and Grand Rapids: Baker Academic, 2001). While some of these studies are critical, several offers qualified support of Sanders's basic conclusions, taking discussions further based on new findings and research. See also the study by Kent L. Yinger, *Paul, Judaism, and Judgment According to Deeds* (Cambridge: Cambridge University Press, 1999), which supports the prevalence of the pattern of covenantal nomism in Judaism based on the study of the recompense motif in Second-Temple Jewish texts. Also of interest is the related discussion of Sanders's expression Common Judaism, which refers to practices and beliefs agreed upon by the priests and the people. Recently, Sanders's reconstruction has received support based on archaeological findings. See discussion in Eric M. Meyers and Mark A. Chancey, *Alexander to Constantine: Archaeology of the Land of the Bible*, vol. 3 (New Haven: Yale University Press, 2012), 47–49. On p. 138, they conclude: "Such commonality in material culture underscores the shared cultural identity held by many Jews throughout the different regions of Palestine."

388. Sanders, *Paul and Palestinian Judaism*, 422.

contemporary with the Gospel, explain the elusive notion of grace in Matthew? And how should Matt 26:28 be understood in this regard?

Let us begin with considering election, which, according to the covenantal pattern described above, is based on God's choice and does not depend on human merits or "works"; election, which is intertwined with peoplehood, precedes and leads to the making of the covenant with Israel, in which the law is given and the people's obligations outlined. We shall proceed in two steps. First, we shall look for signs in the narrative which may reveal whether, in the story world, the election of the people of Israel is presupposed, and if so, functions along the lines of covenantal nomism. Second, we shall focus on specific passages where the terms "elect"/"chosen" are used in order to understand this concept within the larger narrative frame provided by the Gospel.

Let us first state what may be an obvious point: Although the disciples receive special teaching by Jesus on several occasions,[389] the main audience addressed by Jesus in the story is the Jewish crowds.[390] Taking a bird's eyes view, the narrative is about the main character's mission to proclaim the kingdom of God in word and deed to the people of Israel and to save this people (which is his people) from their sins (1:21; 15:24; 9:35–36; cf. 10:5–6). As the proclamation of the kingdom is carried out, twelve disciples—matching the twelve tribes of Israel (19:28)—are chosen and brought in to help (4:17–22; 9:37–10:15), maintaining in the election process, a focus on peoplehood. The disciples are educated for this task, and so, have to receive special teaching, but the aim of their education is to enable them to join Jesus and assist him in achieving a common goal: saving their people, Israel (2:6; 10:5–6; 15:24). The public nature of the proclamation, evidenced by repeated summary statements to the effect that this proclamation was carried out in public synagogues,[391] as well as in specific towns

---

389. E.g., Matt 10:1–42; 16:5–28; 18:1–35; 24:1–25:46.

390. For discussion of "crowds" in Matthew's Gospel, see J. R. C. Cousland, *The Crowds in Matthew's Gospel* (Leiden: Brill, 2001). See also below, chapter 3.2.2.1.

391. Matt 4:17–25; 9:35. His disciples' continued proclamation in public space is evidenced by the fact that Jesus predicts that they will be punished in these synagogue institutions: 10:17; 23:34. Matt 12:9 may be a special case, since it is possible that Matthew aims at portraying this institutional

and villages,[392] shows that Jesus's aim was to reach Israel as a whole, as a people, rather than establishing an exclusive elite group fit for the kingdom.[393] The public nature and inclusive aim of Jesus and the twelve is also made explicit in Matt 10:23: "When they persecute you in one town, flee to the next; for truly I tell you, you will not have gone through all the towns of Israel before the Son of Man comes."

Jesus and his disciples aim, then, at proclaiming the kingdom for and saving a specific people, and there is no evidence in the text that would indicate that the idea of peoplehood has lost its value for the author.[394] This people is identified as "Israel" (2:6; 8:10; 15:24; 19:28; 27:9), and the geographical area where the drama is played out is called either the "land of Israel" (2:20, 21) or just "Israel" (9:33; 10:23; 27:42). Further, based on the fact that tithing is upheld as a necessary, all be it comparatively minor, duty for all (Matt 23:23), we may conclude that the land itself may have been understood as holy by the Matthean Jesus.[395] We may also note that the God of the narrative is called "the God of Israel" (15:31). Importantly, the ethnic and royal identity of the Messiah himself is established already in Matthew's genealogy (1:1–17), including a reference to Abraham (1:1), the forefather of the Jewish people and the person God elected and established the nation-forming covenant with, which included the promise of the land.[396] Abraham,

---

setting as a Pharisaic association synagogue, i.e., a setting which was not public and therefore did not represent the assembly of certain town. For the nature of first-century synagogues generally and those portrayed in the Gospels specifically, see Anders Runesson, *The Origins of the Synagogue: A Socio-Historical Study* (Stockholm: Almqvist & Wiksell International, 2001); idem, "The Historical Jesus, the Gospels, and First-Century Jewish Society: The Importance of the Synagogue for Understanding the New Testament," in *City Set on a Hill: Essays in Honor of James F. Strange* (edited by Daniel Warner and Donald D. Binder; Mountain Home, AR: BorderStone Press, LLC, 2014), 265–97; Lee I. Levine, *The Ancient Synagogue: The First Thousand Years* (second edition; New Haven: Yale University Press, 2005).

392. Matt 11:21–23; 13:54.

393. Jesus's aim was, in this regard, contrary to what we see in the sectarian texts among the Dead Sea Scrolls.

394. We shall return to this below, and also deal with the problem of non-Jews in Matthew more fully in Part II.

395. Tithing, first fruits and other rules pertaining to agricultural produce were restricted to the land of Israel only. The Mishnah states that the reason for this restriction is that "the land of Israel is holier than all the other lands" (*m. Kelim* 1:6). For further discussion of the land, see Anders Runesson, "Purity, Holiness, and the Kingdom of Heaven in Matthew's Narrative World," in *Purity and Holiness in Judaism and Christianity: Essays in Memory of Susan Haber* (edited by Carl Ehrlich, Anders Runesson, and Eileen Schuller; Tübingen: Mohr Siebeck, 2013), 144–80.

396. I have dealt at some length with the religio-political aspects of the infancy narrative, including

then, signals the origin of the people of Israel, and thus, also the mechanism behind its forming as a nation, i.e., God's election.[397] It is hardly possible to understand Matthew's story and focus on Israel without also acknowledging the notion of Israel's election as implied. Indeed, Jesus's proclamation and inclusive approach to the people as a whole may be understood as an expression of God's faithfulness to his election of and covenantal promises to Abraham as the kingdom is drawing near. Election is a given, and functions as the primary criterion behind Jesus's choice of audience. As we can see from how the audience is described, election is not thought of as based on merits or obedience to the law; Jesus talks to and eats with sinners and righteous alike (e.g., 9:9-13; 12:7-14), but restricts his mission to the chosen people only (Israel; 10:5-6; 15:24). In other words, no one in Israel is excluded—except for those who exclude themselves and do not repent—but those beyond the people are not addressed.

The notion of election thus explains Matthew's explicit rejection of the idea that Jesus or his disciples had a mission to fulfill beyond their own people; this distinction itself between Israel and the nations is evidence that election is an active principle in the Gospel's story world with very real consequences for how the narrative develops. This, however, does not mean that the blessings of the kingdom will not reach beyond the ethno-religious boundary established by Israel's status as the people of God, as we shall see in Part II. Suffice it to note here that the rhetorical effectiveness of passages which have sometimes been interpreted as negotiating the ethnic boundaries between the Jewish people, on the one hand, and the nations, on the

---

the focus on the land in Matthew, in Anders Runesson, "Giving Birth to Jesus in the Late First Century: Matthew as Midwife in the Context of Colonisation," in *Infancy Gospels: Stories and Identities* (edited by Claire Clivaz, Andreas Dettwiler, Luc Devilliers, and Enrico Norelli; Tübingen: Mohr Siebeck, 2011), 301-27.

397. It should be noted that Matthew's use of the figure of Abraham differs from Paul's in several ways. For Paul, Abraham is a connecting point between Jews and non-Jews, so that non-Jews may become, "in Christ," children of Abraham, a notion proving how important peoplehood still is for Paul when he addresses non-Jews (cf. Rom 4:1-25; cf. Ps 47:9 [Heb 47:10]). In Matthew, as in most other Jewish texts, Abraham is the father of the Jewish people only. In one instance, though, is the covenant with Abraham (implicitly) referred to by Matthew in a setting involving non-Jews, but the point here is not that non-Jews become heirs of Abraham as Paul has it, nor do they become the people of God; they may benefit, however, as non-Jews, from God's covenant with Abraham in such a way as to allow them salvation (Matt 25:31-46). See further chapter 7.3 below.

other, such as 8:5-13 and 15:21-28, in fact, presupposes and builds on the shared assumption that these ethnic boundaries were valid and operational. Just as many other forms of Judaism, ancient and modern, Matthew's story does not restrict salvation to the Jewish people alone.[398] It is within this primary setting of election, promise, and covenant that Matthew then, more than any other Gospel, emphasizes the law, i.e., what Sanders has referred to as the requirement for remaining within ("staying in") the covenant.

The dynamic between election and law, i.e., the key parameters of covenantal nomism, surfaces in an interesting way in the parable about the wedding feast in Matt 22:1-14.[399] On the level of pattern, the parable, which may be described as an allegory in two parts,[400] displays features typical for covenantal nomism. The "king" (i.e., God) initiates all the action, issuing a total of three invitations for his son's wedding banquet (i.e., the eschatological feast in the kingdom). The invitation is based only on God's generosity, not on human behavior ("grace"). The mechanism excluding people from participation in the banquet, however, is related only to the reaction of the people invited, i.e., their "works," which reveal them as either breaking the most fundamental of laws (bloodshed; 22:7-8), or as more generally being lawbreakers (22:11-13[401]). Invitation to salvation is, thus, by God's grace, if we may use such terms, but exclusion and condemnation are presented as self-

---

398. See Anders Runesson, "Judging Gentiles in the Gospel of Matthew: Between 'Othering' and Inclusion," in Jesus, *Matthew's Gospel and Early Christianity: Studies in Memory of Professor Graham N. Stanton* (edited by Daniel M. Gurtner, Joel Willitts, and Richard A. Burridge; London: T & T Clark, 2011), 133-51. For such notions in other forms of ancient Judaism, see the comprehensive study by Terence L. Donaldson, *Judaism and the Gentiles: Jewish Patterns of Universalism (to 135 CE)* (Waco: Baylor University Press, 2007).

399. For discussion of this parable, see Davies and Allison, *Matthew*, 2.195-208; Nolland, *Matthew*, 884-92. France, *Matthew*, 827-28, interprets the overall meaning of the text within a more traditional replacement-theological paradigm than do Davies, Allison, and Nolland. See also, Karin Hedner Zetterholm, *Jewish Interpretation of the Bible: Ancient and Contemporary* (Minneapolis: Fortress, 2012), 115-21, who reads the parable from a rabbinic comparative perspective and also addresses the issue of how the parable came to be interpreted, after the first century and in non-Jewish Christian settings, as a statement of God's rejection of the Jewish people in favor of Christians and Christianity.

400. Davies and Allison, *Matthew*, 2.197, 203-4.

401. Cf. France, *Matthew*, 827, who interprets the symbolism of the lack of wedding garment as critiquing a "faith without works." Implicitly confirming the pattern of covenantal nomism, France states that: "[e]ntry to the kingdom of heaven may be free, but to continue in it carries conditions."

imposed consequences of human behavior. This pattern confirms what can be seen consistently elsewhere in Matthew, namely, that in judgment, there is no distinction between Jesus's followers and other Jews: the same criteria apply to all, and "all" must be understood, as we have noted above, as the people of Israel.[402] In the narrative and theological logic of the story, Jesus and his followers are part of the larger in-group identified as Israel, in which we also find the crowds (i.e., the unspecified majority of the Jewish people), chief priests, elders, scribes, synagogue leaders, Herodians, Pharisees, and Sadducees. All of them are included in the covenant and the same pattern and rules apply to all, since they belong to the chosen people. This does not mean, however, that all will be saved: heredity is not enough for salvation, as also John the Baptist emphasizes when some Pharisees and Sadducees seek to be baptized by him in Matt 3:7-10.[403]

From within this general perspective and pattern, we need to proceed to ask about the dynamics of the parable on a second level, which addresses the status of the people who accepted the invitation and are in attendance as the banquet begins. This also brings us to the second task outlined above, namely, the question of the identity of "the chosen" (*hoi eklektoi*) in relation to the notion of covenant and grace. The basic problem is this: if all Israel was chosen by God, as we have argued is Matthew's conviction, and God is keeping his promises to the people, which is also clearly stated in the gospel, why is it that a specific group within this larger setting of the people of Israel is addressed as "the elect"? Is this a new covenant, which abolishes the "old" covenant, or should we think about the development of the narrative more in terms of a prophetic perspective, in which a smaller group within the larger group will be saved, based on the same covenant regulations that apply to all?

---

402. E.g., Matt 5:20; 7:21-23; 13:41-43. On "Israel" as understood in these and other contexts in Matthew, see also Bruce J. Malina, "Social-Scientific Approaches and the Gospel of Matthew," in *Methods for Matthew* (edited by Mark Allan Powell; Cambridge: Cambridge University Press, 2009), 154-193, here 190-91.

403. On these verses, see Nolland, *Matthew*, 144-45. As Nolland notes, "We ought not to think that any downgrading of the importance of Abrahamic descent is intended (cf. 1:1). What is being denied is not privilege but immunity from God's outrage at the abuse of privilege" (144). The same pattern is present in Tannaitic literature (Sanders, *Paul and Palestinian Judaism*, 237-38).

Let us consider first the identity of the "elect." The term is used in Matthew only after Jesus and his followers have entered Jerusalem. The first time it appears is in our parable, which is spoken to the chief priests and the elders, as well as to Pharisees (22:14; cf. 21:23, the Pharisees being inserted in 21:45; 22:15). Then, the term reappears in Jesus's apocalyptic discourse, which is delivered to the disciples only (24:22, 24, 31; cf. 24:3). From the context in all of these passages, it is clear that "the elect" refers to individuals who will be admitted into the kingdom, i.e., those who will be saved,[404] although not without suffering (24:22) and threats of distraction and diversion following from the activities of "false messiahs and false prophets" (24:24). If the elect, then, refers to those who are saved, we should be able to find out more about the elect from descriptions elsewhere in the Gospel of those who are saved. In 13:43, those who are saved are labeled "the righteous" (hoi dikaioi) and they are contrasted with those who will perish, who are described as "those who practice that which is against the law," or simply "lawbreakers" (tous poiountas tēn anomian). The implication is, then, that the elects' status as "righteous" depend on them keeping the law.[405]

Another characteristic that identifies people who will perish in the final judgment is that they either refuse to ask forgiveness when at fault (18:15–18; cf. 5:23–26) or refuse to forgive others when asked for forgiveness (6:14–15; 18:21–35). By implication, this means that those who are saved, i.e., those called the "elect" in chapters 22 and 24, are people within Israel who keep the law and ask for/extend forgiveness when the law has been broken. The term "elect" indicates that God has acted first—the saved have been chosen by God or his agent, the Messiah (grace)—but that people need to respond to this election in order to stay within the group of the elect/saved. The pattern of covenantal nomism is thus maintained even when we speak of those within the larger setting of the people of Israel that will be saved. This does not, however, annul the larger group's status as the people of God,

404. Note especially Matt 24:31: "And he will send out his angels with a loud trumpet call, and they will gather his *elect* from the four winds, from one end of heaven to the other."
405. Cf., e.g., Matt 5:17–18; 7:21–23.

as we have also seen earlier in the parable about the wedding banquet; everyone has received the invitation to the kingdom as the eschaton draws near.

Even those who reject the invitation are addressed by the king, based on the previous understanding that they belong within the closest circle around the ruler. In addition to the obvious social logic inherent in the description of a king's invitation to his son's wedding, Matthew indicates this previous relationship with a play on the word *kaleō*, which may mean both "call" and "invite."[406] The king's first order to his slaves in 22:3 (cf. 22:4) is, literally, "to call the called (*kalesai tous keklēmenous*)." The first invitees had thus already been invited (they are "the called ones"), but now when they are finally summoned to the (eschatological) banquet itself they refuse. Their status as "called" before their being summoned may refer to a previous period in the history of Israel, so that the king's slaves would allegorically refer to the prophets, but another interpretation seems more likely, based on specific details in the parable.

First of all, the wedding banquet is for the king's son, and the eschatological setting of this kingdom parable, which is decidedly more political in tone than Luke's related parable in Luke 14:15–24,[407] indicates that we are now being instructed about a situation when the kingdom has come in full, i.e., after the earthly life of Jesus. The "son" is certainly meant to refer to Jesus, just as in the preceding parable (21:37–39), of which theme the present parable is a continuation and extension.[408] In the parable about the vineyard, the slaves who were sent to the vineyard are surely meant to refer to the prophets, but in the parable about the wedding banquet, we are further along in narrative time. The parable about the vineyard describes what is going to happen as the son, Jesus, is killed; the parable about the wedding banquet tells the story about what is happening after Jesus's resurrection at the point when the kingdom is about to be fully realized. The identification of Jesus as the son in our parable is further

---

406. Cf. the use of the word by Paul in Rom 1:1; 6–7; 8:28; 1 Cor 1:1.
407. So also, Nolland, *Matthew*, 885.
408. Nolland, *Matthew*, 884.

supported by the fact that Jesus refers to himself as the bridegroom in Matt 9:15 as well as in the parable of the young women waiting for the bridegroom in 25:1–13. Indeed, the latter parable describes the same context as the parable about the wedding banquet; we are told about how events will unfold at the time of the full realization of eschatological kingdom, at Jesus's return.

If the "son" in 22:2, then, refers to Jesus himself, it follows that the slaves who are sent out by the king should be understood as the followers of Jesus who proclaim the coming of the kingdom after his death. These people are described elsewhere in Matthew as "prophets, sages, and scribes" and it is stated that they will suffer and be killed as a consequence of their proclamation (23:34; cf. 10:16–25). The audience receiving this proclamation is clearly primarily the Jewish people, since punishment will be meted out in "synagogues" (10:17; 23:34), although we also find a reference to "governors and kings" that may refer to non-Jewish persecution of messianically oriented Jews (10:18); we shall return to the latter in Part II. The locations for the proclamation are also primarily identified, before 28:18–20, as "the towns of Israel" (10:23), and it is stated in the same verse that it shall remain so until "the Son of Man comes," i.e., before, as our parable in 22:1–14 would describe it, the wedding banquet is to take place. This means that Matt 28:18–20 does not *replace* the disciples' mission to their own people with a new mission to non-Jews only. Rather, a mission to non-Jews, which had previously, before the resurrection, been explicitly rejected (10:5–6; 15:24), is now, after Jesus has been given all power on earth as well as in heaven (28:18), *added* to a continuing effort to save Israel.[409]

This narrative pattern fits well with the focus on "the crowds" in Matthew's gospel as Jesus's and his disciples' main audience. If we

---

409. This is so despite the fact that the *panta ta ethnē* of Matt 28:19 refers to non-Jews only; the Jewish people are not counted among "the nations," the latter representing a separate category in contradistinction to the people of God in a worldview which divides humanity into two basic categories. On the continued relevance for Matthew of a mission to the Jewish people, focused on "the crowds" (i.e., the majority), see also Terence L. Donaldson, *Jesus on the Mountain: A Study on Matthean Theology* (Sheffield: JSOT, 1985), 205–9. As Donaldson notes, the notion that Israel has been replaced by the 'church,' so that Israel is no longer a relevant category with which to engage in mission, is not present in Matthew.

return to our parable, it seems clear that the third invitation (*kaleō*) allegorically refers precisely to the crowds, among which are found "both good and bad" (22:10). This invitation comes after the king had sent out his soldiers to kill the prominent invitees who refused to come and to burn their city, the Matthean Jesus certainly referring to Jerusalem and its leaders (22:7).[410] Divine judgment turns social expectations up-side-down: the first shall be the last and the last shall be the first, and this goes for everyone who claims any type of power position, even within the movement around Jesus himself (19:30; 20:16; 23:8–12; cf. 20:20–28). God's faithfulness in the covenant relationship with his people is thus maintained, although the outcome of judgment, which is based on peoples' response to God's saving initiative—that leaders are shown to be sinners and those who were perceived as sinners heed the call and will enter the eschatological kingdom (cf. 21:28–31)—is surprising.

The pattern of covenantal nomism is reinforced as the parable ends with a second allegory. The scene is now the wedding banquet itself, and the hall is filled with guests. One of the guests is found not wearing a wedding robe, and, as a consequence of this, is thrown out "into the outer darkness" (22:13). As we have argued above,[411] clothing is most likely to be understood as a metaphor for a person's deeds.[412] The idea that is conveyed is thus that while all are invited, "both good and bad," i.e., without consideration of peoples' (previous) obedience or "works" ("getting in" by grace, in Sanders's terminology), only those who respond with proper action will be allowed to remain at the wedding feast ("staying in" through obedience). Those called "elect" in 22:14 are thus those who display a combination of accepting God's invitation and responding with proper obedience.[413] The covenantal

---

410. So most interpreters; see especially Nolland, *Matthew*, 887–88. This is further emphasized by the story about the two sons in Matt 21:28–32, which Jesus tells to the chief priests and the elders of the people in the temple, as a interpretive "preamble" to the following parables about the tenants in the vineyard (21:33–46) and the wedding banquet (22:1–14). There, Jesus tells the leaders of the temple that "[t]ruly I tell you, the tax collectors and the prostitutes are going into the kingdom of God ahead of you" (21:31).

411. See pp. 171–72.

412. As, e.g., in Rev 19:8; cf. 3:4–5; 16:15.

413. Matthew's use of the term "elect" (*eklektos*) should thus not be understood along the lines of

pattern is clear: salvation is God's initiative and doing, and the aim is all-inclusive ("many are called"), but condemnation cannot be blamed on divine will, only on human attitudes and actions ("few are chosen").[414] In terms of the covenantal pattern, thus, the two parts of the parable are connected and build on the same theology of salvation and judgment.[415] As in other judgment texts in Matthew, there are none among those whom God will save who have not also kept the commandments and repented as well as asked for and extended forgiveness when failing to adhere to the strict standard of the gospel, summarized in the greatest commandments of them all: "'You shall love the Lord your God with all your heart, and with all your soul, and with all your mind.' This is the greatest and first commandment. And a second is like it: 'You shall love your neighbor as yourself'" (22:37–39).[416]

The covenantal pattern as we see it in other Jewish texts is, thus, present also in Matthew's Gospel, and the concept of "grace" follows with it in the form of an invitation to life in the kingdom directed to members of the covenant, regardless of their righteousness or lack thereof, as well as forgiveness when humans repent and forgive others. The question that remains to clarify, then, is *which* covenant it is that permeates the worldview of the narrative.

In the Hebrew Bible and in other Jewish texts that deal with the problem of forgiveness and atonement within a covenant setting, the temple fills a crucial role for the functioning of the Mosaic covenant. Without the temple cult, there would be no means of atonement and

---

some later Christian interpretations suggesting that people are predestined to either salvation or condemnation. Rather, we see both divine and human factors involved in these processes.

414. For discussion of how "works" are conceptualized in Matthew, see above, chapter 2.7.

415. Nolland, *Matthew*, 890, understands the relationship between the two parts of the parable as problematic, suggesting that the person with no wedding robe arrived separately from the group called in Matt 22:9–10. But this ignores the specific comment in verse 10, that both good (*agathos*) and evil (*ponēros*) were invited. From the perspective of divine judgment, while all are invited no person who is found evil will be allowed into the eschatological kingdom (Matt 13:49; note that the same word is used in Matt 5:37 to designate the devil: "the evil one"; cf. 6:13; 13:19; 18:32–35). Thus, while a parable certainly may hold tensions, the theology of covenantal nomism generates the unity here that keeps the two parts of the parable together.

416. On keeping the law in relation to judgment/salvation, see Matt 5:20; 7:21–23; 13:41–43. On repentance in relation to judgment/salvation, see, e.g, Matt 11:20–24. On forgiveness as related to judgment/salvation, see Matt 6:14–15; 18:15–17; 21–35.

the sins of the people would generate guilt that would eventually lead to disaster. In other words, without the temple, the delicate balance in the Mosaic covenant between grace and law would break down, since keeping the law includes atoning for sins committed. Interestingly, in Matthew's story, we see a development from a setting when the temple still stands (e.g., 5:23–24; 23:16–22) to a (predicted) situation when it has been destroyed (e.g., 23:38; 24:1–2; cf. 22:7). How does this development affect the status of the covenant in the narrative? For the sake of clarity, we shall repeat here some of the conclusions previously drawn.

First of all, it should be noted that the covenantal pattern we have outlined above belongs within the theo-ritual logic of the Mosaic covenant, which is indicated not least by the Matthean Jesus's emphasis on the validity of the (Mosaic) law.[417] Indeed, the positive role of the temple in 5:23–24 and 23:16–22 affirms the importance of the temple within the covenantal worldview of the narrative.[418] As is indicated by 5:23–24, the altar needs to be protected from moral impurity, but the leaders—and here, as is typical for Matthew's Jesus, it is primarily the Pharisees and the scribes associated with them who are blamed—defile the temple through heinous crimes, including bloodshed (23:29–35), which will lead to the temple's destruction (23:38–24:2). This is, in fact, part of the core message of the Gospel as a whole, so that chapters 23 and 24 carry key explanatory force with regard to Jesus's ultimate mission as the Messiah, "for he will save his people from their sins" (1:21). As I have argued elsewhere,[419]

---

417. See discussion above, chapter 2.1.2.

418. On the importance of the temple for Matthew, see Daniel M. Gurtner, *The Torn Veil: Matthew's Exposition of the Death of Jesus* (Cambridge: Cambridge University Press, 2007), especially 98–126; idem. "Matthew's Theology of the Temple and the 'Parting of the Ways': Christian Origins and the First Gospel," in *Built on the Rock: Studies in the Gospel of Matthew* (edited by Daniel M. Gurtner and John Nolland; Grand Rapids: Eerdmans, 2008), 128–53. William R. Telford, *The Barren Temple and the Withered Tree: A Redaction-Critical Analysis of the Cursing of the Fig-Tree Pericope in Mark's Gospel and Its Relation to the Cleansing of the Temple Tradition* (Sheffield: JSOT Press, 1982), and Davies and Allison, *Matthew* 3.143, come to similar conclusions, emphasizing that the destruction of the temple in Matthew is a catastrophe in the evangelists eyes; it is described not as God's judgment of the temple as such, but of (corrupt) leaders abusing their privilege.

419. Anders Runesson, "Purity, Holiness, and the Kingdom of Heaven in Matthew's Narrative World," in *Purity and Holiness in Judaism and Christianity: Essays in Memory of Susan Haber* (edited by Carl Ehrlich, Anders Runesson and Eileen Schuller; Tübingen: Mohr Siebeck, 2013), 144–80.

the problem in Matthew's story is not that people, and especially, the Pharisees, keep the law, but that they do not keep it strictly enough (e.g., 5:20; 23:23). This lack of obedience to the law is, with regard to the people (the "crowds"), a result of the lack of guidance that leaders should have provided, but which they have neglected (e.g., 9:36–38) despite the fact that they have access to the Torah (23:2-3).[420] The purpose of the law is, ultimately, to enable God's presence in the midst of the people; holiness[421] is required of the people, and this, in turn, requires obedience and continual repentance and atonement for sins committed, as per the stipulations of the Mosaic covenant.

For Matthew, it is clear that the grave sins of the leaders must lead to the destruction of the temple, and this is precisely why Jesus must die, since without the temple, the people will be destroyed as a consequence of these unatoned sins. Contrary to what many scholars have assumed,[422] the temple will thus not be destroyed because of Jesus's execution (which is ultimately blamed on the chief priests and the elders[423]). The theological logic of Matthew goes in the opposite direction: Jesus must die because the temple will be destroyed. If Matthew's story as a whole is read from this perspective, the relationship between law and grace, the emphasis on the judgment theme, and the place of the covenant as the implied conceptual setting within which Jesus's actions and death make sense falls into place, creating a coherent ritual and theological picture. In brief, since the temple's destruction—an act of divine judgment—is predicted, this would lead to the breakdown of the Mosaic covenant, since the mechanism of atonement would be lost. In such a situation, one would expect that a Messiah whose task has been declared to be to save

---

420. Note here that these verses confirm explicitly what is also said elsewhere, namely, that the authoritative law in Matthew's narrative world is the law of Moses. Cf. Matt 15:3–9.

421. Matthew's Jesus interprets the requirement of holiness, which is found in, e.g., Lev 19:2 ("You shall be holy, for I the LORD your God am holy"), as 'perfection' ("Be perfect, therefore, as your heavenly Father is perfect."). Cf. Luke 6:36 ("Be merciful, just as your Father is merciful").

422. Cf. discussion in Overman, *Church and Community*, 381–84.

423. The Pharisees and the scribes associated with them are blamed for the temple's destruction, but they disappear in the passion story; Jesus's death is thus blamed primarily on the leaders of the temple, the chief priests and the elders. Cf. Gurtner, "Theology of the Temple," 153, who concludes that, "the destruction is necessitated [...] because of the unrepentance of the Jewish leaders." See also further Runesson, "Purity, Holiness, and the Kingdom of Heaven."

his people from their sins would, in one way or another, provide a substitute for this mechanism. This is also precisely what we see in 26:26–28.

We have already dealt with this passage in some detail above and shall not repeat those arguments here.[424] The aspect to be focused on here is, rather, what this passage implies in terms of the theme of covenant in Matthew's story. It is quite clear that the Matthean Jesus refers to sacrificial rituals as he links his own (predicted) death with the covenant. It is noteworthy that Matthew does not say, as Paul and Luke do,[425] that this is a *new* covenant, but rather that this his blood is the "blood of the covenant" (26:8; *to haima mou tēs diathēkes*), alluding to the making of the Mosaic covenant in Exod 34:1–11. This blood, it is stated in the same verse, "is poured out for many for the forgiveness of sins." If we consider the fact that Matthew confirms and emphasizes that the law, i.e., one of the main parts of the Mosaic covenant, is and will remain valid "until heaven and earth pass away" (5:18), the other key component of the covenant, the mechanism of atonement, is here restored after God had abandoned the temple (23:38) in anticipation of its destruction (24:2). What we see in Matthew is thus the restoration of the Mosaic covenant, which is the only setting in which the law and its demands may be balanced by God's mercy and grace, if repentance is at hand. One of the key questions that Matthew's Gospel aims to answer is, thus: "As the world as we know it is coming to an end, how will the Jewish people survive the loss of the temple?" The answer given is, summarized and paraphrased: "In the midst of the suffering that will precede the full realization of the kingdom, Israel will be saved through adherence to the Messiah, who has given the right teaching of the law and has restored the covenant, which had been broken by the leaders of the people, through his atoning sacrifice."

Adherence to the Messiah means keeping the law as he has interpreted it; such obedience has both an individual and a collective dimension to it, which necessitates community formation of some sort.

---

424. See above, chapter 2.4.
425. 1 Cor 11:25; Luke 22:20.

But if this is the human part of the covenant equation, how would it be possible for God to remain among the people—which is part of the covenant promise[426]—when the holy temple, guarded by rules designed to keep the space free from impurity,[427] thereby making it fit as the locus for the divine presence (23:21), is gone (23:38; 24:2)? The fact that Matthew treats these issues more systematically than any of the other Gospels indicates to us that these were questions of vital importance to the storyteller and his intended audience. A brief discussion will show that, just as the rabbis felt a need to affirm and explain God's presence beyond the temple, referring to Israel's experience of exile,[428] Matthew's story provides precisely such covenantal affirmation of God's continued presence in the midst of the community, but partly based on other theo-ritual parameters, more akin to the exclusion mechanisms found in the sectarian texts among the Dead Sea Scrolls.

First, the narrative begins and ends with the explicit reassurance that God will remain among his people through his agent, the Messiah.[429] In 1:23, divine revelation comes to Joseph through an angel's voice in a dream, revealing that the son to be born shall be named Immanuel, which is explained to mean "God with us." This comes after the statement that Jesus will "save his people from their sins" (1:21). As will later be clarified, the removal of sin is essential for the presence of the risen Messiah in the community. Then, in the very last verse of the narrative, Jesus tells his disciples: "remember, I am with you always, to the end of the age" (28:20). Matthew's story of the Messiah is thus book-ended by two paradigmatic statements that God will be, through his Messiah, present among the people.[430]

---

426. E.g., Lev 26:11–12; cf. Jer 7:7; Hos 11:9; Zeph 3:15–17; Zech 2:10 [Heb 2:14].
427. On the issue of purity in relation to the temple, see Jonathan Klawans, *Purity, sacrifice, and the Temple: Symbolism and Supersessionism in the Study of Ancient Judaism* (Oxford: Oxford University Press, 2006).
428. Cf. *b. Meg.* 29a: "Wherever they went in exile, the Shechinah [i.e., God's presence] went with them."
429. For discussion, see D. D. Kupp, *Matthew's Emmanuel: Divine Presence and God's People in the First Gospel* (Cambridge: Cambridge University Press, 1996).
430. One may note that Matthew, just as Mark, lacks the ascension story that Luke – Acts adds (Luke 24:50–51; Acts 1:9–11), and there is no specified Johannine helper (a "Spirit of truth") to be sent instead of Jesus, informing the disciples about true knowledge (John 16:12–15). While Matthew does include a reference to the Spirit of the disciples' "Father," which will support with the right words the persecuted disciples when they must appear in court, Matthew's Gospel construes

Interestingly, in the discourse given just before Jesus begins his journey to Jerusalem,[431] in which the key rules of the community (the *ekklēsia*) that he has laid the foundations for in Galilee are presented, Jesus's presence is again emphasized as it is stated that wherever two or three are gathered in his name, i.e., whenever his followers gather in assemblies dedicated to some form of worship, he will be present (18:20). But in this setting, there is a new element introduced, which is of some importance for our understanding of the Messiah and God's presence in Matthew's Gospel.

While in the story, Jesus constantly teaches among and socializes with what the gospel defines as "sinners," noting to Pharisees and others that he has come specifically to call sinners and not the "righteous," since the latter do not need a "physician," (Matt 9:9–13), this seems to change after his resurrection, when he has been given "all authority in heaven and on earth" (Matt 28:18). In 18:15–20, we are informed about how the *ekklēsia* needs to think about behavior in relation to its membership in the future, the implication being that this applies to the community's life after Jesus's resurrection.[432] The interpretive frame for this pericope is God's care for lost sheep (19:12–14); just as it is the will of the heavenly father that not a single of the "little ones" should get lost, the members of the *ekklēsia* must make sure to admonish repeatedly someone who strays from accepted behavior in order for that person to repent. If no repentance is at hand, after three attempts at reconciliation, the sinning person must be excluded from the community ("let such a one be to you as a gentile and a tax collector"; 18:17). Similarly, Jesus instructs Peter that the

---

divine presence on earth in the time period between the resurrection and the *parousia* in a way different from the latter two Gospels, focusing on the person of Jesus himself. I am grateful to Rebecca Runesson for discussion of this aspect of Matthew in comparative perspective.

431. Chapter 19 introduces the second, post-Galilean phase of Jesus's activities among his people. Although large crowds are still following him (e.g., 19:2; 20:29; 21:8; cf. 21:46), resistance to Jesus increases drastically as he enters Jerusalem, the holy city.

432. Jesus has already, in Matt 16:18–19, announced the building of his *ekklēsia* in the future tense (*oikodomēsō*), with Peter as its future leader with authority to bind and loose (this authority is given to the disciples as a group in Matt 18:18). In Matthew's story, none of this applies to the time before Jesus's death and resurrection.

victim of an injustice must accept a repentant perpetrator and extend forgiveness when asked (18:21–35).

The result of such teaching and the presence of exclusion mechanisms focused on refusal to repent and reconcile with the victim of one's actions is a community in which sin has become powerless; sin—and its consequence, guilt—is, in effect, constantly evaporating as soon as it comes into being.[433] The behavior of asking and extending forgiveness mirrors God's forgiving of all who repent,[434] which, after God's abandonment of the temple, rests entirely on the atoning sacrificial act of the Messiah whose blood "is poured out for many for the forgiveness of sins" (26:28). This mechanism of atonement belongs within the setting of the *ekklēsia*, which postdates Jesus's death and resurrection.[435] Since, in Matthew, sin is defiling ("moral impurity"; 15:18–20), the dynamic of a persistent sharing of forgiveness can be likened with a continuous process of purification. The community itself thus becomes a "space" which is pure, and therefore, acceptable to the presence of a being who shares with God the divine attribute of absolute power in heaven and on earth (cf. 28:18). It is in this setting that the risen Jesus has chosen to be present when two or more community members are assembled.

This theo-ritual logic that applies to the future *ekklēsia* is related to Matthean concerns about moral impurity in relation to the temple, which was the abode of God's presence (23:21) before it was abandoned due to bloodshed and other defiling heinous crimes (23:29–36, 38; 24:2). We see this in 5:23–24, a passage we have discussed above, when Jesus

---

433. It is of some interest to compare this pattern of thought with another first-century Christ-follower's thinking on sin and law. In 1 Cor 15:55–57, Paul writes, "'Where, O death, is your victory? Where, O death, is your sting?' The sting of death is sin, and the power of sin is the law. But thanks be to God, who gives us the victory through our Lord Jesus Christ." Without the sacrifice of the Messiah (what Paul refers to as the "victory through our Lord Jesus Christ"), with the temple regarded as abandoned by God, even Matthew would agree that the law would condemn the people and lead to its destruction, since there would be no mechanism of atonement that those who repented could make use of (so that, as Paul would say, "the power of sin is the law").

434. Cf. e.g., Matt 6:14–15. See also above, section 2.4.

435. Cf. Bruce W. Longenecker, "Rome's Victory and God's Honour: The Jerusalem Temple and the Spirit of God in Lukan Theology," in *The Holy Spirit and Christian Origins: Essays in Honor of James D.G. Dunn* (edited by Graham N. Stanton, Bruce W. Longenecker, and Stephen C. Barton; Grand Rapids: Eerdmans, 2004), 90–102, here 94–95.

advises a person who is about to offer a sacrifice, but remembers that he or she has committed an injustice to someone else, not to enter the temple space until reconciliation has been achieved with the victim of the wrong-doing; then, but not before, the person may return to sacred space and seek communion with God through sacrifice. After his resurrection, Jesus thus seems to have acquired a status akin to the status of the divine, so that his presence is made possible in the assembly when the assembly consists of people who keep the law and engage in a continuous process of reciprocal forgiveness.

While Kupp has argued that with the loss of the temple, the presence of the divine moved to the Matthean community,[436] it is not immediately evident from Matthew's narrative that we find an identification of the Messiah with God, so that the God of Israel and the Messiah are now one and the same.[437] At the very least, it seems clear that Matthew makes a distinction between the pre- and post-resurrection Jesus, so that divine attributes such as absolute power (28:18) apply only to the latter period. As such, however, Matthew's risen Jesus is presented as something more than the angels, whose exclusive presence was claimed by another community, namely that at Qumran, which also carefully guarded the purity of the community through the application of exclusion mechanisms.[438] In any case, it

---

436. Kupp, *Matthew's Emmanuel.*
437. Passages such as Matt 19:17 and 24:36, which refer to the pre-risen existence of the Messiah, at least guards against generalizations of such suggestions. Statements describing Jesus as "embodying" the God of Israel are, consequently, in need of some qualification (cf. Jeannine K. Brown, "Matthew, Gospel of," in *Dictionary of Jesus and the Gospels: A Compendium of Contemporary Biblical Scholarship* [2nd ed; edited by Joel B. Green; Downers Grove: Intervarsity press, 2013], 570–84, here 581).
438. Cf. 1QS 11:7–8; 1QHa 11:21–22, 14:13; see Klawans, *Purity, Sacrifice and the Temple*, 166–67. Klawans emphasizes that there is no evidence in the scrolls for a belief in the divine itself as present in the community. He writes: "It is certainly reasonable to assume that the sectarians believed that the divine presence had already departed from the ritually and morally defiled temple in Jerusalem; presumably they would not have shunned a temple in which the divine presence still resided. But even if God's glory is no longer at the temple, this hardly means that the divine presence now dwells with them at Qumran. Here, too, we find that scholars assume an equivalence between the Qumran community and the temple that is well beyond what is claimed in the Qumran texts themselves." If Timothy R. Carmody, "Matt 18:15–17 in Relation to Three Texts from Qumran Literature (CD 9:2–8, 16–22; 1QS 5:26–6:1)," in *To Touch the Text: Biblical and Related Studies in Honor of Joseph A. Fitzmyer, S.J.* (edited by Maurya P. Horgan and Paul J. Kobelski; New York: Crossroad, 1989), 141–58, is right, the author of Matthew may have had access to the Essene legal code and even written Matt 18:15–17 with the aim of refuting their view of law. While Matthean claims that the risen Jesus's status is such that it must be reckoned to be above even the angels may add to

is clear that Matthew's Gospel presents the Matthean *ekklēsia* as the unique locus of the presence of God's risen Messiah, and that this presence in itself fulfills God's covenantal promises to dwell among his people.

It is thus clear that while Matthew, like Tannaitic literature,[439] does not frequently use the word "covenant," the concept is implied throughout the story and explains much of its teaching on law and judgment, as well as clarifies the otherwise elusive concept of grace.[440] To use one of Ed Sanders's formulations as he describes the rabbinic covenantal conception, for Matthew, too: "[a]tonement implies the restoration to a preexisting relationship, and that relationship is best called covenantal."[441] For Matthew, this is the key meaning of Jesus's sacrifice, since Jesus's blood is said to be "the blood of the covenant," which will atone for the sins of many (26:28). As Jesus's disciples drink from this cup of atoning covenant blood, the relationship to the God of Israel is restored and they are, as Nolland describes the making of the covenant in Exodus 24 when the blood is shared between the altar and the people, "aligned with the holiness of God, and with solemn commitment on both sides."[442] Just as the people heard and accepted the Mosaic law before the making of the covenant with God (Exod 24:3, 7), the disciples have been instructed in Jesus's interpretation of the same law throughout the story before they share the blood of the Messiah. This blood renews and restores the covenant, and makes possible God's continued relationship with the people in the time

---

such an observation, it is beyond the scope of the present study to discuss this further. For the meaning of the 'greater than' expressions in Matthew (Matt 12:6; cf. 26:61; 27:51), which relate that which happens around Jesus to the temple, see discussion above, chapter 2.6.2.

439. See, e.g., Sanders, *Paul and Palestinian Judaism*, 236–37, 420–21.

440. We may also note here with Sanders, *Paul and Palestinian Judaism*, that the frequent mention of the covenant in the sectarian texts among the Dead Sea Scrolls is best explained as a result of the sectarians' need to redefine the covenant and their own special requirements for staying within it. Matthew's Judaism seems to be closer to the heart of what we may call complex common Judaism than the Qumran community is. The notion of complex common Judaism was suggested by Stuart Miller as a further development of the work of E. P. Sanders; see Stuart S. Miller, *Sages and Commoners in Late Antique 'Erez Israel: A Philological Inquiry into Local Traditions in Talmud Yerushalmi* (Tübingen: Mohr Siebeck, 2006), 25–28, and literature referred to there. Cf. Oskar Skarsaune, *In the Shadow if the Temple: Jewish Influences on Early Christianity* (Downers Grove: Intervarsity Press, 2002), 103–29.

441. Sanders, *Paul and Palestinian Judaism*, 236.

442. Nolland, *Matthew*, 1079.

between the divine abandonment of the Jerusalem temple (23:38) and the eschatological final judgment when the kingdom will be established in full (24:31; cf. 13:43).

This overall (eschatological) perspective, in which the covenant plays a key role for how Matthew is telling the story of the Messiah, also explains why the judgment theme has been outlined the way it has in this Gospel. It is precisely because the Mosaic law has remaining validity beyond the death and resurrection of Jesus, "until all is accomplished" (5:18), i.e., until the kingdom has come in full after the "passing away of heaven and earth," the time when the world is "reborn" (19:28),[443] that God's judgment will continue to be exercised and punishment will befall all who do not obey the law and engage in reciprocal forgiveness of other members of the (renewed) covenant. This means that divine judgment in Matthew is not only related to the final eschatological judgment, as is sometimes thought, but also to the period between God's abandonment of the temple and the full realization of the kingdom. This would not have been possible without the renewal of the covenant, since without the covenant and its mechanism of atonement and forgiveness, the people would perish as a result of divine condemnation.

While the focus in Matthew is surely on the eschatological judgment, as David Sim has insisted,[444] the Gospel is also concerned with judgment that occurs on the basis of how the law is or is not obeyed before this happens. Jesus's teaching of the law, both the "extreme" examples of "light" and "heavy" commandments (5:19; 23:23) and commandments that concern everyday life (15:3–6; cf. 15:19), are thus to be understood as taught based on the assumption that breaking them will lead to punishment, although Matthew tends more generally to postpone the outcome of such judgment until the final judgment and in world to

---

443. Variants of this interpretation of a time limit for the validity of the law until the eschatological kingdom comes in full (rather than understanding the reference to say that the law will always remain) has been the prevailing interpretation of the later church, as pointed out by Luz, *Matthew*, 1. 218. Luz regards such an interpretation unlikely. However, if the full realization of the kingdom involves a return to Eden, i.e., to a re-creation of the world, as Matt 25:34 may indicate (cf. Matt 19:28), then there will be no need for the law since all will live in the presence of God and all breakers of law will have been removed (13:41–43).

444. Sim, *Apocalyptic Eschatology*.

come. If we think of rabbinic literature as aiming at addressing the question of how the people should be true to the covenant, how the covenant obligations should be fulfilled,[445] then the Matthean Jesus's aim could be paraphrased in a similar way, but adding the, for Matthew, vitally important eschatological aspect, the central conviction behind and in the text: "How can the people be true to the covenant and fulfill the covenant obligations *as God judges its leaders, abandons the temple, and is about to bring the world to its end and initiate the final judgment?*" Matthew's solution is that God has sent the Messiah, who will teach the right interpretation of the law, which must be observed, and who will also sacrifice himself in order to save his people from their sins as the temple is being abandoned. This is done so that God can remain true to his covenant promises even when the people (through the negligence of its leaders, especially the Pharisees, who are the primary law-breakers in this text) have failed to live according to the standards of the covenant.

If we return to Sanders's pattern of covenantal nomism, listed above in eight points,[446] and compare these points with what we have found in Matthew, the picture that emerges is one of a shared Jewish (theo-ritual) thought pattern. Matching the eight characteristics of covenantal nomism with specific examples from Matthew will provide a convenient summary of the discussion:[447] **[1]** God has chosen Israel (1:1, 21; 10:5–6; 15:24, 31) and **[2]** given the law (5:17–18; 7:12; 19:17; 22:34–39). The law implies both **[3]** God's promise to maintain the election (1:21, 23; 2:6; 3:9;[448] 9:12–13; 24:31) and **[4]** the requirement to

---

445. So Sanders, *Paul and Palestinian Judaism*, 421.
446. See above, p. 179.
447. The examples from Matthew are not exhaustive. Also, some of the passages referred to provide indirect but clear evidence of the characteristic mentioned in Sanders's list, although most passages explicitly address the issue mentioned. As an example of indirect evidence, passages in Matthew that speaks (approvingly) of the people of Israel in contradistinction to all other nations, or of the God of the narrative as the God of Israel, are taken as pointing to a conviction that this people is the people chosen by the God of Israel (election); the mention of Abraham, the ancestor of the Jewish people and the first to be chosen and receive God's promises, functions narratively in the same way as an indicator of the chosenness of Israel, especially in a setting in which the history of Israel is traced from the beginning of peoplehood to the present in the form of a genealogy (Matt 1:1–17).
448. Note that this passage takes as point of departure the validity of the Abrahamic covenant, through which the people of Israel came into being; what is claimed by the Matthean John here is not

obey (3:8–9; 5:20, 48; 7:21–25; 12:50; 13:23; 23:23–28). **[5]** God rewards obedience and punishes transgression (5:6, 19, 20; 6:1, 18, 33; 12:36–37; 13:41–42; 15:3–9, 13–14; 19:17, 29; 23:33, 35–36; 24:12–13). **[6]** The law provides for the means of atonement (5:23–24; cf. 23:17–21; 26:28), and atonement results in **[7]** maintenance or re-establishment of the covenantal relationship (26:28). **[8]** All those who are maintained in the covenant by obedience, atonement, and God's mercy belong to the group which will be saved (13:43, 49; 19:7, 26, 29; 24:12–13, 22, 31; 25:21).

These individual passages and their interpretation have been discussed above over the course of Part I of the present study. Regarding the various characteristics that identify the pattern of covenantal nomism in Second-Temple Judaism, Sanders has noted that "[n]ot every single document studied contains every one of the motifs just listed."[449] He mentions 1 Enoch as an example of a "defective" text and notes that,

> even in the various parts of 1 Enoch one can see enough to justify the assumption that the elements which are not mentioned are presupposed. Thus one can note the requirement of obedience and infer that something must have been given to be obeyed, even though the giving of the law is not rehearsed. Similarly, we may note the existence of the theme that the righteous receive mercy while the wicked are punished strictly for their deeds. This again seems to imply the view that election and salvation as such are not by works of law, although obedience is the condition of remaining righteous.[450]

This is similar to the situation we find in Matthew's Gospel, which contains a variant of each of these characteristics of covenantal nomism. Among the various motifs, we may note especially Matthew's careful avoidance of understanding salvation as a reward for works performed.[451] Whereas Mark and Luke seem to speak of eternal life as

that the covenant or peoplehood is abolished, but that: a) non-Jews can enter (as proselytes) into the lineage of Abraham (i.e., become Jews), and b) that those within the covenant will also be the object of judgment. The proselyte theme is then (actively) dropped until Matt 28:18–20, while the theme of all being subject to divine judgment, including Jesus's disciples (cf. Matt 7:21–23) is repeated throughout the narrative. Matt 3:9 is thus, contrary to many commentators, in fact evidence of God upholding the covenant.

449. Sanders, *Paul and Palestinian Judaism*, 423.
450. Ibid.
451. See also discussion below, chapter 7.3, pp. 420–25.

a reward for obedience,[452] Matthew is cautious to distinguish between rewards for works performed (which he does insist will be delivered), on the one hand, and the process of being given "eternal life," on the other, the latter being spoken of as an "inheritance," not a reward (19:29). As we have discussed above and will return to below in relation to Matt 25:31–46, "inheritance" signals a family relationship[453] as the basis for sharing in the world to come. As with any inheritance, it does not depend primarily on merits, but functions on a different logic of benefitting from the work or initiatives of others without having produced such works oneself, although, of course, there is always the possibility of being disinherited if a person has committed some sort of major insult or atrocity offending the person behind the inheritance.

Matthew's logic of covenant functions in much the same way. The covenant provides the basis for the relationship, within which the members will inherit the kingdom if they have not committed atrocities and broken the law, in which case they will be disinherited. This is emphasized by the Matthean Jesus as he threatens the chief priests, elders, and the Pharisees with the catastrophe of being disinherited in the parable of the Tenants of the Vineyard (21:23, 38, 43, 45).[454] But just as Jesus tells the chief priests, elders, and Pharisees in Jerusalem that "the kingdom of God will be taken away from you and given to a people[455] that produces the fruits of the kingdom" (21:43), he is promising the meek (praus) among the Galilean crowds that they will "inherit" the land[456] (5:5). The use of the inheritance metaphor in these

---

452. Mark 10:29–30; Luke 18:29–30. Both Mark and Luke mentions explicitly that rewards will be paid in this world and then lists eternal life as the reward in addition to these rewards in the present world.

453. Cf. Matt 12:50; 25:40; 28:10.

454. For a historical reading of this parable in its different forms, see John S. Kloppenborg, *The Tenants in the Vineyard: Ideology, Economics, and Agrarian Conflict in Jewish Palestine* (Tübingen: Mohr Siebeck, 2006). Matthew's version of the parable is treated on pages 174–201.

455. On the meaning of *ethnos* in this verse, see p. 50n26.

456. As Nolland, *Matthew*, 212–13, notes, the two interpretive options for translating *gē* here is "land" (cf. Matt 5:5), or "earth" (cf. Matt 5:18). While Nolland suggest "earth" (cf. NRSV) based on the parallel with "world" that follows in Matt 5:14, it seems to me that the parallelism is of an escalating nature, mirroring the larger pattern of the Gospel as a whole; it describes a focus on the people and the land that becomes expanded to include the world and all nations in 28:18–20. In other words, the crowds and the disciples listening to Jesus in the Sermon on the Mount have responsibilities to meet with regard to their own people and the land, which they will inherit (Matt 5:5), as well as to the wider world, which they will eventually be told to make aware of the

settings of eschatological fulfillment suggests not only a pro-Galilean, anti-Judean[457] bias, but also that Matthew's vision of the kingdom has both concrete geographical-political (land) and what we would call "supernatural" (eternal life) aspects to it. What interests us here, however, is the pattern of salvation through belonging, on the one hand, and condemnation based on atrocities committed high-handedly, on the other. This pattern surfaces when Matthew uses the "inheritance" metaphor in eschatological settings relating to salvation, and supports an overall understanding of Matthew's pattern of religion as an example of Second-Temple Jewish covenantal nomism.[458] Interestingly, Matthew maintains the same metaphor when dealing with the salvation of non-Jews in 25:34; we shall therefore return to discuss this text in some detail in Part II.[459]

In sum, as we look closer at the covenant-related theological dynamics of Matthew's Gospel, the narrative emerges as a variant on a Jewish theme, rather than as something that breaks with or goes beyond the phenomena we call ancient Judaism.[460] It would,

universal power and authority of the Messiah. This global rule, however, does not inhibit or make void Israel as a geographic religio-political entity. Further considerations that speak in favor of this translation include the narrative-geographical fact that when Jesus delivers the Sermon on the Mount, he is in the land that he has previously defined as being "the land of Israel" (2:21, 22). The genealogy, too, is (religio-politically) structured with a focus on the land of Israel, since it is explicitly using the exile as a basic dividing point between epochs (1:17).

457. The anti-Judean character of Matthew is also evident in the Gospel's use of *Ioudaioi* in 28:15, as argued by R. T. France, *Matthew*, ad loc. See below, p. 294n206. For full discussion of Matthew's relationship to Jerusalem and Judea, see Runesson, "City of God?".

458. It is interesting to note recent analyses of other texts in the New Testament, as expressing similar forms of "restored covenant" theology. See, e.g., Birger Olsson, "Johannine Christians—Members of a Renewed Covenant? Jewish Christian Identity According to the Johannine Letters," in *The Making of Christianity: Conflicts, Contacts, and Constructions* (edited by Magnus Zetterholm and Samuel Byrskog; Winona Lake: Eisenbrauns, 2012), 174–203. Taking his point of departure in the notion of a restored covenant in other Jewish texts (pp. 179–85), Olsson concludes that the central themes of 1 John come together in and are best explained as growing from underlying traditions of a renewed covenant. Indeed, such ideas about renewed covenant "provides the concept that best holds the entire letter together. [...] Johannine Christians saw themselves as Jews, in fact as *true* Jews" (203). While Matthew takes a different approach, to be sure, a similar conclusion may be drawn for the First Gospel and the followers of Jesus as they are depicted in this narrative world.

459. See chapter 7.3.

460. A similar general conclusion, from various perspectives and based on different investigative foci, has been reached by several other scholars, e.g., Saldarini, *Christian-Jewish Community*; Sim *Apocalyptic Eschatology*; Joel Willitts, *Matthew's Messianic Shepherd King: In Search of 'the Lost Sheep of the House of Israel'* (Berlin: De Guryter, 2007); Daniel M. Gurtner, "Matthew's Theology of the Temple and the 'Parting of the Ways': Christian Origins and the First Gospel," in *Built on the Rock: Studies in the Gospel of Matthew* (edited by Daniel M. Gurtner and John Nolland; Grand Rapids: Eerdmans, 2008), 128–53; Wayne Baxter, *Israel's Only Shepherd: Matthew's Shepherd Motif and His*

consequently, be misleading to call this text a "Christian" text, as is so common in the academy. Such a designation is based on the *reception* of Matthew outside Judaism in the later religion we know as Christianity; Christianity today, in its mainstream forms, is best described as a phenomenon related to but distinct from Judaism. If we aim at a historical understanding of Matthew's Gospel, however, focusing on its inception history,[461] we should take seriously the fact that: a) Christianity as such did not exist as a designation in the first century, when Matthew was authored, and, b) that the pattern of thought evident in the text is, in some key respects, foreign to the thought patterns of later forms of Christianity, as these begin to appear in the second century onwards.[462] Thus, speaking of Matthew's Gospel as a "Christian text" may be as misleading in terms of the nature of the text as it would be to call Isaiah or Ezekiel "Christian texts,'" simply because they are included in a later Christian collection of (sacred) texts. This, of course, in no way invalidates Christian use of any of these texts for specifically Christian purposes, since such concerns are not of a historical, but of a theological and hermeneutical nature, the legitimacy of which cannot be decided through historical analysis alone.[463]

Now, if the Mosaic covenant is what Matthew's Jesus is restoring in order to save his people, and that, as a consequence, the law can now function within a ritual system providing for atonement and forgiveness of sins, what are the limits of salvation, as these are outlined in relation to Jewish characters and collectivities in the

---

Social Setting (London: T&T Clark, 2012); Wolfgang Reinbold, "Das Matthäusevangelium, die Pharisäer und die Torah," *Biblische Zeitschrift* 50:1 (2006), 51–73. Frederick J. Murphy, "The Jewishness of Matthew: Another Look," in *When Judaism and Christianity Began: Essays in memory of Anthony J. Saldarini* (edited by Alan J. Avery Peck, Daniel Harrington, and Jacob Neusner; Leiden: Brill, 2004), 377–403. See also, Matthias Konradt, *Israel, Kirche und die Völker im Matthäusevangelium* (Tübingen: Mohr Siebeck, 2007), who rightly argues that Matthew understands Israel's status as God's people to be permanent and not replaced by the *ekklēsia*.

461. On this term, see above, p. xvi.
462. On problems associated with the use of the terms "Christianity" and 'Christian' in the study of first-century forms of Christ-belief and its adherents, see Anders Runesson, "The Question of Terminology: The Architecture of Contemporary Discussions on Paul," in *Paul Within Judaism: Restoring the First-Century Context to the Apostle* (edited by Mark Nanos and Magnus Zetterholm; Minneapolis: Fortress, 2015), 53–77.
463. For discussion of issues such as these, see the Preface.

narrative? Several scholars have understood Matthew along the lines of Ignatius's and later church fathers' perspective on the relationship between Christianity and Judaism, i.e., that Matthew should be seen as distinct from Judaism.[464] With such claims have followed assertions that the Jewish people as a category have been disinherited and replaced by "the church."[465] The above discussion, however, has problematized generalizing distinctions between two entities, usually talked about as "Judaism" or "the synagogue" or "Israel," on the one hand, and "Jesus followers" or the "church" or "Christians," on the other. Matthew's narrative is more complex and does not conform to such constructions of separate monolithic ("religious") identities.[466]

Rather, as Matthew has Jesus address *his own people*, we need to ask whether he proclaims (the risk of) condemnation and punishment only to individuals or collectivities, or both. Chapter two has been focused

---

464. See Ign., *Magn.* 10.1–3.

465. See, e.g., Kenneth W. Clark, "The Gentile Bias in Matthew" *JBL* 66 (1947): 165–72 ("[T]he assurance that the gentiles have displaced the Jews is the basic message and the gentile bias of Matthew." p. 172). The same conclusion is drawn by Rolf Walker, *Die Heilsgeschichte im ersten Evangelium* (Göttingen: Vandenhoeck & Ruprecht, 1967), e.g., p. 122; cf. Wolfgang Trilling, *Das Wahre Israel: Studien zur Theologie des Matthäus-Evangeliums* (3rd edition; Munich: Köseln-Verlag, 1964), who argues that "die 'Kirche des Matthäus'" is the equivalent to "das *wahre Israel*," and that this "true Israel" replaces the "ungläubige Judentum" (emphasis original; 212–3). See also Meier, *Matthew* ("The death-resurrection marks the end of Israel as the people of God and the founding of the church as the new people of God." p. 343); Michael J. Cook, "Interpreting 'Pro-Jewish' Passages in Matthew," *Hebrew Union College Annual* 54:1 (1983), 135–46; Richard E. Menninger, *Israel and the Church in the Gospel of Matthew* (New York: Peter Lang, 1994); Marguerat, *Jugement.* Jack Dean Kingsbury, *Matthew as Story* (2nd ed.; Philadelphia: Fortress Press, 1988), speaks of Matthew's ties with "contemporary Judaism" as "severed" (p. 160). According to Kingsbury Matthew's longest section, Matt 4:17–16:20, aims at describing "Israel's repudiation of Jesus" as their response to Jesus's ministry (p. 161), a response that displays a contrast between "the disciples" and "Israel" (p. 162). "Israel," Kingsbury concludes, "desires the death of Jesus" and, as a consequence, loses its privilege as "God's chosen people" (p. 162). Paul Foster, *Community, Law and Mission in Matthew's Gospel* (Tübingen: Mohr Siebeck, 2004), understands the Matthean experience as being *extra-muros* and defines that as the Private being outside the 'synagogue,' moving away from 'Judaism.' Douglas R. A. Hare, "How Jewish is the Gospel of Matthew?" *CBQ* 62:2 (2000): 264–77, presents a somewhat ambivalent conclusion, as he argues against the work of Anthony Saldarini, Andrew Overman, and Amy-Jill Levine. While he claims that the so-called "parting of the ways" has already occurred, he notes that this parting is between "Matthean Jews and non-Christian Jews" (p. 276). On the next page, however, Hare speaks of "Matthean Christians" and claims that all scholars should be able to agree that "Jesus has replaced Torah as the key to a right relationship with the God of Israel," apparently misunderstanding the argument that describes the Matthean Jesus not as "replacing" the law in this regard, but as giving the right interpretation of the law, so that it can be fulfilled the way the God of Israel intended it to be from the very beginning. Hare does confirm, though, that "the conceptual world of Matthew is primarily Jewish" (p. 264).

466. Contra, e.g., Sjef van Tilborg, *The Jewish Leaders in Matthew* (Leiden: Brill, 1972), who claims that in Matthew, "[t]he separation between Judaism and Christianity is definitive" (p. 26).

on understanding the criteria of judgment, and we have contextualized these criteria within the concept of the (Mosaic) covenant, which provides the foundational pattern of grace underlying the narrative. Now, as we have a clearer sense of *why* people will be judged and *how* they can be saved, shifting the emphasis and directing our attention to *who* is being judged will allow us to achieve a fuller understanding of the way in which Matthew conceives of the mission of Jesus to his own people. Who are the condemned and who are the saved *within* the Jewish people, as Matthew conjures up the sound of inevitability, the echo of the fast approaching judgment? What is, in other words, the range of the covenant in the world constructed by Matthew's narrative? Whom, more precisely, will it protect?

3

The Limits of Salvation: Jewish Groups and the Judgment of God

As we noted in the Introduction, for Matthew, the basic distinction between groups of people is religio-ethnic in nature, i.e., the line is drawn between Israel and other nations.[1] Matthew's focus is clearly primarily on the Jewish people, although non-Jews also receive their share of judgment-oriented discourse. Putting the situation of the non-Jews on hold for the moment, however, and keeping our focus on Israel, we find that the Jewish people are themselves split into different groups in Matthew's text. We hear of Pharisees, Sadducees, and Herodians, of chief priests, scribes, and elders. Closer to Jesus, we also find John's disciples, the Jewish crowds, as well as Jesus's own disciples, the core of the (future) *ekklēsia*. At times, Jesus also speaks of "this generation" as a collective designation, and "Israel" is mentioned as an all-encompassing entity, referring to all Jews, regardless of any subdivisions.

---

1. For the role played by ethnicity in Matthew's Gospel, see also Anders Runesson, "The Impact of Ethnicity on Salvation in Matthew's Gospel" (in preparation).

Until now, we have discussed the when and why of divine judgment in Matthew, and argued that as these questions are addressed and analyzed, the common Jewish thought pattern of covenantal nomism emerges, which also explains the otherwise elusive aspects of mercy and grace. For the Matthean Jesus, divine judgment affects all Jews, regardless of the groups to which they belong and across related identities, including Jesus's own followers, on an individual level as these individuals belong within the larger entity of the people of Israel. The question I want to ask in this chapter is whether the story also points to any of the Jewish collectivities mentioned in the text as targeted more specifically for punishment/condemnation or reward/salvation.[2]

The task under this heading is thus not to further analyze whether different Jewish groups are judged according to different criteria—they are not: all criteria apply to all Jews within the Mosaic covenant, which is renewed in 26:26–29. Rather, what interests us here is whether, when the Matthean Jesus speaks of judgment, he does so addressing specific groups—some more than others—and if so, how such patterns may be interpreted. Before we take a closer look at divine judgment in relation to such specific groups, we shall say a few words on how Matthew is structuring the narrative world of his Gospel, based on what we know about first-century Jewish society and its institutions. This will then help us to see more clearly which groups, if any, are targeted and what that might imply, based on the nature of these groups.

This question is of some importance, not least since so many scholars in the past have argued that Israel (sometimes identified as "the synagogue") as a whole entity is judged, rejected, and replaced by "the church" in Matthew's Gospel,[3] a conclusion which is at odds with both the thought pattern and the terminology used in the Gospel. In

---

2. We have already dealt with the judgment of specific Galilean towns (Chorazin, Bethsaida, Capernaum; Matt 11:20–24) above and will not repeat that discussion here, although some comments will be necessary. These towns are accused of rejecting Jesus but, as towns, they do not represent a specific social class or occupation, nor a unified teaching or stance on certain matters regarding law as the Jewish groups mentioned here do (cf. Matt 13:57–58). The city of Jerusalem, as the capital of the land, functions in a slightly different way compared to the identified Galilean towns. We shall therefore include some discussion of this city below.

3. For examples of such studies, see p. 204n465 above.

brief, this section will apply the findings of the study so far to specific collectivities mentioned in the narrative in order to see whether any particular patterns emerge, and, if so, what conclusions may be drawn from such patterns, based on the nature of the respective group.

3.1 Collectivities Structuring the World of the Narrative

While it has been common in Matthean studies to speak of the people of Israel as a whole as rejected and condemned, a more recent development in research rather identifies the leaders of the people as the real perpetrators of evil, and therefore, as the ones targeted for divine condemnation. This latter approach is certainly more to the point and marks an important shift in the history of research on the First Gospel. However, while it is certainly true that leading figures, rather than the people ("the crowds"), are targeted, it seems that the narrative attempts to be even more specific with regard to who is singled out for condemnation and why. For example, Sjef Van Tilborg's much quoted study on the Jewish leaders in Matthew suggests a perspective in which different leaders are generalized into one group and analyzed as such.[4] While this attention to greater detail (i.e., distinguishing the leaders from the people at large) is a welcome development of Matthean studies, van Tilborg still confuses the role of the crowds, which he in fact understands as very positive, with the condemnation of the leaders, so that, in the end, "Israel" and the Jewish people are thought to be condemned as a whole.[5] As we shall

---

4. Sjef van Tilborg, *The Jewish Leaders in Matthew* (Leiden Brill, 1972), 6: "It seems evident that Mt did not wish to create any distinction between the various groups [...] In view of the interchangeability of one group for the other, all texts must be put together if one wishes to get some idea of what Mt wishes to make clear to his readers about the representatives of Israel." See also Jack Dean Kingsbury, *Matthew as Story* (2nd ed.; Philadelphia: Fortress, 1988), 115–27, who concludes that "[a]lthough they go by many names—Pharisees, Sadducees, chief priests, elders, scribes, and Herodians—they form a united front against Jesus and hence can be treated...as a single character" (115). This unified "character," he continues, is "flat" and not "round." Cf. Janice Capel Anderson, *Matthew's Narrative Web: Over, and Over, and Over Again* (Sheffield: Sheffield Academic Press, 1994), 97–126; David R. Bauer, The *Structure of Matthew's Gospel: A Study in Literary Design* (Sheffield: Almond Press, 1989), 69. See also, Andrew Overman, *Matthew's Gospel and Formative Judaism* (Minneapolis: Fortress, 1990), 142, who understands all Jewish leadership summed up in the phrase "the scribes and the Pharisees," and David Sim's cautious critique of such a perspective in *Christian Judaism*, 119.

5. van Tilborg, *Jewish leaders*, 166, 170–72.

see, when we distinguish between various Jewish collectivities in
Matthew, such conclusions become difficult to maintain.

If we look at the characters in the narrative in terms of the
collectivities that are represented, we may categorize them in several
ways. On a first level, it is helpful to focus on the institutional setting
with which groups are related. Doing so, it becomes clear that groups
and representatives of groups in Matthew are aligned with two major
aspects of Jewish society: a) public (civic) Jewish institutions, and b)
voluntary associations (association synagogues).[6] The former involves
the Jerusalem temple (5:23–24; 23:16–21), public synagogues (4:23; 6:2),
and local Jewish councils (10:17[7]). Historically, in these public religio-
political settings, we find, primarily, chief priests/the high priest (cf.
2:4; 10:18; 26:3), ordinary priests (8:4; 12:5), elders (16:21; 26:47),[8] and
scribes (7:29; 8:19; 17:10; 26:57).[9] References in Matthew to Jewish

6. For the definition of public and association synagogues, see Anders Runesson, *The Origins of the Synagogue: A Socio-Historical Study* (Stockholm: Almqvist & Wiksell International, 2001); idem, "The Historical Jesus, the Gospels, and First-Century Jewish Society: The Importance of the Synagogue for Understanding the New Testament," in *A City Set on a Hill: Essays in Honor of James F. Strange* (edited by Daniel Warner and Donald D. Binder; Mountain Home, AR: BorderStone Press, LLC, 2014), 265–97.

7. *Synedrion* does not have here the technical meaning which it attracted in later rabbinic literature (cf. *m. Sanh.* 1:6), but rather refers to local (Jewish) courts of justice; see Luz, *Matthew*, 2. 88–89. Such courts were located within the public synagogue institutions. On the synagogue and its function in this regard, see, e.g., Donald D. Binder, *Into the Temple Courts: The Place of the Synagogue in the Second Temple period* (Atlanta: Society of Biblical Literature, 1999), 445–49. Binder concludes that if "the Temple courts served as the central civic center for the Jewish nation, the synagogues could thus function in this manner on a local scale" (449).

8. The elders in Matthew are associated with Jerusalem and the temple (i.e., national administration), and not with local public synagogue institutions elsewhere in the land. For a discussion of the elders in ancient Israel and Early Judaism, see R. Alastair Campbell, *The Elders: Seniority Within Earliest Christianity* (Edinburgh: T & T Clark, 1994), 20–66. Campbell concludes that elders, while politically influential, were not holders of a formal office; they "exercise an authority that is informal, representative and collective" (65). "For most Jewish people in our period," he argues, "it was a term more commonly associated with what we would call the 'civic' community." Such use of the term "elders" matches what we see in Matthew's narrative. In this Gospel, the elders are mentioned together with the chief priests, and sometimes, also with the scribes, but never as being together with the Pharisees. Some Pharisees from Jerusalem, however, are said to sympathize with the traditions of the elders in Matt 15:1–2.

9. With regard to public institutions, scribes are associated both with the Jerusalem temple and with local synagogue institutions (on "village scribes", cf., e.g., Josephus, *BJ* 1.479). They are also associated with non-official groups, such as the Pharisees (23:2) and Jesus's followers (13:52); for the latter, see further below. For a recent discussion of the scribal offices, see Chris Keith, *Jesus' Literacy: Scribal Culture and the Teacher from Galilee* (London: T&T Clark, 2011), chapter 3. See also idem, *Jesus against the Scribal Elite: The Origins of the Conflict* (Grand Rapids: Bake Academic, 2014). Cf. Elias J. Bickerman, *The Jews in the Greek Age* (Cambridge, MA; Harvard University Press, 1988), 161–76; Anthony J. Saldarini, *Pharisees, Scribes, and Sadducees in Palestinian Society: A Sociological Approach* (Grand Rapids: Eerdmans, 2001).

individuals representing political structures and power are limited to the Herodian family: Herod I (2:3), Antipas (14:5), and Philip (14:3).[10] On the other hand, the non-public, or semi-public aspects of Jewish society involve groups such as the Sadducees (22:23), the Herodians (22:16), the Pharisees (9:11; 12:2; 19:3; 22:34), John's disciples (9:14), and Jesus's disciples/the "little ones"/the future *ekklēsia* (10:1; 18:10, 15–20).[11]

While these two aspects of Jewish society, the public and the voluntary, are fundamentally different in nature, the former groups and officials having direct political influence and the latter having only indirect influence on the public sphere, some associations were more closely aligned with political leadership than others. For example, the Sadducees and the Herodians were considerably closer to those having official political or administrative functions than John's disciples.[12] One

10. The reference to "governors and kings" in Matt 10:18 may be understood as indicating the involvement of non-Jews in the persecution of Jesus's followers, although "kings" may have been meant as a reference to Antipas (so Luz, *Matthew*, 2.89). Most commentators would argue that, taken together, 10:17 refers to Jewish institutions and 10:18 to non-Jewish officials (who will be concerned with maintaining law and order for the purpose of ensuring the uninterrupted collection of taxes etc.). This does not necessitate the interpretation, however, that the Matthean Jesus is here speaking of a future worldwide mission of Jesus's disciples to non-Jews (which would contradict 10:5–6; cf. 10:23. As Davies and Allison, *Matthew*, 2.184, notes, the scene may very well be intended to describe the situation in the land, in which non-Jews had many representatives. Cf. W.F. Albright and C.S. Mann, *Matthew: Introduction, Translation, and Notes* (New York: Doubleday, 1971), 124–25; Nolland, *Matthew*, 424. To this, we should add that while "governor" (*hēgemōn*) may refer to non-Jewish political leaders representing Roman interests in the land, we also know of Jewish rulers, local *archontes*, who governed towns and cities (Josephus, *AJ* 4.214; *Vita* 79). Such rulers were active on the national level, where they engaged in legislative and judicial matters of the nation, but the "same pattern played itself out on a local level in Palestine. [...] The Galilean city of Tiberias...was governed by a single *archōn*, who, along with ten principal councilors (*prōtoi*), led a *boulē* or city council of 600 (*Vita* 69, 134, 168, 271, 278, 294, 296; *BJ* 2.639)" (Binder, *Into the Temple Courts*, 346). The public synagogues functioned as the institutional setting for these rulers, as Josephus shows. Interestingly, Matt 9:18 refers to a certain *archōn* who seeks Jesus's help; the parallel in Mark 5:22 has the man's title as *archisynagōgos*, and Luke 8:41 clarifies Matthew's account by adding *archōn tēs synagōgēs*. Doubtless, Matthew intended to say that the man in question was a ruler of a synagogue, i.e., had administrative functions relating to the town in which he lived. When we understand the institution of the public synagogue and its officials in this way, it may seem a small step to use the term "governor" for local Jewish rulers. If this is what Matthew intends, the focus of Matt 10:17–18 is not only on the land, but also on the Jewish rulers of the land. For a similar use of the term *hēgemōn* in Matthew, see Matt 2:6. While seven out of 10 occurrences of *hēgemōn* refer to Pontius Pilate, i.e., a non-Jewish ruler, the word itself lacks a technical sense that would require a specific interpretation or a certain political role (cf. the examples listed in *LSJ*, ad loc).

11. On Jewish groups and their history, see discussion in Albert I. Baumgarten, *The Flourishing of Jewish Sects in the Maccabean Era: An Interpretation* (Leiden: Brill, 1997).

12. Regarding the Sadducees, see the discussion of Anthony Saldarini, *Pharisees, Scribes, and Sadducees in Palestinian Society* (Grand Rapids: Eerdmans, 2001), including the foreword by James C. VanderKam (xi–xxv). See also, John P. Meier, *A Marginal Jew: Rethinking the Historical Jesus, vol. 3: Companions and Competitors* (New York: Doubleday, 2001), 389–487. As to the Herodians, there

should also note, however, that in Matthew, both Pharisees and Jesus's disciples are described as either having influenced, or being in the process of trying to influence, scribes.[13] This means that, in the world of the narrative, both of these groups aim at moving into the public (religio-)political sphere, and the method used to accomplish this is the persuasion of the town and village administrators described as teachers (cf. 7:29; 23:2–3). Indeed, the Matthean Jesus himself is presented as a teacher of the people active in synagogues (4:23; 9:35; 13:54) as well as in the Jerusalem temple (26:55). Jesus is, in the story, thus using public political space on both local and national levels to proclaim his message, which means that he is portrayed as challenging not these institutions as such, but those who run them. The public-political aim of Jesus and his followers is also clearly expressed in 19:28, which essentially describes the twelve as taking over, albeit in an eschatological setting, judicial functions relating to the people of Israel as a whole (the twelve tribes), i.e., on a national scale.

The fact that the Matthean Jesus is not challenging the structure of Jewish society itself is important to note. The various councils and synagogues are used as platforms for his proclamation, and their status and function is, in fact, explicitly acknowledged on several occasions, such as the judicial function of the Sanhedrin (5:22). Even more clearly, and in Matthew alone, Jesus speaks of "the chair of Moses" as a fixed institution related to Torah and teaching (and thus, implicitly to the public synagogues, and therefore, also to the scribal office) in such manner that he even urges the crowds to listen to what his own enemies are saying since they hold authority in this setting (23:2–3).

is not much evidence that will help us to define more clearly who the members of this group were and what their aims were. That there was such a group, however loosely defined, seems clear. For discussion, see Meier, *Marginal Jew*, 560–65, and John P. Meier, "The Historical Jesus and the Historical Herodians," *JBL* 119 (2000): 740–46. (For a brief critique of Meier, see Jonathan Marshall, *Jesus, Patrons, and Benefactors: Roman Palestine and the Gospel of Luke* [Tübingen: Mohr Siebeck, 2009], 189–91). See also Peter Richardson, *Herod: King of the Jews and Friend of the Romans* (Columbia: University of South Carolina Press, 1996), 259–60. Richardson argues convincingly that "Herodians" refers to an "active group coalescing around Herod and the Herodian family," and as such that it had specific political aims (260).

13. Matthew's Gospel is often pairing "the Pharisees" with "the scribes," indicating the former's success in such public settings (e.g., 12:38; 23:13). Matt 8:19; 13:52 indicate that the Matthean Jesus, competing with Pharisees, wants to sway scribes to join his movement.

The Matthean world is thus describing as legitimate the institutional structure of Jewish society, even as the temple is being defiled, and therefore, by necessity, is en route toward its destruction.[14] The narrative portrays Jesus's and his disciples' attempt at moving from the margins—indeed bringing those who inhabit the margins with them—into the public sphere of society, where authority and power resides. We are also told that they will eventually succeed, since God's final judgment will provide the necessary religio-political shift enabling the last to be the first (21:31), the small to be the great (18:4), and the servants/slaves to become servant-leaders (20:26-27; 23:11-12). Matthew's targeted condemnation thus seems not to be directed against public institutions and power *per se*, but against how power is exercised in these institutions; he is against what is being taught (7:29) and against innocent people being judged (12:7).

These two aspects of Jewish society, the political institutions and their officials, on the one hand, and, on the other hand, the non-political groups aiming at influencing the public sphere, are reflected in Matthean references to the history of Israel. Public and political aspects of society are, historically, represented by authorities such as Moses (8:4; 17:3-4; 19:8; 23:2), David (1:1), and Solomon (1:6), all of whom are regarded as legitimate and great, although the Messiah and what happens around him—the kingdom of heaven—are greater than all of them (12:42; 22:41-46). Those not holding political offices are represented by the prophets, either as general references (5:12) or as named individuals (Elijah, Isaiah, Jeremiah, Jonah). As for the prophets, they all aimed at influencing public Jewish society and decision-making.[15] Interestingly, Matthew's Jesus does not mention or elaborate on any of the unrighteous rulers in Israel, despite the fact that he does state that prophets were persecuted and killed (5:12; 23:30-31). We shall return to this below as we discuss how judgment is applied

---

14. Statements regarding the temple's future destruction due to its current defilement are in fact implicit recognition of its status as the legitimate abode of the divine.
15. In one case, Jonah, we find an Israelite aiming at transforming the behavior and worship of non-Jews (Matt 12:41).

to groups narratively contemporary with the Matthean Jesus and his disciples.

While Matthew's story is preoccupied to a large degree with these political and non-political groups aiming at influencing public Jewish society, the narrative world is larger than these groups, which brings us to a second level of categorization of Matthean collectivities. On this level, we should distinguish between: a) the larger entities of a political-geographic nature, and b) collectivities which inhabit these entities.

As to the former, the most important of these entities is Israel. "Israel" refers in Matthew either to the land itself (including Judea, Galilee, and other areas mentioned below; 2:20, 21; 8:10; 9:33; 10:23),[16] or to the people of Israel (2:6; 10:6; 15:24; 19:28); in 27:42, we find a reference to both land and people in the expression "king of Israel." The land of Israel is also referred to simply as "the land" in 5:5 (cf.

---

16. In Matt 4:24 the narrator states that "his fame spread throughout *all Syria* (ἀπῆλθεν ἡ ἀκοὴ αὐτοῦ εἰς ὅλην τὴν Συρίαν)." The use of "Syria" here likely refers to the (non-Jewish) area north and northeast of the land, as it does in the Mishnah, as Davies and Allison, *Matthew*, 1.417, have argued (contra France, *Matthew*, 151). This does not mean, however, that Jesus is portrayed as proclaiming his message there; Matthew insists several times that Jesus and his disciples confined their mission to Israel only (10:6; 15:25). The mention of Jesus's fame in non-Jewish territory, however, echoes the magi's knowledge of Jesus in the infancy narrative (2:1–12) and foreshadows the actions of some individual non-Jews who will later approach Jesus and ask him for help (8:5–13; 15:21–28). On the centripetal force around Jesus as he proclaims his message among his own people, cf. Charles H. Talbert, *Matthew* (Grand Rapids: Baker Academic, 2010), 74. With regard to the story of the Canaanite woman in Matt 15:21–28, Jesus is said to have withdrawn to the area of Tyre and Sidon, i.e., Phoenicia (15:21). No intention is stated on the part of Jesus that he did so in order to interact with non-Jews. As he is there, however he is approached by the woman, who must have heard about his extraordinary powers and now asks him for help. The question is whether Matthew intended this area to be understood as part of Biblical Israel or not. While the area in an extended sense may be considered to have been part of Israel (cf. Luz, *Matthew*, 2.338–39; see also discussion in Terence Donaldson, *Jesus on the Mountain: A Study on Matthean Theology* [Sheffield: JSOT, 1985], 132), if the geographical reference is taken in the more narrow sense, the area was not traditionally part of Israel. (Note, however, that it is unclear exactly where the boundaries were located; see Nils Peter Lemche, *The Canaanites and Their Land: The Tradition of the Canaanites* [JSOT Supplement Series 110; Sheffield: Sheffield Academic Press, 1991].) The area does belong, however, to Ezekiel's vision of the restored land, which relocates the twelve tribes in ways different from the claims in Joshua 13–19 (Ezek 47:13–48:35; cf. Anson F. Rainey and R. Steven Notley, *The Sacred Bridge: Carta's Atlas of the Biblical World* [Jerusalem: Carta, 2006] 269. Based on Matthew's insistence on Jesus and his disciples remaining in the land, it seems reasonable to read this story to mean that, just as in Matt 8:28–34, Jesus is portrayed as visiting areas which he understands as part of what will be the restored Israel. His interaction with non-Jews in these areas only shows how they will have to adapt to the rule of the Messiah. As for the Canaanite woman, she reacts in a way considered appropriate by the narrator, addressing Jesus as Son of David and acknowledging her subordinate status in relation to the Jewish king.

5:13; 10:34; 27:45).[17] The geographic-political entity of Israel is then subdivided into Judea (2:1, 5, 6, 22; 3:1; 4:25; 19:1; 24:16) and Galilee (2:22; 3:13; 4:15, 23, 25; 17:22; 19:1; 21:11; 26:32; 27:55; 28:7, 10, 16), with further areas mentioned, which Matthew understands as part of the land of Israel: the "territory of Zebulon and Naphtali" (4:13–15), the Decapolis (4:25),[18] "the land of the Gadarenes" (*hē chōra tōn Gadarēnōn*; 8:28),[19] "beyond the Jordan" (referring to Perea, ruled by Antipas; 4:25; 19:1).

Regarding the collectivities inhabiting these geographic and religio-politically defined areas, we hear of *Ioudaioi* in the sense of all Jews (2:2; 27:11, 29, 37),[20] as well as in the sense of the inhabitants of Judea (28:15).[21] While Galileans as a group are not explicitly referred to, Jesus is identified as a person who, while originally coming from Judea, is active primarily in Galilee where he is said to have grown up (26:69), and Galilean dialect is noted in relation to Peter in 26:73. Importantly, within both of these geographical-political areas, we find frequent mention of what Matthew calls "the crowds" (*hoi ochloi*). This word refers to people who do not belong to any specific political or non-political group, i.e., it refers to the majority of Jews in any given place.[22] While *hoi ochloi* only refers to crowds, and never to the people of Israel as a whole, *ho laos* can refer to both crowds and the people of Israel.[23] In

17. Cf. Ps 37:11 [LXX 36:11], where *'eretz*/*gē* also refers to the land, not the earth as a whole ("the meek shall inherit the land"). See discussion above, pp. 29n93 and 201–2n456. Regarding the other passages listed, translating *gē* "land" rather than "earth" makes better sense of Matthew's narrative focus on the Jewish people and the development of the story. For example, Matt 5:13 is situated within the logic of destruction that will be unleashed if the law is not followed; the people will be trampled underfoot (by the Romans). Matt 10:34, which is set within a pericope dealing with the land (10:5–6), may, in turn, be understood as referring to the apocalyptic disasters that will soon plague the land.
18. Matthew's understanding of this area as part of biblical Israel is also noted by Nolland, *Matthew*, 185.
19. This area lies within the larger Decapolis area.
20. France, *Matthew*, 68, 1051. Regarding the expression "King of the Jews" (27:11, 29, 37) as referring to Jews generally, cf. Matt 27:42 where chief priests, scribes and elders use "king of Israel," which suggests that this is how the narrator understands *Ioudaioi* when that word is used in relation to Jesus's royal status (contra Bruce J. Malina and Richard L. Rohrbaugh, *Social Science Commentary on the Synoptic Gospels* (2nd ed.; Minneapolis: Fortress, 2003), 136–37, who prefer to translate "king of the Judeans").
21. France, *Matthew*, 1106, rightly argues that in this verse (and in this verse only), the narrator restricts the meaning of *Ioudaioi* to inhabitants of the geographical area called Judea. See below, p. 294n206.
22. Matthew's Gospel contains 50 references to *ho ochlos/hoi ochloi*.

addition to these collectivities, Matthew's Jesus also speaks about "this generation" on several occasions.[24] Finally, the Matthean Jesus refers to specific Jewish cities and their inhabitants as collectivities that are treated in a generalized way as they respond to Jesus: Chorazin, Bethsaida, Capernaum, Nazareth, and Jerusalem.[25] We also find general references to towns (9:35; 10:11; 14:13) and villages (9:35; 10:11; 14:15) in Galilee.[26]

Other collectivities in Matthew refer to spiritual beings, such as angels loyal to the God of Israel (26:53) and to the devil, respectively (25:41; cf. "demons" in 7:22, and "unclean spirits" in 10:1; 12:43).[27] If we now look at how these groups are targeted or not in terms of divine judgment, a pattern soon emerges, which is of importance as we seek to understand Matthew's story from a first-century Jewish horizon.

3.2 The Politics of Divine Wrath: Condemning the Powerful and Saving the Oppressed

As we shall see in this section, different groups are held responsible for different types of sins. Most importantly, while some passages may lead the reader to think that those who will be considered for salvation are few (e.g., 22:14; 24:12–13), Matthew's Jesus is quite clear that he is aiming at saving the many, and, in fact, singles out for condemnation only a few. In the following, we shall discuss, first, the various

23. *Ho laos* is used in the sense of a group of people, or crowd, in Matt 4:16, 23; 26:5; 27:25, 64. In Matt 1:21; 2:4, 6; 13:15; 15:8; 21:23; 26:3, 47; 27:1, the term refers to the Jewish people as a whole. We shall return to this below.
24. Matt 11:16; 12:39, 41, 42, 45; 16:4; 17:17; 23:36; 24:34. See discussion in chapter 3.2.2.1.
25. Other towns mentioned include Caesarea Philippi and Bethany, but these are just used as geographical indicators, with possible political implications in the case of Caesarea Philippi.
26. Matthew often uses the word *polis*, but, compared to Greek usage, does so in a non-technical sense. Cf. Hermann Strathmann, "πόλις," in *TDNT* vol. 6, 516–35: "The use of πόλις in the NT is thus completely non-political. πόλις simply means an 'enclosed place of human habitation' as distinct from uninhabited areas, pastures, villages and single houses" (530). While Strathmann's point is clear enough with regard to *polis*, his use of "political" is less so. One should note that locations such as these did have administrative structures in the form of public synagogues, within which (lower and mid level) scribes worked. These public-assembly institutions were called by many names in the first century, including *ekklēsia*, as we see in, e.g., Josephus, which indicates that they were regarded as local religio-political institutions.
27. The devil goes under several names: "the Tempter" (4:3), "Beelzebub" (10:25; 12:24, 27), "Satan" (4:10; 12:26; 16:23). The "God of Israel" (15:31) is also called the "God of Abraham, Isaac and Jacob" (22:32), "Heaven" (21:25), "the Power" (26:64) or simply, and most frequently, "God" (e.g., 1:23; 4:4; 5:8; 9:8; 22:37).

leadership groups, beginning with politically influential groups, followed by association-like collectivities. Then, second, we shall say a few words about the larger entities in Matthew, such as the crowds and Israel.

3.2.1 Leadership Groups

3.2.1.1 Groups with Direct Political Influence

> From that time on [*Apo tote*], Jesus began to show his disciples that he must go to Jerusalem and undergo great suffering at the hands of the elders and chief priests and scribes, and be killed, and on the third day be raised. (Matt 16:21)

In some ways, this passage, the theme of which is repeated in 17:22–23 and 20:17–19, may be thought of as a summary of the role of the religio-political leaders in Matthew, the elders, the chief priests, and the scribes associated with them; they, and they alone, are responsible for handing Jesus over to the non-Jewish authorities for execution.[28] Still, we need to qualify that statement somewhat in order to do Matthew justice. While the aims of the chief priests and the elders always converge, the role of the scribes is not to be equated with the former two groups.[29] Further, the context that explains the cooperation between these groups is Jerusalem, a location which Matthew contrasts with the more open and complex Galilean environment where the first two groups are not present and scribes may be presented as either negative figures or ideal disciples of Jesus.

Matthew's use of *apo tote* ("from that time on") in 16:21 signals the beginning of the second of two major stages in Jesus's life.[30] The first stage is represented by Jesus's proclamation of the kingdom in Galilee

---

28. While it is stated in Matt 17:22–23 that Jesus will be "betrayed into human hands [*eis cheiras anthrōpōn*]" and killed, it is only in the third prediction of Jesus's suffering (Matt 20:17-19) that it is explicitly clarified that these human hands belong to non-Jews: "See, we are going up to Jerusalem, and the Son of Man will be handed over to the chief priests and scribes, and they will condemn him to death; then they will hand him over to the Gentiles to be mocked and flogged and crucified."

29. On the scribes in Matthew, see esp. David E. Orton's important study, *The Understanding Scribe: Matthew and the Apocalyptic Ideal* (Sheffield: Sheffield Academic Press, 1989).

30. The first stage of Jesus's public life is introduced in Matt 4:17 with the same use of *apo tote*.

after the arrest and imprisonment of John the Baptist, a mission that was largely successful, resulting in great crowds following Jesus, and eventually also in Peter's confession of Jesus's identity as the Messiah, the son of the living God (16:16).[31] The second stage of Jesus's life recounts his journey to Jerusalem and his suffering and death. For Matthew, while the Romans were the ones ordering the execution of Jesus, the responsibility for the death of the Messiah is laid down squarely at the feet of leadership groups working within public Jewish institutions, more specifically, the temple authorities in Jerusalem.[32] Paying attention to Matthew's fine distinctions within this general group of religio-political leaders will shed light on Matthew's understanding of Jewish society and those guilty of betraying the Messiah and having him handed over to non-Jews for torture and execution.

First, we should note that the ordinary priests in the Jerusalem temple are not a concern for the Matthean Jesus. Their work in the temple is legitimate and taken as a given in the logic of the narrative and the rhetoric of arguments made (8:4; 12:4–5). The chief priests, however, are described as the major force behind Jesus's death. The chief priests are mentioned a total of 25 times in Matthew, both by themselves (26:14; 27:6) and together with other groups. When the chief priests appear with other groups, they are almost always mentioned first: with the elders (21:23; 26:3, 47, 57; 27:1, 3, 12, 20; 28:11–12), the scribes (2:4; 20:18; 21:15), and with both the elders and the scribes (27:41; 16:21 is an exception; here, Matthew mentions the elders before the chief priests). They are also mentioned together with the Sanhedrin (26:59), and, interestingly, with the Pharisees (21:45; 27:62); we shall return to the latter connection below as we discuss Matthew's approach to Pharisees and Jewish society. Not surprisingly, the chief priests are always associated with Jerusalem, and therefore, also with Jesus's arrest and subsequent execution. For the Matthean

---

31. The final passages before Jesus is beginning his journey to Jerusalem in Matt 19:1 deal with the disciples and their future, especially their future organization of Jesus's *ekklēsia*.

32. The otherwise so frequently-derided Pharisees disappear when this accusation appears in the narrative. On the role of the Pharisees in the Gospel, see below, chapter 3.2.1.2.

Jesus and the narrator, the chief priests are corrupt[33] and they consistently oppose Jesus from the point in time when he enters the second stage of his mission, from 16:21 onwards, until his death (27:41–42), and even after his resurrection (28:11–12). In all their doings, they fear the people, i.e., the crowds in Jerusalem and the temple, which has the narrative effect of showing that their rule is not supported by the majority of the Jewish people, who understand that Jesus is sent by God (e.g., 21:8–11, 14–16; cf. 21:26, 46). This is the only role of the chief priests in Matthew's narrative: to oppose Jesus and arrange for his execution by the Romans.

One would assume that such characters would be singled out, as a group, for the harshest of divine judgments, and that the author would elaborate extensively on such condemnation. However, while judgment is pronounced and the chief priests are condemned as a group, this is stated in one pericope only, and the punishment meted out is unrelated to their fate in the final judgment. After Jesus's triumphant entry into Jerusalem, and as he speaks with "the chief priests and the elders of the people" (21:23), Jesus reveals, in the parable of the tenants in the vineyard (21:33–46), the coming judgment of these leaders of Israel. We have already dealt with this parable above,[34] and I shall not repeat that discussion. What is important to note here is that what is described is the chief priests and the elders' involvement in, and therefore responsibility for Jesus's death (21:37–39). As Jesus asks them what punishment would be suitable for the crime described, they respond, not yet realizing that they themselves will soon be accused of being the real perpetrators of the offense,[35] that the wrongdoers should be killed and the vineyard should

---

33. They are said to know Scripture, but work with the illegitimate king Herod (2:4); they plan Jesus's death and set in motion an unlawful trial, during which they arrange for false witnesses to step forward and accuse him (26:59). After Jesus's death, they initiate and spread false rumors stating that Jesus's resurrection was faked by the disciples (28:11–12). They are also the key players as they work with Judas when he betrays Jesus; after Judas repented and returned the money, they identify the money received as "blood money," thus implicitly acknowledging that they themselves had been part of unlawful activities, the result of which would defile the temple treasury (26:14; 27:6).

34. See pp. 50n26; 151–52.

35. The Matthean Jesus's rhetorical strategy of using the parable form to provoke self-condemnation

be leased "to other tenants who will give him the produce at the harvest time" (21:41). Jesus then confirms this verdict as the divine judgment that will befall them: The kingdom of God will be taken from them and given to others who will produce the fruits of the kingdom (21:43).[36] If there would be any doubt as to whom the parable was directed against, the narrator confirms in Matt 21:45–46 that the chief priests are the target for this punishment, which is stated to be the loss of leadership based on their corruption and role in the death of the Messiah.[37]

Indeed, this conclusion is already stated in the passage immediately preceding the parable of the tenants, in the story about the two sons in Matt 21:28–32. Here, Jesus explains that the chief priests and the elders of the people are like the son who said he would do what the father had told him but then never followed through. Tax collectors and prostitutes, however, are like the son who rejected the request of the father, but then went on to do his will anyway; the latter will thus be "going into the kingdom of God" ahead of the former. Divine condemnation will, thus, befall only those who do not do the will of the father (cf. 7:21). Still, we may note, Matthew does not explicitly exclude the chief priests and the elders from the kingdom as such, despite their role in the narrative and the hideous crimes they are accused of; what we find here is a reversal of status and roles as the kingdom is set in motion. The Matthean Jesus has saved the ultimate divine punishment for one specific group, to which we shall return in section 3.2.1.2 where we shall also discuss the identity and punishment of the group targeted in Matt 22:1–14.

The second major group with political responsibility in Jewish

---

is similar to Nathan the prophet's as he delivers news of divine judgment to befall king David for the sin he has committed (2 Sam 12:1–12).

36. Note that the death sentence, which is hinted at in Matt 21:44, is not present in all manuscripts and is regarded by many scholars as an interpolation. Cf. Bruce M. Metzger, *A Textual Commentary on the Greek New Testament* (Stuttgart: United Bible Societies, 1975), 58; Reuben Swanson, *New Testament Greek Manuscripts: Variant Readings Arranged in Horizontal Lines Against Codex Vaticanus* (Sheffield: Sheffield Academic Press, 1995), 211.

37. Matthew adds the Pharisees in Matt 21:45, who replace the elders of the people who were Jesus's original conversation partners (Matt 21:23). This is part of Matthew's peculiar but conscious and consistent literary strategy, to which we shall return in the next section.

society is referred to as "the elders of the people" (*hoi prestyberoi tou laou*), or simply, "the elders," and they appear 12 times in the narrative. This group is associated only with Jerusalem, just as the chief priests, and are not portrayed as in charge in local towns and villages in Galilee, although their influence, via the Pharisees, is implicitly claimed to reach beyond the capital (15:1–2). The elders are mostly mentioned together with the chief priests (21:23; 26:3; 26:47, 57; 27:1, 3, 12, 20; 28:11–12), and also a couple of times with the chief priests and the scribes (16:21; 27:41); they are never mentioned together with the scribes only. Not surprisingly, since the elders are mentioned so often together with the chief priests, they are portrayed in a thoroughly negative light; they are afraid of the people, they are corrupt, and they are responsible for the execution of Jesus at the hands of the Romans, as well as of spreading false rumors in Judea after Jesus's death, claiming that Jesus's disciples removed his body from the tomb in order to fake his resurrection. Since the elders are almost always mentioned after the chief priests, they are described as led by them. Still, their punishment will be the same: loss of leadership as the kingdom of God wins ground.[38] While this judgment is firm, Matthew reveals nothing with regard to either the elders or the chief priests that would exclude the possibility of these individuals' future repentance and possible acceptance into the kingdom.[39]

Before we look closer at the third group associated with public religio-political institutions, the scribes, we need to say a few words about Matt 15:1–2. Whatever the "tradition of the elders" (*paradosis tōn presbyterōn*) may mean here,[40] Matthew has connected this tradition with Jerusalem, i.e., with the same geographical-political setting within which all other (negative) references to the elders of the people occur.[41] This is done through the information the narrator provides,

38. The fact that the elders are present in Matt 21:23, but replaced by the Pharisees in 21:45 has less to do with Matthew trying to exonerate them and more to do with the fact that Matthew is aiming at introducing the Pharisees in this public setting, preparing for the following parable and its announcement of divine punishment.

39. As opposed to Matthew's insinuations about the Pharisees.

40. See discussion in Nolland, *Matthew*, 610–11; Luz, *Matthew*, 2.329–30.

41. Josephus, *A.J.* 10.51, provides the only a parallel to this expression. While Josephus is discussing how the young king Josiah was helped by the elders, a topic unrelated to our concerns here, the

namely that the Pharisees and scribes who ask Jesus why his disciples "break the tradition of the elders" come from Jerusalem (15:1). This move creates the impression of a connection between the elders of Jerusalem and Pharisaic interpretation of law, which is reinforced when Jesus launches his counter question: "And why do you break the commandment [*entolē*] of God for the sake of *your* tradition [*paradosis*]?" This tactic of connecting Pharisees with public religio-political figures and authority reoccurs in 22:45, where the Pharisees suddenly replace the elders from 21:23 as targets of divine judgment. The same phenomenon occurs very frequently with regard to scribes. As we shall see below, this is part of Matthew's overall rhetorical strategy in which Jesus is portrayed as involved primarily in a battle against the Pharisees even as he moves from Galilee to Jerusalem, which is the turf of the chief priests, elders, and scribes, trying to implicate the Pharisees with Jesus's suffering and death.

While both chief priests and elders are presented as thoroughly negative groups, responsible for Jesus's death and condemned by God to lose their authority and status as religio-political leaders of the Jewish people, the status and judgment of the scribes is more complex and cannot be generalized.[42] This group changes position as they align themselves with any of the other groups in the narrative. Thus, when scribes are associated with Jerusalem and the chief priests, they are shown to be knowledgeable in holy scriptures, but also, as supporting the illegitimate king Herod (2:4); they are also accused of planning to have Jesus killed (20:18) and they get angry when children call Jesus "Son of David" in the temple (21:15). When scribes are paired with

---

setting of this tradition and education is the same, namely Jerusalem. Note also *m. 'Avot* 1:1, where the (oral) law is said to have been given to Moses on Sinai, who then handed it down to Joshua, who gave it to the elders (the judges), who gave it to the prophets, who in turn handed it on to "the men of the great assembly/synagogue" (לְאַנְשֵׁי כְנֶסֶת הַגְּדוֹלָה, traditionally understood as a body of 120 elders, judges, prophets, sages, teachers, and scribes who returned with Ezra from the exile to Jerusalem). While the historicity of this process as described in the Mishnah is certainly to be doubted, the point is that, in rabbinic literature, we also find this connection between the traditions kept by the rabbis and those handed down to the "great assembly" in Jerusalem.

42. According to Orton, *Scribe*, 161, there are two types of scribes in Matthew: "those with true insight and true teaching of righteousness, and those without." We must thus reject claims that all representatives of leadership in Matthew should be treated as "a single character" (Kingsbury, *Story*, 18) or be seen as "a unity of evil" (David R. Bauer, *The Structure of Matthew's Gospel: A Study in Literary Design* [Sheffield: The Almond Press, 1989], 69).

the elders only, they have gathered together in the palace of the chief priest in order to find a way to condemn Jesus to death (26:57). When all three groups are together in Jerusalem, Matthew presents them as part of an alliance that will inflict suffering on Jesus and have him handed over for execution (16:21); as Jesus hangs on the cross, the Jerusalem scribes mock him together with the chief priests and the elders, calling him "king of Israel" (27:41).

Interestingly, despite this thoroughly negative portrait of Jerusalem scribes, they are not mentioned when Jesus pronounces divine judgment on the other Jerusalem leadership groups, the chief priests and elders.[43] The scribes seem to follow the lead of others, and when they do, they are accused of the same crimes as the more powerful and influential group(s) they are associated with. It seems, however, that they are not evil enough to receive mention as God's judgment is revealed, targeting the chief priests and the elders. The lowest common denominator in these various settings is Jerusalem, the holy city, the corrupt leadership of which will be removed. But Matthew is not blaming the chief priests and the elders for the destruction of the city and the temple. Guilt for this ultimate catastrophe is assigned to another group, one that lacked direct political power: the Pharisees. When scribes associate themselves with this group, they will share that guilt and punishment. In other words: when scribes are mentioned together with chief priests and elders, no specific judgment is pronounced over them, but when they are associated with the Pharisees, they are explicitly condemned in the harshest of ways. But before we deal with these scribes, we must note yet another form in which they appear—namely, as followers of Jesus himself.

Matthew's story presents us with scribes associated with Jesus on three occasions. In 8:19, a Galilean scribe approaches Jesus, and says: "Teacher, I will follow you wherever you go." That this scribe is understood as a disciple, not merely a person more generally sympathetic to Jesus, is confirmed by 8:21, where immediately after

---

43. Contrary to Mark's version of the story (12:1–12), which has the scribes judged along with the chief priests and the elders (Mark 11:27; cf. 12:38–40), but does not mention Pharisees.

Jesus's reply to the scribe's question, "another disciple" (*heteros de tōn mathētōn [autou]*) is introduced with a second question.[44] In 13:52, Jesus is speaking to his disciples (13:36). After they have assured him that they have understood his parables he tells them: "Therefore every scribe who has been trained for the kingdom of heaven [*pas grammateus mathēteutheis tē basileia tōn ouranōn*] is like the master of a household who brings out of his treasure what is new and what is old."[45] Finally, we see confirmation of the success of this educational process involving scribes in 23:34. Here, scribes are already an integral part of the movement around Jesus and they are being sent out as missionaries proclaiming the kingdom to other scribes, who are related to the Pharisees. As they fulfill this task, however, they will be persecuted, flogged, and killed by these other scribes and the Pharisees with whom they are associated: "Therefore I send you prophets, sages, and scribes (*prophētas kai sophous kai grammateis*), some of whom you will kill and crucify, and some you will flog in your synagogues and pursue from town to town."[46]

What we see here is, thus, a battle between different factions, Jesus and his movement on one side, and the Pharisees on the other. The battle takes place in the public synagogue institutions of both Galilee and Judea. Again, this distinction between Galilee and Judea is important for Matthew. In Galilee, the scribes may be described as teachers who teach without power, and who cannot compare to Jesus, according to the crowds hearing the Sermon on the Mount (7:28–29).[47]

---

44. Cf. D. A. Carson, "The Jewish Leaders in Matthew's Gospel: A Reappraisal," *JETS* 25:2 (1982): 161–74, here 169.

45. This passage has led many scholars to assume that the author of the Gospel was himself a scribe (so, e.g., David E. Orton, *The Understanding Scribe: Matthew and the Apocalyptic Ideal* [Sheffield: Sheffield Academic Press, 1989]). As Lamar Cope, *Matthew: A Scribe Trained for the Kingdom of Heaven* (Washington: The Catholic Biblical Association of America, 1976) writes: "The author of Matthew was a Jewish-Christian so thoroughly familiar with the OT *and with Jewish traditions of its interpretation* that it was natural for him often to employ this knowledge as a key to the organization of his Gospel. [...] He probably thought of himself as 'a scribe trained for the kingdom of heaven'" (130; my emphasis). While this is likely correct, this discussion lies beyond the scope of the present study. In the story world, what is important is that Jesus speaks of multiple scribes as being, or being in the process of becoming, disciples of the kingdom. These scribes are, further, presented as the ideal disciples.

46. Luke 11:49 does not mention scribes, but only prophets and apostles.

47. Still, the scribal office is legitimate in and of itself; cf. Orton, *Scribe*, 37.

While some of them are drawn to Jesus (8:19; 13:52), the situation is presented as open-ended with regard to possible outcomes. Thus, on the one hand, some scribes are surprised when Jesus speaks of forgiving sins[48] and understand such talk to be blasphemous (9:3). On the other hand, Jesus confirms that the teaching of the scribes about the coming of Elijah before the Messiah is correct (17:10–11; cf. 11:14); the only problem is that they never recognized John the Baptist as Elijah, and therefore, have difficulties understanding Jesus (17:12).[49] When scribes appear with Galilean Pharisees, they once ask for a sign from Jesus, indicating that they have not, as a group—and certainly not when they are together with Pharisees—accepted Jesus based on what he has done so far.[50]

As long as Jesus is in Galilee and is involved in a "battle" in the public sphere of Jewish society, where both Jesus and the Pharisees are trying to sway scribes, there is only one exception to this general scene of open-endedness in terms of scribal alliances. In 5:20, speaking to Galilean crowds and disciples (5:1; 7:28), Jesus states that if their righteousness does not exceed that of the scribes and the Pharisees, they will "never enter the kingdom of heaven." This view confirms what we see later on when Jesus has left the Galilee and entered Judea and Jerusalem (after 19:1), namely, that whoever associates themselves with the Pharisees will not enter the kingdom. Here, in Galilee, however, this statement functions more as a warning directed toward the crowds and the disciples not to imitate such scribes, since, without Jesus (13:52), their teaching lacks power (7:28–29).[51] The situation

---

48. For the meaning of forgiveness here, see the discussion above, chapter 2.4.

49. The pattern of knowing the scriptures, but not understanding what happens in front of one's eyes is the same as we find in the birth narrative with the Jerusalem scribes (Matt 2:4–6); see discussion in Anders Runesson, "Giving Birth to Jesus in the Late First Century: Matthew as Midwife in the Context of Colonisation," in *Infancy Gospels: Stories and Identities* (edtied by Claire Clivaz, Andreas Dettwiler, Luc Devilliers, and Enrico Norelli; Tübingen: Mohr Siebeck, 2011), 301–27, and the chart on p. 323.

50. Orton, *Scribe*, 37, notes that Matthew still treats scribes with some positive care, removing suggestions that they "tempt" Jesus when they ask questions, turning them into courteous learners and genuine inquirers.

51. Since scribes worked in official public settings in towns and villages, i.e., were involved in administration taking place in public synagogues and thus having significant influence on these towns and villages, we should perhaps mention here also the Galilean cities that are condemned by Jesus because of lack of repentance (Chorazin, Bethsaida, Capernaum; Matt 11:20–24). The

changes after Jesus has entered Jerusalem, where scribes are associated primarily with the Pharisees, and are therefore explicitly and without exception or hesitation condemned.[52]

References to scribes who are associated with Pharisees in Jerusalem are limited to the fierce critique presented in Matthew's twenty-third chapter.[53] While the office of the scribe is legitimate as such, and is not under attack (cf. 23:2),[54] there are two parameters that destine these scribes for condemnation: a) their association with the Pharisees, and b) their location in Jerusalem, and thus, their responsibility for the current state of things in the holy city. For the Matthean Jesus, the combination of these factors leads to the worst possible scenario, the very opposite to the kingdom he, in collaboration with the spirit of the God of Israel (12:28), works to establish as he aims to save his people from their sins.

In brief, the scenario with regard to these Jerusalem scribes can be described as follows. There are two main accusations made against them when associated with the Pharisees. First, their teaching is flawed and has disastrous consequences: it is oppressing the people (23:4; cf. 9:36), and it excludes them from the kingdom (23:13, 15). We also find an example of a key problem in their teaching, which shows how these scribes do not understand the nature of the holiness of the temple (23:16–22); this threatens, by implication, the very existence of the temple, a theme and an accusation which will be made explicit later on in chapter 23. Second, a number of *ad hominem* accusations are delivered against these scribes. They do not practice what they say

---

verdict pronounced on these cities, which will be executed at the final judgment, indicates, implicitly, that the scribal communities of these cities had chosen not to enter into an alliance with Jesus and his movement (cf. Matt 10:14–15).

52. Cf. Orton, *Scribe*, 37, who rightly concludes that only the Pharisaic scribes, who culpably distort the honored picture of the scribe by their hypocrisy and false leadership, bear the full brunt of Jesus's criticism. This does not mean, however, that Matthew conflates the meaning of the terms "Pharisees" and "scribes." Orton continues: "It is precisely because Pharisees are *not* 'scribes' in the ideal sense that Matthew calls them Pharisees rather than scribes; they may be the same people, but the *terms* are not synonymous for Matthew" (37–38).

53. In Matt 15:1, some Pharisees and scribes are said to have travelled from Jerusalem to Galilee to pose halakhic questions to Jesus. This interaction takes place in Galilee, however, and can only be said to foreshadow the condemnation of these Jerusalem-related groups that is to come in chapter 23 (cf. Matt 15:13).

54. So also Orton, *Scribe*.

(23:3), and they are vain, seeking glory from people rather than from God (23:5-7). Third, the scribes of Jerusalem are portrayed as breakers of the law. They neglect the weightier matters of the law, a choice which nullifies the value of the commandments that they do, in fact, keep, making them impure on the inside, i.e., where it really matters, although they appear pure on the outside (23:23; cf. 23:24-28).

The most serious accusation follows directly after the charge of hypocrisy and lawlessness (*anomia*; 23:28): these scribes, who are associated with the Pharisees, are, in fact, murderers, and thus, sons of murderers (23:31-34). As we have discussed above, shedding innocent blood is one of the most serious crimes in Jewish tradition, and it is considered to defile both land and temple. Therefore, when, fourth, the scribes in question are found guilty by the Matthean Jesus of "all the righteous blood shed on earth, from the blood of righteous Abel to the blood of Zechariah son of Barachiah," the latter of whom, Jesus claims, they "murdered between the sanctuary and the altar" (23:35-36), they are pointed to as the very cause behind God's leaving the temple and the city in order for both to be destroyed (23:37-24:2; cf. 22:7). It is precisely because of Matthew's understanding of Jerusalem as a holy city (5:35; 27:53) and the temple as God's abode (23:21), in addition to the fact that these defiling crimes are committed by leaders of the people who are supposed to be teachers of the law (23:2), that the consequences of the law-breaking will be so severe. All of this also means that, for Matthew, the Jerusalem scribes who associate themselves with the Pharisees are part of the problem that lies at the heart of the Gospel—indeed, which likely explains the very production of this Gospel in the first place—namely, that the fall of the temple, blamed on the Jerusalem scribes and the Pharisees, necessitates Jesus's death in order for the covenant to be restored and the people to be saved.

If we summarize the roles of scribes in Matthew's Gospel, the result is quite interesting, as it is unique in comparison with all other groups mentioned in the Gospel. First, when scribes are associated with chief priests and the elders of Jerusalem, they are blamed for the suffering and eventual death of Jesus at the hands of the Romans. Second, when scribes are associated with the Pharisees of Jerusalem, they are blamed for the destruction of the temple and the city itself.[55] Third, when Galilean scribes are associated with Jesus and the kingdom, they are held forth as ideal examples of discipleship (13:52), and they are destined to suffer and even be killed in Judea/Jerusalem (23:34), just as Jesus will be.[56] The scribes are thus portrayed as (mid-level) officials in Jewish society, lacking independent power. They are not leaders in their own right but their understanding of law and their decisions impact the people greatly, since they teach them in local (sabbath) assemblies. This makes them important strategic targets for Jesus's proclamation; *the scribes are the key to reaching and controlling the population at large.*

In relation to groups portrayed as powerful, scribes thus follow the lead of one of these three groups: the chief priests (and the elders of Jerusalem), the Pharisees, and Jesus. Divine judgment will be distributed accordingly, although scribes are removed from explicit condemnation when they are blamed, together with the chief priests and the elders, for the death of Jesus.[57] On the contrary, while chief priests and elders are not blamed for the fall of Jerusalem, scribes who associate themselves with Pharisees are. Finally, as ideal followers of Jesus, scribes will share in the kingdom with the other disciples. The scribes thus represent the only group in Matthew, which is held

---

55. We shall discuss this theme in more detail below when dealing with the Pharisees.

56. Matt 23:34. The interpretation that these scribes are meant to be understood as being from Galilee and sent to Jerusalem is based on the fact that only scribes in Galilee have been mentioned as being Jesus's followers. On the contrary, all scribes mentioned in a Jerusalem setting are portrayed as corrupt, participating in the chief priests' and the elders' plan to have Jesus executed. Thus, when the Matthean Jesus, in Jerusalem, speaks of his scribes as being sent to "the scribes and the Pharisees," who have just been described as murderers destined for Gehenna (23:29–33), and the future of Jesus's scribes involves suffering and crucifixion, just as Jesus will suffer and be crucified, it is reasonable to understand the situation as a Galilee–Judea conflict also with regard to the scribes (although not all Galilean scribes would be on Jesus's side, as noted above). This suggestion is further strengthened when we consider the fact that the disciples are told by the resurrected Jesus to leave Jerusalem and go back to Galilee, just as Jesus himself will do (28:7), and that from Galilee they will also launch their mission to the nations (28:10, 16–19).

57. Cf. Orton, *Scribe*, 37, who notes that Matthew seeks to exonerate scribes from strident opposition to Jesus by characterizing those who do oppose him as unrepresentative of scribes *per se*. This is accomplished through linking opposing scribes with known enemies of Jesus, especially the Pharisees, or qualifying them as representing only "some" of the scribes.

responsible both for the most hideous crimes in Israel's history and for producing ideal disciples for the kingdom of heaven.

If we look at other leading political figures in Jewish society they play, in comparison, marginal roles as far as divine judgment is concerned. An exception is Herod I, who, as an illegitimate king of the Jews who kills the children of Israel (2:16–18), prepares for the portrayal of the Messiah who will save his people (1:21). Herod's son Archelaos is mentioned briefly in 2:22. When Joseph hears that Archelaos had been made king (*basileuō*) in Jerusalem after his father, he decides not to return to Judea, but to relocate to Galilee with Mary and their son. The implied opposition to and anticipated violence against the Messiah by this Herodian ruler sets the stage for Galilee as the home of Jesus, and for the Galilee–Judea tensions that can be seen throughout the rest of the Gospel, up until its very end (e.g., 28:15).

The ruler of Galilee, Herod's second son Antipas, is mentioned in Matt 14:1–12 as the one ordering the execution of John the Baptist, despite being afraid of the people who saw John as a prophet. Contrary to Mark, who claims that Antipas had respect for John and protected him (Mark 6:20), Matthew increases the conflict between Jesus and the ruler of Galilee by stating that Antipas *wanted* to kill John. The effect is that the Herodian family as a whole is presented as (flat) evil characters opposing and killing (or wanting to kill) the heroes of the story, John and Jesus. As for Philip, Herod's third son, he is mentioned only in passing as Antipas' brother, whose marital relationship with Herodias explains why Antipas was accused by John of breaking the law (14:3–4). That passage tells us nothing about Philip's attitude toward John or Jesus. However, it may be of some significance to note that, a couple of chapters later, Matthew has Jesus travel to the area around Caesarea Philippi, Philip's "royal city" rebuilt by him in honor of the Emperor,[58]

58. Josephus, *A.J.* 18.28; *B.J.* 2.168. Commentators variously suggest that Philip rebuilt the city in honor of Augustus and Tiberius, respectively (see, e.g., J. Andrew Overman, *Church and Community in Crisis: The Gospel According to Matthew* [Valley Forge: Trinity Press International, 1996], 237, who claims it was done in honor of Augustus; D. Berhard Weiss, *Das Matthäus-Evangelium* (7th ed.; Göttingen: Vandenhoeck & Ruprecht, 1910], 293, who says the honor was Tiberius's). Josephus states that when Augustus had died and Tiberius had ascended the throne, "Herod (Antipas) and Philip continued to hold their tetrarchies and respectively founded cities: Philip built Caesarea near the source of the Jordan, in the district of Paneas, and Julia in lower Gaulanitis; Herod built

placing there the climactic discourse about Jesus's true identity as the Messiah (16:13–17). Such a setting for this proclamation reminds the reader that Herodian rule—including its support from Rome—is incompatible with the rule of the Messiah. It is, in brief, a claim to that area for the future kingdom under Jesus's rule.[59]

While Matthew portrays the Herodian family as illegitimate rulers irreconcilable with the kingdom of heaven and thus as in the process of being ousted when the Messiah takes up his rule, the negative focus is not on the sons who run Galilee and the areas to the north and northeast (Gaulanitis, Batanea, Auranitis, and Trachonitis[60]), but on Jerusalem and Herod's (and Archelaos's) rule there. It is not only Herod, but "all Jerusalem" (*pasa Hierosolyma*) who reacts with fear (*tarassō*) when news about the new king's birth is announced to them by the Magi from the East (2:3). It is also in Jerusalem that Herod connects with the chief priests and the scribes (2:4)—the groups Matthew will later accuse of condemning Jesus to death (e.g., 20:18)—in

Tiberias in Galilee and a city which also took the name of Julia, in Peraea" (*BJ* 2.168). While Herod I was still alive, he constructed in the same city an Augusteion (Josephus, *AJ* 15.360–64; *BJ* 1.404–5), which has now been partially excavated. On the Greco-Roman cults of the city, see Zvi Uri Ma'oz, *Baniyas in the Greco-Roman Period: A History Based on the Excavations* (Archaostyle Scientific Research Series 3; Qazrin: Archaostyle, 2007); on Philip's rule, see also Eric M. Meyers and Mark A. Chancey, *Alexander to Constantine: Archaeology of the Land of the Bible* (New haven: Yale University Press, 2012), 121–23.

59. Most commentators ignore the territorial-political significance of the place in which Jesus is declared king ("the Messiah, the Son of the living God" [16:16]), Nolland, *Matthew*, 658, explicitly stating that the location probably carries little or no meaning at all since the story is likely based on a memory of a historical episode in Jesus's life. This, however, it seems to me, cannot invalidate possible symbolic meaning, since historical episodes can surely carry symbolic meaning, both at the time when they occur and/or afterwards when described and re-contextualized in a narrative. I find it difficult to imagine that a first-century audience could have ignored the implicit political connection in the passage between this city, Philip, and the Roman emperor, on the one hand, and the identification of Jesus as the Messiah, on the other, especially when one considers the fact that this general area was part of the ideal Davidic kingdom as well as of Ezekiel's later vision of the restored twelve tribes of Israel, and of Alexander Jannaeus' (103–76 BCE) kingdom, and the kingdom of Herod I as well, the latter of which was still in place when Jesus was born. Warren Carter, *Matthew and the Margins: A Socio-Political and Religious Reading* (London: T&T Clark, 2000), 332–33, does mention the political aspect, but stops short of noting the territorial dimension of these political claims. He does say, though, regarding the title "Son of God" and its use for Augustus, that "[t]o designate Jesus as son of God is to contest and challenge those claims of sovereignty and agency" (333). Rudolf Schnackenburg, *The Gospel of Matthew* (trans. Robert R. Barr; Grand Rapids: Eerdmans, 2002) mentions that part of the importance of the location was that "[h]ere was the northern frontier of the land settled by the Jews. Jesus' question to the disciples, the only question uttered by Jesus regarding a judgment of his person, makes good sense and enjoys historical credibility, here on the frontier and at this point in the narrative" (157).

60. Luke 3:1 has Ituraea and Trachonitis, the former not listed by Josephus. For map and discussion, see Rainey and Notley, *Sacred Bridge*, 347–48.

order to find out where the new king was born, so that he can find him and kill him (2:16). While Matthew does not mention specific divine punishments relating to any of the Herodians, it is clear that, based on their resistance to Jesus, the attempt to kill him, and the execution of John the Baptist, they are all rejected by God. Herod's association with the chief priests and Jerusalem scribes further supports the assumption that Herod is as much to blame for the death of Jesus as are they, and his and his sons punishment will be removal from power, although this is not stated explicitly.

In sum, we may conclude that with regard to Jewish leaders in the public sphere of society there is a distinct focus on Judea and Jerusalem as far as divine judgment is concerned. Critique of religio-political leadership in Matthew is set within a wider discourse of tension between Galilee and Judea and cannot be understood without it. As we shall see in the next section, the picture shifts somewhat when we consider groups who do not represent public institutions in Jewish society. Finally, we may note that the behavior of these groups, when negative, certainly falls under the criteria of judgment outlined above and will result in various forms of punishments accordingly, in this world, at the final judgment, and in the world to come. However, when it comes to explicit verdicts associated with these religio-political groups, almost all divine punishment concerns this world, and takes the form of loss of power positions in Jewish society.

3.2.1.2 Groups with Indirect Political Influence

The above discussion has been focused on official representatives of Jewish society on national and local levels, as portrayed by Matthew. We have rejected an approach that generalizes Matthew's opinion about these officials and noted that there are differences between how they are dealt with in terms of culpability for certain offences and the divine judgment that will follow. The same is true for the non-political association-like groups—often, and inaccurately, at least from a sociological point of view, called "sects" in scholarship—described in the text. It is commonplace today, and has been for some time, although its implications for the interpretation of the New Testament have not always been noted, to confirm that Judaism in the first century was diverse.[61] Matthew's narrative world is inhabited by some, but not all, of the Jewish groups we know of from other historical sources. Again, we are not interested in this study in linking Matthew's story to the historical circumstances in either the 30s or the post-70 period when the Gospel was most likely written, and will therefore refrain from discussing whether or not the Gospel's portrayal of the social location, dominance, or lack of influence, of each of the groups mentioned reflects historical reality in Jewish society at the time.[62]

61. E.g., Louis Ginzberg, "The Religion of the Jews at the Time of Jesus," *Hebrew Union College Annual* 1 (1924), 307–21 (republished in *Origins of Judaism, Normative Judaism*, vol. 1, part 2, [edited by Jacob Neusner; New York: 1990], 1–15). As Ginzberg writes, Jewish tradition has acknowledged this diversity from early on, quoting a third-century rabbi recorded in the Jerusalem Talmud (*y. Sanh.* 29c): "Israel went into exile only after it became divided into twenty-four sects" (307). The diversity issue is dealt with in interesting ways by Gabriele Boccaccini, *Middle Judaism: Jewish Thought 300 B.C.E. to 200 C.E.* (Minneapolis: Fortress, 1991), although the terminological question is in need of some further discussion. See also, Andrew Overman, *Matthew's Gospel and Formative Judaism: The Social World of the Matthean Community* (Minneapolis: Fortress, 1990); E. P. Sanders (*Judaism: Practice and Belief 63 BCE–66 CE* [London: SCM Press, 1992], 317–457). Of course, while often not included in standard treatments of first-century Jewish groups, the Jesus movement was yet another example, diverse in itself, of pluriform Judaism. One would assume that this neglect to include Jesus and the Jesus movement (including the New Testament texts) in treatments of first-century Jewish groups has something to do with how university departments and both undergraduate and graduate courses are structured. These administrative and educational structures build on traditional hard-to-overcome confessional boundaries between "Judaism" and "Christianity" that reflect the situation from Late Antiquity until our own days rather than any historical considerations of the nature of first-century Judaism as such. We learn, early on, both directly through textbooks and indirectly from department structures, that studying Jesus and the New Testament is something different from studying ancient Judaism. Daniel Boyarin's *The Jewish Gospels: The Story of the Jewish Christ* (New York: New Press, 2012) represents just one of several recent studies that challenge, on historical grounds, the unstated assumptions underlying such administrative and educational habits.

62. For example, while the Pharisees certainly dominate Matthew's Gospel with regard to their portrayal as Jesus's enemies, their historical influence has been doubted by several scholars, most famously E. P. Sanders (*Judaism: Practice ad Belief 63 BCE–66 CE* [London: SCM Press, 1992], 380–451). See also Hartmut Stegemann, *Die Essener, Qumran, Johannes der Täufer und Jesus: Ein Sachbuch* (4th edition; Freiburg: Herder, 1994), 361–364, who argues that the Essenes were the most influential movement of the time; cf. Günter Stemberger, *Jewish Contemporaries of Jesus: Pharisees, Sadducees, Essene* (Minneapolis: Fortress, 1995). For the view that Pharisees had a high level of influence in Jewish society, see Steve Mason, "Pharisaic Dominance Before 70 CE and the Gospel's Hypocrisy Charge (Matt 23:2–3)," *HTR* 83 (1990): 363–81, here 363–64. Mason's study provides a renewed attempt at arguing for a pre-70 dominance of the Pharisees. See also Peter J. Tomson, *"If This Be from Heaven": Jesus and the New Testament Authors in Their Relationship to Judaism* (Sheffield: Sheffield Academic Press, 2001), 50–55. On the historical Pharisees, see also the recent volume by Jacob Neusner and Bruce D. Chilton (ed.), *In Quest of the Historical Pharisees* (Waco: Baylor University Press, 2007). In my view, all evidence considered, it seems likely that the Pharisees were not a dominant power in the late first century, which triggers interesting questions about why Matthew's Gospel portrays them as such. For discussion of this aspect of Matthew and

What we are interested in here is, rather, how these groups are portrayed in the story world with regard to divine judgment, and thus, how we may understand the socio-narrative dynamics of this constructed world. We shall deal with the groups one by one, beginning with the group most often referred to, the Pharisees, and continuing with the Sadducees, Herodians, and John's disciples. Before concluding the section, we shall also say a few words on Jesus's disciples as a group among other groups in the narrative.

The Pharisees

In Matthew, the Pharisees appear by themselves in Galilee (9:11, 34; 12:2, 14, 24) as well as in Judea (15:12;[63] 19:3; 22:1-14,[64] 15, 34-40, 41). They are also shown to be in conversation with groups with direct political influence, such as the chief priests in Judea (21:45; 27:62) and scribes, both in Galilee (5:20; 12:38) and Judea (15:1;[65] 23:2-3, 13, 15, 23, 25-26, 27, 29-36).[66] They are, further, connected with other groups, which had only indirect political influence, such as Sadducees in Galilee (16:1-12) and Judea (3:7), and Herodians in Judea (22:15-22). The Pharisees are, finally, mentioned as a collectivity in relationship to John the Baptist's disciples, the latter stating that both groups engage in the same practice of fasting, but noting that Jesus's disciples do not (9:14).[67] What does this bird's-eye view communicate to the readers about the Pharisees in terms of divine judgment?

Jewish society, see Anders Runesson, "Re-Thinking Early Jewish–Christian Relations: Matthean Community History as Pharisaic Intragroup Conflict," *JBL* 127:1 (2008): 95–132.

63. While Matthew introduces the conflict with a reference to both scribes and Pharisees, only the Pharisees are said to have taken offence at Jesus's reply.

64. See below for discussion of this parable in this regard.

65. This event is taking place in Galilee, but the Pharisees and scribes in question are said to be from Judea.

66. There is only one passage that connects the Pharisees with the elders: Matt 15:2. Here, however, we have a reference to the traditions of the elders rather than the elders as a narrative group active alongside the Pharisees.

67. Jesus's reply to John's disciples reveals that after Jesus's death, Jesus's disciples will also fast (Matt 9:15). According to the narrative, then, in the time post-dating the narrative itself, all three groups will engage in the same ritual practice of fasting. (As we see in the Didache, a document closely related to the Gospel of Matthew, in such a situation it becomes important for the followers of Jesus to mark their identity by condemning fasting on the wrong days; "hypocrites" fast on Mondays and Thursdays, while Jesus's followers should fast on Wednesdays and Fridays [Did. 8.1].)

The Pharisees, as a group, represent the principal opponents of the Matthean Jesus.[68] This opposition to Jesus, frequently referred to in the narrative, is used to move the story forward and to allow the author to clarify Jesus's teaching on specific laws (e.g., 15:1–20; 23:16–23) as well as establishing the hermeneutical key to his interpretation of the law as such, the hub around which all other interpretations and teachings revolve (22:34–40). As Jesus's primary opponents, the Pharisees, as a collective, also function as a tool used by the author to define the absolute boundaries of salvation. This is done through repeated and consistent condemnation of this group, excluding them from the kingdom (5:20; 15:12–13;[69] 23:13) and speaking of their "proselytes" as "children of Gehenna" (23:15, cf. 23:33). This is the only group in Matthew's Gospel that is condemned in this way. Finally, and perhaps most importantly for our understanding of Matthew's Gospel more generally, the author refers to the Pharisees and the (Judean) scribes associated with them as the cause behind the predicted fall of the temple.[70]

---

68. So also, Martin Pickup, "Matthew's and Mark's Pharisees," in *In Quest of the Historical Pharisees* (edited by Jacob Neusner and Bruce Chilton; Waco: Baylor University Press, 2007), 67–112. While Pickup's analysis is to the point and includes valuable insights, in my view, he downplays the differences between Matthew and Mark that surface when each story is read on its own terms. Matthew's portrait diverts from Mark mainly because of the aim discernable behind Matthew's narrative; even passages taken over verbatim from Mark produce difference nuances of meaning when they are merged with Matthew's overall story. In the end, especially as we focus on judgment discourse, Matthew's message is quite different from Mark's when it comes to describing this specific group. I do agree with Pickup, though, that "Matthew's portrait of the Pharisees is a thoroughly coherent picture" (108). Cf. Mary Marshall, *The Portrayals of the Pharisees in the Gospels and Acts* (Göttingen: Vandenhoeck and Ruprecht, 2015). While this volume was not yet published when the present study was authored, I note that it shares a similar concern, namely, to identify the nuances between how the different New Testament texts deal with and evaluate the Pharisees (see, e.g., p. 16: "It is the contention of this study that the portrayals of the Pharisees in the four Gospels and Acts are complex and individual. It upholds the validity and importance of a trend in recent scholarship to set aside the goal of reconstructing the Pharisees of history and concentrate instead on the way that they are presented in the different texts"). Marshall's detailed book will be an invaluable tool in future research on this topic.

69. Cf. Matt 3:10, which includes judgment on Sadducees too, unless they produce the "good fruit" that follow from repentance. Since the Pharisees are portrayed as breakers of the Mosaic law (e.g., 5:20; 23:23–36), the reference to exclusion from the kingdom in Matt 13:41–42 is directed at them too, as a group. (Note the connection between 23:13 and 13:41–42 with regard to the offences: these people are both breaking the law *and* misleading others. This reinforces the impression that, while individuals other than the Pharisees are certainly to be included in 13:41–42, this threat is most likely also meant to encompass the Pharisees as a group.)

70. As evidenced by the placement of Matt 23:37–24:2 immediately after accusations have been made against these groups in Matt 23:13–36 for not understanding what proper halakhah is (leading to law-breaking), for being "hypocrites," and for, most importantly, being murderers and children

While Matthew constructs the narrative so as to make it appear as if the Pharisees were also involved in Jesus's death,[71] the author stops short of explicitly accusing them of this crime, guilt of which he mainly reserves for the chief priests. A few words need to be said about this in relation to a couple of passages in Matthew. The key pericope is 22:1–14, understood here within the greater context of 21:23–23:39, which presents Jesus's engagement with different Jewish groups within the temple precincts.[72] We have already discussed 22:1–14 above from the perspective of the criteria of judgment in Matthew.[73] Here, we shall look at: a) who, based on the allegorical character of the parable,[74] the wrongdoers of the parable may be identified with in the story world, and b) how the crime and punishment that follows it should be understood.

In the parable, we find a king, his son, his slaves, and his subjects. There is no doubt that the king represents the God of Israel, and that the son represents Jesus. Contrary to the parable of the tenants in the vineyard, the son is not an active participant in this parable; he is not sent out to accomplish anything, but is identified as the reason for the action being taken by the king, i.e., his sending out of his slaves to invite people for the son's wedding banquet. Since the wedding banquet more than likely refers to the eschatological fulfillment of the kingdom,[75] the narrative time of the parable is equivalent to the

---

of murderers, blaming them even for the shedding of innocent blood within the temple precincts (Matt 23:35).

71. We may note, e.g., that there are no Pharisees mentioned in Jesus's predictions of his own death, neither are they present in the passion story (Matthew follows his sources in this regard). However, he inserts a reference to the Pharisees after Jesus's death, connecting them with the chief priests as they visit Pilate to ask for guards for the tomb (Matt 27:62). This narrative strategy results in the impression that the Pharisees have been there all along, without having to insert them into other parts of the passion story where the chief priests are the leading figures as Jesus is handed over to the Roman authorities. On Matthew's insertion of Pharisees in Matt 21:45, see discussion below.

72. On the interpretation of this parable, cf. David C Sim, "The Man Without the Wedding Garment (Matthew 22:11–13)," HeyJ 31 (1990): 165–78.

73. See pp. 171–72; 183–89.

74. As Sim, "Wedding Garment," 165, notes, there is scholarly consensus that the parable represents "pure Matthean allegory."

75. The parable aims at explaining the kingdom of heaven as it takes form, the wedding referring to its eschatological consummation (cf. Matt 9:15; 25:1–13; see also Rev 19:7–8). See discussion in Donald A. Hagner, Matthew 14–28 (Word Books, 1995), 629; Nolland, Matthew, 885. As Nolland notes, the Matthean version of the parable has a political dimension which is lacking in Luke 14:15–22;

larger Matthean narrative's imagined period immediately preceding the eschatological fulfillment, but postdating Jesus's—the bridegroom's—death and resurrection,[76] which marks the beginning of the end in Matthew's story. In Matthew's narrative world, the parable thus intends to inform the audience about events that take place in history, in this world, as the final days are coming to an end.[77]

If the point in time referred to in the parable is clear, then, what about the location where these events are to take place? The key here is 22:7, where it is stated that the king, as a response to the beatings and killings of his slaves, had the murderers' city destroyed. Virtually all commentators agree that this is a reference to Jerusalem and its destruction.[78] Most scholars would, further, understand the author of the Gospel, writing sometime in the 80s, to be referring back to the historical destruction of Jerusalem in 70 CE by the Romans. While this may be correct, our concern here is with the world portrayed in the story, and in the story, Jerusalem has not yet been destroyed. The Matthean Jesus is presented elsewhere as predicting the fall of Jerusalem, however (23:37–24:2), and it seems clear that he is doing so here too, in the form of a parable. The location for the events described in the first part of the parable, i.e., the invitees' ignoring of

---

on the coalescing of theology and politics in Matthew, see also J. Andrew Overman, *Church and Community in Crisis: The Gospel According to Matthew* (Valley Forge: Trinity Press International, 1996), 301.

76. Jesus's death, and the death of the prophets sent before his time, as well as the consequences of these killings, have already been dealt with in Matt 21:33–44.

77. Anticipating the discussion of chapter 7.2, this means that the people finally invited to the banquet in Matt 22:10 may be understood to include both the people of the land and non-Jews (cf. Matt 28:18–20). This, in turn, implies that both of these groups must be wearing the right clothing for the wedding, i.e., the righteousness that follows from obedience to the Torah, leading to the conclusion that non-Jews, to enter the kingdom, must become proselytes (except for under very specific circumstances; see chapter 7.3).

78. See, e.g., D. Bernhard Weiss, *Das Matthäus-Evangelium* (7th ed.; Göttingen: Vandhoeck & Ruprecht, 1910), 374–75; Overman, *Church and Community*, 300; Carter, *Matthew and the Margins*, 435–36 Rudolf Schnackenburg, *The Gospel of Matthew* (Grand Rapids: Eerdmans, 2002), 214–15; Daniel J. Harrington, *The Gospel of Matthew*, 306, 308; Charles H. Talbert, *Matthew* (Grand Rapids: Baker Academic, 2010), 252–53; Francis Wright Beare, *The Gospel According to Matthew: A Commentary* (Oxford: Basil Blackwell, 1981), 435; Davies and Allison, *Matthew* 3.201–2; Ben Witherington III, *Matthew* (Macon: Smyth & Helwys, 2006), 409; France, *Matthew*, 825; Luz, *Matthew*, 3.54. Cf., however, Hagner, *Matthew 14–28*, 630, who is hesitant regarding this identification, and Nolland, *Matthew*, 887, who rejects it. See also Robert H. Gundry, *Matthew: A Commentary on his Handbook for a Mixed Church under Persecution* (sec. ed.; Grand Rapids: Eerdmans, 1994), 436–37, who argues that Matthew is here using the motif from Isa 5:24–25 (cf. Isa 5:1–7), and that the passage should thus not be understood as pointing back in time to the destruction of Jerusalem in 70 CE.

the invitation and the beating and murdering of the king's slaves, is thus to be identified with the Jerusalem of the narrative world, which is elsewhere identified as "the city of the great king" (5:35).

Considering, then, the characters in this part of the parable and who they are meant to symbolize in the larger narrative world of the Gospel, we may conclude that the wrongdoers are Judeans, or more narrowly defined, Jerusalemites; the city that is destroyed is "their city" (22:7), meaning that Jerusalem is the city in which they live. The king's slaves, on the other hand, are sent to these Jerusalemites in order to invite them to the son's wedding banquet. This indicates a distance between those Jerusalemites that causes the city to be destroyed, on the one hand, and the slaves on the other hand; while not a necessary interpretation, this may be understood as an indication that the slaves are presented as coming from elsewhere, such as Galilee. In favor of this interpretation speaks the fact that Jesus's followers, with whom surely the king's slaves are to be identified—the slaves are loyal to the king and their task is to announce the good news of the son's wedding banquet and invite the chosen ones to take part in it—are explicitly told to return to Galilee after Jesus's resurrection (28:7, 10, 16), and from Galilee launch a mission, which also extended beyond the land.[79] Matthew presents Galilee, not Jerusalem,[80] as the place for Jesus's followers to be based between the resurrection and the end of time.

Combining these interpretive results regarding time, space, and characters in the parable, we may draw the following conclusions with regard to what this mini story is meant to say about the future in the larger narrative world. The God of Israel, who dwells in the Jerusalem temple (23:21) until just before its destruction (23:38), will send messengers loyal to the son and the kingdom, i.e., Jesus's followers, to these Jerusalemites (21:37–39). This invitation to the kingdom and the

---

79. On the mission to the nations, and to whom "the nations" refers, see discussion in Part II.

80. Contrary to Luke, who places the center of the Christ-believers in Jerusalem, and refers to that city as the launching pad for their word-wide mission, not even mentioning Galilee in that context (Luke 24:47–53; Acts 1:6–8). For discussion of this contrast between Matthew and Luke, see Runesson, "City of God?"

accompanying call for repentance which began with John the Baptist's work in Judea (3:5–8) and which will lead to persecution and death for Jesus's followers (22:6; 23:34), will take place after Jesus's resurrection and before the full realization of the kingdom, i.e., before the final judgment. But who, more specifically, are those who beat and murder Jesus's followers?

The parable is presented as one of several discourses that Jesus delivers to different groups within the temple precincts (21:23–23:39). Among the groups mentioned, we find the chief priests (21:23, 45), the elders of the people (21:23), the Pharisees (21:45; 22:15; 34, 41), the Herodians (22:16), Jewish crowds (23:1), and Jesus's disciples (23:1). First of all, we should note, as we have also indicated above, that the fact that Jesus addresses several leadership groups does not mean that Matthew is trying to merge their identities into one type of "Jewish leadership," ignoring the social, political, and "doctrinal" differences between them. Rather, each group, representing a distinct position, is targeted even when they are mentioned together.[81] The rhetorical point is that these different groups—except for the crowds, who do not represent a distinct religio-political group or association,[82] and Jesus's own disciples—find common ground in their opposition to Jesus. In terms of our parable, the following can be said.

Jesus's audience shifts as he delivers speeches and engages in dialogues on the temple mount, and it does so according to what seems to be an overlapping pattern focused on targeting primarily the Pharisees. In 21:23, Jesus speaks to the chief priests and the elders of the people, and the meaning of the first parable (21:28–32) is declared to be that tax collectors and prostitutes will enter the kingdom of God ahead of them, since they did not listen to John the Baptist who had shown them the way of righteousness (21:31–32). The divine verdict here concerns, thus, the final judgment and the parable is directed at the religio-political leadership in the temple.

---

81. For discussion of the problematic assumption that differences between groups, e.g., between Pharisees and Sadducees (Matt 3:7; 16:1, 6, 11–12) are ignored in the narrative, see Carson, "Jewish Leaders," especially 167–69.
82. See below, chapter 3.2.2.1.

With regard to 21:33–44, the parable of the tenants in the vineyard, it seems that the audience has remained the same, although the exact identity of those who are answering Jesus in 21:41 is hidden in the verb (*legousin*).[83] There is nothing in the text until this point that would reveal that the audience has shifted. Those who heard the Gospel of Matthew being read for the first time would have concluded that the people condemned by God to be replaced by a new leadership were the chief priests and the elders, i.e., the religio-political leaders in charge of Jerusalem and the temple.[84] The reason for their displacement would be their direct involvement in the beatings and killings of the prophets (the landowner's slaves; 21:35–36), as well as the killing of Jesus himself (the landowner's son; 21:38–39). What the Matthean Jesus communicates is thus a change of national leadership,[85] based on divine judgment as the kingdom is being established.

This is precisely why the inclusion of the Pharisees in 21:45 comes so abruptly and really makes little sense from a religio-political perspective. The Pharisees, as a group, never had the type of political power that the chief priests and the elders had; the nature of their group was on par with that of other associations, including Jesus's *ekklēsia* (16:18). They did not have an official political standing in the administration of the temple, and thus never had any direct political responsibility for the nation as a whole. This also means that the Pharisees, as a group, were not officially responsible for the relationship between the Jewish people and the Romans.[86] Therefore, the Pharisees could not have been threatened with divine condemnation, resulting in them being ousted from this civic level of

83. In Mark's version of the parable (Mark 12:1–12), Jesus's audience, and thus, those who are condemned (12:9), are said to be the chief priests, the scribes, and the elders (Mark 11:27).

84. Interestingly, this reading is so natural that the Swedish translation from 1981 (= *Bibel 2000*) has inserted "the chief priests and the elders" in 21:41, clarifying who Jesus's dialogue partners were (and thus, whom the parable is targeting), although the Greek text does not mention these groups explicitly here.

85. After the death of Herod I and his son Archelaos, the high priests were considered to be the leaders of the nation (cf. Josephus, *AJ* 20.251).

86. This does not mean, however, that individual Pharisees could not be called upon by those in power in order to discuss matters of political importance; cf. *BJ* 2.411–416. I am grateful to Wally Cirafesi, who brought this passage to my attention. This distinction has significant implications for the interpretation not only of Matthew, but also of, e.g., John's Gospel.

governance; one cannot be deposed from a position never held. Since in Matthew, the execution of Jesus is clearly recounted as based on the doings of the chief priests, the elders, and the scribes in Jerusalem, i.e., with the people officially in charge of religio-civic administration and governance, including Jewish–Roman relations, the Pharisees, as a non-civic group, cannot be presented as guilty of this crime in any direct way.[87] What could be done, however, and this is what we see happening in the text, is to imply that the Pharisees were involved in Jesus's death on an unofficial level, behind the scenes.

This impression of shared guilt between Pharisees and chief priests with regard to Jesus's death is achieved through the inclusion of the Pharisees together with the chief priests—but without the elders—in 22:45, and the same strategy is used, as we noted above, in 27:62. The Pharisees enter, out of nowhere, and replace the elders,[88] who were part of the original audience (21:23). After this moment, the Pharisees take centerstage as Jesus is attacked with questions meant to ensnare him in comments that could be used as accusations against him before both the religio-civic authorities, i.e., the chief priests, elders and scribes, and the Romans (22:15). In this scheming, the religio-civic authorities, the chief priests in particular, had no part; they represent the authorities before which a case can be presented; they are not, however, portrayed as the people involved in the asking of devious questions. This all changes when the chief priests and the elders of the people make the decision to arrest Jesus (something which only religio-civic authorities can do), but at that point, the Pharisees had already been gone from the story for two chapters (26:3–4). Indeed, the Pharisees are never mentioned in any of the three predictions of Jesus's soon-to-come suffering and death in Jerusalem; only the religio-civic authorities are (16:21; 17:22; 20:18).

---

87. Mark's version of this parable is, with regard to its audience and target group, thus closer to what could be claimed to be a historical scenario, namely, that the Jewish religio-civic authorities in Jerusalem were responsible for handing Jesus over to the Romans for execution (Mark 11:27). On the political aspects of Jesus's death from the perspective of Jewish civic authorities trying to protect the land and the people, cf. John 11:48–50.

88. Note the connection between the Jerusalem Pharisees and the tradition of the elders in Matt 15:2–3.

The role of the Pharisees in Matthew is thus not to explain Jesus's death (at the hands of the Romans). While they are said to want to "destroy" (12:14; *apollymi*) or to "entangle" or "entrap" (22:15; *pagideuō*) him, they are actually never successful in this; Jesus always wins these debates, and can never be entrapped with words. In fact, no group manages to do this, and it all ends with no one daring to ask him any more questions (22:46). It is not until one of Jesus's own disciples decides to hand Jesus over to the chief priests (26:14–15) that the chief priests can arrest him and set in motion the process leading to the handing over of him to the non-Jews for execution (20:19). In this betrayal of Jesus the Pharisees had no part, according to Matthew, and thus they cannot be directly, but only indirectly and vaguely, accused for being among those causing Jesus's death.

This means that while the Pharisees are mentioned in 21:45, implying a role for them in Jesus's death, a first-century audience being even slightly familiar with Jewish society would hardly have made this connection in any straightforward manner. They would still have thought only of the chief priests and the elders as the authorities guilty of this crime, since they were the only ones that occupied the political offices empowering them to commit it. The insertion of the Pharisees in this verse implies, though, that they have aligned themselves with the chief priests' interests and supported them. The narrative effect of the somewhat unexpected reference to the Pharisees here, replacing the elders, would be rhetorically effective, rather, in relation to what is to come, and thus, would be pointing forward to the next parable to be delivered; this parable's audience within the narrative would, as a consequence, be thought of as consisting of primarily Pharisees. In other words, the reference to Pharisees in 22:45 serves as a bridge over to the parable of the wedding banquet (22:1–14), which message is targeting primarily the Pharisees, who are also claimed to be the only ones reacting to it (22:15).

Taken together, this means that the reference to "them" (*autois*) in 22:1 should be understood as primarily pointing to the Pharisees, not to the previously mentioned chief priests, and that therefore Jesus is portrayed as targeting (Jerusalem-based) Pharisees in this parable. This conclusion is confirmed when we compare the content of the accusation against the subjects in the parable, as well as the king's punishment of the evildoers, with what is later said about Pharisees and the scribes associated with them in chapter 23. Once all attempts by people associated with non-civic groups to ensnare Jesus with questions have failed (22:46), Jesus turns to his disciples and the crowds delivering the harshest possible critique of one of these groups, the Pharisees. Doing so, he associates them with a specific group of religio-civic administrators, the (Jerusalem) scribes. If we read the parable of the wedding banquet in light of Matthew 23, which represents Jesus's climactic reaction to the hostile interactions on the Temple Mount, we may note the following.

Just as the king in 22:3-4 sends his slaves to the invitees (in Jerusalem), in chapter 23, Jesus states that he will be sending his followers, identified as "prophets, sages, and scribes," to the Pharisees and the scribes associated with them (23:34). In the same way, just as the invitees in 22:6 seized the slaves, insulted[89] (*hybrizō*) them, and killed them, in 23:34, Jesus tells the Pharisees and the Jerusalem scribes that they will kill, flog, and persecute these messengers of God. This accusation about the killing of Jesus's followers/missionaries is related directly to the killing of the prophets in Israel's history (23:29-33), guilt for which is, here, transferred to the Pharisees and scribes who were influenced by them (23:35). Further, in 22:7, the outcome of the invitees killing of the king's slaves is that the king has their city—which we have argued above should be understood as referring to Jerusalem—destroyed. In the same way, the result of the killing of Jesus's "prophets, sages and scribes" (23:34) by the Pharisees and their scribes leads to the destruction of Jerusalem (23:35–24:2).

---

89. Cf. Matt 5:11–12, where Jesus speaks of how the people who listen to him (and follow his teachings: 7:21), when they are reviled, persecuted and spoken ill of, should understand this suffering positively, as a sign that they are blessed just as the prophets were before them; their reward will be great in heaven. On speaking evil and the divine judgment that will follow from such destructive behavior, see Matt 12:36–37 and discussion above, chapter 2.7. It may be noted that this teaching on judgment in relation to evil speech is delivered in the context of an encounter between Jesus and the Pharisees (Matt 12:24).

In sum, while we may discern in Matthew's Gospel attempts at associating Pharisees with the death of Jesus through linking them with the chief priests (21:45; 27:62), this remains a limited and underdeveloped trajectory in the First Gospel. It is true that the Pharisees, as a group, are presented as Jesus's archenemies, and that they want to ensnare him (22:15) or destroy him (12:14); however, they are consistently presented as failing to achieve any such aim. In the end, the only person who manages to conspire successfully against Jesus is one of his own, Judas, who works with the religio-civic authorities in Jerusalem, the chief priests, to achieve this goal (26:14–16). Instead, what we see in Matthew's treatment of the Pharisees is an elaborate rhetorical strategy, constructed to accuse them of the fall of Jerusalem and its temple, the very reason why Jesus had to die to save his people from their sins (1:21; 26:28). The fall of Jerusalem is presented as the divine punishment for the shedding of blood throughout Israel's history, even within the temple itself. This punishment thus affects, in this world, the entire Jewish people, but the verdict is not based on the people's guilt; Matthew's Jesus points specifically to the Pharisees and the scribes who align themselves with them as the ones who brought this disaster upon the people. Therefore, God sends his Messiah to save the many (among the Jewish people[90]) as he punishes the few (among the Jewish people; the religio-political leaders and the Pharisees more specifically).[91]

90. Cf. Malina, "Social-Scientific Approaches," who emphasizes that in order to understand Matthew, even when it is not explicitly mentioned one needs to add 'in Israel' to qualify statements and whom they refer to, such as in the following case: "But many [in Israel] that are first will be last, and the last first (Matt 19:30)" (191).

91. It is quite common among scholars to rather point to the execution of Jesus as the cause behind the destruction of Jerusalem. See, e.g., Overman, *Church and Community*, 300–301; "For Matthew the first revolt and destruction of Jerusalem are directly related to the rejection and death of Jesus" (301). See also Talbert, *Matthew*, 253. While Jesus's death is surely part of the filling up of the measure of sin through the shedding of innocent blood, the point in Matthew is, in my view, that it was already too late to stop the temple's destruction *before* Jesus's execution. The overall logic of the story indicates the following theo-ritual understanding of history: When Jesus arrives on the scene in Matthew 1, Israel is already overrun by hardships, such as Roman imperialism and fragmentation of the land. As in the Hebrew Bible and later Jewish texts, disastrous political and economic developments are interpreted as caused by sins committed within the people itself, since everything that happens on earth is connected with cosmic realities; if the God of Israel is then seen as the strongest of all gods, such disasters can only be understood as this God punishing his people for the corruption and sins committed and not atone for. (For obvious reasons, the fall of Jerusalem takes a central position in such texts, both with regard to the first and the second

The Pharisees are thus used in this story to point to the limits of salvation (their teaching and behavior leads to exclusion from the kingdom),[92] but also, to explain the fall of the temple as God's punishment, which will be executed in the period between Jesus's resurrection and his return. This makes the Pharisees extremely important for the author, especially with regard to the latter accusation, since Jesus's mission as it relates to his self-sacrifice cannot be understood without this group. In other words, the two main parts of Matthew's story, Jesus's teaching and his (sacrificial) death, are both provoked by the Pharisees. Jesus's teaching, on the one hand, is done in order to counteract primarily the teaching of the Pharisees, who mislead the people and condemn the innocent (e.g., 5:20; 9:36; 12:7; 15:3, 12–14; 23:15).[93] Jesus's self-sacrifice, on the other hand, is made because of the fall of the temple, which was caused by the Pharisees and the scribes associated with them.

If the Pharisees and the religio-civic scribal administrators in Jerusalem with whom Matthew's Jesus associates them provoke the fall of Jerusalem, and if this group, as the only group in the Gospel, is unequivocally associated with Gehenna and condemnation in the final judgment (23:15, 33), do we hear anything of their possible repentance and salvation, either as individuals or as a group?

Before we answer that question, since scribes are often associated with the Pharisees, it should be noted that the scribes do not represent

---

temple; Isa 10:4–12; Jer 25:3–14; Zech 7:8–14; Pss. Sol. 1:1–2:10; 4 Ezra 3:24–36; 4:22–25; 5:21–30; 2 Bar. 1:1–5; 4:1; 6:9; 32:2–3; Josephus, *B.J.* 4.386–88; 5:559; 6:96–103, 409–11; 7.323–36, 358–60. The rabbis took a similar approach too, as is seen in, e.g., *b. Yom* 9b). For Matthew, the Pharisees are the key people to blame for this state of things, since they influence the teachers of Israel (i.e., the scribes) and mislead the people, including Jesus's own followers (Matt 5:20; 9:36; 15:14; 16:11–12; 18:6; cf. 24:11, 24). Jesus is thus sent to save his people from their sins (1:21), a task which has two components: teaching the Mosaic law as it was intended to be understood, and providing himself as a sacrifice in order to restore the broken (Mosaic) covenant (26:28). These two components provide a way through the apocalyptic disasters that will inevitably befall the people due to their leaders—including the defilement/destruction of the temple and the consequent loss of the means of atonement—and open up for entry into the coming kingdom when God will restore (or "rebirth"; Matt 19:28) everything to the Edenic state of things intended when the world was created.

92. On the interpretation of Matt 23:2–3, see below, pp. 247–52.

93. This is not to say that the teachings of other groups, such as the Sadducees, are presented as within the limits of the acceptable (cf. Matt 16:12; 22:29). There is no doubt, however, that the teaching of the Pharisees is the main target in this narrative.

a specific association such as the Pharisees or the followers of Jesus; being administrators of various kinds, they represent a profession. This means that repentance can be applied in more general terms when scribes are discussed: they, just as much as anybody else, will have to choose sides and repent in order to make it into the kingdom, and Matthew's narrative presents some examples of this. Those who choose to align themselves with Pharisaic teaching, be it in Galilee or even more so in Jerusalem, choose poorly, and will suffer the consequences of divine punishment. Thus, the real question is not about the scribes, but about the Pharisees, who are the dominant characters with whom various other groups and individuals in the story can choose to align themselves.

Matthew's story has two answers with regard to the Pharisees and their possible salvation. While it is clear that repentance is a very powerful concept in the narrative, as we have discussed above,[94] whatever it is that the Pharisees represent, it is condemned to the fullest extent in the First Gospel. However, if individual Pharisees repent, leave behind their old ways, and begin to produce fruits worthy of repentance, they will escape the coming wrath of God, according to the teaching of John the Baptist (3:7–8).[95] This divine wrath refers to the final judgment, and the reader who re-reads the Gospel already knows that, in the story world, they will not repent as long as Jesus is among them, and so will still provoke divine judgment in this world in the form of temple destruction.

Interestingly, this possibility of repentance is also hinted at in 23:39, although there we are dealing with the (Jerusalem) Pharisees as a group. Here, in the context of divine judgment on Jerusalem based on the evil deeds of the Pharisees, Jesus tells the accused: "For I tell you, you will not see me again until you say, 'Blessed is the one who comes in the name of the Lord.'" These words are focusing on Jerusalem's response to Jesus, but do so pointing to the leaders that have just

---

94. See chapter 2.4.
95. The same is true for the Sadducees according to Matt 3:7. While group identity is assumed, the passage speaks of some ("many"), not all, of the Pharisees and the Sadducees (3:7; *pollous tōn Pharisaiōn kai Saddoukaiōn*), emphasizing individual responsibility above collective identity.

been condemned (23:29–36). What is stated is the possibility of the future redemption of the city as these leaders repent at the return of the Messiah.[96] Such salvation will only be possible, however, if the Pharisees and those who align themselves with them join the joyous and triumphant cries of the Galilean and Judaean crowds as they had previously received Jesus when he entered Jerusalem, quoting the same words from Ps 118:26 (LXX 117:26) as they anticipated the redemption of Israel: "Hosanna to the Son of David! Blessed is the one who comes in the name of the Lord!" (21:9)

Thus, despite all the extreme harshness on the part of the Matthean Jesus, including the accusations against the Pharisees of being guilty of all innocent bloodshed in Israel's history, a door is still left open for the salvation of the Pharisees, based on the all-powerful dynamic of repentance, a dynamic which could also avert divine wrath directed against the arch-traitor Judas.[97] While this is true for Matthew, there is also a second aspect of the relationship between the Pharisees and the divine that is more ominous. As we noted in our discussion of "sin against the holy spirit," there is one sin, and one sin only, for which repentance is not effective, either in this world or the next: the sin of rejecting the divine as present in that which happens around and through Jesus (12:31–33).[98] This discourse about the absolute limit of salvation, the point beyond which no redemption is possible, is set within the context of Jesus reacting to Pharisees, who claim that his power to exorcise demons derives from Beelzebub (12:24). While the ruling itself is general in scope (anyone who does this will be beyond salvation), it is related directly to Pharisaic accusations against Jesus. In sum, the rhetorical effect of this passage, if we understand it in the larger setting of Matthew's description of the Pharisees, is condemnation of all that Pharisees do and teach, and those who want

96. Cf. Dale C. Allison, "Matt 23:39 = Luke 13:35b as a Conditional Prophecy," *JSNT* 18 (1983): 75–84. Allison's use of the term "Israel" (e.g., p. 80) for the target of the verse (those who will not see the Messiah until his return) is, however, problematic, as we shall see below, chapter 3.2.2.2. What is referred to here is not "Israel," but Jerusalem, and Matthew makes a very clear and theologically important distinction between these entities.

97. See the above discussion of Judas and his role in the story, pp. 133–34.

98. See above, chapter 2.4.1.

to avoid God's wrath should therefore stay away from this group. Even Pharisees can, however, if they have not "sinned against the holy spirit" (12:31–32) and if they acknowledge Jesus as the Messiah along with the crowds (23:39; 21:9) and produce fruits worthy of repentance (3:8), avoid punishment and be included in the redemption of Israel.[99]

If this is correct, it is all the more interesting to note that the Matthean Jesus can still insist that both the crowds and his own disciples must listen to—and do—what the Pharisees say (23:2–3). Taken at face value—especially when "say" (*legō*) is translated, as it often is, as "teach" (e.g., NRSV)—it would seem that such a command would be equal to a death sentence, since Jesus, having previously explicitly denounced Pharisaic teaching (e.g., 16:6, 11–12), will, just a few verses later, classify any potential Pharisaic sympathizer, or "proselyte" (*prosēlytos*), as a "child of Gehenna" (23:15). Matthew 23:2–3 has, not surprisingly, been the object of much discussion among scholars.[100] Staying within the world of the text, and understanding this passage in the context of what the Matthean Jesus has elsewhere said about the law, on the one hand, and about the Pharisees, on the other, there is, it seems to me, only one among all the interpretations that have been suggested that works hermeneutically within the narrative, does not create unresolvable tension with other sayings in the Gospel, and would make sense to an audience acquainted with first-century Jewish institutional realities. This is the solution suggested by Mark Allan Powell, that what we see here is a reference to what scribes

---

99. It is of some interest to note that, except for a brief mention of a Levite in Acts 4:36 and "many of the priests" in Acts 6:7, other texts included in the New Testament can describe the Pharisees as the only named group that produces believers in Jesus. Acts 15:5 is a case in point, but Paul is, of course, the clearest example of this phenomenon (Phil 3:5; cf. Acts 23:6). (Several other texts in Luke-Acts describe Pharisees as friendly towards Jesus and his followers, even trying to save their lives [Luke 13:31; Acts 5:34–39]). Historically, it is reasonable to assume that, as in physics, nearness creates friction, meaning that Matthew's Gospel was likely produced in a setting in which Pharisees were prominent. See discussion in Anders Runesson "Re-Thinking Early Jewish–Christian Relations: Matthean Community History as Pharisaic Intragroup Conflict," *JBL* 127:1 (2008): 95–132. As for the historical Jesus, cf. Anthony Le Donne, "The Jewish Leaders," in *Jesus Among Friends and Enemies: A Historical and Literary Introduction to Jesus and the Gospels* (edited by Chris Keith and Larry W. Hurtado; Grand Rapids: Bake Academic, 2011), 199–217; here 217: "In sum, both the historical and the literary contexts wherein we find Jesus suggests that Jesus' closest religious/ideological relatives were the Pharisees."

100. For a presentation of the most common interpretations, see Mark Allan Powell, "Do and Keep What Moses Says (Matthew 23:2–7)," *JBL* 114/3 (1995): 419–35, esp. 420–31.

and Pharisees say (*legō*) *when they read from Torah scrolls*, which they have access to, not to what they teach in terms of halakhah (*poieō*).[101] They know the law, but they do not understand it and cannot therefore interpret it correctly, resulting in their breaking of the law (5:20; 15:3; 23:23), their judging of the innocent (12:7), and their misleading of the people when the people "do" what the Pharisees "do" (15:14; 23:13, 15).[102]

"The seat of Moses,"[103] on which the scribes and Pharisees are said to sit,[104] may be taken literally as a reference to an actual chair on which people sat who had authority or status related to Torah in synagogues, likely implying the official status that comes with an office, such as that of the scribes. Or the expression may be understood merely as metaphorical, in which case we would still have to associate it with a position involving privilege in relation to the law of Moses. This is interesting, since the public reading of Torah in synagogues in the first century is a well-established fact, and Matthew (and other contemporary texts) describes one of the duties of the scribes to be teaching (e.g., 7:29).[105] The interpretive implications of 23:2–3 for a first-century Jewish audience would thus be an understanding of Jesus as requiring both his disciples and the crowds to attend public

---

101. Powell, "Do and Keep," 432. As Powell notes, "[t]o 'speak Torah' means to cite accurately what the scriptures say. To 'do Torah' means to demonstrate understanding of Torah through word and deed (5:19)."

102. E.g., 12:2–14; 15:1–9, 14; 19:3–9; 23:13–28. The strength of the rhetoric of these passages lies precisely in the assumption of shared knowledge between Jesus and the Pharisees of the Torah, as well as the recognition of Torah as authoritative for Jewish life. The problem, as Matthew presents it, is not about knowing what the Torah says; it is about the capacity to interpret the Torah halakhically correct as well as being able, based on one's knowledge of the scriptures, to recognize that what is happening around Jesus is in agreement with, and a fulfillment of the promises of, the scriptures. This is also the problem of the Jerusalem chief priests and scribes: they know the scriptures, but they cannot relate what they know to what is happening around them (2:4–6). King Herod, however, is presented as both ignorant of the scriptures and blind to the current moment, and the Sadducees receive a similar treatment (2:3–4; 22:29). For discussion of this latter point, see Anders Runesson, "Giving Birth to Jesus in the Late First Century: Matthew as Midwife in the Context of Colonisation," in *Infancy Gospels: Stories and Identities* (edited by Claire Clivaz, Andreas Dettwiler, Luc Devilliers, and Enrico Norelli; Tübingen: Mohr Siebeck, 2011), 301–27.

103. See Anders Runesson, Donald D. Binder, and Birger Olsson. *The Ancient Synagogue from its Origins to 200 c.e.: A Source Book* (Leiden: Brill, 2008), No. 67, for discussion of this expression in relation to first-century synagogues.

104. On the aorist *ekathisen* as having gnomic, present force, i.e., meaning "sit," see Nolland, *Matthew*, 923.

105. On Torah reading in synagogues, see Runesson, *Origins*, 193–232; Lee I. Levine, *The Ancient Synagogue: The First Thousand Years* (New Haven: Yale University Press, 2005), 146–62.

synagogue assemblies (on sabbaths) in order to listen to the law of Moses, regardless of who is reading it, since local communities were the owners of Torah scrolls, and they were kept and used in these public institutions.[106] However, Jesus's followers are not to accept the halakhic teaching that follows after the reading, an element of synagogue liturgy also well attested for this time. Thus, we would have to assume that what the Matthean Jesus is implying here is that, in public synagogues, his disciples and his sympathizers should question and possibly debate what has been said in the teaching, including formulations of halakhic rulings based on the readings, i.e., what people must do.[107] Such discussions after the teaching are also witnessed in the sources, and the very architecture of first-century synagogues in the land, with stepped benches lining three or four walls, is witness to the fact that interaction was the main purpose of these assemblies.[108] Continued interaction between Jesus's followers and Pharisees in public synagogues is followed up in, and explains Jesus's accusations in 23:34, namely that his followers will be persecuted in such institutional settings, indicating deep involvement of the movement in public Jewish society after Jesus's death. We may also see here, while anticipating resistance and suffering, an aim on the part of the Matthean Jesus that entire local villages, including their scribes (cf. 13:52), may come to understand the law and the current (eschatologically charged) moment as he and his followers proclaim it.

While this addresses the situation regarding the scribes, the seat of Moses, and public synagogues, the situation is problematized by the mention of Pharisees alongside scribes. Historically, neither the Pharisees nor the later Rabbis were leaders of synagogues.[109] How,

---

106. For discussion of Torah scrolls in communal synagogues, see Levine, *Ancient Synagogue.*

107. In Matt 16:19 and 18:18, Jesus's disciples are given the authority to do just this, i.e., determining what is halakhically acceptable. Cf. Powell, "Do and Keep," 433–34, and n. 54.

108. The closest modern analogy to public synagogue architecture would be the British Parliament. For archaeological remains and plans, see Runesson, Binder, and Olsson, *Source Book.* See also the discussion of synagogue space in James F. Strange, "Archaeology and Synagogues up to about 200 CE," in *The Ancient Synagogue from its Origins until 200 C.E.: Papers Presented at an International Conference at Lund University, October 14-17, 2001* (edited by Birger Olsson and Magnus Zetterholm; Almqvist & Wiksell International, 2003), 37–62.

109. For lack of Pharisaic influence in public synagogues, see Shaye J. D. Cohen, "Where the Pharisees and Rabbis the Leaders of Communal Prayer and Torah Study in the First Century? The Evidence

then, should we understand the reference to the "seat of Moses" in relation to this group? First, it is possible to see here a claim that Pharisees were *indirectly* influencing synagogues, via scribes who would accept their teaching and work to implement it through these public institutions. This would not require Pharisees to have an official position in synagogues, which we know from other source they never had, but would still explain what we have noted above, i.e., that Pharisees, on the one hand, and Jesus and his disciples, on the other, are portrayed as trying to win dominance in Jewish society, using these public institutions as a means to reach their goals. But this does not solve the specific issue of the Pharisees as "sitting on Moses' chair," having the necessary access to Torah scrolls that would allow them to read or quote from them to an audience, as per Powell's theory.

In order to solve this problem, we have to assume an additional separate institutional setting beyond the public institutions that were administered and controlled by scribes. In fact, we have, as we have noted above,[110] evidence for such separate institutional contexts, which were not the center of public life in Jewish society, but represented the views of specific interest groups: the associations. While the historical Jesus seems not to have targeted such semi-public institutions as he proclaimed his message, the strong (negative) focus on one specific association in Matthew, the Pharisees, reveals that things were different for the people within whose midst this Gospel was authored.[111] From a first-century Jewish perspective, it is therefore

of the New Testament, Josephus, and the Early Church Fathers," in *Evolution of the Synagogue: Problems and Progress* (edited by Howard C. Kee and Lynn H. Cohick; Harrisburg: Trinity Press, 1999), 89–105; Levine, *Ancient Synagogues*, 40–41n74, 412–498; cf. Runesson, *Origins*, 379–87. As for the later Rabbis, see also Günter Stemberger, *Jews and Christians in the Holy Land: Palestine in the Fourth Century* (Edinburgh: T&T Clark, 2000), esp. 121–60, 277–83. As Levine, *Ancient Synagogue*, concludes, "the truth of the matter is, the Pharisees had little or nothing to do with the early synagogue, and there is not a shred of evidence pointing to a connection between the two" (41).

110. See pp. 210–11 and sources and literature referred to there.

111. It seems clear that Matthew's narrative attempts to transfer some traditions about Jesus interactions to Pharisaic institutional settings, such as the story of the man with a withered hand who was cured. In Matthew, this happens in what seems to be a Pharisaic association synagogue (Matt 12:9–14; Jesus conversation partners here are identified exclusively as Pharisees [12:2, 14], and it is in "their" synagogue that the episode takes place [12:9]). Also unique to Matthew, we find Jesus founding his own association synagogue, under the name of *ekklēsia* (Matt 16:18–19; 18:15–20. For *ekklēsia* as a synagogue term, see most recently the comprehensive study by Ralph Korner, "Before 'Church': Political, Ethno-Religious and Theological Implications of the Collective

reasonable to understand the Matthean Jesus to imply a reference in our passage to Pharisaic association synagogues, institutions in which they themselves were leaders and custodians of Torah scrolls; as such, they sat on the "chair of Moses." Since we know from other sources of Pharisaic Christ-believers who maintained their group identity while also believing in Jesus as the Messiah (e.g., Acts 15:5), there are no socio-religious reasons to doubt that such a reading of our passage may have been intended. Jesus would simply address both institutional settings where the Torah was kept, read, and studied: the public synagogue where scribes were active, and Pharisaic synagogues, which included subgroups of followers of Jesus.[112]

What, then, would be the interpretive outcome of the above discussion in terms of the Matthean Jesus's less than appreciative attitude to the Pharisees and his view on the limits of salvation? First, we may note that institutional belonging is not identified as relevant for salvation, since Jesus requires his followers and sympathizers to attend assemblies, both public and semi-public, that are run by people whose teaching is said to lead to condemnation in the final judgment. Second, Jesus requires the crowds and his disciples to do (*poieō*) what has been read to them from the scriptures, but avoid anything that is taught by the Pharisees after the readings are performed (23:3: "do not do as they do, for they do not do what they say"). This implies a conservative approach to halakhah on the part of Jesus, which rejects adaptations made to what has been written (cf. 15:3; 19:8).[113] The way of and to the kingdom is thus the way of the law as originally intended by God, as this original intent is construed by Matthew.[114] This original

Designation of Pauline Christ-Followers as *Ekklēsiai*," Ph.D. diss., McMaster University, 2014); idem, "*Ekklēsia* as a Jewish Synagogue Term"; cf. Young-Ho Park, *Paul's Ekklesia as a Civic Assembly* (Tübingen: Mohr Siebeck, 2015), 62–97. For discussion of the Gospels and the historical Jesus in relation to synagogues, see Runesson, "Understanding the New Testament."

112. I have argued elsewhere that those who produced Matthew's Gospel were, in all probability, former Pharisees who were in the process of breaking away from the larger Pharisaic network in order to form their own institution, the *ekklēsia*; see Anders Runesson, "Re-Thinking Early Jewish–Christian Relations: Matthean Community History as Pharisaic Intragroup Conflict." *Journal of Biblical Literature* 127:1 (2008), 95–132.

113. Of course, Jesus's own understanding of halakhah is also an adaptation of ancient texts unto his own time. The point here is, however, that this is not the way it is presented in the story: the claim is that Jesus represents the interpretation of the law of Moses as it was originally intended to be understood, even against the background of that which came before the law, i.e., Genesis.

intent has been revealed by Jesus so that his followers can understand the scriptures when they hear it read by those who administer the scrolls and then apply its rulings directly in their lives. In sum, 23:2–3 confirms emphatically the Jewishness of the narrative world portrayed, keeping Moses and the Mosaic Law in focus and maintaining the importance of Jewish institutions, even in a setting in which divine judgment is more pronounced than elsewhere with regard to specific Jewish groups.[115]

One final aspect of the Pharisees' roles in Matthew's Gospel in relation to divine judgment remains to be commented on. As we have noted above, the Pharisees appear alone in the narrative, but also, and more often, in the company of other Jewish groups. The latter characteristic feature has led several scholars to assume that Matthew is treating, in uninformed and/or anachronistic ways, all Jewish groups as one single enemy of Jesus, a group that may be designated simply as "the Jewish leaders."[116] As we have noted above, this is certainly a more accurate approach than previous attempts at understanding Matthew as painting even the crowds and all other Jewish figures in the narrative as opponents of Jesus, leading to the idea that the Jewish people as a whole would be condemned. However, Matthew's Gospel seems to be more specific, even with regard to the distinction between Jewish groups. This is important to note, since it will have implications for how we understand the role of the Pharisees more specifically.

Looking, first, at passages where Pharisees occur by themselves, in both Galilee and Judea, we may note that they are portrayed in a

114. Daniel Boyarin's study of Mark's Gospel has led him to a similar conclusion of a conservative Jesus, opposing innovative groups such as the Pharisees. See his *The Jewish Gospels: The Story of the Jewish Christ* (New York: The New Press, 2012), 104: "Jesus' Judaism was a conservative reaction against some radical innovations in the Law stemming from the Pharisees and Scribes of Jerusalem." Cf. Le Donne, "Jewish Leaders," 217, who notes that the historical Pharisees were "the least legalistic leaders in Israel."

115. We may compare this perspective on interaction within public Jewish society as well as in Pharisaic associations with the more sectarian community at Qumran, evidence of which will have to be decided on a case-by-case study of the Dead Sea Scrolls. While the Matthean narrative world does describe the establishment of a new association to be constituted in the (narrative) time postdating the Gospel itself, i.e., after Jesus's death and resurrection (Matt 16:18; 18:15–20), the perspective we find in Matthew's Gospel is more integrated in Jewish society than what we can see happening in the sectarian texts among the Dead Sea scrolls.

116. So, e.g., Kingsbury, *Matthew as Story.*

thoroughly negative light. In Galilee, they complain about Jesus eating with "sinners" (9:11) and they accuse him of exorcising demons with the help of "the ruler of the demons" (9:34). This accusation is repeated in 12:24, where they claim that "'it is only by Beelzebul, the ruler of the demons, that this fellow casts out the demons.'" In between these key statements, which through the references to the evil powers that oppose God's spirit reveal the core of the conflict (we shall return to this below), Pharisees challenge Jesus regarding halakhah pertaining to the preparation of food (12:2) and to healing (12:10) on the Sabbath. The outcome of these challenges is that Jesus accuses the Pharisees of condemning innocent people (12:7), showing them to be merciless, i.e., failing to fulfill the key components of the law, without which the keeping of any other part of the law will be considered meaningless (cf. 23:23). The response of the Pharisees, as they have been defeated, is to leave the scene in order to plot how to destroy him (12:14), plans which, however, never succeed. The fact that Pharisees are said to fast, just as John the Baptist's disciples fast and Jesus's disciples will fast after his death (9:14–15), has no mitigating effect on this dark portrait; instead, this information is used to indicate that they have not understood that the "bridegroom" is among them, i.e., that they are blind to what is happening in the current moment.

As soon as Jesus has entered Judea, the attacks from Pharisees continue. They ask a halakhic question about divorce to test Jesus (19:3); Jesus's response and their continued discussion reveals that while the Pharisees know the Torah (19:7), they do not understand how to interpret it. Further, in the parable of the wedding banquet (22:1–14), if the interpretation I have presented above is correct, the Pharisees alone are accused of killing Jesus's followers as they proclaim the message of the kingdom after Jesus's death and resurrection; the guilt that is accumulated by the shedding of innocent blood will lead to the fall of Jerusalem. Finally, contrary to Mark, Matthew has a Pharisee ask Jesus about the greatest commandment in the law, i.e., its hermeneutical center (22:34–39). The positive interaction between Jesus and a scribe around this issue in Mark (Mark 12:28–34) is replaced by silence in Matthew. Given the theory of Markan priority, which is, in my view, the theory that best explains the material to which we have access, this silence of Jesus's opponents is intentional on the part of the author. Set within the larger portrait of the Pharisees in the Gospel, it seems that what is communicated by this silence is that the Pharisees agree with Jesus on this principle, but if they acknowledge this, they will not be able to defend their other halakhic interpretations forwarded in the Gospel, which, according to Matthew, contradict the very principle of this double command to love both God and neighbor. This rhetorical technique, or pattern, of trapping enemies with their own words, proving their inconsistent approach to Law, is repeated elsewhere in the Gospel, including in the passage directly following the love command (22:41–46); this short exchange of words silences the Pharisees for the rest of the Gospel.

The critique directed exclusively against the Pharisees, who are mentioned more often and portrayed in more detail than any other group in the Gospel, is thus massive and devastating. When we widen the scope of the analysis to include passages in which Pharisees are paired with other groups, the same type of accusations is maintained. This indicates a rhetorical strategy in which the Pharisees are presented as the key evildoers, and all who align themselves with them will share in their condemnation. Further, while the Pharisees connect with all other groups (Sadducees, Herodians, chief priests, [elders[117]], and Galilean and Judean scribes), no other single group aligns itself

---

117. See Matt 15:1–2. This reference to the "tradition of the elders" signals only an indirect connection, since the Pharisees are portrayed as having a joint purpose here with the Judean scribes. The issue of to whom "the elders" refer is difficult; cf. discussion in Nolland, *Matthew*, 610–11; Davies and Allison, *Matthew*, 2.519–20. While it is clear that these traditions (in this case rules concerning the washing of hands before eating ordinary food) are presented as upheld by the Pharisees, they are also said to be agreed upon by the scribes of Jerusalem, the latter representing religio-civic aspects of Jewish society, rather than any specific association. The mention of these scribes here connects the "tradition of the elders" with the administration of Jerusalem, and thus, implicitly with other leaders on the national scene, such as the elders, who are mentioned elsewhere as enemies of Jesus (note especially Jesus prediction of his own future suffering at the hands of the elders in Matt 16:21 and their involvement in his arrest [Matt 26:3–5]). In other words, regardless of whether we should understand "tradition of the elders" as referring to traditions transmitted by the elders of Jerusalem, or as traditions transmitted by the Pharisees who claim that they uphold the laws affirmed by the generations of old, these traditions are narratively associated with the administrative leaders of Jerusalem.

with all other groups mentioned in the Gospel. The Pharisees thus represent a force which links groups in their resistance against Jesus, sometimes actively provoking hostility by gathering people otherwise unrelated to their own understanding of Jewish life and practice (e.g., 22:15–16).

Returning to the passages referred to above, in which the Pharisees are accusing Jesus of being aligned with the forces of evil as he performs his exorcisms (9:34; 12:24), we may note that, as Jesus is turning the accusation around at the Pharisees themselves, this group is said to be struggling against God's Spirit (12:27), since, ultimately, the struggle to establish the kingdom is presented as a battle between God and Satan.[118] This is also something to which exorcists aligned with the Pharisees themselves will have to agree, since all exorcists are on God's side against Satan and Satan's demons, according to what is presented as general knowledge and irrefutable logic.[119] Thus, when Pharisees challenge Jesus, they align themselves with Satan's aims, which are focused on preventing that which Jesus is bringing, i.e., the kingdom (12:28).[120] In other words, the Pharisees are presented in Matthew as brokers of evil, the source of which is the devil (13:39), who links various groups (but not the Jewish crowds) in a network aiming at hindering the work of God's spirit. Doing so, they function in a way similar to the chief priests, who stand at the center of the religio-civic opposition to Jesus and link other groups in their attempts to stop him from succeeding in his work.

This seems to be the core concern as Matthew molds the Pharisees into Jesus's principal enemies. The form of Pharisaic resistance against the kingdom will take different expressions in various settings as the

---

118. Cf. Acts 5:39 where the author has a prominent Pharisee, Gamaliel, warn the council (*synedrion*) in Jerusalem that "if it [i.e., the Jesus movement] is of God, you will not be able to overthrow them—in that case you may even be found fighting against God!" The same perspective, again associated with Pharisees, is found in Acts 23:9. Such positive depictions of Pharisees, which we also find elsewhere in Luke (Luke 7:39; 11:37; 13:31), are lacking in Matthew's Gospel.

119. The best discussion of this passage is, in my view, that of Luz, *Matthew*, 2.203–4. What is qualitatively different with Jesus's exorcisms compared with the exorcisms of those who sympathize with the Pharisees is the fact that it is Jesus, as the bringer of the kingdom, who performs them; note the emphatic *egō* in Matt 12:28.

120. Cf. Matt 4:1–11.

narrative progresses, but all who align themselves with the Pharisees will share in their condemnation, especially the scribes, who more than other groups represent a link between Jewish interest groups and public Jewish society on a local as well as on a national level. In the final eschatological judgment, the devil and the angels associated with the devil will be condemned to destruction (25:41), along with all breakers of the law, who will be collected and destroyed like weeds by God's angels (13:41–42). The only group identified as destined for "uprooting" (*ekrizoō*) is the Pharisees (15:12–13); to be led by them is, for the Matthean Jesus, to become aligned with evil powers, which, in the end, means sharing their fate (15:14; cf. 23:13).

In sum, in terms of divine wrath, while nothing can stop the destruction of the temple due to the atrocities committed and the guilt that has been accumulated ("the measure has been filled"; 23:32), there is still a door open for Pharisees with regard to the final judgment, which will save them from Gehenna: their repentance as Jesus returns to redeem Jerusalem (23:39). Remaining within, or aligning oneself with the Pharisaic interpretive community will, however, lead to halakhic decisions based on a flawed understanding and weighing of the commandments, and thus, consequently, to exclusion from the coming kingdom based on lack of righteousness.[121]

The Sadducees and the Herodians

In contrast to the Pharisees, the Sadducees receive little attention in Matthew's narrative, and the Herodians even less, the former being referred to seven times and the latter only once. As for the Sadducees, they appear only once by themselves. Interestingly, given the assumption that when groups are mentioned by themselves we receive more specific information about them, we may note here that Sadducees are specifically singled out as a group which does not—contrary to what we know of the Pharisees—accept the idea of the resurrection of the dead (22:23–33). While we find no explicit mention

---

121. Cf. Matt 5:20; 15:3, 13–14; 16:11–12; 23:15, 23, 33.

of divine judgment of the Sadducees here, they are depicted—again contrary to the Pharisees—as being ignorant of the scriptures; they are also said not to understand the power of God (*dynamis tou theou*; 22:29). As Jesus responds to their question about resurrection, the position of the Sadducees is contrasted with the reaction of the crowds, who are amazed by Jesus's teaching (22:33; cf. 7:28), and the Pharisees, who are said to take note of the fact that Jesus had made the Sadducees speechless (22:34). The teaching of the Sadducees is otherwise more generally condemned, alongside that of the Pharisees in the discourse in 16:5–12, after the two groups have joined forces to require a sign from Jesus in order to test him (16:1–4).

Interestingly, while historical considerations would suggest that the Sadducees as a group were attractive to Jerusalem aristocrats, the Sadducees are never mentioned together with any other group, except the Pharisees, effectively divorcing them from religio-civic groups such as the chief priests, the elders, and the scribes. This makes the Pharisees, contrary to what historical reflection would suggest, the only group in Matthew that bridges the gap between a specific Jewish interest group and public Jewish society, via their connection to primarily the scribes, but also, to the chief priests (who in turn, are connected with the scribes and the elders). This, in effect, "neutralizes" the Sadducees, making them less "dangerous" for the Matthean Jesus, since they are not related to the people who have authority to hand him over to the Romans for execution.

While Sadducees—when mentioned together with the Pharisees—are considered "evil" (*ponēros*; 16:4), there is only one explicit text about divine judgment that is directed at them. In this passage, they are again paired with the Pharisees as they are rebuked by John the Baptist, who accuses them for not producing fruit worthy of repentance (3:7–8), making his baptism useless for them in light of God's coming wrath at the time of the final judgment (3:10–12). This verdict, and warning, is contrasted with the reaction of ordinary people, who do not belong within any specific Jewish association or interest group, to John's call for repentance and baptism; they come to him from Jerusalem and Judea and the region along the Jordan and are baptized without any further comments from the author. It is only when the Pharisees and the Sadducees show up that John's anger is triggered and the prophetic utterances about the coming judgment are pronounced.[122]

We may thus conclude that while the Sadducees play a marginal role in the Gospel, they are portrayed as ignorant of the scriptures as well as of God's power, and, when paired with Pharisees, they are considered evil and in desperate need of the type of repentance that produces righteous deeds. Beyond this, they are never said to have caused God's judgment on the people, nor to be destined for Gehenna.

We have noted that Matthew, when referring to the Sadducees themselves without connecting them to the Pharisees, pinpoints a specific characteristic of their teaching, the rejection of the belief in the resurrection of the dead. Similarly, when Matthew mentions the Herodians, although together with the Pharisees, they are presented as playing a role which makes historical and political sense, if, as we have discussed above, this group should be understood as supporters of the Herodian family (22:15–22).[123] While Matthew clearly presents the Herodian rulers as illegitimate,[124] the Herodians have no independent narrative function in our text, but are used to illustrate how the Pharisees try to "destroy" or ensnare Jesus (cf. 12:14; 22:15). Their presence here fills the function of bringing the political aspect of the

---

122. Luz, *Matthew*, 1.137, notes the difference between these groups, on the one hand, and the people more generally, on the other, both here and elsewhere in the Gospel, rightly concluding that the former are those who oppose John and Jesus, not the latter, something which has been obscured in the later reception of the Gospel in which the entire Jewish people has been portrayed as the enemies of the two. However, Luz problematically understands this to shift in the passion narrative, so that "the holy nation" as a whole is identified with its leaders and judged to lose the promise, referring to Matt 21:43 and 27:24–25. We have already dealt with the former passage above and we shall return to discuss 27:24–25 in chapter 3.2.2.2. There is, in my opinion, no reason to read Matthew's story the way Luz does in this regard; in fact, such a reading is counter-intuitive seen from the perspective of the larger narrative and, indeed, is contrary to the very purpose of Jesus as it is portrayed in the Gospel in the first place.

123. Mark, however, has two mentions of the Herodians, the first of which lacks any obvious political context (Mark 3:1–6; cf. Matt 12:9–14).

124. See discussion in Anders Runesson "Giving Birth to Jesus in the Late First Century: Matthew as Midwife in the Context of Colonisation," in *Infancy Gospels: Stories and Identities* (edited by Claire Clivaz, Andreas Dettwiler, Luc Devilliers, and Enrico Norelli; Tübingen: Mohr Siebeck, 2011), 301–27.

Pharisaic aims into sharper focus, namely, to have Jesus charged on what we would call political rather than only halakhic grounds.[125] The focus on the Pharisees in Matthew's version of the story is further emphasized by the fact that Mark, contrary to Matthew, has Jerusalem's chief priests, scribes, and elders initiate this attempt at capturing Jesus by sending Pharisees and Herodians to accomplish their own intentions (Mark 11:27; 12:13–17); in Mark's version of the story, the Pharisees are, like the Herodians, simply tools in the hands of the religio-civic leaders. For Matthew, this is yet another (failed) attempt by the Pharisees to ensnare Jesus, this time through linking themselves with other groups who could potentially help them to achieve their goals. In fact, the Herodians are so marginal that, while critiqued for their evil intensions and for their hypocrisy (22:18), they are not targeted for divine judgment or blamed for any disasters; after their failed deception, they are "amazed" (thaumazō; 22:22) at Jesus's answer and simply walk away.

The Disciples of John

Of all groups mentioned in the narrative, John and his disciples are closest to Jesus and his followers. This is to be expected, since Jesus, although claimed by John to be more important than himself, is baptized by John (3:13–17; cf. 11:11), their message is identical ("Repent, for the kingdom of heaven has come near!"; 3:1; 4:17), both condemn the Pharisees (3:7–8), both are opposed by the religio-civic leaders in Jerusalem, i.e., the chief priests and the elders (21:23, 25), as well as by scribes (16:21; 17:12), and both are supported by partly the same people: prostitutes/sinners and tax collectors (9:10; 21:32), and more generally, the crowds, i.e., the Jewish majority (21:26). Further, Jesus begins his proclamation once John has been imprisoned by Antipas (4:12), suggesting a scenario in which John, who has already

---

125. One should, of course, not make too sharp a distinction between politics and halakhah. As we have noted above, whatever takes place on earth is intertwined with cosmic realities, so that the keeping of the correct halakhah would necessarily have what we would call political implications. Vice versa, political disasters would be understood as symptoms of insufficient or flawed observance of the Torah.

initiated the coming of the kingdom (11:12), hands over the baton to Jesus, who alone will fulfill that with which John can no longer help him. The relationship between the two is so close that Antipas, after he has had John executed, thinks Jesus is John resurrected from the dead (14:2), and some from among the people think the same (16:14). For Jesus, however, John is Elijah (11:14; 17:11–13), which underlines the eschatological urgency of the mission and message of the Messiah, i.e., Jesus himself (16:16–17), as the final judgment draws near.[126]

Although Matthew reports some tension between John and Jesus in that John, at one point, expresses uncertainty about who Jesus really is (11:23), this functions only as a tool for the Matthean Jesus to elaborate on his own identity, as evidenced by what is happening around him, all of which are presented as signs that he is the one who was to come: "the blind receive their sight, the lame walk, the lepers are cleansed, the deaf hear, the dead are raised, and the poor have good news brought to them" (11:5).[127] There is no direct judgment pronounced upon John, although the beatitude that follows the list of signs, "blessed is anyone who takes no offense at me" (11:6), points to the importance of displaying trust in the fact that Jesus is the one. Indeed, the statement in 11:11 that "among those born of women no one has arisen greater than John the Baptist; yet the least in the kingdom of heaven is greater than he" seems to suggest that John, and thus, by implication, his disciples who are portrayed as outsiders in relation to the Jesus group (cf. 9:14) are outside the kingdom. As France has noted, however, this may rather be a reference to John's place in the scheme of salvation history.[128]

In sum, noting that John and his disciples are portrayed as outsiders to the Jesus group, we still do not find any words of judgment pronounced upon them. In fact, not listening to John and rejection of his proclamation leads to negative judgment (21:31–32). Rather, the very strong emphasis on a shared purpose between John and Jesus points toward a continued positive relationship between the two

---

126. Cf. Mal 3:22–24 (LXX 3:22–23, 24; Eng. 4:4–6).
127. Cf. Luke 4:18; Isa 61:1.
128. France, *Matthew*, 425.

groups, even if eventually it may be assumed that John's disciples ideally should, from the Matthean Jesus's point of view, join Jesus's group, just as John himself was portrayed as being of lesser significance than Jesus. Being outside the Jesus group, thus, does not automatically lead to condemnation. Indeed, turning the spotlight to Jesus's own followers, we may reverse that statement: belonging to the Jesus group does not automatically lead to salvation.

The Disciples of Jesus

As we have noted above, the law of Moses must be kept by all, and various forms of punishment will follow for anyone who does not observe the commandments; Jesus's followers are no different than other Jews in this regard.[129] The disciples are, further, often instructed by Jesus along with the crowds, so that the boundaries between the crowds and the disciples are blurred (e.g., 5:1–2; 7:28–29). This reinforces the lack of clear demarcation lines between the disciples and the majority of the Jewish people, i.e., those who are not identified as belonging to a specific group or as holding a particular office in city or state (temple) administration. The indistinct boundaries of Jesus's movement, in turn, gives the impression of a large following, with one inner and one outer circle around Jesus.[130] Narrowing the focus to look specifically at individuals directly identifiable as inner-circle followers of Jesus, i.e., the disciples, we may note the following.

The disciples' loyalty, moral strength, and courage are portrayed as questionable. There is a real risk that they will not acknowledge Jesus before others when in trouble, and, therefore, they have to be warned about the dire consequences of such lack of courage (10:32–33). In fact, despite the serious warning and the threat of ultimate alienation from God at the final judgment, this anticipated weakness in the face of

---

129. See above, chapter 2.1.2.
130. Cf. Talbert, *Matthew*, 74: "The crowds in Matthew can sometimes be regarded as Jesus' disciples (8:19–20; 9:27–29; 14:13; 20:29–34; 21:9–11). In these instances, the crowds are part of the larger circle of Jesus's followers (e.g., 10:24, 25, 42; 27:57)." Commenting on Matt 4:25, Luz, *Matthew*, 1.166, makes a similar point: "the crowds and the disciples [...] may not be understood as two complete separate groups." We shall return to this in chapter 3.2.2.1.

danger turns into reality when Jesus is arrested. In order to save their lives, all disciples abandon their master and Peter, the foremost of all disciples (16:18–19), repeatedly and explicitly denies knowing Jesus at all (26:56, 69–75; cf. 26:31–35).[131]

Indeed, Peter is, at one point, said to be the mouthpiece of God's ultimate enemy, Satan (16:23; cf. 4:1–11). Such a direct accusation is not leveled even at the Pharisees. What is signaled here is that the evil one is never far from Jesus, but tries to ensnare him even when he is among friends who, based on divine revelation, acknowledge him as the Messiah (16:16–17).[132] Further, it is a disciple who succeeds where the Pharisees, the Sadducees, and the Herodians have failed—namely, to have Jesus handed over to the Jewish religio-civic authorities, who, seeking the death penalty, will, in turn, have him delivered to the Romans for execution (26:14–16, 47–50). The weakness of the disciples, to the point of denial and betrayal, function narratively to emphasize Jesus's strength in relation to his opponents, who fail to ensnare and defeat him. It takes a traitor to open the door for those who are in a position to start a judicial chain reaction leading to Jesus's execution, someone who is close to the Messiah and knows him and his habits well.[133]

More generally, the disciples, similarly to the Pharisees, are portrayed as seeking honor. They have to be taught specifically that this is not the way of the kingdom (20:20–28; cf. 18:1–5). Thus, the honor-seeking behavior of the Pharisees can later be used by the Matthean Jesus in order to repeat his instruction about kingdom equality, about how not to behave (23:5–7, 8–12). Proceeding even to the core issue of the fundamentally important concept of trust/faithfulness/loyalty (*pistis*), the disciples are presented as lacking (17:20), leading Jesus to exclaim: "You faithless and perverse

---

131. Cf. Gundry, *Peter*, 43, 45–46. While Gundry is certainly correct in emphasizing the importance of this passage for the portrayal of Peter in this Gospel, in my view, terming this as "apostasy" misses the point of the story, especially with regard to how Matthew has developed his theology of judgment in relation to repentance and forgiveness. See further discussion below.

132. Cf. Matt 4:1–11.

133. For further discussion of Judas, see above, pp. 133–34.

generation, how much longer must I be with you? How much longer must I put up with you?" (17:17)

Is there, then, nothing that positively distinguishes the inner circle of Jesus's disciples from other Jews in terms of divine judgment? To be sure, Matthew's Jesus mentions specific rewards that will be given to those who leave everything behind to follow Jesus, and these followers will also inherit eternal life (19:29). But similar awards will also be given to people who are not among the disciples (10:40–42), and even non-Jews who do not know either Jesus or his followers may, under certain circumstances, inherit eternal life (25:31–46).[134] In other words, while the disciples may receive special teaching from Jesus (e.g., 18:1–35), they must follow the Jewish law just as much as other Jews (5:1–2, 17–20; 7:21–23, 28–29).[135] The risk of their failure, however, is highlighted more than that of the crowds. The danger of falling away from right conduct, or defecting, continue beyond Jesus's death and resurrection since, during the great suffering that will accompany the prelude to the final judgment and the subsequent full realization of the kingdom, their love may grow cold (24:12), and they may be misled by false prophets and Messiah figures (24:24). Indeed, Matthew emphasizes repeatedly that his followers are at great risk and that their true loyalty and obedience will become apparent, and judged, when Jesus returns (13:36–43, 47–50; 22:11–14; 24:48–51; 25:1–13, 14–30).[136]

In the end, to put it plainly, in terms of conduct, there is nothing that positively marks Jesus's disciples as different from other characters in the story in any respect, even when it comes to rewards and the prospect of life in the kingdom, i.e., eternal life. The only characteristic that does distinguish them and make them special is the single fact that Jesus has chosen them for specific kingdom-related tasks, namely to: a)

---

134. See discussion below, chapter 7.3.
135. On divine punishments that follow for anyone who does not observe the rules laid out in the Gospel, see John Kloppenborg, "The Representation of Violence in Synoptic Parables," in *Mark and Matthew. Comparative Readings I: Understanding the Earliest Gospels in their First Century Settings* (edited by Eve-Marie Becker and Anders Runesson; Tübingen: Mohr Siebeck, 2011), 323–51: "Matthew expands the scope and intensity of divine violence so that it is applied both to opponents and to underperforming insiders" (351).
136. Cf. Gundry, *Peter*, 55–56.

travel throughout Israel, proclaiming the good news that the kingdom has come near, curing the sick, raising the dead, cleansing the lepers, and casting out demons (10:1–8);[137] b) establish an *ekklēsia* and be in charge of developing proper halakhah (16:18–19; cf. 18:18) based on Jesus's teachings, which, contrary to the teachings of the Pharisees, have been claimed to conform with God's intentions (15:3–9), and thus, also with the intentions of the law of Moses and the teaching of the prophets (5:17; 7:12; 17:3–4; 22:34–39); c) lead the people of Israel (19:28; cf. 16:18[138]); d) observe a ritual meal effecting atonement (26:26–29);[139] and e) make disciples of the nations, teaching them to keep the Jewish

137. Cf. Matt 4:23; 9:35–38; 11:1. It may be noted that while Jesus until this point in the narrative has limited his proclamation and healing of the afflicted to the Galilee and some of the surrounding areas, the disciples are sent out to "the lost sheep of the house of Israel" (10:6), i.e., they are to travel the entire land of Israel (10:23), including Judea. Narratively speaking, the disciples are thus presented as having proclaimed the message of the kingdom in Judea before Jesus begins his journey to Jerusalem in 19:1. However, at the same time, the disciples are portrayed as always being close to Jesus, traveling with him even after chapter 10 (e.g., 12:1), which reinforces the impression that the speech in 10:1–42 is meant to be understood primarily as a paradigmatic description of Jesus's instructions to the disciples, and their implications; the "Mission Discourse," as this section of Matthew is often called, is thus somewhat detached from the narrative progression and chronology of the Gospel, despite Matt 10:1, 5. The paradigmatic nature of Jesus's instructions to his disciples, together with a few hints in the text, indicate that these tasks are meant to be performed primarily after Jesus's death and resurrection and before his triumphant return (cf. 10:23), rather than before Jesus's journey to Jerusalem, which the narrative chronology otherwise demands. The "Mission Discourse" is thus connected in terms of content—and points forward to—the statements in Matt 22:3–6 and 23:34, which predict the suffering that the disciples will be exposed to in Jerusalem and elsewhere in the land. The discourse is also later to be supplemented by a mission to the nations in Matt 28:18–20, and is therefore, further, connected to the implications of that wider mission in terms of how people around them react when they see them suffering (10:40–42; 25:31–46). This connection, which materializes as rewards or punishments, is explained by the fact that Jesus himself is identified with his disciples in such a way that whatever happens to them happens to him; rewards and punishments will be delivered accordingly. On the relationship between Jesus and the disciples in terms of mission, see also Eung Chun Park, *The Mission Discourse in Matthew's Interpretation* (Tübingen: Mohr Siebeck, 1995), 40.

138. While the establishing of this *ekklēsia* means, institutionally, the creation of an association, i.e., a non-civic institution, the use of this term in the setting of Matthew's Gospel signals an aim to take over the rule of Israel, gathering the people (or citizens) of Israel around the leadership of Peter and the other disciples.

139. It is not clear in Matthew's version of this tradition whether Jesus intends this ritual meal of atonement to be repeated by his disciples (yearly? weekly?), or if this meal is a one-time only enactment of Jesus's sacrificial death, embodying its atoning effects. What is clear, however, is that the sacrifice, i.e., Jesus's death, which is present in the meal, will bring atonement for people beyond the twelve disciples who had gathered with him for the meal; what Jesus is doing will have an atoning affect "for many" (26:28). Since the terms here are sacrificial, and a sacrificial meal usually accompanied the sacrifices in the temple, and certainly the Passover sacrifice, it is likely that this wider applicability of the effects of Jesus's sacrifice enacted in the meal means that the meal itself is meant to be repeated and, as such, provide the atoning benefits associated with a sacrificial meal to those who partake in it. See also discussion in Davies and Allison, *Matthew*, 3. 465, 477, who note that the idea of the repetition of the meal is not discernable in the text, but will have to be assumed by a community who would already be partaking in such meals of atonement.

law (28:19–20). With these tasks come authority and power (10:1; 19:28; cf. 21:21–22), which must not be abused; such abuse, based on the will to power and honor, will be punished (23:11–12).

The key to understanding the position of the disciples in Matthew's Gospel is, thus, their election by Jesus and not the status they might be assumed to have in relation to divine judgment, either positive or negative. The election itself is unrelated to any privileges in this regard; if anything, the disciples are watched more closely than others, based on their anticipated leadership position in Israel as representing the twelve tribes, although this is never stated explicitly in the text.[140] What is interesting, though, is that the disciples themselves comprise a criterion of judgment for others in terms of how they are treated. We noted above that John the Baptist's teaching is presented as a criterion of judgment (22:31–32). While the same is also said about Jesus's disciples (10:14–15), with the latter this notion is taken one step further: it is not only their teaching, but rather they themselves, as individuals belonging to a group, who are placed front and center. We see this both in relation to the Jewish people in 10:40–42 and in relation to non-Jews in 25:31–46. Whatever good is done to the disciples by people not belonging to their group will result in rewards—indeed, will even open up for eternal life for non-Jews—for the people performing these deeds; conversely, whatever good deeds that could have been done by non-Jews to help suffering disciples, but which were never done, will lead to condemnation in the final judgment.

We have already dealt with this pattern of thought above, and we shall return to it below, when we discuss the place of the non-Jews in

---

140. It is a common theme in Jewish texts that, with certain tasks follow greater responsibilities, and therefore, divine judgment will be meted out using a proportionally stricter measure. Cf. James 3:1 (for a concise discussion of this verse, see Richard Bauckham, "James," in *Eerdmans Commentary on the Bible* [edited by James D.G. Dunn; Grand Rapids: Eerdmans], 1483–92, here 1488). A similar principle relates to prophecy in the Hebrew Bible (e.g., Ezek 33:7–9; Jer 1:17). On a more general level, this thought pattern is used to distinguish the Jewish people from non-Jews in Matthew's Gospel; the Jews are expected to know more and are thus judged stricter than non-Jews should they fail to recognize as God's work that which is happening in their midst (see discussion above, pp. 27–28n88). The same basic interpretive paradigm is also found in other Jewish texts, such as the Gospel of John (applied to Pharisees; John 9:41) and Josephus, who states that, since the people is instructed in their law on a weekly basis (in public synagogues), they, contrary to other nations, know their law; if the law is still broken, punishment cannot be evaded based on excuses (*C. Ap.* 2.175–78).

Matthew. What is important for our purposes in this section is that the status of the disciples is based on Jesus's identification with them, so that everything that happens to them is understood as happening to him. The disciples, as a Jewish group comprising the (new) center within the Jewish people, are thus "protected" by, on the one hand, promises of rewards to those who treat them compassionately, and, on the other hand, threats of unleashed divine wrath in the final judgment should they be harmed.[141] As we have noted above, and shall return to in some detail below, this pattern of thought reflects the principle of blessings and curses woven into the Abrahamic covenant in Gen 12:3.[142]

If we understand this Abrahamic pattern as applied to the disciples and the extended body around them, i.e., the *ekklēsia*, which appears to be the intended reading of these passages, the interpretive context in which this pattern has taken form seems to necessitate the idea that this group of Jesus followers constitute the core of the Jewish people, the ones who fulfill, as the salt of the land and the light of the world (5:13–16), their intended purpose as Abraham's descendants.[143] Such a conclusion is further supported by the family relationship that Jesus claims between himself and his disciples, as the latter are identified as those who do his Father's will (12:49–50).[144] Jesus, in turn, is identified

---

141. Cf. Matt 18:6–7; 10:28–31.

142. See chapters 2.3 and 7.3.

143. Abraham is mentioned seven times in Matthew and it is clear that the author thinks of the God of Israel (Matt 15:31) more specifically as the God of Abraham (Matt 22:32). Contrary to Luke, who traces Jesus's ancestry back to Adam, and thus, highlights the aspect of non-Jewish participation in what is often called salvation history (Luke 3:38), Matthew's genealogy emphasizes Abraham as the starting point (Matt 1:1, 2, 17). The perspective of the Gospel is, as a consequence, focused on the Jewish people (on Abraham as primarily a symbol of the Jewish people, not as later Christian tradition has it, as the foundation of non-Jewish forms of Christianity; see Anders Runesson, "Extending or Restricting the Covenant? Abraham and the People of God in Christian Tradition," *Lexington Theological Quarterly*, Vol. XLIV:1 [2011] 1–17, esp. 5–10). Abrahamic descent does not protect from divine wrath, as we have already noted; rather, on the contrary, it intensifies the strictness of the judgment. This also means that Abrahamic descent is never questioned as a key category, as we have argued in relation to Matt 3:9; it represents a foundational principle with implications for divine judgment. Matthew's John and Jesus do not replace Abrahamic descent with an assumed non-ethnic perspective, a "religion" in the modern sense of that word, but emphasize that God has the power to transform stones into children of Abraham, i.e., the people of God is open for non-Jews who want to convert; Matthew's is a theology of addition, not of replacement. We shall return to the issue of proselytes below, chapter 7.2.

144. The family metaphor thus works both ways: Doing the will of God, i.e., keeping the law of Moses as interpreted by Jesus, incorporates the doer into Jesus's family; the shedding of innocent blood, on the other hand, will merge the perpetrators with previous evildoers, so that they become

as the son of Abraham (1:1). The Abrahamic lineage is thus present on two levels, as Jesus is also identifying with his followers both when they are met with compassion and when they suffer (10:40–42; 25:31–46).

In sum, then, Jesus's disciples have special status based on their being chosen by Jesus, but the group's status and boundaries do not constitute the boundaries within which rewards will be exclusively distributed and salvation offered. The permeable boundaries of the core group, the disciples, have no effect with regard to divine rewards and punishment; neither does the wider circle around Jesus, which overlaps with the "crowds,"[145] block access to salvation for those outside it. As will be further discussed in Part II, even the boundary of the Jewish people is porous with regard to one specific aspect, salvation, since non-Jews who have not converted to Judaism and have not related to Jewish law still have a chance to enter the eschatological kingdom based on how they have treated the core group, the descendants of Abraham.

Matthew's Gospel describes a process in which Israel is being charged to fulfill its calling as Abraham's children as the end of the current world order is coming closer (cf. 3:8–9); it needs to fulfill the Mosaic law according to the law's original intent, which is proclaimed by Jesus (Matthew 5–7; 15:3–9; 19:4–9; 23:10, 16–23), and further halakhically elaborated by the disciples (16:19; 18:18). When this is done, the fruits of the kingdom will be produced (cf. 3:10; 7:15–20; 13:18–23; 21:43) and the people will be the salt of the land and the light of the world (5:13–16).[146] The disciples have been entrusted to be custodians of the sacrificial meal (26:26–28), which takes the place of the defiled temple, which in turn is no longer capable of functioning in tandem with the Mosaic law; the atonement to which the meal refers

the children of those who murdered the prophets (Matt 23:31–32). Genealogy is, in Matthew, a powerful theological tool, especially in discourses involving judgment.

145. The disciples are presented in every way as on par with the crowds, although described in greater detail, so that the weaknesses of the disciples are more in focus than those of the crowds. For all, disciples and crowds and all other Jews alike, repentance is the key to salvation. There is no other way.

146. Cf. Isa 42:6; 51:1–4.

will save "many" from their sins, just as the temple had previously done (26:28; 1:21). The disciples represent the twelve tribes and are identified as the new leaders of the Jewish people (21:43; cf. 19:28; 5:5); the Gospel narrative is structured to show how the group, the center within the center—the *ekklēsia*—grows among the crowds, so that the kingdom expands like a mustard seed develops into a great tree, or like the yeast, which is mixed with three measures of flour until all of it is leavened (13:31–33). Thus, the disciples, and the *ekklēsia*, do *not* replace Israel, neither do they render Abrahamic descent meaningless. On the contrary: their task is to *exemplify how ideal Abrahamic descent should materialize, and to work to save the people of Israel from within.*

This task of exemplifying ideal Abrahamic descent and save Israel from within through determining halakhah in accordance with the divine intent of the law, as well as administering and distributing the sacrificial meal that mediates atonement, does not transform the disciples into sinless champions of *pistis.* On the contrary, the disciples, just as the crowds, are a mixed group of people in dire need of continuous repentance and forgiveness (6:14–15; 18:15–17, 21–35). Indeed, as the narrative unfolds, the individuals who pose the greatest threat to Jesus are counted among the disciples; Satan speaks through Peter with the aim of preventing the sacrifice which will save the people (16:22–23), and Judas manages what neither Pharisees nor Herodians or Sadducees manage, namely, to have Jesus handed over to the authorities (26:14–16, 48–50). But this is precisely the point: if those closest to Jesus, those who have been entrusted with the task of continuing the work for the kingdom, are in need of repentance, then everyone needs to repent. It is only those who do not see repentance and forgiveness as necessary who will be condemned, regardless of the group to which such individuals belong (e.g., 3:8; 6:15; 11:20–24; 18:15–17, 33–35). The people who are prepared for the coming judgment are not a people who flawlessly keep the law, in so far as the law is understood in isolation from atonement; Matthew's Gospel contains no illusions about human perfection. Rather, the people prepared for the kingdom is a people who keep the law to the best of their ability, acknowledge their shortcomings and repent of and seek atonement for them; they also forgive others who likewise sin and repent. It is especially the latter who identify what Matthew's Jesus means by perfection: love of God and love of neighbor, and mercy (22:37–40; cf. 12:7; 23:23).[147]

This mixed situation within the people, even within the group of the disciples and the *ekklēsia*, results in an emphasis on the rule that a person must not judge others. This is so not only because judging others may lead to one's own judgment (7:1), but also, more than anything else, because the disciples lack the insight needed for this kind of procedure, and are not able to judge according to God's will.[148] In fact, not even the angels are competent to judge who are to be identified as the children of the kingdom and who are not. As a consequence, they are ordered by the Son of Man to wait until the final judgment before distinguishing between sinners and the righteous, saving the latter and destroying the former (13:24–29, 36–43). In other words, the task of judging who is, in the end, within and who is outside God's mercy is not given to the disciples, nor to the growing *ekklēsia*. This does not, however, weaken their role in deciding what is appropriate halakhah (16:19; 18:18), based on Jesus's teaching; this teaching and the halakhah that follows from it is to be declared even to the nations (28:19–20).

The disciples, a close reading of their status reveals, are, in the end, not that different from most other Jews in Matthew's narrative world *as far as divine judgment is concerned*; in and of itself, their group status has no implications, negatively or positively, as God is about to establish his kingdom. The key is their access to true interpretation of the Torah and the means of atonement provided by Jesus after the temple has been defiled. This impression is confirmed when the focus is shifted from specifically defined and labeled groups to the larger picture, i.e., Matthew's treatment of the majority of those who are included under the umbrella designation "Israel."

---

147. Cf. Luke 6:36.
148. This will change once the kingdom has been established in full: Matt 19:28.

3.2.2 The Larger Picture: "This Generation," the Crowds, and Israel

The above discussion has shown that the group around Jesus, the disciples, is interlinked with other defined Jewish groups with regard to divine condemnation, salvation, and the possibility of repentance. Group boundaries are porous and, with few exceptions, God's judgment pays more attention to how individuals behave than to collective identities and labels, as long as those identities are Jewish. Still, within that which is defined as Jewish, Matthew's Gospel refers to larger collectivities that go beyond religio-political groups and associations, all of which, of course, must be understood as minorities within the Jewish people. In order to understand how Matthew applies his theology of judgment to the majority of the Jewish people, we need to look at terms and expressions that refer to entities that transcend smaller interest groups in the world of the narrative. It is in the dynamic between these larger collectivities and the minority groups dealt with above that the limits of salvation surfaces and can finally be identified.

Within Israel, we find references to people living in specific areas, such as Judeans (e.g., 3:5; 4:25; 28:15) and Galileans (e.g., 26:69). In addition to generalized references to villages and cities in Galilee (4:23; 9:35), Matthew also speaks of certain named cities, four in Galilee and three in Judea: Chorazin (11:21), Bethsaida (11:21), Capernaum (4:13; 8:5; 11:23; 17:24), and Nazareth ("his hometown"; 13:54), on the one hand, and Jericho (20:29), Bethany (21:17; 26:6), and Jerusalem (e.g., 2:3; 4:25; 5:35; 16:21; 21:10; 23:37), on the other. We have discussed most of these above in relation to the analysis of Matthew's criteria of judgment. We also find references in our Gospel, very frequently, to "the crowds," i.e., to the majority present in any given setting. Finally, the Matthean Jesus repeatedly refers to "this generation" in the context of judgment, a somewhat enigmatic expression that has been the object of some scholarly discussion and debate.[149] Adding to

---

149. See especially, Evald Lövestam, *Jesus and 'This Generation': A New Testament Study*, (Stockholm: Almqvist & Wiksell International, 1995). See also the brief discussion in Davies and Allison, *Matthew*, 2. 260–61.

this the designation "Israel," we have here a progression from smaller units to larger: from cities, political areas, and the majority of inhabitants within these various cities and areas, to an expression that seems to encompass the entire population of the land, more or less being equal to "Israel" as a whole, but narrowed down chronologically to the current moment, excluding all previous (and later) generations.

Since "this generation" seems to include all other collectivities, and since it is used in very distinct judgment proclamations, this expression takes interpretive precedence over the other passages and will be dealt with first. Once the nature of this expression and its use in Matthew has been established, the more narrowly defined collectivities will fall into place.

3.2.2.1 "This Generation" and the Crowds

It has been common both in church history and within the academy to understand the expression "this generation" as not only referring to the entirety of the Jewish people, but also as indicating that Israel will, irrevocably, be judged and condemned. An important passage referred to in order to support such an interpretation has been Matt 23:35–36.[150] "This generation" is understood as identical to "Israel" and "Israel" is said to be condemned, without possibility of salvation.[151] Luz writes:

> There is no glimmer of light at the end of the woes discourse. Jesus announces judgment not only on the scribes and the Pharisees but also on all Jerusalem, and that probably means: on all Israel. God will leave his temple. Jesus thereby makes concrete what he had already announced earlier: "the kingdom of God will be taken from you" (21:23).[152]

Such a reading of Matthew must, obviously, understand Jesus's disciples as something other than "Israel," a group not belonging to "this generation." As a reconstruction of a first-century understanding of Matthew, and more specifically, of the meaning of "this generation"

---

150. See Luz, *Matthew*, 3.154–65.
151. This is also how Luz himself interprets Matt 23:35–39; see especially *Matthew*, 3.163–64, where he contrasts Matthew's theology of Israel with Paul's in Romans 9–11.
152. Luz, *Matthew*, 3.164.

as it relates to divine judgment, this type of interpretation is problematic. The kind of reading that Luz represents here, which has its roots in century-old Christian tradition, is very much determined by certain ideas and interpretations, all of which consistently move in one direction and inevitably end in the conclusion that Israel in its entirety (again, excluding the disciples), for Matthew, is condemned, and "the church" is taking its place.[153]

It seems to me, and I hope to have shown above, that such a reading of the text neither does justice to Matthew's many nuances and careful distinctions between different groups, nor takes seriously the emphasis on and nature of Jesus's teaching of the Torah to the disciples and the crowds, teaching that is meant to save the people, not to condemn it (cf. 1:21). This is teaching that the crowds are said to approve of and accept over against the teaching of "their scribes" (7:28–8:1; 19:2; 21:8–11, 14–15; cf. 21:26, 31–32, 46).[154] Indeed, such interpretations also fall short of placing predictions of the fall of the temple within the context of first-century Jewish thought, and rather reflect later (non-Jewish) Christian understandings of what, for Matthew, was a catastrophe, to which he presented Jesus as a solution.[155] Most importantly, if "this generation" is equivalent to all of Israel, and "Israel" is understood as irreversibly lost, this would mean that the disciples, along with the crowds—together with whom they have received instruction in Torah (Matt 5–7)—would also be irrevocably lost, since Matthew never sets them apart from "Israel" and in fact, as we shall see, includes them in "this generation."

A more likely reconstruction of Matthew's first-century pattern of thought and practice is that "this generation" is indeed an all-

153. Rarely, though, do scholars note that such arguments also abrogate God's covenant with Abraham, an interpretive step which few will consider attractive since Abraham has come to fulfill in Christianity a theological function that Moses has not. Nevertheless, any claim that Israel as an entity with theological implications has ceased to be necessitates the view that the Abrahamic covenant is abolished, since peoplehood in Judaism is inextricably linked with Abraham.

154. It is nowhere stated that these crowds ever abandon Jesus's teaching or stop seeking his help, asking for healing and exorcisms, although they, just like the disciples, are sometimes presented as ambivalent and lacking in insight.

155. See above, e.g., p. 163.

encompassing designation for Jesus's (Jewish[156]) contemporaries, which includes the disciples, and that, as such, the expression fills certain functions in the story, all of which are related to the eschatological judgment. In other words, while "this generation" maintains a stable core meaning when read within the larger frame of the Gospel as a whole, the understanding of the expression is, to some degree, dependent on the specific contexts in which it is used.[157]

"This generation" occurs in a variety of settings in Matthew. It is used in contexts where Pharisees and scribes associated with the Pharisees are mentioned (12:39, 41, 42, 45; 23:36), where Sadducees appear together with the Pharisees (16:4), where crowds are mentioned (11:16), and when Jesus's own disciples are referred to (17:17; cf. v. 20).[158] On one occasion, the setting is general and no specific group is targeted as triggering the use of the expression (24:34). In this case, however, the audience is Jesus's disciples (24:3). The rhetorical aim is simply to give the disciples a general chronological time frame, indicating to them when the end will come and the Son of Man will send out his angels to gather his elect; "this generation" will still be alive when it happens. Are the disciples part of "this generation," as the expression is used here?

Since the use of the expression here is chronological in nature only, and no words of condemnation are uttered against the people referred to, it would seem obvious that "this generation" includes Jesus's

---

156. To be sure, we should perhaps note that non-Jews are not part of any of this, and, as is also clear from Matt 12:41–42, are not included in the expression. Matthew's is a story about Israel, its history, its present, and its future. While, as we shall see in Part II, non-Jews are present in the narrative, their role is entirely determined by the function they fill in relation to Israel and its Messiah.

157. Cf. Saldarini, *Community*, 42. See also Gundry, *Matthew*, 472, who, when commenting on Matt 23:36, states that, "[b]y context 'this generation' means the scribes and the Pharisees." Hagner, *Matthew 14-28*, 678, however, does not take into account differences in the contexts within which the expression occurs, and consequently neither the influence on the meaning of the expression that these contexts may have.

158. While Luz, *Matthew*, 2.408, makes an attempt to read Matt 17:17 as not directed at Jesus's disciples, perhaps feeling the interpretive tension this would create in light of his understanding of Matt 23:36, it is beyond doubt that Matthew describes Jesus's outburst as triggered by the disciples' lack of trust/faith and consequent inability to cure the epileptic boy. See Nolland, *Matthew*, 712–13; France, *Matthew*, 660–61; Cf. Davies and Allison, *Matthew*, 2.724; Lövestam, *Jesus and 'This Generation,'* 46–55. The disciples belong within "this generation," and on this occasion they were the ones highlighting the weaknesses and flaws that the Matthean Jesus accuses his contemporaries of.

disciples as well as all other Jews. This conclusion is indirectly supported by 16:28, where Jesus is also addressing his disciples (16:24) and utters a similar chronological prediction of when the end is to come. Here, some of the disciples are explicitly predicted to still be alive when the Son of Man will come with his kingdom (cf. 10:23). In other words, while Matthew's Jesus insists that no specific information can be had about exactly when the end will come—not even the angels or he himself know (24:36)—he does give a general time frame within which these sudden and unexpected developments will take place. This time frame is so important that the disciples are instructed twice about it and assured that while some of them might have died (probably through execution; cf. 10:28, 39; 23:34), they will, as a group, still be alive when it happens. Reading 24:34 against this background, it seems very likely that "this generation" functions as an eschatological chronological marker and refers to all of Jesus's Jewish contemporaries, including the disciples.

Indeed, Matthew shows an interest in the generations of Israel already in the genealogy, counting fourteen[159] of them between Abraham and David, fourteen between David and the Babylonian exile, and fourteen between the exile and the Messiah (1:17). For Matthew, time is not a neutral phenomenon or a label used to define a series of events. Rather, time is something which is invested with theological and revelatory meaning; it can be structured to demonstrate God's plan and intent for the future, revealing the deeper meaning behind the fundamentally important question, "What time is it?" "This generation," as shown by 24:34 and indirectly by 16:28, is a designation that refers to the last generation before the final judgment and the coming of the kingdom, i.e., the time immediately preceding the fulfillment of the promised eschatological salvation to be set in motion by the Messiah. "This generation" refers to the ones who will experience the victory of the Messiah and the salvation of the Jewish people (cf. 1:21). As such, it is clear that this expression must refer to

159. On the number fourteen, see the discussion in Davies and Allison, *Matthew*, 1.161–65, 187.

all of Israel, not just parts of the people, whatever groups we include under the umbrella term "Israel."

On the basis of the above, it is reasonable to conclude that the core meaning of "this generation," which is stable throughout the Gospel, is that it represents a theo-chronological marker, indicating that the present time is the time of the last generation before the eschatological end and the final judgment.[160] Inherent in the expression, wherever it occurs, is the answer to the question, "What time is it?" Now, if someone were to answer this question eschatologically, as Matthew does, we would expect to find a text saturated with warnings of imminent apocalyptic suffering and divine judgment, *if*, that is, the purpose of the text was to save the people of which it spoke and to which it was directed. Having noted that this, in fact, is the stated primary purpose of the Gospel, to save the Jewish people from their sins as the eschaton is approaching (1:21; 4:17), this is also exactly what we find in relation to the expression "this generation." What is it, then, that characterizes "this generation" that makes it so important for them to realize the urgency of the current moment? The fact that they must be saved through the active efforts of the Messiah suggests that something is not right, and that without help, they would be lost (cf. 9:36).

The expression is first used in Galilee. The larger context is this: as Jesus is in the midst of teaching in town and village synagogues all over Galilee, "proclaiming the good news of the kingdom, and curing every disease and every sickness," he realizes how much the crowds are suffering. Then, "he had compassion for them, because they were harassed and helpless, like sheep without a shepherd" (9:35–36). Since the task of helping and saving the people is massive, and all of Israel must be reached (10:5–6), he sends out his disciples and gives them authority over unclean spirits so that they also can do what he himself was doing (Matt 10:1–42). Having sent them off, Jesus is continuing to teach and proclaim in the area when John's disciples confronts him

---

160. Cf. Nolland, *Matthew*, 948, commenting on Matt 23:36: "'This generation' has primarily a chronological thrust: it will all happen in the lifetime of the present generation."

with a question from John, who is now in prison, asking whether Jesus is the one, or if they should wait for another (11:2–6). That is, John has a sense of what time it is, but is not quite able to identify exactly who Jesus is. Jesus's answer confirms what time it is, referring to the deeds he is doing: this is the time when all is going to happen, and he is the one who will bring healing and liberation for the poor.

Turning to the crowds, Jesus then continues to make the same point, referring to John, but he is presented as clearly frustrated that the question needed to be asked at all: his deeds, which are the deeds of Wisdom herself, should be enough for all to understand what is happening around them and with them (11:7–19). The reference to "this generation" (11:16) is triggered by the question raised by John, but also, by the crowds' lack of understanding despite Jesus's teaching, proclamation, and healings, all of which is happening right in front of their eyes. The last generation, the generation that is about to experience what previous generations longed for, but never saw realized (cf. 13:17), though sometimes amazed and intrigued by Jesus's teaching and deeds (7:28–29; 9:33), seems confused and unable to fully realize what is going on (11:16–19).

This confusion and lack of understanding stand in some tension with other passages in Matthew, where it is stated that crowds, contrary to the chief priests and the elders in Jerusalem, understood very well that John as well as Jesus were prophets, and they respected and revered them both (16:14; 21:11, 26, 46).[161] Here, however, they are presented as seeing them as someone possessed by a demon (11:18) and a glutton and drunkard (11:19), respectively. Indeed, crowds, i.e., the majority of the people present in any given locale, are said to have followed Jesus everywhere, even to Jerusalem, and the religio-political leaders were afraid of them due to their loyalty to Jesus (and John; e.g., 8:1, 18, 13:2; 14:13–14; 19:2, 13; 20:29; 21:8–9, 14–15; 23:1; 26:5). The lack of understanding of both John and the crowds, despite the fact that the former had once acknowledged Jesus as being the one they had waited

---

161. Note the transformation of the crowds' interpretation of what they see in Matt 11:5–19 (John is thought to be demon possessed and Jesus is seen as a drunkard and glutton) in Matt 15:30–31 (they are amazed and praise the God of Israel).

for (3:11–15), leads to a general statement that the entire generation was slow to understand, although, as other passages show, not completely unresponsive. This reinforces the impression of the crowds as in dire need of help, and Matthew's Jesus—and his disciples—are there to give it, as they seek out the lost sheep of the house of Israel (9:36; 15:24; 10:6).

A few words need to be added about how we may understand the tension between the crowds' confusion in this passage, and their later conviction that Jesus is, indeed, a prophet and the Son of David. In fact, the sense of tension may be resolved if we read 11:1–19 in conjunction with 13:10–17, 34–35, the latter passage providing a solution to the problem of the former situation.

In Matt 11:7–19, despite the salvific events described in 11:4–6, the crowds hear and see, but they do not understand what is happening and what the full meaning of what transpires in their midst actually is. Matthew returns to this theme of the crowds' seeing and hearing, but not understanding in Matt 13:13–15. Here, he is quoting Isa 6:9–10, although in 13:15, he lets the word *laos*,[162] taken from Isaiah (LXX), designate the Galilean crowds among whom he is working and whom he wants to save. I am suggesting, contrary to the interpretation of Davies and Allison, and several other commentators,[163] that the problem of the crowds' lack of understanding identified in 11:1–19, a problem that is described as generating frustration as it prevents Jesus from fulfilling his mission, is presented as solved in 13:10–15[164] (cf. 13:34–35) through the intentional adoption of a new communication strategy: the use of revelatory parables which explain to the people

---

162. On the meaning of the word *laos* in relation to *ochlos*, see discussion of Matt 27:25 below.

163. Davies and Allison, *Matthew*, 2.392–94.

164. According to Davies and Allison, *Matthew*, 2.393–94, Matt 13:14–15 is likely an early post-Matthean interpolation, despite that fact that these verses (the quote from Isaiah) are present in all manuscripts and versions. They refer to several other scholars who have suggested a similar solution to what they perceive of as a problem, including S. E. Johnson, "The Biblical Quotations in Matthew," *HTR* 34 (1943), 137, and Krister Stendahl, *The School of Matthew*, 129–32. For, in my opinion, convincing arguments against its omission, see Nolland, *Matthew*, 536; Luz, *Matthew*, 2.237–38. Indeed, the quote from Isaiah not only makes sense in the context, it provides the very key to its interpretation.

what the kingdom of heaven is and how it is taking form in the current moment.

According to the traditional interpretation, here represented by Davies and Allison, the parable genre is not intended to help the crowds comprehend the secrets of the kingdom, but the very contrary; Jesus speaks in parables in order for the crowds *not* to understand.[165] This is then contrasted with the insights given to the disciples (13:11, 16–17), so that a sharp distinction is created between the two groups as outsiders and insiders.[166] Such a reading, however, creates a hard-to-resolve tension, not to say a patent contradiction, between 13:13–15 and 13:34–35, as the latter two verses are stating that the purpose of the parables is, indeed, revelatory. This tension is recognized, but not explained or resolved by the traditional reading.[167]

Addressing this issue, a good place to begin is the quote from Isaiah, which Matthew's Jesus provides as an explanation for what is happening and why his new "parable strategy" is needed. We shall also have reason to briefly compare Matthew's version of this passage with Mark's very different approach, which implies a different overall understanding of Jesus's sense of time and purpose with regard to his work among the crowds. If we assume that Matthew, when quoting from Isaiah 6:9–10, also had knowledge about and, in fact, had in mind the rest of that passage (Isa 6:11–13), and if we pay close attention to whom the Matthean Jesus is talking, as well as his general focus on what time it is, then 13:10–17 and 34–35 turn into key texts for understanding the Gospel as a whole. The argument below suggests that 13:34–35, which summarizes the purpose of all parables spoken to the crowds as revelatory, should be given interpretive priority and should be understood as an additional clarification, also supported by a scriptural quote (from Ps 78) of 13:13–15.

---

165. This understanding of Matthew mirrors Mark's version of the tradition (Mark 4:10–12).
166. Cf. Sim, *Christian Judaism*, 195.
167. Davies and Allison, *Matthew*, 2.426 (cf. Nolland, *Matthew*, 555–57), recognize, contra Luz, *Matthew*, 2.265–66, that Matt 13:34–35 claims that Jesus's "parables are revelatory," but do not provide a solution to the tension this creates between the passages in question, both of which exist within the same Matthean discourse, less than 25 verses apart. Luz solves the tension between the two passages by claiming, unconvincingly, that none of them provides an understanding of parables as revelatory.

A reading of Matt 13:13–15 that understands the parables spoken to the crowds to be a solution to the problem of the crowds' lack of insight, rather than an intentional part of the cause behind their lack of understanding, seems to go against the meaning of Isa 6:9–10 in its MT form. Here, God is telling the prophet:

> Go and say to this people: "Keep listening, but do not comprehend; keep looking, but do not understand." Make the mind of this people dull, and stop their ears, and shut their eyes, so that they may not look with their eyes, and listen with their ears, and comprehend with their minds, and turn and be healed.

The purpose of this passage is to prepare the people for God's judgment, which will, inescapably, come. The situation has reached a point of no return, and the prophet's task is to make sure God's judgment can be carried out. God is thus, at this point,[168] the active force behind the dulling of the people's mind, which is done in order to prevent the possibility of the people repenting; repentance, in turn, would have risked influencing God and making him reconsider the coming punishment. The resultant lack of understanding (seeing and hearing) is thus not the people's doing; their crimes had already been committed, generating the guilt which had created this unsustainable situation.[169]

This same sense of setting the stage for comprehensive divine judgment through blocking the minds of people is evident in Mark's reference to Isa 6:9–10 as an explanation for why Jesus is speaking in parables (Mark 4:10–12).[170] Mark's wording is important, as he is

168. But cf. Isa 1:3.
169. The nature of these crimes are revealed already at the outset of the book, when warnings were issued: "Wash yourselves; make yourselves clean; remove the evil of your doings from before my eyes; cease to do evil, learn to do good; seek justice, rescue the oppressed, defend the orphan, plead for the widow" (Isa 1:16–17; cf. 10:1–4). As long as justice is not established in the land, sacrifices and festivals honoring God are meaningless and of no avail: God will not listen to the prayers of a people with hands stained with innocent blood (Isa 1:10–15). It is of some importance to note that Isaiah's accusations are targeting those who have the power to make oppressive decrees and statutes, those who rob the poor of their rights and deprive the people of justice (Isa 10:1–4; cf. Matt 12:7). These are not the people Jesus is speaking to when he is using parables. The Galilean crowds represent those who are abused and downtrodden and in need of God's intervention (Matt 9:34–38; 10:6). Still, as in a war, in both cases, all will suffer because of the sins of the powerful.
170. The Lukan version of this triple tradition follows Mark initially regarding the purpose of the

explicitly distinguishing between the crowds (*ochlos*; Mark 4:1) as outsiders and the disciples as the in-group: "for those outside [i.e., the crowds], everything comes in parables, *in order that* [*hina*] 'they may indeed look, but not perceive, and may indeed listen, but not understand; so that they may not turn again and be forgiven'" (Mark 4:11–12). Mark thus places Jesus and his use of parables within the same time frame of judgment that we find in Isaiah (MT); it is too late, the point of no return has passed, and the time of repentance, if we allow Isaiah to interpret Mark, is no more.[171] Jesus is, as Isaiah was, preparing the crowds for coming judgment, doom and devastation.[172]

If we pay attention to the verses immediately following Isa 6:9–10, however, we see that the prophet hints at a time limit for the people's blindness and deafness and, consequently, for divine punishment (Isa 6:11–13).[173] Isaiah asks God how long this must go on, the blindness and the punishment, and the reply is: *until* cities lie waste and there is only a remnant left, a "stump" (Heb. *matzevet*). This stump is the holy seed (*zera' qodesh*) that will, after further suffering ("it will be burned again"), experience salvation.[174] Elsewhere, Isaiah identifies the remnant as his disciples (8:11–20), and it would seem that Mark's Jesus

---

parables, but then, somewhat inconsistently, excludes Mark's reference to forgiveness at the end (Luke 8:9–10).

171. Despite Mark 1:4, 15, which, however, may be compared to Isa 1:16–20.

172. While Adela Yarbro Collins, *Mark: A Commentary* (Minneapolis: Fortress, 2007), does not address these matters at any length, Joel Marcus, *Mark 1–8* (New York: Doubleday, 2000), 298–307, sees the importance of this passage for our understanding of Mark's Gospel, calling it "one of the most formidable sayings in the entire New Testament" (301). Neither Collins, nor Marcus, however, comment on the specific time-related implications that follow from Mark's choice of approach, and use of *hina*, in relation to divine judgment.

173. There are many textual and other problems in this passage that makes translation and interpretation difficult. One of the questions concerns whether the final words of v. 13 ("The holy seed is its stump"), the words that most clearly indicate that there will be a remnant even after further suffering, were part of the original text; they seem clearly to be a later addition as the language reflects the postexilic period (cf. Ezra 9:2). As Ivan Engnell, *The Call of Isaiah* (Uppsala: A.-B. Lundeqvistska, 1949), 51, and many others have argued, however, the idea of a remnant must have been part of the prophet's call vision, since this idea is found from the very beginning in Isaiah. Cf. Otto Procksch, *Jesaja*, vol. 1 (Leipzig: Deichert, 1930), 60, who states that Isaiah, from the first, believed in the escape of a remnant and that he cannot have found this hope made fruitless by the call vision. Cf. discussion by Ronald E. Clements, Isaiah 1–39 (Grand Rapids: Eerdmans, 1980), 76–78; Margaret Barker, "Isaiah," in *Eerdmans Commentary on the Bible* (edited by James D. G. Dunn and John W. Rogerson; Grand Rapids: Eerdmans, 2003), 489–542, here 504. In any case, regardless of the original form of the text, we are interested here only in the text as it may have been available to Mark and Matthew in the first century CE.

174. Isaiah returns to the theme of the remnant several times, most notably in Isa 10:20–23.

does the same. For Isaiah, as for Mark (Mark 13:3–36; esp. vv. 20, 27), those who remain after the punishment and suffering have ended will see the reversal of darkness into light: "[T]here will be no gloom for those who were in anguish. In the former time he brought into contempt the land of Zebulun and the land of Naphtali, but in the latter time he will make glorious the way of the sea, the land beyond the Jordan, Galilee of the nations".[175] Then, at that time, the prince of peace will rule (Isa 9:6 [MT: 9:5]).

For Mark, then, as his use of *hina* (Mark 4:12) clearly indicates, the parables are part of Jesus's task of making the people's minds dull. Divine punishment is yet to come, and for those who are "outside," there is no escape. There is a close relationship between the meaning of the Hebrew text of Isaiah and Mark's Gospel in this regard. For Matthew, however, Jesus's parables are, contrary to Mark (and, by implication, contrary to the Hebrew text of Isaiah), an attempt to unlock people's minds; their ears (so they can understand Jesus's teaching) and their eyes (so they can understand Jesus's healings). This interpretation is confirmed by the summary statement in Matt 13:34–35.[176]

Contrary to Mark, the author of Matthew, who most likely was bilingual and aware of both the Hebrew and the Greek versions of the Scriptures,[177] provides an almost verbatim quote of the Septuagint version of Isa 6:9–10.[178] The Septuagint, however, contrary to the Masoretic text, does not present God as causing, through his prophet, the people's hearts to grow fat, their ears to stop, and their eyes to shut. Changing the Hebrew text's imperative to a Greek descriptive

---

175. Cf. Matt 4:13–17.
176. "Jesus told the crowds all these things in parables; without a parable he told them nothing. This was to fulfill what had been spoken through the prophet: 'I will open my mouth to speak in parables; I will proclaim what has been hidden from the foundation of the world'" (NRSV).
177. Cf. the recent study by Benedict Viviano, "Who Wrote Q? The Sayings Document (Q) as the Apostle Matthew's Private Notebook as a Bilingual Village Scribe (Mark 2:13–17; Matt 9:9–13)" in *Mark and Matthew II. Comparative Readings: Reception History, Cultural Hermeneutics, and Theology* (ed. by Eve-Marie Becker and Anders Runesson; Tübingen: Mohr Siebeck, 2013), 75–91; cf. Nolland, *Matthew*, 556.
178. The only difference between the LXX version and Matthew is that Matt 13:15 drops *autōn* in the phrase *kai tois ōsin autōn bareōs ēkousan*. Mark's reference to this passage is fragmentary, and does not indicate direct dependence.

aorist, Isaiah LXX describes the situation the people are already in; this is what the people are like, and the responsibility for this is their own.[179] For Matthew, Jesus's parables are not causing this to happen. Matthew chooses to follow the meaning of the Isaiah passage conveyed in the Septuagint, and must, therefore, change Mark's *hina* ("in order that"; Mark 4:12) to *hoti* ("because"; Matt 13:13) when he is explaining why he is talking to the crowds in parables. For Mark, the crowds (those who are "outside") are not only lacking in understanding, they must be further blinded to prepare them for divine judgment, and the parable genre is the tool for this. The point of no return is passed; their blindness and deafness will lead to an inability to repent and a resultant lack of the possibility of forgiveness. For Matthew, the crowds are already blind, deaf, and not understanding, as Jesus also complained in Matt 11:1–19, and the parables do not seem to be meant to add to this situation.

This is a significant difference, since Isa 6:9–10 LXX is treated as a prophecy fulfilled (Matt 13:14). Jesus is presented as experiencing exactly what Isaiah LXX is describing in Matt 11:1–19. This leads him to add to his communication toolbox parables, *because* (cf. *hoti*, 13:13) of the weaknesses of the crowds. The question is now whether *hoti* refers to Jesus's furthering the inabilities of the crowds, as Mark has it, or if the word is part of an explanation of a salvific strategy aiming to deal constructively with their shortcomings. In my opinion, there is nothing in Matthew's pericope that would indicate that he would be following Mark in this regard. Indeed, the changes he incorporates, including the full verbatim quote from the Septuagint, points in the opposite direction, i.e., that Matthew intends to correct Mark's sense of time as well as the consequent interpretation of the nature of Jesus's mission within that time frame. The end is indeed coming, but it is not too late for the crowds to be saved.

Both Mark's version, which aligns with the meaning of the Hebrew text, and Matthew's version, which adopts the perspective of the

---

179. As we have seen, Matthew accuses primarily the Pharisees and scribes associated with them for the state the people is in, since they are said to be blind leaders who mislead the people, i.e., the crowds.

Septuagint, signal, by their very reference to this Isaianic passage, their own time as a time of imminent divine judgment. However, while Mark seems to understand the current moment as building up toward apocalyptic devastation and Jesus as being an active part in bringing about this judgment on all who are "outside," Matthew's Jesus, who will be the eschatological judge (cf. 3:11–12; 13:41–43; 25:31–32), appears to regard his task as saving the crowds from their current downtrodden status, rather than actively solidifying their condemnation through further concealing that which has already been hidden since "the foundation of the world" (13:35). Again, Matt 13:34–35 logically and narratively militates against a reading of 13:10–15 that would imply that parables are part of a strategy of hiding revelation; contrary to Mark, the hiding has already taken place for Matthew, and it makes little sense to hide what has already been hidden. Jesus's task is the opposite: to remove lack of understanding through opening his mouth in order to "speak in parables," and so, eschatologically "fulfill what had been spoken through the prophet" (13:35). Matthew has chosen to reject Mark's sense of Jesus's time as a point of no return for the crowds, since Matthew does not see the crowds as "outsiders" in the same way as Mark explicitly does in Mark 4:11–12.[180]

We may assume that, by incorporating the full quote of Isaiah 6:9–10 LXX, Matthew was, in fact, aware of the entire passage in Isaiah, which encompasses also Isa 6:9–13.[181] The verses that follow after Isa 6:9–10 emphasize further the eschatological interpretation of the current moment in Matthew. If we allow Isa 6:11–13 some interpretive influence on our reading of Matthew, as seems to be Matthew's intention, given his quote, then the use of Isaiah here leads to an

---

180. As noted above (p. 261); cf. Talbert, *Matthew* 74–75; Luz, *Matthew*, 1.166), the boundary between the crowds and the disciples is nebulous and the crowds are sometimes described as disciples. In such cases, the crowds form a larger circle around Jesus, while the disciples constitute the inner core of the movement. Indeed, Matthew addresses this very issue in the parable of the weeds, which follows in Matt 13:24–30, a tradition unknown to, or disliked by, Mark.

181. This, I believe, is a reasonable assumption, one which is readily made as a matter of course by most scholars with regard to other quotes from Scripture in Matthew, such as, e.g., Matt 27:46. It is also likely that Matthew knew these quotes both in Hebrew and in Greek (cf. discussion of Matt 13:34–35 in Nolland, *Matthew*, 556–57).

emphasis on time: Jesus's time is the time of blindness and deafness, but this period of lack of understanding will be a reality only *until this point*; it is now, since John (Matt 11:12), over, so that people may have the opportunity to repent (cf. 3:1–3, 6–12; 9:27–30; 11:15; 12:22–23; 15:30–31; 20:30–34; 21:14), and eventually, if they do, experience salvation.[182] God's "until" (*heōs an*) in Isa 6:11, which responds to the prophet's question, "How long?" (*heōs pote*), is important, since God's reply to the prophet is that this obscuring of revelation to prevent repentance will end when the punishment of the exile and devastation has been fully executed. By then, only a remnant—in the MT designated as "the holy seed" (Isa 6:13; the expression is lacking in LXX)—will be left in the land, a tenth, and even this tenth will have to go through further suffering. This fits Matthew's pattern of exile and exodus quite well; the exile is a key theme for Matthew as he explains the role of the Messiah, which is to end the exile, or rather its consequences,[183] not bring it about (cf. Matt 1:17).

If we return now to Jesus's complaint about the lack of understanding displayed by "this generation" (Matt 11:16), and the context that embeds that complaint, we may see here a pattern according to which Matthew's story develops, a pattern that answers the question of what time it is. Jesus's response to John's question (11:3: "are we to wait for another?") in Matt 11:4–5 is quite straightforward. The answer is this: No. Look around. Something is actually happening right now, through Jesus (and his disciples; cf. Matt 10:1). Despite this, the Galilean crowds (and John) do not seem to understand fully (11:16–19), and so reflect the old order of dull minds, which is described, not caused, by Jesus in Matt 13:13–15.

Since Matthew's Jesus is not causing a lack of understanding among

---

182. This marks Matthew's vision as structured somewhat differently from Mark's. For the latter, Jesus is still participating in the divine strategy of punishment and exile that Isaiah began. For Matthew, the page is turning, Isaiah's time of concealment is over and the eschaton is happening. It is time to change strategy, so that the crowds can be saved.

183. On the one hand, Matthew seems not to envision his own time as still being defined as exile, but on the other, he does not describe it as if exile was over. It is likely that, for Matthew, then, the exilic state of things is not entirely removed until the full realization of the kingdom, which will uproot Roman influence in the land; indeed, remove Rome and its gods completely from the international scene (Matt 28:18–20).

the crowds, he is not presented as engaged in causing exile and punishment to happen, as Isaiah was ordered to do, and as Mark's Gospel claims. For Matthew, as we have seen above, the Pharisees, who are described as blind leaders for those who are blind (Matt 15:14), are the ones causing defilement through judging the innocent (12:7), shedding innocent blood (23:29–35), and misleading the people (23:15); they are the ones causing the destruction of the temple and of Jerusalem (Matt 22:1–15; 24:1–2).[184] In the midst of the ongoing disastrous developments that can only lead to apocalyptic suffering and devastation, Jesus is portrayed as working to save his people.

In fact, Jesus's Messianic work among the crowds in the land (Matt 4:23; 9:35–38; 15:24) is aimed at opening up for the possibility of repentance,[185] ending the remaining consequences of the exile (1:17), and bringing about the kingdom of heaven, i.e., to inaugurate, although through tremendous suffering (Matthew 24), the period envisioned by Isaiah as the realization of God's salvation of a remnant after an extended period of severe divine punishment (Isa 6:13).[186] For Matthew, divine punishment is yet to culminate in the destruction of the temple and apocalyptic suffering in Matthew 23–24. The way to salvation, to the kingdom of heaven, as provided by Jesus through his salvific teaching of Torah,[187] his healing, and the forgiveness of sins through

---

184. See chapter 3.2.1.2 above.

185. Luz, *Matthew*, 2.247n119, also notes that Matthew's version of this tradition allows for repentance as a (necessary) possibility, but this is somewhat inconsistent with his reading of the role of the parables, which he understands more along the lines suggested by Mark's Gospel. Luz, however, replaces Mark's (and Matthew's) explicit concern with the group they call the "crowds" with words such as "the people" and "Israel," thus achieving an interpretive situation in which: a) "Israel"/the "people" is condemned as a whole, and b) the disciples cannot be part of the "people" or "Israel," since the disciples are the ones that will be saved. This opens up for Luz to see in this Matthean passage an explanation of why the "gentiles" will be replacing "Israel" (Luz, *Matthew*, 2.247.) This reading of Matthew, which has deep roots in Christian tradition, as Luz also recognizes, is unconvincing as a historical reconstruction of Matthew, since it disregards both the explicit terms used by Matthew to tell his story as well as the narrative logic of the text, which is interconnected with the terminology used. Indeed, the thought patterns present in Matthew surface also in other contemporary Jewish traditions. These patterns were, however, rarely understood by, nor were they helpful to the later (non-Jewish) Christians in the patristic era when they defined and established their own version of Christ-belief in a process in which rejection of all other forms of Christ-belief, as well as of "Israel" became, for them, necessary.

186. The idea of a remnant comes through also in Matt 22:14; 24:12–13, 22, although Matthew's Jesus aims for a larger entity than other contemporary groups did, who considered themselves to be the remnant of Israel. See further discussion below.

187. On Jesus as saving through teaching of Torah, see, most recently, Thomas R. Blanton IV, "Saved

his sacrificial death, is presented as a way through this suffering, not a way to avoid suffering. This is why the old order (cf. 11:11, 12–13), marked by lack of understanding, must end before the final judgment is carried out. Jesus's experience of the crowds, that "seeing they do not perceive, and hearing they do not listen, nor do they understand" (13:13), leads him to introduce a new strategy—the use of parables—to overcome this obstacle to God's salvation.[188] This new strategy is, indeed, presented as effective, as is clear from 15:30–31, where the crowd see what Jesus is doing and interprets these extraordinary events correctly, praising the God of Israel as a direct result of what they observed.

Despite the fact that the disciples are regarded as part of "this generation," a topic to which we shall return shortly, this strategy was never needed for them, because "the secrets of the kingdom of heaven" had already been revealed to them, as a gift from God (13:11).[189] In Matthew's vision of God's salvific plan for the crowds, this was necessary since the state of the people, the crowds of Galilee, was abysmal, abused and downtrodden as they were, and Jesus was in need of co-workers in order not only to address the Galilean situation, but also the conditions in the entire land of Israel (9:36–38; 10:1–42).[190]

---

by Obedience: Matthew 1:21 in Light of Jesus' Teaching on the Torah," *JBL* 132:2 (2013): 393–413: "Matthew's narrative creates strong thematic and verbal links between the idea of judgment based on one's adherence or nonadherence to the stipulations of the Torah and the theme of salvation" (410).

188. Cf. Nolland, *Matthew*, 533: "Speaking to the crowds in parables is represented as a new move, and the disciples ask for an explanation of this strategy."

189. Cf. Matt 10:1 where Jesus is conferring power to the disciples, so that they can help him save the people through casting out unclean spirits, healing the sick, and proclaim the good news of the kingdom of heaven (10:7); there is more work to be done than Jesus can handle by himself, as noted in Matt 9:37–38.

190. Matthew 13:10–17 is thus not a theological statement about predestination, neither is it a way to talk about the knowledge of the insiders as opposed to the lack of insight of the outsiders (as in Mark), or to argue God's condemnation of "Israel" and a transition of the kingdom over to the gentiles (as Luz would have it). The history of interpretation of this pericope shows how easy it is to over-theologize the text and treat it as if it were not part of a reasonably coherent narrative, but instead, represented a kind of theological tractate answering questions that rather belong in later centuries. In the passage, Jesus is simply explaining for the disciples why the crowds need to hear the message of the kingdom through parables, while they themselves do not have that need; they already sense what time it is (although Jesus will still teach them some additional parables later on, in Matt 13:44–50, probably to equip them to teach the crowds using parables; cf. Matt 13:52—scribes are elsewhere in Matthew described as teachers of the people, see, e.g., 7:29). This knowledge, though, has been given to them by God as a gift, for the specific purpose of equipping

Jesus's task is thus to turn the people of "this generation" around, to initiate the new order in which people again will be able to see, hear, and understand, so that they can be saved in the midst of the apocalyptic calamities that will, irrevocably, befall them all, and then be acquitted in the final judgment.

The parables, then, are meant to break the seal that is binding peoples' minds in blindness, helping salvation to happen as the eschatological process has begun; they are revelatory in nature and proclaim what has previously been obscure (13:34–35; cf. Ps 78:1–8). The parables, *as a genre*, thus answer the question: "What time is it?" As a consequence of Jesus applying this (new) communication strategy, the Galilean crowds as well as some Judeans will eventually realize who Jesus is—a prophet, and more than that, the Son of David (Matt 12:23; 20:30–31; 21:9, 15; Cf. 1:1)[191]—and follow him to Jerusalem. "This generation" is still slow to understand, and that includes the disciples, as we shall see, whose *pistis* is lacking; but those who listen—and not all will listen (cf. 11:20–24)—will eventually have their eyes opened as the narrative progresses (cf. 9:27–31; 20:29–34). Those who refuse to listen will be robbed of whatever little understanding they had before (13:12). Although salvation extends beyond the group called disciples in Matthew, the aim of Jesus's work in Galilee, and the disciples' work all over Israel (cf. 10:23), is to expand the movement around Jesus.[192]

It has been argued by some that Matthew makes a clear and firm distinction between the crowds and the disciples, a distinction which, it seems, is related to a wish to identify the disciples with the "church," i.e., with an entity that is, anachronistically to be sure, seen as something other than "synagogue," and thus, outside of "Judaism." Joining Jesus is, accordingly, understood to mean leaving Judaism, and since the crowds are not leaving Judaism, they are portrayed as outsiders; if some of them are described as repentant, this is seen to

them to help Jesus in his task of saving the people; they have been chosen among the rest of the people for this specific task, to help save, and then rule, the twelve tribes (cf. Matt 19:28).

191. Even a few non-Jews are able to see what is going on: 15:22; cf. 2:1–2; 8:5–13.

192. In Matt 28:19–20, when the disciples are ordered by Jesus to take on the non-Jewish world, this is also defined as "making disciples." Cf. Matt 13:52; 27:57.

imply what is best described as a conversion, from "synagogue" to "church." With such a view, any diversity or mix between good or bad followers of Jesus, a topic treated in several of the parables, has to be played out within the "church," and thus, outside "Judaism."

This type of interpretation is, however, problematized by Matthew 13. As noted above,[193] Matthew's story lacks Mark's clear boundaries between disciples and others, as long as these others are defined as the "crowds." This is further supported by the parable of the wheat and the weeds in Matt 13:24–30, which is aimed at giving the disciples *and* the crowds insight into how, as the kingdom is approaching, divine judgment relates to the crowds.[194]

Matthew has previously presented exactly who the disciples, i.e., the inner circle around Jesus, are, given their number as twelve, and has named them (10:1–4). These twelve disciples are the ones sent out to heal the sick and proclaim the kingdom, just as Jesus has been and is proclaiming the kingdom and healing the sick among the Galilean crowds; doing this work, they are presented as laborers working with God's harvest, which is plentiful (9:37–38). There can be no doubt that the work carried out by Jesus and his disciples is done among the crowds, and not among any of the leadership groups noted elsewhere in the story. The latter are dealt with only as they approach Jesus; he does not seek them out.[195] In the parable about the wheat and the weeds in 13:24–30, the Matthean Jesus returns to the image of harvest. Here, however, the focus is on judgment. The parable is based on the premise that Jesus's (and the disciples') work has been comparatively successful, and that there is a larger movement around him that exceeds by far the number of those designated disciples. In the context in which the parable is given, this larger movement must refer to the

---

193. See the section on Jesus's disciples, chapter 3.2.1.2.

194. Cf. the explanation of the parable in Matt 13:36–43, which is given only to the disciples (v. 36). Matthew 13:34–35 indicates Matthew's view on the revelatory purpose of the parables when addressed to the crowds; cf. Ps 78:1–8 (LXX 77:1–8)

195. The treatment of these leadership groups thus resembles rather closely the Gospel's treatment of non-Jews until Matt 28:18–20. The difference is that, while the non-Jews who approach Jesus are acknowledging his authority, and therefore, receive what they ask for, representatives of the various leadership groups, none of whom acknowledge Jesus's authority, only receive critique and words of condemnation from the Messiah.

crowds who follow Jesus and gather around him (13:2-3), i.e., the same people who are presented as slow to understand (11:7-19; 13:13); these are the people, the majority of Jews at any given locale, to whom Jesus is telling our parable, and the disciples are there to listen too.

Jesus has already delivered and explained the parable of the sower (13:3-9, 18-23), which our parable in vv. 24-30 is meant to further clarify and relate to the theme of divine judgment. This means that among the Galilean crowds—this is not about the disciples, as this group is defined in this discourse—there will be those who respond poorly (13:4-7, 19-22) and those who understand (13:8, 23), and therefore, respond in an exemplary manner to Jesus's proclamation; the latter will produce in abundance the fruit of the kingdom.[196] Thus, we find understanding of what is happening around Jesus outside the group identified as disciples, which anticipates the effectiveness of the parables among the crowds. At the same time, while initially appreciative of the good news about the kingdom, some will eventually leave behind the kind of life required by the kingdom. How do the disciples—and the crowds—judge between who is in and who is out, in a situation such as this? Who will be allowed into the kingdom, and who will perish as a result of the final judgment?

Jesus's answer is that this question is off limits for everyone involved, since no one has the expertise to judge between who is in and who is out within the crowds, i.e., the majority of the Jewish people, excluding the various leadership groups (the latter are clearly marked as out-groups in Matthew, except the scribes, who may be described as both in-group and out-group[197]). This is the message of the parable of the wheat and the weeds: not even the angels are skilled enough to carefully separate the evil from the good without risking destroying the good, and so they are ordered to withhold judgment until the judge himself, the Son of Man (13:30, 41), arrives at the end of time; only then may they remove all who break the law (13:41). Until then, both what eventually turns out to be weeds and the wheat must be left

196. Cf. Matt 3:8; 7:17-23. Cf. also, Matt 25:14-30.
197. See discussion above, chapter 3.2.1.1.

alone, to grow, lest a mistake is made, and wheat is mistaken for weeds (13:28–30).[198]

All of this means that, in terms of divine judgment, not only is Matthew's Gospel outlining the same criteria for all Jews, including the disciples, but the text also avoids any sharp distinction between the majority of the Jewish people (the crowds) and those individuals designated disciples. It is thus not possible to say that the crowds, and even less so "Israel," of which the crowds constitute one part, are, as a group, destined for condemnation; that would simply contradict what Matthew's Jesus is reported as saying and doing. Indeed, it would contradict the entire aim of the Gospel, as stated repeatedly in the text, beginning in 1:21.

Having said this, one more detail remains to be added with regard to the use of parables in Matthew. *Parables proclaiming and explaining salvation are only spoken to the crowds and to the disciples, not to the Pharisees, the chief priests, or the elders.* When these leadership groups are told parables by Jesus, the parables only proclaim the divine judgment that will fall upon them. These are parables that they, in fact, understand and, hardly surprising, that convince them that Jesus must be arrested (Matt 21:28–22:14). Indeed, in addition to not telling them (revelatory) parables about the kingdom, Jesus refuses to provide them even with a sign when they ask for it (Matt 12:38; 16:1). Why is Matthew's Jesus acting in this way?

The Pharisees and the scribes associated with them are portrayed as blind,[199] and those who follow them are also said to be blind (Matt 15:14; cf. the persistent characterization of them as blind in Matthew 23). As such, they will experience divine condemnation and, by implication, are not to be considered as belonging among those who will be saved. Their minds will not be unlocked, a position on judgment that leads one's thoughts back to the theme of the Hebrew version

198. The logic of this approach to judgment is at home in the interpretive trajectory within which we also find Gen 18:16–33 and Matt 24:22. In other words, the parable of the wheat and the weeds further elaborates on a variant of the theme of vicarious righteousness, although limited only to events taking place in this world. See also discussion above, chapter 2.3.

199. On the blindness of the chief priests and the Jerusalem scribes to the current moment, see Runesson, "Matthew as Midwife," 320–25.

of Isa 6:9–10. What Isaiah generalizes to apply to the entire people, despite the fact that Isaiah, too, like Matthew, knows that only the powerful are to blame, Matthew explicitly limits to the leadership groups of Israel. While all of the people belong to "this generation," it is only for them, the leading and influential figures in Israel, that the point of no return has passed. This interpretation, which emphasizes Jesus's mission as focused on saving the people from the influence of leaders that would lead to their destruction (both the leaders and those who follow them will "fall into a pit"; 15:14), receives further support from a close reading of the other passages that mention "this generation."

The frustration Jesus is described as having felt with the crowds' lack of understanding reoccurs later when he experiences yet another setback. This time, it results in an even more harshly worded outburst against "this generation," but now Jesus's reaction is triggered by his own disciples' lack of *pistis* and inability to perform the deeds of the kingdom that he had already given them authority to accomplish (17:17; cf. v. 20).[200] While Jesus, in response to John's and the crowds' lack of understanding, only describes "this generation" as confused, here, as he is responding to his disciples lack of *pistis*, he cries out, "You faithless [*apistos*] and perverse [*diastrephō*] generation, how much longer must I be with you? How much longer must I put up with you?" (17:17) If earlier, we were dealing with a lack of understanding, here we are dealing with a lack of ability, which follows from lack of *pistis*. The context that unites the two passages is the power of the coming kingdom, which should have been obvious to all, and which, for the disciples, should have sparked the trust/faithfulness/loyalty that enables God's spirit (cf. 12:28) to act through them to save the people.

Jesus's frustration stems from the fact that time is short and lack of *pistis* reduces the speed at which salvation can travel through the

---

200. Cf. Nolland, *Matthew*, 712: "Jesus' fierce words can be provoked only by the failure of the disciples. Here, the disciples represent the present generation in its failure to respond to the ministry of Jesus." In fact, while Mark's version of the story (Mark 9:14–29) involves the boy's father's faith, or lack thereof (Mark 9:24), Matthew has redacted his text to focus only on the disciples' inability; it is *their* lack of faith (Matt 17:19–20) that prevents the power that Jesus had already given them (Matt 10:1) to defeat the demon.

land. This slowness to realize what God is doing that characterizes the last generation of the Jewish people before the eschatological end-time liberation is realized is a heavy burden on Jesus's shoulders, just as the generation of the desert wandering was a heavy burden for Moses.[201] The point is, though, that the work carried out by both Moses and Jesus is meant to save the people, not destroy them. Just as it is unreasonable to understand Moses's harsh complaints about the desert generation during the exodus as leading to irreversible condemnation of the people,[202] it is uncalled for to insert such an idea in a passage such as Matt 17:17, which deals with the generation that may experience the kingdom in full, especially since Matthew clearly means to allude to the language used in Deuteronomy.

The reference to "this generation" here is rather meant as a warning to the disciples, that without trust/faithfulness/loyalty, they will not be able to do anything, despite the power over unclean spirits that Jesus had formally bestowed upon them (10:1). This interpretation is confirmed by the fact that the healing episode leads over to a scene in which Jesus is teaching his disciples about what *pistis* is and what can be achieved when God is allowed to work through it (17:19–20). The passage as a whole, Matt 17:14–20, thus serves the purpose of reinforcing the message that *pistis* must be the distinguishing characteristic of those who belong within the kingdom and, especially, of those who have been given the task to spread it. The warning is this: if *pistis* is not present, nothing can be achieved. The good news is this: if *pistis* is present, everything can be accomplished.

If we compare 17:17 with 11:16, we see—just as we did above, when

---

201. The wording of Matt 17:17 clearly alludes to the exodus generation in the desert, as Moses is instrumental in its liberation. See Deut 32:5, 20 LXX. Moses also complains about the people as a burden he has to carry (Num 11:12–14). See discussion in Nolland, *Matthew*, 712; France, *Matthew*, 660–61. As France notes, Jesus's exclamation "how much longer?" resonates with the lament of Ps 4:2 [Hebr. and LXX 4:3] and Jer 4:14; 12:4. See also discussion in Lövestam, *Jesus and 'this Generation,'* 46–47. Note also how Jesus has just come down from the mountain where he was transfigured and had met and talked with Moses and Elijah when this scene is played out (17:1–13). Just as Moses found a disobedient people led by Aaron when he descended from Mount Sinai (Exod 32:1–35; Deut 9:6–29), Jesus finds, when he descended from his mountain, lack of faith with his appointed leaders (10:2–5; cf. 19:28) and their consequent failure to help the people to experience the power of God.
202. Moses, in fact, prays for the people, even voluntarily offering his own life, like Jesus would later do (Matt 20:28; 26:28), to avert God's wrath from them (Exod 32:10–14, 30–32).

discussing the status of Jesus's disciples—that the disciples trigger the use of harsher words and stronger language than the crowds do. If there is condemnation of the crowds, the disciples are even more condemned. If the crowds abandon Jesus when he is later arrested in Jerusalem, so do the disciples, one of them explicitly denying any relationship with Jesus when he is in danger. Indeed, as noted above,[203] individuals among the disciples do more to hurt Jesus than the Galilean and Judean crowds ever do. When these crowds indirectly protected Jesus through having made publicly known their conviction that Jesus was the Son of David and a prophet, like John, so that the chief priests and the elders were restrained in their ability to act against Jesus, one of Jesus's own disciples plotted to betray him and had him handed over to these same leaders at nighttime, when the crowds could not react (26:3–5, 14–16, 47–56).[204]

The only exception to this general picture of the various crowds mentioned in the Gospel as less critiqued than the disciples is the people of Jerusalem, who do not know either who Jesus is or what time it is (21:10; cf. 2:3), and who are present as Jesus is on trial before Pilate (27:15). Contrary to the situation when Jesus was teaching in the temple and the chief priests and the elders feared the pilgrim crowds that had followed him from Galilee and Judea (Matthew 21–22; cf. 19:1–2; 20:29), this Jerusalem crowd, which gathered before Pilate in 27:17, can easily be persuaded by the same religio-political leaders to request Jesus's execution (27:20).[205] While Judas and Peter are described

---

203. See chapter 3.2.1.2.
204. One should perhaps add that even after Jesus's resurrection, at the key moment when the disciples are being sent to the nations to make them disciples, the eleven remaining disciples are described as doubting *distazō* (28:17). On this passage as referring to all disciples, rather than a few of them, see Hagner, *Matthew*, vol. 2, ad loc.
205. While many scholars have understood the crowds mentioned earlier in the Gospel as identical to the crowd now standing before Pilate, this makes "the crowds" into a single character in a way that is not supported by the more dynamic roles played by the people so labeled in the narrative. We simply cannot see "one face," as it were, when we read "crowd" in Matthew. The best definition of "crowd," it seems to me, is that it refers to the majority of people present in any particular location, people that are not described as leaders in any sense of that word. For example, few would identify the "crowd" sent out by the chief priests to arrest Jesus (Matt 26:47) with the crowds who regarded Jesus and John as prophets (Matt 21:11, 26, 46); such an interpretation would violate the logic and complexity of the story. The crowd sent by the chief priests and the elders to arrest Jesus, however, fits narratively rather well the doings of the crowd before Pilate, asking him to have Jesus executed instead of Barabbas. The fault of the other

as repentant, the people of Jerusalem, as much as the leaders upon whom they rely, are portrayed as hostile from the very beginning of the Gospel to its end (2:3; 28:15),[206] and here, before Pilate, as ignorant, and thus, unrepentant in relation to what they are about to do. Trusting the judgment of their leaders, the chief priest and the elders, they are so sure that they are doing the right thing that they are willing to accept any—in their eyes, very unlikely—bloodguilt that may be associated with the death of this Messiah (27:25). This last verse, with its horrible *Wirkungsgeschichte*,[207] requires a few more comments, especially in light of our investigation into the meaning and use of the expression "this generation."

The problem is this: as Matthew has described the crowd gathered before Pilate, asking him to have Jesus crucified, he has used the term

crowds who were present in the temple is, in this situation, rather much the same as the fault of the disciples: they have abandoned the one they believed to be a prophet and more, the Son of David (21:9). We may also add that the people of Jerusalem are explicitly distinguished from the crowds that follow Jesus in Matt 21:10–11. The key content of the word "crowd" in Matthew that remains constant throughout the Gospel is that it refers to people who are not leaders, who need leaders, and who can be manipulated by leaders. But we should not reduce the complexity of Matthew's story by not allowing the author to speak of different crowds, who respond to different leaders in different ways at different times. After all, this is what Matthew does also with other collectivities, such as "scribes," a term that may refer to Jesus's enemies (e.g., 5:20; 23:13), but also, in an exemplary manner, to the ideal disciple (13:52; 23:34).

206. In Matt 28:15, Matthew mentions a hostile rumor, originating with the chief priests and some Roman soldiers, about the disciples stealing Jesus's body, a rumor that is said to be around even in the author's own time, among the Judeans. The word *Ioudaioi* here should not be understood neither translated as Jews, since the reference is clearly geographical. See France, *Matthew*, 1106: "[T]he term is used editorially, by an author who has shown throughout that the distinction between Galilee and Judea is not only very familiar to him but also a matter of some importance. In this context, where the falsehood being spread in Jerusalem contrasts with the proclamation of truth which is about to be launched in Galilee in vv. 16–20, it is likely that Matthew uses the term in its stricter geographical sense: this was a southern propaganda campaign, based in Jerusalem." Thus, for Matthew, while Jerusalem (5:35; 27:53) and the temple (23:19–21) are holy, they have become defiled and have turned into a center of resistance to God's Messiah. Cf. Dunn, *Partings*, 205, who suggests translating *Ioudaioi* as "Jews," noting that the use here is anarthrous: "the story has been spread among Jews in general (not 'the Jews')." Consideration of the overall tension between Judaea and Galilee in the Gospel favors, however, France's interpretation. See also, discussion in Runesson "City of God?"

207. See, e.g., Howard Clarke, *The Gospel of Matthew and Its Readers: A Historical Introduction to the First Gospel* (Bloomington: Indiana University Press, 2003), *ad loc*; Tord Fornberg, *The Bible in a World of Many Faiths* (Tro och Tanke 2000:3; Uppsala: Svenska kyrkans forskningsråd, 2000), 38–40, 58–59; Luz, *Matthew*, 3.506–11; Terence L. Donaldson, *Jews and Anti-Judaism in the New Testament: Decision Points and Divergent Interpretations* (Waco: Baylor University Press, 2010), 30–54; Anders Runesson, "Judging the Theological Tree by its Fruit: The use of the Gospels of Mark and Matthew in Official Church Documents on Jewish-Christian Relations," in *Mark and Matthew II. Comparative Readings: Reception History, Cultural Hermeneutics, and Theology* (edited by Eve-Marie Becker and Anders Runesson; Tübingen: Mohr Siebeck, 2013), 189–228, here 189–94.

ochlos, crowd, to designate these people. However, when he reaches the climax of this episode and Pilate is washing his hands to make clear his innocence with regard to the execution of Jesus, and the crowd exclaims, "His blood be on us and our children!" (27:25), Matthew shifts the word with which they are identified to *laos*, which is usually translated as "people." The question is now whether Matthew wants to convey something theological with this change of word. That is, if *laos*, as so many commentators have argued, is meant to indicate the entire people of Israel, God's people,[208] rather than the local Jerusalem crowd gathered before Pilate, and that therefore what we see here is a self-condemnation, or curse,[209] pronounced by Israel itself, then "Israel" is here, in its entirety, condemning itself.[210] While quite common historically,[211] and until recently certainly the majority reading, such an interpretation is, however, from a historical perspective, extremely unlikely and without support in Matthew's text, as Carter and others have noted.[212]

---

208. This is a very common interpretation throughout church history, from Origen and onwards. So also, Nolland, *Matthew*, 1178; France, *Matthew*, 1057–58.

209. So Luz, *Matthew*, 3.502.

210. Meier, *Vision*, 200, argues that this leads to Israel being replaced by the "church" as the people of God, i.e., condemnation is not only based on peoplehood, but removes peoplehood. This, if correct, would be the first time in Israel's history that God would have acted in this way. A more Jewish approach, if we indeed consider the text as related to first-century Judaism, would have been to talk about a remnant of Israel remaining after severe punishment has been executed. But this is not quite what Meier envisions. We shall return to this issue below.

211. Cf., e.g., Jerome, *Comm Matt* on 27:25: "This imprecation upon the Jews continues until the present day. The Lord's blood will not be removed from them. This is why it says through Isaiah: 'If you wash your hands before me, I will not listen; for your hands are full of Blood.'" As many later commentators, Jerome seems untroubled by the fact that the person washing his hands is Pilate himself (Matt 27:24); the application of Isaiah to the Jewish people rather than to the character doing what Isaiah speaks about is telling, and reveals Jerome's anti-Jewish bias. Indeed, commenting on Matt 27:24, he frees all gentiles of any guilt related to Jesus's death: "Thus, in the washing of his hands, the works of the Gentiles are cleansed, and in some manner he estranges us from the impiety of the Jews who shouted 'Crucify him!'" Jerome continues in the same vein as he comments on Matt 27:26 and the release of Barabbas: "He [i.e., Barabbas] stands for the devil, who reigns in them [i.e., the Jews] until today. It is for this reason that they are unable to have peace." This interpretive trajectory grew strong in Roman Catholic tradition, and lost no momentum in protestant understandings of Matthew (or the church) and the Jewish people. It is not until the Second Vatican Council that we see firm official rejection of this type of theology, which originated with the church fathers. It is somewhat curious that modern scholars have remained, to such a large degree, attached to the general ideas about Matthew's story as exemplified here by Jerome, as if these ideas in fact could find support in the Gospel itself.

212. Carter, *Matthew and the Margins*, 528: "Such attempts [i.e., to interpret the passage as God's permanent rejection of Israel] are textually unsustainable and morally and religiously repugnant." See also Davies and Allison, *Matthew*, 3.591–92. While I agree fully with Carter that such an interpretation is morally and religiously repugnant, such a view is, and must be, beside

The basic assumption behind the argument that *pas ho laos* should be interpreted as referring to Israel as a whole[213] is that, in the LXX, the expression is always used in the same way, as referring to the Jewish people as an entity. This is, as Luz also notes, simply incorrect: "Who in the LXX belongs to πᾶς ὁ λαός is determined in each case by the context."[214] This is also the case in Matthew's narrative, and it includes all uses of the word *laos*, even without the specification *pas ho*.[215] Passages in which *laos* refers to the Jewish people as a whole may be focused on its salvation rather than its condemnation. In 1:21, Jesus's mission, as we have seen repeatedly above, is defined as being to save his own people from their sins. In 2:6, God is speaking through his prophet, identifying Jesus as "a ruler who is to shepherd my people Israel" (cf. 9:36–38). The people's current religio-political leaders include, however, a group called the elders of the people (*presbyteroi*

the point as we try to understand historical texts and movements. We have to be prepared to deal with views and actions that for us are morally objectionable, if our aim is to understand those who are, by necessity in any historical investigation, culturally, politically, and religiously "the other." It seems, though, that the reading of Matt 27:25, which Carter rightly sees as textually unsupported, aligns quite well with the theological needs evident in (non-Jewish) Christian settings from the second century and onwards. This was the time when Christians began to find it necessary to argue that their form of Christ-belief had replaced Israel as the people of God. It is not until this time period that we see, revealingly, the emergence of the term "Christianity," which is formed and defined in opposition to "Judaism" (as shown by of Ignatius Antioch, *Magn.* 10.1–3); cf pp. 5–6n9. This, however, was not a concern for most interested parties in the first century, and certainly, not for Matthew, as we shall also see below when we analyze Matthew's use of the term "Israel." At that time, "Christianity" did not exist as a word, which makes it difficult to accept, contra Stanton, *Gospel for a New People*, 124, a simple distinction between Judaism/synagogue, on the one hand, and Christianity/church, on the other, and consequently, the idea that it was possible to transfer from one to the other.

213. This includes the more nuanced opinion of Luz, *Matthew*, 3.502, who notes that this does not mean every individual belonging to the Jewish people, since Matthew's "own churches are the living proof of the contrary." Aside from the obvious anachronism of speaking of 'churches' in Matthew's context, this is an important point, that attempts to mitigate the Christian view, common from the patristic era onwards, that all Jews everywhere and throughout history are targeted in Matt 27:25. Still, however, Luz's nuancing nevertheless conveys classic Christian replacement theology, which states that while Israel as an entity is rejected by God, individual Jews *who convert* to Christianity (the "church") are accepted. This type of anti-Judaism ("Judaism," or "Israel," is wrong and must vanish as a consequence of divine judgment), which is different in nature from the later anti-Semitism of the nineteenth and twentieth centuries and should not be confused with it, is, in my view, foreign to Matthew's Jesus, who is portrayed as representing the "God of Israel" (Matt 15:31) and who claims 'Israel' for himself (2:6; 10:6; 15:24).

214. Luz, *Matthew*, 3.501.

215. So Carter, *Matthew and the Margins*, 528–29, but cf. Luz, *Matthew*, 3.501, who argues that *laos* consistently in Matthew refers to Israel or God's people, which means that the expression *pas ho laos* would be understood by Matthew's reader as God's people. As we shall see, this apparent difference of opinion may not be as clear-cut as seems to be the case at first.

tou laou; 21:23; 26:3, 47; 27:1), and here, *laos*, although this leadership group is only mentioned in relation to Jerusalem in Matthew, is likely intended to identify the leaders as having influence over the entire people, not only the Jerusalemites; they are included among those who need to be replaced once the kingdom has arrived, since they oppose Jesus's shepherding of the people. As such, it is worth noting that although the people as a whole are implied in the expression, the narrative makes a clear distinction between the leaders of the people and the people themselves, the latter often referred to as "crowds."

Matthew 2:4, which mentions "the chief priests and scribes of the people," uses *laos* in a similar way, but here we find an even stronger connection to Jerusalem, since the people of Jerusalem have just been mentioned as siding with Herod in 2:3. While *laos* identifies these leaders' responsibility for the entire people, it is Jerusalem, both its leaders and its people, who are targeted in this passage. This is further clarified by the fact that Matthew can also use "scribe" to indicate a member of Jesus's movement (13:52; 23:34). While scribes may represent the people of Israel, not all scribes are siding with Jesus's enemies. In Jerusalem, however, all scribes, as well as the chief priests, are consistently presented as Jesus's opponents, and the people of Jerusalem align with them. The meaning of *laos* here is thus double: on a first level, it refers to the fact that the chief priests were the Jewish people's leaders, but on a second, contextual level, the aim is to target specifically the people of Jerusalem.

In Matt 4:16, *laos* occurs in a scriptural quotation, which Matthew uses to identify the people of Galilee as those among whom Jesus will proclaim his message of repentance and the coming kingdom. After John had been put in prison, the narrator tells us, Jesus travels to Galilee in order for the prophecy to be fulfilled, which states that "the people who sat in darkness have seen a great light, and for those who sat in the region and shadow of death light has dawned."[216] Since "the people" (*laos*) are specifically identified as those living in the "Land of Zebulun, land of Naphtali, on the road by the sea, across the Jordan,

---

216. The prophecy is taken, rather freely, from Isa 9:1–2. Cf. 1 Macc 5:15.

Galilee of the Gentiles" (4:15), and Jesus is said to travel precisely to the area so designated (4:13), it is clear that *laos* is here referring to a specific, geographically defined collectivity within the Jewish people: the Jews of Galilee.[217] Set within the larger narrative's depiction of the people Jesus is said to seek out, this makes *laos* identical to the *ochloi*, the crowds of Galilee. This is further supported by the same use of *laos* in 4:23, which occurs in a setting specifying Jesus's target audience geographically to precisely the Galileans. It is among his people, i.e., the Jewish people in Galilee, in "their synagogues," that Jesus works to establish the kingdom of heaven.

The reference to *laos* in 13:15, a passage we have already dealt with extensively above, is, as in 4:16, taken from a scriptural quote. It is triggered specifically by the lack of understanding among the crowds of Galilee that has been identified already in 11:1–19. Again, the Galilean setting described would lead the reader to assume that the Galilean crowds are the ones illustrating the truth of the prophecy. There are simply no other Jews around, except for the disciples who certainly also belong to the Jewish people in this narrative, but are explicitly said not to be among those who fulfill the prophecy; this is the very rationale behind the entire discourse. They, the disciples, have already, for reasons discussed above, received insight into the mysteries of the kingdom (13:11–13). In this passage, *laos* is thus explicitly said to refer to one segment of the Jewish people, the crowds, and not another, the disciples, although the boundary between these groups is deliberately not well-defined in Matthew. The reference is general, though, meaning all of the crowds among whom Jesus has worked, rather than any specific crowd at a specific occasion.

Interestingly, while *laos* in Matthew can refer to the crowds as a specific segment within the Jewish people, the same word is used in

---

217. While Galilee is identified as "gentile," *laos* can only refer to the Jewish people here, since Jesus is explicitly limiting his mission to his own people. As Carter, *Matthew and the Margins*, 115, notes, the land of Zebulon and Naphtali was given to the Jewish people (Deut 34:1–4; Josh 19:10–16, 32–39), but is now under non-Jewish (imperial) influence and control (cf. Josephus, *BJ* 7.216–17). The reference to "gentiles" should not, therefore, be taken as an indication, as some have done, that the area was inhabited primarily by non-Jews. It is a statement that things are not as they should be in Galilee—in Matthew, non-Jews as a collective entity represents a culture that is contrary to God's will (Matt 18:17)—and Jesus's mission is to change this, through shepherding his people.

15:8 to target the Pharisees and the scribes associated with them, a group said to have arrived in Galilee from Jerusalem to seek Jesus out and ask him about his halakhic teaching (15:1). Again, *laos* is part of a passage from Scripture,[218] used by Matthew as a prophecy targeting specifically his interlocutors, who are identified in the previous verse ("You hypocrites! Isaiah prophesied rightly about you [*peri hymōn*] when he said..."; 15:7). This has nothing to do with the crowds, who do not establish or teach halakhah, nor with the disciples, who are themselves later authorized to design their own halakhah (16:19; 18:18). This passage is specifically about people whom the Matthean Jesus accuses of rendering powerless (*akyroō*) the word of God through their traditions, i.e., their halakhah (15:6): the Pharisees and the scribes associated with them. Their inability to form and teach traditions that are fit for the kingdom puts them under God's judgment. They, and here Matthew drops the reference to scribes and maintains only the Pharisees, have not been planted by Jesus's heavenly father and will therefore be uprooted (*ekrizoō*; 15:13).[219] This statement of condemnation and doom is applied also to those who follow these "blind" leaders (15:14).

In a Jerusalem setting, Matt 26:5 is perhaps the clearest evidence of the meaning of *laos*, "people," as identical to *ochlos*, "crowd." Here, the chief priests and the elders of the people agree to conspire with the aim of having Jesus arrested and executed. But they cannot do this; they are presented as saying to one another, "during the festival, or there may be a riot among the people [*en tō laō*]." It goes without saying that chief priests and the elders are not referring to themselves, despite the fact that they too belong to the Jewish people—indeed in their official roles they represent the people before God[220]—but to the pilgrim crowds that visit Jerusalem during Passover. In other words, *laos* refers here to one among several subdivisions within the Jewish people, and since this

---

218. Isa 29:13.
219. Cf. Matt 3:10, where the judgment is also triggered by Pharisees, although at that time in association with Sadducees.
220. It is their failure to do so in a way acceptable to God that has God interfere in history, sending his Messiah and preparing for coming doom.

collectivity represent the majority of the Jews in this particular setting, the chief priests and the leaders of the people fear them.

The same distinction between leaders and crowds is implied in 27:64, where, again, *laos* is used to designate the latter. This time, Matthew, uniquely among the Gospels, reintroduces the Pharisees after Jesus's death and resurrection, combining them with those who had Jesus executed, the chief priests (27:62).[221] The fear they express is that the people (*laos*)—obviously not referring to themselves—may come to believe that Jesus had been resurrected, based on these leaders' assumption that the disciples may come and steal Jesus's body and claim that he had been risen from the dead; therefore, they ask Pilate to put guards in front of the tomb. *Laos* here can only refer to the crowds of Jerusalem, over whom they had asserted control in connection with Jesus's execution.[222]

If we bring all of this together, excluding for a moment 27:25, a certain pattern emerges. First, we should note that, despite the fact that LXX can use *laos* to refer to nations other than Israel,[223] the word is never used of non-Jews in Matthew. When *laos* occurs in Matthew's narrative, it always refers people who are Jewish. Second, *laos* is sometimes used of the Jewish people as a whole. When used this way, it refers to the salvation, not the condemnation, of the people (1:21; 2:6). Third, more often, though, *laos* refers to a specific segment within the Jewish people.[224] When it does, it may refer to the Jewish crowds in Galilee and in Jerusalem, as well as to the Pharisees and the scribes who are associated with them.

While on one occasion, *laos* is used in a setting lamenting the lack

---

221. In this way, the Pharisees are associated with those who conspired against Jesus to have him killed, and even the Roman ruler, Pilate. The same phenomenon occurs in Matt 21:45, where the Pharisees, again, replace the elders of the people in a setting where opposition to Jesus is focused on, as we have discussed above. This is all part of Matthew's overall attempt at targeting the Pharisees for divine condemnation.

222. *Laos* probably refers both to the pilgrim crowds who had thought that Jesus was the Son of David (the chief priests had proven them wrong through having him executed), and the crowds in front of Pilate, the latter probably meant to be thought of as the same as those who were sent out to arrest Jesus in Gethsemane. Such a belief in the resurrection of Jesus would seriously question the authority of the chief priests and the elders of the people, and would vindicate Jesus as the true shepherd of the people, i.e., the Messiah.

223. See, e.g., LXX Gen 23:7; Ps 7:8.

224. Cf. LXX Gen 32:8; 33:15.

of understanding of the Galilean crowds (13:15), all other instances in which *laos* is used as a synonym for *ochlos* are positive in the sense that salvation is to be proclaimed among them (4:16, 23), or the chief priests and the elders of the people fear them since they believe Jesus to be a prophet and the Son of David (26:5), or because they might come to believe that Jesus has been resurrected (27:64). There is only one passage in which the word *laos* is used of a subgroup within the Jewish people that indicates condemnation of those of whom it is used, and that is 15:8, a passage which condemns the Pharisees and those who follow them. This fits the overall pattern of the Gospel, where the Pharisees represent the only group that is explicitly said to be condemned and to be excluded from the kingdom (cf. 5:20; 23:33).[225]

If we now return to the use of *laos* in 27:25, the first thing we can say with certainty is that it was meant to designate people who are Jewish. These Jews are prepared to take responsibility for the shedding of innocent blood and, as such, they are contrasted with the non-Jewish Pilate, the representative of Rome, who refuses to be held responsible. This would seem to make sense in light of Jesus's predictions of the fall of Jerusalem, since, from a Jewish perspective, non-Jews could not be blamed for this catastrophe, since that would imply that the gods of the nations would be stronger than the God of Israel. Guilt had to be found within the people, and the catastrophe construed as punishment, carried out by the God of Israel using the nations as a tool.[226] Most commentators refer to the historical fall of Jerusalem in 70 CE as an explanation for why Matthew has included this verse.[227] While this certainly matches what in many scholars' view, including my own, is the most likely date for the production of the Gospel in the 80s, and that therefore the fall of the temple probably affected the way Matthew wrote his Gospel, in my opinion, the verse should be explained first of all within the narrative itself, as a component of a

---

225. On the Pharisees, see above, chapter 3.2.1.2.
226. This pattern of thought is quite common among other Jewish texts too, from the prophets of the Hebrew Bible to the Rabbis. For sources, see pp. 243–44n91.
227. See e.g., Davies and Allison, *Matthew*, 3.592, who call the passage "an aetiological legend" of the fall of Jerusalem; Carter, *Matthew and the Margins*, 528; France, *Matthew*, 1058.

story that is about to culminate in the death and resurrection of its hero.

Now, to rehearse our conclusions above, according to the Matthean Jesus, Jerusalem and the temple must be destroyed, and he blames the Pharisees and the scribes associated with them for bringing this catastrophe upon the people.[228] They are the ones who are responsible for shedding innocent blood, even within the temple precincts, which pollutes the temple and leads to God's departure from it and, after God has left, its destruction (23:29–24:2[229]). Since, for Matthew, the law is still valid in all its details (e.g., 5:17–19; 13:41–42; 23:23), but the law cannot "function" without the means of atonement provided by the temple cult, Jesus has to die to save the people from their sins, providing the people with the necessary means of atonement that is lost with the temple's pollution and predicted destruction (1:21; 26:28). The moment Jesus dies, the temple veil is torn (27:51), signaling the interconnectedness of the temple and what is happening to Jesus: God is leaving the temple,[230] and Jesus's sacrifice is acknowledged as taking the place of the sacrifices offered there until the end of time and the final judgment. The temple can now be destroyed, without the Jewish people being obliterated at the same time due to the accumulation of un-atoned guilt. According to Matthew, the sins (and the accumulated guilt caused by lack of repentance) that forced all this to happen have already been committed before Jesus is executed (23:35, 38; 24:1–2). Jesus has to die to save his people.

Returning to 27:25, we see the entire city of Jerusalem, *pas ho laos*, corresponding to *pasa Hierosolyma*, "all Jerusalem" in 2:3, taking on responsibility for Jesus's death. This includes all the inhabitants of Jerusalem, not the pilgrim crowds, since they are not related to the capital in the story, but to Galilee and to some parts of Judea that Jesus past through on his way to Jerusalem (20:29), and not the Pharisees, since they are not mentioned in relation to Jesus's death, but primarily targeted as the cause behind Jerusalem's fall. The Pharisees have

228. On the role of the Pharisees in the narrative, see above pp. 233–56.
229. Cf. Ezek 10:1v11:23; see pp. 126–29.
230. Cf. Matt 27:46.

already been accused of the shedding of innocent blood that led to the temple's destruction; they are, then, in Matthew's theo-ritual logic, the reason why Jesus must die. They are responsible for how the story must develop, ending in (temporary) tragedy. The Pharisees are not, however, said to be directly involved in the killing of Jesus himself. These are the players involved and their function in the narrative: the Pharisees are the reason why it must happen; the chief priests, the elders of the people, and the scribes associated with them, are said to arrange for it to happen; Judas is used as the facilitator; the rest of the disciples abandon Jesus (cf. 26:31; Zech 13:7); and so do the pilgrim crowds that had supported him. What we see in 27:25 is the accusation that finalizes the list of guilty parties, forming a kind of inclusio with the capital's rejection of the Messiah in 2:3: the people of Jerusalem take on direct responsibility, together with the chief priests and the elders, for Jesus's death. What Jerusalem failed to do under Herod, they succeed in doing under the rule of the chief priests.

Interestingly, Matthew has never had Jesus directly pronounce condemnation over any crowd of people, only, for different reasons, over the Pharisees, the chief priests, and the elders. Not even now does he depart from this pattern, as he has the people of Jerusalem pronounce judgment on themselves. While all have been described as guilty in one way or another, and eschatological judgment is unavoidable—as is the salvation that the kingdom will bring—we should not generalize the idea of guilt in such a way that it conceals what Matthew is really claiming. Such readings of Matthew easily end up aligning with the historically problematic traditional Christian notion that the Jewish people as a whole are found guilty, Israel is dissolved as the chosen people, and another entity, the "church," takes its place.[231] Matthew's story is more complex than such readings allow for, however natural they may seem from the horizon of the later church history within which they were formed and used. Just as

---

231. This is quite common among scholars. Examples include Marguerat, *Jugement*; France, *Matthew*, 1056–58; Stanton, *New People*; Meier, *Vision of Matthew*; Luz, *Matthew*; Newport, *The Sources and Sitz im Lebel of Matthew, 23*. For a different perspective, see Saldarini, *Matthew Christian Jewish Community*; Andrew Overman, *Matthew's Gospel and Formative Judaism*; David Sim, *Christian Judaism*.

Matthew presents us with scribes who belong to three different people groups—two who oppose Jesus (Pharisees, on the one hand, and chief priests and elders, on the other) and one who supports him (disciples)—he describes the crowds as dynamic collectivities that cannot be generalized in terms of how they act, react, and are judged. This dynamic is related also to the geographical tension between the Galilee and Jerusalem that permeates the Gospel.[232]

If we now return to the expression "this generation" and look at its use in Matt 23:36, the above identified pattern is confirmed. Matthew has used 23:29–35 to describe the shedding of innocent blood, which is, as we have seen, explicitly blamed on the Pharisees and the scribes associated with them. In v. 35, Jesus exclaims: "upon you may come all the righteous blood shed on earth," which includes the blood of Jesus's followers ("prophets, sages and scribes"), whom he will send to them to proclaim the kingdom, but whom they, the Pharisees and their scribes, will persecute; flogging some and killing others (23:34). Previously, we have seen the crowds of Galilee and Jesus's disciples trigger outbursts from Jesus, complaining about the lack of understanding and lack of *pistis*, respectively, that characterizes "this generation." Here, in 23:35–36, Jesus tells the crowds and his disciples (23:1) that the Pharisees are the ones who have shed the innocent blood, which will lead to severe divine punishment.

As in any war, which is also evident in Israel's history, when such punishment is unleashed more people than those who are guilty will suffer. Therefore, Jesus continues from the specific to the general, stating that "this generation," i.e., all members of the Jewish people in Matthew's narrative world alive at the time, including the crowds and Jesus's own disciples, will suffer for what the Pharisees and those who follow them have done and will do (23:36).[233] This apocalyptic suffering

---

232. As France, *Matthew*, 1106, has also pointed out, after the resurrection of Jesus, Jerusalem represents rejection of the Messiah, and the spreading of lies about him; Galilee, on the contrary, is where the truth is proclaimed. It is of some interest to note that rabbinic Judaism also took form in Galilee after the destruction of Jerusalem, although this is not the place to suggest theories concerning possible socio-religious and political implications of these developments.

233. Cf. van Tilborg, *Leaders*, 67: "The scribes and the Pharisees are guilty of all the evil that has happened in the history of Israel. Mt 23,36 therefore receives very specific meaning in Mt. "This generation" is confined to the leaders of the Jewish people. They are the ones upon whom all this

is detailed in Matthew 24 as related to the fall of the temple; this chapter further supports the fact that "this generation," which has to suffer for what the Pharisees brought upon themselves and everybody else, includes Jesus's own people, here referred to as the "elect" (24:22). Indeed, the entire discourse in Matthew 24 is construed as advice to the disciples about what they have to do and how they should react when the time of suffering comes.

What is interesting to note is that the sins of the Pharisees and those who associate with them that are outlined in Matthew 23 are related to Jerusalem, the holy city of the great king (5:35), ruled by illegitimate leaders. The crimes of the Pharisees, more specifically, the accusation of their shedding of innocent blood, are now said to be committed also by Jerusalem (23:37). The result is that the city is presented as in complete agreement with the actions of the Pharisees, and judgment will come as a consequence of their sins too. Jerusalem is, as much as the Pharisees, guilty of shedding innocent blood.

This reminds readers of Jerusalem's resistance to the Messiah in 2:3 (where "all Jerusalem" was "troubled" along with Herod) and prepares them for the reference in 27:25, in which the entire city takes on responsibility for precisely the shedding of innocent blood. At that time, however, the innocent blood that is about to be shed will, rather than just adding to the defilement that already exist, and which in any case will lead to the fall of the temple, have a sacrificial, atoning effect for "many" (26:28). In other words, all who join or relate positively to the movement Jesus has initiated, accepting his teaching of the law and engaging in a praxis of unlimited mutual exchange of forgiveness will have a share of the salvation that results from this atoning sacrifice. Jerusalem is guilty together with the Pharisees for shedding the blood that leads to the temple's destruction, but unlike the Pharisees, the people of Jerusalem are also, unknowingly, instrumental in providing for the sacrificial replacement that will save the people once the temple is destroyed.[234] Regardless, "this generation" will have to go

---

will come down, they are beyond all redemption." While van Tilborg is certainly correct that the Pharisees and their scribes are identified as the guilty party, the punishment that will follow will affect everyone in Israel, in this world; the passage does not deal with the final judgment.

through the suffering that groups within this larger entity have caused; they will also, however, have the option of sharing in the salvation that these developments will bring, due to God's merciful and saving approach to the people, as the kingdom of heaven will be realized in full after a final judgment.[235]

The remaining passages mentioning "this generation" fit well into this overall interpretive frame. Jesus's outbursts in all of these instances are caused by the Pharisees, once together with scribes (12:38–45), and once together with Sadducees (16:4). The trigger is their request for a sign. Referring to the sign of Jonah as the only sign that will be given, Jesus refuses to give them what they ask for, and instead responds, in 12:38–45, with accusations and threats of divine condemnation in the final judgment.[236] The crowds are never condemned in this way, despite their lack of understanding. Further, one may note that Jesus is saying that this "evil and adulterous generation asks for a sign" (12:38); it is, however, only the Pharisees, scribes associated with them, and Sadducees who are reported to have asked for signs, never the crowds. The judgment pronounced should thus be understood to apply to these former groups and those who decide to follow them.

In sum, "this generation" is primarily a chronometric expression indicating the imminence of apocalyptic suffering and the final judgment. Its negative use is triggered by specific groups in the Gospel, including the crowds, Jesus's disciples, the Pharisees, scribes associated

---

234. The shedding of Jesus's blood is thus of a different kind, in terms of its effect, compared to the shedding of the blood of other innocent messengers of God. The latter pollute the temple and forces God to leave his abode, bringing apocalyptic calamity on the people; the former atones for sins and provides a new locus for God's presence among his people (cf. Matt 1:23; 18:20; 28:20). The way Matthew sets things up in terms of the destruction of Jerusalem and the death of Jesus is more complex than seeing the latter as a straightforward explanation of the former, as, e.g., Davies and Allison, *Matthew* 3.592, do. See discussion in Timothy Cargal, "'His Blood Be upon Us and upon Our Children': A Matthean Double Entendre?" *NTS* 37 (1991): 101–12; cf. Catherine Hamilton, "'His Blood Be upon Us': Innocent Blood and the Death of Jesus in Matthew," *CBQ* 70 (2008): 82–100; Amy-Jill Levine, *Social and Ethnic Dimensions*, 269; Carter, *Matthew and the Margins*, 529. As we have argued here, Matthew presents Jesus's death as a solution to the loss of the temple, not its cause. See also Runesson, "Purity and Holiness in Matthew's Narrative World."

235. Cf. Nolland, *Matthew*, 1178–79: "the possibility of forgiveness and restoration remains."

236. In Matt 16:4, when the Pharisees arrive at the scene with the Sadducees, not the scribes, no judgment is pronounced, only reproach. It is only when Pharisees are either alone or with scribes that Matthew has Jesus refer to divine judgment and condemnation.

with the Pharisees, and the Sadducees. While it encompasses the entire Jewish people populating Matthew's narrative world, the accusations, the reproach, and the divine condemnation that follows with references to "this generation" are targeting primarily only the specific groups mentioned in each particular passage.[237] Thus, the warning that this generation will be condemned in the final judgment because of the lack of the repentance that had characterized the people of Nineveh (12:41) does not apply to the disciples, nor to the crowds, since the latter never asked Jesus for a sign, and so have not revealed their insensitivity to Jesus's proclamation of the necessity of repentance.

The full meaning of "this generation" is thus dependent on the context in which it is used. It is thus incompatible with Matthew's narrative to claim that "this generation" would refer to "Israel"—excluding, for unexplained reasons, the disciples—and signal its destruction. "This generation" is presented as confused, lacking in understanding and trust/faithfulness/loyalty (*pistis*), sometimes also as refusing to repent, but this functions as a motivation for, or reason behind, Jesus's mission among his people, an attempt to save them. This brings us, finally, to the issue of the use of the term "Israel" in Matthew.

3.2.2.2 Israel: Land and People

Is "Israel," for Matthew, an entity that has lost or is losing its meaning as the narrative progresses from Jesus's birth to his death as a consequence of divine condemnation, or is it still, at the end of the story, an active category with much the same content as it had in Israel's history and still has in many other Jewish texts contemporary with Matthew? In other words: is Matthew telling his story about Jesus as the story of how the people of Israel came to lose its status as the people of God?[238] Or is the purpose to convey how the people of Israel

---

237. Cf. Saldarini, *Community*, 41: "Jesus does not directly condemn 'this generation' as he does when they are identified explicitly as the Pharisees."
238. So Lloyd Gaston, "The Messiah of Israel as Teacher of the Gentiles," *Interpretation* 29:1 (1975):

can be saved in the midst of the apocalyptic calamities that are soon to be unleashed upon them because of the failures of Israel's shepherds, and then be acquitted in the final judgment?

We have already dealt with some aspects of this problem above in dialogue with Marguerat's work; we can therefore be rather brief here.[239] All that we have said up until this point has consistently pointed in the direction of the latter of the two options given above. Matthew's Gospel portrays Jesus as working to save his people, teaching them how to keep the Torah so that it retains its intended salvific efficacy, healing their wounds and exorcising demons that plagued them, and, finally, as the utmost evidence for his Moses-like commitment to his people,[240] sacrificing his own life to make available a means of atonement for them as God is abandoning his temple due to its defilement.

We have seen how the narrative portrays this mission as a struggle, due to the people's lack of understanding and lack of trust/ faithfulness/loyalty (*pistis*), and due to the fact that Jesus is opposed in his work among the lost sheep of the house of Israel by what is portrayed as illegitimate leaders who, in different ways, primarily through flawed teaching of the Torah, lead the people astray. In the midst of this struggle, the Matthean Jesus outlines the criteria of divine judgment based on his understanding of the Torah, which leads to comprehension of the righteousness demanded by and in the coming kingdom. Doing this, he ensures his audience that these criteria are valid for everyone within the people; disciples, crowds, Pharisees, Sadducees, Herodians, scribes, chief priests, and the elders of the people alike. The question of the redemption or not of the people can thus be re-phrased: did Jesus fail in his mission to save his people Israel—*as a people*—and so, resign himself to the fact that, in the last

---

24–40, here 32: "More than any other Gospel, Matthew emphasizes the utter rejection of Israel." See also discussion of Luz's work below.

239. See pp. 10–12. For context which shed light on Matthew's special use of 'Israel,' see C.T.R Hayward, *Interpretations of the Name Israel in Ancient Judaism and Some Early Christian Writings* (Oxford: Oxford University Press, 2005).

240. Moses refuses replacement theology, i.e., to let the people perish due to their sin, even when it is suggested by God himself (Exod 32:10; Deut 9:14; cf. Exod 32:7–9, 13–14, 32; Deut 9:18–20, 25–29).

two verses of the story (28:19–20), he, as Acts would portray Paul, now has to go to the gentiles *instead*? Although I believe the answer, based on what we have said so far, is a clear "no," Matthew's use of the term "Israel"—which does not cohere with how it was used by the early church, nor, in my opinion, with how many scholars use the term today—will shed further light on this interpretive issue.

The term "Israel" occurs in Mathew in a few different settings, which, with some overlap, may be divided into four thematic categories dealing with: a) salvation, b) the land, c) lack of trust in or rejection of Jesus, and d) guilt relating to the death of Jesus. The majority of mentions fall in the first category, salvation, with only one passage relating the term to Jesus's death. The pattern that emerges when the term is studied in context unfolds as follows.

First of all, Israel plays an important role when Matthew sets the scene for the story of the Messiah. The focus is, from the very start, on the Jewish people, the genealogy beginning with the identification of Jesus as the son of David and the son of Abraham, and ending with the explicit claim that he is the Messiah (1:1, 17). This Messiah's name reveals his task, which is to "save his people from their sins," and be for his people, Immanuel, "God with us" (1:21, 23). This is who Jesus is, what he has been sent to accomplish, and for whom. "His people" is identified specifically as God's people Israel in the prophecy quoted in 2:6.[241] It is precisely as a prophecy about a king chosen to lead Israel that these words worry Herod to the degree that he attempts to kill Jesus. There can be no doubt that Matthew sets the scene for his entire narrative in these early chapters, as also Raymond Brown has argued,[242] and that Jesus's mission is to shepherd and save the people identified as God's people and called Israel: "my people Israel" (2:6).

When Matthew is then telling his story of Jesus, this focus on the people of Israel is explicitly defined not to include any other nations, not even the Samaritans (10:6; 15:24). While the blessings of the kingdom will spill over to also benefit some non-Jews who seek Jesus's

241. Cf. Mica 5:2; 2 Sam 5:2.
242. Raymond Brown, *The birth of the Messiah*, 7; cf. Luz, *Theology of the Gospel of Matthew*, 26–41; Runesson, "Matthew as Midwife," 301.

help (8:5–13; 15:21–28), when Jesus sends the disciples to do what he himself is doing in Galilee, they are told to heal and proclaim the kingdom in "all the towns of Israel" (10:23).[243] The crowds in Galilee are amazed at what he is doing as he is fulfilling his mission, exclaiming that nothing like this has ever happened before "in Israel" (9:33), confirming that Jesus's salvific work maintains a focus on his own people. Indeed, they praise "the God of Israel" when they encounter his power to heal (15:31). Further, Jesus's twelve disciples will be ruling/judging[244] "the twelve tribes of Israel" when the kingdom is established (19:28), which implies that Israel as a people is maintained as a category throughout history, as history is contained and described within the narrative; Jesus's death, which comes before the final judgment, does not affect Israel's peoplehood, neither does the final judgment.

If we look at "Israel" when it is defined as a geopolitical area, we see that the salvation that Jesus's mission will bring to his people is to take form in this area, with a focus primarily on Galilee, and, secondarily, Judea. In Matt 2:20, 21, Jesus returns from Egypt with his parents to "the land of Israel" (gē Israēl), where he grows up in Galilee, which is also where he later begins his mission after a visit to John the Baptist in Judea and a time in the Judean desert (3:13—4:17). As mentioned above, it is to the towns of Israel that the disciples are to travel, and the amazement that the people expresses when they see the power with which Jesus performs his extraordinary deeds results in the claim that never in Israel has anything similar been seen (9:33). "Israel" here refers to both the land and the people, which fits well into the pattern, prevalent in antiquity, to connect an *ethnos* with a land, a law, and a god.[245] Indeed, the same can be said of the crowds' praise of "the

---

243. The fact that Jesus is telling them that they will not be done with this task before the Son of Man comes matters little; the aim is confined to Israel.

244. On the meaning of *krinō* in this verse, see discussion of Matt 19:28 above, p. 46n16. Even if we understand *krinō* to mean "to judge," the word does not imply condemnation, but simply recalls a court setting in which judgment can be either favorable or condemnatory, based on the evidence submitted. Thus, the purpose of the passage is to establish the authority of the twelve disciples to act as judges in Israel at and/or after the final judgment. Previously, they have been given the authority to establish halakhah in accordance with Jesus's teaching (16:19; 18:18); it is on the basis of how Israel has followed this halakhah, i.e., if they have observed the Torah as it was originally meant to be observed, that the nation will be judged.

245. See especially Steve Mason, "Jews, Judaeans, Judaizing, Judaism: Problems of Categorization in

God of Israel" (15:31), since reference to the God of Israel will imply a connection with the people of Israel and the land of Israel.[246]

This connection between land and people comes together in 27:42, an important passage for our purposes in this section. Here, Matthew has the chief priests and the scribes associated with them, as well as the elders of Jerusalem, mock Jesus, ironically stating that Jesus is "the king of Israel." This is, in fact, the claim that Matthew's Gospel has made since 1:1, and which all the different leading groups in Israel have attempted to prove wrong throughout the narrative, beginning with Herod and ending with the chief priests. This is their moment of triumph; this is when they have proven him wrong and showed that he is, in fact, not the king of Israel, contrary to the claims made in 2:6, where it was predicted that Jesus would shepherd Israel. They had now accomplished what Herod failed to do.

It seems to me, based on the very clear declaration of purpose for the Matthean Messiah in the narrative, that if, as researchers claim, "Israel" is indeed rejected as the people of God in Matthew's story,[247] Jesus would have no people to shepherd beyond the final judgment, and one would consequently have to draw the conclusion that the chief priests were right. Jesus was, after all, not the king of Israel, because there will be no Israel to rule.[248] Someone might protest and say that this is just a terminological issue. But the problem lies exactly in how terms are used and how they are allowed to influence the

Ancient History," in *JSJ* 38 (2007): 457–512. Cf. the discussion below on ethnicity in Matthew, Part II.

246. The first time we find an identification of the biblical God as the "God of Israel" is in relation to the exodus, when Moses and Aaron tell the Pharaoh an oracle from their God: "Let my people go" (Exod 5:1). The expression occurs only twice in the New Testament, in Matt 15:31, as we have discussed here, and in Luke 1:68, where John's father Zechariah praises God at the occasion of his son's circumcision on the eight day, saying: "Blessed be the Lord God of Israel, for he has looked favorably on his people and redeemed them."

247. For examples of scholars making this claim, see above p. 204n465.

248. It should be noted that Matthew's Gospel does not operate with concepts such as "new Israel" or "church" as opposed to "Israel," as replacing 'Israel'; these are ideas that came into existence in circles that claimed that they, as (non-Jewish) believers in Jesus, had replaced "Israel" as God's people. But this type of discourse is nowhere to be found in Matthew's text. It is, also, irrelevant to introduce the idea that Jesus was indeed "king of Israel" but "Israel" rejected their king. The result is still the same: If that were true, for Matthew, then Jesus did fail his mission, as the mission is carefully laid out in the genealogy and infancy story, as well as how it is described throughout the narrative. A king who is not accepted by his people is a failed king. But this is not Matthew's message.

conclusions drawn. We build our arguments with words, but words are not innocent neutral servants; they are carriers of meaning, which is more often than not dependent on research that may or may not be outdated. Paying attention to the terms used in historical reconstruction is an important task at the core of the scholarly undertaking.[249]

The point Matthew is making in 27:42 is, of course, that the chief priests were wrong, and that they would soon find out, even if they planned carefully to avoid any, for them, unpleasant surprises even after Jesus's death (27:62–66). The Matthean Jesus was, indeed, what he claimed to be from the very beginning: the Son of David, the king of Israel. And more than that. This Messiah, once resurrected by God, will expand his rule to include all the nations, in essence aiming at creating an empire where God's law, as opposed to Roman law, will be observed.[250]

This pattern of Israel's role in Matthew's story is confirmed in the two last categories mentioned above, the lack of trust in or rejection of Jesus, and guilt related to Jesus's death. In the first of these categories, we find a passage where Jesus tells a centurion whose slave he is about to heal that "in no one in Israel have I found such *pistis*" (8:10). This verse has often been referred to as evidence that Jesus understands Israel as condemned, especially since in 8:12 Jesus states that "the heirs of the kingdom [*hyioi tēs basileias*] will be thrown into the outer darkness, where there will be weeping and gnashing of teeth." But a close reading of these verses in light of how divine judgment is construed in the narrative will yield a different reading.

---

249. On the terminological problem in historical reconstruction, see Runesson, "Inventing Christian Identity"; idem, "The Question of Terminology: The Architecture of Contemporary Discussions on Paul," in *Paul Within Judaism: Restoring the First-Century Context to the Apostle* (edited by Mark Nanos and Magnus Zetterholm; Minneapolis: Fortress, 2015), 53–77.

250. On Matthew and Empire, see Warren Carter, *Matthew and Empire: Initial Explorations* (Harrisburg; Trinity Press International, 2001); John Riches and David C. Sim (eds.), *The Gospel of Matthew in its Roman Imperial Context* (London: T & T Clark, 2005); see also Runesson, "Building Matthean Communities." I do not mean to say that Matthew's primary concern was the Roman Empire; I do not think there is evidence for such a view in Matthew's Gospel. However, it is quite clear, in my opinion, that Roman presence in the land is regarded as a symptom of the fact that something is not right within the nation. Matthew identifies this problem as a lack of proper shepherding, and sets forth to show that Jesus is God's response to the current crisis. Once the crisis is resolved, its symptoms will also disappear.

"Israel" is, in Matthew, the largest entity describing all of the Jewish people, the people Jesus is sent to shepherd and save. This entity is equivalent to "this generation," an expression used by Matthew when he announces what time it is and describes the struggles Jesus encounters when he is carrying out his mission. Since "this generation" includes the disciples, as we have seen above, and since the disciples are certainly to be viewed among those that Jesus is sent to save, "Israel" must include Jesus's closest co-workers.[251] Thus, when Jesus tells the centurion that he has not seen such *pistis* as his in Israel before, this includes Jesus's own disciples. Indeed, one of Jesus's constant complaints against his disciples is precisely their lack of *pistis*, or even their unbelief.[252] As noted above, not even Jesus's resurrection changes this characteristic that Matthew has identified with the disciples. When the resurrected one is speaking to them on the Galilean mountain, sending them out to make disciples of the nations, the disciples are still described as doubting (Matt 28:17).[253] Lack of *pistis* and doubting can thus not be identified as indicating, in Matthew's story, people who will necessarily be condemned and, therefore, Matt 8:10

251. To be sure, as we have noted above, the *ekklēsia* Jesus is telling his disciples that he will establish with them as leaders (Matt 16:18; 18:17; cf. 16:19; 18:18; 19:28 and cannot be seen as a replacement for "Israel," since *ekklēsia*, as a phenomenon and as a term, was an integral part of institutional realities within Israel in first-century Jewish terminology. Historically, the *ekklēsia*, as Matthew envisions it, is to be understood as a Jewish association run by and for Jewish believers in Jesus (other Jews used the same term to describe both their associations and the public assemblies of the land). Theologically and ideologically, the Matthean claim is that this (semi-public) institution represents the assembly of the people of Israel, and that it will rule the nation (and the nations) as the kingdom of heaven is being established. On Jewish usage of *ekklēsia*, see above, pp. 6n9; 11n27.
252. *Oligopistos* ("little trust") is applied almost exclusively to Jesus's disciples as a group (Matt 8:26; 16:8; 17:20) and once to Peter himself, who is to become the leader of the *ekklēsia* (Matt 14:31). Only once is the word used to characterize both the disciples and the Galilean crowds (Matt 6:30). *Apistos* ("lack of trust"/"unbelieving") is used once in Matthew, referring to "this generation" when it is characterized by the disciples' lack of trust and inability to heal (17:17).
253. NRSV has, as many other translations, "but some doubted [*hoi de edistasan*]," i.e., some of the disciples where firm in their *pistis*, others not, and we are not told who belongs to which group. However, the grammar of Matt 28:17 does not require a partitive reading; indeed, as some would argue, the partitive understanding of the sentence is based on an evaluation of the overall content of Matthew, not on the grammar. If we pay close attention to how the disciples are described in Matthew, however, lack of trust, and thus presence of doubt is a key characteristic that follows them throughout the narrative. For discussion, see K. H. Reeves, "They Worshipped Him and They Doubted: Matthew 28:17," *Bible Translator* 49 (1998): 344–49; David L. Turner, *Matthew* (Grand Rapids: Baker Academic, 2008), 688. Hagner, *Matthew*, 2.884–86, argues, correctly in my view, for the inclusive reading, noting that while grammar cannot solve the issue, the author's general use of *hoi de* in the Gospel tips the scale in favor of "and they doubted." Hagner, however, argues for a different understanding of *distazō*, suggesting it refers to 'hesitation' rather than 'doubt.'

cannot be read as an indication that "Israel" will be condemned, based on the criterion of lack of *pistis*.[254]

If this is true, what does Jesus mean to say in 8:12, claiming that the "heirs of the kingdom" will be excluded from the kingdom of heaven? It seems to me that Jesus is here saying precisely what he will be stating in parable form once he has entered Jerusalem and accuses various groups of leaders. While tax collectors and prostitutes—to be sure, also part of "Israel"—are said to enter the kingdom of God, the chief priests and elders, who did not accept John's proclamation and, consequently have not repented, will be rejected and displaced (21:23-32; 33-46). This rejection of those who were supposed to inherit the kingdom is also said to apply to the Pharisees, who, as Matthew has it, now "sit on Moses' chair," and thus have (institutionally based) influence over the people (22:1-15; cf. 23:2-3). "God's kingdom will be taken from them" and will be given to a group—i.e. Jesus's followers[255]—that will be able to produce the fruit that the kingdom requires (21:43).

What is translated in the NRSV as "the heirs of the kingdom," in the Greek text literally "the sons of the kingdom," thus refers not to the entirety of Israel, but to those who lead Israel, those who were, as the parable has it, first invited to the son's wedding (22:1-6). This is confirmed by Matthew's use elsewhere of the exact same expression, translated by the NRSV as "the children of the kingdom," in Greek, again, "the sons of the kingdom" (*hyioi tēs basileias*; 13:38). Here, the expression refers to "the good seed" sown by the Son of Man, those among the crowds who will be called righteous and will, after the final judgment, "shine like the sun in the kingdom of their Father" (13:37-38, 43) as they have inherited the land (5:5) from the displaced leaders (21:43, 45). Again, meaning lies in context; the expression must be understood in relation to how Matthew's Jesus, more generally, is referring to various groups in the Gospel; such considerations should

---

254. On *pistis* ("faith") as a criterion of judgment, see also above, chapter 2.5.

255. The reference to "fruit" here is consistent with other such references to what the kingdom requires, indicating a focus on the correct observance of the Torah, as Jesus is teaching it in the Gospel. Cf. Matt 3:10: "every tree therefore that does not bear good fruit is cut down and thrown into the fire." (See also Matt 7:19; 12:33; 13:8.)

then shed light on how we interpret the specific application of the expression. It is clear that neither in 8:12 nor in 13:38 can the expression be understood as representing the entirety of Israel. In the former verse, it refers to those in Israel who are condemned and displaced; in the latter, it refers to those in Israel who are saved and brought into the kingdom of heaven.

This tension between accepting Jesus and rejecting him is one of the common dynamics in the Gospel, which also comes to the fore when Jesus is preparing his disciples for what they will encounter when he sends them to proclaim the kingdom in the towns of Israel. Some will receive them, and these people will be rewarded by God (10:11–13, 40–42); others will reject them, and those people will be condemned in the final judgment (10:14–15). It is never a question of the entire people of Israel rejecting Jesus and being condemned as a consequence. Such readings of Matthew have simply no textual support in the Gospel and conceal what the text is, in fact, trying to communicate: the kingdom is irrevocably coming, and there will be struggles and suffering in Israel before it is all accomplished.

Indeed, in the final passage that we shall consider in this section, 27:9, this dynamic between those in Israel who reject Jesus's mission and those who accept it is confirmed, precisely when the guilt accumulated by Jesus's death is to be sorted out. In 27:3–5, Judas, realizing that he has betrayed innocent blood is, in an act of repentance, returning the money he was paid to have Jesus handed over to the religio-political authorities in the temple.[256] Then, Matthew has the chief priests buying the potter's field using the blood money (since they would defile the temple treasury if it were put there). This, the narrator tells us, fulfills a prophecy uttered by Jeremiah.[257] When the prophecy is given as referring to the chief priests as those who put a price on Jesus, Matthew is careful to note that the prophet says

---

256. On Judas's repentance and its meaning, see above, pp. 133–34.
257. The quote is, in fact, a rather free, or "targumizing," as Davies and Allison, *Matthew*, 3.570, fittingly phrase it, use of Zech 11:13 (but cf. Jer 32:6–15). For Matthew's use of Jeremiah in his Gospel, see Knowles, *Jeremiah in Matthew's Gospel: The Rejected Prophet Motif in Matthean Redaction* (Sheffield: JSOT Press, 1993).

the price was set by "*some* in the people of Israel."[258] It could hardly be more clearly stated: the source of the guilt generated by the innocent blood that is about to be shed is laid down squarely at the feet of the chief priests, who are said to represent "some" of the people of Israel, not all.[259]

If we are to sum up the results from this reading of "Israel" in Matthew's Gospel, it is clear, in my opinion, that while many scholars use the term to speak about Jesus's opponents, or of those who are condemned, this is not how Matthew employs the word. In the First Gospel, "Israel," understood as people and/or land, refers to the common ground on which Jesus struggles to make known the good news of the kingdom of heaven. While "Israel" defines what is Jesus's aim to save, the narrative refuses to describe the development of the plot in any simplified way as either doomed to fail or destined to succeed. Instead, what we see is a divided Israel. Those who repent belong to the saved and there will be rewards waiting for them depending on their Torah observance. Others are strenuously opposed to the proclamation that the end is drawing near; they continue to break the law and refuse to repent. While some of the latter belongs in Galilean cities such as Bethsaida and Capernaum, resistance to Jesus is epitomized in the attitudes of the Pharisees and the chief priests, and all who align themselves with either of these groups.

Since not all characters in the Gospel are portrayed as condemned, the term "Israel," which is the larger collectivity that embodies these

---

258. *Apo* in the phrase *apo hyiōn Israēl* has partitive meaning, since the verb is in the middle, not the passive form, as also Nolland, *Matthew*, 1157, Luz, *Matthew*, 3.466n3, and other commentators agree. The translation, then, must be "some of the people [or 'sons'] of Israel."

259. As Davies and Allison, *Matthew*, 3.570, note commenting on the partitive force of *apo*, this "harmonizes with Matthew's tendency to distinguish between the Jewish people and their leaders." Nolland, *Matthew*, 1157, agrees and adds, correctly in my opinion, that Matthew "probably has the chief priests specifically in mind." See also Luz, *Matthew*, 3.475, who realizes that this verse will not support his overall interpretation of all Israel as condemned, and consequently must refer to what he believes will happen later on in the story to keep his approach intact, in which Israel is narratively predestined to be lost, i.e., that Jesus's mission to save his people ultimately fails. There seems to be in Luz's reading of Matthew an overarching concern for an explanation of how what we today would call the "church," as an institution distinguishable from Judaism and the synagogue, came into being, a concern that has a certain influence on his interpretation of individual Matthean passages. Whatever the reason, Matthew refuses to answer this question of "church"/synagogue, as we understand these terms today, since it is not relevant to his narrative world.

various groups, cannot be used to refer to the condemned without violating the logic of the plot. Regardless, then, of whether we look at individual groups or characters as they are described in the story, or whether we study specific words or concepts used, such as "Israel," or "*laos*," or "this generation," or covenant, or grace, Matthew resists generalizations and demands careful attention to detail if the text's message is not to be lost in a reception-historical understanding that took, for a variety of reasons, a very different route in the later church.

In Matthew's narrative world, Jesus's mission to save his people Israel is successful in so far as many among them have responded positively to him, recognizing him as the Messiah; these are mostly the Galilean crowds and Jesus's disciples, two groups between whom there are no distinct boundaries, except when the disciples are portrayed as the future leaders of the people. These members of Israel are taught to observe the law as it was originally intended, to practice unlimited mutual forgiveness, and to seek refuge in the forgiveness of sins offered for the sake of "many," as Jesus performs the ultimate sacrifice of offering his own life for his people, and so renews the covenant relationship between God and his people. This, for Matthew, is the portion of Israel that will, *as Israel*, enter the kingdom, and they will enter salvation, as we shall see in Part II, together with individuals from other nations who likewise produce fruit worthy of the kingdom.

3.3 The Critique of Leadership and the Theology of Judgment

The discussion above, in which we have attempted to understand the various collectivities mentioned in the Gospel within the framework of God's wrath and salvation, has led to the conclusion that Matthew is structured to condemn the various leadership groups mentioned and offer salvation primarily to the people of Israel, the latter most often identified with the crowds, i.e., with the majority of people in any given locale. While there is no need to summarize the details of these investigations here, there are, however, a few more words that need to be added with regard to how the Matthean Jesus's relationship to these leadership groups is construed, especially since the criteria of judgment outlined in chapter 2 are not always referred to when these influential groups are targeted for criticism. In order to understand Matthew's critique of leadership, then, we must distinguish between two modes of critique. On the one hand, we may analyze the criteria of judgment, i.e., the method of judgment, to see how these criteria are applied to those who are condemned. On the other hand, we need to pay close attention to the nature of the charges leveled against the leaders when they seem to go beyond the criteria outlined.

With regard to the criteria of judgment that we have discussed in chapter 2, these are all explainable within a first-century Jewish setting as primarily building on the common theme of obedience to the Torah. It is Jesus's understanding of Torah which makes up the foundation for how the people will be judged in the final judgment; Jesus himself is presented both as the teacher of law and as the judge who is going to apply this teaching when he judges the people. Close attention to Jesus's teaching—and the repentance that must necessarily follow—is thus required for all who want to be judged with mercy when the kingdom will come in full. The same criteria are applied to all, disciple or not. The ultimate destiny of the crowds and John's disciples are left open, since they are portrayed as closely related to Jesus and attentive to his teaching, although without explicitly being called disciples of Jesus; especially the boundary between Jesus's disciples and the crowds is blurry, and not meant to distinguish between saved or condemned; the story is in this regard open-ended, which is also shown by passages such as 10:40–42.

There are, however, specific groups that are singled out *as groups* as unresponsive to Jesus, groups that will not repent, but are, in fact, seeking his destruction. Among these groups, all of whom are described as influencing the people of Israel in destructive ways, the Pharisees, as we have argued above,[260] take the front seat, but we also find the chief priests, the elders of the people, and scribes associated with these groups. Sadducees and Herodians are less targeted, but they are portrayed, too, as not heeding the call to repent, but rather,

---

260. See chapter 3.2.1.2.

attempting to ensnare Jesus with questions that will prove him wrong. These various influential groups are not to be conflated into one single group, generalized as "the Jewish leaders." Matthew is making a point of the fact that all these *different* leadership groups have a *common* interest in getting rid of Jesus. What is, then, the charge that Matthew levels against them, which makes the reader understand that aligning oneself with either of these groups is a poor choice if one wants to be among those who survive the apocalyptic suffering and may enter into the kingdom?

If we look first at how Jesus's teaching is portrayed, we may note that Matthew actually presents few real disagreements between Jesus and the leadership groups with regard to the interpretation of Torah. The issues of contention, almost all of which are between Jesus and the Pharisees, are rather quickly summed up as dealing with the washing of hands before meals (15:1–21), the interpretation of what constitutes work on the Sabbath (12:1–8; cf. 24:20), on what basis divorce is acceptable (5:27–32; 19:1–9),[261] and the swearing of oaths (5:33; 23:16–22). In addition to these issues, Jesus, without identifying a group that would be against what he is teaching, builds a fence around the law against murder, stating that anger already breaks the law and defiles the temple (5:21–26). In the same way, the commandment to love is interpreted to extend to enemies (5:38–47).[262] The Pharisees are not explicitly said to be disputing either of these two interpretations, and do not reject Jesus's claim that the key commandment in the Torah which, consequently, must be the point of departure for all understanding of both the law and the prophets, is the requirement to love God and neighbor (22:34–40).

Then, of course, we have the basic agreement between the Matthean Jesus and the Pharisees that prayer is important (6:5–7), as is also almsgiving (6:3–4), fasting (6:17–18; cf. 9:14–15), the wearing of phylacteries and fringes on cloaks (9:20; 14:36; 23:5), the reading of the

---

261. Note that although Jesus states the original intention of the Torah was that no divorce should exist, he, like Moses and the Pharisees, does allow for divorce under certain circumstances.

262. Cf. 2 Chr 19:2. Note that Torah already requires love not only for fellow Israelites (Lev 19:17), but also for immigrants (Hebr. *ger*; Lev 19:34).

Torah in communal settings (cf. 23:2–3), and, more generally, attending synagogue (e.g., 4:23; 9:35; 23:6). Dietary laws are maintained (15:1–20), as are purity laws (8:4, 5–13; 23:25–26). Just like the Pharisees, Jesus teaches a strict rule for tithing, including mint, dill, and cumin (23:23), and he, as all other Jews described in the narrative, celebrates Passover (26:2, 17–35); this gives the impression that Jesus celebrates all festivals according to the law, although this is not, as in John's Gospel, stated explicitly. The temple cult and the practices connected with the temple, including the temple tax, are maintained until the point when the temple is said to have become defiled in Matthew 23–24 (5:23–24; 12:3–5; 17:24–27; 23:19–21). In fact, the Matthean Jesus states that all of the commandments, even the most minor ones, in the Torah remain valid and must be observed in order for the people to produce the fruit worthy of the kingdom (5:17–19; 7:21; cf. 19:17).

With this as a background, are the legal disputes really enough for Matthew to single out the Pharisees as condemned to be sent to destruction in Gehenna (23:33)? After all, legal discussions were a common feature of Second-Temple Judaism, as well as within rabbinic Judaism, and usually did not lead to the type of absolute condemnation of the opponent that we see in Matthew. To be sure, halakhic disagreements were one of the main reasons for the partings of the ways between Jewish groups,[263] but one would expect such differences to be of a more far-reaching character than those presented in Matthew, such as, e.g., disagreements about the calendar. While different Jewish groups could be quite harsh in their portrayal of the Jewish "other,"[264] Matthew singles out the Pharisees as those who will not enter the kingdom (5:20; 23:13, 33). We thus need to look for the reason for such condemnation beyond the legal disputes themselves. When we do, we find that Matthew's Gospel portrays the Pharisees that populate the narrative as wicked and immoral on a general level;

---

263. Cf. discussion in Daniel Patte, *Jewish Hermeneutics*.

264. On the nature of polemic between Jewish groups understood in context, see Luke Timothy Johnson, Luke Timothy Johnson, "The New Testament's Anti-Jewish Slander and the Conventions of Ancient Polemic," *JBL* 108 (1989), 419–41.

they are, from this perspective, contrary to the scribes, the crowds, and John's disciples, flat characters that never surprise the reader.

This theme of the wickedness of, especially, the Pharisees and some of the scribes is developed in various ways in the Gospel (e.g., 9:4; 12:34; 22:18;[265] 23:5–7, 28). Haenchen has argued that the charge of hypocrisy is the sum of all the charges raised against Pharisaism.[266] This, however, has been criticized by Barth: "Haenchen really goes too far, when . . . he pronounces that the theologian Matthew has nothing of which to accuse the Pharisees, apart from their persecution of the church, except their religious hypocrisy."[267] While Barth is correct in noting that there are also other accusations against leadership groups in the Gospel, the charge of hypocrisy is nevertheless the most persistent and fundamental among these. As van Tilborg argues, no other characteristic is being worked out so fully. And, as he continues, this "fits in the over-all plan of Mt's stand."[268]

When we compare Matthew's incessant accusations of hypocrisy leveled against the Pharisees and people associated with them, as well as more general comments on their evil intentions, with what is described as disagreements over halakhic interpretation, the discrepancy that ensues makes clear that the Matthean Jesus cannot be said to be against all of the teachings of these other groups. Indeed, Matthew even maintains such an emphasis on the legitimacy of official authority structures related to Jewish law that, while the individuals and groups that are said to work their influence through these structures are portrayed as wicked, the structures themselves must not be destroyed or removed (23:2–3; cf. 8:4). Now, if Matthew's understanding of authority is intertwined with official structures based on continuity with Moses, and these offices are held by people hostile to the Jesus movement, then Matthew has to undermine their

265. Here, together with the Herodians.
266. Haenchen, "Matthäus 23," 58.
267. Barth, "Law," 61–62n4.
268. van Tilborg, Leaders, 8. For the frequency of the charge of hypocrisy in Matthew's Gospel, see also Bauer, Structure, 68. See also discussion in Christopher Tuckett, "Matthew and Hypocrisy," in Jesus, Matthew's Gospel and Early Christianity: Studies in Memory of Professor Graham N. Stanton (edited by Daniel M. Gurtner, Joel Willitts, and Richard A. Burridge; London: T & T Clark, 2011), 152–65.

authority without destroying the formal structure in order to achieve his goal. The charge of hypocrisy is used as a tool to accomplish this goal.[269]

To be sure, hypocrisy is not to be understood as a discrepancy between word and deed. For Matthew, it consists of the contradiction between outward appearance and inner life (cf. 23:27–28; 21:28–32).[270] Rather than attacking various teachings of the Pharisees on a point-by-point basis, although, as noted above, some of this is also evident, Matthew is telling his story in such a way that the inner character of primarily the Pharisees is asserted as wicked, indeed, impure (23:5–7, 23–28 cf. 6:2, 5, 16).[271] This is what we would call ad hominem attacks, since they are independent of any agreement or disagreement about specific halakhic teachings, or the legitimacy of any official office over which the accused hold influence.

This type of criticism may be used within a larger group to criticize other members of that same group; we see a similar type of accusation against different kinds of Pharisees within Rabbinic literature.[272] In Matthew, however, the issue is not about different kinds of Pharisees; the group is generalized as a single character and attacked as such. When directed at leadership, this type of polemic is more than a warning about flawed behavior, it implies replacement of that leadership, as well as, by necessity, the instatement of a new group that will take over leadership functions defined in new ways (cf. 18:1–4; 23:8–12; 21:43, 45; 19:28).

What is not implied, though, is a change of the authority structure itself; the seat of Moses remains valid, and thus, the communal reading

---

269. One may note that, for Matthew, the line of continuity goes from Moses and Elijah to Jesus (Matt 17:3), implying that the Pharisees, despite claiming such continuity in fact lack it; they have parted ways with Moses through their behavior.

270. Powell, "Do and Keep," 423. See also Barth, "law," 61.

271. Several scholars argue that the condemnation of this type of behavior is indirectly aimed at the Pharisees. See, e.g., van Tilborg, *Leaders*, 8ff, and Baur, *Structure*, 68. Since the same type of behavior is associated with Pharisees elsewhere in the Gospel, and the word hypocrite is used primarily about Pharisees, this is probably correct. The aim here would then be to warn the crowds and the disciples, i.e., the audience of the Sermon on the Mount, against behaving like the Pharisees.

272. For a portrayal of seven types of Pharisees, see *b. Sotah* 22b. See also Weinfeld, "The Charge of Hypocrisy," 52–58. Cf. *m Avot* 1:13, where individuals "who makes worldly use of the crown [i.e. the law]" are criticized.

and teaching of Torah must continue also when the new leadership is in place. Indeed, the Matthean Jesus is presented as educating scribes in the ways of the kingdom, to prepare them to take over once the old leadership is gone.[273] Matthew is thus presenting Jesus's struggles to inaugurate the kingdom as taking place within the society in which they all—friend and foe alike—belong; we do not see a breaking away of either Jesus or his disciples from that world, which is construed as a first-century Jewish world. Therefore, it is impossible to agree with scholars such as van Tilborg, whose general and imprecise statement that in Matthew's Gospel, "[t]he separation between Judaism and Christianity is definitive," does not align with the world the narrative actually describes.[274]

We find, then, that while the Matthean Jesus disagrees with some of the teachings of the Pharisees, there are several halakhic areas where they overlap. Thus, Matthew focuses on attacking the character of this leadership group, more so than their teaching. This means that the real claim in Matthew is not so much that the Pharisees create flawed traditions, and so mislead the people with flawed teachings—although they are certainly accused of doing this (15:7-8; 16:11-12)—but the emphasis is put on the claim that the Pharisees break the law, even in such circumstances where Jesus and the Pharisees would have agreed on the basic principles of the Torah. The problem in Matthew with the Pharisees is not that they keep the law, which became a common opinion in later Christian interpretation of the New Testament; it is the other way around: the Pharisees do not keep the law strictly enough.[275] This is why divine wrath is triggered and will lead to the group's condemnation in the final judgment.

However, the Pharisees have an even more important role to fill in the narrative, beyond functioning as a deterrent for the people who

---

273. On the education of disciples to become scribes, cf. Byrskog, *Teacher*, 241.
274. van Tilborg, *Leaders*, 26. The same is true of the perspective of other scholars discussed above, who draw similar conclusions, including Graham Stanton, Ulrich Luz, Daniel Marguerat, and John P. Meier.
275. Cf. Tuckett, "Hypocrisy," 160, who argues with regard to Matthew 23 that, "the norm presumed is that of the Jewish law itself and the charge made against the scribes and Pharisees is that they themselves have failed to obey the basic demands of the law."

seek righteousness and think it may be found beyond the group around Jesus. Their sin is of such nature that Matthew's Jesus associates it with the shedding of innocent blood in the temple itself (23:35). They are therefore found guilty of polluting the temple, causing its predicted destruction and the apocalyptic disasters that will befall the entire people. The Pharisees, thus, function in the story primarily in two ways: a) to highlight the limits of salvation, serving as a warning for the crowds and the disciples (cf. 23:1), and b) to explain the fall of the temple. While the Pharisees, to some degree, share these two roles with other leadership groups that aligned themselves with them, they are kept at the center of attention throughout the story, except for in the passion narrative, where they take a backseat position. In that setting, the chief priests take over the role as the leading individuals behind Jesus's death. Despite the fact that the Romans were the actual executioners even in the story world, Jesus's death may therefore be explained as the result of an inner-Jewish conflict, without real interference of foreign nations and, importantly, their gods. This, in turn, makes it possible, from a Jewish perspective, to maintain that these foreign gods were still inferior to the God of Israel, even though they appeared to be in control through Roman presence and jurisdiction in the land of Israel.

In sum, looking at all the various collectivities in the Gospel, what Matthew's Jesus is offering the crowds and "this generation," indeed Israel as a whole, is not how to avoid suffering, but how to survive it and be favorably judged by the Son of Man when he comes to execute the final judgment. The key is to keep the Torah as Jesus taught it, extend and receive forgiveness always, and take shelter in the presence of God's Messiah, who represents God's Shekhinah after the temple has been abandoned (23:38; 18:20; 28:20).[276] There is, then, no irreversible condemnation of "Israel" or "this generation" or the crowds, although the Jewish people, including the disciples, have, inevitably, to go through apocalyptic suffering. It is likely this focus on suffering for

---

276. On the Shekhinah as related to Jesus presence among his followers, cf. Lövestam, *Jesus and 'this Generation,'* 55.

all that commentators often mistake for condemnation of Israel as an entity. For Matthew, however, just as in a war, while some in Israel caused the disaster, all have to suffer, including the elect. In the final judgment, though, God's justice means condemnation of the unrepentant powerful, while his covenantal mercy results in liberation and salvation of the oppressed, those who were harassed and helpless like sheep without a shepherd (9:36).

4

———

Conclusion to Part I

Our discussion in Part I of the theme of judgment and salvation of the Jewish people in Matthew's Gospel has led us to several results that challenge, at its core, the traditional view of the Gospel as a "Christian" text promoting a worldview in which Israel as an entity has been dissolved as a consequence of divine disapproval, only to be replaced by a new people, "the church." Instead, what we find in Matthew as we focus on questions of ultimate concern—of divine judgment, salvation and condemnation, punishment and reward—is a narrative landscape belonging firmly within a Second-Temple Jewish theo-ritual world, a world functioning as a matrix, as it were, in which specific responses to these fundamental questions have been shaped in ways rather foreign to later Christian theology.

After brief consideration of when Israel's God will judge his people (i.e., in this world or in or at the threshold of the next), the argument was divided into two main parts. The first of these focused on recovering the criteria of judgment active in the text as well as their conceptual context, i.e., their relationship to key notions which have an impact on how the criteria "move" discursively and effect the story in specific cases; without consideration of such notions, the theme of judgment, including the criteria of judgment, can hardly be understood. Second, in chapter 3, we directed our attention to the question of how the criteria of judgment are applied to named groups and larger collectivities in the Gospel, asking whether such groups are judged in accordance with the criteria outlined, and, if not, why.

Chapter 1 made the case that Matthew continues a general development which is visible already in the texts included in the Hebrew Bible and which continues in later rabbinic Judaism of postponing punishment and reward to the world to come, after the final judgment has been executed and the kingdom is being established in full. A comparison between Matt 19:29 and Mark 10:29-30 further emphasized the Matthean position in this regard. Despite this, we found that there is still evidence in Matthew of the notion that divine judgment is implemented already in this world, the focus being on the punishment of larger collectivities such as Jerusalem and its leaders, the latter of whom will be displaced and replaced with the disciples as the kingdom continues to take form after Jesus's death and resurrection; the meek will, indeed, inherit the land and the disciples will rule (5:5: 19:28). Thus, we find three temporal loci where divine judgment emerges as a (narrative) reality: Punishment and reward will take place: a) in this world, and b) in the world to come. The third and most important locus where the people will be scrutinized and examined is the eschatological final judgment, which either opens up the gate of the kingdom (salvation), where various rewards or punishments will be implemented, or results in exclusion and destruction through fire (Gehenna; condemnation [cf. 10:28]).

With such prospects—no one will escape these judgment processes, neither Jesus's enemies, nor his friends (7:21-23; 23:33)—it would be of some interest to all parties involved to know what it is that will decide their fate. On the basis of which criteria are rewards and punishments meted out, and, most importantly, ultimate salvation or condemnation decided? While some recent studies have suggested that salvation in Matthew is to be understood as payment for work done, i.e., Torah obedience, the present investigation problematizes such conclusions, arguing for a more complex and dynamic picture.

First of all, it should be emphasized that all characters in the narrative who are identified, implicitly or explicitly, as Jewish are judged according to the same standards, on the basis of identical criteria.[1] The disciples of Jesus will be judged along with chief priests, elders, Pharisees, and scribes, regardless of whether these scribes are disciples of Jesus or belong among the Pharisees. There are no distinctions made within Israel; no special rules apply to anybody, no exceptions are made. Not surprisingly, given that this is so, the hermeneutical hub around which judgment discourse perpetually[2] turns is Torah, the law of Moses, as it is given its ultimate interpretation by the Messiah throughout the Gospel, both in terms of overall interpretive keys (7:12; 22:36–40) and its application in specific cases (7:21–22; 12:1–8; 15:20; 19:3–9; 23:16–22).

Since the law carries within it salvific efficacy, affecting punishments and rewards primarily and ultimate salvation and condemnation secondarily (see below), the very nature of sin is defined by it, as we argued in chapter 2.1. Sin, then, is not, for Matthew, a power from which the people need to be saved, a state in which they live, but the result of breaking the Mosaic law. Once this has been established, however, further qualifications have to be made. As in other Jewish texts, Matthew operates with the law in a larger theo-ritual setting which involves cultic mechanisms relevant to law observance (e.g., 5:23–24; 8:4). Intertwined with these mechanisms come a number of nuances, for example, with regard to the severity of offences committed in light of the specific situation at the time when the commandment(s) in question were broken; unintentional sins are judged less severely than intentional sins. Since different sacrifices apply for each type of sin, if the cultic system is upheld, as it is in Matthew (until chapters 23–24; see below), this implies confirmation of such distinctions. While this is not explicitly stated in the Gospel, it is

---

1. Non-Jews, however, are dealt with differently, as we shall see in Part II.
2. There is no distinction in Matthew between the pre- and post-resurrection periods in this regard; the law is valid and retains its salvific importance throughout and beyond the story.

likely that such general sensitivity with regard to intention in relation to Torah observance underlies the Matthean Jesus's active focus on saving the people (the "crowds"); he deals with leading figures only as they approach him. The latter, who know the Torah, have misled the former, whose ignorance of Torah Jesus aims to alleviate (Matthew 5–7). In any case, when words of condemnation are uttered, the focus is primarily on intentional grave sins, such as the shedding of innocent blood (23:31–35).[3]

Another interesting implication of Matthew's focus on the law is the notion that the guilt resulting from sins that are not atoned for fills up a measure, as it were, that eventually will overflow and result in catastrophic (apocalyptic) developments for the people as divine wrath is triggered and unleashed. This process of filling up the measure of sin/guilt is extended transgenerationally, so that guilt is understood to be inherited from generation to generation. This phenomenon further highlights the importance of peoplehood for Matthew. While in the Hebrew Bible, we see a "debate" between conflicting perspectives on such teaching on sin and guilt, involving primarily Exodus, Deuteronomy, Jeremiah, and Ezekiel,[4] Matthew's Jesus makes his own contribution through an important qualification of this notion. In this Gospel, the guilt resulting from sin is indeed inherited, but only by those who commit sins of the same nature. Thus, the guilt accumulated by the leaders of Israel in the past, who "murdered the prophets," are added to by the Pharisees and the scribes associated with them, who are accused of murdering Jesus's own prophets, until the measure is filled and the process of apocalyptic divine judgment is set in motion (23:29–36). Just as allegiance to Jesus creates the equivalent to a family bond between him and his followers within the people of Israel (12:46–50), the grave sins of leadership groups in the narrative's "today" forge a lineage between them and the leaders who shed innocent blood in the past. The division created in the land when Jesus carries out his mission of saving his people (1:21) is thus tied into

3. On Matt 25:31–46, which deals with the final judgment on non-Jewish nations only, see discussion below, Part II.
4. Exod 20:5; 34:7; Deut 5:9; Jer 32:18. Cf. Deut 24:16; Jer 31:29–30; Ezek 18:1–32.

conflicts in Israel's ancient past, Matthew using the latter as a pattern to explain the severity and inevitability of current developments.

While the filling up of this measure of sin within the people—which is done by one specific group within the people (the Pharisees) that is explicitly distinguished from the majority of the Jews (the "crowds")—will result in condemnation of this group in the final judgment, the apocalyptic disasters that they have caused will affect the entire people, including Jesus's own disciples, in this world (Matthew 24). It is important, thus, not to confuse, on the one hand, the final judgment on a particular individual, which affects that individual only and is based on that individual's life choices, with, on the other hand, the divine judgment carried out in this world due to the grave sins of the few, a judgment in which apocalyptic consequences affect all regardless of their level of righteousness. While the suffering ensuing as a consequence of the latter punishment may or may not influence the ultimate destiny of innocent individuals (24:12–13, 24), judgment implemented in this world does not, in and of itself, relate to the outcome of the final eschatological judgment.

If the centrality of the law in Matthew has consequences for how sin is defined and judgment is implemented, the same is true for core concepts such as righteousness (chapters 2.2 and 2.3). Righteousness is a quantitative concept, so that the fulfilling of various commandments will result in different levels of righteousness, some levels not being enough to enter the kingdom (5:20). The Matthean mark of kingdom approval lies in "perfection," which translates the holiness of Lev 19:2 (Matt 5:48; 19:21). "Perfection," however, is required only in relation to a person's ability, and is thus not an absolute measurement (25:14–30). It is, furthermore, dependent on repentance and forgiveness, which implies that perfection is not to be equated with absence of sin, but with sincere dedication to the law, including the means of atonement that comes with the law; this has to do with and is explained by Matthew's notion of covenant, which keeps these aspects together in a functioning theo-ritual system (see below).

Indeed, we find in Matthew evidence of the idea that people may benefit in this world from the higher righteousness of others, called "elect" in the Gospel; for their sake, the apocalyptic suffering is shortened (24:22; cf. 13:29–30). While this type of vicarious righteousness, which resembles the pattern of thought surfacing in Gen 18:16–33, is effective with regard to life in the current world, the notion is taken to a different level as the voluntary suffering and death of the righteous par excellence, Jesus, is understood to produce forgiveness of sins using a sacrificial discourse otherwise belonging within a temple setting. The idea that the suffering of righteous individuals may have an atoning effect on others is present also in other Second-Temple Jewish texts, but here we find such beliefs merging with themes related to the Day of Atonement and the making of the Mosaic Covenant at Sinai, which is, as far as we can tell, an innovation emerging with texts authored by members of the Jesus movement. For Matthew, Jesus's sacrifice, and the forgiveness of the sins of "the many" that results from it, was necessitated because of the previous defilement of the Jerusalem temple which had occurred already in Matthew 23 and which will lead, unavoidably, to God leaving the soon to be destroyed temple.

In Matthew's world, then, Jesus's death is God's response to the destruction of the temple and the people's loss of its mechanisms of atonement. Without access to atonement, the Mosaic covenant would break down, since the law would condemn the people. Because the law remains valid throughout history, pre- and post-Jesus's resurrection, the people's future can only be secured through a mechanism of atonement established beyond the temple, and, for Matthew, Jesus's sacrifice does just this. In this Gospel, then, contrary to later Christian beliefs, Jesus is the solution to the destruction of the temple, not its cause; indeed, his ritualized death is presented precisely as a way of saving the Jewish people *as a people*.

As was the case with individuals accessing atonement through temple sacrifices—as seen also in texts contemporary with Matthew and in later rabbinic writings—forgiveness in Matthew is inextricably linked with repentance (chapter 2.4). This theme is heavily emphasized in the Gospel (3:2; 4:17; 5:23–26; 11:20–22; 12:41; 18:15–17), as repentance is required of everyone, including the disciples. Since no individual is without sin and perfection is defined as keeping the Torah according to one's ability, this implies the willingness of the individual to seek forgiveness and atone for sins committed. The message is clear: without repentance, no atonement; without atonement, no kingdom. There is one sin, however, for which no repentance is effective, and no forgiveness will be given, neither in this world nor in the next: sin against the holy Spirit (12:31–32). Other Jewish texts, including rabbinic traditions, subscribe, too, to the idea that there are actions which are unforgiveable. Matthew defines such ultimate offences against the divine in the singular, as the denial of the work of God's spirit when faced with its power channeled through Jesus. For Matthew, then, there is a clear distinction between the person of Jesus, on the one hand, and God's spirit, on the other, so that offences leveled against Jesus are forgivable, but rejection of the Spirit is not (12:32).

The distinction with regard to divine judgment between Jesus and the Spirit creates an emphasis on continuity with Israel's past, a continuity which is further emphasized through Matthew's numerous references to the scriptures whose authority is taken for granted by all who populate his world, and which can therefore serve as support for the developments and teachings presented. This led us to further questions, though, about the nature of the Jesus event in this Gospel, as it affects judgment processes. While it is clear that Jesus preaches judgment based on (his teaching of) the Mosaic law, and that he is, consequently, toning down the role of his own person in this regard, we may ask what role people's relation to him/the divine plays as expressed in the phenomenon of *pistis* (loyalty/trust/faithfulness). Further, it was necessary to look at the issue of how Jesus's person relates to the kingdom. In other words: does Jesus function as a criterion of judgment in Matthew? Is *pistis* a factor as God judges the nation? These issues, which have been emphasized as crucial within later Christian theology when salvation has been discussed, were dealt with in chapters 2.5 and 2.6.

For Matthew, *pistis* is perhaps best described as a "space" within which, or a medium through which the power of the Spirit can work, and thus, the sphere within which the kingdom can be established on earth (e.g., 12:28). This means that loyalty/trust/faithfulness cannot be regarded as a criterion of judgment in any strict sense of that term. For example, while *pistis* is necessary for healing and exorcism, healing cannot be understood as a "reward" of sorts for the trust displayed, which is made clear by the simple fact that on several occasions, people are healed on the basis of the *pistis* of other individuals (8:5-13; 9:2; 15:21-28). Indeed, when healing/exorcism fails, it is blamed on the persons performing the healing, rather than of the status of the person whose healing is sought (17:14-17, 20). The power of the Spirit and the effects of the kingdom may thus affect people (positively), regardless of their own individual status in this regard; a form of "vicarious *pistis*," as it were.

As *pistis* is related to the law (23:23) and the work of the Spirit, the person of Jesus, despite being in focus and presented as the agent through whom all of this happens, is decentered and attention is directed toward the divine. In Matthew, the kingdom (and the law), not Jesus, is the primary message, and this is true for both John and Jesus as well as for the disciples (3:2; 4:17; 10:7; 28:19-20). *Pistis*, consequently, relates more to the ultimate power behind the kingdom—described by Matthew as greater than even the temple (12:6)—than to the agent through whom this is all accomplished. This is true despite the fact that Jesus is the person who triggers *pistis* defined in this way. Despite being less important than the Spirit (12:32) in the greater scheme of things, the person of Jesus is presented, however, as a criterion of judgment on a secondary level, based on the identification made between the disciples and himself, and between himself and God (10:40-42; cf. 25:31-46), according to the logic that the messenger is to be identified with the person who sends him/her. Consequently, (disproportionately great) rewards will be given to people who are not disciples on the basis of their treatment of the disciples, since the disciples represent, ultimately, the God of Israel. For the disciples themselves, though, it is key not to deny Jesus when confronted by outsiders (10:32–33), like Peter eventually did (26:34–35, 69–74); if not repented for, such denial will have dire consequences in the final judgment.

On the basis of the above conclusions, which indicate that the key criterion of the Jewish law as a criterion of judgment is embedded within several "layers" of concepts that ultimately affect and may modify the outcome of the judgment process, we proceeded to ask how, more exactly, the law is to be fulfilled, i.e., in which ways "works of law" function as criteria (chapter 2.7). Here, we found that Matthew operates with three levels, corresponding to ways in which humans interact with the world around them, in which the law must be fulfilled. These three levels are: a) external deeds (i.e., a person's direct physical interaction with the world, e.g., 5:40–41; 10:40–42), b) verbal deeds (i.e., a person's speech, e.g., 5:22; 12:36–37), and c) internal deeds (i.e., deeds that relate to the world around a person but which are performed only in a person's mind, e.g., 5:28).

If we look at how Divine judgment relates to these three levels of human interaction with the world and God, levels on which the law is either kept or broken, we find that judgment procedures are implemented both in this world and the next, as well as in the final judgment. For example, the shedding of innocent blood will be punished in this world, the fall of the temple being the primary example of such judgment. We also find destruction of other historical cities based on other forms of grave sins (Sodom; 11:23). In the same way, verbal deeds are judged with effects in this world (5:22; 12:32). Internal deeds which break the law are, however, only taken care of in the final judgment. As for the world to come, the majority of the deeds on which judgment is based are external: "physical" deeds carried out in this world. For the final judgment, the most important category for Matthew, all three types of deeds are objects of judgment: external (e.g., 3:7–8, 10; 5:20; 7:19–23; 10:14–15; 11:21–22; 19:16–17; 23:31–33; 24:45–51; 25:14–30), verbal (e.g., 12:36–37), and internal (e.g., 5:27–28; cf. 18:9).

If we bring all of this together and consider the various factors involved in divine judgment as it relates to the Jewish people—the law as well as the related concepts within which it is embedded—it is difficult to avoid the conclusion that what we see operating in Matthew's Gospel is a theo-ritual pattern closely related to other forms of Second-Temple Judaism, where the covenant between the God of Israel and his people is maintained and controls how the narrative and its theology evolves (chapter 2.8). Indeed, Matthew's account of the Jesus event can be read as the story of how the God of Israel saves his people from destruction through Jesus's restoration—not replacement—of the covenantal pattern that had governed their relationship since Sinai, complete with teaching of law and atoning sacrifice. Herein lies the secret to the mystery of the otherwise so elusive concept of grace—of getting something for nothing—in Matthew: Despite the doings of the leaders of the people, which led to God having to abandon the defiled temple—meaning doom for the entire people since the means of atonement must function in tandem with the law within the covenant, lest the law will condemn the people—God decides to send a Messiah filled with his Spirit, not only to teach the people Torah, but also, to restore the broken covenant (26:28) through supplying an alternative means of atonement, replacing the temple until the kingdom is establish in full. This act of divine mercy, based on God's love for the people, defines grace in the first Gospel.[5] The outcome in terms of divine judgment of the restoration of the Mosaic covenant and its ritual system, upon which the notion of mercy is dependent in this Gospel, is that while unrepentant breakers of the law will be condemned as the kingdom is established, the repentant keepers of Torah may access divine grace and will, when that time comes, "shine like the sun in the kingdom of their Father" (13:43).[6]

5. The fact that God's sending of his Messiah takes place before the people have been taught the correct way to keep the law indicates clearly that no merits of the people itself have provoked divine action; just as with the dynamics involved in divine election in the Hebrew Bible (cf., e.g., Deut 7:7–8; 9:5–6), the initiative is God's and it is based on factors independent of Torah observance. For Matthew, then, the giving and teaching of the Mosaic law is the very definition of divine grace, as it is combined with Jesus's atoning sacrifice after the defilement of the temple.

6. It is interesting to note that Nicholas of Lyra interpreted the pattern of religion in Rom 9–11 along similar lines arguing that, "just as it is clear that the elect are called to glory by mercy, so also the condemned are reserved for punishment by justice." (Commentary on Rom 9:21; translation by

Contrary to some recent and not so recent claims,[7] then, salvation cannot ultimately be "earned" through any "works of law" in Matthew, but is the (undeserved) gift of God based on the sacrificial death of the Messiah, which allows the law its salvific efficacy. Without the theo-ritual realities kept together by and functioning within the covenant, no salvation is possible. It is a completely different matter that the keeping of the commandments will result in rewards.

In chapter 3 we moved on to consider in which ways these criteria of judgment were applied to the various groups mentioned in the narrative. Having distinguished between the larger entities in the Gospel, such as "Israel," "this generation," and "the crowds," on the one hand, and groups identified as being in various leadership positions, on the other, the leadership groups were targeted first and divided into those with and without direct political influence, respectively. This investigation showed that Matthew, contrary to common opinion, does not conflate the various leadership groups into one, which he then attacks. Rather, the point in this Gospel is precisely that all these *different* leaders oppose Jesus, and forms what could perhaps best be called an unholy alliance against the Messiah; maintaining differentiation is part of the point in Matthew. This, however, does not mean that all groups are targeted in the same way.

In Matthew, the Pharisees and the scribes associated with them receive the harshest possible treatment; they are, indeed, accused of having caused all the shedding of innocent blood in the history of Israel (23:29–35), and so provoked the defilement and coming destruction of the temple (23:37–24:2), which in turn is the reason why Jesus has to

---

Ian Christopher Levy, Philip D. W. Krey, and Thomas Ryan, *The Letter to the Romans* [Grand Rapids: Eerdmans, 2013], 227). The pattern of thought is, in its broad outline, reminiscent of what E. P. Sanders has termed Covenantal Nomism.

7. Scholars arguing that Matthew presents his audience with a theological pattern where salvation is the result of 'works' include Hans Windisch, *The Meaning of the Sermon on the Mount: A Contribution to the Historical Understanding of the Gospels and to the Problem of Their True Exegesis* (trans. S. McLean Gilmour; Philadelphia: Westminster Press, 1951 [1929]); B. W. Bacon, *Studies in Matthew* (London: Constable, 1930); Bornkamm, "End-Expectation and Church in Matthew"; Siegfried Schultz, *Die Mitte der Schrift: Der Frühkatholizismus im Neuen Testament als Herausforderung und den Protestantismus* (Stuttgart: Kreuz Verlag 1976); Willi Marxen, *New Testament Foundations for Christian Ethics* (Minneapolis: Fortress, 1993); all discussed by Luomanen, *Entering the Kingdom*, 7–13. Cf. most recently Eubank, *Wages of Cross-bearing*.

die. Jesus's death, on the other hand, is blamed on groups with direct political influence, the chief priests and the elders of Jerusalem. Only the Pharisees and all those who associate themselves with them are, however, explicitly stated to be destined for condemnation (5:20; 23:15, 33). There are only vague indications that through (eschatologically provoked) repentance, this group, as part of the people of Jerusalem, will be allowed into the kingdom (23:39).[8]

It is of some interest to note in this regard that Matthew's critique of leadership is so massive that it strikes hard also at his own disciples. In fact, while the Pharisees are said to seek Jesus's destruction, neither they nor any other non-political leadership groups are successful in their scheming; Jesus wins all the arguments and no one can get him into such trouble that he can be handed over to the religio-political leaders, i.e., the chief priests. It takes one of Jesus's own disciples to have Jesus handed over to the authorities, who will eventually see to it that he is condemned to death.[9]

Jesus's mission in Matthew is, however, not primarily concerned with these leadership groups, but rather, with the majority of the Jews, i.e., the crowds; leaders are dealt with only because they interfere in various ways with Jesus's activities among the crowds, as they themselves refuse to repent. It is crucial for the understanding of Matthew to note that no judgment of final condemnation is uttered against the crowds. Indeed, the boundaries between the crowds and the disciples are not clear, and much of the key teaching in Matthew is given to both the disciples and the crowds together, including the Sermon on the Mount (Matthew 5–7) and the critique of the Pharisees (Matthew 23). One could say that Matthew portrays the people around Jesus as belonging within two concentric circles; the one closest to Jesus is designated "disciples," and the outer circle is represented by

---

8. Such an interpretation is dependent, however, on minimizing the influence of the statement on sin against the Holy Spirit, for which there is no forgiveness in this world or the next regardless of repentance (Matt 12:32), as directed against the Pharisees (Matt 12:24). Perhaps 12:32 is best read as a warning directed at the Pharisees, and 23:39 as the door to a future beyond condemnation.

9. One may also note that while the Pharisees are associated with Gehenna (Matt 23:15, 33), only Peter, the foremost among the disciples (Matt 16:18), is said to channel the voice of Satan (Matt 16:23).

the "crowds." Such a rhetorical strategy strongly suggests that Matthew's Gospel is not presenting the Jesus event as a story whose purpose it is to describe the dissolving, through God's judgment, of the religio-ethnic category of the Jewish people. Such an understanding of Matthew is confirmed when the terms "Israel" and "this generation" are analyzed (chapter 3.2.2). In this Gospel, there is no condemnation of the people of Israel; the category is kept intact throughout the narrative and plays an important role for how the discourse on divine judgment is developed. Matthew is a Gospel which primary focus is the critique of leadership in defense of the people, the latter being presented as victims of abuse (9:36).

It should be noted, though, that condemnation of the leaders does not make invalid the structures of authority in Jewish society. Both the law and the authority that its custodians enjoy are protected (23:2–3); indeed, the perfect disciple is described as a scribe, i.e., a person with an official position in Jewish society, trained for the kingdom (13:52; cf. 23:34). This, too, emphasizes further that the narrative world of the Gospel does not present, envision, or aim for a break with either Judaism or Jewish society. Divine judgment is, rather, the process in which God will replace the current leaders, whose suitability as leaders the Gospel undermines, with new leaders, the disciples, who will judge and rule the twelve tribes (19:28; 21:33–46).[10]

If, then, this is how Matthew envisions God's dealings with the Jewish people, among whom Jesus finds both friend and foe, what has this text to say about those who do not belong to the covenant community? If grace is found in Matthew only to the degree that the Mosaic covenant is accepted as restored, how is divine judgment on those outside the covenant construed? Is there any salvation to be had outside the Jewish people, or must those who seek redemption join the people of God as proselytes? To these questions we now turn.

---

10. The language of anti-Judaism, which has been used by several scholars analyzing Matthew, is thus entirely inappropriate and rather belongs to the reception history of the Gospel in the emerging (non-Jewish) Christian church. Cf. Marguerat, *jugement*, 575–80. As Marguerat states: "Il ne paraît pas raisonnable d'imputer à l'évangéliste la responsabilité de ce retournement de l'histoire. Par contre, on est conduit à s'interroger sur la responsabilité de ses lecteurs" (580).

PART II

Judging and Saving
the Nations

5

Preparing the Nations for Judgment

In a recent analysis of how the Gospel of Matthew has been studied, following up on Graham Stanton's widely used and quoted survey of Matthean scholarship between 1945 and 1980, later updated to include studies until 1994,[1] David Sim notes,

> The debate identified by Stanton concerning whether this Christian community was still within Judaism or had separated from it, both physically and ideologically, has intensified considerably and is now without question the dominant theme in Matthean studies.[2]

Analysis of Matthew's view of groups and individuals identified as non-Jewish in the text, focusing on the theme of divine judgment, speaks both directly and indirectly to this topic. While we are concerned in this study with ideological elements that are part of—indeed,

---

1. Graham N. Stanton, "The Origin and Purpose of Matthew's Gospel: Matthean Scholarship from 1945 to 1980," in *Aufstieg und Niedergang der römischen Welt.* II, 25.3 (edited by H. Temporini and W. Haase; Berlin: de Gruyter, 1985), 1890–1951; idem "Introduction: Matthew's Gospel in Recent Scholarship (1994)," in *The Interpretation of Matthew* (edited by Graham N. Stanton; T&T Clark, 1995), 1–26.
2. David C. Sim, "Matthew: The Current State of Research," in, *Mark and Matthew. Comparative Readings I: Understanding the Earliest Gospels in their First Century Settings* (edited by Eve-Marie Becker and Anders Runesson; Tübingen: Mohr Siebeck, 2011), 36.

significantly contribute to construing—a specific narrative world, as we noted in the Introduction, discourses on divine judgment in texts that are given normative status in various communities will tell us a lot about what such communities considered socio-religiously and politically normative and appropriate for their members. We know that Matthew's Gospel was frequently referred to by the church fathers, and that this text, ordered first in the New Testament canon, became the most widely used Gospel as the church took shape in the non-Jewish world.

One of the key issues during this formative time was the relationship between what had become identified as "the church," on the one hand, and, on the other hand, what was classified as "Judaism." While from early on, Matthew's Gospel was seen as having been written within a Jewish setting, a Gospel for the Jews, the Gospel was read from a non-Jewish perspective as countering everything Jewish, proclaiming the truth of "the church." In other words, Matthew was understood to speak in ways Jewish in order to end Judaism from a perspective similar to what we find in medieval disputations between Jews and Christians, in which a Christian, often a convert from Judaism, debates with a representative from the Jewish community using Jewish discourses against Judaism and the Jews.

While removed from the polemical religious settings of Late Antiquity and later periods, the basic components of such readings of Matthew, understanding the Gospel to have been written by a Jew who proclaims irreversible divine condemnation of Israel and declares the "church" to be the new people of God, are still quite common within academia, although they are declining.[3] Such discursive trajectories have become so interwoven with Christian culture—including its secularized variants—that some scholars have even claimed that Matthew was written by a non-Jew for a non-Jewish audience.[4] As we

---

3. For a refreshingly thorough discussion of Israel and non-Jews in Matthew, see Konradt, *Israel, Church, and the Gentiles.*

4. E.g., K. W. Clarke, "The Gentile Bias in Matthew," *JBL* 66 (1947): 165–72. The influence of this article is seen in various forms in many later studies, including widely read encyclopedia articles such as John P. Meier's entry on "Matthew, Gospel of" in *The Anchor Bible Dictionary*, vol. 4 (edited by David Noel Freedman et al.; New York: Doubleday, 1992), 622–41 (cf. Meier, *Vision of Matthew*, 17ff);

have argued in Part I above, however, a first-century reconstruction of the text's thought pattern militates against such understandings of Matthew. There can be no doubt that the discourses of divine judgment that are found in this Gospel are almost exclusively concerned with Jewish groups and individuals and represent expressions of a Jewish thought world, which maintains the status of the Jewish people as God's people.

The question that remains to be addressed is how this text construes the fate of people who are identified as non-Jewish in the story world. Are they judged by the same criteria as the Jewish people? Or do we find here a different approach, a different pattern, with regard to divine rewards, punishments, salvation, and condemnation? If the covenant between the God of Israel and the Jewish people is understood as intact and renewed, and so constituting a "place" for God to exercise mercy and save his people, what does this mean for non-Jews, who are not, and have never been, part of that covenant? Can they be saved, and, if so, will such salvation be based on their "works" only, since the covenantal frame embedding such works within God's mercy is lacking? Furthermore, we have seen that Matthew's Jewish world is populated with various Jewish groups,

---

see also, the similar understanding of the Gospel in Michael Joseph Brown, "Matthew, Gospel of," in *The New Interpreters Dictionary of the Bible* vol. 3 (edited by Katherine Doob Sakenfeld et al.; Nashville: Abingdon, 2008), 839–52. Clarke argues not only that Matthew presents non-Jews in a positive way, but also, that Matthew himself was a gentile. Other scholars, both Jewish and Christian, who read Matthew in a similar way as reflecting a thought pattern which they deem to be non-Jewish, include Samuel Sandmel, *A Jewish Understanding of the New Testament* (Cincinnati: Hebrew Union College Press, 1956; reprinted [with new preface], Woodstock: SkyLight Paths Publications, 2004); Poul Nepper-Christensen, *Das Matthäusevangelium: Ein judenchristliches Evangelium?* (ATDan 1; Aarhus: Universitetsforlaget, 1958); Georg Strecker, *Der Weg der Gerechtigkeit: Untersuchung zur Theologie des Matthäus* (1962; FRLANT 82; 3rd ed.; Göttingen: Vandenhoeck & Ruprecht, 1971); Sjef van Tilborg, *The Jewish Leaders in Matthew* (Leiden: Brill, 1972); David Flusser, "Two Anti-Jewish Montages in Matthew," *Imm* 5 (1975): 37–45; Lloyd Gaston, "The Messiah of Israel as Teacher of the Gentiles," *Interpretation* 29:1 (1975): 24–40; Michael J. Cook, "Interpreting 'Pro-Jewish' Passages in Matthew," *HUCA* 54 (1983): 135–46; Graham Stanton, "5 Ezra and Matthean Christianity in the Second Century," *JTS* 28 (1977): 67–83. Regardless of the assumed identity of the author of Matthew as Jewish or non-Jewish, it is common that scholars see in the Gospel a pattern similar to what we, according to most researchers, find in Acts, namely that the message of the kingdom is first proclaimed to the Jews, and then, when the Jews have rejected it, it is taken to the non-Jews. Often, Matt 28:19–20 is juxtaposed with Matt 10:5–6, the latter passage seen as replaced by the former, to make this point. See, e.g., F. W. Beare, "The Mission of the Disciples and the Mission Charge: Matthew 10 and Parallels," 9; Morna D. Hooker, "Uncomfortable Words: The Prohibition of Foreign Missions (Mt. 105–6)," *Expository Times* 82 (1971): 365.

which are said to react differently to Jesus's proclamation. Do we find a similar interest in the story to distinguish between different groups of non-Jews, in terms of divine judgment? Are all non-Jews treated in a single way, either positively or negatively,[5] or do we find attempts to distinguish between them, so that some are presented as saved and others lost? How are we to understand, comparatively, Matt 10:5–6 and 28:18–20 when we approach these passages from the perspective of divine judgment? Is Matthew's Jesus proclaiming divine judgment as a strategy to promote a non-Jewish mission, creating an *ekklēsia* made up of Jews, and primarily, non-Jews, all of whom practice a form of "Christianity?"

The first thing that needs to be noted, in light of these questions, is that non-Jews, while present in the story, are peripheral. This is so despite the fact that individuals and groups identified as non-Jewish fill important functions in the narrative, as Matthew is telling his story about the Messiah. But filling an important function in the narrative is not the same as being the focus and aim of the story being told. This should be clear from the many hints given in the text, some more explicit than others, that Jesus's aim is, as we have seen above, to save "*his* people" (1:21), to proclaim in word and deed the good news about the kingdom to the "lost sheep of the house of Israel" (cf. 9:36; 10:5–6; 15:24).[6] While non-Jews are, at times, playing significant roles in the narrative, it is, in my opinion, simply impossible to understand them as main characters, or turn them into Jesus's and/or his disciples' target audience without violating the integrity of the story.

5. With regard to Matthew's negative treatment of non-Jews, see David C. Sim "The Gospel of Matthew and the Gentiles," 20–21 for a summary of these views. See also idem, *Eschatology*, 201: "A number of Matthean Pericopae unambiguously betray an anti-gentile perspective. In many scholarly discussions these texts either are explained away as Matthew's conservative retention of traditional material or are conveniently forgotten altogether. Neither approach is fair to the evangelist." Cf. Saldarini, *Community*, 248n2. Referring to S. Brown, Saldarini notes that "Gentiles appear as both good and bad in the narrative."

6. There is, in my view, no support in Matthew for the view expressed by Meier, *Vision*, 38–39, and Charette, *Recompense*, that "Israel is now regarded as merely one among the other nations which need to be evangelized" (Charette, 156). A need for kingdom proclamation (or "evangelization") does not automatically indicate that ethno-religious boundaries must have been abolished. This is a common misunderstanding in scholarship, also with regard to Paul's letters, which builds on later Christian understandings of mission and ethnicity. On the theme of mission, see Runesson, "Was there a Christian Mission Before the Fourth Century?" 205–47.

The passages that deal with non-Jews in Matthew are, in comparison with the focus on the Jewish people and various groups within it, few, especially if we are looking at the theme of divine judgment. In the present chapter, we shall categorize more broadly Matthew's description and use of non-Jews in the story (5.1 and 5.2). The third section, 5.3, will deal briefly with the question of mission to non-Jews in light of the theme of judgment. Chapter 6 will then outline when the nations will be judged, before chapter 7 brings us to the core issue of the criteria of judgment as they apply to people not Jewish in Matthew's story world.

5.1 Beyond the Chosen People: The General View on Non-Jews in Matthew

We have seen above that Matthew refuses to generalize the Jewish people as either good or bad, but rather points to specific groups within the people that are then dealt with in specific ways, either positively or negatively. The closest we get to generalization is Jesus's interaction with the crowds, which represents the majority of the people at any given occasion. These crowds are, as opposed to groups and individuals identified as being leaders in one way or another, never condemned. Indeed, as we have seen, the crowds overlap with the category of disciples, creating a narrative situation in which they are part of the larger movement around Jesus. Revealingly, when Jesus is reported as outlining proper behavior, including how to organize human relationships, he is addressing his disciples *and* the crowds, turning them into one group, which he then distinguishes from the Pharisees and the scribes associated with them:

> Then Jesus said to the crowds and to his disciples . . . you are not [as opposed to alleged Pharisaic practice] to be called rabbi, for you have one teacher, and you are all students. And call no one your father on earth, for you have one Father—the one in heaven. Nor are you to be called instructors, for you have one instructor, the Messiah. The greatest among you will be your servant. All who exalt themselves will be humbled, and all who humble themselves will be exalted. (Matt 23:1, 8–12)[7]

Such concerns about inner Jewish struggles and debates reveal the Gospel's focus as being on the Jewish people. Non-Jews form a separate category, and they are treated differently in the narrative compared to people identified as Jewish; they fill different narrative roles. The question is now, whether all non-Jews are treated the same in terms of divine judgment or whether we find variation within this out-group. In order to determine this, we need to distinguish between non-Jews when they are generalized, on the one hand, and non-Jews when specific individuals are mentioned, on the other. Analysis of passages about the former will inform us of how Matthew's Gospel perceives of non-Jewish culture and behavior as such, and attention to the latter will help us identify specific roles that non-Jews may fulfill—either apart from or as part of their general culture—when they relate to the Messiah and his people. We shall begin with Matthew's perception of non-Jewish culture and behavior as a generalized phenomenon.

Briefly stated, when non-Jewish culture and customs are addressed generally in the narrative, everything non-Jews do must be shunned by Matthew's audience.[8] When Matthew's Jesus is expounding Jewish law, non-Jews function as examples of what not to do (5:47); when Jesus followers are taught to pray, it is explicitly said that they must not imitate non-Jewish practices (6:7), and when Jesus instructs his audience to trust God and not worry about the future, non-Jews are singled out as the opposite of the proper attitude (6:32). As for non-Jewish society, imitation among Jesus's followers of non-Jewish hierarchies and power positions is explicitly forbidden (Matt 20:25–26). Indeed, when Matthew's Jesus establishes the rules for his *ekklēsia*,

---

7. The same strategy is present in the Sermon on the Mount, which is also delivered the crowds and the disciples. They are addressed as a single "you," and set apart from the Jewish "other," the latter identified as the Pharisees and the scribes associated with them (Matt 5:20). Jesus is the teacher of the crowds as much as he is the instructor of the disciples; both of these groups listen to him, although the disciples, who were selected from the same social stratum as that represented by the crowds, are also trained separately as future leaders who are to continue Jesus's work among the crowds. These leadership roles that Jesus claims for himself and for his disciples are rejected by all other current leadership groups, from their own various perspectives. For Matthew, this struggle for leadership is at the heart of the conflict between Jesus and the groups identified as current leaders. This implies that the crowds are never part of the conflict itself; they represent the people over whom these leaders claim authority, the people the Matthean Jesus aims to save as the eschaton is approaching.

8. Cf. the discussion in Sim, *Christian Judaism*, 247–55; Carter, "Systemic Transformation," 280–81.

expulsion from this association[9] results in a change of status of the expelled person, so that he or she is now to be regarded as a non-Jew (Matt 18:17). The "other" is, thus, constructed based on an ethnic criterion. But non-Jews are not the only ones portrayed as the stereotypical outsider. Those who collaborate with them—the tax collectors (18:17; 5:46)—share this disgrace, if, that is, they do not repent. By implication, then, the good insider behaves like a good Jew, that is, someone living within a Jewish context according to the teachings of Jesus, the center within the center.

Against such a background, Jesus's prohibition against expanding the kingdom into the non-Jewish world in Matt 10:5-6, while often regarded as problematic,[10] makes perfect sense. It is no wonder either, that the gentiles of Gadara ask Jesus to leave their territory immediately after he has rid the area of demons and unclean animals, forbidden to Jews, thus claiming for the God of Israel this territory, which, for Matthew, was part of "ideal Israel" (Matt 8:28-34).[11] Indeed, the word *ethnos* is mentioned 15 times by Matthew;[12] except for Matt 21:43, none of these references are positive, but either generalize non-Jewish behavior negatively, claim that they are in need of the Jewish Messiah, or speak of them as guilty of hate, torture, and killing of

---

9. For the historical reconstruction of the Matthean *ekklēsia* as a Jewish association synagogue, see Runesson, "Rethinking Early Jewish–Christian Relations."

10. Hooker, "The Prohibition of Foreign Missions (Mt. 105-6)," 361-65. The solution proposed by Hooker is that this view on mission was limited in time to the period before the resurrection. While this is likely, one still has to explain the Matthean perspective that made such a prohibition both logical and desirable during this period; the resurrection does not abolish the focus on the Jewish people, it just widens the territorial claim.

11. Cf. Luz, *Matthew*, 2.24. While Luz states that "[t]he Jewish-Christian Matthew knows that a large herd of pigs does not belong in the holy land," and he has previously concluded that this area was regarded by Matthew to be part of "biblical Israel," i.e., the holy land (see vol. 1.167), he does not pursue further the ethno-political and national implications of these conclusions. The same avoidance of what for us today would be identified as political aspects of the narrative reoccurs when Luz analyzes the story of the Canaanite woman in Matt 15:21-28. Here, while not contradicting scholars who point out that this area belonged to the "Biblical Holy Land," Luz rejects the idea that Matthew would have intended such an allusion since "the 'gentile' expression 'the region of Tyre and Sidon,' shows that Matthew was not interested in the idea" (2.338). From a postwar, first-century Jewish and non-Jewish perspective, however, it would seem difficult to avoid these dimensions of the story, and therefore also the political claim inherent to it. For maps showing political boundaries, including Ezekiel's vision of the restored tribes (on the tribes, cf. Matt 10:1-4; 19:28), see Anson F. Rainey and R. Steven Notley, *The Sacred Bridge: Carta's Atlas of the Biblical World* (Jerusalem: Carta, 2006), 269.

12. Matthew 4:15; 6:32; 10:5, 18; 12:18, 21; 20:19, 25; 21:43; 24:7, 9, 14; 25:32; 28:19.

the followers of the Messiah (24:9).[13] Non-Jews are also the ones who will mock and kill the Messiah himself (20:19). Such is the culture and behavior of the non-Jews that they will be judged by the Jewish Messiah (12:18), the person embodying the only hope they have (12:21; 28:19–20).[14]

The non-Jewish world seems to have gotten the final word as Roman soldiers torture and mock Jesus as a fake Jewish king, using words such as "Hail, King of the Jews!" (27:27–31) Later, however, the centurion and the soldiers present at the site of the execution are struck by "great fear" as they realize whom they have killed (27:54).[15] Finally, the nations need to be instructed in Jewish law, as Jesus, having received all power in heaven and on earth, sends his disciples to make them all his followers (Matt 28:19–20).[16]

Now, while all of this may be true about the non-Jews when they are treated by Matthew as a generalized group, it may be objected

13. While it is not entirely clear which group it is that will execute the torture and killing (cf. Warren Carter, *Matthew and the Margins: A Socio-Political and Religious Reading* [London: T&T Clark, 2000], 471), the similarity in wording when the same scenario is described as applied to Jesus—in which case it is explicitly stated that non-Jews are the ones guilty of this violence (20:19)—makes it likely that non-Jews are meant here too. Thus, Jesus's followers will be handed over by fellow Jews to suffer at the hands of non-Jews in the same way as Jesus was.

14. For the translation of *krisis* as referring to judgment rather than justice in Matt 12:18, see, e.g., Sim, *Christian Judaism*, 220–22. William R.G. Loader, *Jesus' Attitude towards the Law: A Study of the Gospels* (Grand Rapids: Eerdmans, 2002), 206, notes that *krisis* "can encompass both judgment and justice as the criterion for judgment. Matthew is thus reinforcing Jesus' role as the judge to come who makes known God's justice in the present." Cf. Luz, *Matthew*, 2.193–94, who argues for the translation "judgment," but suggests that this judgment may turn out positively for non-Jews. As Sim notes, however, it is very unlikely that non-Jews as a group could be understood in this way. Matt 12:21, which states that the nations' only hope is the Jewish Messiah, is better read as a statement to the effect that if any non-Jews are going to be part of the kingdom, they must accept the Jewish Messiah and join the Jewish people. On this perspective, see further discussion below, chapter 7. For Matthean rhetoric regarding specific non-Jewish cities as they relate to specific Jewish cities in terms of repentance, see discussion above, pp. 60–61. While these cities will fare better than the Jewish cities mentioned (for reasons discussed above), they will still be judged by the God of Israel.

15. Cf. David C. Sim, "The 'Confession' of the Soldiers in Matthew 27:54," *HeyJ* 24 (1993): 401–24.

16. I find it very difficult to escape the conclusion that what Jesus has taught throughout the Gospel to his disciples and to other Jews, especially in Matt 5–7, is the Jewish law (cf. 5:17–19), and that, consequently, when he commands his disciples to teach all nations what he has taught them, it follows that the content of that teaching is the Jewish law, regardless of how we choose to interpret the content of that law. The point is that the Jewish law is here presented as binding for all nations, not only for the Jewish people. By implication, then, non-Jewish law and culture are rejected as incompatible with the universal rule of the God of Israel. With the idea of mission follows that what is targeted for mission is regarded as somehow inadequate or illegitimate in its present shape. In this case, that inadequacy refers to non-Jewish ways of life, and the solution is Jewish law as interpreted by the Messiah of Israel.

that similar judgments seem to apply to the Jewish people. Does this not mean that, at the end of the day, Matthew makes no distinction between Jews and non-Jews in the Gospel?[17] After all, Matthew insists that the Jews too needed instruction in the law as Jesus interpreted it. In which sense, then, would non-Jewish culture be more condemned than Jewish ways of life? The answer is simple: In the narrative, the Jewish Messiah is represented as the center *within* the center of the Jewish people itself, and is thus described as giving expression to the true interpretation of things Jewish. Matthew's Jesus is not promulgating law as disconnected from the people; it is the Jewish law that is taught and whoever follows that law follows the ways of Judaism in their Matthean-Messianic form. Thus, from Matthew's point of view, those Jews who trusted in and were loyal to Jesus as the Messiah and accepted this form of interpretation of the law lived Judaism to its fullest, the way it was meant to be. If non-Jews were taught the same things as the disciples were, as Matt 28:19–20 says they should be, this would be true of them too, since after the resurrection no distinction is upheld between gentile and Jewish followers of Jesus.[18]

In sum, then, in my view there cannot be any doubt that Matthew uses non-Jewish ethnic identity and culture as a tool when constructing the "other" in relation to the insiders, and warns of behavior not approved by the God of Israel. There is no "gentile bias" in Matthew, other than a negative bias.[19] If this is correct, however,

17. Cf., e.g., Meier, *Vision*, 38–39, 136ff. If Israel loses its status as the people of God, and becomes just one nation among other nations, a new distinction is usually thought to take its place, namely that between "Christians" as the new people of God, and everybody else, including Israel. It should be noted, though, that we do not find in Matthew the expression "new people of God" or even "a new covenant." See also Meier, *Matthew*, 171, where the same opinion is expressed in relation to Matt 15:21–28; the law is understood as abolished, and this means that there is no longer any distinction between Jews and non-Jews. Yet, Meier argues that the mission to the nations, which implies that the law has been abolished and no distinctions remain, is not to begin before Jesus's resurrection, since Jesus earthly ministry is limited to the people of Israel. Such a distinction between Israel and the nations can hardly be made, though, without accepting the validity of the law, since the distinction itself is present in the law and dependent upon it. This view seems to be in tension with the idea, also expressed by Meier, that the law on clean and unclean is abolished already during Jesus ministry, not after the resurrection.
18. There is, however, such a distinction between Jews and gentiles who respond positively to Jesus before the resurrection. See further discussion in chapters 5.2 and 7.
19. Contra Clark, "Gentile Bias"; Lloyd Gaston, "The Messiah of Israel as Teacher of the Gentiles," *Interpretation* 29:1 (1975): 24–40; see esp. 32–34.

what will happen to non-Jews in terms of judgment, salvation, and the kingdom of heaven? Is salvation restricted to the Jewish people (and those non-Jews who join them)? As it turns out, while Matthew, like many other contemporary Jewish texts,[20] rejects non-Jewish identity and culture and maintains the notion of the Jewish people as the people of God, *salvation* is not confined to the Jewish people.[21] In order to make this point, we need first to take a closer look at non-Jews when they appear as individuals in the narrative.

5.2 Categorizing Non-Jews: The Good, the Bad, and the Proselyte

So far, we have concluded that non-Jewish culture and behavior are perceived of as entirely negative in Matthew's story world; this generalized culture represents everything that those whom Jesus teaches, the crowds and the disciples, must avoid. This does not mean, however, that individual non-Jews are always portrayed in negative light. Indeed, it is often the positive portrayal of these individual examples that have made scholars think of Matthew's text as looking favorably upon non-Jews as a whole. Then, when assumptions such as these—based on *individual examples of non-Jews* and ignoring passages condemning non-Jewish culture as such—are contrasted with what Matthew has to say about "the Jews," scholars reading Matthew in this way almost invariably bring forth Matthew's condemnation of specific Jewish leadership groups as if they were representative of the *Jewish people as a whole.*

The result is a reading of Matthew that compares the best among the non-Jews with the worst among the Jews, disregarding the fact that what is compared is the minority among both entities; when results are presented, the minority within both categories are thought of as representative of the whole. Having said this, though, it should be

---

20. Cf. James Carlton Paget, "Jewish Proselytism," 82, who points out that several Second-Temple Jewish groups regarded non-Jews as "inherently wicked." This, he argues "created a condition in which Proselytism seems, in psychological terms, natural." We shall return to the issue of proselytism below in chapter 5.3.

21. The idea that salvation is inextricably and exclusively bound to the status of a person as belonging to the people of God is a theological development within Christianity, foreign to most ancient—and modern—forms of Judaism.

emphasized that Matthew's preoccupation with the Jewish people does lead to a much closer scrutiny of the Jews, including the disciples, who receive more detailed critique than any of the individual non-Jewish characters in the story. This is to be expected if the aim of the text is to describe how its hero is engaged in saving his people from their sins. The question is now how Matthew is categorizing and rhetorically using the non-Jewish individuals and groups as he works to achieve the purpose of his narrative.

5.2.1 Individuals and Groups Exemplifying Negative Stereotypes

First of all, we find several examples of non-Jewish individuals and collectivities that fit the negative overall description of non-Jewish culture and behavior more generally. Examples include the people of Gadara who, when they hear that Jesus has rid their district of pigs, leave their town in order to tell him that he is not welcome; he must leave the region (8:28–34). The message about the exorcism and the drowning of the pigs, animals forbidden to Jews,[22] would have been good news to any Jew, especially considering the fact that the area was, for them, part of "biblical Israel," but for these non-Jews in the Decapolis, Jesus's arrival is unacceptable. It threatened their culture and customs.[23] Other non-Jews also exhibit what Matthew presents as negative behavior toward Jesus.

In 27:27–36, Roman soldiers torture and mock Jesus before the crucifixion. The centurion and the soldiers who had crucified Jesus are struck with fear as they realize what they have done (27:54), and when the soldiers guarding Jesus's tomb encounter God's messenger, who was sent to bring life out of the grave, they shake with fear and became

---

22. For the ruling that pigs are unclean (*akathartos*; LXX) and should not be consumed by Jews, see Lev 11:17; Deut 14:8. Pigs were, however, common sacrificial animals in non-Jewish cults.

23. One may note that Matthew's version of the story, contrary to Mark's (Mark 5:1–20), marginalizes the exorcism and moves on to focus on the pigs and the reaction of the swineherds and the town people; the reaction of the town people is presented as the result of the whole episode and the healed demoniacs are not heard of again. Nolland, *Matthew*, 376, notes that the pericope should not be seen as "a deliberate precursor to the Gentile mission." While this is correct from the perspective of a traditional understanding of mission, what we see here does, in fact, have implications for Matt 28:19–20; when the God of Israel takes over the nations, this is what is going to happen. See further chapter 5.3 below.

like dead (*hōs nekroi*; 28:4). Afterwards, these soldiers co-operate with the chief priests, taking bribes in order to allow for false rumors to spread throughout Judea, rumors that claimed that Jesus was never resurrected (28:11–15). Pilate himself had already earlier co-operated with the chief priests in order to prevent any such rumors about Jesus's resurrection (27:62–66). All of these passages place these non-Jews firmly in the general setting Matthew has designed for them; their behavior is flawed and they are active participants in the attempted destruction of the Jewish Messiah.

There are two special cases that need comment, both of which concern Pilate, either directly or indirectly. Christian interpreters have often painted Pilate in favorable colors, portraying him as insightful when it comes to what is happening around Jesus; he understands that jealousy is behind the attempt to have Jesus executed (27:18), and he tries to set him free (27:15–26).[24] Likewise, Pilate's wife has nightmares and tells her husband not to have Jesus, whom she identifies as righteous, executed (27:19). While these comments seem positive and in favor of Pilate and his wife, portraying them as understanding the situation well, there is a larger theological frame active behind the scenes that undermines any conclusions that elevates the Pilates to a higher religio-ethical standard.

As we have noted above when discussing the chief priests and their guilt in relation to Jesus's death, from a Jewish theo-historical perspective Pilate cannot be considered the guilty party in this drama.[25] Since all that takes place on earth is intertwined with what happens in the cosmos, if Pilate were blamed for the death of the Messiah, it would mean that Israel's God was unable to defeat Rome's gods. Therefore, Jesus's death must be construed in the same way that the fall of the first temple was theologized by the prophets, and the fall of the second temple would soon be theologized by Josephus and the rabbis. Guilt is sought within the Jewish people, so that the

24. While this is true, a comparison with the portrayal of Pilate's handling of the matter of Jesus's execution in Luke 23:1–25 shows that Matthew, like Mark, shows some restraint as he attempts to transfer guilt from Pilate to the chief priests.
25. See pp. 243–44n91.

catastrophe can be construed as God's punishment rather than Roman, i.e., ultimately Jupiter's victory.[26] The Romans, here represented by Pilate, can then be presented as mere tools in the hand of Israel's God; without God's intentions, which are focused on the covenant people, Rome would not be able to achieve anything against God's Messiah.[27] What seems like a way to "save Pilate," based on the common assumption among scholars that the early followers of Jesus would try to appease the Romans out of fear of persecution,[28] is, in reality, an insult to the Roman Empire, whose gods are presented as powerless.

We should also note that, since Pilate in the end agrees to execute Jesus, he is also portrayed as weak and in the hands of a crowd of a conquered nation. Adding to that the fact that Pilate's wife's nightmares must be understood as in the process of becoming realized, since Pilate has, in the end, Jesus executed, the overall picture of these non-Jewish characters is poor indeed.

A final note on non-Jews that fulfill the cultural expectations of them as laid out in the Gospel: In the so-called parable of the sheep and the goats in 25:31–46, which, as we shall argue in chapter 7, deals with non-Jews only, we find individuals who have refrained from assisting Jesus's

---

26. The Romans themselves understood their destruction of Jerusalem and the second temple as a vanquishing of the God of Israel and a victory for Capitoline Jupiter. Cf. Jodi Magness, "The Arch of Titus at Rome and the Fate of the God of Israel," *JJS* 59.2 (2008): 201–17: "In the eyes of the Romans, the destruction of the Jerusalem temple meant that their gods, and in particular Jupiter, had defeated the God of Israel" (207). I am grateful to Wally Cirafesi for drawing my attention to this study in this context.

27. The same theology is at work in John's Gospel, 19:11, where Jesus tells Pilate: "You would have no power over me unless it had been given you from above; therefore the one who handed me over to you is guilty of a greater sin."

28. There are many variants of this hypothesis. See, e.g., Gundry, *Matthew: A Commentary on his Handbook for a Mixed Church under Persecution* (Grand Rapids: Eerdmans, 1994), 561–65, who speaks of the 'Christianization' of Pilate. France, *Matthew*, 1049, critiques Gundry, noting correctly that trying to portray Pilate as innocent is not the same as making him a "Christian"; this did happen in later Christian tradition but such developments are unrelated to the Gospel text. France, however, arguing that, "there is nothing historically improbable in his [i.e., Pilate's] reluctance to allow the Jewish leadership [...] to dictate to him in his own court," misses the theological point that is being made by Matthew (and the other evangelists). The same is true for hypotheses that point to the fact that Pilate's less than flattering character and cruel and impatient habits dealing with his subjects in the land, as described by sources external to the Gospels, militates against the portrayal of him given in the Gospels. Even if it is true that the situation is unlikely historical, which seems to me to be the case based on Pilate's record as a prefect, the reason for Matthew to write as he does is independent of any such historical circumstances. For discussion of the historical Pilate and his reception, see Helen K. Bond, *Pontius Pilate in History and Interpretation* (Cambridge: Cambridge University Press, 1998). See also discussion below, chapter 7.1.

followers when they were suffering and in need of help (25:41–46). This attitude and lack of compassion further adds to the wider portrayal of non-Jews as nurturing a social culture which is opposite to that demanded by the kingdom. There are, however, exceptions to this general rule in Matthew.

5.2.2 Exceptions to the Rule: Non-Jews who Acknowledge Jesus's Authority

A second group of non-Jewish individuals fare better than those described above and breaks through the otherwise compact negative pattern. These passages are not many, but they fill an important function in the larger narrative. Three of the passages describe non-Jewish individuals who acknowledge Jesus's authority in such a way that they themselves are presented as subjects of the Jewish Messiah: 2:1–12; 8:5–13; 15:21–28.[29] We shall begin with the story of the Magi since this pericope sets the (religio-political and narrative) standards for the other two examples.

In 2:1–12, the Magi come from the east because they have "observed his star at its rising, and have come to pay him homage" (2:2), thereby acknowledging their loyalty to the Jewish king.[30] While most scholars studying the birth narrative correctly note how Matthew has composed the story of the Magi, the flight to Egypt, and the return to the land using imagery from the Jewish holy scriptures, it is hard to find a more explicitly political text in the New Testament than Matthew's second chapter. The political theme is what keeps the story of the Magi and the following two episodes in the infancy narrative closely together.[31] It makes explicit what has already been hinted at in the story of the virginal conception,[32] namely, that the Messiah's

---

29. Cf. Paget, "Jewish Proselytism," 82n71: "The belief in the superiority of the Jewish religion is widely evidenced in writers as diverse as Philo, Josephus, *The Sibylline Oracles, 2 Baruch, Joseph and Aseneth* etc." We see the same basic pattern in Matthew's Gospel.
30. For the following argument, set within the general context of the infancy narrative, see also Anders Runesson, "Giving Birth to Jesus in the Late First Century: Matthew as Midwife in the Context of Colonisation," in *Infancy Gospels: Stories and Identities* (edited by Claire Clivaz, Andreas Dettwiler, Luc Devilliers, and Enrico Norelli; Tübingen: Mohr Siebeck, 2011), 301–27.
31. Matt 2:1–12; 13–18; 19–23.

realm of influence includes but is not limited to the land of Israel; it mirrors that of a global empire revolving around a hub—Israel and its Messiah—depicted as the center of the world.[33] Having said that, though, there are a number of surprising details in the narrative, which modify the ethnic focus and give interpretive clues of importance for the rest of the Gospel.

The scenes that follow include as human key players on the Jewish side the king of the Jews, i.e., Herod I, the chief priests and the scribes in Jerusalem, the ethnarch Archelaos, Joseph, and Mary.[34] On the non-Jewish side, we find the Magi, the "wise men" from the east. On the celestial level, "an angel of the Lord" guides the righteous.[35] Matthew's audience knew, of course, that Herod as well as Archelaos could rule only because they were backed by Rome and cooperated with the empire. They also knew that in their own time, this collaboration with Rome had led to the loss of a Jewish ruler in Jerusalem in 6 CE, when Archelaos was discharged by the emperor and replaced by Roman prefects (and later procurators), and, eventually, climaxed in the destruction of the Jerusalem in 70 CE. As presented in Matthew's story, Herodian rule was illegal from a divinely ordained genealogical perspective, proven by Holy Scripture in 1:1–17; this explains the ruler's resistance to the legitimate Jewish king.

It is of some interest to note that the group which is targeted for the most severe criticism in Matthew's Gospel, the Pharisees, is not present in the birth narrative at all. This increases the focus on the

---

32. For discussion of the political aspects of the virgin birth, see Runesson, "Matthew as Midwife," 301–27.
33. Cf. postcolonial studies on how colonized peoples may imitate, consciously and/or unconsciously the discourses of the empire. For the concept of mimicry, see, e.g., H. Bhabha, "Of Mimicry and Man: The Ambivalence of Colonial Discourse," in *Modern Literary Theory* (edited by P. Rice and P. Waugh; London: Edward Arnold, 1989), 234–41; P. Childs and P. Williams, *An Introduction to Post-Colonial Theory* (London: Prentice Hall, 1997), 124–25, 129. On Israel as the center of a renewed world, cf. the perspective of the Book of Jubilees (C.T.R. Hayward, *Interpretations of the Name Israel in Ancient Judaism and Some Early Christian Writings: From Victorious Athlete to Heavenly Champion* (Oxford: Oxford University Press, 2005), 353.
34. Jesus is not yet a player, i.e., he is at this stage a passive character around which events develop.
35. It should perhaps be noted that while an angel is said to instruct Joseph twice in dreams (2.13, 19; cf. 1.20), the Magi are instructed in a dream without the mention of an angel (Matt 2.12). While, as Davies and Allison, *Matthew*, 1.251–252, note, the lack of mention of an angel does not mean that the warning does not come from the divine, it is nevertheless striking that an angel is consistently referred to as Joseph is guided by God, but not when non-Jews are involved.

political[36] and connects the birth of Jesus with his death, since the passion narrative also excludes the presence of Pharisees. Instead, it is the leaders of the temple and Jerusalem, the chief priests and their scribes, who are in focus, i.e., the same groups who move the plot forward in the passion narrative, in collaboration with Rome (who had then taken over Jerusalem, Pilate replacing Herod). Just as Jerusalem is targeted by Matthew in the birth narrative (2:3[37]) because of illegitimate and unjust rule, the city is the scene for the (unjust) trial and death of Jesus in the passion narrative. It is because of the corrupt leaders' blindness to what happens around them, their inability to read the cosmic signs, that they cannot understand that God is now acting. This is so despite the fact that they know the Holy Scriptures well and are able to predict, upon request, the place where the Messiah is supposed to be born (Matt 2:6). This leads us to a comparison between the Jewish leading figures, including Herod, and the Magi; such a comparison will assist us in understanding the role of these particular non-Jews in the narrative.

If we look at how these characters are portrayed in the story, we find that Herod is at the center of the critique, while the chief priests and scribes of Jerusalem are more moderately, but still negatively, depicted. The Magi are, on the contrary, moderately, but positively, described. The Magi are the first in world history (apart from Joseph and Mary) to discover that the Jewish Messiah has been born. They are depicted as attentive to cosmic signs: they both see them and understand them. They travel to Jerusalem since they know that this is the city of the great king (cf. Matt 5:35[38]). However, as they arrive in

36. The Pharisees were not involved on the political level in Jerusalem, neither at the time of Jesus's birth, nor in Matthew's time. This does not mean, however, that there would be no governing officials or scribes that belonged to the Pharisaic party and/or sympathized with them. For discussion of the Pharisees, see above, chapter 3.2.1.2.

37. The expression *pasa Hierosolyma* (Matt 2:3) indicates that the people of the city are ruled by their (illegitimate) leaders in such a way that it is, from Matthew's perspective, not meaningful to distinguish between them and those who impose their flawed rule on them. The holy city is, for Matthew, corrupted and can therefore not recognize its Messiah. The theme is repeated in Matt 27:25, as we have seen above, with the use of *pas ho laos* for the citizens of Jerusalem as they are led astray by their leaders and pronounced guilty of the death of Jesus. What Herod failed to accomplish the chief priests, in direct collaboration with Rome, achieve: the death of the Messiah.

38. Cf. Ps 48:2, with its universal perspective: "beautiful in elevation, is the joy of all the earth, Mount Zion, in the far north, the city of the great King."

Jerusalem it becomes apparent that they do not know how to interpret Jewish holy scriptures. They can see and interpret what the God of Israel is doing from observing creation, but they lack knowledge about revelation as related to scripture, which leads to their failure in finding what they are searching for.

The opposite evaluation applies to the chief priests and the scribes of Jerusalem. The Messiah has been born just a few kilometers south of Jerusalem, but they are not aware of it since they cannot interpret cosmic signs as related to their own time.[39] However, as is shown in 2:5, they know the holy scriptures and how to interpret them. The impression left regarding the "religious experts" is that they are disconnected from reality, despite the fact that they have the knowledge needed to be on top of things. This increases their guilt; at this point in the narrative, one cannot expect non-Jews to be knowledgeable in the Torah,[40] but the chief priests should have known better.

While both shortcomings and skills have been shown for both the Magi and the chief priests and scribes, Matthew's evaluation of Herod is devastatingly and one-dimensionally harsh. Herod, the current king of the Jews, is completely in the dark, since he cannot see or understand cosmic signs, on the one hand, nor, on the other, does he know the holy scriptures.[41] The situation may be described in the form of a chart:

---

39. Cf. Matt 16:3, where this inability is applied to Pharisees and Sadducees.
40. The expectations on non-Jews in relation to understanding of Torah will change in Matt 28:18–20; see further discussion below.
41. The theme of blindness and sight/understanding continues throughout the Gospel. Paradigmatically, it is announced in Matt 5:8 that those with pure hearts will see God. The blindness of Jesus's opponents, especially the Pharisees, is emphasized repeatedly (Matt 15:14; 23:16–17). Regarding responsibility and guilt as associated with knowledge and sight, cf. John 9:41.

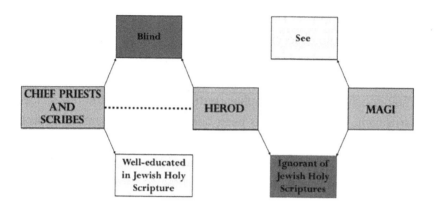

Figure 5.1. Matthew 2: Knowledge, insight, and blindness among Jerusalem's leaders and the Magi.

As a result of his ignorance and inability to rule, Herod reacts on a rumor in the city, but needs to ask both the chief priests and the scribes (2:4), and, deceitfully, the Magi (2:7), in order to know anything about what is going on. And when he has acquired the necessary knowledge, he responds violently by murdering innocent children of Abraham in order to eliminate the (legitimate) son of David and safeguard his own (illegitimate) position on Jerusalem's throne (2:16–18).

Ordering the narrative in this way, Matthew effectively indicates to the audience exactly where the real center of conflict is: it is about who the legitimate king of the Jews is, who is to rule the land and shepherd the people from the throne in Jerusalem.[42] Herod and Jesus are mutually exclusive: the one cannot be in office at the same time as the other. The conflict is not, then, primarily with the chief priests (and by implication, the temple) and the Jerusalem scribes, since their offices and Jesus's rule are not mutually exclusive. Consequently, they

---

42. On the shepherd metaphor (Matt 2:6) and its connection to the land of Israel for Matthew, see Willitts, *Matthew's Messianic Shepherd-King*, esp. 157–76. See also Wayne Baxter, *Israel's Only Shepherd: Matthew's Shepherd Motif and his Social Setting* (London: T&T Clark, 2012).

are rather passive in the story, and do not react as Herod does. They are just a (willing) tool in Herod's hand.[43]

Matthean critique of the Herodian family, and the incompatibility between Herodians and the true lineage of David, is confirmed in Matt 2:22, as Joseph expects Herod's son to act as his father did. As for the Magi, they indicate to the audience yet another contrast between Jesus and Herod. Whereas Herod's rule led to the kingdom's downfall and the fragmentation of the land, the birth of the true Messiah heralds a restored Israel which command worldwide respect and devotion. What is more, the actions of the Magi activate the Abrahamic blessing of Gen 12:3,[44] and signals what John is soon going to announce, namely that God is able to raise up children to Abraham from stones (Matt 3:9[45]).[46] In other words, Herod is killing the children of Abraham, but the Messiah will cause them to multiply.[47] The contrast could hardly be greater and the theological politics of Matthew could not be more intense. The Magi are at the center of these theo-political claims, as Matthew uses them to declare, coterminously, the appropriate response to the arrival of the Messiah into the world, on the one hand, and, on the other, the reaction the legitimate Jewish king will trigger for those who cling to their (illegitimate) power positions in the holy city.

We see this pattern repeated in other parts of the Gospel. While Jewish groups identified in the story as influential and powerful, especially the Pharisees, reject Jesus and work to reduce his influence among the crowds, a Roman centurion (8:5–13) and a Canaanite woman

43. Later in the story, and certainly, in the passion narrative, the chief priests and the Jerusalem scribes and elders take on the leading role as Jesus is attacked, convicted and executed. At this point in the story (and in history), there was no Jewish king ruling from Jerusalem. That political role had now been taken over by Rome. Matthew's message is that whoever rules Jerusalem will oppose Jesus and strive to achieve his elimination.

44. See further chapter 7.3.

45. Cf. Davies and Allison's discussion of this passage, *Matthew*, 1.308–9; see further chapter 5.2.3.

46. Cf. the role of Abraham and Sara in Isa 51:1–2, and how this theme of salvation and the inclusion of people from the nations continues throughout Isaiah to ch. 66 inclusive. Indeed, reading Matthew's Gospel with these Isaiahnic chapters in fresh memory is an intriguing exercise. On Isa 51:1–2, cf. Chrysostom, *Homily on Matthew*, 11.3.

47. Matthew returns to this theme repeatedly in his narrative. Note, e.g., Jesus's reaction to the faith of the centurion in Matt 8:11: "I tell you, many will come from east and west and will eat with Abraham and Isaac and Jacob in the kingdom of heaven, while the heirs of the kingdom will be thrown into the outer darkness, where there will be weeping and gnashing of teeth."

(15:21–28) respond to Jesus in a way similar to the Magi: subordination and, in the case of the Canaanite woman, explicit recognition of the legitimacy of Jesus as the royal Son of David (15:22).[48] As a result of their subordination and trust/faithfulness/loyalty (*pistis*), they receive a share of the blessings of the coming (Jewish) kingdom as their slave and daughter, respectively, are freed from the demons that had taken possession of them. The point of these two passages is precisely that these non-Jews, just as the magi, remain outsiders and still acknowledge Jesus as the rightful Jewish ruler, whose authority extends beyond the Jewish people itself.[49] The trust and loyalty they express bridges the religio-ethnic boundaries, but their "otherness" is maintained,[50] showing the abundance of good things that will overflow when the rightful king arrives.[51]

The status of these non-Jews, who recognize the power of the God of Israel as active in Jesus, but who do not convert, is very similar to the status of the so-called God-fearers described in Acts and elsewhere, i.e., the status of non-Jewish sympathizers present in Jewish synagogues who recognize the importance of the God of Israel, but do not convert.[52] Since the characters in question in Matthew are drawn to

48. While the magi are said to come from the east, the centurion may be said to represent the west; the Canaanite woman represents the historical enemies of Israel, whose land was given to the people of Israel. In other words, we see here how Matthew envisions the ideal response to Jesus from people representing the nations of the known world, including a historical referent that emphasize that even the past enemies of Israel (Babylon in the east, Rome in the West, and the Canaanites in the land) will acknowledge the Messiah.

49. Regarding the Canaanite woman, Margaret Davies, *Matthew*, 115, suggests that "Jesus' healing justified the mission to the Gentiles which the narrative finally gives to the disciples." Cf. Meier, *Matthew*, 171, who claims that the passage indicates that the post-resurrection "church" will include non-Jews in their mission (contrary to the mission during Jesus's earthly ministry), and that non-Jews will have access to the risen Lord through faith and humility. While, as we shall see, there is a narrative trajectory in the Gospel that ends in the direct mission to the nations, there is no straight line between that event and the story about the Canaanite woman (and the centurion and the magi). These stories are not about mission, but about people, outsiders who remain outsiders, who come to Jesus and ask for help; only secondarily and indirectly can we see that they prepare for the adding of a new aspect to the mission of the disciples in Matt 28:18–20, which will transform outsiders to insiders.

50. This is very clearly shown by Matt 15:24, 27.

51. Regarding the theme of abundance that characterize the Messianic rule, see also, the miracles of loaves and fish in Matt 14:13–21; 15:32–38.

52. Evidence for non-Jewish individuals in synagogue settings comes from especially Acts, but we also have sources from outside the New Testament (for sources and discussion, consult the index in Anders Runesson, Donald D. Binder, Birger Olsson, *The Ancient Synagogue From its Origins to 200 CE: A Source Book* [Leiden: Brill, 2008]). See also Louis Feldman, "The Omnipresence of the God-Fearers," *BARev* Sept./Oct. (1986), 59–63. For later inscriptions and non-Jewish authors, see sources and

Israel's God through interaction with the Messiah, and their loyalty is expressed in relation to this Messiah, it may be of some analytical value to use the term Christ-fearers to describe them.[53] As we shall see below, this distinction between Christ-fearers and Jewish followers of Jesus is maintained until after the resurrection of Jesus, but must change as a result of the very last instructions Jesus gives his disciples, based on the global reach of his power that he is then given.

There is also another group of non-Jews in Matthew's story world that is distinguished from the otherwise negative portrayal of the nations. These are not Christ-fearers. In fact, they have never met Jesus or received favor from him, and they are unfamiliar with his teachings. These are people who, as they have encountered Jesus's suffering followers, have shown mercy and compassion, not understanding the wider and deeper significance of what they have done. They are the sheep of 25:33–40. We shall return to this group in relation to divine judgment in chapter 7.3. Before we continue to discuss another category of (former) non-Jews, there are a few other special cases that need comment.

It has been common among scholars who see in Matthew a positive treatment of non-Jews, and, ultimately, divine condemnation of the Jewish people, to point to Jesus's harsh sayings about some Galilean cities, contrasting these cities with some historical non-Jewish cities, which are portrayed in a more favorable light (11:21–24; cf. 12:41–42). In my view, such interpretations misunderstand the rhetorical logic of these passages, as we have also indicated above.[54] Tyre, Sidon, and Sodom were symbols of evil in the Hebrew Bible,[55] and there is no indication that Matthew's Jesus would understand them differently.

discussion in Louis H. Feldman and Meyer Reinhold (eds.), *Jewish Life and Thought Among Greeks and Romans* (Minneapolis: Fortress, 1996), 137–45. For evidence from Late Antiquity, cf. Steven Fine, "Non-Jews in the Synagogues of Late-Antique Palestine: Rabbinic and Archaeological Evidence," in *Jews, Christians, and Polytheists in the Ancient Synagogue: Cultural Interaction During the Greco-Roman Period* (edited by Steven Fine; London: Routledge, 1999).

53. For this terminology, see Runesson, "Inventing Christian Identity," 73. Cf. the special status afforded non-Jews who sympathize with Judaism but do not convert in later rabbinic literature, e.g., *b. Av. Zar.* 3a; *b. San.* 56a-b; *Gen. R.* 98:9; 34:8; 16:6; *Exod. R.* 30:9; *Deut. R.* 2:25; 1:21; *Num. R.* 14:12; cf. *b. San.* 59a; *b. Meg.* 13a; *b. Hull.* 13b.

54. See pp. 60–61.

55. Cf., e.g., Ps 83:7 [Heb 83:8]; Isa 23; Jer 25:15–38; Ezek 28:1–23; Gen 13:13; 18:16–19:29.

They are certainly not going to escape judgment when the final judgment will take place, and they have already been judged in this world through destruction and devastation.

The point being made is that the named Galilean cities will be worse off than even these symbols of evil when the Son of Man comes to judge the world, since they should have known better, based on the deeds of power (*dynamis*) that had been performed in their midst, but to which these non-Jews never had access. Had they seen, they would have repented, goes the argument, emphasizing the guilt of those who see but still do not repent. The same type of argument is present in 8:10–12 (the centurion), and again, in 12:40–41 (the people of Nineveh and the Queen of the South). The logic of the argument is thus, at its heart, demeaning of non-Jews, since the audience-shared point of departure is the very low esteem in which non-Jews are held. This shared view is used by the Matthean Jesus to point out the disgraceful and incomprehensible fact that some Jewish towns responded negatively to Jesus's proclamation.[56]

5.2.3 Proselytes in Matthew's Story World

Finally, there is evidence of a group of non-Jews in Matthew's Gospel who have taken, or will take, the step over to Judaism and become proselytes. This category of non-Jews is signaled already in the genealogy (1:1–17), anticipated in the form of prophetic claims (3:9; 12:18, 21), and culminates in the final verses of the Gospel (28:18–20). The role of the non-Jewish women included in the genealogy is of special importance for the understanding of Matthew's approach to ethnic categories in this regard, and we shall therefore take a closer look at how they function in the immediate setting of the genealogy as well as how they prepare for later developments in the narrative.

The programmatic statement in the title of Matt 1:1 is intriguing and sets the tone for the genealogy, the birth narrative, and the Gospel as a

---

56. In the case of Nineveh and the Queen of the South, the target is the Pharisees and scribes associated with them; they are the ones who trigger Jesus's outburst against "this generation" (12:42).

whole.[57] While it is quite common to interpret the mention of Abraham here as an indication of Matthew's aim to include non-Jews—as non-Jews—in the community of the saved, such an understanding of Abraham should not be assumed without argument. We are easily led astray by seeing Paul's theology as valid also for our understanding of the Gospels. In Second-Temple Judaism, however, to be a child of Abraham, the founding father of the Jewish people, simply meant to be a Jew.[58] With the mention of Abraham, we have the wider interpretive frame for Jesus's identity set: Jesus belongs firmly within the Jewish people and the Jewish world. Within that people, he is the awaited royal Messiah, the Son of David. It is significant that these two individuals, Abraham and David, are mentioned both here and in the summarizing conclusion of the genealogy in Matt 1:17. There, in verse 17, the overall structure of the genealogy (which the audience has already noticed through the clear indicators in vv. 6 and 11–12) is explicitly revealed. It is centered on four key events: Abraham, David, the exile, and the Messiah. These four events are narrowed down to one via the number 14, which, in Hebrew, is the numerical equivalent of the name David.[59]

While much has been said about this structure, which is ideologically and theologically ordered rather than statistically,[60] and most scholars

57. This does not mean that the title refers to more than the genealogy, only that it sets the tone for the perspective that penetrates the Gospel as a whole. For a thorough discussion of the genealogy, see Davies and Allison, *Matthew*, 1.149–60. While they regard, correctly in my view, the genealogy as redactional, i.e., it was composed in the late first century, they understand the title (Matt 1:1) as referring to the whole of Matthew's Gospel, thus preferring a translation of *genesis* as "history" or "genesis" (= new creation; 149–150). Brown, *Messiah*, 57–59, limits the reference of the title to the genealogy itself, thus translating *Biblos geneseōs* as "birth record." This is also the preference of Luz, *Matthew*, 1.103–4 ("Register of the origin"), and of many translations of the New Testament, e.g., the NRSV ("account of the genealogy") and the Swedish translation of 1981 (= Bibel 2000), which has "Släkttavla."

58. For most Jews, this has not changed: Abraham is the forefather of the Jewish people, not of (non-Jewish) Christians or Muslims. On the other hand, several Jewish representatives in inter-religious dialogue are currently reconsidering this traditional position. For discussion, see M. S. Kogan, *Opening the Covenant: A Jewish Theology of Christianity*, Oxford: Oxford University Press, 2008. For an overview of Abraham in Christian tradition with a focus on the New Testament period and the second century, see Anders Runesson, "Extending or Restricting the Covenant? Abraham and the People of God in Christian Tradition," in *LTQ* (2011).

59. So also Brown, *Messiah*, 80n38; Davies and Allison, *Matthew*, 1.161–65, 185; Carter, *Margins*, 65; France, *Matthew*, 75, and many others.

60. From a historical point of view, there are obvious flaws in the list. This makes it all the more

correctly point to the fact that Jesus is emphatically presented as Israel's Messiah here, few have asked for the unifying element of all four events. Such a central theme appears to be intended, since the structure is not only clear from markers in the list, but also commented on explicitly in 1:17. This common element seems to me to be the land, or as Matthew writes a few verses later, the land of Israel (*gē Israēl*; 2:20, 21). The land of Israel was promised to Abraham (1:1, 17) and brought to its religio-politically ideal form under the kingship of David (1:6, 17); the loss of the land followed with the exile (1:11, 17), the disaster which is now going to be triumphantly and fully reversed in a final (cosmic and worldly) battle beginning with the birth of the Messiah (1:16, 17).

Would finding such a strong focus on the land in Matthew be strange? In my view, it is only once we have read the Gospel through the lens of almost 1900 years of non-Jewish Christianity, beginning with Ignatius and later patristic writings, that the importance of the land for Matthew becomes diminished.[61] Christian theology in Late Antiquity, the form of Christianity inherited by modern mainstream Christianity, attempted actively to divorce the Jewish people from their status as the people of God, from their law, as well as from what is, in their own theology, their inherent connection to the land. Indeed, the modern Western de-ethnosized concept of "religion," which is inextricably intertwined with the growing dominance of non-Jewish forms of Christianity in Late Antiquity, was born in this process as the common ancient connection between people, land, god, and law was phased out of history[62] using anti-Jewish and anti-"pagan" rhetoric, political strategies, and violence.[63] But this development post-dates the

---

important to ask why Matthew chose to order the list the way he did. Cf. France, *Matthew*, 17. See also the extensive discussion in Brown, *Messiah*, 57–94.

61. Cf. Willitts, *Matthew's Messianic Shepherd-King*, 157. Willitts predicts that his own focus on the land theme in Matthew will be met with some skepticism by other New Testament scholars. While D. Garlington, review of J. Willitts, *Matthew's Messianic Shepherd-King: In Search of 'The Lost Sheep of the House of Israel*, Review of Biblical Literature [http://www.bookreviews.org] (2010), to some degree, confirms Willitts's prediction, the present study supports Willitts's basic insistence on Matthew's focus on the land from a first-century historical perspective.

62. It should be noted, of course, that from a Jewish (emic) point of view, this divorce between land and "religion" was never accepted; it is still a prominent aspect of most Jewish groups' understanding of their identity today. This may result in support for the modern state of Israel, but also, in radical rejection of this (secular) state, the latter alternative evidenced by several groups among the Haredim ("ultra-orthodox").

first century and may not be applied to the socio-religious and cultural context in which the Gospel of Matthew was written.

If we are aiming at a historical first-century understanding of Matthew's Gospel, we need to take seriously that the genealogy was most likely composed after the catastrophe of the fall of Jerusalem and the temple, when the land was fragmented under the leadership of Agrippa II in the Galilee, on the one hand, and Judea was a Roman province under the direct rule of procurators, on the other. It is in this context that Matthew composes a genealogy that *begins* with the individual to whom the God of Israel promised the land of Israel (Abraham), *continues* with a heavy emphasis on the monarchy through a focus on king David and the disaster of the loss of the land in the exile, and *culminates* with the arrival of the Messiah (who in 1:17 is not even mentioned by name; it is the function that is foregrounded here, and the function is determined by what has been said earlier in the list as well as the list's explicit structure). It seems as if Matthew is indeed rather explicitly and with ideological-mathematical precision announcing the imminent end of the long trajectory of exile and restoration,[64] and the inauguration of the era of the Son of David, in

---

63. For this development, see Runesson, "Inventing Christian Identity." For an in-depth discussion of the connection between land, law, people and god more generally in antiquity, see Steve Mason, "Jews, Judaeans, Judaizing, Judaism: Problems of Categorization in Ancient History," in *JSJ* 38 (2007), 457–512.

64. The idea of exile in Matthew is a much debated issue. Some argue that for Matthew, the Jewish people still live in exile in the first century, despite the fact that they returned to the land several centuries earlier and was, in fact, ruled by a Jewish king at the turn of the era. Others object that it is hardly possible to make such a claim, based on the aforementioned return to the land as well as the fact that the story is taking place in the land itself, the author seemingly being unconcerned with the Diaspora. However, while the historical realities are clear, there are some indications in the text that suggest that, regardless of the factual situation of the Jewish people in the land, Matthew is aiming at portraying the situation before the arrival of the Messiah as part of the larger trajectory of exile, which does not end until the kingdom is fully restored. For example, the genealogy is structured based partly on the criterion of exile, juxtaposing exile with the Messiah (1:17). Herod's rule, which had unified the kingdom, is also considered illegitimate by Matthew, implying that Israel has not yet been fully restored (cf. Acts 1:6–7, where a similar claim is made; restoration of the kingdom still lies in the future). Further, land considered part of the ideal biblical Israel is being claimed by the Matthean Jesus, as we have argued above (8:28–34; see p. 214n16 and p. 349n11), and the message about the coming kingdom is to be proclaimed among Diaspora Jews (24:14; cf. 8:11). Independent rule of the land by a Jewish Messiah seems to be for Matthew a sine qua non for announcing the end of exile in the sense that exile is not fully terminated until the kingdom is restored. It is not over until all is accomplished. Such a perspective also makes sense when Matthew writes, after the destruction of Jerusalem and the loss of temple in 70 CE, events which echo the circumstances surrounding the first (Babylonian) exile, to which Matthew refers repeatedly in the genealogy.

which the Messiah will rule the land of Israel, thereby fulfilling God's promise to Abraham.

This, I would argue, would be the epicenter of meaning in Matthew's genealogy for a first-century Jewish audience, especially, perhaps, if this text was authored, as seems likely, in Galilee. Indeed, even Jesus's name, mentioned immediately in the title of the genealogy before David and Abraham, is an indication in this direction; the Messiah is named after the hero in Israelite history that brought the people into the land after the exodus from slavery in Egypt.

It is in this literary setting that commentators from the patristic era until today have noted challenging irregularities, in particular, the fact that five women of unusual character are included in the list. The explanations for their inclusion have been varied and are often rehearsed in the commentaries.[65] Within the wider interpretive frame given above, the following may be said about these women.

One of the most common interpretations since Martin Luther of why these women are included is that at least four of them seem to be related to non-Jews in various ways. While this is an important observation, a close reading reveals that the gentile connection is not a unifying theme for the five women. First, it is not clear from the biblical story whether Tamar was an Israelite or not, although many commentators assume she was a Canaanite, like Judah's wife, Shuah.[66] Rahab, however, was a Canaanite,[67] and Ruth was a Moabite, first married to an Israelite from Bethlehem, and then, re-married to Boaz, also of Bethlehem.[68] While difficult to determine, it seems that a first-century audience familiar with the biblical stories would understand Bathsheba to be the daughter of an officer in David's army, Eliam, son of Ahitophel of Gilo, the latter of whom had once been David's adviser, but then became a traitor.[69] If this is correct, she was most likely regarded as an Israelite, although she was married to a Hittite:

---

65. See, e.g., Davies and Allison, *Matthew*, 1.170–72; Carter, *Margins*, 59–61. See also Jason B. Hood, *The Messiah, His Brothers, and the Nations (Matthew 1:1-17)* (LNTS 441; New York: T&T Clark, 2011).
66. The story about Tamar is found in Genesis 38.
67. Josh 2; 6:15–25.
68. Ruth 1:4.
69. 2 Sam 23:34; 1 Chr 27:33.

Uriah, an honorable and loyal officer in David's army, according to the story, with extraordinary integrity. She married David after David had murdered Uriah—an act for which David is severely criticized in biblical tradition.[70] The fifth woman, Mary, is clearly depicted as a righteous Jewish woman from Bethlehem, the mother of the Messiah.

Another suggestion by Warren Carter, following Amy-Jill Levine, is that the unifying theme for these women is their marginal status in society, despite of which they are presented as righteous and important figures in Jewish history.[71] Krister Stendahl has put forward a similar interpretation, which focuses on the women's marital relations as scandalous in various ways: still the God of Israel builds his plan to liberate Israel on their active participation.[72] This would mean that anyone who would be tempted to slander Mary (and we know that later sources doubted her status and the virgin birth), would have to acknowledge that the Davidic line was indeed one in which God achieved the unexpected through people in whom society put little or no trust.[73]

It seems to me that these suggestions all point to something that may well have resonated with a first-century Jewish audience. However, it may be the case that the fact that these individuals were women has been over-interpreted by scholars as constituting a unifying element in the list, their gender being thought of as the interpretive key. The genealogy is at its core patriarchal, as has been pointed out by Elaine Wainwright.[74] Within the context and structure of the genealogy itself, the (female) individuals mentioned in Matthew's Gospel (Tamar, Rahab, Ruth, and "the wife of Uriah") should be assigned a more independent role in relation to the woman who gave birth to the Messiah. These women were, in different ways, part

---

70. 2 Sam 11:1–12:25.

71. Carter, *Margins*, 60–61.

72. Krister Stendahl, "Quis et Unde? An Analysis of Mt 1–2", in *The Interpretation of Matthew* (edited by Graham Stanton; 2nd ed.; Edinburgh: T&T Clark, 1995), 69–80.

73. Tamar dresses up as a prostitute and has intercourse with Judah, her Father in Law; Rahab is a prostitute; Bathsheba is forced to commit adultery; Ruth may be interpreted as a seducer; Mary is a young woman who is pregnant before she marries (cf. the problems indicated by Matt 1:19).

74. Elaine Wainwright, *Towards a Feminist Critical Reading of the Gospel according to Matthew* (Berlin: de Gruyter, 1991).

of the conditions necessary for the Davidic line to be kept intact (and, in one case, for the land to be conquered), but Mary's position is exceptional, which is indicated also by the virginal conception that follows in Matthew 2.

We have already noted the centrality of the land in the genealogy, from promise via ideal rule and disaster to fulfillment. We have also remarked that this list was likely composed at a time when the land was fragmented, ruled and taxed directly or indirectly by a foreign power (and its gods). Seen from this perspective, it is important not to ignore the ethnic aspect in the list, and how it is presented.[75] In later Jewish sources, Tamar, Rahab, and Ruth are said to have been proselytes, and it is possible, even likely, that this would also have been Matthew's understanding.[76] But this is not something that, in and of itself, would explain their role in Matthew. The point seems to be the ethnic origin of the women in combination with their good deeds toward Israel and the Jewish people. Tamar, in fact, saves the ancestral line of Judah through her clever trick. Rahab both saves the lives of the Israelite spies and assists Joshua as he conquers the land promised to Abraham. Ruth is the active part in accomplishing the marriage with Boaz, which preserves the Davidic line through Obed, who becomes David's grandfather. This dual focus on ethnicity, in combination with support for the Israelites, may also explain why Bathsheba is not mentioned by name, but only as the "wife of Uriah." The focus is, as a consequence, shifted from her to Uriah, who was a non-Israelite who served Israel's king with utmost loyalty in his military forces, thus protecting the land. In other words, the names of Tamar and Ruth are connected with Davidic lineage, and Rahab and Uriah with the land as ruled by Israelites.

Interestingly, this pattern of ethnic origin and benevolent deeds

---

75. Cf. Hood, *The Messiah*, chs. 6 and 7.
76. Tamar: *b. Sotah* 10a; Rahab: e.g., *Mekhilta Ex.* 18.1; Ruth: *Midrash Ruth* 1.16–17. Part of the explanation for why these women were seen as proselytes in Jewish tradition is surely the interconnectedness we mentioned above between land, people, and God; shifting loyalty from one god to another involved shifting loyalty with regard to national belonging too, and vice versa. This is also why, for the Romans, non-Jewish loyalty to the Jewish "religion" could be understood as treason.

performed toward the chosen people is similar to what we find in the judgment scene in Matt 25:31–46. We can also see a similar pattern in 10:40–42, but then adapted to Jews who do not belong among Jesus's followers. The pattern itself is found in Gen 12:3, where, when Abraham is given the promise of land and of becoming a great nation, it is stated that outsiders will be judged depending on how they relate to Abraham as those promises are being fulfilled. In Matthew's genealogy, we find these non-Jews-turned-proselytes supporting the children of Abraham in various ways, preparing for the coming of the Messiah. The difference between these women, on the one hand, and the magi, the centurion, and the Canaanite woman, on the other, is that the former were thought of as joining the Jewish people (helping them), and the latter are portrayed as outsiders seeking help.

The issue of proselytes surface again in 3:9, when John claims that God can raise children to Abraham out of stones. In other words, Abrahamic descent does not protect from divine wrath when it is abused, and this is, as will be addressed later in the story, true for Jesus's disciples too; all Jews will be judged by the same criteria, based on Torah, and all need to produce fruit worthy of the kingdom (i.e., repentance is key; 3:8; 7:21). John's words here are an attack on "misplaced pride in Abrahamic descent at the expense of genuine righteousness."[77] The people of God is, as a category, kept intact, and that means that the covenant is also upheld, as we have argued above in chapter 2.8. What is happening is not an eradication of Jewishness/ the covenant, but instead, a reaffirmation, in the setting of John's proclamation of divine judgment, of that which most Jews at the time (and later) would agree on,[78] namely, that the covenant is open for non-Jews who want to become proselytes.[79] The faithfulness and loyalty of

---

77. Gundry, *Matthew*, 46. Cf. Nolland, *Matthew*, 144.

78. It is instructive to note that proselytes existed even in the sectarian group at Qumran, according to 1QS 5.6–7. Note that critique against proselytes does exist in later Rabbinic literature; see, e.g., *b Yev.* 47b; *b. Yev.* 24b. Such critique is, however, countered in numerous other rabbinic passages, which welcome proselytes (and are often positive toward a mission to non-Jews; see, e.g., *b. Pes.* 87b; *b. Ber.* 57b; *b. Ned.* 32a; *b. Shabb.* 31a; *Mekhilta* on Exod. 22:20; *Gen. R.* 39:4; 84:4; 90:6; *Eccl. R.* 8:10). On the image of non-Jews in Judaism with a focus on the Noahide commandments (i.e., non-proselyte status) cf. David Novak, *The Image of the Non-Jew in Judaism: The Idea of Noahide Law* (2nd ed.; Oxford: Littman Library of Jewish Civilization, 2011).

possible future proselytes is contrasted with the lack of repentance of those of whom repentance would have been expected. As the kingdom is being restored God can therefore replace some children of Abraham, here understood as referring to Pharisees and Sadducees (3:7), with proselytes, if such proselytes display the same kind of trust and loyalty as the Christ-fearing centurion does in 8:5–13.

As we shall see, though, the status of the Christ-fearer is temporary and will dissolve after Jesus's resurrection; then, non-Jews (*all the nations*) will need to be instructed in Jesus's interpretation of Torah, something that has not happened before at all in Matthew's narrative; this requires that they become proselytes in the process of becoming disciples (28:18–20; cf. 12:18).[80] The lack of Torah knowledge characteristic even of non-Jews who understand that Jesus is the Messiah, such as the magi, as discussed above, will then be overcome through active teaching, as these religio-ethnic outsiders leave their non-Jewish culture behind and cross over into the realm of Judaism. We shall return to this below, when we deal with the criteria of

---

79. Cf. France's early commentary on Matthew, *The Gospel According to Matthew: An Introduction and Commentary* (Grand Rapids: Eerdmans, 1985), where he argues that what John attacks here "is not reliance on race (Gentiles too became *children of Abraham* when they became proselytes), but on status as members of the covenant community" (92; cf. France, *Matthew*, [2007] 111). For a comparative perspective, France refers to Rom 9:6–8, stating that not all are children of Abraham just because they are his descendants, but only those who share Abraham's faith. This use of Romans, however, is slightly misleading in this setting. In Rom 11:26, Paul is stating that *all* Israel will be saved. Such a view should indicate to us that, for Paul, heritage and covenant (i.e., the patriarchs) still matters, even if behavior has been flawed; God's love for the patriarchs is a powerful matrix within which salvation can still be found since God will not revoke his (covenant) promises, regardless of the people's behavior (11:28–29). This does not mean, however, that God will not judge individual members of the people of God; it simply means that judgment in and of itself does not abolish the importance of ethnicity and God's election; these are two different things. Again, this is one of the points where later Christian tradition has tended to confuse some interpreters. In Christian tradition, salvation has been tightly connected to and dependent on belonging within the people of God. In Jewish tradition, however, salvation reaches beyond ethnicity and categorization as God's people. As it happens, this is also the case in Matthew, as we shall see in chapter 7.3.

80. Cf., e.g., Sim, "The Gospel of Matthew and the Gentiles," 44: "[B]y entering his sectarian group they had left the Gentile world and for all intents and purposes had ceased to be Gentiles." See also Frederick J. Murphy, "The Jewishness of Matthew: Another Look," in *When Judaism and Christianity Began: Essays in Memory of Anthony J. Saldarini* (edited by Alan J. Avery-Peck, Daniel Harrington, and Jacob Neusner; Leiden: Brill, 2004), 377–401: "Matthew's community considered itself fully Jewish and Torah observant. They probably insisted on full Torah observance from Gentiles who entered the community" (402). John Painter, "Matthew and John," in *Matthew and his Christian Contemporaries* (edited by David C. Sim and Boris Repschinsky; London: T&T Clark, 2008), 66–86, argues similarly that Matthew's non-Jewish mission was law observant.

judgment for non-Jews. First, however, we need to say a few words about mission in relation to non-Jews, in order to bring some clarity to the situation between the different groups of non-Jews described above, and how Matthew envisions their relationship to the Jewish people.

5.3 Conquering the Nations and Saving the Enemy: Mission and Conversion in Matthew

When the question of the status of non-Jews in Matthew is analyzed, most often, and this is unavoidable, the issue of mission comes up. In brief, the basic problem is this: why is it that the Matthean Jesus, who has explicitly, uniquely among the New Testament texts, restricted his and his disciples proclamation to the Jewish people (1:21; 10:5–6; 15:24) suddenly in 28:18–20 expands their efforts to include all the nations (*panta ta ethnē*)? What does this expanded mission actually entail—what is, more specifically, the aim of such efforts? While a full discussion of mission cannot be undertaken here,[81] it is of some importance to

81. For studies on Jewish mission, see Louis Feldman, *Jew and Gentile in the Ancient World: Attitudes and Interactions From Alexander to Justinian* (Princeton: Princeton University Press, 1993); Martin Goodman, *Mission and Conversion: Proselytizing in the Religious History of the Roman Empire* (Oxford: Clarendon, 1994); James Carleton Paget, "Jewish Proselytism at the Time of Christian Origins: Chimera or Reality?" *JSNT* 62 (1996), 65–103; Scott McKnight, *A Light Among the Gentiles: Jewish Missionary Activity in the Second Temple Period* (Minneapolis: Fortress Press, 1991); Jostein Ådna and Hans Kvalbein, eds., *The Mission of the Early Church to Jews and Gentiles* (Tübingen: Mohr Siebeck, 2000); E. J. Schnabel, *Early Christian Mission* (2 vols.; Downers Grove: Intervarsity Press, 2004); Terence L. Donaldson, *Judaism and the Gentiles: Jewish Patterns of Universalism (to 135 CE)* (Waco: Baylor University Press, 2007). Cf. Elisabeth Schüssler Fiorenza (ed.), *Aspects of Religious Propaganda in Judaism and Early Christianity* (Notre Dame: University of Notre Dame Press, 1976). For additional studies, especially scholars critical to the theory that Jews missionized non-Jews in the first centuries CE, see Schnabel, *Early Christian Mission*, 1:93n8. The Canadian Society of Biblical Studies has produced three recent publications which are relevant to our topic: Terence L. Donaldson, ed., *Religious Rivalries and the Struggle for Success in Caesarea Maritima* (Waterloo: Wilfrid Laurier University Press 2000); Richard S. Ascough, ed., *Religious Rivalries and the Struggle for Success in Sardis and Smyrna* (Waterloo: Wilfrid Laurier University Press, 2005); Leif E. Vaage, ed., *Religious Rivalries in the Early Roman Empire and the Rise of Christianity* (Waterloo: Wilfrid Laurier University Press, 2006). For a recent discussion of Jewish mission, including mission as it appeared in Christ-believing circles and in Graeco-Roman settings, see Runesson, "Was there a Christian Mission Before the Fourth Century?" 205–47. On the mission of Jesus and his disciples in Matthew, see Boris Paschke, *Particularism and Universalism in the Sermon on the Mount: A Narrative-Critical Analysis of Matthew 5–7 in the Light of Matthew's View on Mission* (Neutestamentliche Abhandlungen NS 56; Münster: Aschendorff, 2012). On the issue of terminology and definition of what is usually and problematically referred to as universalism and particularism, see Anders Runesson, "Particularistic Judaism and Universalistic Christianity? Some Critical Remarks on Terminology and Theology," *Journal of Greco-Roman Christianity and Judaism* 1 (2000), 120–44.

provide a brief outline of what is involved and how this relates to the question of divine judgment in Matthew.

Before we can speak of "mission," we need an explanation and classification of the phenomena that are usually referred to as exemplifying mission. I have suggested elsewhere the following working definition of "mission:"[82]

Proselytizing Mission

This refers to attempts by members of one group to convince non-members to join their group. Examples include Eleazar the Galilean, who, contrary to Ananias, insisted on the circumcision of the King of Adiabene (Josephus, AJ 20.34–48). We find also, in this category, the forced circumcision practiced by some of the Hasmonean rulers as they annexed conquered areas.

Ethno-Ethic[83] Mission

This type of mission refers to attempts by members of one group to influence the behavior and/or worship of non-members, without requiring them to join the group as proselytes. Examples would include the thought pattern revealed in the book of Jonah. It seems, also, that Ananias and another anonymous Jew mentioned by Josephus may have engaged in such mission: AJ 20.34–48.24.[84] What is missionized is not the Torah in its entirety, but general (ethically oriented) principles that are considered suitable for non-Jews.[85]

---

82. Runesson, "Christian Mission Before the Fourth Century?" 213–215.
83. The term is intended to communicate that while no conversion or proselyte status is required, the (religio-)ethical standard that is missionized is not "universal," but is dictated by the religio-ethnic standards of the missionizing group or individual belonging to such a group. It should be noted that while in general terms, such standards may be similar to those of the missionizing group, the group may nurture specific requirements applying to itself only, beyond those missionized.
84. For discussion of this passage in relation to Paul, see Mark D. Nanos, "Paul's Non-Jews Do Not Become 'Jews,' But Do They Become 'Jewish'? Reading Romans 2:25–29 Within Judaism, Alongside Josephus," *JJMJS* 1 (2014): 26–53.

Inward Mission

This pattern of mission refers to attempts by a member of a group to influence the behavior and/or worship of other members of the larger group to which they all belong. Examples of this type of mission are countless, both in the Hebrew Bible and the New Testament, as well as throughout Jewish and Christian history.[86]

Each of these three types of mission can be performed either *actively* or *passively*. The former would involve active outreach to targeted individuals or groups, but does not have to be planned and executed by a larger group; individuals could also be active in this regard, without explicit institutional or other authority or financial support behind them. Passive mission refers to a pattern of thought expecting others to change their behavior and/or cultic status as a consequence of the individual missionary's, or group's, way of life and other activities, without direct interaction with those who are expected to change. For example, some Jews in and around the first century expected that non-Jews would join them on their own accord when the time was right and God was about to reinvent the world.[87]

If we summarize the above definition of mission, including passive and active approaches, we will have the following prism through which to read Matthew's text.

---

85. A distant relative to this idea is the rabbinic notion of commandments given to Adam, or, more famously, Noah; for references, see below, p. 419n54.
86. Cf. Goodman, *Mission and Conversion*, 5: "On a social scale broader than that of the household, Jews, Christians, and pagans from time to time, alike took it for granted that within societies religious deviants had to be brought into line, if necessary by force, to avert the hostility of the divine and disaster for all." While this applies to larger societies in which people of different religio-ethnic backgrounds co-exist, it is also valid for cities and groups worshipping the same God.
87. We find such expectations in the book of Isaiah, but also with the historical Jesus, in the Gospel of John, and, as we shall see, partly in the Gospel of Matthew.

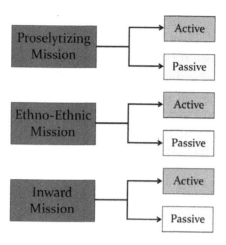

Figure 5.2. "Mission" in Matthew.

Each of these types of mission will have implications for how we may understand the issue of salvation in Matthew. As we have seen throughout this study, Matthew's Gospel presents Jesus (and his disciples) as almost exclusively involved in inward mission, i.e., mission directed at other members of the group to which Jesus himself belong, the Jewish people ("his people"; 1:21), with the aim of having them repent and change their way of life as preparation for the final judgment and the establishment of the kingdom of heaven. The very act of mission represents an aim to save those who are missionized. Do we see other forms of mission represented in the Gospel, and if so, how should we explain such different patterns of thoughts?

As we have seen above, non-Jewish culture and behavior are condemned in generalizing terms in Matthew's Gospel. When non-Jewish individuals and/or groups of people are mentioned, many of these fit well into this overall negative paradigm. The portrayal of some individuals, though, departs from this pattern. We have focused on the magi (2:1–12), the centurion (8:5–13), and the Canaanite woman (15:21–28), and also noted the (for Matthew historical) role played by the Queen of the South as a model for proper behavior (12:42). These figures all have in common that none of them turn to representatives of the Jewish people (Jesus or King Solomon) as a consequence of

any active missionary efforts by either of these sons of David. They have identified that something of importance is happening within the Jewish nation, and interprets this as having value and potential benefits also for themselves, as non-Jews. For this they are commended by the Matthean Jesus, and held up as examples to follow, even for Jews; the events taking place around Jesus should in and of themselves be enough for all, Jews and non-Jews, to seek the kingdom and its promised blessings.

The pattern of thought that provides the matrix within which such ideals are formed is closely related to ideas about the eschatological pilgrimage of non-Jews, a common thought in Second-Temple Judaism.[88] Such pilgrimage will happen without active mission beyond the Jewish people; it is an (anticipated) effect taking place "automatically" when the people fulfill their God-given task of being the salt of the land (*gē*)[89] and the light of the world (5:13–16).[90] We seem to have here, then, in these passages, an ethno-ethic pattern of passive mission, which expects non-Jews to react to the eschatological events that have begun taking place among the Jewish people. In other words, the active inward mission carried out by Jesus and his disciples among their own people is a (passive) witness to those outside of Israel, indicating to these outsiders the importance of what is happening for the whole world.[91] This hermeneutical mechanism also surfaces in a passage like 10:18, where the disciples are described as carrying out their mission to Jews only.[92] It is of some importance to note that there is no requirement for these non-Jews to convert in order to have a share in the benefits that come with the kingdom as it is being

---

88. Cf. Terence L. Donaldson, "Proselytes or 'Righteous Gentiles'? The Status of Gentiles in Eschatological Pilgrimage Patterns of Thought," *JSP* 7 (1990), 3–27. See also idem, *Judaism and the Gentiles*.

89. On the meaning of *gē* here, see above, p. 29n93; cf. p. 266.

90. A similar pattern of thought is expressed in John 13:35; cf. Isa 61:9; 62:1–2.

91. This type of (passive) witness to nations other than Israel may also be signaled in Matt 24:14, although the narrative time here is post-resurrection; thus the disciples are, at this point, involved also in an active mission to non-Jews.

92. That this cannot be an example of active mission to non-Jews is made very clear by Matt 10:5–6. Note also how 10:19 explains how the disciples are going to come in contact with non-Jews: like Jesus, the disciples shall be 'handed over' (*paradidōmi*) to representatives of the nations. No positive responses from the judges of the nations are anticipated, however (10:22).

established during Jesus's lifetime, and nothing is mentioned about them having to observe any part of the Torah, including the least of its commandments, such as the tithing of mint, dill, and cumin, which is required of Jesus's primary (Jewish) audience, the disciples and the crowds (cf. 5:19; 23:23).[93]

On the other side of the spectrum, we find an active proselytizing mission.[94] This type of mission is never portrayed in the Gospel itself, but only announced in the very last verses of the Gospel (28:18–20). The acceptance of proselytes by the movement as portrayed in the story—not all contemporary Jewish groups were in favor of such practices[95]—is indicated already in the genealogy with the mention of non-Jewish women who were most likely regarded as proselytes (1:3, 5),[96] and John's claim that God can raise children of Abraham out of stones (3:9). We have very little information about exactly how Matthean proselytizing mission was meant to be understood by the reader, but we do have some key details from the very last words we hear from the risen Jesus.

93. This pattern differs both from Paul's and Acts' approach to non-Jews. Paul's letters indicate, as the Matthean passages above, no specific Torah requirements for non-Jews, apart from a general command to love, counting that as the fulfillment of the law, but differs from Matthew in that non-Jews are regarded as members of the people of God after a form of conversion that does not imply circumcision. Acts requires non-Jewish believers in Jesus to keep a limited number of laws, not the full Torah, and counts them as part of the movement. Cf., e.g., Rom 13:8–10; Acts 15:13–29.

94. The existence of Jewish mission in the first century has been debated by scholars for some time (see the literature referred to above, p. 373n81). It seems to me, though, that such mission did indeed take place, in different ways; the problem has, to a significant degree, to do with how mission is defined. Cf. Paget, "Jewish Proselytism," 82, who points to the fact that some Jewish groups regarded non-Jews as "inherently wicked," a position, we may add, closely related to how Matthew's Gospel presents non-Jewish culture and behavior (cf. also Gal 2:15). Such an approach to non-Jews, Paget argues, "created a condition in which proselytism seems, in psychological terms, natural." Combined with the view, also expressed by several Jewish groups, that their religion was inherently superior, "the urge to proselytize becomes still more believable" (ibid.). The fact that both of these features, the negative view of non-Jews and the perspective that Judaism, in the form presented in the Gospel, is superior to non-Jewish life and worship, are explicitly present in Matthew, suggests that the mission referred to in Matt 28:18–20 should be understood as proselytizing mission. See further below.

95. This includes the later rabbis, among whom we find different opinions about proselytes, some welcoming them, others rejecting them (for references, see above, p. 371n78). The other major Israelite group at the time, the Samaritans, did not accept proselytes at all. Indeed, when visiting Mt Gerizim in 2010, I was told by a Samaritan priest that they had only very recently begun accepting proselytes into the group, mostly because they are so few (at the time, a total of only ca. 745 individuals) and the population was in a process of further decline. I am grateful to Gary Knoppers for discussion of this issue.

96. See above, pp. 370–72.

First, the mission must take place in the time period between Jesus's resurrection and the end of the age (*tēs synteleias tou aiōnos*), the latter expression referring to the time of the final judgment and the subsequent establishment of the kingdom. Second, the task is to "make disciples" (*mathēteuō*) of "all nations" (*panta ta ethnē*).[97] Third, the method to make disciples out of non-Jews is two-fold: to baptize them and to teach them "to obey/keep everything" that Jesus had commanded his own disciples (as represented in the previous narrative). Taken together, what does this mean in terms of the type of mission referred to here, and how does this affect the status of these non-Jews in relation to the Jewish people? In my view, the following unfolds as a likely first-century interpretive scenario.

First of all, it is clear that Matthew claims that something must change in the status of the non-Jews before the final judgment and the arrival of the kingdom. They cannot remain as they currently are. This change of status has not been indicated or required in any direct way earlier in the Gospel, which means that the Christ-fearers, as we have called them, cannot now remain in their current status; the narrative progression describes a development of thought on this issue, based on the new situation that has occurred after the resurrection (28:18). Matthew is here, for the first time, indicating a ritual, baptism, as a necessary component of a status change that all non-Jews need to go through as a preparation for the final judgment.

There has been a lot of discussion and debate about whether circumcision is also to be understood to be part of this ritual transition. We have already discussed this issue above.[98] While it seems to me very likely that circumcision is meant to be understood as part of

97. This expression excludes the Jewish people in Matthew, and refers only to nations other than the Jews. This does not, however, mean that the mission to the Jewish people, from a Matthean perspective, is cancelled, as some interpreters have claimed. This is clear both from the role of the crowds in the Gospel, among whom the disciples will continue to work after Jesus's death and resurrection, as well as references to the suffering this work will entail for the disciples in synagogue settings (e.g., 10:23; 23:34). What we see here is not a replacement of the people missionized, but an expansion of the people reached. This expansion of the ethnic focus, however, requires a change in the way mission is approached in the case of the non-Jews, as we shall see below.

98. See Introduction, pp. 31–36.

the requirement, the argument being made here is not dependent on this being the case. The reference to the second requirement, the teaching, is crystal clear with regard to the implications of the ritual of transition for non-Jews who are preparing for the kingdom: to be taught to keep everything Jesus has taught his own disciples during his time of proclamation in the land means to live fully as a Jew, keeping the Jewish law as it was originally meant to be kept, including every single detail, moral as well as ritual.[99] It is simply extremely unlikely that Matthew's Jesus would not have been understood by his earliest readers as requiring circumcision by those males who wanted to live according to the principles of this text. Still, for the sake of the argument, even if we were to assume that Matthew for some reason did not see circumcision as part of the details of the law that must be kept—disregarding for a moment that the lighter aspects of the law, such as the tithing of mint, dill, and cumin (23:23), would then have to be considered more important, and "heavier" commandments than circumcision, and that Matthew found no reason why his Jesus would have to explain and justify such a reversal of the weighting of the commandments to his audience—*the ritual effect of baptism would still be identical to the ritual effect that circumcision would have had, namely to make non-Jews Jews.*

With full teaching of Torah, which 28:20 clearly refers to, but without such a ritual—be it baptism or circumcision or both—follows, inescapably, what Christian scholars often refer to as "works righteousness." The law can only be understood, or function, within a covenant context, which offers the necessary means of atonement, as we have discussed above.[100] If such means of atonement are not available within the covenant, righteousness, which Matthew requires of all who wish to enter the kingdom, is impossible, since no one is without sin, measured from the standards established by the Gospel.[101] The righteous person is the one who keeps the law and atones for

---

99. Note especially 5:17–19, exemplified in other parts of the Gospel, including Matthew 5–7; 15:1–20; 18:15–35; 19:17–19; 23:16–23.
100. See chapter 2.8.
101. Cf. Matt 19:26.

his or her sins; without the covenant frame embedding the law, such atonement is unavailable.

This is why the covenant must be renewed after God abandons the temple (before its destruction), and this is why Jesus has to die—to provide the people with a means of atonement in place of the defiled temple so that they would not perish. This theologizing of Jesus's death is ritualized and concretized in what in later Christian tradition has become known as the Eucharist, or the Last Supper, which makes real for its participants the atonement brought about by Jesus's sacrificial death. Thus, those who remain within the renewed covenant will be saved from their sins (1:21). In sum, in a text which maintains the full validity of the Torah, with everything that that implies, and requires obedience of all who want to achieve salvific righteousness, atonement cannot be made available outside the Jewish people's covenant with the God of Israel.[102] Therefore, if there is any interest in Matthew in saving people who do not belong to this covenant between Israel and the God of Israel,[103] it would seem inevitable that the aim and method of a mission to non-Jews must change once Jesus's Messianic task has been accomplished and the covenant has been restored. The question is, now, whether we find indications in the Gospel of a transition from the approach of passive ethno-ethic mission to active proselytizing mission.

While we do not have much to go on, there are a few passages that may shed light on such dynamics of mission in Matthew. First, we have Jesus referring five times, in two specific settings, to the name of Jonah, as he speaks of the sign of Jonah as the only sign that will be given to those who ask for signs, i.e., to Pharisees, regardless of whether

---

102. This is one of the key theological problems that Paul tries to solve in his letters to non-Jewish Christ-believers. His problem was thus much the same as Matthew's (and Acts'), but his solution was quite different. Cf., e.g., Gal 5:3; Rom 4:1–25; 6:1–7:25. The very fact that Paul has to argue his case in most of his letters, and that Acts must present a solution authorized by the highest authorities in the movement (Acts 15:1–35; 21:17–26), shows that there was no single understanding of the place of the non-Jew in relation to the Jewish people within the Jesus movement in the first century. Matthew's position is closest to the one referred to in Acts 15:1, 5.

103. It is notable that the nations are, with the exception of a few individual members among them, portrayed as enemies. While several Jewish texts in or around the first century envisions the destruction of their enemies (e.g., 1QM 6.6; 11.13–18), Matthew departs from this pattern in that it aims at saving them, as indicated by the proselytizing mission described in Matt 28:18–20.

they come with their scribes or with Sadducees.[104] The sign of Jonah is usually interpreted as having two components to it: a reference to Jesus's death (and resurrection) as well as a reference to mission carried out among non-Jews. In my view, those two belong together and one of these aspects should not be emphasized at the expense of the other.

With Jesus's death and resurrection something changes in how the world works, based on Jesus having been given all power in heaven and on earth as a result of his (voluntary) death and God's (cosmic) triumph (cf. 4:8–10).[105] This shift in reality is directly linked in 28:18–20 to an active proselytizing mission to the nations. When the Matthean Jesus refers to the sign of Jonah, the same connection is most likely made. Here, however, we need to note that while Jonah is an example of an active mission to non-Jews, the type of mission described in the biblical book bearing his name is of the ethno-ethic type, and not the active proselyte mission that Matthew 28 envisions. It is possible that Matthew focused more on the active form of mission to non-Jews at this point, though, using the traditions he had available to him, than on the specific type of mission. After all, the big shift in Matthew is from a centripetal (passive) mission dynamic to a centrifugal force sent out from Galilee. In any case, the sign-of-Jonah references provide a bridge over to a shift in missionary strategy.

The second passage of importance here is 8:11, where Jesus predicts, as a consequence of the centurion's extraordinary trust/loyalty, which exceeds even that of his own disciples, that "many will come from east and west and will eat with Abraham and Isaac and Jacob in the kingdom of heaven." The kingdom banquet is to be attended by the key

---

104. Matt 12:38–41; 16:4.

105. At his resurrection, Jesus seems to go through a form of deification, in which his powers are portrayed as on par with God's, although the highest authority is still thought of as belonging with God since God is the one who bestows the power to Jesus. The process of such deification is similar to, but goes beyond, the deification of Moses as presented by Philo in *Mos.* 2.288, as is seen in the description of the consequences of the powers given to him. (For the view that Moses's deification is indeed meant by Philo not as mere metaphor here, but as an ontological claim, see M. David Litwa, "The Deification of Moses in Philo of Alexandria," in *Studia Philonica Annual: Studies in Hellenistic Judaism*, vol. 26 (edited by David T. Runia and Gregory E. Sterling; Atlanta: Society of Biblical Literature, 2014), 1–27.

covenant figures in Israel's history, Abraham, Isaac and Jacob—these figures in fact define the nature of the banquet—and to this banquet there will be non-Jews coming.[106] We may ask, though, how these non-Jews will arrive there, and what kind of mission it is that has preceded their arrival.

We have to pay attention here to the difference in narrative time between the centurion (Jesus's own time) and the eschatological banquet. The latter will take place after Jesus's death and resurrection, and after the proselytizing mission has been carried out by the disciples to all the nations. Thus, what we see is that the centripetal force of Jesus's active inward mission among his own people is understood as a signal that, after his resurrection, this mission will be expanded and turned into a centrifugal force, an equally active proselytizing mission to convert the nations to the God of Israel.[107] Understanding this saying of Jesus within the parameters set up by the narrative chronology thus requires us to interpret these people coming from the east and west as proselytes, as former non-Jews who have turned to the God of Israel seeking refuge as the final judgment approaches.

This interpretation is further supported by another passage about the eschatological banquet: the parable of the wedding banquet (22:1–14).[108] Again, Jesus is speaking of a situation that narratively will postdate his resurrection (the wedding banquet of the king's son), and thus, it also postdates his command to his disciples to actively missionize the nations (cf. 22:9–10). While those who were originally invited (in 22:1–14, this means primarily the Pharisees; cf. 22:15; 5:20;

---

106. There have been some attempts at interpreting this passage as referring to Diaspora Jews rather than non-Jews. While there is, in Matthew, a latent expectation that Diaspora Jews must be reached (cf. Matt 10:18; 24:14), in this specific rhetorical setting the focus is on non-Jews. This does not mean, however, that there has been a transferal of sorts, so that non-Jews now replace Jews in the "ingathering" of people at the end of time. Rather, as is clear from other Matthean passages, non-Jews are now to be added to the Jews who are destined for the kingdom. See, e.g., Nolland, *Matthew*, 357. The question we are concerned with here and in the following chapters is when, how, and on the basis of what criteria this will happen.

107. Cf. Isa 56:1–8. There are several texts in the prophetic literature, not to mention the Psalms, speaking about non-Jews coming to Jerusalem in a similar way; see, e.g., Isa 2:2–3; 25:6–8; Mic 4:1–4; Zech 2:11 [Heb 2:15]; 8:20–23. Cf. Ps 87:4.

108. See discussion of this parable above, pp. 183–89.

23:2, 33) are thrown out into the darkness (8:12; 22:13), others are invited (i.e., actively missionized). The people at the banquet have to wear the right clothes, i.e., they have to be clothed in righteousness, which, in Matthew, is defined in terms of Torah observance. Again, within the narrative chronology set up by the author, this suggests an interpretation in which those present represent people from the lost sheep of the house of Israel as well as of proselytes that have joined them. Those among them who do not live up to the Torah standards set by the Gospel will, however, lose their place in the kingdom.[109] Since Torah observance requires a covenant setting within which the means of atonement are also provided, this suggests an interpretation where Matthew envisions a situation which has been preceded by proselytizing mission, where non-Jews have been instructed in Torah.

Finally, 24:14 provides us with ambiguous wording that can be variously interpreted. Narratively, we are here experiencing the time between the resurrection and the end, which is the time of the great suffering. This should lead us to see this verse as, in some way, reflecting the reality of the proselyte mission mentioned in 28:18–20.[110] However, the wording, especially when noting how Matthew changed his source, Mark 13:10,[111] may suggest that the mission is primarily to the Jewish people (in the Diaspora); only when that inner-Jewish mission is carried out, will it be "a testimony" (martyrion) to the nations that the end is coming. If this is correct, the passage would be an example of an active inward mission, resulting in a (passive) testimony to the nations, which may lead some of them to convert and become proselytes.[112] While the overwhelming majority of commentators have

---

109. This is consistent with the overall presentation of the salvific efficacy of the Torah in Matthew, within the covenant. See, e.g., Matt 5:17–20; 7:21–23; 13:41–43; 19:17; 23:23.

110. For discussion of the relationship between Matt 24 and 28:16–20, see Vicky Balabanski, "Mission in Matthew Against the Horizon of Matthew 24," NTS 54 (2008): 161–75.

111. Virtually all scholars agree that Matt 24:14 copies and rewrites Mark 13:10, but few discuss in which way Matthew's alterations of Mark may signal a change in meaning. Mark 13:10 is quite clear with regard to the object of the active mission described: The gospel must be proclaimed "to," or "for" (eis) "all the nations" (panta ta ethnē). Matthew 24:14, however, changes Mark's sentence so that this clarity is avoided. For Matthew, the Gospel will be proclaimed "in," or "throughout" (en) the entire (inhabited) world (en holē tē oikoumenē). Matthew thus cancels any direct relationship between the proclamation and non-Jewish nations. Only indirectly will this proclamation be a "witness" (martyrion) to all the nations.

ignored this interpretive option, and assumed that Matthew is here basically replicating the message of Mark 13:10,[113] there are, thus, several reasons why we should rethink the assumptions that have led to this conclusion.

It seems reasonable to suggest, then, that Matthew's Jesus is here avoiding the question of an active mission to non-Jews, saving this novelty for the paradigmatic claim in 28:18–20. Further support for this interpretation is found in 10:18, where Jesus speaks of the same time period, and where the active inward mission is explicitly confirmed (10:5–6); it is said here, also, that this inward mission will be a sign for both Jewish rulers and the non-Jews (*eis martyrion autois* [i.e., Jewish rulers] *kai tois ethnēsin*). In Matthew 10, however, the *geographical* extent of this mission is limited to the land of Israel (10:23).

Matthew 24:14 thus differs from the earlier mission command in that it describes an expansion of the inward mission to cover the entire world, which is precisely what the Pharisees have just been accused of being involved in: engaging in mission on a global scale (23:15). Such a scenario matches well Matthew's critique of Pharisees more generally: Jesus's followers and the Pharisees are often said to be keeping the same halakhah, which forces Matthew to claim that the Pharisees are "hypocrites" since they are said to be observing these commandments for the wrong reasons, not being capable of balancing the weightier commandments against the lighter in the right way.[114] In 24:14,

---

112. The thought pattern is somewhat similar to that found in the Sermon on the Mount, but here applied on a global scale and within a setting implying conversion; cf. Matt 5:14–16.

113. See, e.g., Luz, *Matthew*, 3.194–95 (cf. 183–85); Davies and Allison, *Matthew*, 3.344 (explicitly rejecting the option of a mission to Diaspora Jews); France, *Matthew*, 908; Witherington, *Matthew*, 446; Carter, *Matthew and the Margins*, 472 (referring to Matthew 10 but not noticing that this chapter describes mission to Jews only; Schnackenburg, *Matthew*, 239 does the same); Talbert, *Matthew*, 267; Evans, *Matthew*, 404–5. See also, Balabanski, "Mission in Matthew," who understands mission to be directly related to non-Jews in this chapter: both Matthew 24 and Matt 28:16–20 "are concerned with the mission to the nations and the close of the age" (175). While I would certainly agree that the end of the age is tied in Matthew to the worldwide proclamation of the kingdom (so also Overman, *Church and Community in Crisis*, 332–33, who notes that Matthew is the only Gospel which does this), closer attention to the definition of "mission" will add nuance to such claims.

114. Cf., e.g., Matt 12:1–7; 23:5–6, 23. To be sure, there are also instances where Jesus's halakhah differs from that of the Pharisees (e.g., 15:1–20; 23:16–22; the latter of these passages, however, has a lot to do with finding the right balance between what is holier, and therefore, is also a matter of finding the right balance).

Matthew's Jesus is countering their global attempts at generating a following.[115]

The location of 24:14 in the narrative, after 10:18 and before 28:18–20, and the fact that all three passages speak of the same narrative time, after the resurrection and before the end,[116] creates some tension in terms of what type of mission is envisioned here. Perhaps this is an attempt by Matthew to reconcile different traditions about the earliest mission of Jesus and the disciples and later developments among Christ-believers (such as Paul). The reference to non-Jews in a setting which speaks of mission to Jews only in the land of Israel (10:18) and globally (24:14) opens up for the further step of activating a mission explicitly targeting the nations in 28:18–20.[117] Such a scenario may be further supported by the reference to a prophecy by Isaiah in Matt 12:18, 21, in which justice as the basis of judgment is to

---

115. There has been some debate about whether Matt 23:15 is about Pharisaic proselytizing mission, or if it is an expression of a Jewish inward mission aiming at the Jewish people only. For example, Salo W. Baron, *A Social and Religious History of the Jews*, vol. 1 (New York: Columbia University Press, 1952), 173, understands this passage as reflecting historical realities, since the phenomenon of peripatetic preachers and philosophers were not uncommon in antiquity; it would be natural to assume that there were Jews, also, involved in such activities. However, he adds: "there is not the slightest evidence that Pharisaic leaders ever made an *organized attempt* to spread Judaism among the nations, but [...] they did not discourage individual efforts" (my emphasis). Lois H. Feldman, *Jew and Gentile in the Ancient World: Attitudes and Interactions From Alexander to Justinian* (Princeton: Princeton University Press, 1993), 298, 332, interprets the Pharisees in a similar way. "To be credible," Feldman argues, "polemic, like satire, must be based on reality" (298). Goodman, *Mission and Conversion*, 69–70, argues that *prosēlytos* refers, in Matt 23:15, to a Jewish person who joins the Pharisaic group, i.e., what we would call inward mission. McKnight, *Light Among the Gentiles*, 106–7, advances the argument that what we see referenced in Matthew are Pharisaic attempts at converting so-called god-fearers, i.e., persuading non-Jews sympathetic to Judaism to take the next step and go through full conversion, including, for males, circumcision. For support, he refers to the story about the conversion of Izates, and how a certain Eleazar from Galilee persuades Izates, who was sympathetic to Judaism, but had not converted, to go through circumcision (Josephus, *AJ* 20.38–48). Paul, the Pharisee, had also been involved in similar activities among non-Jews, if Gal 5:11 is read as referring to his life before the Damascus experience.
116. Cf. Hagner, *Matthew*, 2.694.
117. Such a process is, in fact, what Acts is describing Paul to be involved in: mission in synagogues, in which non-Jews are also present, thus being exposed to the same message. In Acts, however, the solution to the gentile problem is not that they become proselytes, but that they keep a minimum of four commandments. As we have noted above, Matthew seems indeed to share the views of those Pharisaic believers in Jesus, which Acts describes as enemies of Paul and the Jerusalem leaders (Acts 15:1, 5). On tensions between Matthew and Jerusalem (and the Jerusalem leaders of the Jesus movement), see further Anders Runesson, "City of God or Home of Traitors and Killers? Jerusalem According to Matthew," in *Cities of God? An Interdisciplinary Assessment of Early Christian Engagement with the Ancient Urban Environment(s)* (edited by Steve Walton, David Gill, and Paul Trebilco; Grand Rapids: Eerdmans, 2016; forthcoming).

be proclaimed to the nations, a process that is said to give them hope. Since divine judgment and justice are based on the Torah in Matthew, the mission envisioned in this prophetic quote should be seen in the context of an active proselytizing mission, aiming, as 28:18–20, at the conversion of the nations to worship of the God of Israel within the covenant established between God and his people.

The impression created by these three passages when they are read within the chronological parameters set up by the author, which guide the interpretation of the narrative as a whole, is of an expansion of a pre-resurrection inward mission to the Jewish people in the land only, with indirect consequences for some non-Jews, to a post-resurrection global active mission to both Jews and non-Jews.[118]

In sum, then, we find an overall shift in missionary strategy in Matthew as the narrative develops toward its climax. While Jesus's activities among his own people triggers a pattern similar to eschatological pilgrimage traditions, portraying some, but not all, non-Jewish individuals as loyal to the Jewish Messiah and seeking the blessings of the kingdom without converting, this type of indirect, passive ethno-ethic mission to non-Jews is replaced by a new form of mission in the last verses of the Gospel. Once Jesus has been given all authority in heaven and on earth, the disciples must expand their efforts to make disciples of all nations, which entails the latters' conversion to the form of Judaism proclaimed and taught by the Matthean Jesus. One could perhaps say that the triggering of the eschatological pilgrimage pattern prepares a setting in which non-Jewish individuals can be brought to conversion, once Jesus has expanded his cosmic powerbase and extended his claim to involve all nations.[119]

---

118. Contra Lloyd Gaston, "The Messiah of Israel as Teacher of the Gentiles," *Interpretation* 29:1 (1975), 24–40, who claims that "the Church is no longer engaged in a mission to Israel" (33). Gaston builds his interpretation too much on a specific reading of the pattern of Luke – Acts in which the mission to non-Jews is dependent on the mission to the Jews having failed. While one may certainly see and understand the use of such an overall theological idea in the later church, this mode of thinking is foreign to, and directly contradicted by, Matthew's story of Israel and the nations.

119. Such a paradigm for the story would match well a socio-institutional setting in which non-Jewish God-fearers were present among Jews, i.e., a synagogue setting. As Acts describe the mission of

While mission strategies will tell us a lot about how divine judgment and salvation are construed, there are, in Matthew, passages which speak of salvation and condemnation as applied to non-Jews beyond such missionary discourses, and which are not the result of any missionary efforts. We shall deal with these below in chapter 7. Before doing so, however, we need to say a few words about when Matthew envisions non-Jews to be judged; timing, too, will tell us something about the status of non-Jews in this Gospel.

Paul and others, missionary activities almost exclusively take place in such synagogue settings, where people who are not Jewish are also affected by the message proclaimed. From a socio-historical perspective, Matthew would thus be arguing that such Christ-fearers, who are loyal to Jesus, but have not converted, should be instructed in the Torah and convert fully to the messianic form of Judaism proclaimed in the Gospel. Such a claim would be similar to the approach that Paul condemns in Galatians, attacking such missionaries directly in Gal 5:12; it would also be similar to the standpoint of the Messianic Pharisees of Acts 15:1, 5. Indeed, it seems to me that the Gospel of Matthew in fact may preserve in some detail a variant of the stance that characterizes Paul's opponents, and so give voice to the voiceless in Paul's letters. From a canonical and theological perspective, this should, in my view, inspire a more critical view not to Paul but to the way in which he speaks about those who do not share his convictions. At the very least, it should cause theologians to pause and reflect deeper before uncritically adopting and perpetuating attitudes that do not constructively engage the rather profound diversity of ritual and theological praxis that exists even within the canon itself.

6

When Will Israel's God Judge the Nations?

As we have seen above, Matthew's Gospel is working with an overall idea of divine judgment, applied to the Jewish people, as taking place in this world, at the final judgment, and, as a result of the final judgment, in the world to come.[1] Are we to assume that the same is the case for non-Jews in the Gospel? We have very few passages to work with here that would help us answer this question, but there are a few hints that, when categorized according to certain definitions of what judgment means, will shed light on this issue.[2]

If we understand Jesus's activities as they are expressed in healings and exorcisms as being part of God's judgment, condemning demons and evil powers, and saving the people who have been oppressed by them, we must conclude that some non-Jews, just as individuals within the Jewish people, are judged (favorably) already in this world (8:5–13; 15:21–28).[3] In addition to such saving activities, we have one passage that speaks of God's punishment of non-Jews carried out in this world,

1. See chapter 1.
2. The lack of material shows, in and of itself, that Matthew's main concern lies not with non-Jews, but with Jews and Judaism.
3. While such a reading may be reasonable from a certain perspective, Jesus's dealings with demons may also be understood more along the lines of cosmic warfare enacted on earth.

namely, in the form of the destruction of Sodom, as described in the Hebrew Bible and referred to in Matt 11:23.

This, however, does not mean that those who have been judged in the past will not be judged again, positively or negatively, in the final judgment. Indeed, with the nations as with the Jewish people, divine justice will primarily be administered in the final judgment at the end of the age. In 11:21–24 and 12:41–42, this focus on the final judgment, also hinted at in 12:18, 21, is construed so that non-Jews are used rhetorically in order to shame those Jews who have not repented. Interestingly, this tactic of shaming results in a comparative perspective that negotiates and relativizes the otherwise absolute outcomes of the final judgment: condemnation or salvation. In 11:22 and 24, we find that, while Tyre, Sidon, and Sodom will be judged, they will receive a verdict that is said to be less harsh than those of Chorazin, Bethsaida, and Capernaum. It may be that one should simply understand this as a result of the comparative rhetorical strategy, but the fact remains that these cities, symbols of evil, are said to be treated less harshly than other cities in the final judgment. One may therefore assume that there are options beyond the either/or in terms of condemnation and salvation for non-Jews as much as for Jews.[4] If so, these passages would give expression to the same idea about judgment that we have seen above with regard to the Jewish people, namely, that

---

4. The thought pattern behind this type of theology may well be related to the idea, present also in other forms of Judaism, including rabbinic Judaism (e.g., *Sifre Deut.* 307 on 32:4; *t. Pe'ah* 1:2–3), that judgment executed in history will pay off some of the guilt, the "debt," as it were, accumulated by certain sins, thus mitigating the outcome of the final verdict. Cf. 2 Macc 6:12–16. Here, the author understands punishment of Jews in history as a sign of mercy, since such punishment will prevent the people from fulfilling their measure of sins and be severely punished in a final act of judgment. For the nations, however, the procedure is the reverse: lack of punishment in history will result in condemnation when their sins have reached their height. Matthew, thus, seems to share a basic pattern of thought with 2 Maccabees, but applies it equally, in this case, to non-Jews as well as to Jews. This results in a theology of judgment that allows for the presence of non-Jews in the world to come, along the lines of a major interpretive trajectory also found in Tannaitic literature, a theology of the other that has become mainstream in Jewish thought ever since, as also noted by Svante Lundgren, *Particularism and Universalism in Modern Jewish Thought* (Binghamton: Global Publications, 2001), 30; see, e.g., *t. Sanh.* 13:2; cf. *Sifre Num.* 88 on 11:6–7 and cf. Benno Przybylski, *Righteousness in Matthew and his World of Thought* (Cambridge: Cambridge University Press, 1980), 48–49. On sin as debt, see the recent comprehensive study of Nathan Eubank, *Wages of Cross-Bearing*.

the result of the final judgment may imply punishment or reward in the world to come, even for non-Jews.[5]

With regard to the final judgment, we also have to ask whether the same idea is present in Matthew that we also see in some other contemporary Jewish texts, namely, that there are to be two judgment proceedings: one for Jews, and, after that process has been completed, one for non-Jews.[6] Based on Matt 25:31–46, the interpretation of which we shall return to in chapter 7.3, this seems to me to be the case; this final judgment scene is concerned with the nations only, excluding the Jewish people. This, however, does not mean that there is no final judgment for the Jewish people, of course, as we have also argued at some length in Part I of this study (cf. 24:31; 19:28). This dividing of the final judgment between the Jewish people, on the one hand, and the nations, on the other, in Matthew, has to do with how the narrative is structured; the status of non-Jewish Christ-fearers, as we have called them, changes as the story progresses, so that in the narrative time after 28:18–20 (i.e., between the resurrection and the final judgment) they should convert fully and keep the entire Torah in accordance with Jesus teaching. This will make them, for all intents and purposes, Jewish believers in Jesus, and they will, as proselytes, therefore be judged along with the rest of the Jewish people, just as the disciples will be. But this process does not cover all individuals among the nations, and Matthew has included, alone among the Gospels, the so-called parable of the sheep and the goats to deal with those who do not belong; they too will be judged in the final judgment, but after the judgment of Israel has taken place.

In sum, based on the few passages in Matthew that shed light on the

---

5. Cf. above, chapter 1.
6. In several Jewish texts, the difference between the Jewish people and the nations in terms of timing is that the Jewish people, including Jesus's followers and proselytes, will be judged first. Then, as in some other contemporary Jewish traditions, with some variation (cf., e.g., *T. Benj.* 10:8–10; *1 En.* 91:12–16; 4 Ezra 12:31–34; *T. Abr.* 13:1–8), there will be a second judgment following immediately after the first, which concerns only the nations (Matt 25:31–46). (The pattern is somewhat similar to Paul's repeated insistence on "the Jew first, but also the Greek"; cf. Rom 1:16; 2:9–10.) Harrington, *Matthew*, 358–59, argues that Matthew divides the judgment into two events, based on the categories Jews and non-Jews. For Matthew, Jesus's followers belong within the Jewish people (there is no third category called "Christians") and are judged accordingly.

question of when the nations will be judged, we may conclude that, while we find a chronological pattern similar, but not identical to that applied to the Jewish people, the evidence is fragmentary. This is yet a further indication that Matthew's focus rests firmly on the Jewish people, and deals with non-Jews almost exclusively to make specific theological points about Israel. In the end, as Jesus's disciples are to launch the worldwide mission to make disciples of all nations, those who do convert will become disciples on the same conditions as those among the Jewish people who join the movement. This, in turn, means that they will receive the same treatment in the judgment as all other Jews, based on their keeping of Torah within the (restored) Mosaic covenant. Matthew's theologizing about non-Jews goes further than this, however, as we shall see below when we turn to the criteria of judgment that are applied to those who do not belong, as these are construed at various points in the narrative sequence of the Gospel.

7

The Criteria of Judgment for Those Who Do Not Belong

Based on the general portrayal of non-Jewish culture and the categorization of non-Jewish individuals and groups in Matthew, we are now in a position to address more directly the question of the criteria of judgment as they apply to the nations at different points in the narrative. We shall do this under three headings, responding to the categories we identified in chapter 5, beginning with the group we have called the Christ-fearers.

As we shall see, Jesus's death and resurrection proves to be a crucial key to unlock the meaning of Matthew's changing view of what the nations must do to be saved. After reluctantly allowing non-Jewish individuals a share of the blessings of the kingdom, without extending to them an invitation to join God's people as disciples, in the end, Jesus's post-resurrection position of unlimited cosmic and earthly power solves the "gentile problem" by inviting the nations into the Jewish people, where they can practice the Torah within the covenant. Thus, rather than removing Jewish identity markers and requirements for salvation in preparation for the kingdom, which in effect, would be turning Jews who want to be part of the world to come into non-Jews, Matthew's Jesus opens up the Mosaic covenant for non-Jews, allowing them entry as proselytes. The eschatological process is, thus, an ingathering of the nations to the people of God, not an expulsion of Jews, as Jews, from the kingdom.[1]

Still, there is some hope for those who never joined the movement, those who are not part of the people of God. Matthew would never have understood, even less accepted, Cyprian's famous dictum *extra ecclesiam nulla salus*,[2] and the reason for this is precisely his Jewish approach to matters of salvation.

7.1 Accepting the Rule of the Messiah in the Land: The Christ-Fearers

If we remove, for the time being, the last four verses of the Gospel (the post-resurrection setting) as well as the "parable" of the sheep and the goats (the eschatological final judgment on the nations immediately preceding the realization of the kingdom), and focus on what Matthew claims Jesus taught while he was walking the land which he calls Israel (excluding Samaria), we are in a position to reconstruct a rather coherent, but embryonic, set of criteria, which apply specifically to non-Jews as they appear: a) in Israel's holy scriptures, and b) in descriptions of encounters with Jesus himself, in the narrative here and now. There is nothing explicitly stated about non-Jews on these matters, but based on how they are treated and what is said about them, we may identify a basic pattern of thought that can be used to isolate the criteria that either allow or deny non-Jews access to the benefits that follow with the kingdom. It should be noted from the outset that we are here dealing with non-Jews who remain

---

1. The latter scenario is, however, what follows from a traditional Christian reading of Matthew, a type of reading which has been quite influential not only in the churches, but also in Matthean scholarship. In such readings, Jews can be part of salvation only if they leave behind their Jewish identity and Torah, i.e., if they, for all intents and purposes, cease to be Jews and adopt non-Jewish ways of being. A historical reading of Matthew unveils, in my opinion, a story arguing for the exact opposite process.
2. So also, Davies and Allison, *Matthew*, 3.423.

outsiders—i.e., they are not members of the people of God, and are thus, not part of the covenant between God and his people—but who relate to the Jewish people and Jesus in specific ways with specific results. What we are interested in are these encounters and their evaluation and outcomes in discourses that allude to, or explicitly deal with, the process of divine judgment.

The relevant passages can be divided into two basic groups of sayings, which in turn subdivides into two further groups. First, Matthew refers to examples from Israel's history in order to make his point. These examples reveal patterns of thought that the author applies to the narrative present, i.e., Jesus's own time. The sayings that are embedded in the narrative here and now constitute the second basic group. Each group of pronouncements then describes: a) "real" encounters between members and non-members of God's people, and b) potential (imagined) encounters. To the latter group belong rhetorical sayings, spoken to Jews, suggesting that *if* the miracles performed here *would have been* performed before the eyes of "the other," they *would have* understood and reacted differently than you are currently doing. We also have a few special cases concerning non-Jewish individuals and groups in the narrative present, such as Pilate, his wife, and groups of Roman soldiers, which require special attention; we shall save these for last, before we summarize our observations in a table that will provide an overview of Matthean criteria of judgment as they relate to Christ-fearers.

If we begin with the category consisting of examples from Israel's past, and focus first on encounters between Israelites and non-Israelites that the author understood as having occurred in history, the story of Jonah and the people of Nineveh provides us with some details of interest. For us, the important verse is Matt 12:41: "The people of Nineveh will rise up at the judgment with this generation and condemn it, because they repented at the proclamation of Jonah, and see, something greater than Jonah is here!" Assuming that the author knew the basics of the story of Jonah, the following can be said in terms of the criteria of judgment that he intends to signal to his audience.

There are two keywords in this verse: repentance and proclamation. The larger setting of the story of Jonah must be understood, namely, that the proclamation concerned the imminent destruction of Nineveh as a consequence of the evil ways[3] of the inhabitants of the city; the God of Israel has power over and is judging not only his own people, but also the cities of the nations (Jonah 1:2; 3:4). In light of later Christian theologies of salvation and their impact on the reception history of the biblical texts, both the Hebrew Bible and the New Testament, it may be of some importance to state the obvious here, since this applies both to Jonah and Matthew: the people of Nineveh are not judged because they are non-Israelites; they are condemned because they break or disregard fundamental principles of acceptable behavior that apply, in the author's mind, to the entire world, not only to Israel. Implied in such claims is that the standards of behavior that are revealed to God's people, in the Torah and/or through Israel's prophets, are valid also for, and must be followed by, non-Israelites; the whole world belongs, in the final analysis, to the God of Israel, as the Psalter and the prophets also repeatedly make clear, and evil cannot be tolerated wherever it occurs; after all, the claim is that Israel's God created the whole world.[4] Needless to say, such a perspective on divine rule and judgment does not, neither in Jonah nor in Matthew, in any way negotiate or remove the boundaries between the people of God and the rest of the world. Rather, the people of Israel—here in the form of one of its prophets—have a task to fulfill in relation to the world, whether they like it or not.[5]

Based on these basic observations regarding Israel's God's relationship to the world and the nations, we may conclude that the foundational principles of acceptable behavior as they are revealed to Israel constitute the criteria on which the nations will be judged; "evil"

---

3. The Book of Jonah does not define more closely what "evil" refers to, other than mentioning the "violence" (*hamas*) that "is in their hands" (Jonah 3:8).

4. See, e.g., Pss 24:1; 96:10. Cf. the judgment on the nations in the prophetic literature, such as, e.g., Amos 1:3–2:3; Isa 34:1–17, which implies Israel's God's global rule and right to act as judge beyond his own people. Such claims involving Israel's God's right to global rule are often related to statements about creation. We shall return to this theme when dealing with Matt 25:31–46.

5. Jonah 1:3; 4:1–3; cf. Isa 42:1, 5–6; Matt 5:14–16; 12:18, 21.

is, in other words, defined as the opposite of the proper values as they are stated in the Torah. Neither Jonah nor Matthew will give us further details regarding which specific values we are dealing with; the point is that "evil" has been committed, and God will punish whoever carries out such deeds.

What, then, will save non-Israelites, or non-Jews in Jesus's days, from destruction? The only answer we are given is: repentance. Why is repentance enough? Because, as Jonah says, disappointed that the city will be spared: the God of Israel is "a gracious God and merciful, slow to anger, and abounding in steadfast love, and ready to relent from punishing" (Jonah 4:2).[6] But for Matthew, the interpretive key lies in *why* they repented at all. The reason that they did repent was that they trusted that Jonah proclaimed what this powerful God was actually going to do (Jonah 3:5); they believed that this God had such power and that he had sent Jonah. The work of the Spirit of God through Jesus is then, in the form of a *qal va-homer* argument, compared to what God accomplished through Jonah. Matthew thus emphasizes that if already the Ninevites, who did not know anything about God's ways (Jonah 4:11), would trust in God's messenger and repent, how much more should not the Pharisees and the scribes associated with them (Matt 12:38), who have access to the Torah *and* encounter Jesus first-hand, understand that divine judgment in imminent, and so repent from their evil ways.[7]

From this verse (Matt 12:41), we learn, then, that the forerunners of the Christ-fearers, as they are presented by Matthew, are judged based on their behavior, as measured against the standards of the Torah and prophetic proclamation. Their salvation from condemnation and punishment, which is taking place in this world, depends on their willingness to listen to the prophets of Israel, their repentance and turn from evil, as well as on the fact that the God of Israel is merciful. Conversion is irrelevant to the process. For Matthew, the fact that the Ninevites trusted in God's messenger, repented, and changed their

---

6. Cf. Exod 34:6.
7. Regarding the interpretation of this passage as directed against the Pharisees, and the judgment on Pharisees, see above chapter 3.2.1.2.

evil ways not only saved their city, but will also have a positive effect for them in the final judgment. These "righteous gentiles" will have a share in the world to come, while the (unrepentant) Pharisees and scribes associated with them will not, based on their maltreatment and neglect of the Jewish people ("the crowds"/"the lost sheep of the house of Israel").

The above basic pattern of thought is repeated in other passages mentioning "the other" in Israel's history. Immediately after our Jonah reference, Matthew's Jesus turns to "The Queen of the South" (i.e., the Queen of Sheba):[8] "The queen of the South will rise up at the judgment with this generation and condemn it, because she came from the ends of the earth to listen to the wisdom of Solomon, and see, something greater than Solomon is here!" Here, we find that, contrary to the Ninevites, the Queen takes the initiative and travels to Israel's king Solomon to learn from his wisdom, which she realizes is from God.[9] Again, assuming that the author of Matthew is familiar with the story he is referring to, we may take into account a couple of basic points made in that story as we interpret its use in the Gospel. Importantly, the result of the Queen's meeting with Solomon is that she blesses Israel's God and acknowledges that God works through Solomon, that Solomon rules through God's power (1 Kgs 10:9 = 2 Chr 9:8). This insight and recognition of the rule of God through David's son, Solomon, and the fact that she listens to and learns from his wisdom, is enough to identify her as an example of acceptable behavior and claim her inclusion in the coming kingdom, which is implied in the verse.

Her actions are exemplary. Not only do they mirror what the so-called God-fearers were doing in Jesus's time, she does more than the Pharisees and the scribes associated with them manage to do as they encounter Jesus, despite the fact that the Pharisees should have been able to recognize that God's Spirit was at work in that which was happening around Jesus;[10] the works of the Spirit through Jesus were, after all, even more than what Solomon could achieve. The Queen's

---

8. 1 Kgs 10:1–13 (= 2 Chr 9:1–12); Matt 12:42.
9. The movement is thus, as in the case of the Magi, centripetal, not centrifugal as in the case of the Ninevites and in Matt 28:16–20.

understanding of God's ways and God's agents on earth and in Israel will, therefore, condemn the Pharisees in the last judgment.[11] There is no repentance involved here, since the Queen is described as doing all the right things and praising the God of Israel. She represents a "righteous gentile," and as such, she will be part of the coming kingdom. Again, conversion is irrelevant to this type of discourse, and the boundaries between the people of God and "the other" are not negotiated; salvation/condemnation are not correlated with ethno-religious boundaries.

Remaining within Israel's history, but moving on to a saying that deals with a potential, or imagined, encounter between non-Israelites and representatives of the people of God, we have, finally, the judgment on Sodom, together with Gomorrah, the ultimate symbol of unrighteousness,[12] as it is contrasted against the future fate of Capernaum (Matt 11:23–24). Since this case is, in the narrative, hypothetical, the evidence is indirect; nevertheless, the picture is clear. The criteria of judgment here can be compared with those outlined above as applied to the people of Nineveh. In the imagined scenario Matthew's Jesus invokes, he suggests that if the extraordinary deeds that he has done in Capernaum had been done in Sodom, the people of that city would have repented (as the Ninevites repented as a consequence of Jonah's proclamation), and the city (as Nineveh) would still be standing. Because Sodom did not have the privileged position of Capernaum, namely, to have been able to encounter first-hand the work of the Spirit through the Messiah, the final judgment on Sodom will be less harsh.[13] In other words, the example of Sodom supports the above list of criteria of judgment and salvation.

What is demanded of "the other," then, is the recognition[14] that the divine (Israel's God) is at work through Israel's representatives,

---

10. Matthew, after all, does place them on the Seat of Moses and as being in control of Torah (Matt 23:2).

11. Cf. Rom 2:27.

12. On Gomorrah, see Matt 10:15; cf. Deut 29:32; Isa 1:9; 3:9, 13:9; Jer 23:14; Lam 4:6; Ezek 16:48–50.

13. On divine judgment as dependent on a person's (or group's) ability to keep the law, based on factors beyond the person's control, see above chapter 2.2.1 and pp. 85–86. The leniency on Sodom in the final judgment expressed in Matthew echoes the prophecy in Ezek 16:53.

14. Such recognition is best thought of as an expression of *pistis*.

be they a prophet (divine voice), a king (divine wisdom and rule), or the Messiah himself (divine power, as indicated by extraordinary deeds); that he or she submits to the authority of Israel's leadership, which is divinely inspired; that he or she repents and lives according to the principles for acceptable behavior outlined in the Torah and/or through prophetic proclamation (repentance will evoke divine mercy and lead to various forms of deliverance in history or salvation at the final judgment, since Israel's God is "merciful, slow to anger, and abounding in steadfast love, and ready to relent from punishing"[15]).

If we proceed now to the other main category of sayings—which concerns encounters, narratively "real" or hypothetical and imagined, between Jesus and non-Jewish individuals and cities in the here and now of the story—not surprisingly, a very similar pattern unfolds so that Israel's past and present emerge as ideologically and theologically intertwined, based on the continuous work of the divine (the Spirit) in God's representatives on earth (prophet, king, and Messiah).

Jesus is still a child when the first encounter takes place as the Magi from the east arrive in Bethlehem to prostrate (*proskyneō*; 2:2, 11) before and pay tribute to him as loyal subjects would. While the passage describes the ideal behavior of the "other," just as the example with the Queen of the South does, there is nothing explicit here about criteria of judgment. It is clear, however, that Matthew wants his readers to understand that the subordination of the nations under the legitimate Jewish king is required as the kingdom of heaven takes form. The same basic approach to Christ-fearers is taken in the stories about the centurion in 8:5–13 and the Canaanite woman in 15:21–28. In order to receive a share of the blessings of the kingdom, non-Jews must subordinate themselves to the Jewish Messiah; this is shown quite explicitly by how these non-Jews, a Roman and a Canaanite, argue to get what they want (8:8–9; 15:27). In all three cases, the interpretive key lies in the fact that these non-Jews recognize the work of the divine in that which Jesus does; in the case of the centurion and the Canaanite woman, this is said to be expressed in *pistis*, i.e., the form of trust that

15. Jonah 4:2.

merges with loyalty, the result of which is the defeat of demons that cause illness.

Pistis, loyalty, and subordination thus go hand in hand as these non-Jews display proper behavior in their encounters with Jesus, behavior that will affect their standing in the eyes of the God of Israel. While the centurion and the Canaanite woman experience the result of God's warfare against evil demons in the here and now, only in relation to the centurion is the final judgment brought up (8:11). We have already dealt with how this passage plays out in terms of judgment on the Jewish people and shall not repeat here those conclusions.[16] Through the story about the centurion, however, it becomes clear that Matthew envisions *pistis* and subordination to the Messiah to have a positive effect not only in this world, but also, in the final judgment. Since the same characteristics are mentioned in relation to the Canaanite woman, there is no reason to understand the latter passage as not also being a carrier for the same theology of the last judgment, and we may generalize this thought pattern to apply to the Magi too. Just as in the cases of the Ninevites and the Queen of the South, these three stories are examples of "righteous gentiles," i.e., non-Jews who will be included among those who enter the coming kingdom, based on the fact that they recognize the divine, i.e., the Spirit,[17] in that which Jesus does, and act accordingly.

If we proceed to sayings that build on hypothetical reactions in non-Jewish settings in the narrative here and now, we find references to two cities, Tyre and Sidon (11:21–22). The argument is of the same type as we have noted above for the Sodom and Gomorrah sayings, and the rhetorical point of departure is an assumed agreement between author and audience that the contemporary cities in question were particularly sinful. Again, a *qal va-homer*: if already these sinful non-Jewish cities would have repented if they had encountered the

---

16. See above, chapter 5.2.2.
17. For Matthew, all that Jesus does is to channel the power of the Spirit of God as he defeats the demons on earth; cf. Matt 12:28. While Jesus has extraordinary abilities due to his extraordinary birth (through the Spirit; Matt 1:18), the Spirit can also be channeled through his disciples (Matt 10:1).

extraordinary deeds that Jesus had performed in Chorazin and Bethsaida, how much more should not these Jewish cities have repented, which had had the privilege to experience the work of the Spirit through Jesus first-hand? As in the case of Sodom, certain criteria of judgment for non-Jews are revealed, implicitly, in this statement: (Hypothetically assumed) recognition of God's power as active in Jesus's deeds, which leads to repentance and change in way of life to conform with the principles of behavior laid down in the Torah, as Jesus interprets it. Again, subordination to the Jewish Messiah as having authority also over them as non-Jewish cities is implied.

Overall, we may conclude that regardless of whether the Christ-fearers or their forerunners are located in Matthew's ideal land of Israel (the centurion; the Canaanite woman, Sodom, Gomorrah, [Tyre, Sidon][18]), or outside (the Queen of the South, the Magi, the Ninevites), in order to have a share in the blessings of the kingdom and/or be saved in the final judgment, they must, as non-Jews, accept subordination under the Jewish Messiah. The image that emerges is that of an empire, in which all provinces, as well as all resident aliens, must pledge loyalty to the emperor and the god through whose power he rules. As we shall see below, this image of empire is confirmed and developed further in the post-Easter "Great Commission" (28:18–20). Here, we may note, additionally, that the importance of recognizing the work of the Spirit in that which happens around Jesus is something that brings together Jews and non-Jews in a common criterion of judgment. Sin against the Holy Spirit is precisely the rejection of such a claim about the Spirit, and for this sin, there is no forgiveness either in this world or the next (12:28, 31–33). The saying about sin against the Holy Spirit is part of Jesus's critique of the Pharisees (12:24), but it is quite clear that this sentiment lies behind Matthew's view of

---

18. The inclusion of Tyre and Sidon here is based on Ezekiel's vision of the restored territory of the twelve tribes (Ezek 47:13–48:35; cf. Anson F. Rainey and R. Steven Notley, *The Sacred Bridge: Carta's Atlas of the Biblical World* [Jerusalem: Carta, 2006] 269), on the assumption that Matthew, who speaks of a restored land precisely referring to the twelve tribes (Matt 10:1–4; 19:28), and who has likely based his general description of Jesus's task on Ezekiel (cf., e.g., Ezekiel 34; Matt 2:6; 9:36; 10:6; and Baxter, *Israel's Only Shepherd*, 163), nurtures a similar eschatological vision. David's and Salomon's (historical) kingdoms never included any of the two cities, their north-western boundaries ending just south of Tyre.

non-Jews too; while critique of Jesus is judged less harshly and will be forgiven, those who do not accept that the Spirit is ultimately the active force behind Jesus's healings and exorcisms, and thus, the power establishing the kingdom, be they Jew or non-Jew, will have no chance of surviving the final judgment.

Before proceeding to the problem of proselytes and conversion as these phenomena relate to criteria of judgment in Matthew, we need to say a few words on the judgment on non-Jews as they appear in the passion narrative. The following characters are of importance, especially in light of how they have been dealt with in later Christian interpretation: Pilate (27:11–26), Pilate's wife (27:19), the Roman soldiers who carry out the torture and execution of Jesus (27:27–36), and the Roman centurion who is present at the cross as Jesus dies (27:54).

While the Roman soldiers who tortured and executed Jesus have never filled a positive role in Christian tradition, Pilate and his wife have both been understood not only as converts to Christianity, but even as saints.[19] The Roman centurion at the cross has met a similar fate, as he, under the name Longinus, was turned into a convert and martyr in Christian tradition, thus attaining sainthood too. For Luz, such traditional Christian interpretations of the centurion's reaction to the crucifixion, which are closely related to Luke's version of the story (Luke 23:47), are not far from the historical intention of Matthew.[20] But is this a reasonable interpretation of Matthew's narrative, in light of

---

19. Both Pilate and his wife, the latter to whom tradition has given the name Claudia Procula, came to be regarded as converts to Christianity and were made saints in several branches of Christianity, for example, in the Abyssinian (Ethiopian) and Coptic Churches. Already Origen suggested in his commentary on Matthew that Pilate's wife is "saved" and "blessed" (*Comm. ser. Matt.* 122). In *Acts of Pilate* (= Gospel of Nicodemus; ca. 5th/6th century), Pilate's wife is a "fearer of God," one who observed some of the Jewish customs (2.1; cf. 11.2). Cf. Luz, *Matthew*, 3.499. On the anti-Semitism that has followed in the footsteps of Christian portrayals of Pilate, see Colum Hourihane, *Pontius Pilate, Anti-Semitism, and the Passion in Medieval Art* (Princeton: Princeton University Press, 2009); cf. Helen K. Bond, *Pontius Pilate in History and Interpretation* (Cambridge: Cambridge University Press, 1998). The posthumous career of Pilate in Christian imagination is all the more astonishing when one considers how he was portrayed by other Jewish authors contemporary with Jesus and the Gospels: Philo, *Legat.* 299–305; Josephus, *B.J.* 2.169–77; *A.J.* 18.35, 55–62, 85–89. (The only non-Jewish literary source mentioning Pilate is Tacitus, *Ann.* 15.44.4; this passage, however, simply states that Pilate was the one ordering Jesus's execution and gives no further information on his career.)

20. Luz, *Matthew*, 3.569–70.

what has been stated above regarding the criteria of judgment on non-Jews? I think not.

As we have already discussed with regard to the centurion and the soldiers who were with him at the cross, Sim has convincingly argued that this is not a "confession" at all, but an exclamation of fear; they were terrified (*ephobēthēsan sphodra*) as they realized that they had just executed "the son of God."[21] Contrary to Judas's reaction when he realizes what he has done,[22] we do not find even a hint that the centurion and these soldiers repent. Neither do we see them praise God, as the centurion does in Luke 23:47. In fact, this passage does not contain any of the positive characteristics that we have isolated in relation to those non-Jews in Matthew of whom Jesus approves. On the contrary, the soldiers who were struck with fear at Jesus's death are narratively meant to be understood to be the same soldiers who tortured Jesus and mocked him as "king of the Jews" (note esp. 27:27, 31, 32, 36, 54). They cannot claim, therefore, not to have known what they were doing, since they very clearly and repeatedly identified him as "king" (27:29, 37).

Their actions should be compared to the Canaanite woman, who also identifies Jesus, albeit implicitly, as king of the Jews, through calling him "Son of David" (15:22); she, just as the majority of the Jewish people, i.e., the crowds,[23] knows who it is she has encountered and

---

21. See David C. Sim, "The 'Confession' of the Soldiers in Matthew 27:54," *HeyJ* 24 (1993), 401–24, and discussion. As is the case in other New Testament passages, both in the Gospels and beyond them, to recognize a truth about the divine or about a messenger of the divine is not the same as being aligned to, or be on the same side as God: even demons know that Jesus is God's son (Matt 8:29; cf. Jas 2:19;). It is also of some interest to note that Jesus as the Son of God is referred to at the moment Jesus dies, just as it is claimed that Jesus was born as Son of God, through the Spirit, at the beginning of the Gospel (Matt 2:18). If one takes seriously the political dimension of the virgin birth, and notes that rulers of global empires, such as Alexander and Augustus, were also said to have been born without the assistance of human fathers, which in effect turned them into sons of gods, then the reaction of the centurion and the soldiers with him emerges as even more logical. They now realize that the person whom they just executed was a legitimate king with claims to a global empire, something which is later confirmed in Matt 28:16–20. For further discussion of the virgin birth in political context, see Runesson, "Matthew as Midwife," and literature referred to there.

22. Matt 27:3–10.

23. The crowds, the blind both in Galilee and Judea, and the children in the Jerusalem temple all recognize Jesus positively as the Son of David, the king of the Jews: Matt 9:27; 12:23; 20:30–31; 21:9, 15. This is precisely why the soldiers mock him using these words as they know that they have now removed a threat to Rome.

understands what her position in relation to the king should be. Her reaction is subordination and she receives a share of the blessings of the kingdom. The reaction of the centurion of Matt 8:5–13 is the same (subordination), and the result is the same (healing). Pilate's soldiers' reaction is, on the contrary, that they torture and execute him. Thus, according to the criteria of judgment that are applied to non-Jews in the pre-resurrection period, they have failed to recognize the work of the Spirit in Jesus; they have also radically failed to subordinate themselves to the Jewish king; indeed, what they have done is the very opposite to subordination. In light of all this, it is, in my view, narratively almost impossible to interpret what happens with these executioners at the cross in a positive way. There is simply no evidence in the Gospel that can support such a reading, but there is significant evidence that directly contradicts it.

Similarly, the position of Pilate in Matthew is, measured against the backdrop of what the rest of the Gospel has to say about righteous non-Jews, quite negative. He is presented as understanding, to some degree, that what he is about to do is unjust; his wife even tells him explicitly that Jesus is righteous and thus innocent, and that disasters will follow if this man is executed (27:19). Still, Pilate goes ahead and has him executed. This should be compared not only to the reactions of the righteous non-Jews in the Gospel (the Magi, the Centurion, and the Canaanite woman), but also to what Jesus's (Jewish) disciples must anticipate as they, as a consequence of their convictions (they know who Jesus is), proclaim the kingdom. Regardless of whatever suffering will befall them, including torture and death, they must stand firm, or otherwise they will not be recognized by Jesus before his Father in heaven (10:32–33; cf. 10:17–24, 28, 37–39). How does Pilate's actions compare with such criteria of judgment, even if we would allow that he is presented as caught between his duty to Rome and a potential riot among a colonized people?

While Matthew must place the guilt generated from Jesus's death on a group of people within the people of God in order to construe Rome as a tool in the hands of the God of Israel,[24] there is nothing here that even remotely connects Pilate with the ideal of the righteous non-Jew in Matthew. Indeed, as in the case of Judas and the betrayal of Jesus, what happens in the trial must happen, and we may paraphrase Matt 26:24 to suggest more clearly the Matthean perspective: it must indeed happen, "but woe unto the person by whom the Son of Man is executed; it would be better for that one if he had never been born." As with the soldiers and the centurion at the cross, Pilate refuses to subordinate himself to the king of the Jews, the person who will soon become elevated to the status of world ruler (i.e., replacing the emperor and the gods by whose will the emperor ruled), and thus, rob Rome and its gods of their power (28:18). Any hint of repentance is conspicuously absent.[25] On the contrary, Pilate continues after Jesus's death to work against the divine plan, in that he willingly allows for a guard to be placed outside the tomb (27:62–66). There is no *pistis* here, only empire politics. Based on the criteria of judgment outlined above, non-Jews so characterized will face condemnation in the final judgment. In sum, Pilate, the centurion at the cross, and the soldiers who carried out the torture and execution of Jesus—far from being portrayed as the saints Christian tradition morphed them into—provide the narrative pattern, the blueprint for how Jesus's followers, who will be hated by all nations (24:9; cf. 10:22), shall be persecuted and killed.[26]

The only non-Jew in the passion story who comes close to a status of righteousness, measured on the Christ-fearer scale outlined above, is Pilate's wife. Her words to her husband as he is about to sentence Jesus to death, are instructive: "Have nothing to do with that innocent

24. See above, pp. 127n236; 354–55.
25. It is interesting to note that Eusebius, perhaps also aware of this lack of repentance of the Roman Prefect in the Gospels, pondering what would happen to a man who would sentence Jesus to death, claims that Pilate (like Judas) committed suicide (*HE* 2.7). The reason given by Eusebius for the suicide is, in light of our discussion of Judas above (see pp. 133–34), worth noting: "[Pilate] fell into such great calamity that he was forced to become his own slayer and to punish himself with his own hand, for the penalty of God, as it seems, followed hard after him." While Eusebius claims that Pilate's suicide is noted by Greek writers, there are no other sources that can confirm this. What we do know is that after many complaints had been leveled against Pilate's rule Lucius Vitellius, governor of Syria, removed him from office in 36 CE (cf. Josephus, *A.J.* 18.89).
26. Cf. Matt 10:24–25, 38–39. Since no repentance is noted by Matthew for these characters, the outcome of the final judgment will be disastrous, as is clear based on the criteria of judgment outlined in Matt 25:31–46. On this judgment scene, see further below chapter 7.3.

[*dikaios*] man, for today I have suffered a great deal because of a dream about him" (27:19). She is thus presented as realizing indirectly, as did the Magi of Matthew 2, the centurion of Matthew 8, and the Canaanite woman of Matthew 15, that Jesus is righteous and innocent of the crime he is accused of. Since Jesus is claimed to be innocent, the sign that is put on the cross saying that he is "King of the Jews" (27:37) can be understood in two ways by the reader who tries to think with Pilate's wife. Either Jesus never claimed to be "King of the Jews," and thus, that which happens to him is the result of a conspiracy, or Jesus did claim this title, and therefore, must not be crucified, but rather, recognized by Rome as the rightful ruler of the Jewish people. It is not difficult to see that Matthew would have promoted the latter of these two understandings of the situation, especially since the other Christ-fearers of the story all subordinate themselves to Jesus, recognizing his power and legitimate status among the Jews.[27] In any case, the story of Pilate's wife increases the reader's sense of outrage at the unjust trial of Jesus even as it applies to Pilate, who is otherwise stuck in a narrative web that demands his innocence to preserve intact the power of the God Israel over Rome.

The situation as it applies to Christ-fearers in Matthew's narrative can be summarized in Table 7.1. The Judgment on Christ-Fearers and Their Forerunners:

---

27. The Magi, too, receive revelation from the divine in a dream, aimed at saving Jesus's life (Matt 2:12). If Pilate had listened to his wife, Jesus's life would have been saved; this, however, is an impossible development of the story in Matthew, since Jesus must die to save his people from their sins, which can no longer be atoned for in the defiled and soon to be destroyed temple.

CHRIST-FEARERS AND THEIR FORERUNNERS: THE PRE-RESURRECTION PERSPECTIVE

Examples From Israel's History				The Narrative Here and Now			
Encounters Between Non-Israelites and Israelites		Hypothetical (Imagined) Encounters Between Non-Israelites and Israelites		Encounters Between Non-Jews and Jesus		Hypothetical (Imagined) Encounters Between Non-Jews and Jesus	
Passage	Criteria	Passage	Criteria	Passage	Criteria	Passage	Criteria
Jonah – The People of Nineveh (12:38-41)	Righteous behavior as defined by Torah and Prophetic proclamation; accepting divine voice through Israel's prophets; repentance. Subordination to Israel's God and his prophet.	Sodom (11:23-24; 10:15)	Righteous behavior as defined by Torah and Prophetic proclamation; accepting divine power as working through Israel's Messiah; repentance. Subordination to Israel's God and his Messiah; Receiving Jesus' disciples and listening to their proclamation	The Magi (2:1-12)	Subordination under Jewish king [Other criteria implied; cf. previously on the Queen of the South]	Tyre (11:21-22)	Righteous behavior as defined by Torah and Prophetic proclamation; accepting divine power as working through Israel's Messiah; repentance. Subordination to Israel's God and his Messiah
Solomon – The Queen of the South (12:42)	Righteous behavior, recognition of divine rule through and wisdom in Israel's king Solomon. Subordination to Israel's king	Gomorrah (10:15)	Receiving Jesus' disciples and listening to their proclamation [cf the Jonah story above]	The Centurion (8:5-13)	*Pistis*, subordination	Sidon (11:21-22)	Righteous behavior as defined by Torah and Prophetic proclamation; accepting divine power as working through Israel's Messiah; repentance. Subordination to Israel's God and his Messiah
				The Canaanite Woman (15:21-28)	*Pistis*, subordination		
				Special Cases			
				Pilate (27:11-26, 62-65); Pilate's wife (27:19); Roman Soldiers (27:27-37, 54); Roman Centurion at Cross (27:54)	Criteria related to salvation lacking in all cases except Pilate's wife, where they can be understood as implied based on Matthew's treatment of other Christ-fearers		

As we can see from this table, a certain pattern of thought emerges when the spotlight is put on divine judgment, a pattern that applies to both the historical and the contemporary characters and cities in the story. In brief, non-Jews described in a positive light are those who accept and act on Israel's prophetic oracles of judgment (Matt 12:38–41; implied in 11:21–22, 23–24; cf. 10:15); those who come to the Son of David to seek the wisdom and healing that only the God of Israel can provide, recognizing the divine power active through appointed leaders (12:24; 8:5–13; 15:21–28); those outside of the land of Israel who subordinate themselves more generally to the rule of the Jewish Messiah (2:1–12). Judgment is carried out in this world, both in Israel's history (when cities are destroyed) and in the narrative here and now (when exorcism and healings are performed). For Matthew's pre-resurrection Jesus, it is also clear that Christ-fearers and their forerunners will receive the positive treatment in the final judgment that secures a place for them in the coming kingdom. Contrary to 28:18–20, there is no teaching required, no baptism, no conversion. They are judged, it seems, based on their "intuitive" realization that the God of Israel rules the world and that through this God's people, or rather, through the legitimate rulers of this people, they may receive a share of the blessings that such power brings with it.

What distinguishes the Christ-fearers and their forerunners from other non-Jews, those that are presented as examples of everything a good Jew must not be or do,[28] is that they, when they encounter Israel's prophets and kings, experience and understand what happens around these prophets and kings is the work of God's Spirit. It is in this realization (and the resulting *pistis*) we find the key to Matthew's positive treatment of this group. For Matthew's Jesus, accepting that what happens around him is the work of the Spirit is of utmost importance, even to the degree that rejecting that this is the case is unforgiveable. The latter is exactly what the Pharisees, contrary to the Jewish crowds (12:23), are accused of doing (12:24, 31–32).

Ultimately, then, we can deduce a criterion of judgment that is

28. See discussion above, chapter 5.2.1.

active for both Jews and non-Jews: to recognize the work of the Holy
Spirit in that which happens around Jesus (and through the people
from Israel's history that Jesus points to as divine messengers). In
Israel's past and present, Matthew claims, the Spirit channels the
divine voice (Jonah and Jesus), wisdom (Solomon and Jesus), and power
(Jesus's extraordinary deeds), and this is precisely what the Jewish
crowds and the Christ-fearers and their forerunners perceive. The fact
that those who should have been able to understand this—those who
sit on Moses's seat (23:2) and are skilled interpreters of Jewish history
and law—do not see what these uneducated people understand (cf.
11:25), increases the harshness of the judgment as it applies to the
them as leaders. Consequently, the Christ-fearers, together with the
Jewish crowds, function as narrative tools used to shame the various
leadership groups in the story and point to the seriousness of the
situation for the Jewish people in a *qal-va-homer*-style argument.[29] In
the end, thus, Matthew's interest lies in addressing the Jewish people,
not the non-Jews.[30] This will become all the more obvious when we look
at how the Matthean Jesus understands the situation in which non-

29. The logic goes as follows: "If even non-Jews, who do not have access to the law, are being held
responsible for their actions and are requested to repent and do repent, how much more is not
repentance required of you who are (learned; this is spoken to Pharisees and their scribes) Jews
and have access to the law, and how much more severe will not your judgment be since you do
not repent?"

30. Matthew's story involves a lot more detail when he narrates events taking place among the
Jewish people; non-Jews are there to support points made about Jews. One may compare Matthew
with the rabbis in this regard: Rabbinic ideas about laws for non-Jews, such as the Noahide
commandments, do exist in this body of literature, but they occupy a miniscule amount of space
in the larger whole compared to the detailed treatment of Jewish law for Jews. In a similar
way, Matthew's theology of divine judgment on non-Jews is rather embryonic. Indeed, overall,
Matthew's disinterest in non-Jews is also seen in his redaction of Mark when he speaks about as
central an institution as the temple. In Mark, the temple's purpose was supposed to be "a house
of prayer for all the nations" (Mark 11:17); in Matthew, who removes "for all the nations," thus
modifying the focus of both Isa 56:7 and Mark 11:17, the temple's function is only to be "a house
of prayer" (21:13). Seen against the background of Matt 28:18–20, this change of meaning may
be explained by the fact that Matthew envisions non-Jews to become Jews. Explanations taking
their point of departure in a specific dating of Matthew after 70 CE, such as Harrington, *Matthew*,
294, arguing that the temple would not be relevant after 70 in any case, are not convincing; the
rabbis, too, had a lot to say about the temple and how it should be run, not a decade but *centuries*
after its destruction. Konradt, *Israel*, 322–23, however, proposes an interesting interpretation
based on the juxtaposition of temple and *ekklēsia*, although, in my view, he does not fully develop
the implications for non-Jews of joining the covenant and the likelihood that Matthew assumes
circumcision as a requirement for them to join the *ekklēsia* (idem, *Israel*, 320–21). Cf. discussion
above, chapters 5.2.3, and 5.3, and below, chapter 7.2.

Jews find themselves after he has been given "all authority in heaven and on earth" (28:18).

7.2 Joining God's People Before it is Too Late: The Proselytes

If the criteria of judgment isolated above in relation to Christ-fearers allow for non-Jews to have a share in the benefits of the kingdom without requiring of them any knowledge of the Torah/Jewish law, conversion/baptism, or membership in the people of God, how do we explain the fact that the Matthean Jesus, in the very last verses of the Gospel, demands precisely all of these things from non-Jews, implying that the nations would otherwise be excluded from salvation? In my view, this seeming contradiction is not possible to resolve as long as we ignore aspects of narrative progression and treat the Gospel as if it could provide us with some kind of synchronic outline of various important theological doctrines, ethical advice, or cultic dos and don'ts. In other words, the dynamic of divine judgment is intertwined with certain historical realities (as such realities are construed in the narrative world of the Gospel), so that when narrative-historical circumstances change, new requirements are introduced which meet the demands of the new situation.

There are a few such key moments, or turning points, in the narrative when conditions are presented as transformed, and, as such, change the game rules. First, the arrival of John marks the end of the pre-eschatological period and prepares for the new (Matt 11:11–13); a baptism of repentance is introduced (3:5–6, 11).[31] Second, overlapping with John, the birth of the Messiah initiates the eschatological age, a period which requires special attention to Jewish law as a way to prepare for the day of judgment (the Gospel then moves on to describe

---

31. One may note that this requirement, after Jesus's own baptism, seem to be dropped, at least as it applies to the Jews in the story (neither Jesus nor his followers baptize anyone before the resurrection). We do not hear of baptism again until rules for non-Jewish conversion are introduced in 28:18–20. Perhaps Matthew understands John's baptism as superseded by the baptism of "Holy Spirit and fire" (which evidently does not require water) that will be administered by Jesus (Matt 3:11; cf. Ezek 37:14). If so, the baptism of non-Jews in Matt 28:18–20 is a different kind of baptism, combining water and Spirit as it aims to change the status of non-Jews as they become proselytes. These are issues, however, that require fuller discussion than can be given here.

411

in which way the law must be interpreted and kept within that eschatological time frame, as indicated by the beatitudes, and what deeds of power that will follow in the footsteps of the kingdom). Third, as we have argued above, the Jerusalem temple is described as defiled, and therefore, as inadequate for the Divine presence; this means the loss of the mechanism of atonement that had been available in the Gospel until this point (Matthew 23–24). Fourth, with Jesus's death, a new form of atonement is supplied, so that the Jewish people can be saved (1:21; 26:26–28; 27:52–53; cf. Ezek 37:11–14). Fifth and finally, once Jesus's sacrificial death has provided the cultic mechanism to save the people, his resurrection means that he has now been given even more power than the devil promised him in 4:8–9, which was limited to the kingdoms of the world (*pasas tas basileias tou kosmou*; 4:8), and which he refused. The God of Israel is now giving the Messiah authority over all the nations as well as over all the powers in the cosmic realm (*pasa exousia en ouranō kai epi [tēs] gēs*; 28:18; cf. 6:10).

This last change of the conditions under which human life is conducted even exceeds the magnitude of the Spirit's work as the Messiah arrives in Matthew 1, although the virginal conception, echoing myths surrounding the births of Alexander the Great and Augustus,[32] does indicate that this person will become a world ruler. Something unprecedented has happened in history as it is described in the story world, which changes, fundamentally, the rules of the game for individuals and collectivities not Jewish. They and their gods are now under the direct influence and ultimate authority of the Jewish Messiah. Implied in the so-called Great Commission, which is presented as the logical consequence of this change of power dynamics in the universe, we find the new requirements that apply under these new circumstances.

In brief, as we have also noted above, all nations must "become disciples," a change of status which is connected with knowledge of Torah and conversion (28:19–20). Regardless of how we understand

---

32. The birth of Alexander is recounted by Plutarch, *Alex.* 2–3; see discussion in Collins and Collins, *King and Messiah as Son of God* (Grand Rapids: Eerdmans, 2008), 48–49. On the birth of Augustus without the involvement of a human father, see Suetonius, *Aug.* 94.3–4.

the conversion process—if it involved circumcision and baptism or just baptism—the change required of the nations is the adoption and keeping of the Torah as Jesus taught it to the disciples in the Gospel (*didaskontes autous tērein panta hosa eneteilamēn hymin*; 28:20).[33] The narrative turning point provided by the resurrection does thus not affect the Jewish people other than indirectly; their Messiah is now the ruler of the entire cosmos, and non-Jews must adapt to their law and their God.[34] For Matthew, keeping the Torah can only be done within the Mosaic covenant, which provides for the necessary means of atonement; after the defilement of the temple, Jesus's self-sacrifice offers the forgiveness of sins needed for the law to function (26:26–28). In other words, just as the Pharisaic believers in Jesus referred to in Acts 15:5, the Matthean Jesus rules that non-Jews must cease to be non-Jews and become Jews if they are to be among the saved; they need to prepare themselves for the coming judgment just like other Jews in the story.

This means that at this point in the story, after the resurrection, the criteria of judgment on those non-Jews who convert to the eschatological form of Jesus-oriented Judaism that Matthew's Jesus proclaims will be the same as for any other Jews; there is no distinction made between Jews and proselytes. Saving the nations, thus, involves offering them the shelter that the Jewish *ekklēsia* provides as the Day of Judgment approaches. For those who sympathize and believe in the power of the kingdom, like the Christ-fearers, what is offered is a gracious opportunity for them to attain equal status with the Jews within the people of God,[35] something akin to Roman citizenship, but

---

33. For the expression, cf. 1 Chr 22:13.
34. On Israel's/the righteous' rule over the nations, cf. Jub 32:19; Wis Sol 3:8 (cf. Isa 34:1–17). On the conversion of non-Jews in the land as Israel resettles its tribal areas, see Ezek 47:22. On the changing status of non-Jews after the arrival of the Messiah, cf. Gen R. 98:9.
35. Matthew's Gospel thus proclaims equality within the people of God in a way that differs from Pauline theology. According to the latter, in which non-Jews must remain non-Jews as they join the movement, Jews like Paul constituted the center and non-Jews were only "a wild olive shoot" grafted in to share "the rich root of the olive tree" (Rom 11:17). In the same way, the theology of non-Jews in Acts differs significantly from Matthew. As can be seen in Acts 15:1–29, non-Jews constitute a separate group within the Jesus movement, which is never invited to join Israel and is thus subject to a different set of laws; for Acts, contrary to Matthew, the criteria of judgment for Jews and non-Jews are different even after the resurrection.

far beyond its narrow confines, inferior gods, and ultimately, doomed religio-political structures. As proselytes, they will no longer be outsiders, no longer "dogs" in Jesus's eyes (15:26); they will be full members of Israel.

But does this mean that, according to Matthew, only Jews (including proselytes) will have a share in the world to come? Such a perspective on judgment would surely align with what we have seen above regarding how this Gospel generalizes non-Jews negatively as outsiders and examples of everything that good Jews must not do or be.[36] There are, however, exceptions to this general rule, which indicate that Matthew's theology of judgment is quite closely related to an interpretive trajectory that we find also in later Rabbinic writings, but which is absent from Christian interpretations of the First Gospel. To this theme, we now turn: the judgment on non-Jews in the period after the resurrection.

7.3 Offering Salvation Beyond the In-Group: The Benevolent Other

Since the pre-resurrection centripetal movement of approved non-Jews around Jesus (they search for him, he does not go looking for them, but restricts his mission to Jews only[37]) is centrifugally reversed in 28:19–20 (Jesus actively takes on the known world through his disciples), and Jewish law is now to be taught to all, which implies the abolishing of the very "otherness" that marked the Christ-fearers, as we have argued above, the time of the Christ-fearers is now over and non-Jews can, based on Jesus's new universal powers (28:18), be incorporated into Israel. What was a closed-ethnic[38] approach for Jesus as long as he was confined by parameters associated with what we call history has thus changed into an open-ethnic perspective based

36. See chapter 5.2.1.
37. Matt 10:5–6; 15:24; cf. 9:36.
38. On this and related terminology, see above chapter 5.3, and Runesson, "Universalistic Christianity?" 131–32. On genealogy and Jewishness, see Matthew Thiessen, *Contesting Conversion: Genealogy, Circumcision, and Identity in Ancient Judaism and Christianity* (Oxford: Oxford University Press, 2011), esp. ch. 4 (pp. 87–110).

on the Matthean understanding of the cosmic implications of the resurrection; proselytes are welcome, as John the Baptist also prophesied in 3:9. As Jesus receives "all authority [*exousia*] in heaven and on earth" (28:18), the transformation of the world has begun and all need to live in accordance with even the most minor of the commandments in the Jewish law in order to prepare for the coming judgment (Matt 5:19; 23:23; 28:20; cf. 13:41[39]).

In terms of salvation, this open-ethnic position seems to lead to a salvation-exclusive stance, since salvation appears now to be limited to the in-group. Formerly, the position of the Christ-fearers indicated that, as in many other forms of ancient (and modern) Judaism, the boundary between the people of God and those outside is not the same as the boundary between those who shared in the benefits brought about by the kingdom and those who were left out. Should we assume, then, that Matthew's understanding of salvation and condemnation as related to the outsider changes after the resurrection? It certainly does, but this does not mean that Matthew abandons the idea that the "other" among the nations can be saved. Rather, what we see is a transformation of that very notion in a way that may strike modern readers as unexpected and contrary to how Christianity has traditionally understood the requirements for inclusion among the saved. We have one text in particular that sheds light on this issue, outlining the criteria of judgment as they apply to the non-Jewish outsider in the period between the resurrection and the final judgment: Matt 25:31–46.

The so-called parable[40] of the sheep and the goats in 25:31–46 is, arguably, contra Marguerat, not a synthesis of how the author has

---

39. Note that many translations conceal the fact that this verse refers specifically to the people who break the law (*tous poiountas tēn anomian*) as those who will be gathered and removed from the kingdom; NRSV, e.g., has the more general "evildoers." The Swedish translation, Bibel 2000, however, identifies those who are cast out as "all those who mislead people and break the law" ("alla som förleder människorna och *bryter mot lagen*").

40. Davies and Allison, *Matthew*, 3.418 prefer the designation "word-picture," but cf. Sherman W. Gray, *The Least of My Brothers. Matthew 25:31–46: A History of Interpretation* (Atlanta: Scholars Press, 1989), 351–52, who argues for the parabolic nature of the pericope. Strictly speaking, the passage is not, in my view, a parable, but, as France, *Matthew*, 960, has argued, a judgment scene in which a simile is inserted in two of the verses (25:32–33).

presented God's judgment in the Gospel.[41] This text deals specifically with the "outsider," regardless of any ethnic or other identity markers, and spells out the criteria of salvation for those who *do not* belong among Jesus's followers.[42] In modern terminology, one might say that we find here, implicitly, an indication of Matthew's theology of the other.[43]

There are two key interpretive issues in this parable, the answer to which determine how the text is understood: the identity of *panta ta ethnē* (25:32) and of the *elachistos* (25:40, 45). As Sherman Gray has shown, interpretations have varied through the centuries.[44] From a perspective which understands the parable within the narrative frame of the Gospel of Matthew as a whole, it seems difficult to avoid the conclusion that: a) "the least" are not the same as or included in "all the nations," and b) "the least" refers to followers of Jesus, i.e., the insiders.[45] While there has been some debate about whether Jews who

---

41. Marguerat, *jugement*, 118–20. Cf. Jones, *Matthean Parables*, 226, who understands this pericope to be an example of a summary parable. In my view, Luz, *Theology of the Gospel of Matthew*, 129–32, seems too interested in making the parable "work" from a Christian perspective to appreciate the very clear differences between other judgment texts (related to the Jewish people, including the disciples) in the Gospel and this parable.

42. So also, Talbert, *Matthew*, 275: "In view here is the judgment of the nations, those not of the people of God." As Talbert notes, the judgment of the people of God has been taken care of in 24:36–25:30. See further below.

43. From a modern perspective, the text is thus of importance not only, as has been the case from the nineteenth and twentieth century onwards, for the Church's social work, as theologically based on a specific understanding of the "parable" (see, e.g., discussion by Overman, *Church and Community*, 351–52), but even more so for the church's understanding of the religious other, i.e., for its theology of religion. Cf., however, the hermeneutics applied by Ulrich Luz, as he adapts what he understands as the historical meaning of the text for modern use, against its original meaning: "The Final Judgment (Matt 25:31–46): An Exercise in 'History of Influence' Exegesis," in *Treasures New and Old: Contributions to Matthean Studies* (edited by David R. Bauer and Mark Allan Powell; Atlanta: Scholars Press, 1996), 271–310, here 308–10. Luz argument may be compared with Luomanen's historical reading of the text and its origin, as Luomanen theorizes about an early narrow understanding of "the least" and suggests that, in the context of Matthew's Gospel, a more universalistic interpretation is more likely: *Entering the Kingdom*, 184–90. On the church's reception of Matt 25:31–46, see also John R. Donahue, S.J., "The 'Parable' of the Sheep and the Goats: A Challenge to Christian Ethics," *Theological Studies* 47 (1986), 3–31.

44. Gray, *Least of My Brothers;* cf. Luz, "Final Judgment."

45. On "the least" as Jesus followers, see Jacques Winandy, "La scène du jugement dernier," *Sciences ecclésiastiques* 18 (1966), 169–86; Gray, *Least of My Brothers,* 357–58; Lamar Cope, "Matthew XXV:31–46, 'The Sheep and the Goats' Reinterpreted," *NovT* 11 (1969): 32–44; J. Mánek, "Mit wem identifiziert sich Jesus? Eine exegetische Rekonstruktion ad Matth 25:31–46," in *Christ and the Spirit in the New Testament: In Honor of C. F. D. Moule* (edited by B. Lindars and B. S. Smalley; Cambridge: Cambridge University Press, 1973), 15–25, here 22; Overman, *Church and Community*, 349; Luz, "Last Judgment," 308; Stanton, *New People*, 207–31; France, *Matthew*, 957–58; Talbert, *Matthew*, 276–77. As France, *Matthew*, 958, argues, the reference is clearly inclusive of any disciples, and does not point

have not recognized Jesus as the Messiah are included in "all the nations," or if this expression refers only to nations other than Israel, it seems to me that the Jewish people, including Jesus's followers (who in the period after the resurrection are Jews or proselytes in this story), are not part of this judgment scene.[46] It is very likely that what we see surfacing here is a belief, not uncommon in other forms of Judaism contemporary with Matthew, in two separate judgments: one for the Jewish people and one for the nations; the "parable" of the sheep and the goats deals with the latter, and thus excludes Israel.[47] It should perhaps be emphasized, again, that the fact that Israel is still understood as the people of God does not mean that it will avoid judgment. This is true both of those Jews who have joined the Jesus movement and those who have not. This interpretation is supported by the fact that "the least" are not judged in this text, despite the fact that the Gospel states clearly that Jesus's followers will also be judged.[48]

Having isolated the identity of the judged (all non-Jewish nations) in relation to "the least" (Jesus's followers), we may note that a central point of the pericope is the fact that neither "the sheep" nor "the goats" knew Jesus or his teaching during their lifetime; if they had, they would have understood the connection made between the people they either helped or did not help, and Jesus.[49] Instead, they are

to a specific group among the disciples, such as missionaries; cf. Luomanen, *Entering the Kingdom*, 185; Levine, *Social and Ethnic Dimensions*, 236.

46. Contra Hagner, *Matthew*, 2.742. For discussion, see, e.g., France, *Matthew*, 957–61. Stanton, *New People*, 212–14, argues that those judged cannot include "evangelized Christians."

47. Gray, *Least of My Brothers*, 358; cf. Harrington, *Matthew*, 357–59; Reuman, *Variety*, 54; Luz, *Theology of the Gospel of Matthew*, 131n21 (cf. 139–40). Contra Marguerat, *Jugement*, 506; Bornkamm, "End-Expectation," 23–24; Jones, *Matthean Parables*, 245–51. Matthew 25:31–46 does thus not describe the judgment on all humanity. In Matthew's narrative world, this is all the more clear, since: a) Jesus followers are Jews and Matthew's judgment relating to Jews makes no difference between the disciples and other Jews; b) "the least," who are clearly Jesus's followers, are thus Jews (cf. Overman, *Church and Community*, 349: "[C]ertainly Matthew did not mean these people represented a new religion apart from Judaism. The people who are to be served and aided are fellow Matthean Jews. These people are fulfilling the will, law, and plan of the God of Israel."); c) the least are evidently not judged in this parable, but constitute a criterion which determines the divine judgment on outsiders. Looking beyond the parable, we also find that the elect have already been gathered separately (Matt 24:31).

48. See, e.g., Matt 7:21–27; 13:24–43; 25:1–30. Cf. Nolland, "The Gospel of Matthew and Anti-Semitism," in *Built Upon the Rock: Studies in the Gospel of Matthew* (edited by Daniel M. Gurtner and John Nolland; Grand Rapids: Eerdmans, 2008), 154–69, here 163, who notes that Matthew is as critical of Jesus's disciples as he is of the Pharisees in terms of certain types of behavior.

49. Cf. Matt 10:40; 10:32–33. Some scholars have speculated about whether the reader is meant to

presented as completely unaware of what they had done (or not done) and how that relates to the judge before whom they now stand. Ultimately, what outsiders have done to the judge himself is *the* criterion of judgment on which the nations are judged, since the insiders and their master cannot be thought of in isolation from one another.

This thought pattern is found also in the Hebrew Bible, as we have argued above, where in Genesis, the fate of the outsiders is determined by how they treat Abraham and his descendants (Gen 12:3).[50] In fact, some of the language in Matthew relates quite closely to Genesis 12. The sheep to the right are said to be blessed (*eulogeō*; 25:34) as a consequence of their positive treatment of "the least," just as those who bless Abraham will be blessed (LXX: *eulogeō*). The goats to the left are *cursed* (*kataraomai*; 25:41) on the basis of an absence of good deeds when they encountered the suffering followers of Jesus; in the same way those who curse Abraham will be cursed (LXX: *kataraomai*).[51] There is, thus, a divinely ordained mechanism of blessing and cursing already in place, so to speak, based on God's covenant with and promises to Abraham, which is activated when outsiders relate in one way or

---

understand as implicit in this text that the "little ones" are in fact missionaries, and that therefore the sheep and the goats must have known whom they were helping or ignoring. Such speculation diverts attention, however, from the fact that it is the unawareness of the judged that stands in focus as judgment is pronounced. Cf. France, *Matthew*, 959: "They have helped, or failed to help, not a Jesus recognized in his representatives, but a Jesus *incognito*." The unawareness is in and of itself is a carrier of theological meaning.

50. Cf. Charette, *Recompense*, 155–59. See also Joel 3:1–3 (MT and LXX: 4:1–3); Deut 30:7; *Jub.* 31:17.

51. On the imagery of right and left in a judgment scene, cf. *Ap. Ab.* 22:3–5. The pattern of judgment in which the in-group constitutes the criterion on which the out-group is judged is found in many other texts contemporary with Matthew, and the reason behind these theologies of the other is the same: the identification of the suffering of the in-group with the suffering of their deity. For Graeco-Roman texts, see Euripides, *Bacch.* 784–95; Achilles Tatius, *Leuc. Clit.* 8.2.2–3; 7.14.6. The motif is even more common in Jewish texts; see, e.g., 2 Bar. 72.4–6; *Ap. Ab.* 31.2; 1 Enoch 62.11. For the identification between the divine and the suffering, see Philo, *Decal.* 119; cf. *Midrash Tannaim* on Deut 15:9 (= *Mekhilta on Deuteronomy*: "my children, when you gave food to the poor, I counted it as though you had given it to me"). For discussion, see Talbert, *Matthew*, 277, which includes New Testament texts other than Matthew, which reveal a similar thought pattern (e.g., 2 Thess 1:6–7; cf. 1 Cor 8:11–12; Luk 10:16). These texts, however, concern condemnation of those who mistreat Jesus's followers, not the salvation of those who treat them well. In the same way, most of the Jewish and Graeco-Roman texts referred to deal with the condemnation, not the salvation of the other (note, however, the positive outcome for nations who have not "trodden down the seed of Jacob" in 2 Bar. 72.4–6). Rabbinic literature reveals, finally, a pattern of thought similar to Matthew's, as Melinek, "Reward and Punishment," has argued: "In fact, a blessing comes to anyone, whether Jew or Gentile, who extends hospitality to the righteous" (310).

another to the chosen people. The question is now whether Gen 12:3 is in fact providing us with a blueprint for how to understand Matt 25:31–46, when on the Day of Judgment individuals from the nations arrive either blessed or cursed, and this status decides whether they are allowed to enter the kingdom or not. There are several details that seem to support such a view, in which God's dealings with Abraham are alluded to by Matthew in order to make sense of the future destiny of non-Jews.[52]

If we begin in 25:34, we may note that the sheep to the right are related to the creation of the world, the time when the kingdom was prepared for them. Read together with the *panta ta ethnē* of 25:32, this supports an understanding of the parable according to which we are dealing only with non-Jews, since in Jewish theo-historical narratives, Jewish foundations go back not to the creation story but to the story of Abraham and Sarah (cf. Matt 1:1).[53] Does this reference to the creation of the world also signal that Matthew considers non-Jews to be involved in a covenant-like relationship, based on the notion of a covenant between God and Adam, as some later Rabbinic traditions would have it?[54] Such discourses related to the foundation of the world were formulated to answer questions regarding the status of the "other," of the non-Jew. Keeping within the bounds of such a covenant would enable non-Jews to enter the kingdom, i.e., to achieve the status of righteous gentiles. While I have previously entertained this interpretive possibility,[55] a different theological scenario, based on

---

52. As the following will make clear, I have modified my thinking on this topic beyond the argument made in my "Judging Gentiles."

53. Cf. the discussion in Davies and Allison, *Matthew*, 3, ad loc., and the six possible interpretations mentioned there. The idea that non-Jews *as non-Jews* should be able to be counted as Abraham's children is a Pauline thought which does not exist in Matthew. For Matthew, to become a child of Abraham requires conversion to the form of Judaism that his Jesus lives and proclaims (Matt 3:9; 28:19–20). This does not mean, however, that Abraham has no function to fill in relation to the judgment of non-Jews in Matthew.

54. Texts mentioning a covenant with Adam (listing 6 commandments) include, e.g., *Genesis Rabbah* 16:6; *Deuteronomy Rabbah* 2:25; *Numeri Rabbah* 14:12. Cf. *Exodus Rabbah* 30:9, where different collections of laws were given to key figures in the Hebrew Bible (6 commandments to Adam, 7 to Noah, 8 to Abraham, 9 to Jacob, and "all" to Israel). Cf. Acts 15:20. Eventually, the tradition of the seven Noahide commandments won the day and became the standard Jewish way of understanding criteria for a righteous life among non-Jews.

55. Runesson, "Judging Gentiles," 148–49.

what appears to be a direct allusion to the covenant with Abraham and Matthew's use of the word *klēronomeō*, now seems to me more likely.

Beginning with the latter, Matthew's use of *klēronomeō* (usually translated "inherit") in my view indicates a wider frame of reference for what is to come than an understanding of the requirements for entry into the kingdom based simply on the idea of recompense for work performed (i.e., good deeds) would allow for. In light of recent research, such a claim requires, however, some discussion. Nathan Eubank has argued that *klēronomeō* should rather be read as a synonym for "acquiring," i.e., that the word indeed only indicates payment for work done and does not signal the idea of inheritance; such an understanding of the word is possible, based on context, although its primary meaning in Greek literature is related to inheritance.[56] While Eubank is certainly correct that Matthew's Gospel frequently uses the language of debt and wages as a way of speaking about sin/good deeds and punishment/reward, in my view Matthew is quite particular in his use of this specific term and differentiates, through its use, between receiving rewards in this world and the next on the one hand, and the process of entering the kingdom on the other. This has to do with more general discourses, found in other contemporary Jewish texts—including some of those in the New Testament—in which ideas about salvation are connected with Abraham, Isaac, and Jacob in such a way that God's dealings with and promises to the Patriarchs are (genealogically) activated in the here and now and function as a prerequisite for entry into the world to come. In other words, salvation does not exist in a chronologically isolated place coterminous with the individuals and groups concerned, but is stretched out through history and so makes redemption dependent on factors other than those produced or controlled by the people of the here and now of the text. Since the people of God are a (religio-) ethnic category, which traces its lineage back to Abraham, salvation and kingdom cannot be divorced from covenant and inheritance.[57]

---

56. Eubank, *Wages of Cross-Bearing*, 70–71. Cf. *LSJ, ad loc*, which comments on some of the same passages that Eubank discusses.

57. On covenant in Matthew, see also discussion above, chapter 2.8.

Therefore, in a first-century Jewish setting, speaking about salvation (and related ideas) triggers the notion of inheritance, which in turn, activates the concept of covenant, and vice versa. We would do well, therefore, to consider such notions, especially when Matthew applies a word whose primary meaning relates to inheritance when he discusses that which we call salvation. Let us first take a look at the other passages where Matthew uses *klēronomeō*, which happen to be concerned with precisely land and life in the world to come, before we return to 25:34. A close reading of these passages will, to my mind, supply evidence that Matthew uses the word only in such a way that it is understood that what is being "inherited" cannot be bought or simply earned. It is owned by someone else and has already been promised to previous generations, the descendants of whom may inherit it if certain conditions, as outlined in the ancient past, are met.

In Matt 5:5 the meek, who are identified as "blessed" (*makarios*[58]), are said to be about to inherit the land (*gē*[59]). The giving of land, of course, was part of the covenant agreement between Abraham/Israel and the God of Israel (e.g., Gen 12:1–2; 15:6–21; Exod 19:5; Deut 7:12–13; 11:8–12). Therefore, the eschatological notion of being given the land needs to be understood within a larger covenantal frame, and thus, also as something that will happen "within the family," as the descendants of the patriarchs inherit God's promise to Abraham (and the people as a whole after him); ultimately, while conditions must be fulfilled, taking possession of the land cannot be understood, therefore, as a process based solely on the people's achievements (cf. Deut 8:1; 9:5–6). In Jewish traditions relating to land (and salvation, more generally), inheritance comes with specific requirements: if the law is not kept, exile will follow. But is Matthew speaking specifically into a context where all of these notions are relevant? Would the reader have understood?

Based on the conclusions reached in Part One above, this seems indeed likely to have been the case. In Matthew, the focus is on

---

58. Cf. *LSJ, ad loc.*
59. On the meaning of *gē* as "land" rather than "earth" here, see above p. 29n93. On Israel as land and people, see also pp. 307–17.

precisely the God of Abraham/Israel (Matt 22:32/15:31) and the descendants of Abraham/members of the people of Israel (Matt 1:1; 2:6; 10:6; 15:24). It is to the latter Jesus addresses his proclamation, even if: a) some will fail to fulfill the conditions attached to the covenant, and so, be disinherited, and b) some who were originally not members of the family, as it were, may be incorporated, or adopted, and so, share in the inheritance (Matt 3:9; 8:11–12; 28:20).[60] In the same way, when Matthew speaks of "inheriting" (*klēronomeō*) life in the world to come in 19:29, after having listed rewards that will be paid to those who suffered loss for the sake of Jesus's name in the present world, this wider covenantal frame is signaled. While Torah obedience, and, more generally, good deeds, will certainly result in rewards in the world to come, the act of *entering* the kingdom, taking possession of the kingdom, is associated with being given the land, and thus, inextricably intertwined with notions of (religio-ethnic) lineage and, consequently, covenant.

It is, ultimately, Israel's history and the active role in the narrative present of the ancestors and God's promises to them, which are still operational,[61] that militates against a translation of *klēronomeō* as simply synonymous with "acquiring." For Matthew, fulfilling what the law requires triggers the promises made to the ancestors, so that what God promised them is now given to (inherited by) God's people in the present (and future). Without God's doings in the past, there would be nothing for the present generation to acquire or inherit, regardless of how many good deeds a person has performed; if the covenant and its promises were removed from discourses of salvation, such good deeds could not be defined as meeting any previously agreed-upon requirements, signed into law, as it were, alongside mechanisms of atonement, and would therefore only produce hollow echoes in an otherwise empty cosmos void of an agreeable counterpart.

In sum, a translation of *klēronomeō*, which does not reflect the

---

60. Cf. Paul's use of inheritance language in Gal 4:7: if a son, then also an heir. Paul, rather than abolishing the importance of family ties for salvation, thus aims at expanding the privileges of family beyond traditional ideas of belonging.
61. Cf. Matt 22:32.

cultural as well as the literary setting in which the text was produced is, ultimately, unsatisfactory, and we should therefore retain in Matthew the primary meaning of the word as "inherit."[62] What is striking in Matt 25:34 is that the notion of inheriting the kingdom is associated with *non-Jews*, who cannot trace their lineage along with Israel and who are therefore not considered to exist in a covenantal relationship with the God of Israel. Quite naturally, it should not be possible to consider them as heirs, since they are not part of the "family," and, consequently, not mentioned in the "testament." How are we to explain this? Does this mean that Matthew's notion of covenant breaks down at this point, and that the final judgment is, in the end, independent of it? That *klēronomeō* loses its primary meaning, since the lineage that would be required for an heir is non-existent? I think not, and the solution to this problem lies precisely in Gen 12:3, when this passage is understood as an intertext alluded to by Matthew as he interprets the future for those who do not belong to the people of God.

God's covenant with Abraham, i.e., with the Jewish people, often referred to in other texts included in the New Testament when the status of non-Jews is discussed,[63] provides Matthew with a ethno-

---

62. Eubank, *Wages of Cross-Bearing*, 68–70, is correct, however, with regard to the translation of *misthos* and *apodidōmi* as related to wages and repayment. In none of the verses where *misthos* is used, however, does this word refer to the taking over of the kingdom (Matt 5:12, 46; 6:1, 2, 5, 16; 10:41, 42); instead, the word is used to convey the message that certain deeds will be repaid with corresponding wages in the world to come. The one exception is the special case of Matt 22:8. In the latter case, the use of *misthos* is explained, however, by how a parable can turn on their head the expectations of an audience. The point here is precisely that *misthos* is *not* what the workers (and readers) think it is, since all workers receive the same wages despite having worked a different number of hours. The audience's attention is caught through the setting up of an outrageous scene, which evokes feelings of unfairness, in order for the point of the parable to stand out more clearly, namely that entrance into the kingdom *cannot* be understood as the receiving of (fair) wages. The situation regarding *apodidōmi* is similar to that of *misthos*. When the issue is about human guilt, humans must repay what they owe (Matt 5:26; 12:36; 16:27; 18:25–34; cf. 21:41). When Matthew speaks about the world to come, God will repay humans for the good they have done (6:4, 6, 18; 16:27). (On 20:8, see above on *misthos*.) Never, however, is entering into the kingdom in and of itself construed as God *repaying* humans for work done. The result is that those who are not allowed into the kingdom can only blame themselves, while those who are accepted must acknowledge God's mercy as based on the covenantal promises made to the patriarchs. It is thus possible to say that judgment is based on deeds, since deeds play a role both in cases of condemnation and salvation; in the latter case they correspond to the covenantal agreement between God and Israel, and thus, trigger God's mercy, which is a *sine qua non* for salvation.

63. Paul's letters are of course the first to come to mind, as they construe a theology of the non-Jew (see esp. Romans 4). While Paul's notion of the Abrahamic covenant differs from Matthew's, he

theological pattern in which Jewish identity and lineage, and its importance for the salvation of the people, can be maintained at the same time as an opening for non-Jews can be forged. For the Matthean Jesus, while non-Jews who never joined the Jewish people are excluded from the kingdom, based on genealogy (no promises apply to them), through acts of loving kindness performed toward members of the chosen people, they will—based on God's promise to Abraham that all who treat Abraham and his descendants well be blessed—share in the inheritance that God has promised Abraham's descendants. Thus, there is no salvation to be had for non-Jews, except in relation to the chosen people and its Messiah. Matthew's criteria of judgment for non-Jews who have not converted, i.e., the construal of the conditions that apply for the salvation of the outsider, are thus simultaneously moving beyond the ethno-religiously defined boundary of the Jewish people *and* maintaining a sharp focus on the people and their Messiah as the center of the world and the gate through which non-Jews must pass to enter the kingdom. It is, after all, a Jewish kingdom, proclaimed and ruled by a Jewish Messiah (and his Jewish disciples; 19:28), all of whom are sent by and derive their authority from a Jewish God.

Through this way of theologizing Abraham, Matthew manages to maintain a focus on the covenant and its promises even in relation to those who do not belong within the covenant. The inheritance (*klēronomeō*; 25:34) that "the sheep" will share with "the least" (who belong within the Jewish people) is based on a logic within which good deeds done to specific people trigger God's mercy, as based on promises made in the ancient past. There is thus no reason to think (or fear), as many Christian interpreters seem to do, that Matthew here outlines criteria of judgment based exclusively on deeds, i.e., that he would proclaim what is usually called "work righteousness."[64] The fact

still regards Abraham as the ancestor of the Jewish people, not of the non-Jews (Rom 11:1), even though he too, recognizes the fact that even as a Jew one can forfeit one's place in the world to come. As a people, though, Israel still has a right to its inheritance, i.e., salvation, based on God's love for the patriarchs (Rom 11:28–29). For other ways of construing God's dealings with Abraham and their consequences for the criteria of judgment, see Jas 2:18–26.

64. Examples of these types of concerns are legion in the scholarly literature. For a condensed form of what is thought to be at stake, see Talbert, *Matthew*, 277. See also discussion above, chapter 2.7. It is true, though, that the type of compassionate deeds that result in salvation for these non-

that non-Jews can enter the kingdom is, ultimately, God's doing; it is an act of benevolence as God took upon himself to protect the people he began to form with Abraham.[65] The salvation of these non-converted non-Jews may thus be understood as a theological "bi-product," as it were, of God's primary strategy of shielding and caring for Abraham and his descendants, among whom we find "the least" in the "parable" of the sheep and the goats. "The least," in turn, represent the cosmic judge, who himself is genealogically identified in the Gospel as the son of Abraham (Matt 1:1). Therefore, when Stephen Wilson notes that for Matthew, "the only salvation offered was through Christ," this statement is only partly true. Salvation is indeed said to be bound to the Messiah (via his followers), but there are—in ways that are unknown to the outsider—those outside of the circle of disciples that will have a share in the kingdom, based on the divine grace once shown to Abraham.[66] The theological claim can be drawn as a chart, Figure 7.1. Divine judgment and the Outsider in Matt 25:31–46:

Jews is consistent with what the Matthean Jesus demands of his own people, as indicated by his interpretation of Jewish law; see William R. G. Loader, *Jesus Attitude towards the Law: A Study of the Gospels* (Grand Rapids: Eerdmans, 1997), 248–49.

65. The way Matt 25:34 is worded, with reference to creation as a way to indicate that we are dealing with non-Jews, may signal to some a sense of predestination: the kingdom has been waiting for these individuals since they themselves (as a people category) were created. While there are other contemporary Jewish texts that seem to hint at the idea of saved non-Jews as "chosen" (T. Benj. 10:10), this does not seem to be the main idea here. The point Matthew is making is simply that God has pre-arranged things for these non-Jews; the kingdom has been prepared since the foundation of the world. If anything, we might see an implicit claim that God has known all along that some among the nations will act in such ways toward Abraham's children that they will inherit the kingdom together with his own people. It is *as if* they too had been chosen.

66. Stephen G. Wilson, *Related Strangers: Jews and Christians 70-170 C.E.* (Minneapolis: Fortress, 1995), 55. Wilson's argument is, however, based on an analysis of the Gospel as a whole, and not only on Matt 25:31–46. It should be noted that, contrary to the interpretation argued in the present study, Wilson reads Matthew as having cancelled Israel's special status, aligning her destiny with that of all other nations. As I have tried to show above in both Part I and Part II, I believe Matthew's theology of judgment makes better sense if understood as evolving from and relating to the basic ethno-religious distinctions that were common to most ancient Mediterranean societies.

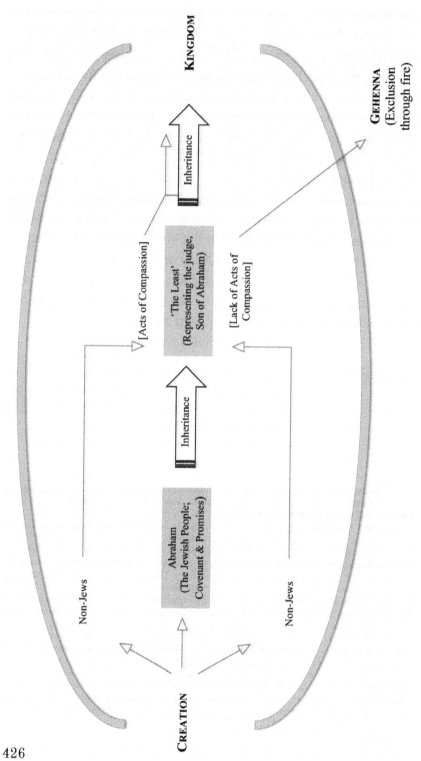

A theology of judgment that allows for an outsider to be part of salvation may, to Christian readers who consider Matthew's Gospel to be part of Holy Scripture, sound strikingly modern and pluralistic since it opens up for people who are not Christians to be included in the kingdom and thus seem to contradict more traditional particularistic Christian claims that salvation is to be found only within the Church.[67] However, understood within a Jewish interpretive frame, such salvation-inclusive theology goes back to antiquity and is still, in its basic form, an active principle in mainstream Jewish thought today; the boundary of the people of God is not the same as the boundary between the saved and the lost.[68] This type of theology is rarely a desk-product written by the powerful. It is the kind of theology that grows from a reality of persecution, in which a minority is harassed by the surrounding majority. Those within the majority who depart from the pattern of persecution and help and even save the lives of those who suffer can rarely be ignored theologically by those who were helped and saved.

Perhaps this salvation-inclusive principle receives its clearest modern analogy in the criteria governing the identification of righteous gentiles at the Yad Vashem in Jerusalem.[69] Matthew 25:31–46 follows the same basic theological logic, although on a much smaller

---

67. *Extra ecclesiam nulla salus*, as Cyprian would phrase it. One should perhaps add that the mainstream churches have developed theologies of religion that reaches far beyond Cyprian's claims. One trajectory of these developments includes the idea of so-called "anonymous Christians," a notion referred to in some discussions of Matt 25:31–46 (see, e.g., France, *Matthew*, 959). Since commentators use this modern theological notion as an analogy to explain Matthew's perspective, it should be noted that a historical reading of Matthew's Gospel hardly lends support to such a theology. The very point in Matthew is that "the sheep" (as well as "the goats") are indeed "the other" in an absolute sense of the word, and that therefore they cannot be identified using terminology connected with the in-group. The blessing with which they have been blessed (Matt 25:34) is dependent on their otherness in relation to the people of God in order for it to be intelligible within the logic of the Abrahamic principle. "The sheep" cannot be appropriated for the church, claimed as their own, without contradicting the point the Matthean Jesus is trying to make. Indeed, the idea itself of "anonymous Christians" shows just how uncomfortable the churches can be, just as Cyprian was, with the thought of salvation as under certain circumstances unrelated to the criteria of judgment governing its own communities.
68. One should note, however, that such Jewish theologies of "the other" are usually more open than what we have seen in Matthew, since they do not relate salvation only to how "the other" has treated them, as the notion of the Noahide commandments shows. In some cases, though, modern Jewish ideas about righteous gentiles are quite similar to Matthew; see further below.
69. For basic information about the identification of righteous gentiles, see the official website of the Yad Vashem: http://www.yadvashem.org/yv/en/righteous/about.asp.

scale, building its case on contrasting the otherness of the outsider with his or her acts of mercy toward the insider. While it is beyond the scope of the present study to discuss at length the historical setting in which the Gospel was authored,[70] it may be at least briefly noted here that a location in post-70 Galilee, devastated by war and now plagued by an increasing permanent presence of the Roman military, would make sense, as stories of persecution in Matthew relate to both Jews and non-Jews.[71] Salvation, then, is from and primarily for the Jewish people, including proselytes, but does not exclude those who do not belong among them as long as they, knowingly or unknowingly, fulfill the criteria laid out by God as he made his covenant with Abraham and his children, namely, to bless in deeds rather than only in words the people of God. It seems to me that as long as this parable is read from a later (non-Jewish) Christian perspective, in particular when understood as part of traditional Christian theologies of salvation, its imagery and message will be found to be in one way or another inconsistent, resisting "logical" readings.[72] Such inconsistencies, however, tend to dissolve when the parable is read within a Jewish interpretive frame. This brings us to a few concluding remarks on how Matthew construes the judgment and salvation of the nations.

---

70. I plan to return to the topic of the provenance of Matthew's Gospel in a future study.
71. For the origin of the judgment scene as a Matthean composition, see Robert H. Gundry, *Matthew: A Commentary on His Literary and Theological Art* (Grand Rapids: Eerdmans, 1984), 511. But cf. Davies and Allison, *Matthew*, 3.417–18, who argue that Matthew wrote the parable using previously existing oral tradition. Interestingly, they note on p. 418n10 that Bultmann considered the pericope to be a Jewish parable reworked by Christians. In any case, if this type of theology can indeed be related to harsh realities in which the author(s) live, we may deduce, on the basis of Matt 10:40–42 and 25:31–46, that the people among which this text was produced experienced persecution from both fellow Jews and non-Jews.
72. This is shown not least by the history of interpretation of the parable, from antiquity to the twentieth century; see Gray, *The Least of My Brothers*.

8

Conclusion to Part II

In Part II, we have aimed at isolating and analyzing the way in which Matthew construes divine judgment as it relates to the non-Jewish outsider. While the material is meager—Matthew's interest is focused on the Jewish people—it is still possible to say a few things about this text's approach to divine wrath, justice, and salvation as it applies to what is depicted as the out-group. Importantly, the tension that many scholars have observed between different ways of treating non-Jews in the Gospel are, it has been argued, resolved when the narrative progression of the story is taken into account.

For the Matthean Jesus, the non-Jewish world, in general, is at odds with how the God of Israel wants life to be lived. Non-Jews are generalized negatively, as examples of everything a good Jew must not be or do (e.g., 5:47; 6:7, 32; 20:25–26; cf. 18:17; 24:9; 20:19). There is thus nothing in Matthew that would support the idea, launched in the 1940s and repeated many times since then, that this Gospel would be biased in favor of "the gentiles." Such (mis-) understandings of the text, however, may be explained by the existence in Matthew of *exceptions* to the general negative view. These exceptions praise specific non-Jewish individuals or groups for their trust/loyalty (*pistis*) in the Jewish Messiah and their willingness to subordinate themselves to his authority. The best-known examples are the Magi from the East (2:1–12), the centurion (8:5–13), and the Canaanite woman (15:21–28), as well as the narrative-historical examples of the people of Nineveh (12:38–41) and the Queen of the South (12:42). Matthew also mentions non-Jewish cities, both historical ones and some that are contemporary with the narrative's here and now: Sodom, Gomorrah, Tyre, and Sidon (10:15; 11:23–24; 11:21–22).

It should be noted, though, that the positive light in which these individuals and groups are portrayed is deceptive. Indeed, the function of these specific non-Jews in the narrative is, fundamentally, to shame the Jews who do not recognize the Messiah through whom the Spirit is working in their midst to establish the kingdom. What we have in such instances is a *qal va-homer* type of argument: if even some non-Jews, who do not have the Torah, who do not know the God of Israel and who, generally, live lives contrary to the law of God, if even some such non-Jews are able to identify what is happening around Jesus as a sign of the kingdom, how much more should not these Jews, who have the Torah and know their God, have been able to recognize their Messiah? Such arguments rest, ultimately, on the negative understanding, shared between author and intended audience, that one cannot expect anything from non-Jews, and thus, in fact, adds force to the other passages mentioned, which speak in generalized negative terms of non-Jews and their culture. Nevertheless, these positive exceptions, we have called them Christ-fearers, are construed in such a way that the blessings of the kingdom will benefit them too, even if the Matthean Jesus, during his pre-resurrection lifetime, explicitly and strictly limits his and his disciples' mission to the Jewish people alone, and thus exhibit a closed-ethnic attitude combined with a (reluctant) salvation-inclusive approach (10:5–6; 15:24).

An open-ethnic turn is soon to come, however, and it is prepared for already in the genealogy with the mention of the non-Jewish women who joined the people of Israel at crucial moments in its history (1:3, 5; cf. 1:6), and John's prophecy in 3:9 that God is able to raise children of Abraham (i.e., Jews) from stones (i.e., non-Jews). It is not until after Jesus's resurrection, however, that this transformation is implemented, and the basis for this change in "salvation history," if the term be allowed, is that Jesus is now, for the first time, given all power and authority in heaven as well as on earth, indicating universal (imperial) rule (28:18). What the so-called Great Commission is really saying is that all non-Jewish nations must now be actively engaged and made to adopt Jewish law as Jesus taught it (28:19–20). As we have noted, while it is highly likely that the author meant circumcision for males to be understood as a ritual requirement in this conversion process, since not a single iota of the law must be lost and all matters of law must be followed (5:17–20; 23:23), the argument made here is not dependent on this to be true. Indeed, Matthew is quite clear that whatever the ritual requirements are for joining the people of God, circumcision and baptism or just baptism, the end result is the same: non-Jews must become Jews, leave their old status as non-Jews behind, and adhere to Jewish law. To the closed-ethnic inward mission of the pre-resurrection period is thus added an open-ethnic active proselytizing mission.

With this follows a change in the criteria of judgment for non-Jews, since the open-ethnic approach now taken implies a salvation-exclusive position. Jesus's previous (reluctant) acceptance of allowing the benefits of the kingdom to be shared with the outsiders who acknowledge his authority and power (but who were never baptized and had no knowledge of Torah), the Christ-fearers, is now cancelled. Matthew's vision is, ultimately, that of a single people of God following God's law on a global scale, since the God of Israel is the ruler of the whole world, heaven as well as the earth—a kind of Eden restored, when humanity as a whole is united and under God's rule. Contrary to Acts and Paul's letters,[1] this is a vision in which no distinctions are made between Jew and non-Jew within the people of God, between those who must keep the entire law and those who should keep only four commandments or none at all. It is, indeed, a vision that matches

1. See e.g., Acts 15:19–21; 21:20–25; 1 Cor 7:18.

quite well that of the Pharisaic believers in Jesus who are identified as enemies in Acts 15:5, as well as of others whom Paul attacks in his various letters, especially in Galatians.[2] In brief, the criteria of judgment in the post-resurrection period, a period which leads up to the return of Jesus and the final judgment, are universal: together with the Jewish people, all nations must keep the Jewish law. God has therefore opened up the covenant so that non-Jews may be included (as proselytes), share in the mechanism of atonement offered within it (26:28), and be saved on the day of the final judgment.

Interestingly, this salvation-exclusive approach is balanced with, even perforated by a theology of the other that in the period between the resurrection and the final judgment, and under specific circumstances, allows for the outsider, *as outsider*, to enter the coming kingdom. In an interpretive trajectory that finds its continuation in later mainstream forms of Judaism, but lacks reception history in mainstream (non-Jewish) Christianity, Matthew, alone among the Gospels, builds on Abrahamic traditions (Gen 12:3) to claim salvation for those who act with compassion toward (Jewish) believers in Jesus, including proselytes, who suffer (25:31–46).

In sum, Matthew's Gospel describes a development in which Jesus's resurrection is the turning point for the non-Jews, so that they end up under his direct authority and must follow his law. This changes nothing for the Jewish people, however. They have already been instructed in some detail about what is required of them (esp. in Matthew 5–7). The mission of the disciples will continue among them too until Jesus returns to judge Israel and the world (10:23; 23:34). There are, in fact, several clear indications that Matthew's Jesus perceives of the people (the "crowds," as opposed to leadership groups) in positive terms as potential followers.[3] The proselytizing

---

2. Gal 2:3–4; 5:11–12.

3. On the continued mission to the Jewish people in Matthew's narrative world, see also Hans Kvalbein, "'La hans blod komme over oss og våre barn!' Var Matteusevangeliet jødefientligt?" *Religio* 48 (1997), 55–69. Kvalbein understands Matt 28:19–20 as directed only to non-Jewish nations, but emphasizes, contrary to Luz, that this in no way implies that the mission to the Jews is over for Matthew. We do not find in this Gospel a pattern, in which the offer of salvation first goes to the Jews, and once they have rejected it, it is handed over to the non-Jews. In addition to referring to Matt 10:23, Kvalbein suggests that Matt 23:39 indicates the future eschatological

mission launched in 28:18-20 is thus not triggered, as commonly assumed, by any disappointment due to a lack of Jesus-followers, real or potential, within the Jewish people. It represents, rather, the eschatological process caused by Jesus's resurrection and the universal authority associated with it. In this way, then, 28:18-20 interprets the universal claims of 12:18-21 (Isa 42:1-4). Jesus will, as the cosmic ruler, judge all nations (12:18) and the only hope they have is in him (12:21). They must therefore adjust to Jewish law since this law now constitutes a universal criterion of judgment. Matthew thus picks up the longstanding theme of Israel's God's universal rule that surfaces, time and again, in his holy scriptures—a theme that requires not only Israel, but all the peoples of the earth to worship this God—and uses it to infuse the resurrection with global eschatological meaning.[4]

salvation of the Jewish people. While this must remain an interpretive option, I would suggest that this reference is limited to the Jewish leaders, since it is the leaders who are addressed here and not the people as a whole. Indeed, it seems that Matthew sees a potential for a large following within the people before the parousia, as we have discussed in Part I. In favor of such an interpretation is the fact that Matt 23:39 echoes precisely what the Galilean and Judean crowds have already said in Matt 21:9 as Jesus was about to enter Jerusalem. What the leaders cannot see even the blind among the crowds perceive (Matt 9:27; 20:30).

4. The motif of the universal worship of Israel's God is found not least in the prophetic books (e.g., Hab 2:14 [cf. Num 14:21] Isa 42:6-7; 49:6; 55:4-5; 56:6-7; 66:18-23) and, especially, in the Psalter (e.g., Pss 22:29 [NRSV 22:28]; 47:8-10 [NRSV 47:8-9]; 48:11 [NRSV 48:10]; 57:12 [NRSV 57:11]; 72:19; 113:3-4; 117:1-2; 119:90-91; 138:4-5; 148:11-13). Indeed, according to the Psalter, everything that lives and breathes must praise Israel's God (Ps 150:6). God's judgment of and rule over the nations is especially addressed in Pss 82:8; 98:2-9; cf. 67:2-8 [NRSV 67:1-8].

Conclusion: Divine Wrath and Salvation in Matthew's Narrative World

What, then, has this study accomplished? There is no need to repeat in detail the results of our investigation; summaries have already been given at the end of Parts I and II, respectively (chapters 4 and 8). Instead, we shall limit ourselves here to some general comments on the overall historical reconstruction of Matthew's story world and its meaning in terms of divine judgment as it has emerged as a result of our findings.

The narrative world in which Matthew's characters, both as individuals and as groups, live and move and have their being is a complex place full of oppression, pain, scheming, ill will, hate, fear, frustration, confusion, betrayal, and helplessness. It is also, however, a world of hope, repentance, resistance, kindness, compassion, love, mercy, gladness, determination, and ultimate defeat unexpectedly turned into irreversible victory. On the surface, the story line is rather straightforward. The main character, Jesus, is a Judean born in Bethlehem as the rightful heir to the throne in Jerusalem. When the illegitimate ruling king attempts to kill the child, the family flees and they become refugees, first in Egypt, and then, having returned to the land of Israel, in Galilee. Having grown up in Galilee, the legitimate king, soon to be revealed as the Messiah himself, returns to Judea and joins John's prophetic apocalyptic-eschatological movement, preaching the need for one and all to repent from their evil ways and prepare for the kingdom, which is about to be established through God's judgment; divine wrath will soon sweep the land and finally rid it of all breakers of the law. When John is arrested by the ruler of Galilee and Perea, the son of the former king of the Jews, Herod, Jesus returns to Galilee and sets in motion his own movement with a core of twelve disciples working as his closest partners, preaching in the north what John had urged in the south: "Repent, for the kingdom of heaven has come near!" (3:2; 4:17). Despite meeting some resistance from local civic administrators and authorities of Torah, Jesus gathers a large following in Galilee by proclaiming the message in public synagogues and in open-air settings (4:23–25; 9:35; 19:1–2), teaching God's judgment through law and exorcising demons (5:1; 15:29–31). After having organized the disciples (16:18–19; 18:1–35), the Messiah then leads the Galilean crowds to Judea, where yet more people band together with them as they aim at Jerusalem (21:8–9), the capital where the royal throne is vacant but where the presence of God still dwells in the temple (21:12–16; 23:21).

In Jerusalem, however, corrupt religio-political authorities, who have abandoned the Torah, and thus, also the covenant with the God of Israel, have replaced the former illegitimate king and now rule by the power of Rome (and its gods). Protecting its own position and privilege, Jerusalem does not receive the Davidic Bethlehemite as he returns from Galilee with crowds steeped in messianic fervor (21:8–9). Instead, the leaders of the city seek to achieve through irregular judicial procedures what Herod once failed to accomplish: the death of the legitimate heir to the throne. Murder, torture, and persecution are rampant in the capital as the sins of ancient Israelite rulers, iniquities for which no atonement had been sought or given, are invoked from the shadows of the past by the transgressions of the leading figures of the present generation (23:29–36), defiling the temple so severely that the point of no return is reached. God, whose holiness cannot coexist with the impure, departs from his dwelling and prepares to unleash apocalyptic calamities as he leaves the city susceptible to destruction by soldiers (23:37–24:2; 22:7; 24:7–21).

What began as a triumph (21:7–11) is turned into tragedy as the Messiah, betrayed by one of his own disciples, is finally caught, and then, executed by the foreign imperial powers. The God of Israel, however, brings Jesus out of Hades on the third day and, unexpectedly, bestows upon him universal powers in heaven and on earth. Having returned to Galilee, the disciples, awaiting the final apocalyptic suffering that will lead to the end of all unrighteousness (13:41–42), and eventually, bring on new beginnings in a kingdom in which they will judge and rule the twelve tribes of Israel (13:43; 19:28), are sent out to all the nations of the world with the task of turning them too, before it is too late, into Torah-observing disciples of Israel's risen Messiah.

The first-time reader of Matthew does not know until chapters 23 and 24 that the crowds' perfect observance of the commandments will not be enough to prevent disaster, since the temple will become so defiled by unrepentant leading Jerusalemites that its destruction is inevitable. The question of *why* Jesus has to die is left until the end of the story. The issue of his death as such is signaled by three predictions (16:21; 17:22–23; 20:18–19). From a Galilean and early Judean, pre-Jerusalem horizon, however, such predictions align, theo-historically, with stories about the death of prophets at the hands of corrupt political leaders, rather than prompt ideas about mechanisms of atonement.[1] With the devastating disclosure of the soon to happen loss of the temple comes new insight into what 1:21 really meant. Not only will the people be saved through being shepherded by true teaching of the law; the shepherd himself (2:6; 18:12–14) will voluntarily give up his own life as a sacrifice, substituting for the means of atonement no longer available through the now abandoned temple (26:28). In this way, the Mosaic covenant, broken as a consequence of flawed leaders, is restored; here, within the revived covenant, the Jewish people may

---

1. Note, however, the isolated hint to death as related to atonement in Matt 20:28, just before the entry into Jerusalem.

find refuge as Jerusalem is destroyed and the final judgment approaches (chapters 24–25).

From a Second-Temple perspective, such developments make theo-ritual sense as an attempt at saving the Jewish people from the divine judgment that would otherwise inevitably have befallen them (since the law is valid until heaven and earth disappear and will condemn anyone who does not have access to cultic means of atonement). Few readers, however, would likely have been able to predict that after law had been taught and atonement achieved, Jesus's post-resurrection status would become so transformed that all the nations of the world would now come under his cosmic control.[2] Indeed, that Israel's God would aim to bring the nations *into his covenant* in order to save as many as possible of them too as the world is about to be reborn is narratively quite unexpected. A previously explicitly stated closed-ethnic approach (10:5–6; 15:24) to judgment and salvation is replaced by a just as explicitly proclaimed open-ethnic stance to the nations in the final verses of the book (28:18–20).[3]

As the plot develops toward its climax, the modern-day reader realizes that the worldview that controls how events are shaped, presented, and explained in this Gospel is religio-culturally quite foreign to most Western ideas about how the world works. The story is, on one level, construed as warfare, as it were, between the God of Israel and his Spirit working through the Messiah, on the one hand, and the devil and demons and unclean spirits related to him, which roam the land of Israel and afflict the people in various ways, on the other. It is a world in which the cosmic and spiritual, gods and demons, are inextricably intertwined with the earthly and political, so that, ultimately, what is played out on the ground is experienced as a struggle between the kingdom of Satan and the kingdom of heaven (12:26–29).[4] This leads to an overall perception of reality in which

---

2. Thus in effect removing the control of the nations from the devil (Matt 4:8–9).

3. For the terminology of open- and closed ethnic approaches, see above, chapter 5.3. To be noted is that a non-ethnic stance is completely foreign to the First Gospel.

4. Cf. Matt 4:8–9. See also, Luke 10:17–20 and Rev 12:7–12; these texts express the same basic conviction with regard to the inseparability of things cosmic and earthly, but construes the events involved somewhat differently.

causality is turned on its head; what seems to be a problem originating in socio-political and imperial mismanagement and violence is, in reality, a mirror image of cosmic disorder, caused, in turn, by poor worship and life choices on earth. We find a causal system of connections that follows an A–B–B–A pattern:

A. Plight in the land leads to realization that there is
  B. Disorder in the cosmic/spirit world. Thus,
  B. Plight must be addressed on the cosmic/spirit level, so that
A. Suffering in the land can be eliminated.

There are some complicating factors, though, to this pattern. Jews, as all other religio-ethnic collectivities, recognized the existence of a multitude of gods and lesser demonic beings.[5] Contrary to other people groups, however, they worshipped only one God, the God of Israel, whom they were convinced was stronger and mightier than any other divine or demonic powers, including Jupiter, by whose will Rome had conquered and now ruled the world. For Matthew, though, Rome ruled on the authority of the devil. Because the devil had all the kingdoms of the world in his hand he could assign their rule to anyone he wished (4:8–9); since Rome ruled, it follows that they must have received their dominance from the evil power *par excellence*, the same power Jesus was fighting as he worked to establish the kingdom of heaven (12:25–30). The question of politics is, thus, ultimately, a question of worship and vice versa (4:10); for the Matthean Jesus, as for other Jews, worship (and politics) is summed up in Torah observance (5:17–19; 28:16–20).

Based on the conviction that Israel's God stands tall in the midst of other gods and can never be defeated, any calamity that befalls

---

5. On the god-congested universe of ancient societies, see Paula Fredriksen, *Augustine and the Jews: A Christian Defense of Jews and Judaism* (New Haven: Yale University Press, 2010), 3–103. The case for abandoning traditional definitions of "monotheism" is made also in, eadem, "Mandatory Retirement: Ideas in the Study of Christian Origins whose Time has Come to Go," *Studies in Religion/Sciences Religieuses* 35 (2006), 231–46. On the cosmology of judgment, see already J. Arthur Baird, *The Justice of God in the Teachings of Jesus* (London: SCM Press, 1963), 75–151, esp. 75–93.

the people must be explained in terms of guilt originating within the people. Therefore, suffering is construed, partly, as divine punishment. When temples in Jerusalem fall, the prophets of the Hebrew Bible point to the shedding of innocent blood and oppression of the defenseless; Josephus blames rebellious thugs and bandits in the city, and the rabbis trace the guilt back to baseless hatred and lack of unity. Matthew's Jesus, on his part, blames Jewish leadership groups for the poor state in which the fragmented land and its people exist. Something must be done. False leadership must be replaced by the rightful Messianic ruler and his closest followers so that the people can be liberated and the land healed (21:43; 19:28). For this to happen, though, demonic powers, invigorated and strengthened by unsound human worship and life choices, need to be defeated.

This is the ominous and troubled situation that Matthew has written into his world, and to which he provides a solution as he aims to save his people from perishing along with the ruins of Jerusalem. The eschatologically dense mood of the story, so intensely focused on God's wrath and judgment, is well-captured by a quote from Zephaniah's second chapter:

> Gather together, gather, O shameless[6] nation, before you are driven away like the drifting chaff, before there comes upon you the fierce anger of the Lord, before there comes upon you the day of the Lord's wrath. Seek the Lord, all you humble of the land, who do his commands; seek righteousness, seek humility; perhaps you may be protected on the day of the Lord's wrath.[7]

Matthew's focus is firmly on the people of the land, the "crowds," as he calls them. They are the ones who are suffering, mislead and abused by all the leading groups in society, groups who do not understand or teach Torah as it should be taught (9:35–36; 12:7; 15:13–14; 16:11–12; 23:13–25). The crowds see and understand the difference between Jesus's teaching and that of their scribes (7:28–29), as they can also see and understand the power that is channeled through him in healings

6. LXX has *apaideutos* ('ignorant').
7. Zeph 2:1–3 (NRSV, slightly modified).

and exorcisms (9:33; 15:31). Part of the importance of these stories about Jesus's activities lies in the fact that they reveal that this text aims primarily at saving the Jewish people—as opposed to other nations—from the coming judgment. The eschatological judgment is approaching, and the people must be prepared if they are to survive the apocalyptic suffering that precedes it. While rejection of the need to repent and failure to return to full observance of Torah, as it was originally intended by God, will lead to condemnation and exclusion from the coming kingdom through fire (Gehenna), the salvific effectiveness of the law is dependent on the divine mercy, grace, and forgiveness that is found within the Mosaic covenant, given to Abraham's children and restored by Jesus. Keeping the commandments is thus a necessary, but not sufficient means to escape destruction and pass through the gates of the kingdom.

Since Torah obedience is relative to a person's ability (25:14–30), perfection, which is required for the kingdom (5:48; cf. 5:20), means to observe the law *and* atone for transgressions; such behavior will keep Abraham's children within the covenant where access is given to divine grace. Keeping intact the notion of lineage (ethnicity) through the upholding of the Abrahamic and Mosaic covenants, while a person's condemnation in the final judgment can always be referred to as based on the unrighteousness of the individual, salvation is ultimately dependent on ancestry (the promises to the Patriarchs), and can therefore only be inherited (*klēronomeō*), never earned. Matthew thus retains the basic theo-ritual logic of Second-Temple Judaism as he shows his people a way forward after the defilement and future destruction of God's dwelling.

Matthew's Second-Temple Jewish understanding of socio-religious and political life also helps explain the salvation-inclusive approach to the outsider discernable in the Gospel. The Christ-fearers' position, which excludes the requirement of conversion to receive a share of the blessings of the kingdom, makes perfect sense in Galilean settings narratively predating the defilement of the temple. The post-temple abandonment and eschatologically motivated cancelling of this status as well as its replacement with an open-ethnic approach to save the non-Jew through proselyte conversion is more unexpected, perhaps. If we note, however, that other temple-critical and eschatologically oriented associations such as the sectarians at Qumran accepted proselytes as members of their group and, at the same time, nurtured the idea that only they would be victorious in the final war against the sons of darkness (i.e., all other Jews and non-Jews), it makes more sense to connect temple-less end-of-time expectations with the exclusive salvific efficacy of a restored or reinvented covenant relationship.

In addition to such exclusive claims to a restored saving covenant, open to non-Jews who accept full conversion, Matthew also accepted a version of the notion of the possible salvation of the outsider, *as outsider*, under certain circumstances (25:31–46). Contrary to the more open later rabbinic notion of a separate Noahide covenant for non-Jews, Matthew used the logic of the Abrahamic covenant (Gen 12:3) and made such salvation dependent on the other's treatment of the suffering (messianic-Jewish) in-group. For Matthew, in the end, salvation is, whatever the approach, from the Jews, and therefore, dependent on the Jews.[8] Although not explicitly related to the Abrahamic covenant, a similar theological dynamic still exists in modern forms of Judaism alongside the notion of the Noahide covenant, and may be observed (on a much larger scale) in the rules governing the identification of righteous gentiles at the Yad Vashem memorial in Jerusalem.

The reconstructed Matthean thought pattern presented in this study sheds light on a specific eschatologically-oriented variant of Second-Temple Judaism, in which the prospect of imminent divine judgment has led to a focus on perfect Torah observance and intense attention to atonement and forgiveness within the context of a restored Mosaic covenant. We are dealing with, as Daniel Boyarin would phrase it,[9] a

8. Matthew would thus agree with both John's Gospel (4:22) and Paul (Rom 11) regarding the basic conviction of where the center is located, even though there would be considerable disagreement between them as to how this conviction should be realized in concrete terms.
9. Cf. Daniel Boyarin, *Borderlines: The Partition of Judeo-Christianity* (Philadelphia: Pennsylvania University Press, 2004).

"dialect" of Judaism that finds its closest comparative material in other Second-Temple and later rabbinic Jewish "dialects." Redirecting our attention beyond the Gospel's inception history to its later reception history, two main trajectories are discernable: one in which this Jewish "dialect" is developed further locally,[10] and another, in which Matthew was used as a contribution to the creation of a new language, Christianity.[11] The reason why the former has been so neglected in the history of research, and the latter so prominent that historians often still think of Matthew as a "Christian" text—despite the fact that "Christian" or "Christianity" do not exist as categories in the world of this text and are foreign to it—is likely that there is some truth to the saying that a language is "a dialect with an army." Indeed, had Matthew's Gospel been written a century or so later, it would probably have been identified as a heretical text.[12]

In any case, this complex and entangled inception and reception history suggests that the First Gospel should be approached as a topic

---

10. The earliest such reception of Matthew, probably even part of its inception history, is found in the Didache (see discussion in Huub van de Sandt and David Flusser, *The Didache: Its Jewish Sources and its Place in Early Judaism and Christianity* [Assen: Royal van Gorcum, 2002]; Alan J. P. Garrow, *The Gospel of Matthew's Dependence on the Didache* [London: T & T Clark, 2004]; Huub van de Sandt and Jürgen K. Zangenberg (eds.) *Matthew, James, and the Didache: Three Related Documents in Their Jewish and Christian Settings* [Atlanta: Society of Biblical Literature, 2008]). Later key examples include, e.g., *Rec.* 1.27–71 (see discussion in F. Stanley Jones, *An Ancient Jewish Christian Source on the History of Christianity: Pseudo-Clementine "Recognitions" 1.27–71* [Texts and Translations 37, Christian Apocrypha Series 2; Atlanta: Scholars, 1995]); the Pseudo-Clementine Homilies (cf. Annette Yoshiko Reed, "'Jewish Christianity' After the 'Parting of the Ways': Approaches to Historiography and Self-Definition in the Pseudo-Clementines," in *The Ways that Never Parted: Jews and Christians in Late Antiquity and the Early Middle Ages* [Tübingen: Mohr Siebeck, 2003], 189–231); and the Didascalia Apostolorum (cf. Charlotte Elisheva Fonrobert, "The Didascalia Apostolorum: A Mishnah for the Disciples of Jesus," *Journal of Early Christian Studies* 9.4 [2001], 483–509). See also, Karin Hedner Zetterholm, "Jesus-Oriented Visions of Judaism in Antiquity" in *Scripta Instituti Donneriani Aboensis no. 27: Jewish Studies in the Nordic Countries Today* (2016): 37–60. For general discussion of Jewish uses of Matthew, see James Carleton Paget, "Jewish Christianity," in *Cambridge History of Judaism, vol. 3, The Early Roman Period* (ed. William Horbury et al.; Cambridge: Cambridge University Press, 1999), 731–75.
11. While disputed, it is likely that Ignatius of Antioch presents us with the earliest such use of Matthew's Gospel. For discussion, see Édouard Massaux, *Influence de l'évangile de saint Matthieu sur la littérature chrétienne avant saint Irénée* (Universitas Catholica Lovaniensis, Dissertationes, Ser. 2, 42; Leuven: Leuven University Press, 1950; 2nd ed., 1986; Eng. trans., part 1, 1990); Helmut Koester, *Synoptische Überlieferung bei den Apostolischen Vätern* (TUGAL 65; Berlin: Akademie,1957); Wolf-Dietrich Köhler, *Die Rezeption des Matthäusevangeliums in der Zeit vor Irenaeus* (WUNT 24; Tübingen: Mohr Siebeck, 1987); D. Jeffrey Bingham, *Irenaeus' Use of Matthew's Gospel in Adversus Haereses* (Traditio Exegetica Graeca 7; Louvain: Peeters, 1998); Jean-François Racine, *The Text of Matthew in the Writings of Basil of Caesarea* (New Testament in the Greek Fathers 5; Boston: Brill, 2004).
12. So also Reinbold, "Das Matthäusevangelium, die Pharisäer und die Tora," 71.

443

of key importance within the larger fields of Jewish origins and Christian (canonical) reception of Jewish texts, perhaps with a special focus within both fields on how text is produced and used in the process of identity construction and community formation. In the end, it is clear that both Jews and Christians found revelatory value in this eschatological narrative, saturated as it is by an uninterrupted flow of judgment sayings that mark the boundaries of a community of equals fiercely critical of self-serving leadership. From a hermeneutical perspective, and referring back to the discussion in the Preface, one may conclude that only to the degree that later uses of Matthew converge upon the conviction that the proclamation of divine judgment brings hope of salvation to the marginalized and the compassionate, but constitutes a threat to the unrepentant powerful, do they emerge as being in interpretive contact with the aims of the Matthean Jesus.

Bibliography

Primary Sources and Translations

Aberbach, Moses and Bernard Grossfeld. *Targum Onkelos to Genesis: A Critical Analysis Together with an English Translation of the Text (Based of A.Sperber's Edition)*. New York: Ktav Publishing, 1982.

Alexander, Philip S. *The Targum Lamentations: Translated, with a Critical Introduction, Apparatus, and Notes*. Collegeville: Liturgical Press, 2008.

The Apocrypha and Pseudepigrapha of the Old Testament in English. With Introduction and Critical and Explanatory Notes to Several Books. Translated by Robert H. Charles. Vol. 2. Oxford: Clarendon Press, 1913.

'*Avot de Rabbi Nathan. The Fathers according to Rabbi Nathan*. Translated from the Hebrew by Judah Goldin. New Haven: Yale University Press, 1955.

The Babylonian Talmud. Vols. 1–17. Translated by Rabbi Dr. I. Epstein. London: Soncino, 1961.

תלמוד בבלי. The Vilna edition. Jerusalem, 1973.

Biblia Hebraica Stuttgartensia. Edited by K. Elliger and W. Rudolph. Stuttgart: Deutsche Bibelgesellschaft, 1987.

Clarke, Ernest G. *Targum Pseudo-Jonathan of the Pentateuch: Text and Concordance*. Hoboken: Ktav Publishing, 1984.

The Dead Sea Scrolls in English. Translated by G. Vermes. London: Penguin, 1995.

The Dead Sea Scrolls Reader. Vol. 1 *Texts Concerned with Religious Law, Exegetical Texts and Parabiblical Texts*. Vol 2 *Calendrical texts and sapiental texts, Poetic and liturgical texts, Additional genres and unclassified texts*. Edited by Donald W.

Parry and Emanuel Tov in association with Geraldine I. Clements. 2nd rev. and enl. ed. Leiden: Brill, 2014.

The Dead Sea Scrolls Translated. The Qumran Texts in English. Translated by F. Garcia Martinez. 2nd ed. Leiden: Brill, 1996.

The Dead Sea Scrolls Uncovered: The First Complete Translation and Interpretation of 50 Key Documents Withheld for Over 35 Years. Edited by R. Eisenman and M. Wise. New York: Penguin, 1992.

The Holy Bible containing the Old and New Testaments. Revised Standard Version. New York: Oxford University Press, 1971.

The Holy Bible containing the Old and New Testaments with the Aprocryphal/ Deuterocanonical Books: New Revised Standard Version. New York: Oxford University Press, 1989.

The Holy Bible: New International Version. London: Hodder & Stoughton, 1982.

Jerome, St. *Sancit Hieronymi Presbyteri. Commentariorum in Mathaeum libri iv.* Edited by D. Hurst and M. Adriaen. CCSL 77. Turnhout: Brepols, 1969.

———. *Commentary on Matthew.* Translated by Thomas P. Scheck. Washington: The Catholic University of America Press, 2008.

Josephus. Translated by Henry St. J. Thackeray et al. 10 vols. LCL. Cambridge: Harvard University Press, 1926–1965.

Mekilta de-Rabbi Ishmael. Vols. 1–3. Edited by J. Z. Lauterbach. Philadelphia: The Jewish Publication Society of America, 1933–1935.

Meyer, Marvin W., and Harold Bloom. *The Gospel of Thomas: The Hidden Sayings of Jesus.* San Francisco: HarperSanFrancisco, 1992.

Midrash Rabbah. Midrash Rabbah translated into English with notes, glossary and indices under the editorship of Rabbi Dr. H. Freedman and Maurice Simon. Vols. 1–10. London: Soncino, 1961.

מדרש רבה על חמשה חומשי תורה וחמש מגלות. The Vilna edition. Jerusalem, 1961.

Mishnayoth. Pointed Hebrew Text, English Translation, Introductions, Notes, Supplement, Appendix, Indexes, Addenda, Corrigenda. Edited by P. Blackman. 2nd ed. Vols. 1–7. Gateshead: Judaica Press, 1990.

Novum Testamentum Graece. Nestle-Aland. 28th ed. Stuttgart: Deutsche Bibelgesellschaft, 2012.

Old Testament Pseudepigrapha. Edited by James H. Charlesworth. 2 vols. New York: Doubleday, 1983, 1985.

Origen. *Fontes Christiani: zweisprachige Neuausgabe christlicher Quellentexte aus Altertum und Mittelalter : Bd. 2 4: Commentarii in epistulam ad Romanos, Liber septimus.* Freiburg: Herder Verlag, 1991.

Philo. Translated by F. H., Colson, J. W. Earp, R. Marcus, and G. H. Whitaker. 10 vols. and 2 supplement vols. LCL. Cambridge, MA: Harvard University Press, 1927–1962.

Septuaginta. Vetus Testamentum graece auctoritate Societatis Göttingensis editum. Göttingen: Vandenhoeck & Ruprecht, 1931–.

The Tosefta. Translated from the Hebrew by J. Neusner. Vols. 1–6. New York 1977–1986.

תוספתא. Based on the Erfurt and Vienna codices. Edited by M.S. Zuckermandel. With Supplement to the Tosephta by S. Liebermann. Jerusalem, 1960.

The Apostolic Fathers. Vol 1: *1 Clement, 2 Clement, Ignatius, Polycarp, Didache.* Edited and translated by Bart D. Ehrman. LCL 24. Cambridge, MA: Harvard University Press, 2003.

Secondary Literature

Aalen, Sverre. *Gud i Kristus: Nytestamentlige studier.* Oslo: Universitetsforlaget, 1986.

Ådna, Jostein and Hans Kvalbein, eds. *The Mission of the Early Church to Jews and Gentiles.* WUNT 127. Tübingen: Mohr Siebeck, 2000.

Albright, W.F. and C.S. Mann. *Matthew: Introduction, Translation, and Notes.* AB 26. New York: Doubleday, 1971.

Allen, W. C. *A Critical and Exegetical Commentary on the Gospel According to Saint Matthew.* 2nd ed. ICC. Edinburgh: T&T Clark, 1907.

Allison, Dale C. *The New Moses: A Matthean Typology.* Minneapolis: Fortress, 1993.

____. *Studies in Matthew: Interpretation Past and Present.* Grand Rapids: Baker Academic, 2005.

____. "Matt 23:39 = Luke 13:35b as a Conditional Prophecy." *JSNT* 18 (1983): 75–84.

Anderson, Arnold A. *The Book of Psalms.* Vol. 1. London: Oliphants, 1972.

Anderson, Gary A. "From Israel's Burden to Israel's Debt: Towards a Theology of Sin in Biblical and Early Second Temple Sources." Pages 1–30 in *Reworking the Bible: Apocryphal and Related Texts at Qumran. Proceedings of a Joint*

Symposium by the Orion Center for the Study of the Dead Sea Scrolls and Associated Literature and the Hebrew University Institute for Advanced Studies Research Group on Qumran, 15-17 January, 2002. Edited by Esther G. Chazon, Devorah Diman, and Ruth A. Clements. STDJ 58. Leiden: Brill, 2005.

Anderson, Janice Capel. *Matthew's Narrative Web: Over, and Over, and Over Again.* JSNTSup 91. Sheffield: Sheffield Academic, 1994.

Argall, Randal A. *1 Enoch and Sirach: A Comparative Literary and Conceptual Analysis of the Themes of Revelation, Creation and Judgment.* SBLEJL 8. Atlanta: Scholars Press, 1995.

Ascough, Richard S., ed. *Religious Rivalries and the Struggle for Success in Sardis and Smyrna.* ESCJ 14. Waterloo: Wilfrid Laurier University Press, 2005.

Avemarie, Friedrich. "Erwählung und Vergeltung: Zur Optionalen Struktur Rabbinischer Soteriologie." *NTS* 45 (1999): 108–26.

Bacon, B. W. *Studies in Matthew.* New York: Henry Holt; London: Constable, 1930.

Baird, J. Arthur. *The Justice of God in the Teachings of Jesus.* NTL. London: SCM, 1963.

Balabanski, Vicky. "Mission in Matthew against the Horizon of Matthew 24." *NTS* 54 (2008): 161–75.

Banks, Robert. *Jesus and the Law in the Synoptic Tradition.* SNTSMS 28. Cambridge: Cambridge University Press, 1975.

Barker, Margaret. "Isaiah." Pages 489–542, in *Eerdmans Commentary on the Bible.* Edited by James D. G. Dunn and John W. Rogerson. Grand Rapids: Eerdmans, 2003.

Baron, Salo W. *A Social and Religious History of the Jews.* Vol. 1. New York: Columbia University Press, 1952.

Barth, Gerhard. "Matthew's Understanding of the Law." Pages 58–164, in *Tradition and Interpretation in Matthew.* Edited by Günther Bornkamm, Gerhard Barth, and Heinz Joachim Held. NTL. London: SCM, 1963.

Bauckham, Richard. "James." Pages 1483–92 in *Eerdmans Commentary on the Bible.* Edited by James D. G. Dunn and John W. Rogerson. Grand Rapids: Eerdmans.

Bauer, David R. *The Structure of Matthew's Gospel: A Study in Literary Design.* JSNTSup 31. Sheffield: Almond Press, 1989.

Baum, Armin. *Der mündliche Faktor: Analogien zur synoptischen Frage aus der antiken Literatur, der experimentalpsychologie, der Oral Poetry-Forschung und dem rabbinischen Traditionswesen.* Texte und Arbeiten zum Neutestamentlichen Zeitalter 49. Tübingen: Franke, 2008.

_____. "Matthew's Sources – Written or Oral? A Rabbinic Analogy and Empirical Insights." Pages 1–23 in *Built Upon the Rock: Studies in the Gospel of Matthew.* Edited by Daniel M. Gurtner and John Nolland. Grand Rapids: Eerdmans, 2008.

Baumgarten, Albert I. *The Flourishing of Jewish Sects in the Maccabean Era: An Interpretation.* Leiden: Brill, 1997.

Baxter, Wayne. *Israel's Only Shepherd: Matthew's Shepherd Motif and His Social Setting.* LNTS 457. London: T&T Clark, 2012.

Bazzana, Giovanni Battista. "*Basileia* and Debt Relief: The Forgiveness of Debts in the Lord's Prayer in the Light of Documentary Papyri." *CBQ* 73 (2011): 511–25.

Beare, Francis Wright. "The Mission of the Disciples and the Mission Charge: Matthew 10 and Parallels." *JBL* 89 (1970): 1–13.

_____. *The Gospel according to Matthew: A Commentary.* Oxford: Blackwell, 1981.

Bernier, Jonathan. Aposynagōgos *and the Historical Jesus in John: Rethinking the Historicity of the Johannine Expulsion Passages.* BibInt 122. Leiden: Brill, 2013.

Bhabha, H. "Of Mimicry and Man: The Ambivalence of Colonial Discourse." Pages 234–41 in *Modern Literary Theory.* Edited by P. Rice and P. Waugh. London: Edward Arnold, 1989.

Bickerman, Elias J. *The Jews in the Greek Age.* Cambridge, MA; Harvard University Press, 1988.

Binder, Donald D. *Into the Temple Courts: The Place of the Synagogues in the Second Temple Period.* SBLDS 169. Atlanta: Society of Biblical Literature, 1999.

Bingham, D. Jeffrey. *Irenaeus' Use of Matthew's Gospel in Adversus Haereses.* Traditio Exegetica Graeca 7. Louvain: Peeters, 1998.

Blanton IV, Thomas R. "Saved by Obedience: Matthew 1:21 in Light of Jesus' Teaching on the Torah." *JBL* 132 (2013): 393–413.

Boccaccini, Gabriele. *Middle Judaism: Jewish Thought 300 B.C.E. to 200 C.E.* Minneapolis: Fortress, 1991.

Bockmuehl, Markus. "The Noachide Commandments and New Testament Ethics." *RB* (1995): 72–101.

_____. "IQS and Salvation in Qumran." Pages 383–414, in *The Complexities of Second Temple Judaism*. Vol. 1 of *Justification and Variegated Nomism*. Edited by D. A. Carson, Peter T. OBrien, and Mark Seifrid. Tübingen: Mohr Siebeck; Grand Rapids: Baker Academic, 2001.

Bond, Helen K. *Pontius Pilate in History and Interpretation*. SNTSMS 100. Cambridge: Cambridge University Press, 1998.

Bornkamm, Günther. "Der Lohngedanke im Neuen Testament." Pages 69–92, in *Studien zu Antike und Urchristentum*. Gesammelte Aufsätze. Band II. Edited by Günther Bornkamm. BEvT 28. Munich: Chr. Kaiser Verlag, 1959.

_____. "End-Expectation and Church in Matthew." Pages 15–51, in *Tradition and Interpretation in Matthew*. Edited by Günther Bornkamm, Gerhard Barth, and Heinz Joachim Held. NTL. London: SCM, 1963.

Boyarin, Daniel. *Borderlines: The Partition of Judeo-Christianity*. Philadelphia: Pennsylvania University Press, 2004.

_____. *The Jewish Gospels: The Story of the Jewish Christ*. New York: New Press, 2012.

Brandenburger, Egon. "Gerichtskonzeptionen im Urchristentum und ihre Voraussetzungen. Eine Problemstudie." Pages 289–338, in *Studien zur Geschichte und Theologie des Urchristentums*. Edited by Egon Brandenburger. SBAB 15. Stuttgart: Verlag Katholisches Bibelwerk, 1993.

Bright, John. *Covenant and Promise: The Prophetic Understanding of the Future in Pre-Exilic Israel*. Philadelphia: Westminster Press, 1976.

Brown, Jeannine K. "Matthew, Gospel of." Pages 570–84, in *Dictionary of Jesus and the Gospels: A Compendium of Contemporary Biblical Scholarship*. Edited by Joel B. Green. 2nd ed. Downers Grove, IL: InterVarsity, 2013.

Brown, Michael Joseph. "Matthew, Gospel of." *NIDB* 3:839–52.

Brown, Raymond E. *The Birth of the Messiah: A Commentary on the Infancy Narratives in the Gospels of Matthew and Luke*. ABRL. New York: Doubleday, 1993.

_____. *The Churches the Apostles left Behind*. New York: Doubleday, 1984.

Brown, Raymond E. *The Death of the Messiah: From Gethsemane to the Grave. A Commentary on the Passion Narratives in the Four Gospels*. 2 vols. London: Geoffrey Chapman, 1994.

Brown, Schuyler. "The Matthean Community and the Gentile Mission." *NovT* 22 (1980): 193–221.

Bryan, Steven. *Jesus and Israel's Traditions of Judgment and Restoration.* SNTSMS 117. Cambridge: Cambridge University Press, 2002.

Buchanan, George W. *The Consequences of the Covenant.* NovTSup 20. Leiden: Brill, 1970.

Byrskog, Samuel. *Jesus the Only Teacher: Didactic Authority and Transmission in Ancient Israel, Ancient Judaism, and the Matthean Community.* ConBNT 24. Stockholm: Almqvist & Wiksell, 1994.

Campbell, R. Alastair. *The Elders: Seniority within Earliest Christianity.* SNTW. Edinburgh: T&T Clark, 1994.

Caragounis, Chrys C. *The Son of Man: Vision and Interpretation.* WUNT 38. Tübingen: Mohr Siebeck, 1986.

Cargal, Timothy. "'His Blood Be upon Us and upon Our Children': A Matthean Double Entendre?" *NTS* 37 (1991): 101–12.

Carleton Paget, James. "Jewish Proselytism at the Time of Christian Origins: Chimera or Reality?" *JSNT* 62 (1996): 65–103.

Carlston, Charles E, and Craig A. Evans. *From Synagogue to Ecclesia: Matthew's Community at the Crossroads,* WUNT. Tübingen: Mohr Siebeck, 2014.

Carmody, Timothy R. "Matt 18:15–17 in Relation to Three Texts from Qumran Literature (CD 9:2–8, 16–22; 1QS 5:26–6:1)." Pages 141–58, in *To Touch the Text: Biblical and Related Studies in Honor of Joseph A. Fitzmyer, S.J.* Edited by Maurya P. Horgan and Paul J. Kobelski. New York: Crossroad, 1989.

Carson, D. A. "The Jewish Leaders in Matthew's Gospel: A Reappraisal." *JETS* 25 (1982): 16--74.

Carson, D. A., Peter T. Obrien, and Mark Seifrid, eds. *The Complexities of Second Temple Judaism.* Vol. 1 of *Justification and Variegated Nomism.* Tübingen: Mohr Siebeck; Grand Rapids: Baker Academic, 2001.

Carter, Warren. *Matthew and Empire: Initial Explorations.* Harrisburg: Trinity Press International, 2001.

____. *Matthew and the Margins: A Socio-Political and Religious Reading.* London: T&T Clark, 2000.

____. "Matthew and the Gentiles: Individual Conversion and/or Systemic Transformation?" *JSNT* 26 (2004): 259–82.

Charette, Blaine. *The Theme of Recompense in Matthew's Gospel.* Sheffield: Sheffield Academic, 1992.

_____. *Restoring Presence: The Spirit in Matthew's Gospel.* Sheffield: Sheffield Academic, 2000.

Childs, Peter and Patrick Williams. *An Introduction to Post-Colonial Theory.* London: Prentice Hall, 1997.

Chow, Simon. *The Sign of Jonah Reconsidered: A Study of Its Meaning in the Gospel Traditions.* ConBNT 27. Uppsala: Almqvist & Wiksell, 1995.

Clark, Kenneth W. "The Gentile Bias in Matthew." *JBL* 66 (1947): 165–72.

Clarke, Howard. *The Gospel of Matthew and Its Readers: A Historical Introduction to the First Gospel.* Bloomington: Indiana University Press, 2003.

Clements, Ronald E. *Isaiah 1–39.* NCB. Grand Rapids: Eerdmans, 1980.

Cohen, Shaye J. D. "Were the Pharisees and Rabbis the Leaders of Communal Prayer and Torah Study in the First Century? The Evidence of the New Testament, Josephus, and the Early Church Fathers." Pages 89–105, in *Evolution of the Synagogue: Problems and Progress.* Edited by Howard C. Kee and Lynn H. Cohick. Harrisburg: Trinity Press, 1999.

Collins, Nina L. *Jesus, The Sabbath, and The Jewish Debate: Healing on the Sabbath in the 1st and 2nd Centuries CE.* LNTS 474; New York: T&T Clark, 2014.

Cook, Michael J. "Interpreting 'Pro-Jewish' Passages in Matthew." *HUCA* 54 (1983): 135–46.

Cope, O. Lamar. "Matthew XXV:31–46, 'The Sheep and the Goats' Reinterpreted." *NovT* 11 (1969): 32–44.

_____. *Matthew: A Scribe Trained for the Kingdom of Heaven.* Washington: The Catholic Biblical Association of America, 1976.

_____. "To the Close of the Age: The Role of Apocalyptic Thought in the Gospel of Matthew." Pages 113–24, in *Apocalyptic and the New Testament: Essays in Honour of J. Louis Martyn.* Edited by Joel Marcus and Marion L. Soards. Sheffield: Sheffield Academic, 1989.

Cousland, J. R. C. *The Crowds in Matthew's Gospel.* NovTSup 102. Leiden: Brill, 2001.

Crossley, James G. *The New Testament and Jewish Law: A Guide for the Perplexed.* London: T&T Clark, 2010.

Davies, Margaret. *Matthew.* Sheffield: Sheffield Academic, 1993.

Davies, W. D. and Dale C. Allison. *The Gospel According of Saint Matthew.* 3 vols. ICC. London: T&T Clark, 1988–1997.

Davison, James E. "Anomia and the Question of an antinomian Polemic in Matthew." *JBL* 104 (1985): 617–33.

Deines, Roland. "Not the Law but the Messiah: Law and Righteousness in the Gospel of Matthew: An Ongoing Debate." Pages 53–84, in *Built on the Rock: Studies in the Gospel of Matthew.* Edited by Daniel M. Gurtner and John Nolland. Grand Rapids: Eerdmans, 2008.

Dobbeler, Stephanie von. "Wahre und falsche Christen oder: An der Frage der Orthopraxie scheiden sich die Geister." *BZ* 50 (2006): 174–95.

Donahue, John R., S.J. "The 'Parable' of the Sheep and the Goats: A Challenge to Christian Ethics." *TS* 47 (1986): 3–31.

Donaldson, Terence L. *Jesus on the Mountain: A Study on Matthean Theology.* JSNTSup 8. Sheffield: JSOT, 1985.

_____. *Jews and Anti-Judaism in the New Testament: Decision Points and Divergent Interpretations.* Waco: Baylor University Press, 2010.

_____. *Judaism and the Gentiles: Jewish Patterns of Universalism (to 135 CE).* Waco: Baylor University Press, 2007.

_____. *Paul and the Gentiles: Remapping the Apostle's Convictional World.* Minneapolis: Fortress, 1997.

_____. "Proselytes or 'Righteous Gentiles'? The Status of Gentiles in Eschatological Pilgrimage Patterns of Thought." *JSP* 7 (1990): 3–27.

_____, ed. *Religious Rivalries and the Struggle for Success in Caesarea Maritima.* Waterloo: Wilfrid Laurier University Press 2000.

Dresner, Samuel H. *The Zaddik: An Inspired Study of the Mystical Spiritual Leader of 18th Century Hasidism.* New York: Aberlard-Schuman, 1960.

Dunn, James D. G. *Christology in the Making: A New Testament Inquiry into the Origins of the Doctrine of the Incarnation.* 2nd ed. London: SCM, 1989.

_____. *Jesus and the Spirit: A Study of the Religious and Charismatic Experience of Jesus and the First Christians as Reflected in the New Testament.* London: SCM, 1975. Repr., Grand Rapids: Eerdmans, 1997.

_____. *The Partings of the Ways: Between Christianity and Judaism and their Significance for the Character of Christianity.* 2nd ed. London: SCM, 2006.

_____. "A Response to Peter Stuhlmacher." Pages 363–68, in *Auferstehung/ Resurrection: The Fourth Durham-Tübingen Research Symposium: Resurrection, Transfiguration and Exaltation in Old Testament, Ancient Judaism and Early*

Christianity. Edited by Friedrich Avemarie and Hermann Lichtenberger. WUNT 135. Tübingen: Mohr Siebeck, 2001.

Ebeling, Gerhard. *Wort Gottes und Tradition: Studien zu einer Hermeneutik der Konfessionen.* Göttingen: Vandenhoeck and Ruprecht, 1964.

Elliott, Neil. *The Arrogance Nations: Reading Romans in the Shadow of Empire.* Minneapolis: Fortress: 2008.

Engnell, Ivan. *The Call of Isaiah: An Exegetical and Comparative Study.* UUA 4. Uppsala: A.-B. Lundeqvistska, 1949.

Eubank, Nathan. *Wages of Cross-Bearing and Debt of Sin: The Economy of Heaven in Matthew's Gospel.* BZNW 196. Berlin: de Gruyter, 2013.

Evans, C. F. *Saint Luke.* London: SCM, 1990.

Evans, Craig A. "The Jewish Christian Gospel Tradition." Pages 241–77, in *Jewish Believers in Jesus: The Early Centuries.* Edited by Oskar Skarsaune and Reidar Hvalvik. Peabody: Hendrickson, 2007.

____. *Matthew.* New Cambridge Bible Commentary. Cambridge: Cambridge University Press, 2012.

____. "Predictions of the Destruction of the Herodian Temple in the Pseudepigrapha, Qumran Scrolls and Related Texts." *JSP* 10 (1992): 89–147.

Feldman, Louis H. *Jew and Gentile in the Ancient World: Attitudes and Interactions from Alexander to Justinian.* Princeton: Princeton University Press, 1993.

____. "The Omnipresence of the God-Fearers." *BAR* 12 (1986): 59–63.

____. *Studies in Hellenistic Judaism.* AGJU 30. Leiden: Brill, 1996.

Feldman. Louis H. and Meyer Reinhold, eds. *Jewish Life and Thought among Greeks and Romans.* Minneapolis: Fortress, 1996.

Fine, Steven. "Non-Jews in the Synagogues of Late-Antique Palestine: Rabbinic and Archaeological Evidence." Pages 224–42, in *Jews, Christians, and Polytheists in the Ancient Synagogue: Cultural Interaction during the Greco-Roman Period.* Edited by Steven Fine. London: Routledge, 1999.

Fitzmyer, Joseph, S.J. *The Gospel according to Luke.* 2 vols. AB. New York: Doubleday, 1970–1985.

Flusser, David. "Two Anti-Jewish Montages in Matthew." *Imm* 5 (1975): 37–45.

Fonrobert, Charlotte Elisheva. "The Didascalia Apostolorum: A Mishnah for the Disciples of Jesus." *JECS* 9 (2001): 483–509.

Fornberg, Tord. *The Bible in a World of Many Faiths.* Tro och Tanke 2000:3. Uppsala: Svenska kyrkans forskningsråd, 2000.

_____. *Matteusevangeliet 1:1-13-52.* Kommentar till Nya Testamentet 1 A. Uppsala: EFS-förl, 1989.

_____. "Matthew and His Readers: Some Examples from the History of Interpretation." [in Swedish] *Religio* 48 (1997): 25–39.

Foster, Paul. *Community, Law and Mission in Matthew's Gospel.* WUNT 177. Tübingen: Mohr Siebeck, 2004.

France, R. T. *The Gospel According to Matthew.* NICNT. Grand Rapids: Eerdmans, 2007.

_____. *The Gospel According to Matthew: An Introduction and Commentary.* TNTC 1. Leicester: InterVarsity, 1985.

Fredriksen, Paula. *Augustine and the Jews: A Christian Defense of Jews and Judaism.* New Haven: Yale University Press, 2010.

_____. "Mandatory Retirement: Ideas in the Study of Christian Origins whose Time Has Come to Go." *SR* 35 (2006): 231–46.

_____. *Sin: The Early History of an Idea.* Princeton: Princeton University Press, 2012.

Gagné, Renaud. *Ancestral Fault in Ancient Greece.* Cambridge: Cambridge University Press, 2013.

Garlington, D. review of *Matthew's Messianic Shepherd-King: In Search of 'The Lost Sheep of the House of Israel,* by J. Willitts. *RBL* [http://www.bookreviews.org] (2010).

Garrow, Alan J. P. *The Gospel of Matthew's Dependence on the Didache.* LNTS 254. London: T&T Clark, 2004.

Gaston, Lloyd. "The Messiah of Israel as Teacher of the Gentiles." *Int* 29 (1975): 24–40.

Gathercole, Simon J. *Where is Boasting? Early Jewish Soteriology and Paul's Response in Romans 1-5.* Grand Rapids: Eerdmans, 2002.

Gerhardsson, Birger. *The Ethos of the Bible.* Translated by Stephen Westerholm. London: Darton, Longman and Todd, 1982.

_____. *"Hör, Israel": Om Jesus och den gamla bekännelsen.* Lund: LiberLäromedel, 1979.

_____. "Sacrificial Service and Atonement in the Gospel of Matthew." Pages

25–35, in *Reconciliation and Hope: New Testament Essays on Atonement and Eschatology Presented to L. L. Morris on His 60th Birthday.* Edited by Robert J. Banks. Exeter: Paternoster, 1974.

———. "De sju liknelserna i Matteus 13." *SEÅ* 34 (1969): 77–106.

———. *The Testing of God's Son [Matt 4:1–11 & Par]: An Analysis of an Early Christian Midrash.* Lund: CWK Gleerup, 1966. Repr., Wipf & Stock, 2009.

Gerstenberger, Erhard S. *Leviticus: A Commentary.* OTL. Louisville: Westminster John Knox, 1996.

Ginzberg, Louis. "The Religion of the Jews at the Time of Jesus." *HUCA* 1 (1924): 307–21. Repr. pp. 1–15 in *Origins of Judaism, Normative Judaism.* Vol.1. Part 2. Edited by Jacob Neusner. New York: 1990.

"Global Christianity—A Report on the Size and Distribution of the World's Christian Population." *PewResearch Center.* Published Dec 11, 2011. http://www.pewforum.org/2011/12/19/global-christianity-exec/.

Goodacre, Mark. *The Case against Q: Studies in Markan Priority and the Synoptic Problem.* Harrisburgh: Trinity Press International, 2002.

Goodman, Martin. *Mission and Conversion: Proselytizing in the Religious History of the Roman Empire.* Oxford: Clarendon, 1994.

Gowan, Donald E. "Repentance in the OT." *NIDB* 4:764–65.

Gray, Sherman W. *The Least of My Brothers: Matthew 25:31–46: A History of Interpretation.* SBLDS 114. Atlanta: Scholars Press, 1989.

Griffiths, J. Gwyn. *The Divine Verdict: A Study of Divine Judgment in the Ancient Religions.* SHR 52. Leiden: Brill, 1991.

Griswold, Charles L. and David Konstan, eds. *Ancient Forgiveness: Classical, Judaic, and Christian.* Cambridge: Cambridge University Press, 2012.

Grundmann, Walter. "ἁμαρτανω." *TDNT* 1:302–316.

Gundry, Robert H. *Matthew. A Commentary on His Literary and Theological Art.* Grand Rapids: Eerdmans, 1982.

———. *Matthew: A Commentary on His Handbook for a Mixed Church under Persecution.* 2nd ed. Grand Rapids: Eerdmans, 1994.

Gurtner, Daniel M. "The Gospel of Matthew from Stanton to Present: A Survey of Some Recent Developments." Pages 23–38, in *Jesus, Matthew's Gospel, and Early Christianity: Studies in Memory of Graham N. Stanton.* Edited by Daniel

M. Gurtner, Joel Willitts, and Richard A. Burridge. LNTS 435. London: T&T Clark, 2011.

———. "Matthew's Theology of the Temple and the 'Parting of the Ways': Christian Origins and the First Gospel." Pages 128–53, in *Built upon the Rock: Studies in the Gospel of Matthew*. Edited by Daniel M. Gurtner and John Nolland. Grand Rapids: Eerdmans, 2008.

———. *The Torn Veil: Matthew's Exposition of the Death of Jesus*. Cambridge: Cambridge University Press, 2007.

Haenchen, Ernst. "Matthäus 23." *ZTK* 48 (1951): 38–63.

Hägerland, Tobias. *Jesus and the Forgiveness of Sins: An Aspect of his Prophetic Mission*. SNTSMS 150. Cambridge: Cambridge University Press, 2012.

Hagner, Donald A. "Apocalyptic Motifs in the Gospel of Matthew: Continuity and Discontinuity." *HBT* 7 (1985): 53–82.

———. *Matthew 14–28*. WBC. Dallas: Word Books, 1995.

Hahn, Scott W. *Kinship by Covenant: A Canonical Approach to the Fulfillment of God's Saving Promises*. New Haven: Yale University Press, 2009

Hahn, Ferdinand. *Mission in the New Testament*. Translated by Frank Clarke. SBT 47. London: SCM, 1965.

Hamilton, Catherine. "'His Blood Be upon Us': Innocent Blood and the Death of Jesus in Matthew." *CBQ* 70 (2008): 82–100.

———. "Innocent Blood Traditions in Early Judaism and the Death of Jesus in Matthew." PhD diss., Wycliffe College, Toronto School of Theology, 2013.

Hare, Douglas R. A. "How Jewish is the Gospel of Matthew?" *CBQ* 62 (2000): 264–77.

Harrington, Daniel J. *The Gospel of Matthew*. SP. Collegeville: Liturgical Press, 1991.

———. *Meeting St. Matthew Today: Understanding the Man, His Mission, and His Message*. Chicago: Loyola Press, 2010.

Hayward, C. T. R. *Interpretations of the Name Israel in Ancient Judaism and Some Early Christian Writings*. Oxford: Oxford University Press, 2005.

Hill, David. *The Gospel of Matthew*. London: Oliphants, 1972.

Hilton, Michael and Gordian Marshall. *The Gospels and Rabbinic Judaism: A Study Guide*. London: SCM, 1988.

Holowerda, David E. *Jesus and Israel: One Covenant or Two?* Grand Rapids: Eerdmans, 1995.

Hood, Jason B. *The Messiah, His Brothers, and the Nations (Matthew 1:1–17).* LNTS 441. New York: T&T Clark, 2011.

Hooker, Morna D. "Uncomfortable Words: The Prohibition of Foreign Missions (Mt. 105–6)." *ExpTim* 82 (1971): 361–65.

Hourihane, Colum. *Pontius Pilate, Anti-Semitism, and the Passion in Medieval Art.* Princeton: Princeton University Press, 2009.

Hyatt, J. Philip. *Exodus.* Grand Rapids: Eerdmans, 1980.

Jeremias, Gert. *Der Lehrer der Gerechtigkeit.* SUNT 2. Göttingen: Vandenhoeck & Ruprecht, 1963.

Johnson, Bo. *Rättfärdigheten i Biblen.* Göteborg: Gothia, 1985.

Johnson, Luke Timothy. "The New Testament's Anti-Jewish Slander and the Conventions of Ancient Polemic." *JBL* 108 (1989): 419–41.

Johnson, S. E. "The Biblical Quotations in Matthew." *HTR* 36 (1943): 135–53.

Jones, F. Stanley. *An Ancient Jewish Christian Source on the History of Christianity: Pseudo-Clementine "Recognitions" 1.27–71.* Texts and Translations 37. Christian Apocrypha Series 2. Atlanta: Scholars, 1995.

Jones, Ivor H. *The Matthean Parables: A Literary and Historical Commentary.* NovTSup 80. Leiden: Brill, 1995.

Kampen, John I. "'Righteousness' in Matthew and the Legal Texts from Qumran." Pages 461–87, in *Legal Texts and Legal Issues: Proceedings of the Second Meeting of the International Organization for Qumran Studies, Cambridge, 1995: Published in Honour of Joseph M. Baumgarten.* Edited by Moshe J. Bernstein, Florentino García Martínez, and John Kampen. STDJ 23. Leiden: Brill, 1997.

Kampling, Rainer. *Das Blut Christi und die Juden: Mt 27,25 bei den lateinischsprachigen christliche Autoren bis zu Leo dem Großen.* Münster: Aschendorf, 1984.

Kee, Howard C. *Christian Origins in Sociological Perspective.* London: SCM, 1980.

Keith, Chris. *Jesus against the Scribal Elite: The Origins of the Conflict.* Grand Rapids: Baker Academic, 2014.

―――. *Jesus' Literacy: Scribal Culture and the Teacher from Galilee.* LNTS 413. London: T&T Clark, 2011.

Kellermann, D. "עלה." *TDOT* 11:96–113.

Kennedy, H. A. A. "The Significance and Range of the Covenant Conception in the New Testament." *The Expositor* 8 (1915): 385–410.

Kieffer, René. "'Mer-än'-kristologin hos synoptikerna." *SEÅ* 44 (1979): 134–47.

Kilpatrick, George Dunbar. *The Origins of the Gospel according to Saint Matthew.* Oxford: Clarendon, 1946.

Kim, Kyong-Shik. *God Will Judge Each One according to Works: Judgment according to Works and Psalm 62 in Early Judaism and the New Testament.* BZNW 178. Berlin: de Gruyter, 2011.

Kingsbury, Jack Dean. *Matthew as Story.* 2nd ed. Philadelphia: Fortress, 1988.

____. *Matthew: Structure, Christology, Kingdom.* Philadelphia: Fortress: 1975.

Klawans, Jonathan. *Impurity and Sin in Ancient Judaism.* Oxford: Oxford University Press, 2000.

____. *Purity, Sacrifice, and the Temple: Symbolism and Supersessionism in the Study of Ancient Judaism.* Oxford: Oxford University Press, 2006.

Kloppenborg, John S. "The Representation of Violence in Synoptic Parables." Pages 323–51, in *Mark and Matthew. Comparative Readings I: Understanding the Earliest Gospels in the First-Century Settings.* Edited by Eve-Marie Becker and Anders Runesson. WUNT 271. Tübingen: Mohr Siebeck, 2011.

____. *The Tenants in the Vineyard: Ideology, Economics, and Agrarian Conflict in Jewish Palestine.* WUNT 195. Tübingen: Mohr Siebeck, 2006.

Knowles, Michael P. *Jeremiah in Matthew's Gospel: The Rejected Prophet Motif in Matthean Redaction.* Sheffield: JSOT Press, 1993.

____. *The Unfolding Mystery of the Divine Name: The God of Sinai in Our Midst.* Downers Grove, IL: IVP Academic, 2012.

Koester, Helmut. *Synoptische Überlieferung bei den Apostolischen Vätern.* TUGAL 65. Berlin: Akademie, 1957.

Kogan, M. S. *Opening the Covenant: A Jewish Theology of Christianity.* Oxford: Oxford University Press, 2008.

Köhler, Wolf-Dietrich. *Die Rezeption des Matthäusevangeliums in der Zeit vor Irenaeus.* WUNT 24. Tübingen: Mohr Siebeck, 1987.

Konradt, Matthias. *Gericht und Gemeinde: Eine Studie zur Bedeutung und Funktion von Gerichtsaussagen im Rahmen der paulinischen Ekklesiologie und Ethik im 1 Thess und 1 Kor.* BZNW 117. Berlin: de Gruyter, 2003.

____. *Israel, Kirche und die Völker im Matthäusevangelium.* WUNT 215. Tübingen: Mohr Siebeck, 2007.

Konstan, David. *Before Forgiveness: The Origins of a Moral Idea.* Cambridge: Cambridge University Press, 2010.

Korner, Ralph. "Before 'Church': Political, Ethno-Religious and Theological Implications of the Collective Designation of Pauline Christ-Followers as *Ekklēsiai.*" Ph.D. diss., McMaster University, 2014.

____. "*Ekklēsia* as a Jewish Synagogue Term: Some Implications for Paul's Socio-Religious Location." *JJMJS* 2 (2015): 53–78.

Kratz, Reinhard G. and Hermann Spieckermann, eds. *Divine Wrath and Mercy in the World of Antiquity.* FAT 33. Tübingen: Mohr Siebeck, 2008.

Kuck, David W. *Judgement and Community Conflict: Paul's Use of Apocalyptic Judgment Language in 1 Corinthians 3:5–4:5.* NovTSup 66. Leiden: Brill, 1992.

Kümmel, Werner G. *The Theology of the New Testament.* London: SCM, 1974.

Kupp, D. D. *Matthew's Emmanuel: Divine Presence and God's People in the First Gospel.* SNTSMS 90. Cambridge: Cambridge University Press, 1996.

Kvalbein, Hans. "'La hans blod komme over oss og våre barn!' Var Matteusevangeliet jødefientligt?" *Religio* 48 (1997): 55–69.

Lachs, Samuel Tobias. *A Rabbinic Commentary on the New Testament: The Gospels of Matthew, Mark and Luke.* Hoboen: Ktav Publishing House, 1987.

Langer, Ruth. *Cursing the Christians? A History of the Birkat Haminim.* Oxford: Oxford University Press, 2011.

Le Donne, Anthony. "The Jewish Leaders." Pages 199–217, in *Jesus Among Friends and Enemies: A Historical and Literary Introduction to Jesus and the Gospels.* Edited by Chris Keith and Larry W. Hurtado. Grand Rapids: Baker Academic, 2011.

Lemche, Nils Peter. *The Canaanites and Their Land: The Tradition of the Canaanites.* JSOT Supplement Series 110. Sheffield: Sheffield Academic Press, 1991.

Levine, Amy-Jill. *The Social and Ethnic Dimensions of Matthean Salvation History: 'Go Nowhere among the Gentiles...' Matt. 10:5b.* Lewiston: Mellen Press, 1988.

Levine, Lee I. *The Ancient Synagogue: The First Thousand Years.* 2nd ed. New Haven: Yale University Press, 2005.

Levy, Ian Christopher, Philip D. W. Krey, and Thomas Ryan. *The Letter to the Romans.* The Bible in Medieval Tradition. Grand Rapids: Eerdmans, 2013.

Liddell, Henry George, Robert Scott, Henry Stuart Jones. *A Greek-English Lexicon.* 9th ed. with revised supplement. Oxford: Clarendon,1996.

Lieberman, Saul. *Hellenism in Jewish Palestine: Studies in the Literary Transmission, Beliefs and Manners of Palestine in the I century B.C.E.- IV Century C.E.* 2nd ed. Texts and Studies of the Jewish Theological Seminary of America 18. New York: Jewish Theological Seminary of America, 1962.

_____. "Some Aspects of Afterlife in Early Rabbinic Literature." Pages 103–40, in *Origins of Judaism: Normative Judaism.* Vol. 1. Part 2. Edited by Jacob Neusner and William Scott Green. New York: Garland, 1990.

Litwa, M. David. "The Deification of Moses in Philo of Alexandria." Pages 1–27, in *Studia Philonica Annual: Studies in Hellenistic Judaism.* Volume XXVI. Edited by David T. Runia and Gregory E. Sterling. Atlanta: Society of Biblical Literature, 2014.

Ljungman, Henrik. *Guds barmhärtighet och dom: Fariséernas lära om de två 'måtten'.* Lund: Gleerup, 1950.

Loader, William R. G. *Jesus' Attitude towards the Law: A Study of the Gospels.* Grand Rapids: Eerdmans, 2002.

Lohmeyer, Ernst. *Das Evangelium nach Matthäus: Nachgelassene Ausarbeitungen und Entwürfe zur Übersetzung und Erklärung.* KEK. Göttingen: Vandenhoeck and Ruprecht, 1956.

Longenecker, Bruce W. "Rome's Victory and God's Honour: The Jerusalem Temple and the Spirit of God in Lukan Theology." Pages 90–102, in *The Holy Spirit and Christian Origins: Essays in Honor of James D. G. Dunn.* Edited by Graham N. Stanton, Bruce W. Longenecker, and Stephen C. Barton. Grand Rapids: Eerdmans, 2004.

Lövestam, Evald. *Jesus and 'This Generation': A New Testament Study.* Stockholm: Almqvist & Wiksell International, 1995.

_____. "Logiet om hädelse mot den helige Ande." *SEÅ* 33 (1968): 101–17.

_____. *Spiritus Blasphemia: Eine Studie zu Mk 3,28f par Mt 12,31f, Lk 12,10.* Lund: Gleerup, 1968.

Lundgren, Svante. *Particularism and Universalism in Modern Jewish Thought.* Binghamton: Global Publications, 2001.

Luomanen, Petri. *Entering the Kingdom of Heaven: A Study on the Structure of Matthew's View of Salvation.* WUNT 101. Tübingen: Mohr Siebeck, 1998.

461

Luz, Ulrich. *Das Evangelium nach Matthäus*. 2. Teilband, Mt 8–17. Zürich: Benzinger, 1990.

———. "The Final Judgment (Matt 25:31–46): An Exercise in 'History of Influence' Exegesis." Pages 271–310 in *Treasures New and Old: Contributions to Matthean Studies*. Edited by David R. Bauer and Mark Allan Powell. Atlanta: Scholars Press, 1996.

———. *Matthew: A Commentary*. 3 Vols. Hermeneia. Minneapolis: Fortress, 2001–2007.

———. *The Theology of the Gospel of Matthew*. Translated by J. Bradford Robinson. Cambridge: Cambridge University Press, 1995.

MacLennan, Robert S. and A. Thomas Kraabel. "The God-Fearers – A Literary and Theological Invention." *BAR* 12 (1986): 47–53.

Magness, Jodi. "The Arch of Titus at Rome and the Fate of the God of Israel," *JJS* 59.2 (2008): 201–17.

Malina, Bruce J. "Social-Scientific Approaches and the Gospel of Matthew." Pages 154–93, in *Methods for Matthew*. Edited by Mark Allan Powell. Cambridge: Cambridge University Press, 2009.

Malina, Bruce J., and Richard L. Rohrbaugh. *Social Science Commentary on the Synoptic Gospels*. 2nd ed. Minneapolis: Fortress, 2003.

Mánek, J. "Mit wem identifiziert sich Jesus? Eine exegetische Rekonstruktion ad Matth 25:31–46." Pages 15–25, in *Christ and the Spirit in the New Testament: In Honor of C. F. D. Moule*. Edited by B. Lindars and B. S. Smalley. Cambridge: Cambridge University Press, 1973.

Maʿoz, Zvi Uri. *Baniyas in the Greco-Roman Period: A History Based on the Excavations*. Archaostyle Scientific Research Series 3. Qazrin: Archaostyle, 2007.

Marcus, Joel. *Mark 1-8*. AB 27. New York: Doubleday, 2000.

Marguerat, Daniel. *Le jugement dans l'évangile de Matthieu*. 2nd ed. Geneva: Labor et Fides, 1995.

Marshall, John W. "John's Jewish (Christian?) Apocalypse." Pages 233–-56, in *Jewish-Christianity Reconsidered: Re-Thinking Groups and Texts*. Edited by Matt Jackson McCabe. Minneapolis: Fortress, 2007.

———. *Parables of War: Reading John's Jewish Apocalypse*. Waterloo: Wilfrid Laurier University Press, 2001.

Marshall, Jonathan. *Jesus, Patrons, and Benefactors: Roman Palestine and the Gospel of Luke.* WUNT 259. Tübingen: Mohr Siebeck, 2009.

Marshall, Mary. *The Portrayals of the Pharisees in the Gospels and Acts.* Göttingen: Vandenhoeck and Ruprecht, 2015.

Marxen, Willi. *New Testament Foundations for Christian Ethics.* Minneapolis: Fortress, 1993.

Mason, Steve. "Jews, Judaeans, Judaizing, Judaism: Problems of Categorization in Ancient History." *JSJ* 38 (2007): 457–512.

———. "Pharisaic Dominance before 70 ce and the Gospel's Hypocrisy Charge (Matt 23:2–3)." *HTR* 83 (1990): 363–81.

———. "Pollution and Purification in Josephus's Judean War." Pages 181–207, in *Purity, Holiness, and Identity in Judaism and Christianity.* Edited by Carl S. Ehrlich, Anders Runesson, and Eileen Schuller. WUNT 305. Tübingen: Mohr Siebeck, 2013.

Massaux, Édouard. *The Influence of the Gospel of Saint Matthew on Christian Literature before Saint Irenaeus.* Vol. 1. Translated by Norman J. Belval and Suzanne Hecht. Edited and with an introduction and addenda by Arthu J. Bellinzoni. New Gospel Studies 5/1. Mercer University Press, 1991. Translation of *Influence de l'évangile de saint Matthieu sur la littérature chrétienne avant saint Irénée.* Universitas Catholica Lovaniensis, Dissertationes, Ser. 2,42. Leuven: Leuven University Press, 1950. 2nd ed., 1986.

Mbabazi, Isaac K. *The Significance of Interpersonal Forgiveness in the Gospel of Matthew.* Eugene: Wipf & Stock, 2013.

McKnight, Scott. *A Light among the Gentiles: Jewish Missionary Activity in the Second Temple Period.* Minneapolis: Fortress Press, 1991.

Meier, John P. *Companions and Competitors.* Vol. 3 of *A Marginal Jew: Rethinking the Historical Jesus.* New York: Doubleday, 2001.

———. "The Historical Jesus and the Historical Herodians." *JBL* 119 (2000): 740–46.

———. *Matthew.* Collegeville: Liturgical Press, 1980.

———. "Matthew, Gospel of." *ABD* 4:622–41.

———. *The Roots of the Problem and the Person.* Vol. 1 of *A Marginal Jew: Rethinking the Historical Jesus.* New York: Doubleday, 1991.

_____. *The Vision of Matthew: Christ, Church, and Morality in the First Gospel.* Eugene: Wipf & Stock, 1991.

Melinek, A. "The Doctrine of Reward and Punishment in Biblical and Early Rabbinic Writings." Pages 297–312, in *Origins of Judaism: Normative Judaism.* Vol. 1. Part 2. Edited by Jacob Neusner and William Scott Green. New York: Garland, 1990.

Mendels, Doron. *The Rise and Fall of Jewish Nationalism: Jewish and Christian Ethnicity in Ancient Palestine.* Grand Rapids: Eerdmans, 1992.

Menninger, Richard E. *Israel and the Church in the Gospel of Matthew.* New York: Peter Lang, 1994.

Metzger, Bruce M. *A Textual Commentary on the Greek New Testament.* Stuttgart: United Bible Societies, 1975.

Meyer, R., "ὄχλος." *TDNT* 5:582–90.

Meyers, Eric M. and Mark A. Chancey. *Alexander to Constantine: Archaeology of the Land of the Bible.* Vol. 3. New Haven: Yale University Press, 2012.

Miller, Stuart S. *Sages and Commoners in Late Antique 'Erez Israel: A Philological Inquiry into Local Traditions in Talmud Yerushalmi.* TSAJ 111. Tübingen: Mohr Siebeck, 2006.

Modéus, Martin. *Sacrifice and Symbol: Biblical Šhĕlāmîm in a Ritual Perspective.* ConBOT 52. Stockholm: Almqvist & Wiksell International, 2005.

Moffitt, David M. "Righteous Bloodshed, Matthew's Passion Narrative, and the Temple's Destruction: Lamentations as a Matthean Intertext." *JBL* 125 (2006): 299–320.

Montefiore, C. G. *The Synoptic Gospels: Edited with an Introduction and a Commentary.* 2 vols. 2nd ed. London: Macmillan, 1927.

Montefiore, C. G., and H. M. J. Loewe, eds. *A Rabbinic Anthology.* London: Macmillan, 1938; Repr., Cambridge: Cambridge University Press, 2012.

Montgomery, Eric. "A Stream from Eden: The Nature and Development of a Revelatory Tradition in the Dead Sea Scrolls." PhD diss., McMaster University, 2013.

Moore, George Foot. *The Age of the Tannaim.* Vol. 1 of *Judaism in the First Centuries of the Christian Era.* Cambridge: Cambridge University Press, 1927.

Moses, A. D. A. *Matthew's Transfiguration Story and Jewish-Christian Controversy.* LNTS 122. Sheffield: Sheffield Academic Press, 1996.

Mouton, Elna. *The Pathos of New Testament Studies: Of What Use Are We to the Church?* Stellenbosch: University of Stellenbosch, 2005.

Müller, Mogens. "Mattæusevangeliets messiasbillede." *SEÅ* 51 (1986–7): 168–79.

Murphy, Frederick J. "The Jewishness of Matthew: Another Look." Pages 377–401, in *When Judaism and Christianity Began: Essays in Memory of Anthony J. Saldarini.* Edited by Alan J. Avery-Peck, Daniel Harrington, and Jacob Neusner. JSJSup 85. Leiden: Brill, 2004.

Nanos, Mark D. *The Irony of Galatians: Paul's Letter in First-Century Context.* Minneapolis: Fortress, 2002.

____. "Paul's Non-Jews Do Not Become 'Jews,' But Do They Become 'Jewish'? Reading Romans 2:25–29 Within Judaism, Alongside Josephus." *JJMJS* 1 (2014): 26–53.

Nepper-Christensen, Poul. *Das Matthäusevangelium: Ein judenchristliches Evangelium?* ATDan 1. Aarhus: Universitetsforlaget, 1958.

Neusner, Jacob. *The Idea of Purity in Ancient Judaism.* Leiden: Brill, 1973.

____. "Preface" to *Origins of Judaism: Normative Judaism,* vol. 1. Edited by J. Neusner. New York: Garland, 1990.

____. *Vanquished Nation, Broken Spirit: The Virtues of the Heart in Formative Judaism.* Cambridge: Cambridge University Press, 1987.

Neusner, Jacob and Bruce D. Chilton, eds. *In Quest of the Historical Pharisees.* Waco: Baylor University Press, 2007.

Newport, Kenneth G. C. *The Sources and Sitz im Lebel of Matthew 23.* JSNTSup 117. Sheffield: Sheffield Academic, 1989.

Niederwimmer, Kurt. *The Didache: A Commentary.* Hermeneia. Minneapolis: Fortress, 1998.

Nolland, John. *The Gospel of Matthew: A Commentary on the Greek Text.* NIGTC. Grand Rapids: Eerdmans, 2005.

____. "The Gospel of Matthew and Anti-Semitism." Pages 154–69, in *Built upon the Rock: Studies in the Gospel of Matthew.* Edited by Daniel M. Gurtner and John Nolland. Grand Rapids: Eerdmans, 2008.

Novak, David. *The Image of the Non-Jew in Judaism: The Idea of Noahide Law.* 2nd ed. Oxford: Littman Library of Jewish Civilization, 2011.

Novik, Tzvi. "Wages from God: The Dynamics of a Biblical Metaphor." *CBQ* 73 (2011): 708–22.

Oliver, Isaac W. *Torah Praxis after 70 CE: Reading Matthew and Luke-Acts as Jewish Texts.* Wissenschaftliche Untersuchungen zum Neuen Testament 2. Reihe 355. Tübingen: Mohr Siebeck, 2013

Olsson, Birger. "Johannine Christians—Members of a Renewed Covenant? Jewish Christian Identity according to the Johannine Letters." Pages 174–203, in *The Making of Christianity: Conflicts, Contacts, and Constructions.* Edited by Magnus Zetterholm and Samuel Byrskog. Winona Lake: Eisenbrauns, 2012.

Orton, David E. *The Understanding Scribe: Matthew and the Apocalyptic Ideal.* JSNTSup 25. Sheffield: Sheffield Academic, 1989.

Overman, Andrew J. *Church and Community in Crisis: The Gospel according to Matthew.* Valley Forge: Trinity Press International, 1996.

_____. *Matthew's Gospel and Formative Judaism: The Social World of the Matthean Community.* Minneapolis: Fortress, 1990.

Paget, James Carleton. "Jewish Christianity." Pages 731–75, in *The Early Roman Period.* Vol. 3 of *The Cambridge History of Judaism.* Edited by William Horbury, W. D. Davies, and John Sturdy. Cambridge: Cambridge University Press, 1999.

Painter, John. "Matthew and John." Pages 66–86 in *Matthew and his Christian Contemporaries.* Edited by David C. Sim and Boris Repschinsky. London: T&T Clark, 2008.

Park, Eung Chun. *The Mission Discourse in Matthew's Interpretation.* WUNT 2.81. Tübingen: Mohr Siebeck, 1995.

Park, Young-Ho. *Paul's Ekklesia as a Civic Assembly.* WUNT 2.393. Tübingen: Mohr Siebeck, 2015.

Paschke, Boris. *Particularism and Universalism in the Sermon on the Mount: A Narrative-Critical Analysis of Matthew 5-7 in the Light of Matthew's View on Mission.* Neutestamentliche Abhandlungen NS 56. Münster: Aschendorff, 2012.

Patte, Daniel. *Early Jewish Hermeneutic in Palestine.* SBLDS 22. Missoula, MT: Scholars Press, 1975.

_____. *The Gospel according to Matthew: A Structural Commentary on Matthew's Gospel.* Valley Forge: Trinity Press International, 1987.

Pesch, Wilhelm. *Der Lohngedanke in der Lehre Jesu vergleichen mit der religiösen Lohnlehre des Spätjudentums.* Munich: Karl Zink, 1955.

Pickup, Martin. "Matthew's and Mark's Pharisees." Pages 67–112, in *In Quest of the Historical Pharisees.* Edited by Jacob Neusner and Bruce Chilton. Waco: Baylor University Press, 2007.

Porten, Bezalel. *Archives from Elephantine: The Life of an Ancient Jewish Military Colony.* Berkeley: University of California Press, 1968.

Powell, Mark Allan. *God with Us: A Pastoral Theology of the Gospel of Matthew.* Minneapolis: Fortress, 1995.

_____. "Do and Keep What Moses Says (Matthew 23:2–7)." *JBL* 114 (1995): 419–35.

Procksch, Otto. *Jesaja: Kaptial 1–39.* KAT 9. Leipzig: Deichert, 1930.

Przybylski, Benno. *Righteousness in Matthew and His World of Thought.* SNTSMS 41. Cambridge: Cambridge University Press, 1980.

Racine, Jean-François. *The Text of Matthew in the Writings of Basil of Caesarea.* NTGF 5. Boston: Brill, 2004.

Rad, Gerhard von. *Genesis: A Commentary.* 2nd ed. OTL. London: SCM, 1972.

Rainey, Anson F. and R. Steven Notley. *The Sacred Bridge: Carta's Atlas of the Biblical World.* Jerusalem: Carta, 2006.

Reeves, K. H. "They Worshipped Him and They Doubted: Matthew 28:17." *BT* 49 (1998): 344–49.

Regev, Eyal. "Moral Impurity and the Temple in Early Christianity in Light of Ancient Greek Practice and Qumranic Ideology." *HTR* 97 (2004): 383–411.

Reinbold, Wolfgang. "Das Matthäusevangelium, die Pharisäer und die Tora." *BZ* 50 (2006): 51–73.

Reiser, Marius. *Jesus and Judgment: The Eschatological Proclamation in its Jewish Context.* Minneapolis: Fortress, 1997.

Repschinski, Boris. *Nicht Aufzulösen, sondern zu erfüllen: Das jüdische Gesetz in den synoptischen Jesuserzählungen.* FzB, 120. Würzburg: Echter Verlag, 2009.

_____. "Purity in Matthew, James, and the Didache." Pages 379–95 in *Matthew, James, and Didache: Three Related Documents in Their Jewish and Christian Settings.* Edited by H. van de Sandt and J. K. Zangenberg. SymS. Atlanta: Society of Biblical Literature, 2008.

_____. "Re-Imagining the Presence of God: The Temple and the Messiah in the Gospel of Matthew." *ABR* 54 (2006): 37–49.

Reumann, John. *Variety and Unity in New Testament Thought.* Oxford: Oxford University Press, 1991.

Richardson, Peter. *Herod: King of the Jews and Friend of the Romans.* Columbia: University of South Carolina Press, 1996.

Riches, John and David C. Sim, eds. *The Gospel of Matthew in its Roman Imperial Context.* LNTS 276. London: T&T Clark, 2005.

Runesson, Anders. "Building Matthean Communities: The Politics of Textualization." Pages 379–408, in *Mark and Matthew. Comparative Readings I: Understanding the Earliest Gospels in their First-Century Settings.* Edited by Eve-Marie Becker and Anders Runesson. WUNT 271. Tübingen: Mohr Siebeck, 2011.

____. "City of God or Home of Traitors and Killers? Jerusalem according to Matthew." In *Cities of God? An Interdisciplinary Assessment of Early Christian Engagement with the Ancient Urban Environment(s).* Edited by David Gill, Paul Trebilco, and Steve Walton. Grand Rapids: Eerdmans, forthcoming, 2016.

____. "Extending or Restricting the Covenant? Abraham and the People of God in Christian Tradition." *LTQ* 44 (2011): 1–17.

____. "Giving Birth to Jesus in the Late First Century: Matthew as Midwife in the Context of Colonisation." Pages 301–27, in *Infancy Gospels: Stories and Identities.* Edited by Claire Clivaz, Andreas Dettwiler, Luc Devilliers, and Enrico Norelli. WUNT 281. Tübingen: Mohr Siebeck, 2011.

____. "The Historical Jesus, the Gospels, and First-Century Jewish Society: The Importance of the Synagogue for Understanding the New Testament." Pages 265–97, in *A City Set on a Hill: Essays in Honor of James F. Strange.* Edited by Daniel Warner and Donald D. Binder. Mountain Home, AR: BorderStone, LLC, 2014.

____. "The Impact of Ethnicity on Salvation in Matthew's Gospel" in *Matthew Within Judaism.* Edited by Anders Runesson and Daniel M. Gurtner. In preparation.

____. "Inventing Christian Identity: Paul, Ignatius, and Theodosius I." Pages 59–92 in *Exploring Early Christian Identity.* Edited by B. Holmberg. WUNT 226. Tübingen: Mohr Siebeck, 2008.

____. "Judging Gentiles in the Gospel of Matthew: Between 'Othering' and Inclusion." Pages 133–51, in *Matthew's Gospel and Early Christianity: Studies in Memory of Professor Graham Stanton.* Edited by Joel Willitts and Daniel M. Gurtner, and Richard A. Burridge. London: T&T Clark, 2011.

———. "Judging the Theological Tree by its Fruit: The Use of the Gospels of Mark and Matthew in Official Church Documents on Jewish – Christian Relations." Pages 189–228, in *Mark and Matthew. Comparative Readings II: Hermeneutics, Reception History, Theology.* Edited by Eve-Marie Becker and Anders Runesson. WUNT 304. Tübingen: Mohr Siebeck, 2013.

———. "Judgment." *NIDB* 3:457–66.

———. "Kunskap, dårskap och intighet i nytestamentlig frälsningsteologi: Jesus, Paulus och Första Johannesbrevet." ["Knowledge, Madness, and Nothingness in New Testament Theologies of Salvation: Jesus, Paul, and First John."] Pages 43–65, in *Sōteria och gnōsis: Frälsning och kunskap i den tidiga kyrkan. Föreläsningar hållna vid Nordiska patristikermötet i Lund 18–21 augusti 2010. [Sōteria and Gnōsis: Salvation and Knowledge in the Early Church. Papers given at the Meeting of the Nordic Society for Patristic Studies in Lund August 18–21, 2010.]* Edited by Benjamin Ekman and Henrik Rydell Johnsén. Patristica Nordica VIII. Skellefteå: Artos & Norma, 2012.

———. "Matthew, Gospel According to." Pages 2:59–78, in *The Oxford Encyclopedia of the Books of the Bible.* Edited by M. D. Coogan. 2 vols. Oxford: Oxford University Press, 2011.

———. *O That You Would Tear Open the Heavens and Come Down! On the Historical Jesus, Jonas Gardell, and the Breath of God.* [In Swedish.] Örebro and Skellefteå: Libris and Artos, 2011.

———. *The Origins of the Synagogue: A Socio-Historical Study.* ConBNT 37. Stockholm: Almqvist & Wiksell International, 2001.

———. "Particularistic Judaism and Universalistic Christianity? Some Critical Remarks on Terminology and Theology." *JGRChJ* 1 (2000): 120–44.

———. "Purity, Holiness, and the Kingdom of Heaven in Matthew's Narrative World." Pages 144–80, in *Purity, Holiness, and Identity in Judaism and Christianity: Essays in Memory of Susan Haber.* Edited by Carl Ehrlich, Anders Runesson, and Eileen Schuller. WUNT 305. Tübingen: Mohr Siebeck, 2013.

———. "The Question of Terminology: The Architecture of Contemporary Discussions on Paul." Pages 53–77, in *Paul within Judaism: Restoring the First-*

Century Context to the Apostle. Edited by Mark Nanos and Magnus Zetterholm. Minneapolis: Fortress, 2015.

____. "Re-Thinking Early Jewish–Christian Relations: Matthean Community History as Pharisaic Intragroup Conflict." *JBL* 127 (2008): 95–132.

____. "Was There a Christian Mission before the Fourth Century? Problematizing Common Ideas about Early Christianity and the Beginnings of Modern Mission." Pages 205–47, in *The Making of Christianity: Conflicts, Contacts, and Constructions.* Edited by Magnus Zetterholm and Samuel Byrskog. Winona Lake: Eisenbrauns, 2012.

Runesson, Anders, Donald D. Binder, and Birger Olsson. *The Ancient Synagogue from its Origins to 200 C.E.: A Source Book.* AGJU 72. Leiden: Brill, 2008.

Ruzer, Serge. *Mapping the New Testament: Early Christian Writings as a Witness for Jewish Biblical Exegesis.* Jewish and Christian Perspectives Series 13. Leiden: Brill, 2007.

Sahlin, H. "Chassidismen och Nya testamentets Kristusbild." *SEÅ* 17 (1953): 119–43.

Sakenfeld, Katharine Doob. *The Meaning of* Hesed *in the Hebrew Bible.* Missoula: Scholars Press, 1978.

Saldarini, Anthony. *Matthew's Christian-Jewish Community.* Chicago: Chicago University Press, 1994.

____. *Pharisees, Scribes, and Sadducees in Palestinian Society.* Grand Rapids: Eerdmans, 2001.

Sanders, E. P. *Jesus and Judaism.* London: SCM, 1985.

____. *Jewish Law from Jesus to the Mishnah.* London: SCM, 1990.

____. *Judaism: Practice ad Belief 63 BCE–66 CE.* London: SCM, 1992.

____. *Paul and Palestinian Judaism: A Comparison of Patterns of Religion.* London: SCM, 1977.

Sandmel, Samuel. "Herodians." *IDB* 2:594–95.

____. *A Jewish Understanding of the New Testament.* Cincinnati: Hebrew Union College Press, 1956. Repr., with new preface, Woodstock: SkyLight Paths Publications, 2004.

Sandt, Huub van de, and David Flusser. *The Didache: Its Jewish Sources and its Place in Early Judaism and Christianity.* CRINT. Assen: Royal van Gorcum, 2002.

Sandt, Huub van de, and Jürgen K. Zangenberg, eds. *Matthew, James, and the*

Didache: Three Related Documents in Their Jewish and Christian Settings. SymS 45. Atlanta: Society of Biblical Literature, 2008.

Schechter, Solomon. *Aspects of Rabbinic Theology.* Introduction to new edition by Louis Finkelstein. New York: Schocken Books, 1961 [1909].

Schnabel, E. J. *Early Christian Mission.* 2 vols. Downers Grove, IL: InterVarsity Press, 2004.

Schnackenburg, Rudolf. *The Gospel of Matthew.* Translated by Robert R. Barr. Grand Rapids: Eerdmans, 2002.

Schrenk, Gottlob. "δίκαιός, δικαιοσύνη." *TDNT* 2:182–210.

Schultz, Siegfried. *Die Mitte der Schrift: Der Frühkatholizismus im Neuen Testament als Herausforderung and den Protestantismus.* Stuttgart: Kreuz Verlag 1976.

Schüssler Fiorenza, Elisabeth, ed. *Aspects of Religious Propaganda in Judaism and Early Christianity.* Notre Dame: University of Notre Dame Press, 1976.

Schweitzer, Albert. *Out of My Life and Thought: An Autobiography. Postscript 1932-1949 by Everett Skillings.* Translated by C. T. Campion. New York: Mentor Books, 1953.

Seidl, T. "שלמים." *TDOT* 15:105–16.

Senior, Donald. *The Gospel of Matthew.* IBT. Nashville: Abingdon, 1997.

Sigal, Phillip. *The Halakhah of Jesus of Nazareth according to the Gospel of Matthew.* Lanham: University Press of America, *1986.*

Sim, David C. *Apocalyptic Eschatology in the Gospel of Matthew.* SNTSMS 88. Cambridge: Cambridge University Press, 1996.

_____. "The 'Confession' of the Soldiers in Matthew 27:54." *HeyJ* 24 (1993): 401–24.

_____. *The Gospel of Matthew and Christian Judaism: The History and Social Setting of the Matthean Community.* SNTW. Edinburgh: T&T Clark, 1998.

_____. "The Gospel of Matthew and the Gentiles." *JSNT* 57 (1995): 19–48.

_____. "Introduction." Pages 1–10, in *Matthew and His Christian Contemporaries.* Edited by David C. Sim and Boris Repschinski. LNTS 333. London: T&T Clark, 2008.

_____. "The Man without the Wedding Garment (Matthew 22:11–13)." *HeyJ* 31 (1990): 165–78.

_____. "Matthew: The Current State of Research." Pages 33–51, in *Mark and Matthew. Comparative Readings I: Understanding the Earliest Gospels in the First-*

Century Settings. Edited by Eve-Marie Becker and Anders Runesson. WUNT 271. Tübingen: Mohr Siebeck, 2011.

Sjöberg, Erik. *Gott und die Sünder im palästinischen Judentum. Nach dem Zeugnis der Tannaiten und der apokryphisch-pseudepigraphischen Literatur.* BWANT 27. Stuttgart: W. Kohlhammer, 1939.

Skarsaune, Oskar. *In the Shadow of the Temple: Jewish Influences on Early Christianity.* Downers Grove, IL: InterVarsity Press, 2002.

Snodgrass, Klyne. "Reading to Hear: A Hermeneutics of Hearing." *HBT* 24 (2002): 1–32.

Spieckermann, Hermann. "Wrath and Mercy as Crucial Terms of Theological Hermeneutics." Pages 3–16, in *Divine Wrath and Mercy in the World of Antiquity.* Edited by Reinhard G. Kratz and Hermann Spieckermann. FAT 33. Tübingen: Mohr Siebeck, 2008.

Stanley, Alan P. *Did Jesus Teach Salvation by Works? The Role of Works in Salvation in the Synoptic Gospels.* Eugene: Pickwick Publications, 2006.

_____, ed. *Four Views on the Role of Works at the Final Judgment.* Grand Rapids: Zondervan, 2013.

Stanton, Graham N. "5 Ezra and Matthean Christianity in the Second Century." *JTS* 28 (1977): 67–83.

_____. *A Gospel for a New People: Studies in Matthew.* Edinburgh: T&T Clark, 1992.

_____. "The Gospel of Matthew and Judaism." *BJRL* 66 (1984): 264–84.

_____. "Introduction: Matthew's Gospel in Recent Scholarship (1994)." Pages 1–26, in *The Interpretation of Matthew.* Edited by Graham N. Stanton. 2nd ed. Studies in New Testament Interpretation. T&T Clark, 1995.

_____. "The Origin and Purpose of Matthew's Gospel: Matthean Scholarship from 1945 to 1980." Pages 1890–951 in *Aufstieg und Niedergang der römischen Welt.* II, 25.3. Edited by H. Temporini and W. Haase. ANRW 2. Berlin: de Gruyter, 1985.

Stegemann, Hartmut. *Die Essener, Qumran, Johannes der Täufer und Jesus: Ein Sachbuch.* 4th ed. Freiburg: Herder, 1994.

Stemberger, Günter. *Jewish Contemporaries of Jesus: Pharisees, Sadducees, Essence.* Minneapolis: Fortress, 1995.

_____. *Jews and Christians in the Holy Land: Palestine in the Fourth Century.* Edinburgh: T&T Clark, 2000.

Stendahl, Krister. "Quis et Unde? An Analysis of Mt 1–2." Pages 69–80, in *The Interpretation of Matthew*. Edited by Graham Stanton. 2nd ed. Studies in New Testament Interpretation. Edinburgh: T&T Clark, 1995.

____. *The School of St. Matthew: And Its Use of the Old Testament*. Lund: Gleerup, 1954.

Strange, James F. "Archaeology and Synagogues up to about 200 CE." Pages 37–62, in *The Ancient Synagogue from its Origins until 200 C.E.: Papers Presented at an International Conference at Lund University, October 14–17, 2001*. Edited by Birger Olsson and Magnus Zetterholm. ConBNT 39. Almqvist & Wiksell International, 2003.

Strathmann, Hermann. "λαός." 4:29–39, 50–57.

____. "πόλις." *TDNT* 6:516–35.

Strecker, Georg. *Der Weg der Gerechtigkeit: Untersuchung zur Theologie des Matthäus*. 3rd ed. FRLANT 82. Göttingen: Vandenhoeck & Ruprecht, 1971.

Streeter, Burnett Hillman. *The Four Gospels: A Study of Origins*. London: Macmillan, 1924.

Stuart, Douglas. "Exegesis." *ABD* 2:682–88.

Suggs, M. Jack. *Wisdom, Christology, and Law in Matthew's Gospel*. Cambridge, M.A.: Harvard University Press, 1970.

Swanson, Reuben. *New Testament Greek Manuscripts: Variant Readings Arranged in Horizontal Lines against Codex Vaticanus*. Sheffield: Sheffield Academic, 1995.

Talbert, Charles H. *Matthew*. Paideia. Grand Rapids: Baker Academic, 2010.

Tennant, Frederick R. *The Sources of the Doctrines of the Fall and Original Sin*. New York: Schocken Books, 1903. Repr., 1946 with an Introduction by Mary Frances Thelen.

Telford, William R. *The Barren Temple and the Withered Tree: A Redaction-Critical Analysis of the Cursing of the Fig-Tree Pericope in Mark's Gospel and Its Relation to the Cleansing of the Temple Tradition*. Sheffield: JSOT Press, 1982.

Thayer, Joseph Henry. *A Greek-English Lexicon of the New Testament*. Grand Rapids: Baker Book House, 1977.

Thiessen, Matthew. *Contesting Conversion: Genealogy, Circumcision, and Identity in Ancient Judaism and Christianity*. Oxford: Oxford University Press, 2011.

Thomas, John Christopher. "The Kingdom of God in the Gospel according to Matthew." *NTS* 39 (1993): 136–46.

Thompson, William G. "Historical Perspective in the Gospel of Matthew." *JBL* 93 (1974): 243–62.

Tilborg, Shef van. *The Jewish Leaders in Matthew*. Leiden: Brill, 1972.

Tomson, Peter J. *"If This Be from Heaven": Jesus and the New Testament Authors in Their Relationship to Judaism*. BibSem 76. Sheffield: Sheffield Academic, 2001.

Trilling, Wolfgang. *Das Wahre Israel: Studien zur Theologie des Matthäus-Evangeliums*. 3rd ed. SANT 10. Munich: Köseln-Verlag, 1964.

Tuckett, Christopher. "Matthew and Hypocrisy." Pages 152–65, in *Jesus, Matthew's Gospel and Early Christianity: Studies in Memory of Professor Graham N. Stanton*. Edited by Daniel M. Gurtner, Joel Willitts, and Richard A. Burridge. LNTS 435. London: T&T Clark, 2011.

Turner, David L. *Matthew*. BECNT. Grand Rapids: Baker Academic, 2008.

Ulfgard, Håkan. "Rättfärdighetens lärare och Qumranförsamlingens historia." Pages 129–57, in *Dødehavsteksterne og Bibelen*. Edited by Niels Hyldahl and Thomas L. Thompson. København: Museum Tusculanum, 1996.

Urbach, Ephraim E. *The Sages: Their Concepts and Beliefs*. Translated by Israel Abrahams. Cambridge, MA: Harvard University Press, 1979.

Vaage, Leif E., ed. *Religious Rivalries in the Early Roman Empire and the Rise of Christianity*. Waterloo: Wilfrid Laurier University Press, 2006.

VanLandingham, Chris. *Judgment and Justification in Early Judaism and the Apostle Paul*. Peabody: Hendrickson, 2006.

Varkey, Mothy. "Salvation in Continuity: A Reconsideration of Matthew's Soteriology." PhD diss., Murdoch University, 2014.

Vaux, Roland de. *Ancient Israel: Its Life and Institutions*. 2nd ed. London: Darton, Longman & Todd, 1965.

Viviano, Benedict. "Who Wrote Q? The Sayings Document (Q) as the Apostle Matthew's Private Notebook as a Bilingual Village Scribe (Mark 2:13-17; Matt 9:9-13)." Pages 75–91, in *Mark and Matthew II. Comparative Readings: Reception History, Cultural Hermeneutics, and Theology*. Edited by Eve-Marie Becker and Anders Runesson. WUNT 304. Tübingen: Mohr Siebeck, 2013.

Wainwright, Elaine. *Towards a Feminist Critical Reading of the Gospel according to Matthew*. BZNW 60. Berlin: de Gruyter, 1991.

Walker, Rolf. *Die Heilsgeschichte im ersten Evangelium*. FRLANT 91. Göttingen: Vandenhoeck & Ruprecht, 1967.

Wassén, Cecilia. "Do You Have to be Pure in a Metaphorical Temple? Sanctuary Metaphors and Construction of Sacred Space in the Dead Sea Scrolls and Paul's Letters." Pages 55–86, in *Purity and Holiness in Judaism and Christianity: Essays in Memory of Susan Haber.* Edited by Carl S. Ehrlich, Anders Runesson, and Eileen Schuller. WUNT 305. Tübingen: Mohr Siebeck, 2013.

Watson, Francis. *Gospel Writing: A Canonical Perspective.* Grand Rapids: Eerdmans, 2014.

Weinfeld, Moshe. "The Charge of Hypocrisy in Matthew 23 and in Jewish Sources." *Imm* 24–25 (1990): 52–8.

Weiss, D. Bernhard. *Das Matthäus-Evangelium.* 7th ed. Göttingen: Vandenhoeck & Ruprecht, 1910.

Westerholm, Stephen. "Grace." *NIDB* 2:655–60.

____. "Hearing the Gospel of Matthew and Mark." Pages 245–258 in *Mark and Matthew. Comparative Readings II: Hermeneutics, Reception History, Theology.* WUNT 304; edited by Eve-Marie Becker and Anders Runesson; Tübingen: Mohr Siebeck, 2013.

____. *Understanding Matthew: The Early Christian Worldview of the First Gospel.* Grand Rapids: Baker Academic, 2006.

Williamson, H. G. M. *Ezra, Nehemiah.* WBC 16. Waco: Word Books, 1985.

Willitts, Joel. *Matthew's Messianic Shepherd-King: In Search of 'the Lost Sheep of the House of Israel'.* BZNW 147. Berlin: de Gruyter, 2007.

Wilson, Stephen G. *Related Strangers: Jews and Christians, 70-170 C.E.* Minneapolis: Fortress, 1995.

Winandy, Jacques. "La scène du jugement dernier." *ScEcc* 18 (1966): 169–86.

Windisch, Hans. *The Meaning of the Sermon on the Mount: A Contribution to the Historical Understanding of the Gospels and to the Problem of Their True Exegesis.* Translated by S. McLean Gilmour. Philadelphia: Westminster, 1951.

Winninge, Michael. *Sinners and the Righteous: A Comparative Study of the Psalms of Salomon and Paul's Letters.* ConBNT 26. Stockholm: Almqvist & Wiksell International, 1995.

Witherington III, Ben. *Matthew.* Macon: Smyth & Helwys, 2006.

Witmer, Amanda. *Jesus, The Galilean Exorcist: His Exorcisms in Social and Political Context.* LNTS 459. London: T&T Clark, 2012.

Yarbro Collins, Adela. *Mark: A Commentary*. Hermeneia. Minneapolis: Fortress, 2007.

Yarbro Collins, Adela and John J. Collins. *King and Messiah as Son of God: Divine, Human, and Angelic Messianic Figures in Biblical and Related Literature*. Grand Rapids: Eerdmans, 2008.

Yinger, Kent L. *Paul, Judaism, and Judgment according to Deeds*. SNTSMS 105. Cambridge: Cambridge University Press, 1999.

Yoshiko Reed, Annette. "'Jewish Christianity' after the 'Parting of the Ways': Approaches to Historiography and Self-Definition in the Pseudo-Clementines." Pages 189–231, in *The Ways that Never Parted: Jews and Christians in Late Antiquity and the Early Middle Ages*. Edited by Adam H. Becker and Annette Yoshiko Reed. Tübingen: Mohr Siebeck, 2003.

Zetterholm, Karin Hedner. "Alternative Visions of Judaism and Their Impact on the Formation of Rabbinic Judaism." *JJMJS* 1 (2014): 127–53.

_____. "Jesus–Oriented Visions of Judaism in Antiquity." In *Jewish Studies in the Nordic Countries Today - Scripta Instituti Donneriani Aboensis* 27 (2016): 37–60.

_____. *Jewish Interpretation of the Bible: Ancient and Contemporary*. Minneapolis: Fortress, 2012.

Ziesler, J. A. *The Meaning of Righteousness in Paul: A Linguistic and Theological Enquiry*. SNTSMS 20. Cambridge: Cambridge University Press, 1972.

Ancient Sources Index

Didascalia Apostolorum
6:5:7......127

Acts of Pilate (= Gospel of Nicodemus)
2:1......403
11:2......403

John Chrysostom
Homily on Matthew
11:3......361

Jerome
Comm. Matt.
5:4......29
5:19......77
19:20......95
27:25......295

Nicholas of Lyra
Comm. Rom.
9:21......336

Origen
CER
7:13......177

Eusebius
HE
2:7......406

Graeco-Roman Sources

Achilles Tatius
Leuc. Clit.
7:14:6......418
8:2:2–3......418

Euripides
Bacch.
784–95......418

Plutarch
Alex.
2–3......412

Seutonius
Aug.
94:3–4......412

Tacitus
Ann.
15:44:4......403

Subject Index